Firearms in
Colonial America

1492–1792

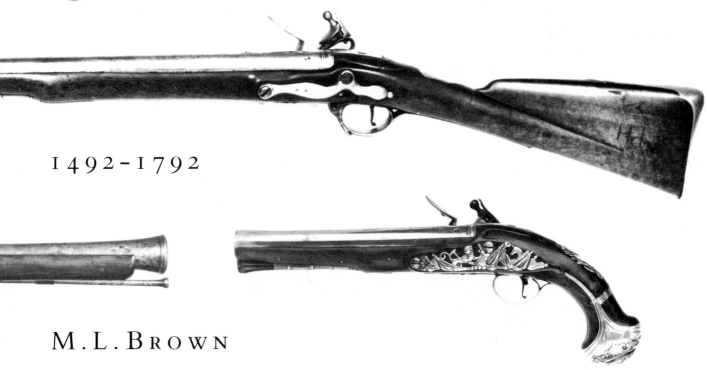

M. L. BROWN

WASHINGTON CITY · 1980

Parts of this book previously appeared in these articles written by the author and are used with the publisher's permission:

"Early Gun Makers Met War Woes," *The American Rifleman* (January 1971), Centennial ed.

"Firearms in Frontier America: The Economic Impact, Part I - 1560 to 1800," *The Gun Digest,* 1976.

"Matchlocks in Spanish Florida," *The Gun Digest,* 1978.

"Muskets for Liberty," *Ordnance* (July-August 1973).

"Muskets, Powder and Patriots," *The Gun Digest,* 1973.

Library of Congress Cataloging in Publication Data

Brown, M.L., 1934—

Firearms in Colonial America.

Bibliography: p.

Includes index.

1. Firearms—United States—History—16th century. 2. Firearms—United States—History—17th century. 3. Firearms—United States—History—18th century. 4. United States—History—Colonial period, ca. 1600-1775.

I. Title.

TS533.2.B76   683.4'00973   80-27221
ISBN 0-87474-290-0

DEDICATION

To

Carolyn, my wife,
from whom I learned that woman is all things to man.

And To

Walter Elbert Brown (1900-1954), my father,
from whom I learned a deep and abiding respect for all creatures wild
and their environment before ecology became a popular *and* social issue,
and who also taught me the proper respect for firearms
and how to properly use them.

CONTENTS

FOREWORD

As the author notes in his preface to this book, he has closely examined the interlocking relationship of firearms and economics—a partnership, if you will—through the course of history. He has done exactly that, in the process coining a word to describe the dual growth—*techonomics*.

This monumental volume has been over seven years in the making. In that time, M.L. Brown traveled thousands of miles, and visited or corresponded with scores of sources here and abroad—archives, museums, libraries and individuals. Here you will find a fascinating text, clearly and simply written; over 400 illustrations—photographs, maps and drawings, plus important tables, an extensive bibliography, and an invaluable index.

I've known the author of the book for many years, during which time I published several articles he wrote for *Gun Digest*. I know, therefore, a good deal about the intensive care with which Lee Brown puts together a story, the exhaustive research he pursues to enhance his knowledge and, thereby, to insure the accuracy and depth of his work.

The tools of the trade and the accouterments used in operating firearms are well covered in this book—materials heretofore, for the most part, much neglected. Pictured and described are: powder flasks, early bow drills, cartridge boxes, bullet extractors and moulds, powder testers, rifling guides, mandrel lathes and many more.

I can unhesitatingly recommend this book to students of firearms development during our colonial period, and also to all researchers in the history of the industrial revolution in the United States.

JOHN T. AMBER

John Amber is Editor Emeritus of *Gun Digest*.

PREFACE

This is a book about firearms. It is also a book about people and technology, for the dramatic role of the firearm as an efficient, effective tool which evolved during humankind's continuing struggle for survival cannot be minimized in any history of civilization.

Firearms have been an integral part of technological evolution since the early fourteenth century and there is a strong link between firearms technology and the technology in other, often unrelated fields, an influence clearly evident throughout the centuries.

Any investigation seriously devoted to the technological evolution of firearms in Colonial America cannot be divorced from an inquiry into European achievements in that endeavor, nor can it be separated from coeval accomplishments in fields such as chemistry, metallurgy, manufacturing techniques, and the evolution of hand tools and machine tools.

A distinct product of Old World technology, firearms performed a significant part in the astonishingly rapid conquest, colonization, and techonomic* development of the New World, and nowhere was that performance more crucial or decisive than in the vast wilderness of North America which subsequently became the United States.

This book is fundamentally concerned with the Old World firearms evolution as it relates to the influence of firearms in colonial America during the period 1492 to 1792; a complex sphere of influence spanning three centuries, and intricately woven into the colorful and diverse fabric of our distinctive national heritage.

The utilization of machines to manufacture firearms and gunpowder began in fourteenth-century Europe, reaching a relatively sophisticated plateau of development in the late eighteenth century when combined on a limited scale with the then radical concepts of mass production and interchangeable components; concepts which originated in Classical antiquity and subsequently flourished with a startling intensity to transcend the sphere of firearms technology and create innovative manufacturing techniques which altered forever the course of human aspiration.

It is my intention to present an accurate techonomic history of firearms in colonial America during an epoch when most crafts remained essentially within the grasp of the individual and were characterized by a lack of standardization, though leavened with a generous amount of ingenuity and improvization; traits which were especially evident in the infant American firearms industry from its inception and which were responsible for creating a viable enterprise and a burgeoning mechanization virtually unknown in other fields of technology until the late nineteenth century.

I have attempted to retain a balanced measure of objectivity and have supported my interpretation with documented evidence; however, if I am derelict in this presentation the full onus of responsibility rests upon myself.

M.L. BROWN
Tampa, Florida

---

*A word coined by the author and combining *tech* (nology) with (ec) *onomic,* describing an economic system based on technological achievement.

The Colonists in America
were the greatest weapon-using people
of that epoch in the world.

CHARLES WINTHROP SAWYER
Firearms in American History

Liber Ignium (9th/13th Century): The *Liber Ignium ad Comburendos Hostes* (M S Latin 7156, Folio 65) preserved various formulae for incendiaries and explosives such as *ignis volans* (flying fire): "Take one pound of sulphur, two pounds of willow charcoal, and six pounds of saltpeter [6:1:2], which three things grind finely on a marble stone. Then put as much as you wish into a paper case to make flying fire or thunder." The formula is identical to English gunpowder ca. 1350. Courtesy of the *Bibliothèque Nationale*, Paris.

THE ADVENT OF THE RENAISSANCE in the fourteenth century stripped away the repressive shroud of the Dark Ages enveloping western Europe, and it was during that enlightened resurgence of European science and technology that firearms gradually emerged to exert a profound influence on the affairs of humankind.

Edward Gibbon (1734-1794), in his *Decline and Fall of the Roman Empire,* observed that "The precise era of the invention and application of gunpowder is involved in doubtful traditions and equivocal language. . . ."[1]

Gibbon's statement is as valid now as when written, for what is currently known of early chemical explosive compounds and the first primitive guns is largely conjectural. There are, however, ancient manuscripts revealing a limited knowledge of incendiary substances and several of those works make oblique references to explosives used to propel crude missiles from rudimentary weapons.

Though we now live in a nuclear age characterized by unprecedented technological achievement, it is presumptuous to imagine that the ancients were completely ignorant about technological developments or less well informed about many other accomplishments conceived before the dawn of recorded history.

At some undetermined time between the Fifth and Fourth Millennium, the ancients discovered numerous techniques for mining, smelting, and forging non-ferrous metals like copper, gold, lead, tin, and silver. They also invented and perfected an alloy of copper and tin which introduced the Bronze Age ca. 4000 B.C.

Iron-making was known as early as 3000 B.C., and by 1400 B.C. the industry flourished throughout the Near East, India, and elsewhere in the Orient, while casting techniques devised in the Bronze Age were used for making iron weapons and other utilitarian articles. Ferrous iron supplanted bronze as a major influence in metallurgical technology in the Middle East ca. 1200 B.C. and spread to western Europe through the loosely federated Celtic cultures shortly thereafter.

Steel was produced on a limited scale in India ca. 1200 B.C., while daggers and swords with iron handles and blades fashioned from steel appeared in the Fertile Crescent ca. 800 B.C. The introduction of the Iron Age in western Europe was of monumental significance, for the quality of tools and weaponry dramatically improved.

By 2000 B.C. the Assyrians recognized many of the properties of potassium nitrate (saltpeter/niter), while various ancient cultures utilized sulphur for medicinal purposes and relied on charcoal for fuel; those chemical substances essential to the composition of what came to be known as gunpowder.

The ancients also recorded the use of incendiary substances derived from animal fats, vegetable oils, and numerous petroleum products. Greek chronicler Herodotus of Halicarnassus (ca. 484-425 B.C.) related in his *Histories* (IV, 119) that the Persians processed asphalt, salt, and oil from a substance called *rhadinace* procured from wells in the Black Sea region.

The crude, earthen ore reduction kiln, the charcoal kiln, the bellows, the forge, the hammer, the anvil, the bow drill, the potter's wheel, the pole lathe and other hand tools and primitive machines were all known to the ancients and, in the light of those diverse technological achievements, it is not inconceivable that chemical compounds capable of generating an explosive force were known in classical antiquity.

Over the centuries innumerable theories have been advanced attempting to explain the origin and evolution of explosive compounds. Edward A. Dieckmann, Sr., for instance, has presented a plausible supposition, suggesting that Druid (Celtic) priests learned to make a chemical explosive at some undetermined time and that it was passed from one generation of those erudite clerics to the next.[2] Wandering throughout the Old World during the Hallstatt period (ca. 800-500 B.C.), Druid priests contacted their counterparts elsewhere and the arcane knowledge spread, exclusively preserved among the powerful holy men to maintain their inordinate influence over a populace struggling to survive in a morass of ignorance, poverty, superstition, and nearly perpetual warfare.

Dieckmann supports his contention with the assertion that Herodotus unwittingly recorded the first use of an extremely volatile explosive when relating the attempt of the Persian king, Khashayarsha (Xerxes), to conquer Delphi in 481 B.C. According to Herodotus (*Histories:* VIII, 37) the Greeks were spared when the narrow pass between Mount Parnassus and Mount Carphis inexplicably and thunderously erupted when the Persians stormed through it during the attack.

The grateful Hellenes attributed their good fortune to the timely intervention of the sacred Delphic oracle though modern scholars believe the eruption was caused by a strikingly propitious earthquake. Dieckmann ascribes the event to Delphic priests who deliberately "mined" the pass, bolstering his theory by pointing out that the supposedly coincidental eruption was repeated in 279 B.C. when the Gauls assaulted the treacherous defile. Substantial credence can be given to Dieckmann's interpretation of those events, for it is difficult to imagine the intervention of a natural phenomenon at Delphi the precise moment of each threat; particularly when separated by nearly two centuries.

Thucydides (ca. 470-393 B.C.), in his perceptive *History of the Peloponnesian War* (IV, 100), mentioned that the Boetians used incendiary compounds at the siege of Delium in 424 B.C. References to similar flammable concoctions abound in other ancient manuscripts, and they are now collectively termed Greek fire; its origin conjectural, though it is usually ascribed to the ancient Hellenes.

Greek fire was indiscriminately employed with devastating results in Classical antiquity and thereafter, hurled by catapults and other engines of war including a huge prototype of the modern flamethrower called a *siphon* and attributed to the Greek scholar and inventor Archimedes (ca. 287-212 B.C.).

An early allusion to an unidentified explosive apparently employed to propel missiles of an equally unknown kind from some sort of destructive engine was made by the Athenian scholar Philostratus (ca. A.D. 170-245) in his biography of Apollonius Tyanaeus:

These truly wise men (the Oxydracae) dwell between the rivers of Hyphasis and Ganges. Their country Alexander [the Great, 356-323 B.C.] never entered, deterred . . . I suppose, by religious motives, for had he passed the Hyphasis he might doubtless have made himself master of all the country round them; but their

cities he never could have taken . . . , for they come not out to the field to fight those who attack them, but these holy men, beloved by the gods, overthrew their enemies with tempests and thunderbolts shot from their walls. . . .[3]

Equally intriguing as the mysterious Oxydracae of India is the still impressive and controversial feat performed by Carthaginian general Hannibal (ca. 247-183 B.C.). His mighty army, including thirty-seven armored elephants, broached the frigid alps at a yet undisclosed location in fifteen days when invading Roman territory from Spain in 218 B.C. As Dieckmann notes, an imprecise explanation of Hannibal's expeditious passage was given by Col. Eugene Hennebert, *Histoire d' Annibal* (Paris: 1870).[4]

Col. Hennebert contended that Hannibal's engineers used a chemical compound called *oxus* to demolish any formidable obstacles hindering the march, though he revealed no clue to the origin or ingredients of that apparently remarkable substance. Considering the size of the Carthaginian army and the swift crossing, *oxus* was obviously some kind of explosive because anything less volatile could not have removed impassable barriers in such short order.

There is no doubt that Greek fire and other flammables survived Classical antiquity though the same cannot be said of explosives, for as yet there is no concrete proof that they existed during that distant epoch. There is, however, the possibility that what knowledge the ancients acquired about explosives was subsequently lost like many other early technological achievements, only to be resurrected centuries later; but when, where, and by whom remains obscure even under the scrutiny of modern scientific and scholarly investigation.

While most of Europe struggled under Christianity following the collapse of the once powerful Roman Empire, science and technology flourished across the sparkling *Mare Mediterraneum* among Semitic and oriental cultures, and there was also a vigorous, lucrative commerce between those cultures via India, presupposing a covert if not deliberate exchange of knowledge.

Arabic culture spilled over into Hispanic Europe ca. A.D. 700 when the powerful North African Moors entered the Iberian peninsula, bringing an enlightenment to Spain which was lacking elsewhere on the Continent and simultaneously engendering a pernicious struggle between Islam and Christendom; an irreparable breach exemplified by the savagery of the Crusades (ca. 1095-1291).

In the Orient, meanwhile, the detailed Chinese *Wu Ching Tsung Yao* of A.D. 1044 mentioned crude incendiaries containing saltpeter,[5] yet that illuminating work was no more explicit than the *Alexiad* of 1118 ascribed to Byzantine princess Anna Comnena

(1083-1148) which listed various formulae for Greek fire and other flammables, for neither ancient treatise described a true chemical explosive.[6]

Significantly, there were at that time in western Europe countless individuals attempting to unravel the mysteries of the universe, relying on the pseudo science of alchemy and also invoking the powers of magic. A number of those mystical practitioners delved into the secrets of chemistry, producing ineffectual explosive concoctions which were scrupulously recorded.

The *Liber Ignium ad Comburendos Hostes* (Book of Fires for Consuming the Enemy), purportedly written A.D. 846 by the Byzantine Marcus Graecus (Mark of Greece), is thought by modern scholars to be a composite more reliably dated ca. 1200 and featuring the works of several unidentified authors transcribed into Latin from an earlier Arabic manuscript produced in Spain.[7] The *Liber Ignium* disclosed formulae for at least 35 incendiaries and several explosive compounds, though the latter are believed to have been surreptitiously added to the text somewhat later.

Working in Spain, Moorish scholar Abdallah Ibn al-Baythar (1197-1248) was apparently familiar with Chinese, Hindu, and Persian manuscripts dealing with incendiaries and he referred to saltpeter as *thalj al-Sin* (snow of China). He wrote ca. 1240 of various processes for refining saltpeter and sulphur.[8] His contemporaries in Spain, Nedj-iddin Hassan Abrammah, Yussuf-ibn Ismail, and the erudite monk Ferrarius, are also believed to have experimented with incendiaries and rudimentary explosives.[9]

In England the inquisitive Franciscan philosopher Roger Bacon (ca. 1214-1294) of Ilchester, Somerset, recorded the formula for a true explosive between 1248 and 1252 in his somewhat convoluted *Epistola de Secretis Operibus Artis et Naturae et de Nullitate Magiae* (A Treatise Concerning the Marvelous Power of Art and Nature, and Concerning the Nullity of Magic).[10]

Friar Bacon, possibly to avoid a conflict with stringent papal doctrine regarding scientific inquiry as heretical, concealed the formula in an anagram, giving the proportions as 41.2 percent saltpeter, 29.4 percent sulphur, and 29.4 percent charcoal. Most firearms historiographers accept Bacon's cryptic text as the source for the initial introduction of a true chemical explosive to Western culture.

The astute Bacon, a contemporary of Ferrarius, mentioned "Tagus Sand" in several of his later works and it is probably euphemistic, indicating the origin of his formula in that the river Tagus *(Tejo)* flows through central Spain and the finely granulated ingredients resembled grains of sand; however, the foregoing is purely conjectural.

A similar formula appeared in *Opus de Mirabilibus Mundi,* attributed to Bishop Albertus Magnus (1193-1280) of Ratisbon, and it is believed that he and Friar Bacon exchanged correspondence.[11] In any event neither Bacon nor his European contemporaries suggested that the various incendiaries or explosives known to them be used for anything more potent than crude pyrotechnics.

No less nebulous and speculative as the origin of a true explosive is when, where, and by whom it was initially employed to propel a crude missile from an equally primitive gun. Again, numerous theories suggest the origin of the first gun, though whether cannons predate firearms or vice versa remains moot because various factors combined with conflicting archaeological and documentary evidence prevent a definite conclusion.

Many of the hypotheses concerning the initial appearance of the gun remain in the realm of fantasy, exemplified by the persistent legend attributing it to the mythical fourteenth-century German monk Berchtoldus Niger (Black Berthold or Berthold Schwarz), and several are "educated" suppositions based on interpretations of uncorroborated, often conflicting evidence.

In 1776 English philologist Nathaniel B. Halhed (1751-1830) translated a Persian copy of the ancient Hindu *Code of Manu,* placing the origin of gunpowder and guns in India ca. 1200 B.C. As Col. Henry Hime revealed in *Gunpowder and Ammunition: Their Origin and Progress* (London: 1904), Halhed inadvertently rendered the "fire-weapons" of the Persian text as "firearms," thereby imparting substantial confusion to a subject already obfuscated by the ages.[12]

Compounding the confusion was another Englishman, Sir George Staunton (1737-1810), who wrote in *Embassy to the Emperor of China* (London: 1798), that in that country "the knowledge of gunpowder seems to be coeval with . . . the most distant historic events."[13] Later scholars relying on Halhed perpetuated the India myth and those accepting Staunton's comment or basing their interpretations on oriental manuscripts of dubious origin and date, steadfastly ascribed the invention of gunpowder to the Chinese ca. A.D. 900 and further asserted that rudimentary cannon were produced there ca. 1200.

Chinese history during those three centuries is amply documented and the available literature makes no concrete reference to either gunpowder or guns. Equally significant is that of all the varied artifacts surviving the ages in China prior to the fourteenth century, none remotely resemble cannon or firearms barring a single exception of doubtful authenticity.[14]

Notwithstanding the venturesome Marco Polo (ca. 1245-1324) whose exaggerated autobiography related that he returned to Venice from the opulent court of Kubla Khan bearing the gift of an explosive compound, there is no conclusive proof that gunpowder or guns were known in China prior to the late Yuan Dynasty (ca. 1325-1368); a time when it was possible that both technological innovations were introduced to the Orient, rather than vice versa, via the overland trade routes earlier established by Arab and eastern European merchants.[15]

The Five Ceremonies, a Korean military compendium of ca. 1475 purportedly containing data from more ancient sources, mentioned short bamboo tubes firing arrow-like projectiles by means of a fuze.[16] Similar weapons made of copper are depicted in the *Wu Pei Chih,* a Chinese martial treatise of ca. 1628 which also described *fa* powder.[17] Neither work is of sufficient antiquity to substantiate the oriental theory concerning the origin of black powder, nor do they describe firearms more sophisticated than those emerging in fourteenth-century Europe.

In 1885, the controversial English adventurer, diplomat, and orientalist, Sir Richard Francis Burton (1821-1890), published an illuminating sixteen-volume opus which investigated the origins of the tales comprising the *Arabian Nights.* The work was promptly branded obscene in Victorian England and it was subsequently placed on the *Index Librorum Prohibitorum* because part of the text candidly discussed Moslem sexual customs. In the initial volume Burton commented on the introduction of gunpowder and guns to Western culture thusly:

We ignore the invention-date and the inventor of gunpowder, as of all old discoveries which have affected mankind at large: all we know is that the popular ideas betray great ignorance. . . .[18]

* * *

Passing over the Arab sieges of Constantinople (A.D. 668) and Meccah (A.D. 690) we come to the days of Alphonso the Valiant [Alfonso VI of León, d. 1109] whose long and short guns, used at the Siege of Madrid in A.D. 1040, are preserved in the Armeria Real [Royal Armory, Madrid]. Viardot has noted that the African Arabs [Moors] first employed cannon in A.D. 1200, and that the Maghribis defended Algeciras near Gibraltar with great guns in A.D. 1247, and utilised them to besiege Seville in A.D. 1342. This last feat of arms introduced the cannon into barbarous Northern Europe, and it must have been known to civilised Asia for many a decade before that date.[19]

Burton's assertion that "long and short guns" were employed in Spain by Alfonso the Valiant in 1040 cannot be verified, nor can all the thirteenth-century dates given by Viardot. Present research has determined that any eleventh-and twelfth-century literature referring to gunpowder and guns is suspect. Nevertheless, those familiar with historical research are aware that a distinct chronological lapse often separates the actual date of an invention and when its use was first recorded.

In 1949 historian Albert Manucy stated with some equivocation that the Moors used cannon at Saragossa in A.D. 1118 (the date curiously coinciding

CANNON (1404): The art and science of European gun-founding progressed at an astonishing rate as illustrated by this huge cannon cast at Innsbruck Arsenal. The muzzle inscription translates: "My name is Catherine, beware of me, I punish injustice. Georg Endorfer cast me." Slightly more than ten feet long, "Catherine" weighs five tons and has a bore diameter of almost 15 inches. Courtesy of the *Musée de l'Armée,* Paris.

MORTAR (15th Century, ca. 1480): Weighing 7,330 pounds, this cast-bronze mortar fired a ball weighing 575 pounds. It is inscribed "F PETRUS DAVBUSSON M HOSPITALIS IHER," referring to its maker, Peter d' Aubusson. Courtesy of the *Musée de l'Armée,* Paris.

with the appearance of Anna Comnena's *Alexiad*) though he unhesitatingly declared that the Spaniards employed some form of cannon against the Moors at Cordova in 1280 and again at Gibraltar in 1306.[20]

Presently available evidence indicates that a now anonymous savant, either by accident or design, harnessed the awesome power of black powder to hurl an unidentified projectile from an unknown vessel in either North Africa or Spain ca. 1250; thus completing the metamorphosis of black powder into gunpowder proper and the unknown vessel into the first gun. There remains, however, the real possibility that that portentous technological innovation occurred elsewhere in the Old World at about the same time.

There is no current evidence indicating that cannon were known beyond the borders of Hispanic Europe prior to the fourteenth century though there is little doubt, as Viardot noted, that cannon were utilized at Seville in 1342, for there is undeniable proof that they were known in England and Italy at least 20 years earlier; thus disputing Burton's contention that the assault on Seville introduced cannon "into barbarous Northern Europe."

The cannon available in North Africa and Spain during the late thirteenth century were crude, mortar-like weapons called *madfaa* which were bucket-shaped, made of wood rather than metal, and reinforced by strips of leather, rope, or bands of bronze or iron. The *madfaa* employed roughly hewn stone projectiles propelled by an inferior black powder and its performance left much to be desired.

The first conclusive archival evidence that cannon and projectiles were fabricated beyond the Islamic sphere in Europe indicates that both were metal. A segment of the Italian *Riformagioni* of 1324-1326 notes that the Council of Florence decreed *"pilas seu palloctas ferreas et canones de metallo"* (iron balls and metal cannon) should be made for the defense of the republic.[21]

In 1326 Walter de Milemete, chaplain and tutor to young Edward III of England (1327-1377) produced an illuminated manuscript titled *De Nobilitatibus, Sapientiis, et Prudentiis Regum* (Concerning the Nobility, Wisdom, and Prudence of Kings).[22] Although the text does not mention cannon, it provides the first corroborative pictorial evidence, depicting in color a large, bulbous, vase-like cannon with a missile similar to an arrow protruding from it. The design leaves no doubt that the cannon was cast, yet whether of bronze or iron cannot be determined.

Edward II (1284-1327) purportedly employed small wrought iron cannon against the Scots at Berwick in 1327 though the authenticity of that account has been seriously challenged.[23] In any event the wrought iron cannon appearing in England shortly thereafter were forged from longitudinal bars hammer welded to form a cylinder which was reinforced by shrinking iron bands around it.

French chronicler Jean Froissart (ca. 1333-1400) related that *"canons et bombardes"* (cannon and bombards) firing arrow-like projectiles were used against the English at Quesnoi in 1340 during the devastating Hundred Years' War (1337-1453).[24] The French in turn faced Edward III's crude cannon at Crécy on August 23, 1346. The decisive factor in that murderous contest, however, was the extremely powerful, rapid-firing longbow in the steady hands of stalwart English yeomen; an efficient, long-range weapon tracing its ancestry to prehistory.

Cannon fabricated at Tournai were the first to be mounted aboard sailing vessels, accompanying the mightly fleet of Louis de Male in an attack on heavily fortified Antwerp in 1336.[25] Two years later Genoese galleys serving in the French fleet were provided with cannon of the design depicted by de Milemete, while wrought iron cannon were carried on English vessels in 1345.[26] Spanish ships mounted cannon prior to 1360 and Venetian merchant vessels carried them for protection from Mediterranean pirates as early as 1380.[27]

Various kinds of bronze and iron cannon in a wide range of calibers and design innovations including breech-loading specimens appeared in Europe by 1350 and, as the century progressed, their number rapidly increased as did their prodigious size.[28] That the use of cannon was widespread in the Old World prior to the fifteenth century is attested to by the Italian bard and philosopher Petrarch (1304-1374) who somewhat cynically remarked in *De Remediis Utriusque Fortunae* (lib. I, dialog 99):

> . . . these instruments which discharge balls of metal with most tremendous noise and flashes of fire . . . were a few years ago very rare and were viewed with greatest astonishment and admiration, but now they are become as common and familiar as any other kind of arms. So quick and ingenious are the minds of men in learning the most pernicious arts.

Firearms

Unlike cannon and other early forms of artillery, the first firearms were crude, portable weapons primarily designed for individual use and, to distinguish them from artillery and subsequently developed small arms employing mechanical ignition systems, they are termed hand cannon. Less frequently encountered is the descriptive cannon lock, a somewhat misleading term, for in the broad sense it refers to artillery and implies that some form of mechanical ignition (lock mechanism) was used. Equally deceptive is that cannon lock is employed by some firearms historians to describe a breech sealing device for cannon and there is a distinct physical resemblance between those devices and early forms of hand cannon.

The hand cannon was initially a short tube (barrel) cast of bronze or iron and provided with an ignition vent (touch-hole) bored through the barrel wall near the closed end (breech). The powder charge was merely poured down the open end of the barrel (muzzle), leaving sufficient space for the projectile which followed. There was neither a front nor a rear sight and nothing to support the barrel or to hold when pointing the weapon.

The manual application of a glowing wire or piece of smouldering tinder to the vent passed through the vent channel (hole bored through the barrel wall) to ignite the powder in the chamber (interior of the breech); thus forcing the projectile out of the bore (interior of the barrel).

A common denominator characterizing hand cannon and most firearms for nearly three centuries was a lack of standardization regarding barrel length, caliber (bore diameter), overall length, weight, and design.

The chronological lapse evident in determining the origin of gunpowder and the first gun is also obvious regarding the initial appearance of firearms. What is purportedly the first literary reference to European firearms is found in an Italian manuscript unreliably dated A.D. 1281 and cited by Maj. Angelo Angelucci, *Documenti Inediti per la Storia della Armi de Fuocco Italiane* (Edited Documents Concerning the History of Italian Firearms [Turin: 1869]). The passage reads: "*Une squadra grande de Balestrieri e scoppettieri del conte Guido di Montefeltro*" (A large company comprised of the *Balestrieri* and *scoppettieri* of Count Guido of Montefeltro).[29]

As rendered by Maj. Angelucci the *scoppettieri* were firearms bearers though no description of their weapons has survived, yet some doubt is cast on his interpretation because the Latin *sclopo, scolop, scoppo*, and other variants of the word from which *scoppettieri* is derived, refers to either cannon or hand cannon in fourteenth-century Italian manuscripts.

The aforementioned volume also described a cast-bronze *scloppo* embellished with oak leaf engraving and a Greek cross. The *scloppo* was marked P P P F and bears the Arabic numerals 1322, possibly signifying the date. No further identification was given by Maj. Angelucci and verification remains speculative, for the weapon subsequently vanished from the Monastery of St. Orsola in Mantua.[30]

A cast-bronze hand cannon excavated near Loshult, Sweden, in 1861 has been assigned an early fourteenth-century date and it is similar to the de Milemete cannon though measuring a mere eleven inches.[31] A vent is provided at the bulbous base and the bore is approximately .75 caliber, i.e., twelve bore (see Appendix I). There are no sights and the muzzle is surrounded by a protruding annulus, possibly ornamental. The Loshult hand cannon is considered one of the earliest firearms and nothing suggests that it was held by anything other than the hand.

As far as it can be determined the first pictorial evidence of European hand cannon appeared in a series of frescoes executed ca. 1340 by Paolo Neri.[32] The frescoes were commissioned by the church of the former Monastery of St. Leonardo near Lecetto, Italy, and depict *scoppettieri* firing smooth, round missiles from short metal tubes attached to long wooden poles. Though the hand cannon scenes could have been added later, the frescoes nevertheless depict the earliest known technological innovation in firearms evolution: the wooden shaft (tiller) to which the barrel was mounted; forerunner of the gunstock proper.

In England ca. 1344 Robert de Mildenhale, Keeper of the King's Wardrobe (personal property), noted in his accounts *"gunnis cum telar"* (guns with tillers), probably the initial reference to hand cannon in England and consistent with the contemporaneous Italian fresco illustrations.[33] Similar weapons were described as *handgonnes* in a list of arms delivered to the Chamberlain of Berwick in 1371 by John Halton, Keeper of the Tower of London; the Tower serving as a repository for arms and armor since the eleventh century.[34]

Ugonino di Chatillion (fl. 1345-1350), an Italian armorer of Val d' Aosto, Turin Province, made four bronze *schioppi* (hand cannon) for the Marquis of Montferrato ca. 1347 though the weapons are not described,[35] while a Perugia Arsenal inventory of 1364 listed *"500 bombarde una spanna longhe"* (500 bombards one span long); a span measuring approximately nine inches.[36]

Early Firearms Innovations

The foregoing evidence clearly indicates that by 1350 various kinds of cast-bronze hand cannon were common throughout Europe and it is apparent from available records that bronze was preferred to iron for barrel-making, probably because it was easier to cast. In any event hand cannon early illustrated a number of design innovations and some of them were quite sophisticated, displaying an understanding of chemistry, metallurgy, and physics not generally associated with the corporate body of scientific acumen available during that distant epoch.

One of the earliest and most significant documents relating to firearms evolution and technological innovation is the *Anleitung Schiesspulver zu bereiten. Büchsen zu laden und zu beschiessen* (Directions for the Preparation of Gunpowder. How to Load Guns and Discharge Them).[37] The manuscript, known also as the *Codex Germanicus 600* and dated ca.

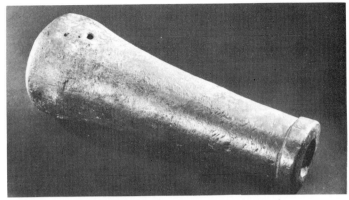

LOSHULT GUN (14th Century): This famous handcannon found in Loshult parish, Småland, Sweden, is similar to the large, vase-like cannon depicted by De Milemete in 1326. Note the simple vent near the base and the muzzle ring. Courtesy of the *Statens Historiska Museum*, Stockholm.

1350-1370, describes three technological developments and the first known loading data for firearms.

The *Codex* suggests that three-fifths of the bore be filled with firmly tamped gunpowder, that an air space to provide oxygen for combustion remain between the powder charge and a wooden sabot (disc-like plug), and that the missile be snugly fitted against the sabot. The *Codex* infers that early gunpowder was a weak or at least an occasionally unreliable concoction, for the recommended charge nearly filled the bore, while it also indicates that the powder charge was no longer merely poured down the bore, denoting the knowledge that tamping the charge increased its explosive force.

In addition, tamping the powder signified the introduction of the ramrod which was also employed to properly seat the sabot and the projectile. The sabot separating the powder charge from the projectile was another innovation and the earliest known reference to obturation, i.e., preventing the escape of the powder gases around the projectile by sealing the bore immediately behind it with a plug readily discharged by the thrust of the gases.

Early black powder was a moderately effective propellant, though the scientific principles of how the ingredients created the explosive force to propel the projectile were not entirely explained until the late eighteenth century. When combined and confined in the chamber of a firearm the ingredients performed specific functions invoking a spontaneous chemical reaction. Saltpeter provides the oxygen to burn the sulphur and charcoal, sulpher lowers the temperature at which ignition occurs and furnishes density, while charcoal also adds bulk and serves as the oxidizing (burning) agent.

When ignited black powder instantly generates extreme heat, releasing energy in the form of powerful gases. The gases compressed in the breech of the firearm rapidly expand, exerting uniform pressure in

TANNENBURG *Büchse* (14th Century, ca. 1399): One of the earliest, reliably dated firearms, the Tannenburg gun has two significant technological innovations: breech-chambering and the stock (tiller). Note the shallow priming pan surrounding the vent. Courtesy of the *Germanisches Nationalmuseum,* Nuremburg.

DIAGRAMATIC: (1) Muzzle. (2) Muzzle Collar (reinforcing ring or annulus). (3) Barrel. (4) Bore. (5) Breech. (6) Chamber, smaller than bore diameter (breech-chambering). (7) Vent (Touch-hole). (8) Tiller Socket. (9) Tiller (pole-type stock). Author's sketch.

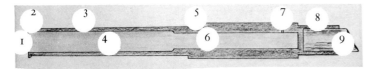

all directions simultaneously and violently forcing the projectile from the bore, i.e., the point of least resistance, and driving the weapon sharply upward and to the rear (recoil) because the breech is sealed, effectively blocking the movement of the powerful gases to the rear. The amount of powder used and the purity and the ratio of the ingredients determined the intensity of the explosive force which was sufficiently powerful to overcome the inertia (weight) of the projectile and accelerate its velocity (speed) in flight.

Technologically superior to all known fourteenth-century hand cannon is the Tannenberg *Büchse* (gun), the earliest extant German firearm.[38] There is no doubt concerning its antiquity because it was excavated in 1849 from the ruins of *Festung* Tannenberg in Hess, a haven for criminals destroyed in 1399.

The cast-bronze Tannenberg gun is hexagonal, measuring nearly 13 inches, and it weighs approximately two and three-quarter pounds. The short breech section is somewhat thicker than the remainder of the slightly tapered barrel; an innovation strengthening it to withstand the pressure generated by the powder charge. Tapering the barrel was another innovation designed to reduce its weight.

The bore diameter (caliber) of the Tannenberg gun is 1.43 inches, the muzzle has an annulus, and there are no sights. The vent is located atop the breech and is approximately 1/10th inch in diameter, encompassed by a shallow detent serving as a rudimentary priming pan (flashpan). Unlike the Loshult hand cannon, the Tannenberg gun is provided with a tiller socket directly behind the breech.

The Tannenberg gun illustrates the first known example of breech chambering; an innovation wherein the powder chamber located in the breech is smaller than bore diameter. The narrow chamber neck, functioning like the sabot, prevented the projectile from compressing the propellant because it had been discovered that powder too tightly tamped failed to properly ignite.

Because the powder gases were strictly confined in the narrow chamber they expanded with greater force; thus increasing chamber pressure which accelerated the velocity of the projectile, thereby improving its range and its kinetic (striking) force. A deliberate innovation, breech chambering illustrates an advanced knowledge of physics.

Another design innovation peculiar to the Tannenberg gun is the shallow depression surrounding the vent. After the powder and projectile were loaded a small amount of powder was sprinkled in the cup-like detent and some of it filled the vent channel leading to the chamber. When ignited that primary or "priming" charge flashed through the vent channel, ensuring positive combustion.

Though differing in several respects from the Loshult and Tannenberg guns, a fourteenth-century hand cannon recovered from the sea near Mörkö, Sweden, ca. 1900 is also cast of bronze and retains the hexagonal design of the latter. The Mörkö gun measures seven and one-half inches and the bore is approximately .65 caliber.[39] A tiller socket is provided at the breech though the weapon has no sights and is not breech-chambered.

The priming pan of the Mörkö gun is more developed than the shallow depression serving the Tannenberg gun. Resembling an inverted pyramid, the pan is wider and deeper and surrounded by a slight lip; an innovative design increasing powder capacity and more efficiently directing ignition flash into the chamber which improved combustion. As in the Tannenberg gun the breech section of the barrel is thicker. Both the breech and barrel flats of the Mörkö gun display an engraved inscription.

The Mörkö gun also has two integrally-cast breech projections, each a technological innovation. The upper projection appears to be an ornamental bust of Jesus Christ and it possibly served as a flash deflector (fence), directing priming flash away from the eyes and hands. The lower protrusion is a hook curving slightly rearward.

MÖRKÖ GUN (14th Century, ca. 1350): Note the barrel hook and the hexagonal breech and barrel similar to the Tannenburg gun design. The firearm was recovered from the sea near Mörkö, Bälinge parish, Södermanland, Sweden.

The barrel and the breech flats are inscribed "MARIA PLEA" from the Latin *Ave Maria gratia plena* and "Hielp. Got. Help. Uns."

The figure immediately behind the priming pan is believed to represent Jesus. The interior of the pan is shaped like an inverted pyramid, forcefully directing ignition flash into the powder chamber. Courtesy of the *Statens Historiska Museum*, Stockholm.

Several functions have been ascribed to the hook found on the Mörkö gun and other European firearms dating to the early seventeenth century; the most plausible suggesting that the hook was forced against an embrasure or parapet to minimize the heavy recoil shock (kick) when the weapon was fired. Considering the diminutive size of the Mörkö gun, recoil would have been negligible and the hook apparently superfluous. In larger firearms, however, recoil was more severe.

Archaeologists have discovered numerous holes drilled in the masonry along the course of the parapets in several Old World fortifications and it is possible that the barrel hook was designed to fit them, supporting the weapon, though other explanations for the holes are equally convincing. Also possible is that the barrel hook served as a hand grip or was designed to fit into a socket or other fixture attached to a portable wooden staff *(fourquine)* to assist in controlling and supporting the barrel. Whatever the purpose, German hand cannon displaying the hook early received the appellation *hakenbüchse,* derived from *haken* (hook) and *Büchse* (gun); literally "hook gun."

Gunpowder Manufacture

Early fourteenth-century black powder was essentially the same unrefined, unstable, and unreliable compound it had been since Friar Bacon recorded the formula, though by ca. 1350 the ratio of the ingredients had been gradually altered. English gunpowder was then formulated of six parts saltpeter, one part sulphur, and two parts charcoal (6:1:2), while in Germany the ratio fluctuated between 4:1:1 and 8:1:1.

During the fourteenth century and considerably thereafter gunpowder, like cannon and firearms, was made by hand, even though during that early epoch several technological innovations assisted in the preparation of the ingredients. Various methods for refining saltpeter and sulphur were early devised in China, India, Persia, and North Africa and they eventually spread to Europe.

The following process for refining saltpeter is described in the *Liber Ignium:*

Note that saltpeter is a mineral of the earth and is found as an efflorescence on stones. This earth is dissolved in boiling water, then purified and passed through a filter. It is boiled for a day and night and solidified, and transparent plates of salt [nitrate] are found at the bottom of the vessel.[40]

Sulphur was distilled by an evaporation process. Mixed with water, the sulphur was boiled in a large covered vat provided with a flue. Sulphur-laden steam passed through the flue to a sealed condensing chamber where it cooled, leaving purified sulphur crystals. The distillation and refining techniques early utilized were little altered throughout the centuries though as technology progressed the equipment employed became more sophisticated.

Willow, hazel, birch, alder, or beech in that order were the most suitable wood for making charcoal and it was cut into footlong lengths about an inch thick. The wood was then carefully stacked in an earthen kiln and baked under controlled flame (dry heat) to prevent complete combustion; a method used until the early nineteenth century.

After a few days the color of the smoke emanating from the kiln indicated that the wood had been sufficiently carbonized. The kiln was then dismantled and the charcoal spread to cool. Using the simple mortar and pestle, the harvested charcoal was pulverized. Depending on the kind of wood and the time it was baked, charcoal ranged in color from dark brown to black.

Considerable caution was observed when mixing the saltpeter, sulphur, and charcoal during the powder-making process; not only to prevent a disastrous explosion, but to make certain that the ratio of the ingredients remained reasonably constant. Any radical change in the proportions resulted in powder too weak to be effective or so powerful it frequently shattered the weapon.

After mixing and further pulverizing the finished gunpowder was characterized by its exceedingly fine granulation which made it easier to ignite. Permeating the other ingredients, the color of the charcoal gave rise to the appellation "black" powder.

CHARCOAL KILN (10th/19th Century): For centuries charcoal was vital to iron and gunpowder manufacture. Charcoal kilns were operated in the rural United States until the late nineteenth century. Courtesy of the American Iron and Steel Institute, Washington, D.C.

Powder was usually stored in barrels, casks, or kegs until needed though in some instances artillerists, to ensure potency, mixed the ingredients immediately prior to use.

When stored for long periods early black powder either solidified through dampness and chemical deterioration or settled in layers in relation to the specific gravity of each ingredient, the latter circumvented by merely inverting the storage containers at regular intervals; a practice continuing long after the necessity had been eliminated by the appearance of corned powder in the fifteenth century.

Black powder early came to be called serpentine powder, the term either derived from a small cannon of the same designation popular during the late fourteenth century or a kind of hand cannon then emerging. Serpentine powder was extremely hygroscopic and the ingredients contained various impurities because of crude refining techniques; thus exhibiting several disadvantages.

Damp or wet powder caused misfires and even under perfect conditions all the powder was not consumed when ignited. The unburned residue (powder fouling) frequently caused misfires by clogging the vent channel and it made loading difficult or impossible because it accumulated in the bore after a few shots, preventing the free passage of the powder and projectile.

Powder fouling also contained corrosive salts produced by the combustion of the ingredients. The acidic salts fostered rust and metal erosion which, if neglected, eventually weakened the barrel or chamber to the extent that it ruptured unexpectedly to shatter the weapon and its user. Powder fouling remained a major problem limiting the efficacy of firearms for nearly six centuries, i.e., until black powder was supplanted by nitrocellulose propellants in the late nineteenth and early twentieth century.

Projectiles

Missiles of various geometric designs made from equally diverse materials were early used in firearms and among the first were rough or polished stones and arrows similar to that illustrated in the de Milemete manuscript. Hand cannon arrows were either made of iron or had wood shafts with iron points and fletched with iron or tin vanes (fins) for stability in flight. The shaft was bound with leather or other suitable materials, acting like the sabot to provide adequate obturation. Arrow-like projectiles were sporadically used in several kinds of firearms until the late sixteenth century; a Tower of London inventory of 1589 listing "musket arrows, 892 shefe."[41]

GUNPOWDER MANUFACTURE (14th/18th Century): This illustration from Allain Manesson Mallet, *Les Travaux de Mars ou l'Art de Guerre* (Paris, 1684), depicts a common powder-making method used from the 14th to the 18th Century despite the introduction of superior techniques in the interim. After weighing the ingredients (scale, foreground), they were crushed with a wooden pestle. The two figures (right) determine the grain size with sieves and the third figure is collecting the powder from the graining bin. Courtesy of the University of North Carolina Library, Chapel Hill.

Bronze, copper, lead, iron, pewter, tin, gemstones, and precious metals were also used for projectiles, frequently appearing in every conceivable shape including cones, cubes, hexagons, octagons, pyramids, spheres, teardrops, religious symbols, and those representing witchcraft. The design of the bore often corresponded to the shape of the projectile and experimentation with other projectile forms continued throughout the centuries. As late as 1718 it was seriously suggested in England that round bullets be used against Christians and square ones against infidels (see p. 239).

Trial and error, comprising the entire body of small arms ballistics during the fourteenth century and considerably thereafter, eventually led to the conclusion that lead projectiles were more suited to firearms because the metal was readily procured, inexpensive, could be easily cast, rolled, or swedged into myriad shapes and, being softer than bronze or iron, it did no damage to the bore despite prolonged use.[42]

It was also found that spherical (ball) projectiles were easily and rapidly loaded and performed less erratically in flight; the latter known to Balearian slingers at least as early as 300 B.C., for they employed cast lead balls up to two inches in diameter purportedly hurled with sufficient velocity to penetrate heavy bronze shields.[43] The lead ball was accepted by 1350, and even then multiple-ball loads (shot) were effectively used. Significantly, the lead ball in various sizes remained preeminent as a projectile for nearly five centuries.

The soft lead projectile presented a minor problem when fired, for some of the lead was stripped away as it passed down the bore and it left a residue called leading. Leading made loading difficult and impeded the passage of the projectile which adversely effected its flight. The problems of leading and powder fouling were circumvented by the frequent and meticulous cleaning of the bore.

Accessories and Accouterments

Many of the accessories and accouterments designed for firearms came to be as elaborately and elegantly decorated as the weapons they complemented and their number and variety proliferated and were improved upon as the centuries progressed and firearms became more sophisticated.

Gunpowder and projectiles were early carried in cloth or leather drawstring pouches, though ca. 1350 powder containers made of bone, horn, leather, shell, wood, metal and other materials appeared, often in combination. The early powder container or flask varied in capacity though it usually displayed a simple pour spout with a stopper and a carrying thong.

Made of like materials and used in conjunction with the powder flask was a small charger designed to simplify loading. The powder was poured into the charger from the flask and it held only enough for a single shot. Powder chargers in various forms served throughout the six centuries that firearms were usually loaded at the muzzle and some firearms historians believe that the charger inspired the design of the first practical cartridges.

POWDER FLASKS (16th Century, ca. 1565): Center, Danish leather-covered martial flask with spring-closure pour spout featuring a cutoff to throw a predetermined charge, ca. 1570. Left, Danish leather flask ca. 1565. Right, Danish leather-covered flask for priming with spring-closure spout, ca. 1570. Courtesy of the *Tøjhusmuseet,* Copenhagen.

The early appearance of the cast projectile for use in firearms presupposed the prior evolution of the mould, the aforementioned Balearians casting lead balls. Initially designed to cast a single projectile, the single cavity mould was of two-piece construction and made of several materials including baked clay, bronze, hardwood, iron, or soft stone-like sandstone and soapstone.

Each half of the mould was hollowed out to the desired diameter of the ball or other projectile shape and a small pour channel was provided. Positioning studs aligned the mould halves and they were simply bound or clamped when used. Cast-iron pots and ladles for melting and pouring lead were common accessories.

Moulds designed to cast more than one projectile emerged by ca. 1350 and both single cavity and multiple cavity moulds were subsequently hinged and provided with metal handles; a hook and clasp securing the halves. Multiple cavity moulds simultaneously casting projectiles of various sizes and shapes appeared before the turn of the century. With the evolution of more sophisticated firearms each was customarily provided with the proper caliber mould.

Simple procedures were followed to ensure the quality of the cast lead ball. Impurities found on the surface of the molten lead were skimmed before pouring and as each cavity was filled the mould was

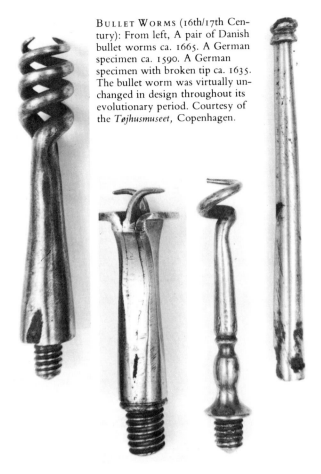

BULLET WORMS (16th/17th Century): From left, A pair of Danish bullet worms ca. 1665. A German specimen ca. 1590. A German specimen with broken tip ca. 1635. The bullet worm was virtually unchanged in design throughout its evolutionary period. Courtesy of the *Tøjhusmuseet*, Copenhagen.

lightly tapped to prevent air pockets (bubbles) from forming because weight changes altered the balance of the ball. Once sufficiently cool the mould was opened, exposing the tail or sprue formed on the ball by the pour channel. The sprue was trimmed to preserve the concentricity of the ball, for improper balance and conformation resulted in an erratic flight pattern.

Powder horns and flasks, chargers, and bullet moulds can be considered technological innovations of the first rank, comparable to the wooden ramrod, the tiller, the sabot, the barrel hook, the flashpan, the fence, and breech-chambering. In addition, the problems of leading and powder fouling inspired the origin and evolution of other accessories.

The frequency of misfires caused by powder fouling clogging the vent channel saw the early introduction of the vent pick or priming wire as it was often termed and the connotation is obvious. With the development of the priming pan the innovative pan brush emerged. Provided with stiff bristles, the pan brush removed powder residue from the priming pan and it was subsequently used to clean other parts of the firearm. The vent pick and the pan brush were usually carried in conjunction, attached to a leather thong or small chain for convenience.

It was also early apparent that some form of cleaning implement was needed to remove powder

fouling and leading from the bore. Serving that purpose was the scower or wipe, usually made of iron and provided with a slot to hold a cloth patch or swab and sharp tines designed to loosen and scrape encrusted fouling and lead residue.

The problem of removing the ball and powder charge from muzzle-loading firearms was solved with the worm. Shaped like a corkscrew in its early form, the worm was merely screwed into the soft lead ball and it was then easily extracted, while the sharp prongs readily removed the powder charge even if it had solidified after remaining in the bore for a prolonged period. The worm was a common accessory throughout the muzzle-loading era. In their earliest form scowers and worms were forged integral with an iron rod, though by ca. 1425 they were provided with a threaded tang which screwed into a metal sleeve at the end of the wooden ramrod.

As barrels became longer in the last half of the fourteenth century the sabot was discarded because it was difficult to seat properly. Flax fibers, wool scrap, or similar materials collectively called tow were used instead of the sabot and performed the same function. In addition, tow was used to keep the projectile from rolling out of the bore (the ball cast slightly smaller than bore diameter to facilitate loading) and it was particularly effective when multiple-ball loads or small shot was used. Parenthetically, the difference between the diameter of the bore and that of the projectile came to be termed windage.

The glowing wire or smouldering tinder initially used as the ignition agent in firearms was applied by hand to the vent or the priming pan, exposing the gunner to dangerous priming flash. At some undetermined time in the fourteenth century implements known as fire sticks were designed to hold the ignition agent, diminishing the chance of injury. Fire sticks were made of various materials and measured about a foot long, similar to the linstock used with early artillery.

Most of the accessories designed for the use and maintenance of firearms were carried in or suspended from accouterments devised for the purpose, including the knapsack, waist belt, and cloth or leather shoulder strap. Accessories and accouterments fluctuated widely in design and ornamentation and they were improved upon throughout the various stages of firearms evolution.

Problems and Technological Progress

Italian historian Pierino Belli, commenting on the siege of Lucca by the Florentines in *De Re Militari*

VEDELSPANG GUN (15th Century, ca. 1420): Recovered from the ruins of a Schleswig fortress destroyed in 1426, the Vedelspang gun has an overall length of 32 inches; the barrel measuring 7¼ inches from vent to muzzle. Bore diameter is 1.06 inches at the muzzle and .71 inches at the breech. The hook *(haken)* was added after the barrel was cast. Courtesy of the *Tøjhusmuseet,* Copenhagen.

et Bello Tractatus (Venice: 1563), wrote that in 1430 the Lucanese were armed with "a sort of club, about three feet in length, to which they had fastened iron pipes . . . which threw small iron balls by force of fire. The impact meant certain death, and neither armor nor shield was effective against them. Not infrequently a single ball penetrated a file of two or three men. . . ."[44]

Considering the rudimentary state of the hand cannon in the early fifteenth century and the tendency of many early chroniclers to exaggerate, Belli's statements should be met with considerable skepticism. There is, however, available data which attests to the efficacy of at least one kind of hand cannon and it was gathered by Tage Lasson between 1932 and 1940 in a series of experiments conducted under the auspices of the Royal Museum of Arms in Copenhagen and the Danish Society of Arms and Armours.[45]

An exact replica of the cast-iron Vedelspang gun dated prior to 1426 was used in the experiment in addition to two black powder formulae, both of the latter taken from German manuscripts: the first dated ca. 1330 with a ratio of 35:35:30, and the second dated ca. 1380 with a ratio of 80:10:10 (8:1:1). Each formula conformed as close as possible to the original in the texture and the quality of the ingredients. Used with the powder charge was a lead ball weighing 802 grains (437.5 grains equals one ounce avdp.).

In the initial test Lasson used 750 grains of powder (35:35:30) which produced a considerable volume of thick, black smoke and failed to propel the heavy ball more than 60 feet. The following test saw the Vedelspang copy loaded with 600 grains of powder (8:1:1), a superior mixture. At 30 yards the lead ball penetrated a two-inch pine board and a suit of light armor. Using the same formula at 50 yards, penetration was limited to a one-inch pine board. Lasson reported that in the experiments the vent, located atop the barrel, made aiming impossible because of priming flash and he concluded that hand cannon were more effective as defensive than offensive weapons.

Lasson's data indicates that the common hand cannon was practically useless beyond 60 yards through when loaded with quality gunpowder it

could penetrate light armor and kill up to about 40 yards; thus Belli's comment that two or three men were pierced by a single ball defies credulity.

Despite the relatively poor performance of the hand cannon it is likely that anyone struck by a lead ball, if not instantly killed, died horribly shortly thereafter from lead poisoning, for in the realm of early medical practice the treatment of wounds and infection was perfunctory as well as ineffectual. As any cursory study of military casualty figures will substantiate, infection and disease produced a vastly greater mortality rate than all the known weaponry of that truculent era; a phenomenon apparent as late as the nineteenth century.

Several firearms historians have suggested that while hand cannon were not effective beyond a few yards, the flash and noise associated with them engendered severe psychological trauma among the uninitiated. Considering the few hand cannon used in warfare and the constant din produced as the adversaries hacked and slashed *en masse* as was customary in the rigorous combat of the era, it is extremely doubtful if early firearms produced any immediate or lingering mental disorder; certainly not of sufficient magnitude to be responsible for the wholesale desertion of entire armies as has been suggested.

In addition to the inadequate ballistics performance of hand cannon and other early firearms, weather was a prime factor in limiting their efficacy for centuries and one reason, in conjunction with logistics problems, why military campaigns were usually suspended in winter. Even as late as the nineteenth century battles ground to a halt when snow or rain rendered powder and ignition agents useless.

HANDCANNON (15th Century): This three-barreled hand cannon was designed to increase firepower and has several technological innovations including a flash deflector circumscribing the .40 caliber barrels, sliding priming pan covers, an iron ramrod secured by two thimbles, and what appears to be a belt hook situated between the covered pans though a pole-type tiller could be attached to the base. Courtesy of the *Musée de l' Armée,* Paris.

If inclement weather were not enough, the hand cannoneer was plagued with other difficulties. Aiming the smoothbore, single-shot, muzzle-loading hand cannon with any appreciable degree of accuracy was virtually impossible and rarely attempted; and, in any event, most early hand cannon had no sights. Pointing the weapon at the enemy, the gunner could only do his best to control the unwieldy tiller with one hand as the other frantically manipulated the fire stick toward the vent.

Extremely vulnerable when tediously reloading, the hand cannoneer was often given protection and, frequently, his guardians also prevented him from taking to his heels when danger threatened. Priming flash was another hazard and there was the possibility that the weapon could shatter when fired.

And *if* the hand cannoneer somehow managed to stay alive and *if* he mastered the enervating chore of loading and firing under the stress of combat, he still could not be certain that the missile would strike where intended or, if it did, have sufficient force to inflict serious damage. Further contributing to the confusion was the dense smoke generated by artillery and hand cannon, for it frequently obscured the battlefield.

While there were certainly numerous disadvantages associated with the use and performance of hand cannon, even during the earliest stages of firearms evolution technological innovation flourished, frequently transcending the practical limits of existing technology. The imagination and ingenuity of the first gunmakers knew no bounds; a trait characterizing the craft throughout the centuries. Significantly, it was during the fifteenth century that the now seemingly perpetual armament race began to rapidly escalate.

By 1425 various kinds of hand cannon were produced in the arsenals and forges scattered across the Old World, and there were noticeable design improvements. Barrels became longer, tapering toward the muzzle, and the breech was thicker. Front and rear sights were evident, frequently found in conjunction and cast integral with the barrel. The introduction of sights presented a better method of pointing the weapon, though firearms were not aimed in the modern sense.

Manually operated priming pan covers were introduced, preventing an errant wind from scattering the priming powder. The long, cumbrous tiller was gradually supplanted by a shorter, broader support cut from a single piece of wood which made the weapon easier to manipulate. Forestocks, i.e., the part of the stock extending beneath the barrel, became more prevalent and firing from the shoulder in the manner of modern long arms was uncommon but not unknown.

Hand cannon were often used as clubs following

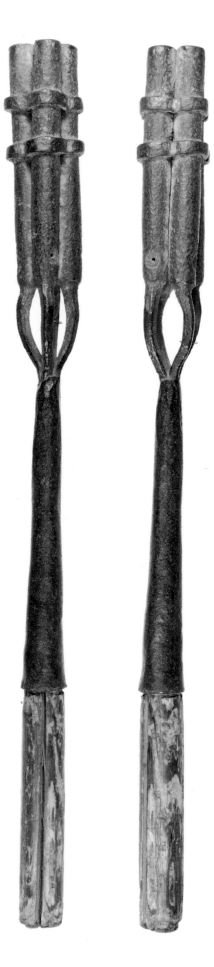

HANDCANNON (15th Century, ca. 1450): Like the handcannon depicted on page 14, this four-barreled specimen was also designed to increase firepower though it is a less sophisticated weapon. The barrels appear to be welded to the tiller socket rather than cast integral. Courtesy of the Winchester Gun Museum, Olin Corporation, New Haven, Conn.

the initial shot because in many instances there was not time to reload in the heat of battle, while they were also frequently combined with traditional battering and slashing weapons like the mace and battle axe. During the late fourteenth century hand cannon designed to be used by two men appeared and there were also cavalry versions.

The term *culverin* was collectively applied to both small hand cannon served by one man and specimens weighing 60 pounds and more served by two; those massive firearms using a two to three ounce lead ball and displaying a barrel six feet or longer. The *collinator* pointed the large *culverin* and supported the heavy barrel on his shoulder and the *incendiarus* ignited the powder charge, while each assisted in loading, cleaning, and transporting the ponderous weapon.

With the appearance of the large *culverin* the *fourquine* or barrel rest became popular, displacing

HUSSITE WAR WAGONS (14th/ 15th Century): The Hussite soldier (bottom center) is firing a hand-cannon from the shoulder like a modern long arm. Bohemian Gen. Jan Zizka (1360?-1424) employed war wagons in a defensive circle, a tactic emulated by 19th-Century American pioneers on the western frontier. From M S *Codex 3062* (1437). Courtesy of the National Library, Vienna.

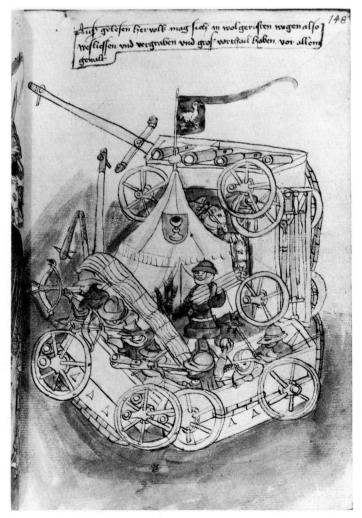

the *collinator*. The *fourquine* was simply a pole about four or five feet long, displaying at one end a U-or Y-shaped fixture designed to hold the barrel, while the opposite end had a sharp point stuck into the ground to steady and support the massive weapon. A wrist cord for additional support and carrying the *fourquine* was often provided. *Fourquines* served as accessories for large firearms until ca. 1700; their modern counterparts are exemplified by the bipod and the tripod used with some sporting and martial firearms.

The *petronel* was a cavalry weapon cast entirely of metal including the stock and it was relatively short, ranging from about 24 to 36 inches, while caliber fluctuated between .75 and .80. A shoulder sling was usually provided though centuries would pass before that innovation would be employed in the modern sense of supporting the firearm to assist in aiming. The term *petronel* survived the hand cannon era and in the sixteenth and seventeenth century it was generally applied to what came to be known as the carbine.

In addition to the *culverin* and the *petronel* there were hand cannon displaying two barrels, either superimposed or arranged side by side. Some specimens appeared with three or more barrels incorporating sliding priming pan covers. Also devised were single-and multi-barreled hand cannon firing projectiles in rapid succession, forerunners of modern repeating firearms. The firing cycle emulated the roman candle principle in single-barreled, repeating hand cannon, while in multi-barreled specimens each vent was connected by a single ignition channel filled with powder. Weapons using either system continued to discharge until empty.

Several hand cannon designs, including a few breech-loading specimens with and without separate loading chambers, existed only in the fertile imagination of early firearms inventors who meticulously transferred their novel creations to simple sketches depicted in a number of manuscripts surviving that ancient epoch. Significantly, the aforementioned technological innovations in firearms evolution were extremely slow to develop, emerging gradually in more than a century of achievement.

Hand cannon were neither sufficiently sophisticated to drastically influence the traditional concepts of fourteenth-and fifteenth-century European warfare, nor were they capable of altering existing cultural patterns in the socio-economic sphere or the political sense of violent armed rebellion, for what small quantities that were available were strictly controlled and their manufacture stringently regulated by an omnipotent aristocracy. Not until the late sixteenth century, with the introduction of more advanced weapons systems, did firearms emerge to engender startling changes in human affairs.

Metallurgical Developments and Barrel-Making

Fourteenth-century European metallurgical technology was minimal, though more advanced than generally supposed; a technological legacy inherited from the ancient Celts who dispersed a knowledge of the art throughout Europe long before the Roman conquest.

During the La Tène period (ca. 500-50 B.C.) Celtic iron forgers can be credited with inventing most of the common hand tools currently employed and the iron-making techniques utilized during the Middle Ages (ca. A.D. 476-1450). The technology spawned in the Middle Ages produced moderately efficient power systems and a number of primitive machine tools which were subsequently improved; some of them early applied to the manufacture of firearms and affiliated products.

Iron was initially produced by reduction, i.e., the ore worked in the cone-or pyramidal-shaped earthen kiln was reduced to a molten rather than liquid state. Further refining was a matter of reheating and chafing (hammering) the molten mass or bloom which reduced slag intrusions though a considerable amount of carbon remained; thus producing a brittle iron suitable for casting a variety of useful articles.

Iron-making was substantially improved with the introduction of the superior masonry furnace ca. 1350-1375. The masonry furnace had a larger capacity which increased production and it displayed a tall flue or tunnel which improved its draught, while a larger bellows introduced more oxygen; the latter innovations intensifying the heat required to liquify the ore which then could be readily cast. Adding large amounts of charcoal (carbon) to the liquified ore produced a low-grade carbon steel of sufficient quality to cut non-ferrous metals.

Wrought iron was produced by repeatedly heating and chafing the bloom which significantly reduced the carbon content; thus making less brittle iron. Large quantities of wrought iron were produced by the triphammer; an important contribution to technology which appeared in eleventh-century Europe.[46] The triphammer rapidly chafed the carbon out of the bloom and was also used to shape it into various practical forms.

The iron triphammer head was attached to one end of a horizontal beam pivoting around a stationary shaft mounted in a vertical wooden frame. The rapid tripping action of the hammer was accomplished by a revolving shaft usually driven by a waterwheel and provided with a series of cams which intermittently struck (tripped) the beam, violently forcing the hammer head down to strike the bloom against the face of a huge anvil. A counterweight on the opposite end of the beam raised the hammer for another stroke as the hammerman manipulated the bloom.

While low-grade carbon steel was readily made by adding carbon to iron, a superior, high-grade steel was produced by intensifying the temperature of the iron in a process called cementation, producing what

IRON-MAKING KILN (11th-16th Century): Diagramatic of a typical European kiln. The molten iron, heavier than the impurities, settled to the bottom of the kiln and was drained into ingots. Courtesy of the American Iron and Steel Institute, Washington, D.C.

TRIPHAMMER (11th/17th Century): The first triphammers reached colonial America ca. 1645, though more than a century would pass before they were used to make gun barrels. Courtesy of the American Iron and Steel Institute, Washington, D.C.

is known as crucible or blister steel. The ordinary furnace failed to produce the high temperatures required to make crucible steel, so small pieces of iron were densely packed in a clay crucible (hence the name) with a suitable quantity of carbon. The tightly sealed crucible was then subjected to extremely high temperature in a small, bellows-operated, charcoal-fired kiln for 72 hours or more; the intense heat distributing the carbon particles throughout the molecular structure of the iron creating a blistered effect. Because intense, prolonged heat was required, only limited quantities of crucible (blister) steel were produced and its quality was inconsistent.

Bronze was relatively easy to cast, resisted corrosion, and was more ductile than the cast-or wrought-iron of that early period. Bronze was also readily managed with existing hand tools and machines, while the technique of casting in clay moulds was sufficiently advanced and thoroughly familiar, for bronze had been widely used for millennia in making a variety of weapons and utilitarian articles, including such large objects as bells and statuary.

Fourteenth-century armorers devised three barrel-making techniques: casting, forging (hammer welding), and boring. Obviously, there were slight variations in each technique because the craftsman brought his idiosyncrasies to the work. Early gunmakers also devised specialized hand tools and adopted from other crafts boring and grinding machines which they adapted to their needs; those machines initially operated by hand crank and foot treadle, though subsequently employing water, wind, or animal power.

The first barrels for firearms were cast, and the armorer apparently preferred bronze to iron, as exemplified by the Loshult, Tannenberg, and Mörkö hand cannon. Few early fourteenth-century armorers had the knowledge or experience to make reliable cast-iron barrels, for slag intrusions and other impurities weakened the molecular structure of the iron, while the early reduction kiln failed to produce sufficient heat to completely liquify the ore; consequently cast-iron barrels had a propensity to fracture when subjected to the inordinate stress generated by the explosive force of gunpowder.

Bronze or iron barrels were cast in a one-piece mould, the cylindrical bore shaped and centered in the mould by an iron rod (mandrel) slightly smaller in diameter than the desired caliber. The mandrel was then covered with a thin layer of clay and then several layers of either tallow or wax to the proper thickness and dimensions of the breech and barrel with the final layer reflecting the finished pattern. A simple cylinder or vase-like pattern was common early in the century, though hexagonal barrels were later evident as expressed in the design of the Tannenberg and the Mörkö hand cannon.

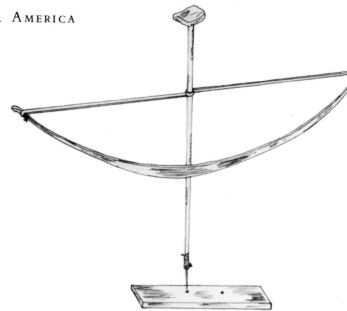

BOW DRILL (Prehistory/18th Century): Derived from the ancient fire-making drill, the bow drill was used for boring holes in various materials and not until the early 18th Century was it displaced by the bitstock. The palm rest atop the bit shaft protected the hand from friction burn. Author's sketch.

A thick layer of clay was applied after the final tallow or wax coating, forming the mould proper. The mould was then fired in a kiln, the heat hardening the exterior clay and the layer covering the mandrel while melting out the tallow or wax in a process known as the lost wax method. Allowed to cool, the mould was then buried in a box of damp sand; the sand firmly tamped around it to preserve the configuration. Molten bronze or iron was poured into the mould. Once set and cool, the mould was then removed from the sand, broken open, and the mandrel extracted; the thin layer of clay having prevented it from adhering to the molten metal.

Whether bronze or iron, the exterior and the interior of the cast barrel was roughly textured. The exterior was smoothed with files or polished on a grinding wheel and the vent was bored through the breech wall by a bow drill; a technological innovation appearing in various forms and surviving prehistory. The bow drill continued to be used for boring small holes until the late eighteenth century.

The interior of the barrel was then bored to the desired caliber; the smaller mandrel allowing for the removal of some of the metal. Initially performed by hand, barrel boring was a difficult, time-consuming process. In the fourteenth century and considerably thereafter the boring tool was either an iron or hardwood rod with a T-shaped handle at one end and a sharp, steel bit attached to the other. Forced into the bore with a twisting motion, the bit removed only a small amount of metal with each turn. To attain the proper bore diameter the process was repeated several times and each time a slightly wider bit was required.

Substantial changes in the shape of the cast barrel came with design improvements as seen in the innovative Tannenberg and Mörkö hand cannon, while subsequent developments rendered cast barrels impractical. Additional modifications occurred when the tiller was supplanted by the gunstock, for barrels were then often cast with integral lugs, though bands were still used occasionally. The stock was mortised to receive the barrel and secured to it by small iron pins transversing the lugs; a method commonly used until the early nineteenth century though others emerged in the interim.

Hand cannon barrels with integrally-cast sights appeared in the late fourteenth century. The front sight was merely a post located at the muzzle and the rear sight a simple protrusion situated atop the breech with a small v-notch filed in the center. It was also during that period that hand cannon emerged displaying the priming pan cast integral with or welded to the right side of the breech; an innovation of major significance which involved relocating the vent. It is likely that the introduction of the rear sight inspired the move because the eye would have been placed in proximity to the vent and priming pan if it had remained atop the breech; a potentially hazardous situation.

Wrought iron, easily worked when reheated in a charcoal forge, was especially suited for barrels because it was softer and more ductile than brittle cast-iron; thus less susceptible to rupturing when sub-

jected to the explosive force of gunpowder. By ca. 1350 European armorers adopted for their barrel-making a method used by the Romans in fabricating lead water pipe which produced a barrel with a longitudinal seam; the interior open from end to end.

In hammer welding (forging) a barrel with a longitudinal seam, a procedure more expeditious and less difficult than casting, the armorer selected several rectangular slabs of wrought iron approximately an inch thick, three to three and a half inches wide, and about 18 inches long; the slab used for the breech slightly thicker to withstand the force of the powder charge.[47]

The breech slab was heated to a malleable state and, for convenience in handling, it was welded to a discarded barrel. The slab was then vigorously hammered in two to three-inch sections around a tapered iron mandrel somewhat smaller than the desired bore diameter. Constantly reheated and hammered, the breech slab was deftly welded to another slab or slabs (depending upon the length of the barrel desired) until they were all drawn into a reasonably cylindrical tube. Throughout the forging process the barrel was worked on an anvil with a number of semi-circular grooves cut into its face; the grooves corresponding to the exterior shape of the breech and barrel.

After the rough forging, during which great care was taken to ensure the integrity of the seam, the exterior of the barrel was dressed (smoothed) using

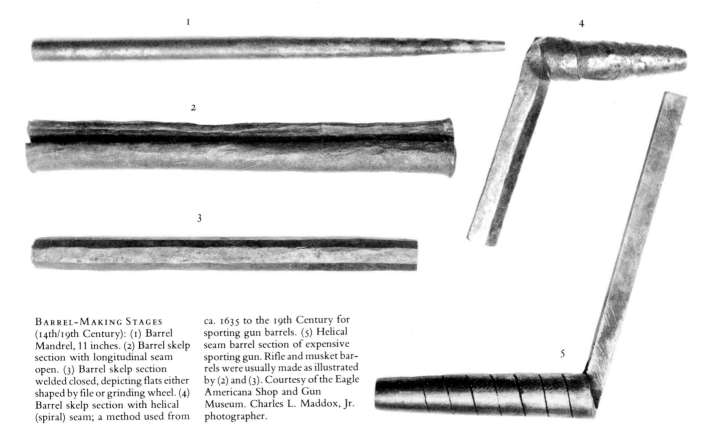

BARREL-MAKING STAGES (14th/19th Century): (1) Barrel Mandrel, 11 inches. (2) Barrel skelp section with longitudinal seam open. (3) Barrel skelp section welded closed, depicting flats either shaped by file or grinding wheel. (4) Barrel skelp section with helical (spiral) seam; a method used from ca. 1635 to the 19th Century for sporting gun barrels. (5) Helical seam barrel section of expensive sporting gun. Rifle and musket barrels were usually made as illustrated by (2) and (3). Courtesy of the Eagle Americana Shop and Gun Museum. Charles L. Maddox, Jr. photographer.

the same methods as described in finishing cast barrels, the vent was drilled, and the interior bored to the desired caliber. The priming pan was then welded to the breech and sights were added in the same manner, followed by the barrel lugs and the barrel hook if required.

While it was easier to drill the bore of a barrel which was open from end to end, it also presented the problem of sealing the breech to prevent the escape of the powder gases. In cast barrels the breech was solid, the closure integral with the mould design. Wrought iron barrels were initially sealed by merely welding the breech; however, at some undetermined time during the late fourteenth or early fifteenth century a solid iron plug was heated and then hammer welded into the breech opening. The solid iron breech plug continued to be used in poor quality firearms until the early nineteenth century, though other breech closures appeared in the interim.

Once the barrel had been completely finished it was mounted on the stock, either secured by bands or the lug-pin arrangement previously noted. Now it remained only to be fired.

A third barrel-making technique emerged in the late fourteenth century and, though failing to survive the first quarter of the fifteenth century, it was resurrected just prior to the mid-nineteenth century. According to German scholar F.M. Feldhaus, barrels were bored through solid wrought iron rods ca. 1370.[48] That method was exceedingly more difficult, expensive, and time-consuming than casting or forging, particularly when considering the rudimentary state of boring technology, and it was probably because of those reasons that boring solid rods was not widely practiced and only briefly employed during that period.

Precisely when cast barrels were supplanted by forged barrels cannot be determined though the transition is believed to have transpired during the first quarter of the sixteenth century. Other barrel-forging techniques appeared as the centuries progressed and they were successfully employed until machines had largely replaced the hammer-forging technique during the late nineteenth century. Wrought iron continued to be the most popular material used for making barrels until the early twentieth century with only minor metallurgical refinements incorporated in the interim.

During the early stages of firearms evolution barrels were finished "bright," i.e., burnished to the natural color of the metal whether bronze or iron. Though bronze was susceptible to corrosion it did not oxidize (rust) like iron. Oxidation produced a surface patina which gradually darkened as it continued to permeate the iron components and it was observed that it ceased after a long period of exposure, leaving a dark, russet finish which came to be called russeting and is now referred to as browning. Prior to the end of the fifteenth century European armorers artificailly induced russeting with an acidic chemical solution which also accelerated the process; however, once treated and inhibited no further oxidation occurred. Russeting provided a pleasing, durable finish which was used until the early twentieth century.

With the advent of the fourteenth century, European armorers had also devised heat treatment techniques to prevent oxidation on body armor and, like russeting, they were subsequently applied to firearms components, though imparting a blue or blue-black finish. Bluing, as it is presently termed, also came to be artificially induced by a chemical solution early in the sixteenth century and it was primarily used on elegant and expensive sporting firearms; however, not until the nineteenth century did the bluing of firearms become a widespread practice.

Most sixteenth-century martial and utilitarian firearms were varnished to preserve the russet finish, though in some instances black paint was applied to the iron components as well as the stock. Rendered from flax seed, linseed oil was also early used as a preservative on gunstocks and it is currently popular.

Corned Powder

The innovative technology early characterizing firearms evolution was also exhibited in powder-making. Cautious experimentation eventually resulted in changing the powder-making process as well as the ratio of the ingredients, e.g., the German formula for serpentine powder ca. 1350 was 4:1:1, though by the turn of the century it had been radically altered to 22:4:5. Variations in the ratio subsequently emerged and some of them produced a more potent propellant.

A partially successful solution to the obvious disadvantages of serpentine powder was found ca. 1425 when it was discovered that the ingredients were more thoroughly blended by adding either water, alcohol derived from distilled spirits, or human urine rich in nitrate.

Combining any of those liquids with serpentine powder produced a viscous paste which was further mixed by constant kneading and pounding. Once blended, the powder paste was moulded into large cakes and dried. The cured powder cake was then judiciously pulverized with a mortar and pestle and the resultant granules or grains were graded according to size by sifting them through a series of fine, wire-mesh sieves; the large grains used in artillery and the small in firearms.

Gunpowder made in that manner came to be called corned powder; an innovation of major significance first described in 1429 by Konrad von Schöngau in his *Feuerbuch* (Fire Book).[49] The "corned" appellation derived from the fact that the small kernels of powder resembled in size the cereal grains like barley, rye, and wheat which were and are collectively referred to as corn in Europe and not, as some writers have suggested, the size of corn kernels in the Western Hemisphere, for Indian maize was unknown in the Old World until the sixteenth century.

The corning process completely amalgamated the ingredients of serpentine powder and thereby produced a superior propellant, for it reduced hygroscopicity and the tendency of the ingredients to solidify, eliminated gravity separation, improved combustion, and distinctly enhanced the explosive force.

Serpentine powder, easier to ignite because of its finer granulation, continued to serve as priming powder while the more potent corned powder was used for the propellant charge. Consequently a loading and a priming flask became necessary accouterments and something of an inconvenience; particularly when firearms came to be widely accepted as martial weapons. And despite the corning process, black powder still produced a generous amount of fouling.

Between 1475 and 1500 European powdermakers devised relatively sophisticated stamping mills for blending the ingredients of gunpowder and equally innovative machines for pulverizing the powder cake. The stamping mill had largely supplanted the simple mortar and pestle prior to the end of the sixteenth century, thereby increasing powder production commensurate with the demand, because during that epoch artillery and firearms became an integral part of warfare.

Like most early machines the first stamping mills were constructed of wood and manually operated. In the stamping mill a large flywheel was attached to a horizontal axle displaying short cams. As the flywheel turned the axle, the cams alternately and intermittently raised and lowered in sequence a series of vertical pestles with bronze heads. The pestles were aligned with corresponding mortar cavities in the mill base. The cavities were filled with moist powder and constantly battered by the pestles which thoroughly mixed the ingredients. The innovative stamping mill performed the work of several powder-makers faster and more economically.

Coeval with the introduction of the stamping mill was the tumbling machine; a simple innovation utilized for pulverizing the powder cake and also adapted to crushing charcoal. First broken into large pieces, the powder cake was loaded into a large barrel transversed by a long shaft connected to a power source. The barrel, rotating in conjunction with the shaft, reduced the powder cake into small granules with its tumbling action.

In some instances several metal balls were placed in the barrel with the powder cake, accelerating the tumbling process. Iron balls were initially used, though they produced dangerous sparks when they struck each other; a hazard eliminated by substituting non-ferrous balls.

Though the machines and techniques employed in powder-making became larger and more sophisticated as the centuries progressed, and while gunpowder underwent innumerable changes in the ratio of the ingredients, no substantial improvement in either occurred until the latter half of the eighteenth century.

POWDER-STAMPING MILL (17th Century): This engraving from Georg Andreas Boeckler, *Theatrum Machinarum Novum* (Noribergae, 1661), depicts a water-powered stamping mill which amalgamated the ingredients of gunpowder by heavy pestles (D) raised and lowered via a series of cams (C) arranged on the horizontal shaft (B) driven by the waterwheel (A). An attendant (foreground) mixes the ingredients in the mortar boxes comprising the mill base, while another (background) sifts the powder granules. Courtesy of Eleutherian Mills Historical Library, Wilmington, Del.

Armorers, Gun-Founders and Gunsmiths

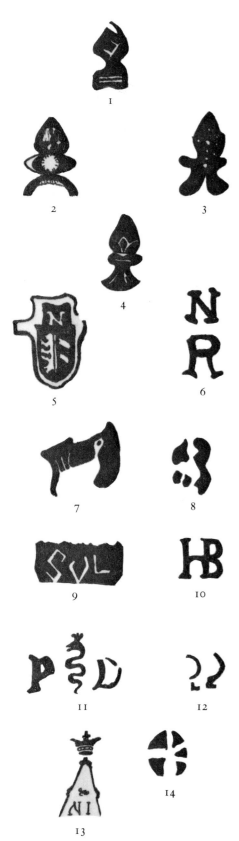

CONTROL AND GUNSMITHS' MARKS (15th/16th Century): (1) Augsburg (Ger.) city control mark ca. 1480 is thought to be the earliest used. (2) Augsburg city control mark ca. 1550. (3) Augsburg city control mark for muskets ca. 1590. (4) Augsburg city control mark on a wheellock pistol ca. 1590. (5) Nuremburg (Ger.) city control mark with split eagle ca. 1585. (6) Nuremburg city control mark ca. 1595. (7) Suhl (Ger.) city control mark for martial muskets ca. 1570. (8) Suhl city control mark for martial muskets ca. 1590. (9) Suhl city control mark ca. 1590. (10) Signature mark of gunsmith H. Bahr, Dresden and Nuremburg ca. 1585-1627. (11) Signature mark of gunsmith Peter Dauer, Nuremburg ca. 1595; snake symbol is Nuremburg city control mark. (12) Double sickle signature mark of gunsmith Simon Marquart (fl. 1519-1540) who was brought to Madrid from Augsburg by Carlos I of Spain; Simon's brother and sons used similar marks. (13) Signature mark of Negroli family of Milan (It.) armorers ca. 1498-1561. (14) Mark on a 16th Century combination snaphaunce pistol and battle axe. Author's sketch, not to scale.

There was no readily discernable distinction between the armorer, gun-founder, and gunsmith during the early stages of firearms evolution. The ancient armorer was essentially a blacksmith who began to specialize in making weapons and armor; ranking among the few professional, technologically-oriented craftsmen of Classical antiquity. With the advent of gunpowder weapons the armorer continued in that important techonomic role.

European armorers began to diversify early in the fourteenth century and by ca. 1350 several specialized in gun-founding, producing crude cannon, mortars, and firearms. Gunsmithing in the presently accepted sense, however, was not firmly established as an independent craft on the Continent until the early sixteenth century and considerably later in England and Scotland.

The gun-founder early occupied a unique position in the rigid social structure characterizing the Feudal Age. Gun founders not only designed and cast heavy ordnance and firearms, but were involved in powder-making, while in many instances they served as gunners for the weapons they made. Consequently, as the European armament race accelerated, the diverse and specialized talents of the gun founder were eagerly sought.

Subsidized by a host of assorted emperors, kings, princes, *petit* barons, and not a few aspiring despots, the mercenary gun founders commanded and received more than adequate compensation for their sundry skills, not the least of which included the choicest plunder following a victorious campaign as well as the "right to the bells," which gave them first claim to any captured bronze or iron bells, for during that epoch there was often a scarcity of suitable gun-making metal.[50]

Exorbitant sums and equally generous promises were lavishly expended to lure master gun founders from their employers and, often as not, such blandishments were readily accepted. If captured, gun founders were generally spared because of their expertise, though in some instances they preferred to switch allegiance. Neither was it unheard of for Christian gun founders to accept employment from what was then considered the "infidel" Moslem. Flemish, German, and Italian gun founders developed the craft into a fine art during the late fourteenth century and they were in great demand throughout the Old World.

Guilds were early established to protect, preserve, and perpetuate the invaluable skills of the gun-founder and many of the technological innovations characterizing the craft were jealously guarded secrets. Like the venerated and highly skilled armorer of Classical antiquity, the Renaissance gun-founder was among the first to feel the burgeoning influence of governmental regulation concerning the quality, quantity, and distribution of his products.

The powerful ruling houses of Europe as well as a number of city-states, independent principalities, and self-proclaimed republics early enacted legislation dealing with arms manufacture and procurement, including provisions for identifying the gun-founder and the quality of his work.[51] Those provisions introduced the control mark. Control marks were used as early as 1450, usually appearing in the form of heraldic crests, official seals, or other appropriate symbols which were stamped or engraved in the breech or elsewhere on the barrel by authorized officials. In some instances the gun-founder signed his work with a personal mark.

Harsh penalties, even death, were prescribed for gun-founders making inferior weapons or selling them without authorization, yet poor quality weapons continued to be made and a profitable clandestine commerce in ordnance emerged.

The gunsmith, like his gun-founder predecessor, also profited from his extraordinary technical skills and many of the most gifted received lifetime appointments to the royal court or the crown; an enviable position with several attendant benefits often including free lodging, clothing and food allowances, and a pension which, in some instances, continued to be paid to his heirs. Gunsmiths were also early represented by guilds and came under government regulation.

Like the gun-founder, the gunsmith early identified his work with his initials, signature, or other suitable symbols; frequently combining them. Signature marks were usually stamped or engraved on the breech of the firearm and they are frequently mistaken for control marks or proof marks; the latter a special designation also varying in design and indicating that the barrel had been tested at a guild or government proofhouse and found acceptable under established quality standards.

Though quality standards varied throughout Europe, the strength of the barrel was usually determined by firing it with a double charge of gunpowder and a single ball. If the barrel remained intact, the proofmaster or his representative applied the official proof mark. Penalties, including fines and imprisonment, were levied against those who sold unproved barrels, while some gunsmiths not only counterfeited official proof marks but signature marks as well.

HANDCANNONEERS (15th Century, 1469): The handcannoneer (center) in this illumination (*Burney M S*, No. 169, Folio 127) depicting an attack on a fortress is manually applying a firestick to the vent. Courtesy of the British Museum, London.

Match Ignition

A more convenient ignition agent appeared in Europe prior to the end of the fourteenth century though when and where it was initially employed in firearms remains speculative. Called slow match, matchcord, or simply match, it was a novel innovation possibly derived from the quick-burning fuze (quick match) early used as the ignition agent with pyrotechnics and some forms of artillery. The glowing wire or smouldering tinder initially employed as the ignition agent in firearms was not immediately supplanted by matchcord, for the *Burney Manuscript* of 1469 depicts hand cannoneers still using the fire stick.[52]

Slow match was a cord made of cotton, flax, or hemp fibers soaked in a saltpeter/water solution, twisted, and then dried. Properly made matchcord burned slowly and evenly, producing a hard, pointed tip and leaving a fine ash. Matchcord was consumed at a rate of four to five inches per hour, determined by fiber density and the amount of saltpeter in the solution.

ANCIENT FIREARMS (14th/15th Century): Top to bottom. (1) Arrow-firing handcannon or rocket gun with copper barrel using a fuze for ignition depicted in the Chinese *Wu-Pei-Chih*. (2) Serpentine with front sight and flash deflector, German ca. 1420. (3) Serpentine with pivoting arm mounted at left, from *Codex 3069* dated 1411. (4) Cast-iron handcannon with breech and barrel flats, European ca. 1430. (5) Hand culverin (serpentine) with pivoting arm mounted at the right in conventional manner; priming pan at the side of the breech, European ca. 1440. Author's sketch.

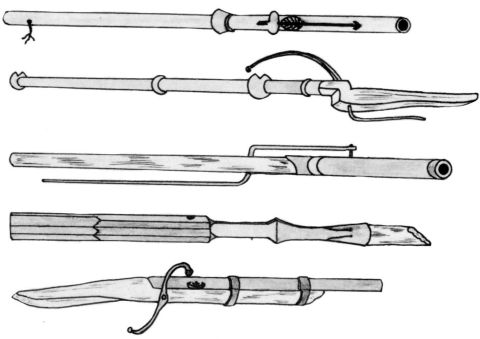

Serpentine Firearms

The evolution of any practical invention is normally accompanied by an evaluation period during which its potential is examined and improvements made where applicable and possible. Hand cannon were no exception and, by the dawn of the fifteenth century, they had reached a relatively high plateau of development.

The potential for improving hand cannon was obvious and the technology available, yet the catalyst remains unknown. In any event there appeared in Europe ca. 1400 a form of hand cannon incorporating match ignition; a radical technological innovation now known as the serpentine. The use of matchcord in serpentine firearms eliminated the fire stick and provided more control when firing; a positive accomplishment leading to further exploitation and innovation.

An S-shaped metal arm, termed a serpentine because of its obvious snake-like form, pivoted freely on a pin set into the right side of the hand cannon stock at the breech. The short, upper curve of the S had a loop or notch which held a suitable length of smouldering match. The longer, lower curve stabilized the arm, keeping the match away from the priming pan mounted on the breech, and also served as a firing lever or what can be described as a rudimentary trigger.

When the lower curve of the serpentine arm was manually drawn rearward, the upper curve with the match rotated forward, igniting the priming powder in the pan. It has been suggested that the innovative serpentine arm inspired the relocation of the priming pan from the top to the side of the breech though hand cannon without the serpentine often display the pan at the side.

Dated 1411, the *Codex 3069* in the Vienna National Library depicts what is possibly the first example of a serpentine firearm.[53] The weapon displays an extremely long arm attached to the left side of the stock, the lower segment passing beneath the barrel to the right. A contemporaneous Froissart manuscript in the Breslau City Library illustrates a satyr holding a serpentine firearm though the S-shaped arm is much smaller and mounted conventionally on the right side of the breech.[54]

Serpentine firearms had become more complex by midcentury. Sketches in the *Codex 1390* of ca. 1450-1460, preserved in the Erlangen (Germany) University Library, depict specimens incorporating sights and flash deflectors.[55] The innovative serpentine arm, combined with matchcord, was a significant factor in the subsequent development of the first gunlock and therefore serpentine firearms can be considered a transitional link between firearms with mechanical ignition and those without.

The Gunlock

Much supposition surrounds the origin and early evolution of the first mechanical ignition system which, in conjunction with the barrel and the stock, was the third basic firearms component: the gunlock or, simply, the lock. The term *lock* is a misnomer when referring to firearms emerging prior to the sixteenth century because the first gunlock was designed to convey the ignition agent to the priming pan rather than restrain or "lock" any part of the mechanism. More appropriate is the term *ignition mechanism* though both appellations are used here for clarity and convenience.

Identifying firearms by the ignition agent or mechanism is common practice. The first ignition mechanism, designated the matchlock because it used matchcord, is believed to have been devised in Germany ca. 1440-1470, though it is possible that it originated elsewhere in western Europe during that period.

The matchlock mechanism is similar in design to the pivotal sear arrangement devised for releasing the string of the powerful crossbow; a mechanism which can be traced to the eleventh century, though the crossbow is a resurrected variant of the much larger *scorpio* known to Classical antiquity. The serpentine arm, combined with the bowstring release mechanism (sear), emerged as the matchlock.

The first matchlocks were of the pressure type or so-called C pattern; a remarkably simple though revolutionary device with two operating parts: the serpentine arm and the pivotal sear. Those components were incorporated in a flat, rectangular plate (lockplate) mortised into the right side of stock and usually retained by three transverse screws.

Parenthetically, the screws securing the lockplates of the various firearms mentioned in the text bear no relation to the now common helically-threaded (spiral) wood screw; rather they are more akin to the threaded bolt known in Europe as early as A.D. 60 (see p. 32).

In the C pattern matchlock the serpentine arm was altered to an inverted C. Facing the breech, the upper curl of the serpentine was provided with jaws to hold the match; the jaws subsequently displaying a small turnscrew for securing the match and adjusting it when preparing to fire. The lower serpentine curl had a short shank transversing the lockplate at the forward end; the shank attached to a stationary, slotted tumbler.

The nose of the elongated, pivotal sear engaged the tumbler slot inside the lockplate and an L-shaped firing lever was screwed into the sear heel, passing through a slot in the stock and protruding beneath it. An internal leaf spring exerted constant pressure on the pivotal sear either from above or below, maintaining its stability which prevented the serpentine from moving until the firing lever was squeezed.

Squeezing the L-shaped firing lever lifted the sear heel, pivoting the nose down and simultaneously rotating the tumbler attached to the serpen-

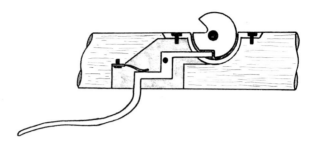

CROSSBOW MECHANISM (10th/15th Century): The bow string was held in the groove of the rotating "nut." The sear nose, engaging a notch in the nut, prevented it from turning. Raising the pivotal lever disengaged the sear nose, thereby releasing the bow string. The sear lever is similar to that employed with the matchlock mechanism. Author's sketch.

MATCHLOCK MECHANISM (15th/18th Century): Top, common C pattern matchlock mechanism with lever trigger. Bottom, a matchlock variant called a sear lock. A short, L-shaped tang at the end of the sear bar extended to contact a conventional trigger. Author's sketch.

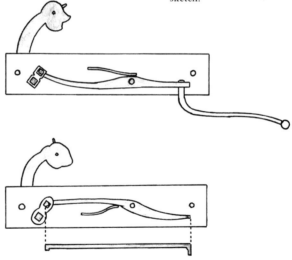

tine shank. As the tumbler was forced to the rear it took with it the serpentine, dropping the lighted match into the priming pan to effect ignition. When the firing lever was released, spring pressure on the pivotal sear lifted the nose attached to the tumbler and the serpentine returned to its former position.

While the position of the sear spring and the size and shape of the lockplate and its components varied, owing to geography and the idiosyncrasies of the craftsman, the functioning cycle was identical in the majority of the C pattern matchlocks produced in Europe for more than two centuries.

Though it was a distinctly radical innovation, the simplicity of the C pattern matchlock rendered it easy to make and repair and it was also inexpensive, sturdy, and fairly reliable despite the disadvantages of matchcord. Significantly, the matchlock mechanism engendered several design changes which made firearms easier to operate and control than its immediate predecessor or the venerable hand cannon. Those considerations were responsible for the lasting popularity of matchlock firearms, particularly as martial weapons, despite the subsequent introduction of more reliable ignition systems.

Matchcord did not entirely satisfy the requirements for an adequate ignition agent because, like gunpowder, it was subject to the caprice of the natural elements, had a distinctive odor, visibly glowed at night, and in daylight the smoke it produced was often readily detected. Usually provided in two to three foot lengths, matchcord was lighted at each end when any immediate action was anticipated; thus ensuring ignition if one end of the cord was extinguished. Matchcord was either carried coiled in the hand or looped around the stock wrist for convenience, one end always secured in the serpentine jaws. Despite its obvious disadvantages, matchcord served as the ignition agent in firearms for nearly three centuries.

The diversity of design innovation conspicuous throughout the evolution of the hand cannon was also evident in matchlock firearms and additional innovations subsequently emerged. Dated ca. 1470-75 the *Codex Germanicus 599* (Munich State Library) depicts a matchlock firearm displaying several design innovations and it is attributed to Martin Merz (Mercz), the most renowned firearms authority of his time.

In the Merz matchlock the serpentine faced the muzzle, opposite of the common C pattern though characterizing most oriental matchlocks and some European variations; each appearing somewhat later. There was no firing lever, the functioning cycle of the lock initiated by pressing a button-head rod concealed in the forestock; a device noted in earlier crossbows and subsequently used in firearms during the early sixteenth century. The Merz matchlock was also provided with an iron rather than wooden ramrod, anticipating the widespread adoption of the former by nearly three centuries.

BREECH PLUGS (14th/19th Century): Top to bottom. (1) Solid iron breech plug welded in wrought iron barrel ca. 1425. (2) Solid iron breech plug with tang ca. 1440. (3) Threaded breech plug with tang ca. 1455. (4) Top view of threaded breech plug depicting notch cut for vent clearance. Author's sketch.

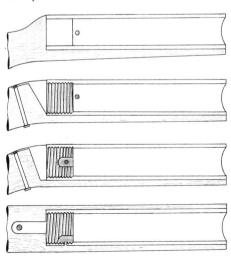

Firearms similar to the Merz matchlock and several other contemporary weapons are color-illustrated in the *Codex Monacensis 222* (Munich State Library), part of the nineteen-volume *Zeügbucher* (arsenal books) prepared by various artists at the behest of Maximilian I, Emperor of the Holy Roman Empire (1459-1519). Maximilian expressed a profound interest in firearms technology and maintained at Innsbruck one of the largest arsenals in fifteenth-century Europe.

Shortly after the introduction of matchlock firearms an improved breech-sealing method appeared in the form of a threaded breech plug. Screwed into the breech rather than welded, the breech plug subsequently featured a short tang (extension) mortised into the upper stock wrist. The tang was secured by a long screw transversing the stock wrist from below; further strengthening the bond between the barrel and the stock and also subsequently serving as the rear trigger guard screw.

The threaded breech plug could be readily removed and it was therefore reusable. A significant innovation, the threaded breech plug made it easier to rebore the barrel if necessary or remove an obstruction. Not until the mid-eighteenth century would the threaded breech plug see substantial improvement, further enhancing the efficacy of firearms.

Throughout the various stages of firearms evolution a transition period occurred during which existing weapons systems were eventually replaced by more efficent systems. The transition was neither immediate nor simultaneous owing to economic conditions, the state of technology, the dissemination of technical knowledge, and the skill exhibited by the artisan.

The lack of standardization in firearms manufacture was also influenced by those variable considerations, as well as the idiosyncrasies of the craftsman; factors preëminent in firearms evolution until the late nineteenth century when machines had generally replaced the human element involved.

When hand cannon and serpentine firearms were gradually supplanted by various kinds of matchlock weapons during the transition period ca. 1475-1525, the Teutonic descriptive *hakenbüchse* (hook gun) or its variants were often interpreted as firearms with or without a lock mechanism; thus creating almost insurmountable identification problems among historians. Meanwhile, the hook from which *hakenbüchse* had been derived became less evident, disappearing entirely by the beginning of the seventeenth century.

In Spain *hakenbüchse* was borrowed almost intact, appearing as *hacabuche*. The Italians knew the term as *archibuso*, and in England it was called a *hakbut, hagbutt, harkbutte,* or similar variants. The

French equivalent of hook, *arque,* became a prefix for the corrupted German *Büchse* (—bus), emerging as *arquebus* or *harquebus.* The French employed *arquebusier* or *harquebusier* to describe a gunsmith or one who used firearms and the Spanish equivalent was *arcubucero;* however, the French terms transcended the centuries to enter the modern English lexicon.

The first quarter of the sixteenth century saw the matchlock arquebus emerge as a martial weapon, while thereafter the role of firearms continuously escalated in domestic and military affairs; primarily as hunting or utilitarian weapons in regard to the former. And it was in the sixteenth century, as the Renaissance blossomed, that firearms technology advanced at an unprecedented rate.

MULTI-SHOT FIREARMS (15th/16th Century): This water color plate from Maximilian's *Zëugbucher* depicts two kinds of early multi-shot firearms. Top: Armorers firing a four-shot handcannon, each barrel independently mounted at the corner of a simple board stock. Note the firestick holding the match. Bottom: Armorer supporting a three-barreled *hakenbüchse* (arquebus) with a fourquine wedged against the hook. The serpentine is provided with a piece of tinder rather than match. Courtesy of the *Kunsthistorische Museum,* Vienna.

MATCHLOCK ARQUEBUSES (15th/16th Century): Another plate from the *Zëugbucher,* illustrated by Nicolaus Glockenthon, depicts an armorer firing a matchlock arquebus. Note the absence of a discernable trigger, indicating that a button-head trigger concealed in the forestock released the sear. Similar firearms are displayed on the wall rack. Armorer (foreground) appears to be loading or cleaning an arquebus. Courtesy of the *Kunsthistorisches Museum,* Vienna.

Rifling

Like many early achievements in firearms evolution the appearance of rifling is also obscured by the mists of time. What precise logic inspired that radical departure from smoothbore firearms cannot be determined; however, it is generally attributed to fifteenth-century armorers attempting to eliminate the inherent problem of powder fouling.

WALL [PARAPET/RAMPART] GUN (15th/16th Century): This *Zëugbucher* illustration depicts two armorers firing a heavy arquebus supported by a wooden tripod wedged against the barrel hook perhaps designed for the purpose. As one armorer aims, the other applies the firestick to the vent to effect ignition. Courtesy of the *Kunsthistorisches Museum,* Vienna.

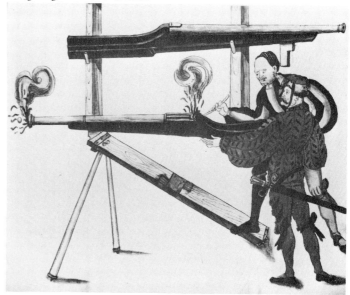

Der Büchsenmacher (THE GUNSMITH, 17th Century): This engraving from Christoff Weigel, *Abbildung der gemein-nutzlichen Haupt-Staende* (Illustrations of the Most Useful and Important Crafts [Augsburg, 1698]), depicts a master gunsmith's shop. The gunsmith (foreground) secures a barrel in the boring engine as an apprentice cranks the large wheel which rotates the boring tool.

Another apprentice (background) is rifling a barrel using a T-handle rifling rod. A bow drill or barrel straightening bow hangs from the wall as does a combination matchlock/wheellock firearm (extreme right). Note the screw plate on the workbench (left), used for cutting the threads on gun screws as early as ca. 1480. Courtesy of the *Bayerische Staatsbibliothek*, Munich.

In any event there appeared in southern Germany ca. 1460 a number of matchlock firearms with eight to ten wide, parallel grooves cut into the bore; the grooves apparently designed to trap the fouling below the bore surface which would permit more shots to be fired before cleaning it. Although it was an effective solution, there was room for improvement and a now anonymous savant reasoned that helical (spiral) grooves would present more surface area in which to trap the fouling, with the result that the ball flew farther and faster with much greater accuracy.

That early artisan had reproduced a phenomenon first observed in Classical antiquity, for it was then recognized that fletched arrows rotated in flight and went farther than those without vanes; the spinning motion imparting greater stability. And that was the possible reason why the arrow-like missile continued to be used in firearms for nearly two centuries.

Despite the rudimentary science of ballistics explored by Nicola Fontana Tartaglia (1500-1557) and Galileo (1564-1642), the phenomenon of the spinning projectile was not satisfactorily explained until 1747 when English mathematician Benjamin Robbins (1707-1751) presented his *Observations on the Nature and Advantages of Rifled Barrel Pieces.*

There is little doubt that rifles were known beyond the borders of Germany by 1475, for Maj. Angelo Angelucci mentioned in his *Catalogo della Armeria Reale* (Catalog of the Royal Armory, [Turin: 1890]) a 1476 inventory listing a *"sclopetus unus ferri factus lumage"* (a firearm with a spiral grooved barrel).[56] Thereafter references to rifles and rifling frequently appeared in European literature, most of them suspect regarding the inventor or precisely when that portentous technological achievement occurred.

For many years European rifle-making was centered in the alpine regions of southern Germany and northern Switzerland, and it was there that rifles were developed as sporting firearms, sufficiently sophisticated by 1487 to participate in a *Scheibenschiessen* (target match) at Eichstaedt, competing at a distance of 200 meters; a respectable challenge for the modern rifle.[57]

Organized shooting matches, a form of practice as well as entertainment, were an integral part of the social scene in Europe and elsewhere long before firearms were invented. Firearms competition was separated from archery during the latter half of the fifteenth century, and prior to the end of that epoch it was found that the smoothbore arquebus was no match for the accuracy of the rifle and the latter was banned from competition with the former.

What is believed to be the earliest extant example of a rifle is a bronze-barreled matchlock made for Emperor Maximilian I by an unknown riflesmith between 1493 and 1508,[58] and the powerful Hapsburg ruler also described using firearms for the chase in his *Hunting Book* of ca. 1499-1500.

That rifles existed in the late fifteenth century presupposes the evolution of specialized tools designed to cut the parallel or helical grooves in the bore and demonstrates the advanced technological expertise attained by the German gunsmiths specializing in the craft; because they developed the tools and techniques capable of cutting uniform groves in bronze or iron.

Rifling the bore was a precision task initially performed by hand and even more difficult than boring, requiring an exceptional amount of patience, skill, and mathematical ability. The innovative rifling rod was derived from the boring rod, though unlike the latter with its straight, double-edged bit, the rifling rod was provided with a flat, serrated bit or saw; the sharp teeth arranged in a single line on the bit surface. When cutting the grooves for spiral ri-

Der Büchsenschiffter (THE STOCKMAKER, 17th Century): Also from Weigel, this engraving depicts a master stockmaker skillfully finishing the stock where the trigger will be fitted.

An apprentice is perfecting his skills at the workbench and a workman is delivering a supply of rough-hewn stock blanks. Courtesy of the *Bayerisches Staatsbibliothek,* Munich.

fling the bit was forced to describe a helical path from the breech to the muzzle. The rifling rod was also provided with a T-shaped handle.

It is likely that the invention of rifling inspired the relocation of the bit from the end of the boring rod to the surface, for in rifling the saw was mortised into a hardwood rod and a thin material of some sort was inserted beneath it, i.e., a shim. To reach the desired depth of the groove, additional shims were inserted under the saw after each pass through the barrel; thus a single saw could be used rather than increasing its size as necessitated with boring bits.

The riflesmith found it extremely difficult to properly control the rifling rod and at some undetermined time, probably between ca. 1485 and 1525, a machine was devised which eliminated the problem. The rifling engine as it came to be known was constructed of wood and mounted in a horizontal wooden frame now referred to as a rifling bench (see p. 271).

The pre-bored barrel was rigidly clamped to the rifling bench and the rifling rod was inserted in the barrel with the saw at the breech and the opposite end fastened to a cylindrical guide into which a series of helical grooves were mortised (straight grooves for parallel rifling). The grooved guide was mounted in a sliding frame with a T-shaped handle and encompassed by an index plate provided with a series of notches corresponding in number to the cylinder grooves. An alignment stud (finger) extended from one of the index plate notches to the guide groove.

When the T-shaped frame handle was turned it rotated the cylindrical guide and rifling rod simulta-

neously, the movement of the guide directed by the index plate finger engaging the spiral groove which determined the twist (pitch) of the cut, usually making one and a half turns from the breech to the muzzle. The guide reproduced successive cuts exactly like the first; the riflesmith adjusting the elevation of the saw with a shim prior to each cut until reaching the desired groove depth. The width of the groove corresponded to the saw width.

After the first groove was cut the riflesmith readjusted the index finger, aligning it with another groove in the guide cylinder, and the process was repeated until the desired number of grooves had been cut into the bore; the space between the guide grooves preserving the proper alignment of the corresponding bore grooves. The spaces separating the grooves in the bore came to be called lands.

A competent riflesmith could machine-rifle a barrel in ten to twelve hours depending upon the number and the depth of the grooves, which was about half the time consumed in the hand method. Bores with as many as ten or as few as two grooves were early known, though the usual number was six to eight, while in some instances an odd number was cut. In early rifles the grooves were deep and square-shouldered. The horizontal rifling engine was also adapted for drilling smoothbore barrels and it served continuously until superseded by more sophisticated, power-driven machines in the nineteenth century.[59]

Fifteenth-century small arms ballistics remained a problematical, hit-or-miss proposition, consequently the early riflesmith devoted considerable time and effort conducting numerous experiments to determine the most effective twist to apply to the rifling; that factor influencing the spinning motion of the ball inside the barrel (internal ballistics) and its stability in flight (external ballistics).

Numerous theories were devised and applied regarding the number and the design of the lands and grooves as well as how barrel length effected the range and accuracy of the ball. Experiments were also conducted to determine the proper powder charge because sufficient force was required to overcome the inertia and the friction of the lead ball pressed into the rifling while preserving the velocity needed for accuracy and range. Several kinds of rifling emerged as a result of those experiments, some discarded as impractical and others reflected in current designs.

That the revolutionary concept of the rifle failed for many years to transcend the boundaries of Germany and Switzerland is as difficult to understand as why the military potential of the rifle was so obviously ignored, with minor exceptions, for more than three centuries.

Denmark was the first nation to employ the rifle for military use though it was restricted to the King's Bodyguards, issued in limited numbers ca. 1600,[60] and while it subsequently emerged to participate in warfare later in the century it was not considered a practical martial firearm.

The immediate, widespread acceptance of the rifle as a military firearm was limited by a combination of factors, principally the scarcity of skilled riflesmiths, the fact that they were difficult to make and consequently expensive, and the financial burden caused by rearmament and retraining during the great number of wars disrupting Europe over the centuries. The most formidable barrier to the popular use of the rifle, however, was the inordinately tedious loading procedure.

Because the bore was rifled, the term believed to be derived from the Middle High German *riffeln* (to cut or groove), the soft lead ball had to grip the lands and grooves tightly in order to obtain the full benefit of the spinning motion imparted by the twist, as well as to provide sufficient obturation for maximum velocity. Consequently, the ball was cast slightly larger than bore diameter and was, with some difficulty, literally pounded down the bore with a ramrod and mallet rather than merely dropped in as exemplified with smoothbore firearms.

A solution was found ca. 1590-1600 with the introduction of the greased, cloth bullet patch.[61] To compensate for the thickness of the lubricated patch the rifle ball was cast slightly undersize and was more easily loaded though some force was still necessary. While the patched ball was a significant technological improvement, the rifle could not as yet be loaded as rapidly as smoothbore firearms and the latter continued to reign supreme for more than four centuries.

The leading problem was more severe in rifles than smoothbore firearms because the soft ball was vigorously forced into the rifling when loading and firing. The lubricated patch partially solved the problem though a number of purists refused to use it, asserting the bare ball was more accurate because it directly gripped the rifling.

After considerable experimentation it was found ca. 1625 that adding tin and antimony to the lead when casting produced a hard ball less inclined to strip in the bore; the degree of hardness determined by the amount of tin and antimony alloyed with the lead.[62] Though a step in the right direction, that technological innovation was not a positive solution.

The accuracy of the rifle was to a large extent dependent upon several factors, including the pitch of the rifling, the fit of the ball in the bore, the strength of the powder charge, and the ability of the rifleman to judge distance and wind velocity correctly. Most important, however, was the concentricity of the bore in relation to the axis of the barrel, i.e., whether the barrel was as absolutely straight as the riflesmith could make it.

In cast barrels the mandrel centered the bore in the mould, though in forged barrels the vigorous hammer welding distorted the metal. Little attention was early given to whether smoothbore barrels were perfectly straight, for hand cannon and serpentine firearms were relatively short-barreled and accuracy was no criterion for efficacy. A crooked rifle barrel, however, was inaccurate no matter how precise the grooves were cut.

Obviously, the barrel was straightened before the bore was rifled and the method devised was an important technological innovation probably introduced by late fifteenth-century riflesmiths. The barrel straightening technique was subsequently adopted for smoothbore firearms though not until the late nineteenth century were machines devised to perform the task. Parenthetically, the ancient method is currently employed by a select handful of master gunsmiths engaged in making custom shotguns.

The initial step in straightening the barrel was to polish the bore and that was accomplished by what is now termed lapping. During the early stages of firearms evolution the bore was lapped with a wad of tow moistened with oil and saturated with fine emery powder. The tow was affixed to a scower (wipe) attached to a long wooden rod which was then repeatedly thrust through the bore until the abrasive emery powder produced a mirror-like finish.

The bore was then scrupulously cleaned and transversed with a fine silk thread stretched between the points of a wooden bow to keep it taut. With the bow held to prevent the thread from touching the bore, the barrel was raised to a natural light source. The thread cast a readily detected shadow on the polished bore surface and any irregularities were revealed if the shadow deviated from a straight line.

Once any irregularities in the bore had been detected, the exterior of the barrel was chalk-marked to correspond with their position, the thread removed, and the barrel placed in an anvil groove and struck at the marked areas sufficiently hard with a hammer to straighten the bore at those crucial points. The entire process was then repeated, several times if necessary, until it was determined that no irregularities remained.

Straightening a barrel was an onerous, time-consuming chore entirely dependent on the skill and perseverance of the craftsman and many of them failed to master the technique. Consequently, the art of straightening a barrel early became a specialized craft and, by virtue of their extraordinary talent, barrel straighteners were in great demand with their uncommonly high wages reflecting their skill.

Change and Challenge

The burgeoning demand for heavy ordnance (artillery), firearms, and gunpowder during the fourteenth century and thereafter engendered a complex pattern of socio-economic and technological change in feudal Europe. The monopolistic enterprise early established by the gun-founder gradually succumbed to a trend toward specialization which saw powder-making and gunsmithing emerge as separate crafts in the following century with the gunsmithing craft even then reflecting a measure of diversity as exemplified by the riflesmith and barrel straightener.

The rapid growth of the military armament industry prior to the sixteenth century also inaugurated the establishment of permanent arsenals and armories employing a stable cadre of loyal, experienced artisans, while vigorously stimulating the development of a lucrative, widespread commerce in all kinds of weaponry and the various commodities and services either directly or indirectly vital to the support of the armament industry.

A large, diversified, and continuously expanding labor force was required to support the growing armament industry and it was subsidized by the various ruling powers and supervised by the increasingly powerful network of guilds spreading over the Continent. Significantly, guilds sponsored rigorous apprentice programs which provided the skilled craftsmen essential to the future of the fledgling industry.

Skilled and semi-skilled laborers constructed arsenals, armories, magazines, powder mills, furnaces, forges, and other industry-related installations, as well as the requisite boring, grinding, hammering, rifling, stamping, and tumbling machines which proliferated during and after the late fourteenth century. In addition, heavy machinery like waterwheels, windmills, and treadmills were built to supply the power for those early machine tools.

Laborers were also needed for mining and refining saltpeter and sulphur, as well as providing the huge quantities of lime, iron, copper, tin, and lead required by the industry, while there were a host of menial chores and a wide range of ancillary tasks like making accessories, accouterments, projectiles, and associated articles. And it was also the laborer who transported and distributed those commodities.

Essential to the survival of that early military-industrial complex, however, was charcoal. Charcoal had been and remained for centuries the most vital element in the European economic system because it was the basic energy source. Not only was charcoal requisite for the manufacture of iron, steel, and gunpowder, but it served as fuel for the forge and furnace. The vast forests of continental Europe provided sufficient quantities of wood suitable for making charcoal throughout the centuries though that was not the rule in England.

By the late sixteenth century the huge amounts of wood consumed for making charcoal seriously depleted English forests, resulting in protests from early environmentalists, the armament industry, and a host of others lamenting the exorbitant cost of charcoal and the wide range of products made by or with it.[63] Significantly, deforestation hastened the use of fossil fuels in England much earlier than elsewhere in the known world.

The often profligate fiscal expenditures attending the accelerated European armament race frequently stripped already depleted national treasuries, while the demand for raw materials threatened national resources; however, the latter produced several positive reactions because it forced further investigations into the undiscovered secrets of chemistry and metallurgy, inspired technological innovation and improvization, sparked the search for and exploitation of additional sources of raw material, and expanded trade relations with other nations.

There were also a number of negative aspects involved in the armament race, for it escalated inflation, created burdensome taxation, and fostered unbridled human exploitation, while often intensifying national rivalries which frequently exploded into devastating warfare; thus engendering a variety of socio-economic ills during a restless epoch distinctly characterized by both beauty and incandescence, and by brutality and injustice.

Either unconsciously overlooked or deliberately ignored by many historians is that the factory system, believed to have originated with the proliferation of the late eighteenth-century British textile industry which supposedly gave birth to the misnamed Industrial Revolution, was clearly discernable in Europe by the first half of the fifteenth century.[64]

Factories by any other name were the flourishing arsenals, armories, and powder mills representative of the fifteenth-century armament industry, for they were central locations where skilled and unskilled labor, raw materials, rudimentary science, power-driven machines, and innovative technology were all cohesively and intelligently combined under controlled management and supervision to make specific products for a continuously expanding market.

One of the first and largest arms-making factories emerging in Europe was the Perugia Arsenal established in Italy prior to 1364. At the beginning of the fifteenth century the foremost arsenal in southern Europe was located at Venice, and the Venetians also operated a cannon foundry at Brescia, while Maximilian I subsidized the then famous Innsbruck Arsenal.

The Venice Arsenal was exceptionally well organized and the Venetians had early devised a surprisingly efficient system of preparing their war galleys for immediate action. The following passage is a contemporary account of the Venetian system, and the analogy to assembly line production is obvious:

And as one enters the gate [lock] there is a great street [canal] on either hand, and [on] one side are windows opening out of the houses of the Arsenal, and the same on the other side, and out came a galley, towed by a boat, and from the windows they handed out to them, from one the cordage, from another the bread, from another the arms, and from another the balista [cannon] and mortars, and so from all sides everything which was required, and when the galley had reached the end of the street all the men required were on board, together with the complement of oars, and she was equipped from end to end. In this manner there came out ten galleys, fully armed, between the hours of three and nine.[65]

Fifteenth-century Venetians were then using a method commonly employed in the present industrial system, however, emerging much earlier were the radical innovations of mass production and interchangeable components currently utilized by all modern industry.

Those novel technological concepts were first intimated in the *dioptra* (theodolite and level), a surveying instrument similar to the modern transit, and it was conceived by the imaginative Hero (Heron) of

Alexandria ca. A.D. 60.[66] Hero was also actively involved in the development and application of catapults, hydraulic systems, the screw press, and the threaded bolt to name but few of his varied interests.

The *dioptra* was provided with a vertical shaft supporting a metal base plate. The base plate had three holes set in a triangular pattern around a vertical pivot. The hollow column supporting the *dioptra* proper fit over the pivot and had three short pegs which engaged the corresponding holes in the base plate. At least 3,000 *dioptras* are known to have been made (mass production) and any *dioptra* would fit any base plate (interchangeable components). The *dioptra* is the single example of those revolutionary manufacturing techniques to survive that ancient epoch and more than seventeen centuries would pass before those novel concepts were resurrected and, significantly, they were initially applied in the armament industry.

The genesis of the gun irrevocably altered the established patterns of European culture, for it can be said with some precision that the technological innovations of gunpowder and guns were as much responsible for the eventual demise of the already decaying Feudal Age as the virulent Black Death. The heavily armed and armored knight was suddenly vulnerable to a lead pellet weighing no more than a few ounces, and the once nearly impregnable walls of the mighty fortress crumbled under the onslaught of massed cannon.

The increasing knowledge of chemistry, mathematics, and metallurgy gleaned from the widespread manufacture of gunpowder and guns distinctly influenced the development of other technology, for destructive agents tend to produce constructive reagents. Nor can it be denied that the burgeoning armament industry directly stimulated the European economic system.

Comprised of church and state, the spiritual and temporal fifteenth-century European power structure eventually recognized that an expanding economy was entirely dependent upon the strong support of labor contributed by a willing rather than coerced populace; a populace devastatingly reduced by the infectious plague. The survivors of that prolonged pestilence came to be afforded more humane treatment, though by no means were they completely free from socio-economic exploitation and religious persecution.

The grandeur, opulence, and intellectual curiosity spawned by the Renaissance not only rekindled the flame of scientific inquiry but revitalized the sagging spirit of humankind. New ideas, rooted in concepts and principles already old in Classical antiquity, stalked abroad during that luminous epoch, invading the minds of men just as men invaded and conquered the New World.

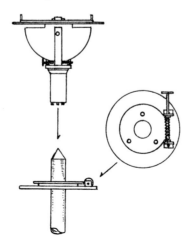

Dioptra AND BASE PLATE (2nd Century): Invented by Hero of Alexandria, the *dioptra* employed a base with three holes corresponding to an equal number of tines or pegs located on the edges of a hollow column which slid over the shaft supporting the base plate. The *dioptra* introduced the concept of interchangeable components during the first century of the Christian era. At least 3,000 *dioptras* were made, initiating the concept of mass production. Author's sketch.

Notes

(In all chapter notes paperbound books and monographs are indicated in the reference by the publisher's name.)

1. 3 vols., Modern Library edn. (New York, n.d.), 3:685.
2. "Those Thundering Clerics," *Gun Digest* (Chicago, 1965), p. 113.
3. W.W. Greener, *The Gun and its Development,* 9th edn. (New York, 1967), p. 13.
4. Dieckmann, see n. 2 above, p. 113.
5. Howard L. Blackmore, *Guns and Rifles of the World* (New York, 1965), p. 1.
6. Gibbon, see n. 1 above, 3:219 n. 22.
7. James R. Partington, "Gunpowder," in *Encyclopedia of Firearms,* ed. Harold L. Peterson (New York, 1964), p. 147.
8. Ibid., p. 148.
9. W.H.B. Smith and Joseph E. Smith, *The Book of Rifles* (Harrisburg, 1963), p. 5.
10. Robert Held, *The Age of Firearms* (New York, 1957), p. 17.
11. Smith and Smith, p. 5.
12. Dudley Pope, *Guns* (New York, 1965), p. 18; Held, p. 16.
13. Held, p. 15.
14. Pope, p. 21.
15. Ibid., p. 18.
16. Blackmore, p. 2 n. 5.
17. Ibid., p. 2 n. 1.
18. Kenneth Walker, ed., *Love, War and Fancy* (New York: Ballentine Books, Inc., 1964), p. 49.
19. Burton's acknowledgement refers to Louis Viardot, *Histoire des Arabes et Maures d'Espagne* (History of the Arabs and Moors in Spain [Paris: 1832]).
20. Albert Manucy, *Artillery Through the Ages* (Washington: National Park Service Interpretive Series History No. 3, 1949), p. 3.
21. Smith and Smith, p. 8; Blackmore, p. 4.
22. MS 92, Christ Church Library, Oxford.
23. Pope, p. 27.
24. Ibid.
25. Carlo M. Cipolla, *Guns, Sails and Empires: Technological Innovation and the Early Phases of European Expansion 1400-1700* (New York, 1965), pp. 75-76.
26. Pope, p. 43.
27. Cipolla, pp. 75-76.
28. I have not emphasized artillery development because it is beyond the scope of this work. The reader more than casually interested is directed to Cipolla's excellent discourse previously cited; especially the bibliography.
29. Clement Bosson, "Hand Cannon," in *Encyclopedia of Firearms,* p. 158.
30. Smith and Smith, p. 9.
31. Blackmore, pp. 5-6.
32. Held, p. 23.
33. Pope, p. 31.
34. Held, p. 23.
35. Col. Robert E. Gardner, *Small Arms Makers: A Directory of Fabricators of Firearms, Edged Weapons, Crossbows and Polearms* (New York, 1962), p. 245. (hereafter cited as *Small Arms Makers*).
36. Held, p. 20.
37. Smith and Smith, p. 9.
38. Ibid., pp. 10-11.
39. Blackmore, p. 6.
40. Partington, "Gunpowder," p. 148.
41. Smith and Smith, p. 23.
42. Ballistics (sing. and pl.) is the science of projectiles in flight.
43. Harold Lamb, *Hannibal: One Man Against Rome* (New York: Bantam Pathfinder edn., Doubleday and Company, Inc., 1958), p. 50.
44. Held, p. 24.
45. Tage Lasson, "Hand Cannon to Flintlock," *Gun Digest* (Chicago, 1956): pp. 34-36.
46. Lynn White, Jr., "Technology in the Middle Ages," in *Technology in Western Civilization,* eds. Melvin Kranzberg and Carroll W. Pursell, Jr., 2 vols (New York and London, 1967), 1:78.
47. The barrel slabs came to be called scelps or skelps in England, attaining a measure of uniformity ca. 1675.
48. *Die Technik* (Berlin and Leipzig, 1914), p. 391.
49. Held, p. 32.
50. Charles Ffoulkes, *The Gun-Founders of England* (Cambridge, 1937), p. 26.
51. An outstanding study of European control marks, proof marks, and gunsmiths' marks is provided by Johan F. Støckel, *Haandskydevaabens Bedømmelse* (Copenhagen, 1938-45), 2 vols.
52. MS 139, fol. 127. Oxford University Library, Oxford.
53. Smith and Smith, p. 32.
54. Blackmore, p. 9.
55. Greener, p. 51, illus. 52.
56. Smith and Smith, p. 32.
57. Ibid.
58. William G. Renwick, "The Earliest Known Rifle," *American Rifleman* (March 1953): 15-18, 75.
59. Variations of those ancient, hand-operated boring and rifling engines are currently used in the U.S. by a handful of purists. Lucian Cary, *Guns & Shooting* (Greenwich, Conn.: Fawcett Book 170, Fawcett Publications, Inc., 1952): 4-9, noted that Appalachian gunsmith Wyatt Atkinson of Wayne Co., Ky., made rifles with a similar engine in the early 1950's.
60. Smith and Smith, p. 32.
61. Harold L. Peterson, *The Treasury of the Gun* (New York, 1962), p. 134, refers to lubricated cloth patches of that era found in the butt traps of rifles now in the Dresden Royal Armory. The rifle and the patched ball was also mentioned by contemporary Spanish gunsmith Alonso Martinez de Espinar, *Arte de Ballestería y Montería* (The Art of Shooting and Horsemanship [Madrid: 1644]).
62. Antimony was isolated by Valentine in the fifteenth century.
63. Cipolla, pp. 62-63.
64. The term Industrial Revolution was introduced by some late eighteenth-century French writers to describe industrial mechanization and subsequently popularized by English economist, historian, and sociologist Arnold Toynbee (1852-1883) who applied it to that phenomenon occurring in Great Britain ca. 1760-1840; however, more appropriate would be the terms Techonomic Revolution or Technological Revolution, for technology was coeval with human evolution and remains a continuing marvel of human aspiration.
65. John B. Rae, "The Rationalization of Production," in *Technology in Western Civilization,* 2:38.
66. A.G. Drachmann, "The Classical Civilizations," in *Technology in Western Civilization,* 1:51-54.

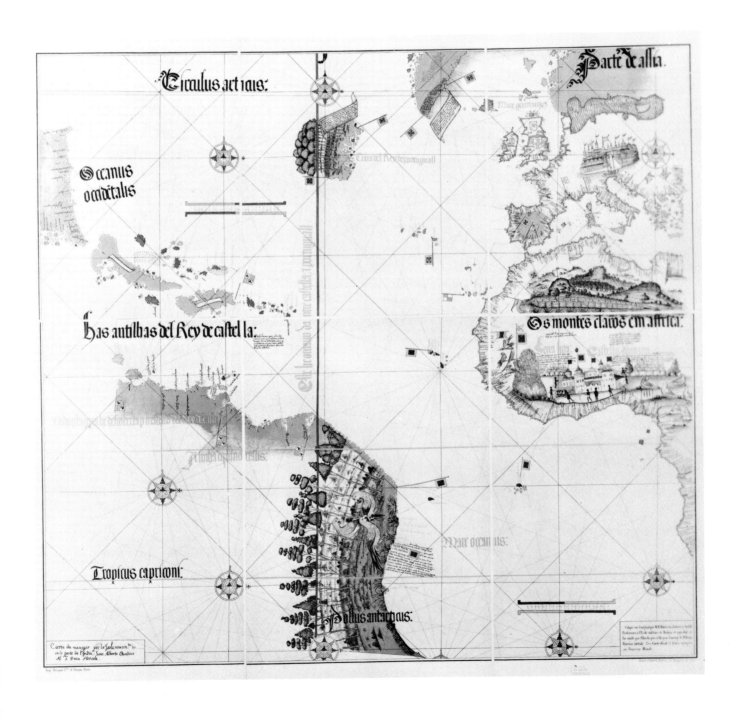

FOR CENTURIES THE PARAMOUNT concern of western Europe was the threat from the East, magnified in 1453 when Constantinople fell to the Turks. Significantly, innovative European weapons technology incorporated in the framework of advanced naval architecture created a superior maritime force which balanced the scales of power. Exploiting the seas, the West decisively outflanked the East and reached toward new horizons.

As the shifting winds of change swept violently across the face of Europe in the final decade of the fifteenth century, Spain emerged to exercise an increasingly strong influence on the course of history. In January, 1492, the Christian armies of Ferdinand and Isabela crushed the Moors at Granada to climax nearly eight centuries of Islamic dominance; and on March 15, 1493, Genoese navigator Christopher Columbus triumphantly sailed into bustling Palos harbor with the astounding revelation that he had discovered a New World.

Coeval with the European invasion of the New World was the inevitable collision of a relatively sophisticated Old World culture with that of the premordial Native Americans and, as history tragically records, the once isolated inhabitants of the Western Hemisphere lost much more than they gained in the exchange.

Woefully disorganized, Native American resistance to Spanish incursions and subsequent encroachments by other European powers prompted immediate and uncompromising retaliation as the expanding Old World powers violently struggled for ascendancy; yet neither were the Native Americans themselves immune from avarice, and in many instances they willingly assisted the invaders to the detriment or destruction of their own kind.

Firearms of the Columbian Expeditions

Among the limited inventory of defensive and offensive weapons aboard the *Niña, Pinta* and *Santa Maria* sailing from Palos harbor with the early morning tide of August 3, 1492, were the ships' cannon, a few crossbows, a Turkish bow, and one hand cannon; vestige of a vanishing age.[1]

If Columbus brought more sophisticated firearms to the New World on his initial voyage he either failed to record it or the documentation has been lost to history. In 1493, however, upon his return to the *La Navidad* settlement on Hispaniola, he brought a minimum of 100 firearms and soon discovered the need for more. During his absence the once docile Tainos destroyed the fort at *La Navidad* and slaughtered its small garrison, infuriated by the Spaniards' lust for their women and desirous of what little gold they possessed.

The firearms accompanying the second expedition of Columbus were a form of the *hacabuche* (arquebus). Prior to ca. 1520 *hacabuche* was an ambiguous term and it has been synonymously though incorrectly identified with *espingarda*. Existing evidence suggests that the *hacabuche* and the *espingarda* were separate entities, neither of them matchlock firearms.

James D. Lavin has described an early fifteenth-century *hacabuche* with a barrel cast of iron which has a simple form of breech chambering and a tiller-like stock similar to the Tannenberg gun. He

DEMARCATION LINE (15th Century, 1493): Pope Alexander VI, attempting to avert hostilities between Spain and Portugal over conflicting territorial claims in the Western Hemisphere, established the 1493 demarcation line permitting Spain to colonize the land to the left and Portugal that to the right of the line, as depicted in this Alberto Cantino map of November 19, 1502. Courtesy of the Library of Congress.

also noted a later specimen, also cast of iron, and though it is not breech-chambered it displays a front and a rear sight, an integrally-cast priming pan at the breech, and a pin-fastened forestock; the large barrel lug near the muzzle serving as the hook. Neither of those venerable Spanish firearms has a lock mechanism.[2]

By January 30, 1495, relations with the Tainos had deteriorated to the extent that Columbus, fearing retaliation, drafted an order for 100 crossbows, 200 cuirasses (breastplates), 100 espingardas and an unspecified amount of gunpowder to bolster the defenses of the Isabela settlement.[3] He dispatched Antonio de Torres with the order in February, much too late to return from Spain with the needed weapons, for he learned that the Tainos were preparing to attack.

The outnumbered Spaniards, aware that attack was their only defense, surprised the Tainos in late March. Two hundred infantry, half of them armed with the hacabuches brought by Columbus in 1493, devastated the Tainos in the first major contest between Europeans and Native Americans in the New World; a bloody confrontation continuously repeated when the Spaniards and other Europeans subsequently penetrated the interior of the hemisphere. And what began in the West Indies at the close of the fifteenth century would not be concluded in North America until the final decade of the nineteenth century.

There is little doubt that the 100 hacabuches Columbus employed against the Tainos and the 100 espingardas he requested from Spain in 1495 were hand cannon, for while his 1495 order mentioned gunpowder, matchcord (mecha or cuerda) was conspicuously absent. That in itself is not conclusive evidence, for the Spanish munitions supply at Isabela could have included sufficient match.

Further supporting the contention that the espingarda was a hand cannon is that during the conquest of Puerto Rico in 1508, Juan Ponce de León purchased 26 espingardas de hierro (iron espingardas)

and 200 pounds of polvora (gunpowder) for his campaigns against the Caribs.[4] Again, there is no mention of matchcord.

That the espingarda was a firearm distinct from the hacabuche is inferred by Pedro Arias de Avila, for on May 31, 1513, he ordered from the artillery factory at Málaga 200 espingardas for infantry use, supplemented by 35 hacabuches "each of thirty lb." to serve as wall guns.[5] In specifying the use and the weight of the hacabuche, Arias indicated that the infantry espingarda was somewhat lighter though he failed to note whether either firearm incorporated an ignition mechanism.

While no definitive description of the hacabuche or the espingarda has thus far emerged, they have been described by some recent historians as matchlock firearms during the Columbian era; an assumption probably stemming from the fact that during the transition from hand cannon to matchlock hacabuche was also rendered arcabuche and the terms were used interchangeably. By ca. 1520 arcabuche also appeared as arcabuz and by that time it had become a matchlock, yet there is insufficient evidence to consider all early forms of the Spanish arquebus as matchlock firearms.

Compounding the confusion is the use of the term escopeta by contemporary Spanish soldier-historian Bernal Díaz del Castillo (ca. 1492-1581) in his Historia Verdadera de la Conquista de la Nueva España (A True History of the Conquest of New Spain). Díaz made no mention of the espingarda, describing the escopeta as a matchlock firearm, and he made no distinction between the escopeta and the hacabuche.[6]

Lt. Col. Luis Martínez Mateo, Servicio Historico Militar, Madrid, says that the escopeta "was used for the first time by the Gran Capitan, Gonzalo de Cordoba, about 1500 . . .," i.e., approximately two years after the third Columbian expedition.[7] He also cites Spanish historiographer Antonio Herrera (1559-1625) who mentioned escopetas which "as they were fired from the arm [shoulder] must have been esmeriles or as it is said today [1601] 'postas' muskets."[8]

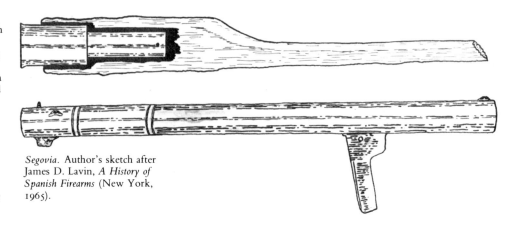

Espingardas (15th Century):
Top—Early 15th-Century Spanish espingarda has innovative breech-chambering as in the Tannenburg gun (see Page 8). This specimen, in the Real Armeria, Madrid, has a breech diameter of .94 caliber and a bore diameter of 1.61 caliber; it was originally stocked in oak. Bottom—Late 15th-Century Spanish espingarda is not breech-chambered, though it has sights and a priming pan. The barrel hook also served as a lug for securing the stock, now missing. This specimen is in the Alcazar de

Segovia. Author's sketch after James D. Lavin, A History of Spanish Firearms (New York, 1965).

Col. Mateo is of the opinion that the early *escopeta* "was a smoothbore shoulder arm, *probably** matchlock, fired offhand."[9]

Herrera's account was published 105 years after his death and it is not clear what *esmeriles* then meant, which leaves uncertain the definition of *postas* muskets. The current translation of *postas* is either a small bullet (ball) or wager and, by inference, *postas* muskets were probably firearms using a ball smaller than musket caliber, i.e., arquebuses.

Christopher Columbus, *Almirante del Mar Océano* (Admiral of the Ocean Sea), died destitute and nearly forgotten on May 20, 1506, unaware of the magnitude of his discovery, and his death ushered in the brutal and bloody Age of the Conquistador. From the tenuous Spanish lodgement on Hispaniola other hardy, determined adventurers set forth seeking gold and glory. Among the first was Juan Ponce de León, former governor of Puerto Rico, whose search for Bimini inadvertently led to the discovery of Florida on April 2, 1513.

There is presently no direct evidence that Ponce de León or his chroniclers made any concrete reference to firearms either regarding his initial Florida expedition or the disastrous 1521 colonization attempt which cost his life. That he was aware of firearms is uncontested, for he had served his country in Europe, accompanied the second Columbian expedition, and employed firearms in conquering Puerto Rico.

Despite an encounter with the aggressive Ais on the east coast of *La Florida* on April 21, 1513, and another with the fierce Calusas on the west coast on June 11, Ponce de León mentioned only ships' cannon and crossbows. A man of his time, he either preferred the efficient, traditional crossbow or took the use of firearms for granted as did many early historians.

During the course of de León's Florida explorations of 1513 his successor in Puerto Rico, Gov. Juan Cerón, faced a Carib uprising led by cacique Daguao. Daguao launched a surprise attack on the village of Caparra in June.[10] Several settlers were killed or wounded and the Caribs burned the church, the bishop's residence, 29 straw houses, and the mansion deserted by de León's family at the outset of hostilities.

The attack coincided with the arrival at San Germán of Admiral Diego Colón and Cristobal de Mendoza, the newly appointed lieutenant governor, accompanied by a small body of troops commanded by Captain General Juan Enriquez. Enriquez momentarily repulsed the Caribs and Admiral Colón sent to Hispaniola for additional arms and munitions.

The weapons arrived in September, primarily

*Italics added.

PONCE DE LEON (16th Century): This portrait of Juan Ponce de Leon initially appeared in Antonio de Herrera y Tordesillas, *Description de las Indias Occidentales* (Description of the West Indies [Madrid, 1726-1730]). The figures (extreme left) depict the Spaniards fighting the Native Americans (probably Calusas) in *La Florida*. The soldier (center) is shooting what could be interpreted as an *espingarda*. Lack of detail prevents identification of the firearm as a handcannon or matchlock and the late date of the 1726 edition tends to discredit the accuracy of the illustration like the buildings and mountains in the background though it was probably copied from the 1601 version of Herrera appearing eighty years after De Leon's death. Courtesy of the Library of Congress.

consisting of crossbows and lances though six firearms were included. Royal factor Miguel Díaz noted how the firearms and munitions were dispersed, reporting that Enriquez received "four *arcabuces* [arquebuses] and a barrel of gunpowder and three dozen *pelotas* [balls] . . . and four *atacadores* [wooden ramrods] of the aforementioned and two *espingardas* and ten balls for them."[11]

It is apparent from Díaz' account that the *arcabuce* and the *espingarda* were distinguished not only by terminology but by caliber, for he recorded the identity of each firearm and the number of bullets provided. Unfortunately, he did not specifically describe either firearm.

Following the Carib uprising and for reasons known only to himself, Captain General Juan Enriquez buried four *arcabuces con falsera* in Caparra. A literal translation of *arcabuce con falsera* refers to an arquebus without a lock, i.e., a false arquebus; however, what the term then meant remains unknown. It is probable that the arquebuses were the four he had received from Díaz, though the fate of the two *espingardas* cannot be determined. Enriquez subsequently returned to claim the arquebuses and found it impossible, for during his absence acting lieutenant governor Bishop Alonso Manso had ordered a fort constructed on the burial site.[12] The journey was not entirely wasted, for Enriquez retrieved a barrel of gunpowder hidden in the ruins of Ponce de León's estate.[13]

In October, 1513, de León returned to Puerto Rico from Florida, found his family safe, and almost immediately sailed for Spain and an audience with Ferdinand V (II of Aragon, 1452-1516). His grateful sovereign elevated him to a knighthood with the title *Adelantado* and rewarded him with the governorship of Bimini and Florida. He was then ordered to return to Puerto Rico to subdue the still hostile Caribs.

Three caravels were purchased for de León's expedition and they were outfitted with arms and munitions from Seville. An inventory was prepared on September 1, 1514, by Sancho Matienzo, *testorero de la Casa de la Contractacíon* (treasurer of the contracting house). Ponce received for his ships' cannon 409 pounds of gunpowder valued at 2000 *maravedis** per *quintal* (cwt.) and 200 pounds of *espingarda* powder worth 2875 *maravedis* per *quintal* with a surcharge of 12 *reales* put on the six *carriles* (casks) in which it was packed. He also received 240 pounds of bullet lead at 550 *maravedis* per *quintal* and six *alcabuzes del campo* with their copper moulds and their iron ladles for casting valued at 3750 *maravedis*.[14]

It can be noted from the Matienzo inventory that cannon powder cost less per hundredweight than *espingarda* powder, the disparity doubtlessly resulting from manufacturing techniques because the latter was more finely granulated. Also, Matienzo described the firearms propellant as *espingarda* powder rather than arquebus powder which could have been a personal idiocyncracy, though it is more likely that the *espingarda* was then a more common and popular firearm than the apparently larger *arcabuce*. Regarding the six *alcabuzes del campo* mentioned in Matienzo's accounts, it is possible that the words *del campo* referred to the place of manufacture, i.e., the Royal Arsenal at Medina del Campo in Castile.

Similar to Columbus' request for arms in 1495, there is no mention of matchcord in either Matienzo's inventory at Seville or Díaz' records in Puerto Rico. The glaring omission of matchcord by two individuals charged with keeping royal accounts cannot be dismissed as a mere oversight, for Spanish accounting procedures were then well defined and, for the most part, meticulously and scrupulously followed; again bolstering the contention that the *arcabuce* and *espingarda* employed in Spanish America during the late fifteenth and early sixteenth century were not matchlock firearms.

Early Spanish Gun-Founding

With the defeat of Islam, gun-founding momentarily languished in Spain, and considering the rudimentary state of the armament industry during the reign of Ferdinand and Isabela (1479-1504) it is not surprising that the one hundred *espingardas* Columbus ordered in 1495 could have been hand cannon or that they accompanied other early Spanish explorers in the Caribbean and elsewhere. It must be pointed out, however, that the devastating conflict with the Moors had wreaked havoc with even the most insignificant industries and the nation was then in dire economic straits.

Of all western Europe, Spain was least prepared to meet the vigorous challenge of power politics and overseas expansion suddenly thrust upon her by the rediscovery of the New World. A mighty armada was desperately needed to continue exploration and effectively maintain and protect an efficient line of communication to and from her emerging American colonies. The demand for ships alone severely strained all of Spain's limited resources; a demand continuously escalating when these large, heavily-laden treasure fleets began to sail regularly from the West Indies and were systematically plundered by assorted pirates and privateers.

No less an economic burden was the demand for cannon and firearms, for Spain lagged far behind her major European rivals in cultivating sources for raw materials, providing skilled craftsmen, establishing proper manufacturing facilities, and procuring the essential financial resources for producing those vital weapons. Despite the enormous tonnage of precious metals exhumed from the bowles of Spanish America at a horrendous cost of human life, never in the course of Spain's colonial aspirations would she muster the accouterments of war in sufficient quantity, or would she fully support the basic needs of her distant, struggling colonists.

Prior to the sixteenth century Spanish gun-founders were recruited from ranks of iron forgers when the situation demanded, and the emphasis was on artillery rather than firearms. Production levels were consistently low and the weapons made were of poor quality compared to those of other European nations.

Some progress was made in the armament industry under the united banner of Castile and Aragón, for by 1495 three arsenals had been established; each in a different province: Barcelona (Catalonia), Baza (Andalusia), and Medina del Campo (Castile).[15] With the threat of French invasion in 1497, the Baza Arsenal was relocated at Málaga and there the Royal Artillery Factory flourished for nearly a century, though during that epoch Medina del Campo Arsenal steadily declined.[16] Those facilities also pro-

---

*The established sixteenth-century Spanish currency was the *maravedi* (sing.), the *real,* and the *ducado;* the latter of greatest value. Thirty-four *maravedis* equalled one *real* and eleven *reales* equalled one *ducado.* The precise U.S. equivalent at present is conjectural at best.

duced firearms, for as yet Spain had developed no commercial firearms industry.

In 1519 the armament industry received considerable impetus, stimulated by the ascension of Carlos I (1500-1558) as Holy Roman Emperor Charles V (1519-1556). Charles ruled as His Royal and Imperial Majesty, King of Spain and the Netherlands, Ruler of Germany and Austria, King of Naples and Sicily, and Lord of the Americas. With most of western Europe marching to the authorative beat of Charles' royal drum, Spain enjoyed a sustained period of militant expansion in the Old and New World.

Charles generously subsidized Spanish gunfounding and gunsmithing and also imported Flemish and German masters. He purchased large quantities of cannon, firearms, gunpowder, and the raw materials needed for their manufacture from England, Germany, Hungary, Italy, and the southern Low Countries, while by ca. 1550 Cuban copper was utilized to make bronze for casting cannon.

It was also during Charles' reign that Spain became the first European power of consequence to discover the military potential of the matchlock arquebus when on February 25, 1525, her *arcubuceros* penetrated the strong French flank at Pavia (Italy), capturing Francis I during the first of several conflicts involving the Hapsburgs and the House of Valois.[17]

Under Charles' cohesive and energetic leadership Spain quickly emerged as a major European power, her military strength sustained by the seemingly boundless stream of treasure beginning to flow across the Atlantic and the dedication of her venturesome conquistadors. However, if Spain was to preserve her equilibrium in the Old and New World she had to provide ordnance of sufficient durability and efficacy to support and defend her scattered dominions.

To ensure an adequate supply of quality ordnance Spain implemented and enforced a stringent military proof system. The proof system was inaugurated ca. 1520-1525, shortly after Charles assumed the emperor's mantle. An arms contract preserved in the Simancas Archive and cited by Lavin is believed to be the first documentary evidence referring to the Spanish proof system.[18] The contract also provides an excellent description of a martial matchlock arquebus and relates specific technological data concerning the manufacturing and loading techniques established for firearms. Accepted in 1535 by Antón de Urquizu, a Biscayan *arcubucero* (gunsmith) of Orio Province, the contract provided for:

> . . . the manufacture of two thousand arquebuses of the length and shape and walnut stocks and powder flasks and priming flasks and [bullet] mould and ramrod and barrel cleaner and bullet worm and all other tools as had the sample [pattern] arquebus that was given him [de Urquizu] at the time he took with him the contract that was made at moncon [Monzón] the past year of five hundred and thirty-three [1533] for the four thousand arquebuses which he took to malaga [Málaga] which [pattern] weighs fourteen pounds and three-quarters weight of castilla [Castile] which are sixteen ounces to the pound the said arquebuses must be well and cleanly bored and the ball for each three-quarters of an ounce and half a silver *real* weight of castilla and the lock of the said arquebuses as the same as those that he delivered in malaga and each one of them must carry seven turns to the breech plug which must be very tight and well made at the time the said anton de urquicu receive the said arquebuses from the masters who are to make them he must prove each with two charges [a double charge] of fine arquebus [serpentine] powder and its ball of lead and each charge must be of the weight of its ball for in this manner they are used and all must be made in the same way with charge and ball conforming to the said sample so that in time of necessity the charges and balls of one arquebus can be used in others. . . .

According to the contract it is apparent that master Biscayan *arcubuceros* were capable of handling large firearms orders, for in 1533 Antón de Urquizu delivered 4,000 arquebuses to Málaga and they were undoubtedly satisfactory because he was offered the contract cited. De Urquizu apparently acted as an

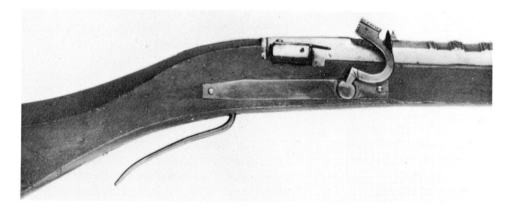

MATCHLOCK ARQUEBUS (16th Century, ca. 1525): The simple lockplate and straight stock of this .65 caliber Spanish *hacabuche* reflects its other plain characteristics. The priming pan is welded to the breech and has a flat, pivotal cover. Spanish arquebuses of the period displayed front and rear sights and weighed approximately 12 to 14 pounds. This specimen, from the ducal house of Medinaceli, is in the *Museo del Ejército* (Army Museum), Madrid. Courtesy of Dr. James D. Lavin.

agent and a gunsmith, for while he was awarded the contract it stipulated that the 2,000 arquebuses were to be obtained "from the masters who are to make them," indicating that several gunsmiths were involved. Gunsmiths acting as agents for other gunsmiths in contract negotiations or sub-contracting gunsmithing work was common throughout Europe by ca. 1550.

The contract also indicates that as early as 1533 Spain attempted to simplify manufacturing techniques and had successfully standardized martial firearms caliber, for the number of turns to the threaded breech plug was specified as seven and "the charges and balls of one arquebus can be used in others." Unless earlier documentation is unearthed, it is evident that the standardization and the interchangeability of martial caliber in continental Europe was first accomplished in Spain.

The 1535 contract noted in addition that "each charge must be of the weight of its ball." That rule-of-thumb method for determining the proper powder charge for long arms was nearly universal throughout the muzzle-loading era. By ca. 1575, however, when gunpowder had become more powerful through the corning process, an amount equal to one fifth of the weight of the ball was also used. Another commonly used method was to place the ball in the palm of the hand and cover it with powder; an estimate approximating the aforementioned practice which persisted well into the nineteenth century.

The proof technique described in the contract was used as early as 1538, for that year Juan Orbea and Juan Ermúra of Eibar received a contract for 15,000 martial arquebuses to be proved at the Royal Arms Factory in Placencia.[19] That Spain established proof facilities at Placencia doubtlessly stemmed from the fact that nearby Eibar had been an arms-making center since ca. 1520. While martial firearms barrels continued to be proved at government installations, it was not until January 31, 1915, that official proof of all firearms was made mandatory in Spain.[20]

The various methods employed by Charles V to stimulate effectively Spanish arms-making produced positive results while he remained in command of his vast, consolidated dominions, but when illness forced his abdication in 1556 the armament industry gradually deteriorated. One reason was a lack of experienced craftsmen, for in 1557 Venetian ambassador Badoer remarked, "I do not think there is another country less provided with skilled workers than Spain."[21] By 1590 even the Royal Gun Foundry at Málaga had perceptibly declined and two years later a contemporary historian noted that because Spain had failed to develop a successful gunpowder industry she was forced "to beg for gun-powder abroad."[22]

While Spain was occupied in the Caribbean, Venetian mariners John and Sebastian Cabot sailing under the Tudor standard of Henry VII explored Newfoundland and Nova Scotia in 1497-1498 and possibly visited Florida prior to Ponce de León. In 1501 Portugese slavers raided Labrador and by that time Dutch, English, French, Irish, Portugese, Scandinavian, and Spanish fishermen had visited the extensive North American coast seeking fresh water and provisions. Those European seafarers also engaged in a limited barter with the Native Americans even before many official expeditions were launched; expeditions upon which were based bitterly contested claims to the vast land mass ultimately known as North America.

During that early period of sporadic and disorganized European activity along the Atlantic littoral it is probable that the Native Americans of the Eastern woodland culture first became aware of firearms, though as yet no substantial evidence has been found to verify that contention.

Some historians state that the Native Americans were first astonished and then terrified when confronted by cannon and firearms. While there is some truth in the assertion, they quickly overcame their fear as Columbus experienced on Hispaniola, Diego Velásquez found in Cuba, and Ponce de León discovered when conquering Puerto Rico and during his later Florida expeditions.

In 1514 Mayans along the Yucatan coast repulsed Spanish slavers in the face of cannon fire, yet broke when charged by mounted lancers because they were unable to comprehend the strange apparition of man and horse combined. When invading Mexico in 1519 Captain General Hernando de Cortés learned to his regret that the fierce Tlaxcalans and their Otomi allies "far from panicking at the explosion of gunpowder, drowned its noise with their shrill whistles and threw dust in the air while they rushed the dead and wounded away so no one could see the damage the . . . cannons had done."[23]

Nor were the cultured Aztecs reluctant to stand against shimmering Spanish swords and brightly burnished *escopetas*. In July, 1520, they drove Cortés from the gilded hall of Montezuma at Tenochtitlan (Mexico City). Cortés had invaded Mexico with 11 ships carrying a crew of 110 and, in addition, 508 soldiers of whom 32 were crossbowmen and only 12 *escopeteros;* a mere handful considering the numerical strength of the Aztecs.[24] Parenthetically, Cortés had earlier supplemented his defenses at Segura de la Frontera with a wall gun. The weapon weighed 17 pounds and the 34½-inch, .34 caliber barrel was "fastened to a point-ended stock by clamps."[25]

Despite overwhelming odds, dissention among his ranks, and interference from his superiors, Cortés conquered Mexico in 1522; an impressive feat of arms substantially assisted by the Native American allies he had actively cultivated and virtually impossible without them. Yet perhaps more impressive was Francisco Pizarro's bloody conquest of Peru in 1533, for his "army" consisted of 177 men: twenty armed with crossbows and only three with firearms.[26]

Even a cursory investigation of the initial European involvement in the Western Hemisphere indicates that neither cannon nor firearms were entirely instrumental in subjugating the Native Americans, for the few cannon then available were transported with great difficulty through the rough and hostile terrain or mounted in static fortifications limiting their mobility. Though more abundant and portable, even firearms were subordinate to traditional weaponry like the halberd, lance, pike, sword, and crossbow.

The smoothbore, muzzle-loading single-shot matchlock arquebus representing the acme of fifteenth-century firearms technology remained inferior to projectile weapons like the crossbow and the longbow in accuracy, missile penetration, range, and rapidity of fire while also suffering the inherent disadvantages of match ignition. Despite the poor and often unreliable performance of the matchlock arquebus, however, it supplanted the crossbow in the Americas by ca. 1550 though the transition was more gradual in the Old World.

The Matchlock Comes of Age

It was not that matchlock firearms suddenly became superior to the crossbow or the longbow in performance or reliability, but from the military standpoint of tactical employment and training it was much easier and faster to teach men to use firearms, for it often required several years of practice to produce an experienced archer while massed ranks firing at point-blank range eliminated the need for accuracy and at that meager distance firearms were equally lethal.

That matchlock firearms rapidly superseded crossbows in the Americas can be explained by examining the unorthodox aspects of Native American warfare in comparison to standard European methods and the nature of the terrain encountered in the New World. Native Americans employed highly successful hit-and-run guerilla tactics and preferred the ambuscade to an open confrontation despite their numerical superiority; a system of warfare ideally suited to their primitive weaponry and usually conducted at close quarters. Shooting massive flights of arrows at great distances across generally open ground chosen for manoeuver was customary in European warfare, though virtually precluded in the Americas by the dense forests and jungles which obscured visibility and hampered mobility, notwithstanding the fact that logistics prevented the invaders from fielding large armies during the initial period of conquest and colonization.

Neither the crossbow nor the longbow were immediately discarded in the Old World, and though the longbow peculiar to Britain was never employed in the Americas it was not considered obsolete as a martial weapon until 1638.[27]

From the beginning all firearms were made by hand, reflecting the idiosyncracies as well as the skill attained by the craftsman, and despite a superficial similarity between the various kinds in a single group no two firearms were exactly alike. Design characteristics often fluctuated because of locale, tradition, specialized use, and consumer preference. Innovations also flourished and those of merit eventually supplanted previous developments to spread slowly beyond their immediate sphere of influence; a factor evident throughout the various stages of firearms evolution and in other fields of technology. Considering those variables, any description of early firearms is necessarily a composite drawn from typical specimens unless specific examples are cited.

The common C pattern European matchlock arquebus of ca. 1520-1535 weighed 14 to 18 pounds and had an overall length of 55 to 65 inches. The bronze or iron barrel measured about 48 inches, taking a .65 to .75 caliber ball backed by three to four drams of corned powder. Sights, if any, were similar to those found on hand cannon. The thick, hexagonal breech extended about a third of the way down the barel which was thereafter round, delineated from the breech by a decorative annulus. The muzzle often displayed a baluster moulding also common among cannon of the period. In atypical matchlock arquebuses the barrel was fully round with no breech delineation and the muzzle was slightly swamped, i.e., it displayed a funnel-like flare ostensibly introduced to facilitate loading.

Early smoothbore long arms often had crooked barrels; a defect particularly evident in most martial long arms for many years because accuracy was no criterion for efficacy. Also reducing the efficacy of smoothbore firearms throughout the centuries embracing this study was the phenomenon of chattering. The ball, cast slightly undersized to facilitate loading and varying in some instances as much as 1/24th of an inch, literally bounced down the bore, losing much of its velocity and kinetic energy because the powder gases escaped around it (blow-by). Although chattering was partially alleviated by paper or tow wadding, it also caused the ball to leave the muzzle at various angles which was not conducive to accuracy or range.

While those ballistics deficiencies were common to the matchlock arquebus it was also found that the firing lever, screwed into the sear heel, had a propensity to loosen and fall out so a cord was usually tied around it, secured to the stockwrist. And neither was the early matchlock arquebus provided with a sideplate (screwplate or counterplate) opposite the lock mechanism.

The early matchlock arquebus also displayed several technological innovations, among them an improved pan cover. Rather than sliding forward as in some sophisticated forms of the hand cannon, the pan cover was provided with a finger piece and pivoted to the side around a vertical post mounted on the rear of the pan. In addition to offering slight protection from the natural elements, the pan cover now functioned as a safety, preventing the lighted matchcord or sparks from it inadvertently reaching the priming powder and causing accidental, premature ignition.

The innovative fence found on some hand cannon and serpentine firearms had been improved and spanned the breech behind the pan, the fence bridge often v-notched for sighting, and in some instances it secured the novel match guide. The match guide was a short metal tube through which the matchcord was threaded to prevent it from fouling the serpentine arm and the firing lever. It has been suggested that the match guide was the progenitor of an early form of the peep sight, i.e., a rear sight with an extremely small aperture.

The typical matchlock arquebus stock had a thick wrist (hand grip) and the comb or upper surface dropped abruptly from the breech, terminating in a wide, flat butt. The usually slim forestock extended nearly to the muzzle and was pin-fastened to the barrel. Beech, birch, oak, and walnut were generally used for stocking, though other varieties of wood became popular.

The sharply curved buttstock which had evolved throughout most of early sixteenth-century Europe necessitated firing the arquebus with the butt resting atop the shoulder and the comb pressed to the cheek, or with the butt held against the center of the chest; neither position conducive to adequate control when pointing or firing.

In Spain the arquebus buttstock was atypically straighter and provided positive control, for the butt was pressed into the cup of the shoulder. The Spanish buttstock design was subsequently adopted by most European powers, particularly in martial firearms, and the Spaniards can be credited with introducing the method by which long arms are currently aimed and fired.

Several methods for attaching the wooden ramrod early emerged. Typically, as in some late forms of the hand cannon, the ramrod was supported by one or two metal loops (thimbles or pipes) welded to the underside of the barrel. In the matchlock arquebus the thimbles were often pinned through the forestock. In atypical specimens the ramrod was secured by a thimble on the left side of the forestock near the muzzle and the threaded rod tip was screwed a few turns into an L-shaped hook mounted opposite the lockplate. In some martial arquebuses the vent pick was carried in a recess near the forestock end.

Loading and firing matchlock firearms was difficult and tedious. When action was anticipated the ramrod tip was often stuck in the ground because it could be manipulated faster than if returned to the thimbles after each shot, while by sixteenth-century standards loading and firing two shots in three minutes was exceptional.

After pouring the proper charge of corned powder into the muzzle and firmly tamping it with the ramrod, loading and tamping the ball and the tow, blowing the accumulated ash from the smouldering match and properly adjusting it in the serpentine jaws, and lastly as a safety precaution priming the pan with fine serpentine powder, the weapon was finally prepared for firing. After the priming pan cover was introduced the pan was primed first, for the cover acted as a safety and prevented the priming from falling out of the pan. In some instances the pan edges were sealed with tallow to protect the priming from humidity or precipitation.

On a clear, calm day the effective range of the early matchlock arquebus was approximately 125 yards though the ball carried much farther. The ball could penetrate heavy armor at about 80 yards and light armor at 100 yards, though accuracy and penetration beyond effective range was dismal even with quality gunpowder and a reasonably straight barrel.

Matchlocks in Spanish Florida

Juan Ponce de León died in Cuba in 1521, victim of a Calusa arrow while attempting to plant a colony near present Charlotte Harbor on the Florida west coast. On November 28, 1525, an inquiry was made by *albacea* (executor) García Troche concerning the disposition of the firearms and other supplies the adventurer had received when engaging the Caribs in Puerto Rico; a prerequisite for probating his estate.

Testimony heard by Troche included various references to the firearms used against the Caribs and while *espingarda* was prevalent there was no mention of the *hacabuche,* though the witnesses frequently employed *escopeta,* apparently using it as a synonym like Bernal Díaz (see p. 36). Again, there was no mention of matchcord. The witnesses also noted that none of the firearms used against the Caribs were recovered, explaining that they had virtually rusted away because of the extremely high tropical humidity.[28]

De León's legendary explorations and the fabulous wealth accumulated by Cortés and other adventurers stimulated additional excursions and in 1526 Lucas Vásquez de Ayllon sailed from Hispaniola with five hundred colonists, establishing a settlement near present Winyah Bay, S.C. The colony failed that same year when he and two-thirds of the expedition succumbed to starvation and hostile Native Americans.

In April, 1528, Panfilo de Narváez marched north from the vicinity of Boca Ciega Bay on the Florida west coast with 400 men and 80 horses, leaving among the Native Americans in his wake a legacy of intense hatred fostered by inhumane treatment. The nearly exhausted and disillusioned Narváez expedition reached the Florida panhandle, wintering near present Tallahassee, and subsequently perished in an attempt to sail for Mexico in a number of frail, handmade boats. Of five survivors, two were rescued many years later.

Little is known of the firearms accompanying those early Spanish explorers, for theirs was a transition period in firearms evolution and documentation is either non-existent, fragmentary, or yet only superficially investigated. The attrition of the ages has relinquished but few bits and pieces of the firearms they carried; those now painstakingly excavated and studied by dedicated archaeologists examining known Spanish camp sites, trails, and shipwrecks in the gulf region extending from Florida to Mexico. All that can be said of those firearms is that they were probably similar to the arquebuses described in the 1535 arms contract preserved at Simancas (see p. 39).

Eleven years after the Narváez disaster, Captain General Hernando de Soto arrived in *La Florida* and struck north from Tampa Bay, almost continuously attacked by the Calusa, Timucua, Ocali, and Apalachee who were freshly reminded of his predecessor. As offensive or defensive weapons both crossbow and matchlock arquebus left much to be desired, for as one anonymous Portugese survivor of the beleaguered expedition lamented, the Native Americans "never stand still, but are alwaies running and traversing from one place to another: by reason whereof neither crossbow nor arcubuse can aime at them: and before one crossbowman can make one shot, an Indian will discharge three or foure arrowes; and he seldome misseth what he shooteth at."[29]

With that acerbic comment the unknown Gentleman of Elvas whose narrative survived the ages succinctly described the prevailing pattern of Native American warfare in sixteenth-century North America, and it remained basically unchanged from prehistory to the final, tragic challenge of the late nineteenth century.

In 1541 Antonio de Mendoza, Viceroy of *Nueva España* (New Spain), dispatched Francisco Vásquez de Coronado into the interior of the continent in search of the fabled seven golden cities of Cibola. Penetrating what is now Texas and marching northeast to Quivera (central Kansas), at one point Coronado was less than 500 miles from the De Soto party in present northwest Arkansas. Both expeditions fought climate, terrain, and the Native Americans and brought many of them their first, often fatal knowledge of firearms and, perhaps more significantly, the horse.

Spain early proscribed Native American firearms procurement in all her New World dominions for reasons more self-serving than altruistic. Inaugurated by Ferdinand II in 1501 to preserve Spanish dominance and subsequently embraced by the church which recognized that warfare with the Native Americans interfered with proselyzation, the stringent crown policy was initially successful. During the late seventeenth century and thereafter, however, the policy frequently backfired, for the English and the French armed their Native American allies and began to challenge seriously Spanish authority in *La Florida.*

La Florida, as the early Spaniards knew it, was a vast wilderness extending from present Key West to Labrador and from the Atlantic strand to New Spain; but despite determined assaults by de León, Narváez, Coronado, De Soto and others it remained largely unexplored and it successfully resisted colonization.

In 1559, past failures notwithstanding, another attempt was made to colonize the Florida peninsula proper and the venture was mounted from Vera Cruz. Led by Tristán de Luna y Arrellano, 1,000 settlers and 500 soldiers reached what is now Pensacola Bay on August 14. Though the colony was abandoned in 1561, significant data relating to the firearms and accouterments used is revealed in the correspondence of Luís de Velasco, Viceroy of New Spain, who dispatched the following to de Luna at Pensacola Bay on May 6, 1560:

. . . Luís Daza is taking [to the colony] two hundred helmets covered with tin. I think they will be stronger and last longer than those you took with you. He is also taking one hundred and ten or one hundred and twenty horn flasks [powder horns] which will preserve the powder better in a damp cold country than wooden ones; they will last longer, and be useful for loading and priming. If they work well let me know, and I will send more. He is also taking I do not know how many *arrobas* [approximately twenty-five pounds] of matchcord. It did not turn out as well as I . . . wished. It will [need to be] twisted and pulled again there, and if this is done, it will serve. It pained me to learn what you write me about the little care which the men take to conserve their offensive and defensive arms, for, aside from the fact that they are necessary, they cost a great deal and much time and labor is spent in making them. You will give strict orders how to care for and preserve the arquebuses which came from Spain. I have ordered that one hundred of them be given to Luis Daza in Vera Cruz, together with their powder horns and small flasks and iron helmets. They [authorities in Spain] write me that these are very good munitions. . . . Please tell me whether more munitions . . . are needed, that they may be sent.

* * *

You ask me to send you two Indians who know how to make arquebus stocks. Until now I have not been able to finish with two or three who are making them here, and not one of them wants to go. I think they may be excused for the time being, considering the munitions now being sent which have come from Spain. . . . If there is no one who knows how to make stocks or who can repair the broken ones . . ., you will order them sent here and they will be repaired or others will be sent.[30]

Spain, like other European powers subsequently involved in the New World, exploited Native American labor in various enterprises and Velasco's correspondence reveals that arms-making was no exception, for Native Americans apparently had been making and repairing arquebus stocks in Mexico prior to May, 1560. Velasco also mentioned problems with making matchcord there, while ob-

viously discovering that powder horns were superior to wooden flasks.

Native Americans, though often abused by the early Spaniards, were the object of much concern from chruch and crown. By ca. 1550 reform measures were instituted to relieve the burden of the Native American slave worker. Velasco, an able administrator, displayed admirable compassion when discussing the Native American stock-makers; an attitude reflecting the official policy and one more prevalent than generally supposed.

Philip II (1527-1598) assumed the Spanish crown in 1556 and displayed little of the ability and tact which distinguished his father, Charles V. De Luna's unfortunate colonization effort and prior failures prompted Philip to terminate all attempts to colonize *La Florida* on September 23, 1561, though events in strife-torn Europe influenced by various socio-economic factors earlier initiated by the Protestant Reformation soon dictated a reversal of crown policy.

Breton navigator Jacques Cartier established the French claim to North America in 1534-1535 while exploring the St. Lawrence region for ambitious Francis I, and in 1541 he founded the ill-fated Quebec colony. The discord prompted by the Reformation delayed further French explorations until shortly after midcentury when persecution reached intolerable proportions. As a result Admiral Gaspard de Chatillon Coligny, leader of the Huguenot faction, sent Jean Ribault to North America seeking a haven for the religious dissidents.

Ribault's initial expedition consisted of two ships and 150 men, half of them arquebusiers, and they departed from Dieppe on February 18, 1562.[31] Arriving off the Florida peninsula on April 30, Ribault cruised north, making his first landfall that evening near present Jacksonville and claiming the territory for Charles IX. The Timucua inhabiting the region quickly established an amicable relationship with the Huguenots.

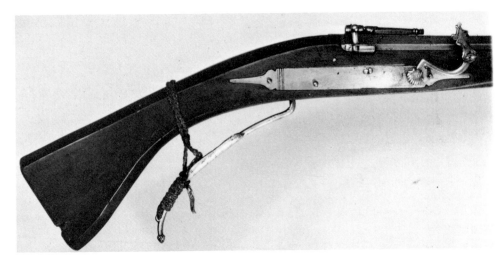

MATCHLOCK ARQUEBUS (16th Century, ca. 1550): The simple lines of this Spanish *arcabuz* made during the reign of Carlos V exemplifies the craftsmanship of Spanish gunsmiths. The 39½-inch, .69 caliber barrel has an octagonal breech. Overall length is 55 inches and it weighs 12 pounds. Note the match guide and vertical pivot of the priming pan cover. The firing lever is secured by a cord. The scallop design at the serpentine base was common in Spain and the Netherlands. Courtesy of Dr. James D. Lavin.

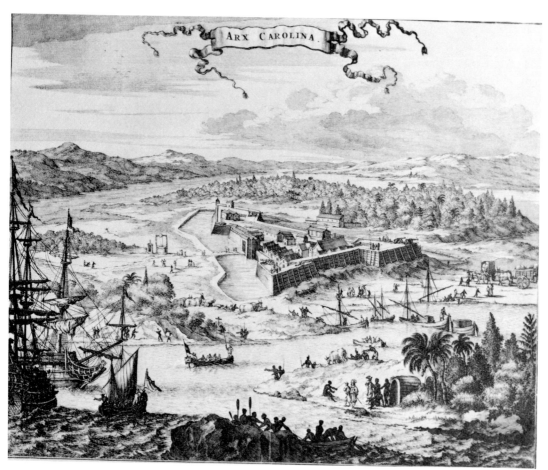

FORT CAROLINE (17th Century): The broad A plan of the French fort on the St. Johns River, Florida, is compatible with Spanish descriptions after it was captured in 1565 and renamed San Mateo. The mountainous background derived from artistic license. From *Arx Carolina* (Amsterdam, 1671). Courtesy of the Chicago Historical Society.

NATIVE AMERICAN WARFARE (ca. 1564): Shortly after establishing Fort Caroline the French assisted Timucua chief Outina in defeating his rival Saturioa (right) as depicted by Jacques Le Moyne de Morgues and engraved by Theodor de Bry. De Bry faithfully delineated the flared (swamped) muzzles of the French arquebuses, though omitting the matchcord needed for ignition. From *India Occidentale* (Amsterdam, 1591). Courtesy of the Library of Congress.

Nearly a month later Ribault sailed farther north and on May 26 landed at what is now Parris Island, South Carolina, and there built Charlesfort. Leaving 25 colonists under the command of Capt. Albert de la Pierria, Ribault sailed for France on June 11, promising reinforcements and additional provisions. Reaching France, he was at once swept up in the fervid religious discord then ravaging the country and his return was considerably delayed.

Short of supplies and almost continuously raided by the Native Americans, the Charlesfort garrison mutinied, murdered de la Pierria, and sailed for France in a small boat. Reduced from short rations to none, the starving mutineers killed and ate one of their companions and were subsequently captured by the English.

A momentary lull in the religious war inspired Coligny to make another colonization attempt, and on April 22, 1564, three ships commanded by René Goulaine de Laudonniéré sailed from France, arriving near Ribault's first landfall on June 22. Five days later on the banks of Florida's St. Johns River construction began on Fort Caroline.

Relations with the Timucua rapidly deteriorated when the French interfered in a tribal dispute and meanwhile provisions ran short. Laudonniéré was soon faced with mutinous settlers who carried

their dissatisfaction to the ultimate point of booby-trapping his quarters with a keg of gunpowder.[32] He escaped that grisly trap because the powder failed to ignite, though shortly thereafter he was confronted by the wrath of the Spaniards.

Philip II viewed the French incursions in *La Florida* with considerable alarm, for not only had

Huguenot apostates encroached upon Catholic soil, but the thought of a hostile Protestant colony situated on the vulnerable flank of the Spanish treasure fleet route from the West Indies was more than intolerable. He immediately dispatched *Adelantado* Pedro Menéndez de Avilés with 500 soldiers to eliminate the French and subsidized 2000 settlers in yet another colonization effort.

Sighting the Florida coast on August 25, 1565, Menéndez located a suitable harbor on the twenty-eighth (St. Augustine's Day), reaffirmed Spain's title to the land de León had investigated, and disembarked at what he proclaimed St. Augustine in honor of the day; the site destined to become the first permanent European settlement within the present limits of the United States.

Menéndez shortly thereafter sailed north attempting to locate the French enclave and on September 4 encountered Ribault's relief expedition to Fort Caroline. After a brief exchange of cannon fire the outnumbered French cut their cables and scattered and Menéndez returned to St. Augustine.

Though there is no accurate method for computing the present equivalent U.S. dollar value of the sixteenth-century Spanish *ducado* (ducat), some idea of the cost of arms can be calculated by comparing the prices of various commodities available at St. Augustine during the period 1565-1572:

Ship biscuit (600 lbs.)	3 ducats
Beef (half side)	5 ducats
Arquebus (matchlock)	3 ducats
Crossbow	2 ducats
Bow & 24 arrows	2 ducats
Coat of mail	50 ducats[33]

The primary disadvantage of match ignition was graphically demonstrated during Menéndez' dawn attack against Fort Caroline on September twentieth. Five hundred Spaniards, at least two-thirds of them *arcubuceros,* made a four-day forced march through a severe hurricane to reach the French position. Though torrential rain had ruined both powder and match, the attack was vigorously pressed with the sword and the surprised French were slaughtered.

Laudonnieré and 25 others escaped, eventually returning to France. Not so fortunate was Ribault who had earlier put to sea planning to strike the Spanish fleet. The violent storm destroyed most of the French ships, casting Ribault and more than 200 ashore south of St. Augustine. All but 16 of them who renounced their religion were put to the sword by the Spaniards, including Ribault, at a small inlet not far from St. Augustine thereafter appropriately known as *Matanzas* (massacre).

With that debacle French colonial aspirations were again temporarily suspended in North America, resuming under different circumstances early in the seventeenth century with the main thrust centered in the St. Lawrence region previously investigated by Cartier.

Having learned to distrust the French, many of the Timucua extended the animosity toward the Spaniards. Exploring Guale* in 1566, Menéndez withdrew from an encounter with them because a sudden shower doused his *arcubuceros'* match. That same year a Timucua night attack on the wooden fort at St. Augustine failed although a few sentries were killed when betrayed by their glowing match and flaming arrows destroyed the powder magazine.

Some indication of the firearms, munitions, and related ordnance available at St. Augustine and Fort San Felipe at Santa Elena (Parris Island, S.C.) during the 1565-1572 period is derived from testimony presented by several witnesses questioned in a crown investigation of the Florida provinces held in Madrid on February 4, 1573:

... On being questioned as to how many arms, and how much artillery and ammunition there are in the said two forts and in the said province, and in what order and with what care they keep them, he [Alonzo Ruíz] said that in the fort of St. Augustine there are about twenty pieces of artillery, large and small, some of bronze and others of iron; and, as it appeared to this witness, there were a quantity of powder, fuzes [match] and balls, that which was necessary for its defense; and there may be an extra supply of about twenty or thirty arquebuses, *of the large ones,** and all the soldiers had their complete outfits of arms and arquebuses. And this witness knows that in the fort of Santa Elena there were about four pieces of mounted artillery, and there were others to be mounted which were in an old fort [Charlesfort]; and this witness does not know how many were there, nor how many arquebuses, nor how much ammunition they had, further than . . . that the soldiers . . . had the needed supply of arms and ammunition, and it was well managed and in good order.[34]

Another witness, Pedro Gonzales of Escalona, stated that in addition to the artillery at St. Augustine there were "sixteen large arquebuses, thirty small ones, all in good condition . . . and much powder and lead, many balls and fuzes, and other things in good order and well guarded. . . ."[35] Testimony from Juan Lopez de Paredes disclosed that there were at St. Augustine as many as "twenty-four arquebuses for a reserve supply. . . ."[36]

The 1573 investigation revealed that large and small arquebuses were available at St. Augustine and

*A region encompassing a large part of present northeast Florida and southeast Georgia.

*Italics added.

it is apparent that the large arquebus was a distinct entity, possibly a true musket not then known by that designation. Precisely when *mosquete* (musket) was introduced to the language remains difficult to determine, though it is frequently encountered in late sixteenth-century Spanish literature.

Modern scholars have consistently attributed the origin of the term musket to the Italian *moschetto* (sparrow hawk), stemming from the traditional practice of naming cannon and firearms for birds of prey. In France it came to be called a *mousquet*, while in England it subsequently appeared as *mousquit*, *muskitt*, *muskett* and, finally musket.

The origin and a brief description of the matchlock musket was given by Spanish historian Sebastián de Covarrubias, *Tesoro de la Lengua Castellana o Española* (Madrid: 1611), who wrote of it as "a type of reinforced *escopeta* [arquebus], a terrible arm and heavy to the one who carries it; but with the employment of forks [a *fourquine*] its use has been facilitated. It is called a *mosquete, quasi-muscovete,* for having invented it, so it is understood, the Muscovites."[37]

While Covarrubias ascribed the invention of the matchlock musket to Russian technology it is thought to have been introduced in western Europe by Fernando Alvarez de Toledo (1508-1583), the infamous Duke of Alva, during the sanguinary Spanish adventure in the Netherlands (1565-1581) which ultimately resulted in the emergence of the Dutch Republic in 1609.

The matchlock musket, or at least its prototype as made in Spain, is known to have been employed in *La Florida* prior to the 1573 investigation, for both Alonzo Ruiz and Pedro Gonzales mentioned large arquebuses in their testimony about the arms at St. Augustine. It is possible that the matchlcok musket served Pedro Menéndez de Avilés in 1565, for a number of the witnesses testifying at the 1573 investigation in Madrid had accompanied the Menéndez expedition and did not return to Spain until 1572.

The firearms and munitions intended for the Florida provinces either came directly from Spain or were transferred via Mexico, Cuba, Hispaniola, or other West Indies ports. Gov. Diego de Velasco, writing to the crown from St. Augustine in August, 1575, complained that "there is such a need of providing the pay and sustenance of the soldiers . . . at present, that I doubt if they can be maintained in conformity with what your Majesty commands; because as the supplies and munitions wherewith they are provided, are bought in Havana and other parts of these Indies, they are so expensive. . . ."[38]

A primary cause of the fiscal problems plaguing *La Florida* throughout the first Spanish period was that the crown, of necessity, subsidized St. Augustine and subsequent settlements with the *situado;*

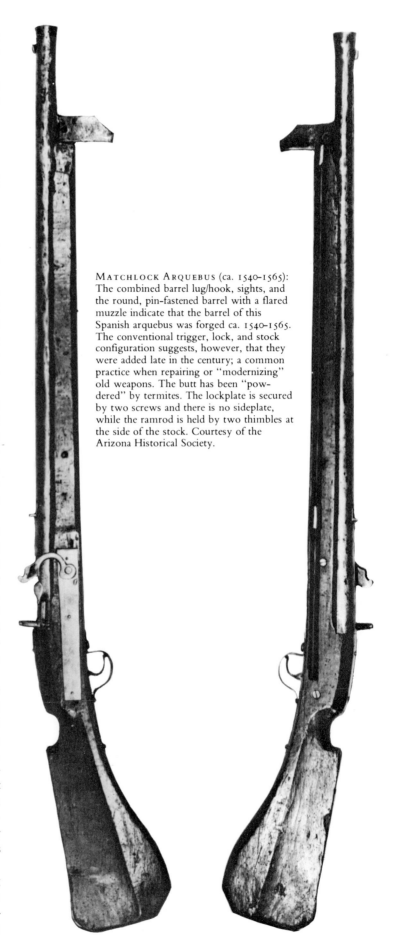

MATCHLOCK ARQUEBUS (ca. 1540-1565): The combined barrel lug/hook, sights, and the round, pin-fastened barrel with a flared muzzle indicate that the barrel of this Spanish arquebus was forged ca. 1540-1565. The conventional trigger, lock, and stock configuration suggests, however, that they were added late in the century; a common practice when repairing or "modernizing" old weapons. The butt has been "powdered" by termites. The lockplate is secured by two screws and there is no sideplate, while the ramrod is held by two thimbles at the side of the stock. Courtesy of the Arizona Historical Society.

an annual payment disbursed from the royal treasury in Havana. A budget enumerating the expected expenditures for food, clothing, salaries, defense, and the other vital needs of the settlements was submitted to the treasury by the *tenedors de bastímentos y municíones* (keepers of the foodstuffs and munitions).[39]

Subject to the whim of treasury officials the *situado* was often inadequate, late in arriving, or failed to arrive at all, and embezzlement among the *tenedors* was not unknown, while many accounts were lost, overlooked, destroyed by accident and, in some instances, stolen or burned as a result of enemy action. Without the *situado* the defensive posture of *La Florida* was considerably weakened and the settlers as well as colonial officials were frequently reduced to abject poverty.

The defenses of *La Florida* were the object of great concern to the crown and *Visitador** Alvaro Flores arrived in St. Augustine on September 27, 1578, to inspect the fort and garrison, and he visited Santa Elena for the same purpose on October twelfth. Flores was an ordnance expert authorized by the crown to report on the number and condition of the weapons and accouterments used and stored at those installations and his inspection was executed with typical Spanish thoroughness.

At St. Augustine Flores found "at the door . . . whereby one enters this platform and the fort, twenty-five arquebuses, primed and loaded, laid on a long table . . . [and] . . . in the sentry-box of the said platform . . . [were] . . . two pikes and his arquebus in order that with it, if need be, he can give the alarm; with its fuze lighted, as it is, by day and by night."[40] Hanging from the walls of the guard room where the sentries slept were "twelve muskets, and many other arquebuses of the soldiers; there were fourteen arquebuses. . . ."[41]

An inspection of the magazine in the fort disclosed "a house built of boards where the powder and arquebus fuzes are kept, with its key and sliding door, wherein were twelve barrels each containing one *quintal* of powder for arquebuses, ten *quintals* of fuzes for arquebuses from Palnuch [Palmicha, Spain?] and New Spain; six bars of lead, four of them weighing five *arrobas* and two of them, six; and one thousand five hundred bullets made for arquebuses, and five hundred for muskets."[42]

Flores' inspection of the St. Augustine garrison determined that the soldiers were provided with "an arquebus, a sword, powder flasks, and bullets. . . ."[43] His inspection of the Santa Elena garrison disclosed the soldiers armed with "swords, powder-flasks, bullets, and munitions pouches."[44]

Entering Fort San Felipe at Santa Elena the *Vis-itador* perceived "thirty soldiers, and a table on which were the arquebuses of the said soldiers, primed and loaded."[45] In a bastion on the south side of the fort he saw "six muskets, eight pikes, sixteen half-pikes, and one dozen arquebuses. . . ."[46] Proceeding to the magazine Flores found "eight barrels, each of the capacity of one *quintal* of arquebus powder; eight *quintals* of fuzes . . . six bars of lead weighing five or six *arrobas* each one, five hundred bullets of lead for muskets and one thousand for arquebuses."[47]

Though muskets were available and referred to as such in the Flores report, it can be seen that in 1578 the arquebus was preponderant in *La Florida*. There was also a distinction regarding the caliber of the arquebus and the musket, though it was not specifically mentioned by the author of the report who referred only to the number of bullets for each kind of weapon and not the size. Parenthetically, the ratio of arquebus to musket balls at St. Augustine was four to one, while at Santa Elena it was three to one; thus further indicating the popularity of the arquebus.

The demand for artillery and firearms continued to escalate as Spain began to be seriously challenged in Europe and North America in the latter half of the sixteenth century and during that epoch several arms-making centers were active in the mother country, principally Barcelona, Baza, Biscay and Cordova; Eibar, Madrid, Málaga and Medina del Campo; Orio, Placencia, Ricla, and Ripoll; Salamanca, Seville, Soria, and Toledo.

By the end of the sixteenth century the smooth-bore, single-shot, muzzle-loading matchlock musket had emerged as the principal martial long arm in Spain and her New World dominions and it served in that capacity for nearly two centuries; long after most other European nations of consequence had adopted firearms with more advanced ignition systems.

Old World Technological Innovation

European technology gradually expanded during the vigorous sixteenth century and the innovative machines and manufacturing techniques developed previously were continuously improved; thus the technological revolution was carried forward into yet another age of inspired growth which included more sophisticated achievements in firearms evolution.

The advent of printing with moveable type in the fifteenth century significantly enhanced the dissemination of technical knowledge and recorded it

*A crown representative akin to the military rank of inspector general.

for posterity with the publication of such sixteenth-century classics as Agricola's (Georg Bauer) *De Re Metallica* (metals and metallurgy), Vanoccio Biringuccio's *De La Pirotechnia* (explosives and incendiaries), Lazrus Ercker's *Beschreibung Allerfurnemsten Mineralischen Ertzt und Berckwercksarten* (mineralogy and manufacturing techniques), Flavius Vegetius Renatus' *De Re Militari* (weapons and tactics), Leonardo da Vinci's *Il Codice Atlantico* (chemistry, weapons, and military fortifications), and numerous other treatises concerned with technology.

The dawn of the sixteenth century saw a significant improvement in the matchlock mechanism which would have a profound impact on firearms evolution, for it subsequently influenced the development of several radical ignition mechanisms. As far as it can be determined, the first example of the innovative matchlock appeared in southern Germany ca. 1493-1508 where it was known as a *lütenschnappschloss* (light snapping lock).[48]

Though there were subsequent variations the *lütenschnappschloss* initially incorporated a lateral sear, i.e., the sear pivoted horizontally rather than vertically as in the C pattern matchlock. The rectangular sear nose protruded through a corresponding slot in the lockplate, engaging a projection on the toe of the serpentine arm which had been repositioned at the rear of the lockplate with the jaws facing the muzzle; a system opposite of the C pattern mechanism and one profusely copied in the Orient.

Depressing a small, button-head trigger extending from the side of the lockplate disengaged the sear nose from the serpentine arm. The serpentine, activated by a spring, carried the match to the priming pan. The *lütenschnappschloss* was occasionally encountered in some martial arquebuses prior to midcentury and it can be considered a true lock mechanism because the sear restrained the serpentine.

A variation of the *lütenschnappschloss* emerged ca. 1540 and was known as the *schwammschloss* (tinder lock). The *schwammschloss* was less frequently encountered and it is identified by an intermediate link between the sear and the sear release (trigger). Disengaged by pulling a short cord or pushing a button concealed in the forestock, the intermediate link was activated by a leaf spring and struck the sear a sharp blow, releasing it from the serpentine arm in the manner of the *lütenschnappschloss*.

It is probable that the intermediate sear link of the *schwammschloss* originated ca. 1500-1525 in some sophisticated variation of the hunting crossbow mechanism and it is undoubtedly the precursor of what is currently known as the set-trigger. Some historians claim that the set-trigger mechanism was invented in 1543 by Nuremburg master gunsmith Wolf Danner (fl. 1540-1592), then serving Emperor

Charles V, though it is likely that Danner adapted the mechanism for use in a gunlock.[49]

The *lütenschnappschloss* employed matchcord in the prescribed manner, though in the *schwammschloss* the priming powder was ignited from a bit of tinder or small piece of match held in the serpentine jaws and lighted from a separate match or other combustible agent immediately prior to firing; thus the appellation tinder lock. Matchlock firearms incorporating either snapping mechanism were not found in abundance until ca. 1565 and their distribution was limited to Germany until ca. 1575-1580.

The success of the Spanish matchlock musket in the Netherlands campaigns inspired its rapid acceptance by other European powers. A massive weapon, the typical martial matchlock musket displayed a 45 to 55 inch wrought iron barrel with an hexagonal or octagonal breech and it was loaded with an .80 to .90 caliber ball backed by three and one half to four drams of *grosse corne* (corned powder). Overall length was approximately six feet and the musket weighed 18 to 20 pounds, though there were heavier exceptions. The *fourquine*, formerly used with the obsolete *culverin*, was resurrected to support the ponderous weapon.

The large ball employed in the martial musket was capable of penetrating heavy armor up to 175 yards and could readily drop man or beast at 200 yards if it found its mark. Parenthetically, body armor fluctuated considerably in its ability to withstand the kinetic energy generated by an iron crossbow quarrel, a steel-tipped arrow, or a lead ball propelled by a large powder charge.

By ca. 1525 full armor had been discarded throughout most of Europe, though the cuirass was retained for several reasons, including the quality and the density of the metal which ranged in some instances from 0.040 to 0.175-inch.

Tage Lasson also tested matchlock firearms and clarifies some of the confusion regarding their efficacy (see p. 14). The gunpowder used in his experiments conformed to a formulae recorded by Pietro Sarti in 1621 with a ratio of 71.4:14.3:14.3. The powder charge weighed 310 grains and the ball 616 grains.

The martial matchlock musket employed in the test was made in Suhl, Germany, ca. 1590-1600, weighed 11 pounds, and displayed a 52.4-inch barrel

WALL GUN (16th Century, 1562): This snapping matchlock wall gun made in Germany has an octagonal, 53¾-inch barrel of .85 caliber. The stock is ¾ length. Note the barrel hook, external mainspring, swamped muzzle, and the serpentine arm facing the muzzle; an innovation dictated by the lock design. The snapping matchlock was the immediate precursor of the snapping flintlock. British Crown Copyright. Reproduced with permission of the Controller of Her Britannic Majesty's Stationery Office.

MATCHLOCK ARQUEBUS, Revolving
Breech (15th/16th Century): Made in
Germany ca. 1490-1530, this ten-shot,
matchlock arquebus incorporated a
radical technological innovation: the
revolving cylinder breech. The
mechanical principles illustrate one of
the attempts by early gunsmiths to
increase firepower and it can be
considered an advanced approach to the
evolution of practical breech-loading,
repeating firearms. From *Quellen zur
Geschichte de Feuerwaffen*
(Leipzig, 1872).
Author's sketch.

MATCHLOCK ARQUEBUS (17th
Century, 1607): This C pattern
matchlock arquebus made in
Suhl, Germany, has a 42-inch barrel of approximately .55 caliber.
Note the post-type rear sight,
lever trigger, and butt trap with
sliding wooden cover. The lockplate indicates that the arquebus
was originally provided with a
wheellock. Courtesy of the
Tøjhusmuseet, Copenhagen.

of .71 caliber. The specifications differ radically from the martial matchlock muskets produced nearly 50 years earlier, for interim technological innovation had reduced the characteristic bulk of those firearms though performance was comparable.

Lasson reported that the chronographed velocity of the ball was measured at 1,650 feet per second, and that it readily penetrated the heaviest body armor. He reduced the powder charge by 100 grains and velocity measured 1,280 fps; comparable to a modern 40 grain, .22 caliber long rifle bullet or a 100 grain, .32-20 bullet. Muzzle (kinetic) energy was recorded at 2,000 foot-pounds per square inch as compared to 2,090 psi for a modern 100 grain, .243 bullet. At about 500 feet the .71 caliber musket ball penetrated a thin breastplate and a two-inch pine board. Firing the musket, Lasson noted, produced severe recoil and he received a face full of smouldering matchcord embers; discomfitures doubtlessly experienced by all arquebusiers and musketeers.

The C pattern matchlock mechanism displayed a number of innovative improvements by ca. 1580. The firing lever had been generally supplanted by a shorter, curved projection (trigger) pin-fastened to the lockplate and a square-backed or rounded trigger guard was provided; the rear tang frequently displaying a finger rest. The sear bar was redesigned with a lateral, L-shaped heel to provide a bearing surface for the upper part of the trigger.

A flat, iron plate (sideplate) or small washers installed opposite the lockplate were introduced to support the lock screws, relieving the strain formerly sustained by the stock alone. Buttstocks were generally straighter, emulating the Spanish pattern, and some terminated in a wide, flaring butt now termed a fishtail, while the wrist was thicker and displayed a deep thumb notch. By ca. 1600 the wooden ramrod was almost exclusively carried beneath the forestock; a shallow channel for the purpose often mortised into the wood.

Design innovations in matchlock firearms emerged gradually and occasionally illustrated a large measure of technological sophistication well in advance of prevailing concepts. This is exemplified by the singular design of a matchlock arquebus presumed to have been made in Germany by an unknown gunsmith-inventor ca. 1490-1530, and it represents the first known example of the revolving breech principle. Once part of a private collection, the radically innovative firearm subsequently vanished, though it is depicted in *Quellen sur Geschicte der Feuerwaffen* (Source Material for the History of Firearms [Leipzip: 1872]).[50]

This revolving breech firearm is particularly significant because it apparently emerged nearly a century before similar specimens, and while the rotating breech concept sporadically appeared during the seventeenth century and thereafter it failed to reach its full potential until the second quarter of the nineteenth century.

The revolving breech matchlock arquebus was also a breech-loading firearm, the breech appearing as a cylinder and in this instance ten chambers were bored into it, each separately loaded. The cylinder was manually rotated around a central axis pin positioning it slightly forward of the serpentine arm which faced the muzzle, indicating that it was a snapping matchlock though there is no conclusive evidence supporting that contention. A spring catch integral with the rear sight and mounted atop the round barrel snapped into a detent on the face of each chamber, locking it in alignment with the barrel. Each chamber also had a vent and a priming pan with a sliding cover. A front sight was mounted near the muzzle and a pin-fastened rather than lever trigger was used.

In addition to the ignition system the revolving cylinder arquebus displayed several disadvantages and consequently failed to transcend the experimental category to become a popular martial or utilitarian firearm. The firearm was difficult to manipulate, for the cylinder was rotated by hand and each pan cover had to be opened independently and immediately prior to firing, otherwise the priming powder would have fallen from the chamber pans not aligned with the barrel. Reloading the ten-shot cylinder significantly reduced the rapid-fire capability of the arquebus, while the relatively complex design made it difficult and expensive to manufacture.

Though by 1535 Spain had successfully standardized the caliber of the martial matchlock arquebus and its ball to permit interchangeability, the same cannot be said of other European powers; nor were commercial (utilitarian) firearms brought to that degree of tolerance in Spain or elsewhere on the Continent. Various measuring systems were employed throughout Europe and what standards there were not only fluctuated between countries, but even from village to village; a problem largely unresolved until the widespread acceptance of the metric system devised in France and adopted there in 1791.

In Spain the caliber of the martial matchlock arquebus was based on the measuring system used in Castile, while other firearms employed systems familiar in the place where they were made. In England, however, a practical system of weights and measures employed throughout the nation evolved ca. 1540 during the reign of Henry VIII (1509-1547) when the standard inch and the 16-ounce pound were adopted; a significant advantage stemming from England's isolation and the political hemogeny imposed by her powerful monarch. Parenthetically, the pound weight of Castile was also 16 ounces, as earlier noted in the 1535 martial arquebus contract.

In English firearms the number of balls which could be cast from a pound of lead determined the bore size (caliber), e.g., a pound of lead produced 16 one-ounce balls. The number of lead balls per pound was expressed as *bore number* rather than caliber, and a bore taking a ball 16 to the pound was a 16 bore; eight to the pound an eight bore; and four to the pound a four bore (see APPENDIX I). In English-speaking nations the current system used to determine the bore size of shotguns is based on a modified version of the early Tudor method, though by ca. 1880 the term bore size was supplanted by the now common gauge.

Throughout the sixteenth century there appeared in Europe additional accessories and accouterments designed for firearms. Carrying a length of matchcord in the hand or wrapped around the stock was inconvenient and also exposed it to the elements. A solution was found with the match case. Precisely where the match case originated is unknown though it was popular ca. 1530 and it remained in use among grenadiers long after match ignition had been rendered obsolete.

The match case was a cylinder nearly a foot long and made of tin or other metal into which a two-foot length of lighted match was coiled. Provided with a

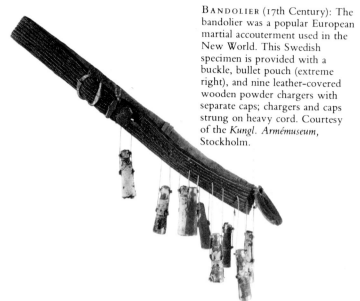

BANDOLIER (17th Century): The bandolier was a popular European martial accouterment used in the New World. This Swedish specimen is provided with a buckle, bullet pouch (extreme right), and nine leather-covered wooden powder chargers with separate caps; chargers and caps strung on heavy cord. Courtesy of the *Kungl. Armémuseum*, Stockholm.

ARCUBUCERO & ACCOUTERMENTS (16th/17th Century): The detail of the Spanish arquebusier (*arcubucero*) is from a late 16th Century mural in the *Sala de Batallas* of the *Escorial*, Madrid. Flanking the arquebusier (clockwise) are an aiming fork or rest *(horquilla)* and bullet pouch, a powder flask with a belt hook and a powder horn, a vent pick and a pan brush; a tin match case, paper cartridges depicting the method of attaching the ball: the paper tied to the casting sprue (right) and the paper tied to an integral flange incorporated in the bullet mould (left); a bore scraper (scower) and bullet worm, and a loading flask *(estuche)* and a priming flask *(frasquillo)*. Author's sketch.

tight cap, the match case was perforated to provide oxygen and exhaust vents, while it was usually carried suspended from the belt by a short chain or thong.

In addition to the waist belt or *hanger* serving to support and carry edged weapons like the sword and cutlass, there was the wide leather or cloth shoulder strap known as the *baldric* and used for the same purpose. With the widespread acceptance of the martial arquebus by ca. 1550 there was introduced in the Netherlands an accouterment similar to the baldric and known there as the *bandelier*; the term subsequently anglicized to *bandoleer* or *bandolier*.

The bandolier is believed to have been designed to make it easier for the arquebusier to load, because strung from it on heavy cords and within easy reach were a dozen or more wood or leather containers each provided with a cap and filled with a single, predetermined powder charge. The small powder containers can be considered the progenitor of the paper cartridge and were probably inspired by the fourteenth-century powder charger.

By 1575 the bandolier was extremely popular in western Europe, though it found little favor in Spanish America. Unlike the Old World where most battles were fought in open terrain, the Spaniards struggled against the Native Americans in dense forests and jungles. The bandolier had a predilection to tangle in the foliage, the chargers rattled when any stealthy movement was attempted, and they were unusually susceptible to priming flash because the caps were easily opened; often jarring loose by ordinary body movement or catching in the undergrowth.

There is also the possibility that the bandolier was used sparingly in Spanish America because a less troublesome means of carrying ammunition had been introduced to complement yet another radical technological innovation. Though the evidence is flimsy, the 1578 Flores report on the Florida provinces mentioned "munitions pouches" (see p. 48) as part of the garrison equipment, indicating that something other than loose powder and ball was available and carried in a special pouch. It can be surmised that the "something" was paper cartridges though supportive evidence has not been found. There is, however, substantial documentation confirming the concept of the paper cartridge.

A thin paper tube containing both powder and ball for convenience in loading and priming had been suggested for military use by Leonardo da Vinci (1452?-1519) when ca. 1482-1499 he served as a military engineer for Ludovico Sforza, Duke of Milan. Precisely where, when, or by whom the paper cartridge was first introduced has not been determined, though there remains the remote possibility that it was used in La Florida by 1578.

It has been suggested that paper cartridges containing only powder were used ca. 1550 by German cavalry to facilitate loading when mounted.[51] Paper cartridges containing both powder and ball probably emerged in Denmark or the Netherlands ca. 1575 and it is known that they were employed in England prior to 1590, for that year Sir John Smythe described "cartages with which [musketeers] charge theyr peeces both with poudre and ball at 1 time."[52]

In some early forms of the cartridge the ball was cast with an integral flange and tied to the paper wrapper, though the most common method was to wrap the ball with the powder; a string securing the ball end of the paper and the other end merely twisted and folded. When loading the wrapper was torn or bitten open and the predetermined charge, less a small amount for priming, was poured down the bore with the ball and paper driven after it; the paper used as wadding instead of tow.

The paper cartridge was a significant technological innovation which greatly simplified and accelerated the heretofore lengthy and tedious loading process. Despite the advantages, paper cartridges were not immediately adopted for military use nor did they find popular acceptance, while they were then never seriously considered for rifled firearms because of the substantially different loading techniques involved. With the widespread military acceptance of paper cartridges ca. 1640-1650 they thereafter exclusively served in that capacity until rendered obsolete by metallic cartridges in the late nineteenth century.

Self-igniting Gunlocks

European gunsmiths and inventors, frequently one and the same, early sought to eliminate the disadvantages of matchcord and devised a number of innovative ignition systems which did not rely on it to deliver the requisite spark, and they can be considered self-igniting gunlocks, i.e., rather than being extraneously applied as with matchcord, the ignition spark was produced by mechanical means.

It is believed that the earliest self-igniting gunlock appeared in Germany ca. 1480. Known as the Monk's Gun because of some vague notion that it was made by the mythical Friar Schwartz who is also erroneously credited with inventing gunpowder and guns, it is preserved in Dresden's Historisches Museum.[53] A number of firearms historians have suggested that the Dresden specimen is the surviving example of the few produced and others say that it is the only firearm of its kind ever made. And if the controversy surrounding the date of its introduction can be satisfactorily resolved, the Monk's Gun could claim the distinction of being the first pistol, notwithstanding the diminutive Loshult hand cannon.

The Monk's Gun has no sights or stock, displays an eleven-inch, round iron barrel, and both hands were required to fire it. One of the novel innovations represented in the Monk's Gun is the hook attached beneath the breech which allowed it to be conveniently carried on the belt and, as far as it is known, it is the first example of the belt hook subsequently found on a variety of firearms.

Attached to the left side of the Monk's Gun

breech is a rectangular box about five and one-half inches long with a small compartment at the rear, open at the bottom, which serves as the priming pan. Transversing the box is a serrated bar with a finger piece at the rear; the serrated edge of the bar protruding into the pan opening.

Mounted atop the pan box and facing the breech is a pivotal serpentine arm held by spring tension. A piece of iron pyrites (marcasite) clamped in the serpentine jaws rests upon the serrated bar exposed in the pan. Loaded and primed conventionally, the Monk's Gun was fired by a sharp, rearward pull on the rasp-like bar. The serrations sliding against the marcasite produced the requisite ignition spark. A finger piece beneath the barrel was held in one hand when the other pulled the serrated bar; thus the Monk's Gun was extremely difficult to control when fired.

A possibly unique technological achievement, the Monk's Gun failed to be further exploited because of its control disadvantage and it is extremely doubtful, as some writers have suggested, that it influenced the development of other self-igniting mechanisms like the innovative wheellock which emerged at the same time.

The origin of the wheellock is bound in as much obscurity and controversy as many other early firearms innovations. The first known illustration of the self-igniting wheellock appears in Leonardo da Vinci's *Il Codice Atlantico,* presumably written ca. 1485–1510, and it is accompanied by a sketch of a self-igniting tinder lighter used for starting fires; probably to delineate the mechanical affinity.[54]

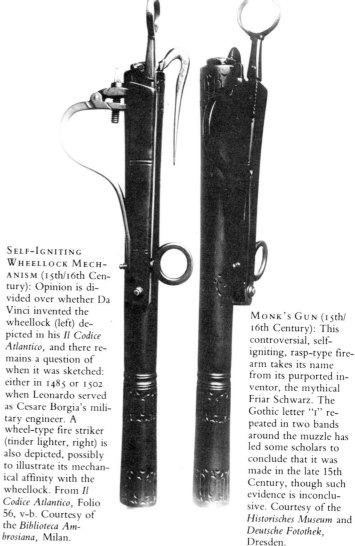

SELF-IGNITING WHEELLOCK MECHANISM (15th/16th Century): Opinion is divided over whether Da Vinci invented the wheellock (left) depicted in his *Il Codice Atlantico,* and there remains a question of when it was sketched: either in 1485 or 1502 when Leonardo served as Cesare Borgia's military engineer. A wheel-type fire striker (tinder lighter, right) is also depicted, possibly to illustrate its mechanical affinity with the wheellock. From *Il Codice Atlantico,* Folio 56, v-b. Courtesy of the *Biblioteca Ambrosiana,* Milan.

MONK'S GUN (15th/16th Century): This controversial, self-igniting, rasp-type firearm takes its name from its purported inventor, the mythical Friar Schwarz. The Gothic letter "I" repeated in two bands around the muzzle has led some scholars to conclude that it was made in the late 15th Century, though such evidence is inconclusive. Courtesy of the *Historisches Museum* and *Deutsche Fotothek,* Dresden.

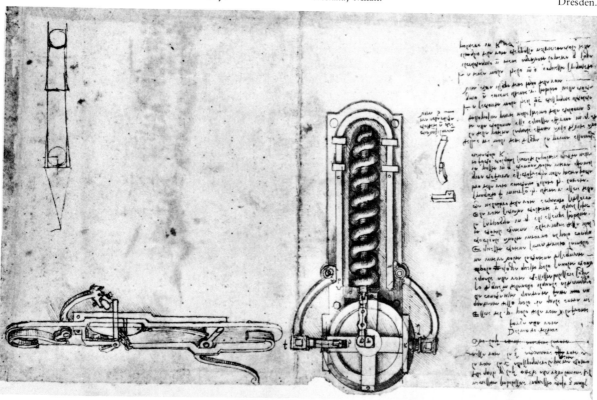

Da Vinci's detailed sketch does not conclusively determine where the wheellock originated or the identity of its inventor and it is likely that it was known in Germany and Italy before 1500, though the earliest authenticated references indicate that it emerged in southern Germany prior to 1510. Tinder lighters similar to that sketched by da Vinci were depicted in a 1505 manuscript now lost though attributed to Martin Loffelholtz of Nuremburg, and it is possible that the wheellock was derived from those spark-producing mechanisms.[55]

In *Schuss and Waffe* (Shooting and Firearms) F.M. Feldhaus avers that in 1506 the statutes governing the shooting range at Geisslingen prohibited the use of wheellock firearms, though the reference has been recently discredited.[56] It is known, however, that in 1507 Cardinal Ippolito d'Este I, Archbishop of Zagreb, purchased from Germany *"unam piscidem de illis que incenduntur cum lapide"* (a firearm kindled by a stone).[57] There is also an undisputed reference to Goslar gunsmith Hans Luder who made wheellocks in 1509.[58]

Within the time frame of this study the wheellock was the most complex ignition mechanism invented and it came to be applied to a variety of firearms, and of all the ignition mechanisms produced the wheellock dramatically exemplifies the extraordinary technical expertise of the gunsmith as well as the expanding technology representative of that magnificent epoch in firearms evolution.

Prior to ca. 1550 the few gunsmiths capable of forging the intricate wheellock were also engaged in making clocks and scientific instruments and they were usually Flemish, German, or Italian masters. Several kinds of wheellock mechanisms emerged and they were all variants of four basic designs,

primarily distinguished by the location of the distinctive serrated wheel which gave the lock its name and the relationship of the other components incorporated in the usually large, flat lockplate.

In the first and less complex wheellock variant the wheel is positioned outside the lockplate and completely exposed except for a shoulder or lip protecting the serrated wheel edge. The wheel is also mounted externally in the second lock variation, though it is provided with a cover. The third lock version has the wheel entirely enclosed in the lockplate, while in the fourth variant the wheel and most of the other components are exposed.

The functioning cycle of the basic wheellock is similar to the variations except in minor detail. As in most wheellocks the wheel is externally mounted on a short shank transversing the large lockplate. The lockplate displays an integrally-forged priming pan open at the bottom to expose a portion of the serrated wheel; the design expressed in several kinds of tinder lighters and the Monk's Gun.

A pivotal arm (doghead) facing the breech is attached by a screw to the forward end of the lockplate. The doghead heel rests on the upper leaf of a v-shaped feather spring externally mounted beneath it. The doghead spring in the lock sketched by da Vinci is a single, u-shaped bar passing under the wheel, though the design was early discarded. In some wheellock variations the doghead faced the muzzle.

The doghead jaws were adjusted by a vertical (jaw) screw. In early wheellocks the jaws held a piece of marcasite, but chert or flint were later substituted because marcasite was too brittle and easily broken.

A short chain with linkage similar to the common bicycle chain was attached to the end of the

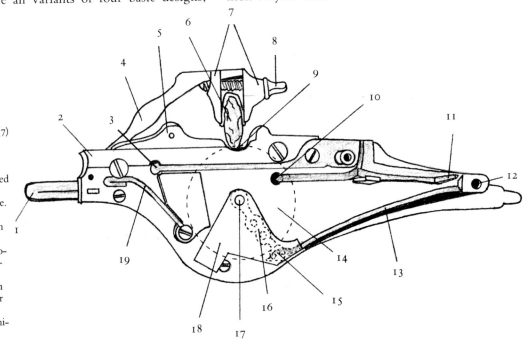

WHEELLOCK MECHANISM (ca. 1485-1502): (1) Doghead spring. (2) Lockplate. (3) Priming pan cover plunger. (4) Doghead. (5) Priming pan cover. (6) Pyrites. (7) Cock jaws. (8) Cock jaw screw. (9) Priming pan. (10) Sear nose. (11) Sear heel. (12) Mainspring. (13) Mainspring leaf. (14) Serrated Wheel. (15) Mainspring hook. (16) Wheel links. (17) Wheel axle. (18) Bridle. (19) Priming pan cover spring. Trigger bearing on (11) causes (10) to pivot out of recess in (14), permitting it to rotate under pressure from (15) attached to (16), simultaneously pushing (3) to activate (5) which slides forward to expose powder in (9) to the spark generated by (6) held in (7); thus effecting ignition. Author's sketch.

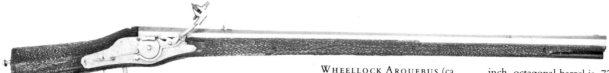

WHEELLOCK ARQUEBUS (ca. 1535): The slightly flared (swamped) muzzle of this German arquebus was common to many 16th-Century firearms. The full-length, pin-fastened stock is veneered with stag horn and the rounded butt projection is a screw-in vent pick; an innovation seen on Scottish pistols. The 37- inch, octagonal barrel is .72 caliber and provided with sights. Note the U-shaped dog-head spring and trigger guard with finger rests. British Crown Copyright. Reproduced with permission of the Controller of Her Britannic Majesty's Stationery Office.

wheel shank inside the lockplate, while a hook on the internal mainspring engaged a toggle at the opposite end of the chain. A wheel spanner (key or wrench), fitting the square shank head, was used to turn (span) the serrated wheel in the manner of winding a clock; thus the chain was wound around the wheel shank which exerted considerable tension on the powerful mainspring.

The sear, moving laterally as in the *lütenschnappschloss* and under pressure from the sear spring, engaged a detent in the inner wheel face, locking it in firing position. The doghead was manually positioned, the marcasite in its jaws contacting the serrated wheel edge exposed in the priming pan. In most early wheellocks a manually operated, sliding pan cover was provided; the cover withdrawn prior to lowering the doghead to the pan. Later wheellocks displayed a pan cover which automatically exposed the pan when the doghead was lowered.

Pressure on either a button-head protruding from the lockplate or the conventional pin-fastened trigger initiated the firing cycle, pivoting the sear nose out of its detent in the wheel surface. The wheel then rapidly rotated counterclockwise under mainspring pressure, the serrated edge contacting the marcasite to generate the ignition spark. The distance spanned by the wheel determined the duration and intensity of the spark. Depending on the kind of lock construction, the wheel generally spanned between 270-355°.

In some instances the number of components performing the intricate functioning cycle engendered a relatively difficult trigger release, i.e., inordinate trigger pressure was needed to disengage the sear and that interfered with the control of the firearm. After 1545 the problem was often circumvented with a set-trigger (intermediate sear) which released the sear crisply and smoothly with minimal disturbance to the aim.

The first set-triggers such as found in the *schwammschloss* were single-stage types, i.e., only one sear release was used. By midcentury double set-triggers emerged employing two stages, while prior to 1600 compound set-triggers evolved with some incorporating three intermediate stages. Subsequent variations used as many as six stages. Set-trigger mechanisms were sporadically used throughout the centuries, and they are currently evident.

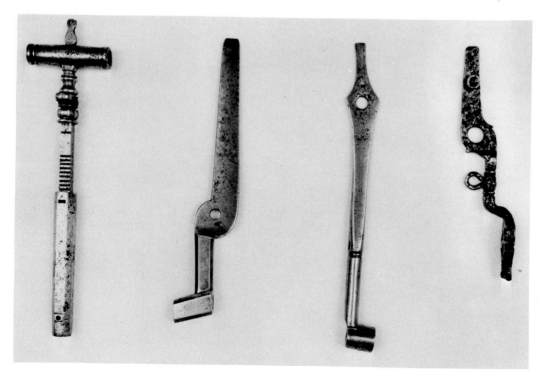

WHEELLOCK SPANNERS (16th/17th Century): From left. German spanner ca. 1575 includes an adjustable powder measure (charger). German spanner of ca. 1570 incorporates a screwdriver blade; an early form of the so-called combination tool for firearms disassembly and assembly. Danish spanner of ca. 1585 also has a screwdriver. German spanner of ca. 1625 has an offset screwdriver and loop for a carrying thong. Courtesy of the *Tøjhusmuseet*, Copenhagen.

The set-trigger as applied to the wheellock was provided with a relatively straight trigger bar extending beneath the stock and usually situated forward of the primary (lock) trigger. The set-trigger was adjusted by a tension screw also extending beneath the stock and regulating the amount of pressure necessary to release the sear when the primary trigger was squeezed. Pressure on the trigger bar "set" the intermediate sear and the tension could be so precisely adjusted that the slightest pressure on the primary trigger discharged the weapon, subsequently giving rise to the expression *hair trigger;* an exaggeration implying that pressure on the trigger equal in weight to a hair was sufficient to release the sear.

The wheellock mechanism was so well developed in Germany by 1515 that it had been applied to an innovative firearm which could be readily held and discharged by one hand, for that year Wilhelm Rem of Augsburg related in his *Chronica Newer Geschicten* that a prostitute had been accidentally wounded by a wheellock pistol.[59] Some scholars say that the word *pistol* derived from the Italian arms-making center of Pistoia, often erroneously referred to as the birthplace of the wheellock, though it also has been suggested that it evolved from *pistole,* an Italian coin of the period approximating the circumference of a pistol ball, or from the Czech *pist'ala* (tube).[60]

The compact, readily concealed wheellock pistol had become available in such numbers by the second decade of the sixteenth century that it was considered a threat to public and, more disturbing, sovereign safety. Consequently, in 1517 emperor Maximilian banned wheellock pistols throughout the Hapsburg Empire and in so doing enacted the first anti-firearms legislation. A year later he proscribed the use of self-igniting mechanisms in all firearms. In Italy similar prohibitions were initiated by the Duke of Ferrara in 1522.

By 1525 various kinds of smoothbore and rifled wheellock firearms were known throughout Europe and there was as much diversity in the design of those firearms as in the wheellock mechanisms they displayed. Prior to midcentury there were wheellock firearms with interchangeable barrels, superimposed barrels, multiple barrels, and barrels loaded at the breech. Wheellock firearms displayed dual locks set in a single lockplate or locks mounted on either or both sides of the breech. There were also wheellock firearms combined with crossbows, lances, battle axes, matchlocks, maces, knives and forks, sundials, and sundry other articles both useful and impractical.

The earliest dated firearm incorporating the wheellock is currently in the *Bayerische Armeemuseum,* Munich, and it was expressly made for Ferdinand I (1503-1564) who became Holy Roman Emperor upon the abdication of his brother, Charles V. Charles had chosen Ferdinand to rule Germany in 1521 and that year he also married Anna, daughter of King Vladislav III of Hungary and Bohemia. A combination wheellock arquebus and crossbow, the weapon parallels the design of several similar crossbow-firearms of Italian origin now in the Palazzo Ducale (Ducal Palace), Venice.

Marked FERDINANDUS on the upper breech flat, the arquebus displays a coat of arms indicating that it was made after Ferdinand assumed the German crown in 1521, though before he became king of Bohemia in 1526. The bow has a 21 inch span and overall length of the weapon is 28¾ inches. The .36 caliber, smoothbore barrel is 15¾ inches long and the stock is painted red and gold with the initials F (Ferdinand) and A (Anna) continuously repeated in the decorative motif. The arquebus and the bow are each provided with a button-head trigger.

Dated with more precision is an *arcabucillo de arzon* (short wheellock saddle carbine) made in 1530 for Charles V and now in the Royal Armory Museum, Madrid.[61] A signature mark identifies the

SET TRIGGER MECHANISMS (16th Century): Top. Single set trigger ca. 1540. Similar devices were used earlier in sporting crossbows and subsequently adapted to firearms. Bottom. Compound set trigger ca. 1575.

Set screws regulated the spring tension of the intermediate set trigger which reduced the amount of pressure needed to release the sear when the primary trigger was pulled. Author's sketch.

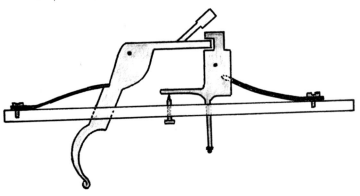

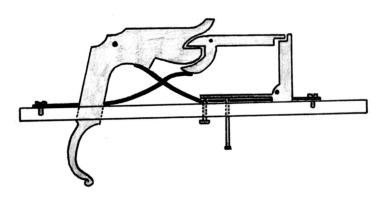

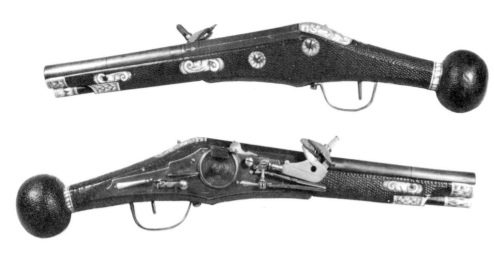

carbine as the work of Augsburg master gunsmith Bartholme Marquart (fl. 1527-1552) whose sons, Siegmund and Peter, subsequently went to Madrid and were employed as journeymen gunsmiths in the court of Philip II.

Charles V also possessed a wheellock pistol made ca. 1540 by Munich master gunsmith Peter Pech (1503-1596).[62] It was an unique handgun with .46 caliber, superimposed barrels. The upper barrel measures ten inches and the lower seven and ⅝ inches; each served by a separate lock incorporated in a single lockplate. A cherry grip carved in a twist pattern extends straight back from the breech in the usual fashion of wheellock pistols, though the curved butt displays a metal cap atypical of the period. The pistol weighs five pounds and ten ounces and it is poorly balanced because of the superimposed barrels and the large lockplate supporting dual locks.

Unlike his grandfather Maximilian, Charles V had no qualms regarding innovative firearms. Having advantageously employed Spanish *arcubuceros* at Pavia in 1525, he armed his German *Reiters* (cavalry) in 1544 with wheellock pistols then commonly known as dags.[63] Dags were single-shot pistols issued in pairs to increase firepower and in some instances a single horseman carried two pairs; one pair in specially designed leather holsters attached to the front saddle skirts and the other pair merely thrust into the belt or sash or wide boot top. The characteristically straight grip design of the dag was dictated by the fact that, like the short sword, it was thrust directly at an adversary at extremely close range, for as Lasson notes, the accuracy of the dag was minimal beyond twenty yards.[64]

It is believed that the popularity of the dag as a cavalry weapon inspired the development of the paper cartridge for convenience in loading when mounted. Charles V might have been instrumental in the adoption of the paper cartridge and he could have learned of that innovation from his grandfather, Maximilian, for in 1494 the then emperor married Bianca Maria Sforza, niece of Ludovico Sforza. Maximilian and Ludovico often discussed military matters and the latter was generous in his praise of his pragmatic military engineer, Leonardo da Vinci, who had suggested the use of paper cartridges (see p. 52).

The acceptance of paper cartridges for cavalry use spawned the development of the *patron*, a sheet metal container designed to carry five or six pistol cartridges in separate compartments which protected them from the elements and physical damage. The *patron* had a hinged cover with a spring latch, its name probably derived from *patronen*, the German and Scandinavian word for cartridge. By ca. 1590 the *patron* was a common cavalry accouterment though whether it was used in the New World remains moot.

The primary advantage of wheellock ignition was that the firearm was instantly available for use because it could be safely carried fully primed and loaded. Another advantage was design latitude, for the wheellock inspired the development of the first practical handguns. Wheellock firearms also became popular for sporting purposes in both smoothbore and rifled versions with many of the latter superbly accurate, though the cost limited their procurement to the aristocracy.

Wheellock arquebuses and muskets were comparable to corresponding matchlock firearms in range, accuracy, and missile penetration, yet the complexity of the mechanism rendered it susceptible to malfunctions; especially when continuously fired or exposed to the elements for prolonged periods. While component failure was a problem, most malfunctions were caused by powder fouling which

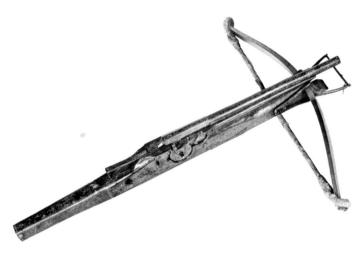

CROSSBOW/WHEELLOCK (ca. 1521-1526): One of the earliest reliably dated wheellock firearms is this combination crossbow/wheellock made for Ferdinand I (1503-1564), successor to Emperor Charles V, between 1521 and 1526. The top breech flat is marked FERDINANDUS. The steel bow has a 21-inch span and the overall length of the firearm is 28¾-inches. The 15¾-inch barrel is .36 caliber. The doghead jaws are missing.

Top view depicts breech flat marking. Note the v-notch rear sight at the rear of the breech flat and the right and left button-head triggers; the former releasing the wheellock sear. Courtesy of the *Bayerisches Nationalmuseum,* Munich.

clogged the mechanism and it was particularly severe in wet weather. Cleaning the bore and the lock was mandatory after as few as five shots.

A distinct though unpredictable safety hazard was discovered by Lasson during his wheellock performance tests, for he found that a jammed wheel was often unexpectedly released and the firing cycle completed by merely jostling the weapon.[65] The complexity of the wheellock made it difficult and consequently expensive to make and repair and, combined with an inherent safety hazard, those disadvantages limited its application in martial firearms.

In addition to graphically illustrating the technical expertise of the master gunsmith, wheellock firearms magnificently reflected the exquisite and elegant craftsmanship exhibited by a host of other, equally talented artisans; thus in most instances wheellock firearms were not the product of a single, skilled artificer. Considerable time, effort, and painstaking attention to detail were lavishly expended when chasing, carving, engraving, and deftly inlaying those estimable firearms. Particularly impressive was the masterfully expressive inlay work incorporating a mélange of exotic wood, ivory, bone, horn, mother of pearl, priceless gems, and precious metals either singly or combined in a wide range of elaborate, intricate, and often erotic motifs. Many of the wheellock firearms currently reposing in museums were chosen for display not because of their esoteric technological characteristics, but for their esthetic appeal as majestic works of art.

By 1550 even a rather plain wheellock arquebus cost the equivalent of $800 to $1000 at present inflation value, and the more sophisticated and vermiculated specimens were accordingly priced higher. Utilitarian and martial wheellock firearms with few or no embellishments were less expensive, though more costly than matchlock firearms. In Spain a common matchlock arquebus was priced at four ducats in 1593, while a comparable wheellock arquebus cost fifteen.[66]

Wheellock firearms spread through most of Europe and were employed in the New World prior to the end of the sixteenth century. Spanish gunsmiths, however, did not become proficient in making wheellocks until ca. 1575 and the popularity of the lock was relatively brief in Spain and her overseas dominions, lasting until ca. 1630 when supplanted by more efficient and less expensive ignition systems.[67]

With the advent of wheellock firearms several terms emerged to distinguish them from other firearms. Many of those appellations were ambiguous and interchangeable; thus further contributing to the problem of proper identification among contemporary and subsequent chroniclers.

In Spain ca. 1535 the matchlock arquebus was referred to as an *arcabuz de cuerda* (—cord) or *arcabuz*

CROSS, SWORD AND ARQUEBUS

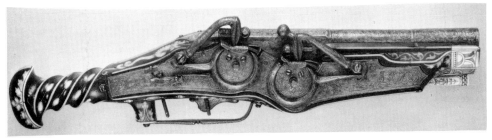

WHEELLOCK PISTOL, Superimposed Barrels (ca. 1540): This unique handgun, made by Munich gunsmith Peter Pech for Emperor Charles V, incorporates a dual lock and the helical stock is inlaid with carved ivory, while the metal components are engraved. Courtesy of the Metropolitan Museum of Art, Gift of William H. Riggs, 1913.

de mecha (—match), while the wheellock arquebus was termed an *arcabuz de pedernal* (—flint). Sixteenth-century Italians knew the wheellock arquebus as an *archibusi da ruota* (—wheel). In Germany the wheellock was known as a *feuerschloss* (firelock) and *firelock* was commonly used in England, while the wheellock pistol was called a *faustrohr* (fist tube). The French referred to the wheellock as a *platine à rouet*.

In the Netherlands the wheellock was known as a *vuerroer* though in the seventeenth century it came to be called a *radslot,* while a wheellock pistol was then termed a *radslotpistol*. While distinguishing the wheellock from the matchlock, the English term *firelock* was subsequently employed as a catch-all describing any self-igniting lock and it is comparable to the Spanish phrase *con su llave* (with a lock) which was popular ca. 1625.

CAVALRY CARTRIDGE BOXES (ca. 1580): Depicted are two examples of German engraved cartridge boxes (patrons) with hinged covers. The patron was a popular cavalry accouterment and served in colonial America. Courtesy of the *Tøjhusmuseet,* Copenhagen.

DOUBLE WHEELLOCK MECHANISM (ca. 1540): Interior view of disassembled lockplate from Charles V's pistol (top) and the lock components. The exemplary workmanship characterizes the technical expertise attained by early 16th-Century German gunsmiths as well as the innovative technology then extant. Courtesy of the Metropolitan Museum of Art, Gift of William H. Riggs, 1913.

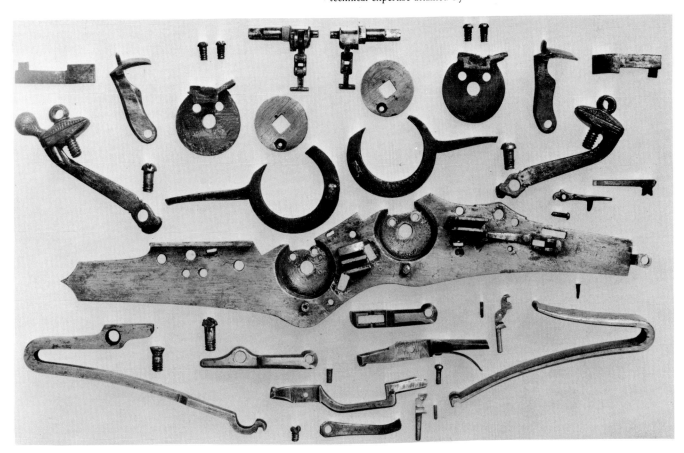

Machine-Tool Innovations

The ancient windmills, waterwheels, and treadmills serving as the primary power sources in sixteenth-century Europe had undergone centuries of innovative change, yet they were only as reliable as their dependence on the capricious natural elements or as animal and human energy would permit, nor did they produce sufficient power in relation to their prodigious size. Though inadequate, such machinery was the prime mover of what little heavy industry then existed in the Old World and remained so until the widespread application of steam power in the nineteenth century.

The elementary machine tools emerging in fifteenth-century Europe were basically employed for boring, grinding, and cutting; initially relying on the foot treadle and hand crank, though subsequently adapted to use the primary power sources. A number of those machine tools can trace their origin to the ancient bow drill and the potter's wheel of prehistory.

Augsburg and Nuremburg began to garner reputations as arms-making and machine-producing centers in late fourteenth-century Germany and it was in Germany that the innovative rifling engine was devised, while ca. 1475-1500 the crank-operated stamping mill was used there for powder-making. A relatively sophisticated stamping mill appears in Joseph Furtenbach, *Mannhaffter Kunst Spiegel* (Mirror of the Manly Arts [Augsburg: 1663]).

While those early machine tools directly contributed to the innovative manufacturing techniques emerging in firearms technology there existed an imperative need for large quantities of gunscrews in addition to those used in the various navigating, surveying, and scientific instruments devised and developed during that expansive epoch.

Screws were initially made by laboriously filing helical grooves (threads) into suitable wrought iron stock; a difficult and time-consuming task. At some undetermined time prior to the advent of firearms the innovative screw plate appeared, serving as a die to cut the helical threads. The flat surface of the steel screw plate was perforated with a series of holes varying in size with the internal cutting edge corresponding to the width and diameter of the helical threads desired. The soft iron stock was forced into the die hole with a twisting motion; the threads cut by the sharp, internal edge.

While the screw plate cut the external (male) threads for the various component screws used in firearms, including the breech plug, equally innova-

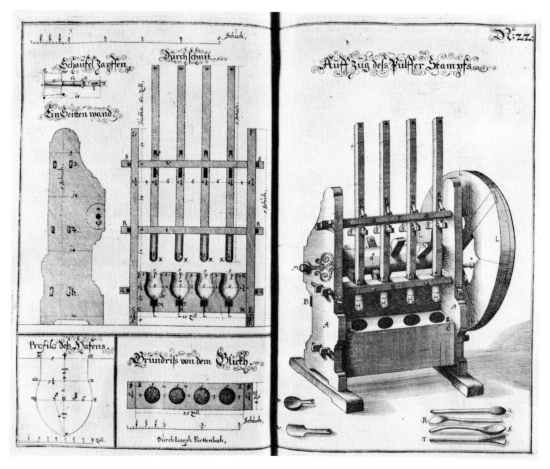

POWDER-STAMPING MILL (1663): Hand-and-water-powered stamping mills were used in European powder mills since the early 16th Century. This specimen is depicted in Joseph Furtenbach, *Mannhaffter Kunst-Spiegel* (Mirror of the Manly Arts), Augsburg, 1663. Courtesy of the Smithsonian Institution, Washington, D.C.

tive steel taps were employed to cut the internal (female) threads in the screw holes. Resembling the screw, the tap was forced into the screw hole with a twisting motion and the external cutting edges produced threads corresponding to those made by the screw plate; thus the threads of the screw fit the hole threads.

Nor can it be dismissed as a distinct possibility that gunscrews were turned (cut) on a lathe, for machine-tool technology had progressed to the point where it was feasible by ca. 1550. Though it has been frequently stated that the pole lathe and the mandrel lathe of that early epoch were exclusively employed for woodworking, either machine could be used to cut soft bronze or mild wrought iron because steel of sufficient durability was then available and already in use for making boring and rifling bits in addition to taps and screw plates.

One of the first machine tools capable of cutting screw threads was the pole lathe, believed to be a horizontal adaptation of the vertical potter's wheel initially appearing in the Fertile Crescent ca. 3250 B.C. An illustration dated A.D. 1395 confirms the early use of the pole lathe in Europe, and it was subsequently improved.[68]

The pole lathe used a resilient sapling (spring pole) as a power source. A long, stout cord was attached to the spring pole then looped around the horizontal work piece and connected to a foot treadle. The pumping treadle action was reciprocated by the spring pole, rapidly rotating the work as the operator manipulated a variety of cutting tools against it while simultaneously pumping the treadle.

Leonardo da Vinci, the Renaissance man of catholic interests, counted an innovative file-making machine among his myriad inventions and he also sketched a rudimentary, water-powered mandrel lathe. The horizontal mandrel lathe reproduced screw threads in wood from a handmade pattern, though like the pole lathe, it was incapable of originating the thread.[69]

The *Mittelalterliche Hausbuch* of ca. 1480 depicts a superior mandrel lathe, for it incorporated an adjustable cross-slide to hold the cutting tools; a portentous innovation permitting a precisely controlled cut. The improved mandrel lathe, however, still could not originate a thread. By ca. 1530 the cross-slide was applied to the pole lathe and it was further improved ca. 1550 with the addition of a drive spindle to which the cord was attached; the spindle securing the work rather than the cord.

Though the pole lathe and the mandrel lathe were certainly incapable of precision work, and while there were no established thread standards, it is not beyond reason to assume that gunscrews were turned by machine at least as early as 1550-1575 though whether the method persisted remains moot.

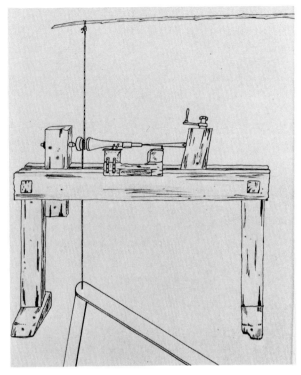

POLE (MANDREL) LATHE (Classical Antiquity/19th Century): Emerging ca. 1500 B.C., the pole lathe is an horizontal adaptation of the vertical potter's wheel. The first European illustration of a pole lathe appeared in 1395 and the specimen depicted is similar to those used in colonial America. Author's sketch.

MANDREL LATHE (ca. 1480): By 1450 mandrel lathes such as this specimen appearing in *Mittelalteriche Hausbuch* ca. 1480 were capable of cutting coarse screw threads in wood, copying a master model made by hand. Gun screws were handmade until late 17th-Century lathes were capable of making metal screws; some machines then designed to originate a thread. Courtesy of the Smithsonian Institution, Washington, D.C.

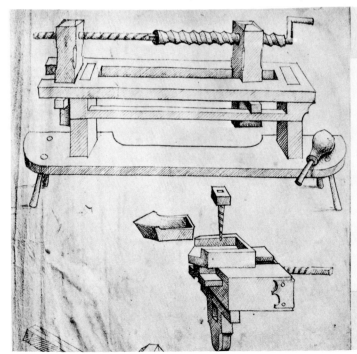

The innovative wheel-and-pulley drive system was introduced in Europe ca. 1550 and it was initially supplied with a human power source.[70] First depicted in 1568, the system incorporated a large flywheel mounted in a wood frame. The flywheel axle was provided with a pulley. A thick rope usually describing a figure eight extended from the flywheel pulley to a corresponding pulley or spindle attached to a machine. The speed of the machine spindle was regulated by the amount of energy applied to the flywheel. The wheel-and-pulley drive system is currently used.

Sights

Sixteenth-century firearms continued to use the post front sight and the v-notched rear sight earlier introduced and there were interim innovations. While early sights were usually integral with the barrel, many sixteenth-century sights were either brazed or soldered on or provided with a dovetailed base; brazing is a form of welding with brass, and soldering is the same although using a tin-lead alloy.

In rifled firearms the sights were more sophisticated because aiming was a criterion for accuracy. The use of the dovetailed slot cut in the barrel of rifled firearms rendered precision sight alignment practicable, permitting sufficient latitude for lateral adjustment because the sight base could be readily moved either to the right or left.

Trial and error determined the proper lateral and vertical sight adjustments, each related to correct bore alignment on the intended target because the sights had to correspond with the bore to achieve accuracy. The weapon was fired at a suitable target until the proper lateral and vertical adjustments had been made. If the ball struck low a higher front sight was used and vice versa, while if it struck to the right or left of the target the rear sight was moved in the dovetail slot to compensate.

When the sights were correctly aligned an index mark was usually scribed on the sight base and the barrel surface, making alignment easier if either sight was knocked awry. The sight base was generally *staked* in the dovetail slot, i.e., the edges of the slot were struck with a hammer and punch which forced them against the sight base, providing a tight grip.

Staking made it more difficult to knock the sights out of alignment; the front sight was more susceptible because it was usually mounted at the end of the barrel. The problem was circumvented by moving the front sight an inch or so to the rear. The rear sight was mounted on the breech flat about a foot from the eye when aiming, for it was found to be the optimum distance permitting a clear view of both sights.

Though the v-notch rear sight continued to be used and is currently evident, the sixteenth century

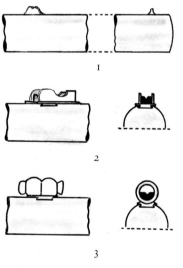

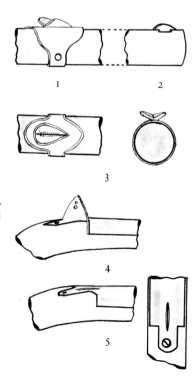

METALLIC SIGHTS (14th/18th Century): Left (top to bottom). (1) Post-type front sight and vertical, v-notch rear sight. Welded or cast integral with the barrel, early sights were fixed, i.e., not adjustable. (2) Panel-type rear sight. Fixed, dovetailed into the breech flat. Two flat panels enclosed a v-notch rear sight; used with some matchlock and wheellock firearms. (3) Tube-type rear sight (peep sight). Fixed, dovetailed and similar to match guide, some specimens had v-notch or peep aperture inserts. (4) Leaf-type rear sight. Fixed, dovetailed, and consisting of two leaves, one of which pivoted; each leaf regis-tered for a specific range. Found on rifled firearms. Right (top to bottom). (1 & 2) Saddle-type rear sight and knife-blade front sight. (3) Top and rear view of saddle-type sight. Fixed, attached to breech by a band or a pin and band. Primarily a Dutch innovation found on sporting guns. (4) Vertical, dual aperture rear sight. Fixed, one aperture smaller for finer sighting. Popular in Near East. (5) V-groove musket sight cut into top of breech as an aiming guide. Bottom center. Knife blade sight mounted on front barrel band, popular on some martial firearms; late 17th Century and thereafter, fixed. Author's sketch.

saw the introduction of three additional rear sights: the panel sight, the leaf sight, and the tube sight. Also introduced was the so-called knife-blade sight, longer and more narrow than the post-type front sight.

The panel sight had two short, parallel plates separated by a v-notched lead spacer. The leaf sight, usually found on rifled firearms, displayed two v-notched leaves with each serving a specific range. The separate leaves pivoted on pins in the sight base and lay flat against the barrel until raised for use. The tube sight was similar to the match guide purportedly inspiring it (see p. 42) and it was provided with disc-like insert plates either displaying a v-notch or small hole (aperture), i.e., a peep sight. Tube sights often had lids to facilitate changing the insert plates. Sights, like other technological innovations, were continuously improved and innumerable variations appeared.

The Emergence of Hunting Firearms

The firearm was initially a weapon of war, though not confined to that purpose, and as technology progressed it caused the demise of the crossbow and the longbow as martial and hunting weapons. Hunting was for the Old World aristocracy a traditional, often highly ritualistic sport, though for countless centuries it had been recognized by the peasantry as a prerequisite for survival.

By ca. 1490 simple, inexpensive matchlock firearms found their way into the calloused hands of the peasantry who successfully used them to supplement their meager fare with a variety of game. Because most of the land and its bounty was the property of the aristocracy, poaching continued as a way of life for the impoverished and remained a thorn in the flesh of the landlords who had for centuries attempted to regulate hunting with a plethora of odious and oppressive legislation. The poor ignored the law, for a growling belly had no respect for rules and regulations.

In England a peasantry long accustomed to certain liberties and especially contemputous of aristocratic prerogatives quickly embraced firearms; a dangerous precedent as seen by the aristocracy because it discouraged the use of the longbow which had been the mainstay of English military prowess since Edward III's decisive victory at Crécy (see p. 5).

Firearms had become so popular among the peasantry by 1508 that an alarmed Henry VII elicited from Parliament an act forbidding the use of cross-bows and firearms for hunting unless granted by royal permission.[71] In 1511 a proclamation from his son, Henry VIII, ordered all males under age forty to arm themselves with a longbow and practice daily.[72] Those royal pronouncements were directed toward regulating hunting with firearms as much as promoting the military use of the longbow.

The perceptive Tudors were aware that a dissatisfied peasantry increasingly recognizing the efficacy of firearms posed a powerful threat to present and future crown sovereignty; thus they attempted to protect the so-called inherent right of kings by discouraging the use of firearms without overtly confiscating them, consequently avoiding a political confrontation involving a popular emotional cause.

Continental aristocracy also attempted to prohibit the use of firearms among the peasantry with as little success. Whether for sport or sustenance, hunting with firearms was firmly established in western Europe prior to 1550 and legislation concerning licenses, seasons, bag limits, and protected land was difficult or impossible to enforce.

Despite the disadvantages of match ignition and firearms with irregularly bored barrels, peasant hunters managed to put extra meat on the trestle table. Most of it was large game because wildfowl and other small game was difficult to bag with a single ball unless the prey remained motionless while the hunter crept as close as possible, hoping that his presence would not be betrayed by a disturbing sound or the smouldering match and that shooting conditions were at least nearly perfect.

In the late fifteenth century it was discovered by a now unknown savant that a large number of small lead balls widely scattered when fired, increasing the chance of success when hunting wildfowl and other small game. The small pellets came to be known as birdshot or simply shot and distinctly improved the efficacy of hunting firearms.

Shot pellets were initially cast, though by ca. 1520 sheet lead cut into small cubes was also used, while shortly thereafter the cubes were tumbled after the manner of crushing powder cake or charcoal; friction rounding the edges to produce spherical shot.[73] In Spain ca. 1545 lead wire was cut into small pieces which were pelletized with a shot roller; a technological innovation consisting of a cast-iron plate mounted on a hardwood disc provided with a handle.[74] The roughly cut lead wire was gathered on a hard, flat surface and rolled into spherical form by the plate.

English peasantry early used *swan drops* (pellets shaped like teardrops) or *hayle* [hail] shot which was somewhat larger. A pound of shot contained 200 to 250 pellets, depending upon their size. There emerged in England ca. 1525-1550 a matchlock firearm with an exceptionally long barrel and massive breech designed specifically for bird hunting and it came to be called a long fowler. A pound of shot was often crammed down the muzzle of those early fowling pieces, frequently backed by a powder charge exceeding four drams. Judged by modern standards, fowling was then rather unsportsman-like because the hunter fired into the flock before the birds chanced to fly; a practical expedient dictated by survival.

Emerging with the widespread acceptance of shot was the shot flask, early specimens consisting of a large, leather pouch provided with a pour spout and stopper, though later flasks were similar in construction and design to the common powder flask. By ca. 1580 shot flasks and powder flasks were often provided with a spring-actuated stopper with the spout delivering a predetermined charge.

After ca. 1550 shot was made in volume by a process which continued to be used in the Old and New World until the end of the eighteenth century,

SHOT-MAKING (14th/18th Century): This shot-making method was widespread in Europe during the period indicated and it is similar to that described by Prince Rupert. From a woodcut in Vita Bonfadini, *La Caccia Dell' Arcobugio* (Hunting With the Arquebus), Venice, 1691. Author's sketch.

though there were more sophisticated interim methods. While there is no adequate contemporary description of the sixteenth-century shot-making technique, it is detailed in a seventeenth-century manuscript titled *Micrographia or Some Physiological Descriptions of Minute Bodies Made by Magnifying Glasses, with Observations and Inquiries thereon.*

Micrographia was published in 1665 by the noted chemist, mathematician, and inventor Robert Hooke (1635-1703) also known as the Father of Microscopy in England. Included in the treatise is a paper on shot-making written by Prince Rupert (1619-1682), son of Frederick V, Elector Palatine. Rupert manifested a scientist's curiosity, experimenting with metal alloys, gunpowder, and boring cannon barrels. He described the shot-making technique:

. . . Take lead out of the Pig what quantity you please, melt it down, stir and clear it with an iron Ladle, gathering together the blackist parts that swim at top like scum, and when you see the colour of the clear Lead to be greenish but no sooner, strew upon it Auripigmentum [arsenic trisulphide] powdered according to the quantity of Lead, about as much as will lye upon a half Crown piece will serve for eighteen to twenty pounds weight of some sorts of Lead; others will require more, or less. After the Auripigmentum is put in, stir the Lead well, and the Auripigmentum will flame: when the flame is over, take out some of the Lead in a Ladle having a lip or notch in the brim for convenient pouring out of the Lead, and with a stick make some single drops of Lead trickle out of the Ladle into water in a Glass, which if they fall to be round and without tails, there is Auripigmentum enough put in, and the temper of the heat is right, otherwise put in more. Then lay two bars of Iron (or some more proper Iron-tool made on purpose) upon a Pail of water, and place upon them a round Plate of Copper, of the size and figure of an ordinary large Pewter or Silver Trencher, the hollow whereof is to be about three inches over, the bottom lower then the brims about half an inch, pierced with thirty, forty, or more small holes; the smaller the holes are, the smaller the shot will be; and the brim is to be thicker then the bottom, to conserve the heat better.

The bottom of the Trencher being some four inches distant frum the water in the Pail, lay upon it some burning Coles [coals], to keep the Lead melted upon it. Then with the hot Ladle take Lead off the pot where it stands melted, and pour it softly upon the burning Coles over the bottom of the Trencher, and it will immediately ran through the holes into the water in small round drops. Thus pour on new Lead still as fast as it runs through the Trencher till all be done; blowing now and then the Coles with hand-Bellows, when the Lead in the Trencher cools so as to stop from running.

Whilst one pours on the Lead, another must, with another Ladle, thrusted four or five inches under [the] water in the Pail, catch from time to time some of the shot, as it drops down, to see the size of it, and whether there be any faults in it. The greatest care is to keep the Lead upon the Trencher in the right degree of heat; if it be too cool, it will not run through the Trencher, though it stand melted upon it; and this is to be helped by blowing the Coles a little, or pouring on new Lead that is hotter: but the cooler the Lead, the larger the Shot; and the hotter, the smaller; when it is too hot, the drops will crack and fly; then you must stop pouring on new Lead, and let it cool; and so long as you observe the right temper of the heat, the Lead will constantly drop into very round Shot, without so much as one with a tail in many pounds.

When all is done, take your Shot out of the Pail of water, and put it in a Frying-pan over the fire to dry them, which must be done warily, still shaking them that they melt not; and when they are dry you may separate the small from the great, in Pearl Sives [sieves] made of Copper or Lattin [latten, i.e., brass] let into one another, into as many sizes as you please. But if you would have your Shot larger then the Trencher makes them, you may do it with a Stick, making them trickle out of the Ladle, as hath been said.

If the Trencher be but toucht a very little when the Lead stops from going through it, and be not too cool, it will drop again, but it is better not to touch it at all. At the melting of the Lead take care that there be no kind of Oyl, Grease, or the like, upon the Pots, or Ladles, or Trencher.

The Chief cause of this Globular Figure of the Shot, seems to be the Auripigmentun; for, as soon as it is put in among the melted Lead, it loses its shining brightness, contracting instantly a grayish film or skin upon it, when you scum it to make it clean with the Ladle. So that when the Air comes at the falling drop of the melted Lead, that skin constricts them every where equally; but upon what account, and whether this be the true cause, is left to further disquisition.

The emergence of superior shot-making techniques and the appearance of firearms designed expressly for hunting accelerated firearms distribution among a larger segment of the populace and those factors, combined with the development and refinement of self-igniting gunlocks and paper cartridges, engendered significant socio-economic changes in sixteenth-century Europe. And during the final decades of the century Spain began to be seriously challenged in the Old and New World.

Beyond the Spanish Sea

Since Columbus' voyage to the New World the Atlantic had literally become a Spanish sea, and by 1575 Spanish America boasted a population of approximately 152,000, though it was widely scattered in remote settlements and protected by meager military forces exercizing only minimal control and by no means capable of defending the vast territory increasingly threatened by Native Americans and rival European powers. Spain nevertheless responded to those incursions with what limited resources she could muster.

In 1576 a new fort, San Marcos, was built at Santa Elena in the Florida provinces. Near there Spanish avarice coupled with Native American perfidy precipitated a full-scale conflict when Ensign Hernando Moyano and 21 *arcubuceros* recklessly entered a Cusabo village, seizing provisions needed at the fort. The wily Cusabos promised to coöperate if the soldiers would smother their match. Despite protests from his men, Moyano agreed, and of the detachment only Andreas Calderon escaped to warn the Santa Elena settlement.

The Cusabo incident and other confrontations with the Native Americans in Apalachee, Axacan, Guale, and Orista provinces forced the abandonment of Santa Elena in 1587, while a decade later another Guale uprising terminated missionary activity there. In addition fiscal ineptitude and increasingly devastating raids by pirates and privateers in *La Florida* and the Caribbean brought Spain to the threshold of disaster.

Despite those tribulations, the English learned to respect Spanish zeal and determination when in 1586 Sir Francis Drake attacked St. Augustine, partially burning the settlement with flaming musket arrows and destroying Fort San Juan de los Pinillos. Thoughout the night Juan de Contreras harassed the raiders, intermittently discharging his arquebus at their positions, and as an English patrol entered the stricken town the following morning he shot and killed Sergeant Major Anthony Powell and managed to elude his pursuers.

The bold, dramatic exploits of Sir John Hawkins, Sir Walter Ralegh, Sir Francis Drake and other aggressive English sea dogs aroused Elizabethan interest in the Americas and several other European powers began to perceive the economic potential of a

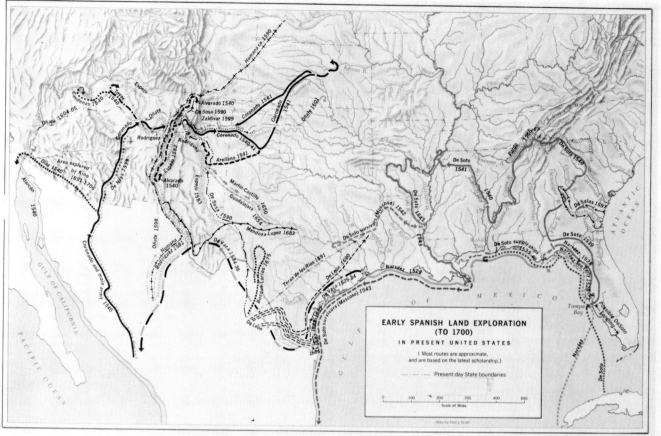

Early Spanish Land Exploration Within the Present Limits of the United
States (16th/17th Century). Courtesy of the National Park Service, Washington, D.C.

virtually pristine continent beckoning from beyond
the Spanish sea.

The startling defeat of the seemingly invincible
Spanish armada off the English coast during July and
August, 1588, was less an inspired tactical or strategic
victory than a triumph of English technology and it
marked the beginning of Spain's decline as a world
power.

While aggressive English commanders, spirited
gunners, and a violent, unexpected storm indisputably contributed to the devastating Spanish defeat, the
fact of not having enough seasoned wood to make
suitable storage barrels for food, fresh water, and
gunpowder foreshadowed the debacle, for sea water

contaminated those essentials when they were most
needed.

Britannia emerged to rule the waves at the end
of the volatile sixteenth century, sustained by
superior technological innovations in naval architecture and in the manufacture of stronger, more reliable cast-iron cannon shooting harder and farther
than those made on the Continent.

The advent of the seventeenth century saw the
pace of militant colonialism rapidly accelerate with a
corresponding demand for cannon and firearms as
yet another wave of European invaders sought to
establish permanent colonies on the first frontier of
North America.

Notes

1. Harold L. Peterson, *Pageant of the Gun* (New York, 1967), p. 12.
2. James D. Lavin, *A History of Spanish Firearms* (New York, 1965), p. 43.
3. Ibid., pp. 41, 43.
4. Vincente Murga Sanz, *Juan Ponce de León* (San Juan, 1959), p. 75, n. 10.
5. Lavin, p. 46.
6. Ibid., p. 44.
7. Lt. Co. Luis Martinez Mateo, "Guns of the Conquistadors," *Guns* (April 1961): 37, 63, 65.
8. Ibid., p. 37.
9. Ibid.
10. Sanz, p. 132.
11. Ibid., p. 135.
12. Ibid., p. 137.
13. Ibid.
14. Ibid.
15. Carlo M. Cipolla, *Guns, Sails and Empires: Technological Innovation and the Early Phases of European Expansion 1400-1700* (New York, 1965), p. 33n.
16. Ibid.
17. W.W. Greener, *The Gun and its Development* (New York, 1967), p. 54.
18. Lavin, pp. 48-49n.
19. A. Baron Englehardt, "The Story of European Proof Marks," *Gun Digest* (Chicago, 1957): 29.
20. Ibid.
21. Cipolla, p. 33.
22. Ibid., p. 35n.
23. William Brandon, *The American Heritage Book of Indians* (New York, 1961), p. 83.
24. Mateo, p. 37.
25. Ibid., p. 65.
26. Ibid.
27. W.H.B. Smith and Joseph E. Smith, *The Book of Rifles* (Harrisburg, 1963), p. 13.
28. Sanz, pp. 346-347.
29. [Gentleman of Elvas], *Virginia Richly Valued,* tr. Richard Hackluyt, London, 1609, Peter Force, comp. *Tracts and Other Papers,* 4 vols. (Washington, 1836-1846) 1:22.
30. Herbert Ingram Priestly, ed. and tr., *The Luna Papers,* 2 vols. (De Land, 1928) 1:107-109, 117.
31. Woodbury Lowery, *The Spanish Settlements Within the Present Limits of the United States,* 2 vols. (New York, 1905) 2:30.
32. Ibid., p. 70.
33. Charles W. Arnade, *Florida on Trial* (Coral Gables: University of Miami Press, 1959): v.
34. Jeanette Thurber Conner, ed. and tr., *Colonial Records of Spanish Florida,* 2 vols. (De Land, 1925 and 1930) 1:89-91.
35. Ibid., 97.
36. Ibid., 101.
37. Lavin, p. 48n.
38. Conner, 1:307.
39. Paul E. Hoffman and Eugene Lyon, "Accounts of the *Real Hacienda,* Florida, 1565 to 1602," *Florida Historical Quarterly* (July 1969): 57-59.
40. Conner, 1:125-127.
41. Ibid., 127.
42. Ibid., 131.
43. Ibid., 137.
44. Ibid., 153-155.
45. Ibid.
46. Ibid., 159.
47. Ibid., 161.
48. Smith and Smith, p. 18. Maximilian's rifle was a snapping matchlock *(lütenschnappschloss).*
49. Stephen V. Grancsay, "The Emperor's Pistol," *Gun Digest* (Chicago, 1957): 3.
50. Robert Held, *The Age of Firearms* (New York, 1957), p. 43.
51. Herschel C. Logan, *Cartridges* (Harrisburg, 1955), p. 1.
52. Held, p. 39.
53. Claude Blair, *Pistols of the World* (New York, 1968), pp. 2, 22; Held, p. 46.
54. Fol. 56 v-b, *Ambrosiana,* Milan.
55. MS 132, *Staatsbibliothek,* Berlin.
56. Torsten Lenk, *The Flintlock: Its Origin and Development* (New York, 1965), pp. 11-12.
57. C[laude]. Blair, "A Further Note on the Early History of the Wheellock," *Journal of the Arms and Armour Society* (April 1964): 187-188.
58. Lenk, p. 12.
59. Howard L. Blackmore, *Guns and Rifles of the World* (New York, 1965), p. 21, n. 3.
60. Held, p. 55.
61. Lavin, p. 72.
62. Grancsay, p. 3.
63. Ibid., p. 2.
64. "Hand Cannon to Flintlock," *Gun Digest* (Chicago, 1956): 38.
65. Ibid.
66. Lavin, p. 46.
67. Ibid., p. 69.
68. W. Steeds, *A History of Machine Tools 1700-1900* (Oxford, 1969), p. 1.
69. Silvio A. Bedini and Derek J. De Solla Price, "Instrumentation," in *Technology in Western Civilization,* eds. Melvin Kranzberg and Caroll W. Pursell, Jr., 2 vols. (New York and London, 1967), 1:180.
70. Steeds, p. 3, n. 3.
71. Held, p. 63.
72. Ibid.
73. Ibid., p. 67.
74. Lavin, p. 93.

AS THE WORLD CHURNED into the seventeenth century western Europe was plunged into a period of crises, and the Americas were thrust into an unprecedented era of colonization; while in firearms evolution that explosive epoch became the century of the flintlock.

An atmosphere conducive to colonial expansion prevailed in Europe at the dawn of the century. The rapid growth of commerce engendered a prosperous, proliferating middle class and a burgeoning mercantile establishment supported by crown acquiescence, protected by professional military forces, and given enormous latitude with the expansion of aggressive merchant fleets.

The monopolistic trade concessions granted by sovereign dispensation to the enterprising merchant-adventurers seeking to enhance their fortunes in North America were sustained by nearly unlimited financial resources and the unconstrained application of military force; thus economic rivalry in the Old and New World escalated to even greater intensity and proportion, creating an unparalleled demand for firearms, munitions, and a wide variety of trade goods which effectively stimulated the economy and innovative technology.

The bold colonization experiments directed toward wilderness North America throughout the seventeenth century and thereafter involved enormous risks in terms of human life and finance; yet the commercial exploitation of the new continent was welcomed by hundreds and then thousands of the displaced, dispossessed, and purely adventurous seeking surcease from the intolerable socioeconomic conditions throughout Europe.

Coeval with the demand for firearms and related material to support the second European invasion of North America was the emergence of several ignition mechanisms far superior to the simple matchlock and less expensive and more reliable than the complex wheellock. Most of those innovative ignition mechanisms appeared in the final half of the sixteenth century and all of them were self-igniting, related by technology to the snapping matchlocks earlier conceived in Germany, and they produced the requisite ignition spark by the then common method of striking a piece of chert or flint against a piece of steel; thus initiating a technological revolution in firearms evolution.

The Snaphaunce

The origin and early evolution of the first self-striking flintlock or what is now termed the snaphaunce remains obscure, although available evidence suggests it emerged in southern Germany ca. 1530, shortly after the introduction of the snapping matchlock (*lütenschnappschloss*).

Snaphaunce development in Germany was inhibited by two factors: (1) Emperor Maximilian had proscribed the use of self-igniting gunlocks in the Hapsburg Empire, and (2) Teutonic gunsmiths had brought the C pattern matchlock and the wheellock to a relatively high degree of perfection which minimized the need for an improved ignition system there.

Those negative aspects vanished, however, when in 1519 liberal Charles V assumed the emperor's role, for he encouraged firearms innovation, and beyond Germany many gunsmiths were receptive to the concept of a more simple, efficient lock because they recognized the disadvantages of match ignition while the majority had yet to master the necessary skills to make the intricate wheellock.

The early German snaphaunce was characterized by the position of the serpentine and the functioning of the sear, both emulating the *lütenschnappschloss* (see p. 49), though the mechanism was otherwise substantially altered. The transformation included substituting chert or flint for the match

in the serpentine (cock) jaws and adding opposite the cock a pivotal arm similar to the wheellock doghead, though instead of jaws it was provided with a slightly concave strike plate or steel, now usually referred to as the battery or frizzen.

Tracing the development and the dispersal patterns of the various kinds of snaphaunce mechanisms appearing in Europe from ca. 1535 is no simple task because contradictory documentation invites abundant supposition and equally broad interpretation. It is known, however, that by 1542 German gunsmiths were producing self-igniting flintlock firearms in sufficient quantity to supply Swedish rebel leader Nils Dacke, clandestinely shipping them from Lübeck.[1]

The German snaphaunce was apparently known in Italy by 1547, for a Florentine ordinance of that year cited by Maj. Angelucci in *Catalogo della Armeria Reale* mentioned an arquebus fitted with a mechanism akin to the self-striking flint tinder lighter: an *"archibusi . . . da fucile."*[2] The use of the term *fucile* (flint), however, does not preclude the possibility that the mechanism was a wheellock employing flint rather than marcasite.

It was also in 1547 that the Swedish Royal Accounts referred to firearms incorporating a *snapplås* (snapping lock), the word describing a pecking fowl (cock) to which the action of the serpentine striking the steel was compared.[3] In 1556 armorers at the Swedish Royal Armory in Arboga fitted 35 Nuremburg matchlock arquebuses with the *snapplås* and it is known that several German gunsmiths familiar with snapping locks were then employed there.[4]

By ca. 1570 German gunsmiths were fabricating firearms incorporating match and flint ignition in a single lock, i.e., a dual-ignition lock with match available if the flintlock malfunctioned, and several variations of the dual-ignition lock subsequently emerged in Europe; one of them believed to have been used in North America.

Four distinctive snaphaunce variations evolved from the German lock by ca. 1580: Baltic, Scan-

SNAPHAUNCE ARQUEBUS (ca. 1556): A city control mark on the barrel identifies this arquebus as made in Nuremburg. The barrel is also marked CK. This specimen is believed to be one of the German arquebuses fitted with the first form of the Swedish snaphaunce at the Royal Armory, Arboga, Sweden. Courtesy of the *Livrustkammaren,* Stockholm.

SNAPHAUNCE LOCK (ca. 1580): (1) Priming pan fence. (2) Priming pan. (3) Cock jaws. (4) Cock jaw screw. (5) Cock. (6) Tail of cock. (7) Sear heel. (8) Sear nose. (9) Tumbler. (10) Priming pan cover plunger. (11) Priming pan cover lever. (12) Mainspring. (13) Priming pan cover. (14) Battery (steel) arm. (15) Face of the steel. Trigger bearing on (7) pivots (8) away from (6), permitting (5) to fall forward, rotating (9) which activates (10) to move (11), exposing (2). Pressure on (9) from lower leaf of (12) provides sufficient force to ensure adequate spark from the flint held by (3) when it strikes (15), directing the spark into (2). Author's sketch.

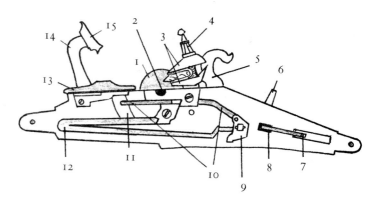

dinavian, Mediterranean (Italian), and what can be termed the Channel region snaphaunce because it was distributed in England, Scotland, Flanders (modern Belgium), and France; all adjacent to the English Channel.

Developed in the countries bordering the Baltic Sea east of Germany, the Baltic snaphaunce subsequently influenced snapping flintlock design in European Russia. The Scandinavian snaphaunce, originating in Sweden and patterned after the German mechanism, was reflected in snapping flintlocks made in Denmark, Finland, and Norway.

Reaching Italy from Germany, the snaphaunce was further refined and spread west to Spain through

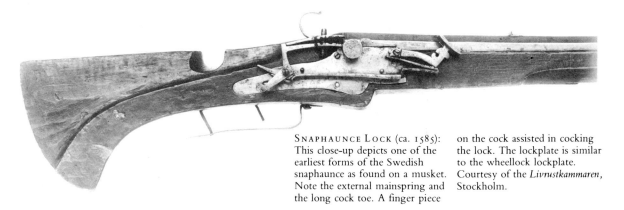

SNAPHAUNCE LOCK (ca. 1585): This close-up depicts one of the earliest forms of the Swedish snaphaunce as found on a musket. Note the external mainspring and the long cock toe. A finger piece on the cock assisted in cocking the lock. The lockplate is similar to the wheellock lockplate. Courtesy of the *Livrustkammaren*, Stockholm.

her commercial ties with Naples, thence south to North Africa, and then east from Genoa and Venice to the Balkan states and Asia Minor, subsequently making its way to India and the Far East via the long-established caravan and maritime routes.

The German snaphaunce arrived in Flanders ca. 1550 and it was probably introduced in England by 1575, considering the proximity of the Flemish coast. The earliest known reference to the snaphaunce in England dates from 1588 when "Henry Radoe, smythe," was paid for a snaphaunce pistol by the Chamberlain of Norwich, though it cannot be determined whether the pistol was indigenous or imported.[5]

The snaphaunce had made its way to Scotland prior to the turn of the century and it was incorporated in the prototype of a radically innovative handgun developed there. The first examples of the Scottish snaphaunce are dated 1598, the locks gracing a pair of pistols preserved in the *Staatliche Kunstsammlungen*, Dresden.

The four snaphaunce variations incorporated distinctive design innovations owing primarily to geography, and other variants subsequently appeared, especially in the Italian snaphaunce often known as the Mediterranean snaphaunce because of its extremely wide distribution in that region.

The snaphaunce failed to make any immediate or lasting impression in Spain though it was doubtlessly known there through German gunsmiths sent by Charles V. It is likely that the apathy displayed toward the snaphaunce in Spain was engendered by the development of an even more sophisticated flintlock there during the final decades of the sixteenth century. Similar circumstances inhibited the acceptance of the snaphaunce in France, for while it was introduced there from Flanders ca. 1570 it was not made in substantial numbers because an infinitely superior flintlock emerged shortly after the turn of the century.[6]

Echoing the venerable and persistent hypothesis that the snaphaunce originated in the Netherlands ca. 1550-1580, many firearms historians have apparently chosen to ignore available evidence to the contrary. Thorough investigations by Dutch historiographers have determined that there is little reason to believe that the snaphaunce existed in the Netherlands or Holland proper before 1600.[7]

Despite the relatively late introduction of the Netherlands snaphaunce it is the Dutch term for the lock, *schnapp-hahn* or *schnapp-haan* (literally "pecking cock" and similar to the meaning of the Swedish *snapplås),* which is currently employed, though anglicized to snaphaunce or snaphance. The

SNAPHAUNCE PISTOLS (16th Century, 1598): These pistols display an early form of the snaphaunce and are believed to be the first snaphaunce firearms made in Scotland. The locks are stamped I K and 1598 is found on the priming pan fence. Exquisitely engraved, the pistols have flat grips of the fish tail pattern. The 16-inch barrels are of .55 caliber. The lock of the left-hand pistol (top) is mounted on that side. The top jaw screw and the top jaw are missing from the right-hand pistol. Courtesy of the *Staatlich Kunstsammlungen,* Dresden.

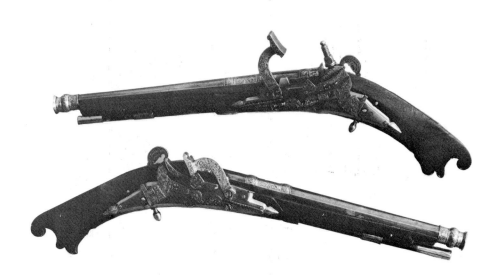

English translation of *schnapp-hahn* (snapping cock) was applied to the modified serpentine arm, while the action of drawing the serpentine to the rear when preparing to fire came to be known as *cocking* the lock. Unlike the Dutch, English, and Swedes who compared the striking action of the lock to a pecking fowl, the Italians referred to the flint *(fucile)* when describing the snaphaunce and the French called it a *fusil* (steel) because of the strike plate on the separate arm.

Snaphaunce lockplates were initially flat, emulating the wheellock design, though the few components were more compact than the wheellock, and by ca. 1600 the lockplate was reduced in size, tapered somewhat, and rounded at each end. In most German, Scandinavian, and Baltic snaphaunces the flat, v-shaped mainspring was externally mounted on the lockplate, serving as the cock and the battery (steel) spring. Channel region and Italian snaphaunces displayed a separate, externally-mounted battery spring and the mainspring was enclosed in the lockplate.

In most early snaphaunces the pan cover was manually operated, though sliding covers subsequently emerged, moving forward with the momentum of the cock to expose the priming powder in the pan. The outer edge of the pan in Channel region snaphaunces usually displayed a fence, often seen as a disc, though there were variations as in the later Netherlands lock where it frequently assumed the shape of a scallop shell. In most snaphaunces the forward cock movement was arrested by a small buffer screwed to the lockplate in front of the cock base.

In Channel region snaphaunces the cock shank transversing the lockplate was provided with a tumbler; the lower leaf of the mainspring resting on the tumbler shoulder. When the cock was drawn to the rear the tumbler raised the mainspring and the cock heel was caught by the nose of the lateral sear protruding through the lockplate as with the *lütenschnappschloss*. The sear spring provided sufficient tension to hold the cock in firing position.

Squeezing the trigger disengaged the sear nose from the cock heel, permitting the cock to fall forward under mainspring pressure. Positioned over the priming pan, the concave battery face received a hard, glancing blow from the sharp chert or flint in the adjustable cock jaws. The battery arm, held in position by the tension of the battery spring, provided adequate resistance which caused the flint to produce the necessary ignition spark.

With the snaphaunce cocked and the pivotal battery in firing position over the priming pan, an accidental touch of the trigger or merely jostling the firearm if the sear nose was worn resulted in premature ignition. A positive safety feature of the snap-

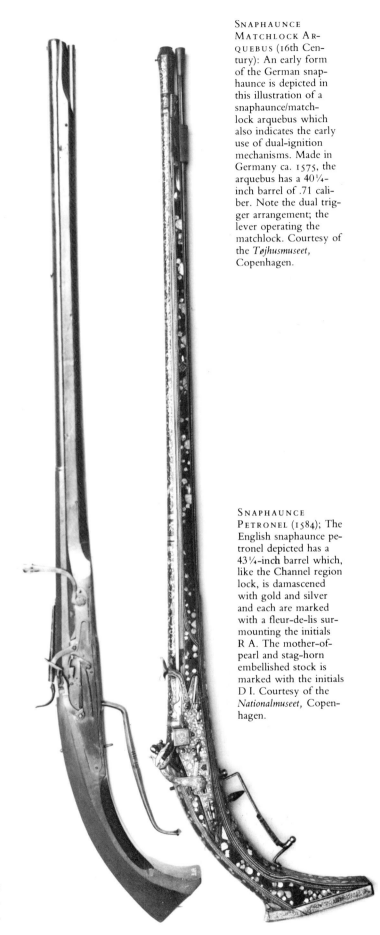

SNAPHAUNCE MATCHLOCK ARQUEBUS (16th Century): An early form of the German snaphaunce is depicted in this illustration of a snaphaunce/matchlock arquebus which also indicates the early use of dual-ignition mechanisms. Made in Germany ca. 1575, the arquebus has a 40¼-inch barrel of .71 caliber. Note the dual trigger arrangement; the lever operating the matchlock. Courtesy of the *Tøjhusmuseet*, Copenhagen.

SNAPHAUNCE PETRONEL (1584); The English snaphaunce petronel depicted has a 43¼-inch barrel which, like the Channel region lock, is damascened with gold and silver and each are marked with a fleur-de-lis surmounting the initials R A. The mother-of-pearl and stag-horn embellished stock is marked with the initials D I. Courtesy of the *Nationalmuseet*, Copenhagen.

haunce, however, was that ignition could not be effected until the battery arm was lowered into firing position.

The snaphaunce, like previous ignition systems, was not immune from misfires caused by adverse weather, and a worn battery face and a dull, misaligned, or broken flint also caused misfires in the snaphaunce and all flint-ignition locks. In snaphaunces with the separate battery spring misfires frequently occurred because of improper timing, i.e., achieving an inadequate tension balance between the mainspring and the battery spring.

Timing was a prerequisite for proper ignition in all flintlock mechanisms. If the springs were made of quality steel, precisely tempered for tension balance, ignition was practically instantaneous. In the snaphaunce a weak mainspring did not give the cock sufficient impetus to produce ignition spark when the flint struck the battery face, while a weak battery spring did not provide enough resistance when struck by the flint, giving the same result. If the mainspring was too powerful it forced the battery arm away from the pan prematurely; thus insufficient spark reached the priming powder.

By ca. 1600 the snaphaunce and its variants were familiar throughout Europe, distributed via the extensive and flourishing arms commerce identified with Augsburg, Frankfort, Lübeck, Marienburg, Munich, and Nuremburg (Germany); Amsterdam, Antwerp, Delft, Dinant, Dordrecht, Launnoy, Liége, Malines, Mons, Namur, Rotterdam, Utrecht, and The Hague (Flanders and the Netherlands); Abbeville, Autun, Blamont, Cherbourg, Dijon, Epinal, Fontenay, Grenoble, Lisieux, Luneville, Metz, Montmirail, Nancy, Paris, Rouen, St. Brieuc, St. Étienne, St. Mâlo, Sedan, and Turenne (France); Bergamo, Brescia, Florence, Gardone, Genoa, Milan, Naples, Pistoia, Rome, and Venice (Italy); Arboga, Jönköping, and Stockholm (Sweden); Doune, Edinburgh, and Glasgow (Scotland); and London, Bern, Vienna, and Oslo, as well as Tula in Russia.

The Italian Flintlock

The basic design and therefore the functioning cycle remained intact through the respective evolutionary periods of the Baltic, Scandinavian, and Channel region snaphaunce. After ca. 1570, however, Italian gunsmiths contributed several significant innovations which altered the functioning of the snaphaunce, consequently producing a superior mechanism which merits consideration as an independent lock form or what could be called the Italian flintlock.

There were four fundamental refinements which transformed the Italian snaphaunce to the Italian flintlock: (1) the vertical sear, (2) the cock shoulder buffer, (3) the manual (dog) safety, and (4) the combined battery face and priming pan cover. All of those innovations distinctly improved the snaphaunce and were later incorporated in the true or French flintlock.

In the Italian flintlock the lateral snaphaunce sear was supplanted by a vertical sear working in conjunction with the tumbler. The sear nose, rather than protruding through the lockplate, engaged a simple notch in the tumbler face (full-cock notch) to hold the cock to the rear. When the trigger was squeezed the vertical sear pivoted out of the full-cock tumbler notch and the mainspring forced the cock forward.

A shoulder cut into the inner face of the cock neck struck the upper edge of the lockplate to arrest its forward movement; an innovation eliminating the external cock buffer common to northern European snaphaunces.

The most important innovation, however, consisted of a single, L-shaped component combining the strike plate (face) of the snaphaunce battery arm with the priming pan cover; a radical concept appearing ca. 1580 which eliminated the separate battery and independent pan cover.

SNAPHAUNCE PISTOL (ca. 1630-1650): This elegantly chased Brescian pistol is provided with a *patilla*-type lock common in Spain ca. 1600 and thereafter; the *patilla* similar in many respects to the Italian snaphaunce. Courtesy of the Metropolitan Museum of Art, Rogers Fund, 1928.

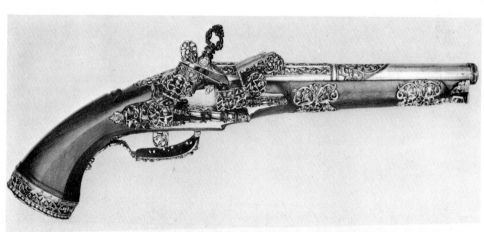

The vertical part of the L-shaped battery served as the strike plate and the horizontal portion corresponded to the pan cover; the entire component freely pivoting around a screw attaching it to the lockplate. A short tang on the bottom of the pan cover rested against the upper leaf of the battery spring. The force of the falling cock against the strike plate overcame the inertia of the battery spring and the L-shaped battery pivoted upward as it was struck, directing the ignition spark into the priming pan.

Eliminating the battery arm necessitated another safety arrangement and a manual safety was provided, appearing as a small hook or *dog*. The dog pivoted on a screw located behind the cock and engaged a corresponding notch in the cock body; an innovation which prevented the cock from falling until the hook was released.[8]

Several kinds of self-striking flintlocks subsequently employed the positive dog safety and it persisted in various forms until the early nineteenth century. In some instances those locks are referred to as dog locks, implying that the dog represents an entirely independent lock development whereas it was simply a technological innovation.

While the vertical sear, cock shoulder buffer, and dog safety were significant innovations, it was the radical L-shaped strike plate and pan cover combination which transformed the Italian snaphaunce into a flintlock proper. Variations of the Italian flintlock spread throughout the Continent and were known in England prior to 1600. Earlier forms of the snaphaunce continued to be used, however, and enjoyed considerable popularity in the New World as well.

The Spanish Flintlock

Two self-striking flintlocks appeared in Spain during the latter half of the sixteenth century: the first an indigenous lock emerging ca. 1570-1580 though failing to gain acceptance;[9] the second a variation of the Italian flintlock developed during the period 1590-1625 and achieving substantial and lasting popularity.[10] Both locks were superior to the venerable matchlock, the complex wheellock, and the snaphaunce.

The earliest extant self-striking Spanish flintlocks are a pair incorporated in a double-barreled firearm combined with a lance and they are currently preserved in the Royal Armory, Madrid. The locks are unique and Lavin suggests that the design emerged in Spain shortly after the German wheel-

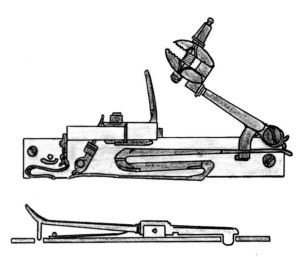

SNAPPING FLINTLOCK (ca. 1580): This unique snapping flintlock preceded the *patilla* in Spain and it was likely an indigenous innovation. The doghead (cock) faces the breech. A manual safety was provided at the rear of the lock. The sear (side view, below) is a pivotal arm displaying the sear nose (right) and the tang (left) engaging the manual safety. Author's sketch, after Lavin.

lock was introduced and before Spanish gun-makers began producing variants of the complex mechanism.[11]

The lance-gun locks employ the lateral sear. The sliding pan cover is combined with the battery and the cock faces the breech. The rectangular lockplate is flat except for a slight hump where the cock is attached and, of all the components, only the elongated sear is mounted internally. The similarity of the lance-gun locks to the wheellock is indicated by the cock, corresponding to the wheellock doghead, and the use of a sliding pan cover. The battery strike plate is combined with the sliding cover rather than pivoting as in the Italian flintlock; an innovation further indicating indigenous development, though German and Italian influence on Spanish arms-making was evident during the sixteenth century and shortly thereafter.

In the lance-gun locks the nose and the heel of the pivoting, lateral sear transverse the lockplate, the nose catching the long cock toe and the sear heel engaging a small, manual safety (dog) at the rear of the lockplate when desired. The elongated, S-shaped mainspring exerts pressure on the cock heel and the toe of the sliding pan cover retaining link. Squeezing the trigger withdraws the sear nose from the cock toe, permitting the cock to strike the vertical battery face, simultaneously forcing the sliding pan cover to override the retaining link and expose the priming powder to ignition spark.

The lance-gun locks had no significant technological impact on firearms evolution and cannot be considered intermediate mechanisms, i.e., locks spanning an evolutionary period in the development of technologically-related mechanisms, and neither are the characteristics of the locks reflected in the evolution of the popular *patilla* or *llave española*

(Spanish lock), for the *patilla* illustrates specific design features found in the Italian flintlock.

The *patilla* was a simple, efficient flintlock continuously employed in Spanish firearms until the second quarter of the nineteenth century and it is presently known as the *miquelet* or *miguelet* though neither term was contemporary, being introduced by some late nineteenth-century historians.

Apparently unaware of the Italian influence the Germans recognized the *llave española* as an indigenous achievement because they referred to it as a *spanische Schnappschloss* (Spanish snaplock). The *llave española* derived its name from the curved foot (*patilla*) at the cock base and subsequently influenced the evolution of three additional Spanish flintlocks: the *agujeta*, the *invención*, and the *calzo atrás*. [12] Design imperfections limited the development and popularity of the latter three mechanisms and they were not widely employed in Spain or her New World dominions.

Alonzo Martínez de Espinar (1594?-1682), in his *Arte de Ballestería y Montería* (Madrid, 1644), remarked that of all contemporary Spanish flintlocks "the best are the *patilla* . . ., for they have fewer parts, and run less risk of breaking, and are less prone to fire accidentally, being better regulated [timed]." [13] Few Spaniards were more qualified to judge the *patilla*, for Espinar served three monarchs as royal *ballestero* (huntsman) and was as intimately acquainted with

Patilla (Miquelet) LOCK (17th Century): Top. Priming pan steel with removable, dovetailed, striated strike plate. Center. Interior view of lock depicting primary (full-cock) sear with integral sear spring (rectangular face) and secondary (half-cock) sear (round face) with pivotal trigger tang. Bottom. Exterior view of the cock illustrating the mainspring resting against the cock heel. The cock toe or foot (*patilla*) engages the notch in the secondary sear. Author's sketch.

the firearms of the period as he was with the techniques of the royal gunsmiths.

Like the design of most Spanish firearms and gunlocks that of the *patilla* was purely functional; a pragmatic approach exemplified by the lockplate which provided only enough surface area to secure the components. The *patilla* was distinguished from the snaphaunce by the innovative, L-shaped battery found in the Italian flintlock though retaining the lateral sear.

Other, indigenous features setting the *patilla* apart from the snaphaunce and the Italian flintlock included a large ring surmounting the cock jaw screw which remained typical throughout its evolutionary period, a striated (grooved) strike plate dovetailed into the battery face and also secured by a screw, and a secondary (half-cock) sear. The primary and secondary sears were the only internal lock components and the elongated sear spring incorporated the primary (full-cock) sear nose.

The upper cock jaw was fixed, transversed by the jaw screw which passed through the adjustable lower jaw. The cock foot curved forward, the toe catching the primary and the secondary sear. The cock heel rested against the upper leaf of the long, powerful, externally-mounted mainspring. The L-shaped battery was held by the battery screw and the pan cover tang abutted the battery spring. The priming pan was usually secured to the lockplate by an internal screw. The strike plate in the battery face was readily replaced when worn; early speciments displaying shallow striations, though grooves were deeper in later plates which less frequently needed to be replaced.

The mainspring and the battery spring were secured to the flat lockplate by integral lugs attached by *fieles*, i.e., small, tapered wedges transversing the lugs. [14] The *fiele* was also used to secure lock screws and it was commonly employed until the second quarter of the eighteenth century when it was discovered that the threads were sufficient to hold the screws and tension alone secured the mainspring. The battery spring continued to be retained by a *fiele* until ca. 1675 when it was replaced by a pin.

In addition to the *fieles* the mainspring and the battery spring were retained by a bridle, i.e., a metal plate. The cock body served as the mainspring bridle and the battery spring bridle was held by the battery screw and a small projection at its forward end which engaged a hole in the lockplate.

Working in conjunction with the primary sear and the elongated sear spring, the secondary sear displayed a rounded nose located at the short end of an L-shaped, lateral sear extension engaging the trigger; the extension secured by a small pin to a bracket mounted inside the lockplate.

When the cock was partly drawn rearward, the

secondary sear nose transversed the lockplate, pivoting under sear spring pressure, and the notch in its nose engaged the cock foot (half-cock); at full-cock the rectangular nose of the primary sear protruded through the lockplate to catch the cock foot. The secondary sear was disengaged when the cock was drawn to the full-cock position; a vertical tang at the base of the L-shaped sear extension, overridden by the primary sear, camming the secondary sear away from the cock foot.

Squeezing the trigger pivoted the L-shaped sear extension, and the sear spring, bearing on the tang, withdrew the primary sear nose from the cock foot, permitting the cock to fall forward. The flint struck the striated battery face a glancing blow, simultaneously flinging the pan cover upward to expose the priming powder to the ignition spark.

With the appearance of the snapping *patilla* and subsequent Spanish flintlocks there were gradual changes in terminology distinguishing them from the matchlock and the wheellock. The Spaniards likened the glancing blow of the *patilla* cock against the battery face to the action of a rake or comb *(rastrillo, rastrillar)*; hence the term was applied to the battery and came to be used to describe firearms employing flint ignition, e.g., *arcabuz de rastrillo* or—*rastrillar.*

Pedernal (flint) was applied to Spanish flintlocks as early as 1614.[15] *Pedernal* should not be confused with *pedrenal,* the latter describing sixteenth-century wheellock *pistoletes* (pistols), while *pistolete* was transformed into *pistola* by ca. 1620. Early in the seventeenth century the ambiguous catch-all phrase *llave de chispa* appeared, used to describe any self-striking flintlock, while *escopeta* was resurrected from the early sixteenth century as *escopeta de rastrillo;* generally designating a smoothbore sporting firearm though referring to a type of martial firearm as well. When flintlock firearms became popular in Spain the *rastrillo* designation was commonly disregarded.

The French Flintlock

The emergence of the Italian and Spanish flintlocks directly influenced the development of another flintlock superior in design and efficacy and the prototype of the flint ignition system subsequently employed in most firearms for nearly two centuries: the French or *true* flintlock.

Most of the outstanding technological developments related to firearms evolution prior to the introduction of the French flintlock cannot be at-

MARIN LE BOURGEOYS (16th/17th Century, 1550?-1634): Artist, art dealer, and maker of mechanical marvels, Marin Le Bourgeoys was also a gifted gunsmith in the service of the first Bourbon king, Henry IV, and his successor Louis XIII. Henry was assassinated May 14, 1610, by religious fanatic Ravaillac. Courtesy of the Holland Press Limited, London.

tributed to a specific individual, geographically delineated, or positively dated with any degree of certainty. There is, however, documentary and physical evidence identifying the locale and the individuals involved in the origin of the French flintlock and it was revealed in 1939 by the late Dr. Torsten Lenk in his masterly *Flintlåset, Dess Uppkomst och Utveckling* (The Flintlock, Its Origin and Development).

Dr. Lenk's detailed analysis of self-striking flint ignition systems led him to ascribe the invention of the true flintlock to the brothers Jean and Marin le Bourgeoys, members of a family dynasty flourishing in the sixteenth-and seventeenth century at Lisieux, Department of Calvados, Normandy, where they were engaged in making crossbows, clocks, and firearms.[16]

Marin le Bourgeoys (1550?-1634) embraced myriad interests like Italian genius da Vinci, his talents expressed in painting, sculpting, engraving, and making musical instruments, mobile globes, and other intricate mechanical contrivances as well as firearms. In 1589 Marin was in the service of François de Bourbon, Duke of Montpensier and governor of Normandy. Nine years later Marin became court

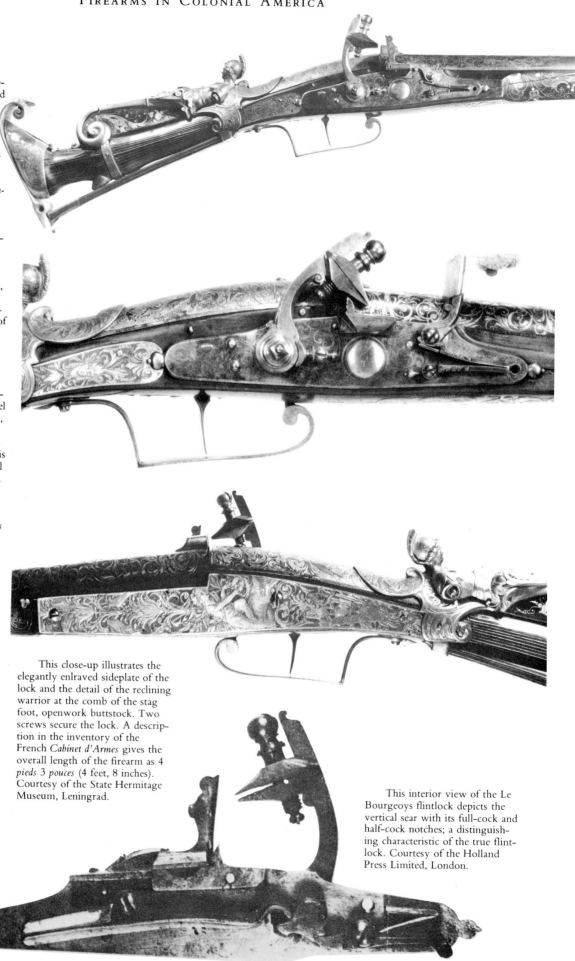

FLINTLOCK AR-
QUEBUS (ca. 1605–
1610): This ornate fire-
arm has been identified
by the late Torsten
Lenk as made by the
master French gun-
smith Marin Le
Bourgeoys. It displays
the first true flintlock.
E. Lenz, *Collection
d'armes de l'Ermitage im-
périal* (St. Petersburg,
1908), describes it as
from the armory of
Prince Condé at Chan-
tilly, noting that the
blued barrel is embel-
lished with gold, the
stock inlaid with brass,
silver, and mother-of-
pearl, and a plate bear-
ing the coats of arms of
France and Navarre.
Courtesy of the State
Hermitage Museum,
Leningrad.

This close-up of
the French flintlock de-
picts the combined steel
and priming pan cover,
one characteristic of a
true flintlock. The for-
ward cock movement is
arrested by the external
buffer at the cock base.
The trigger plate ex-
tending in front of the
trigger guard is en-
graved *M. Le Bourgeoys
à Liseul.* Courtesy of
the State Hermitage
Museum, Leningrad.

This close-up illustrates the
elegantly enlraved sideplate of the
lock and the detail of the reclining
warrior at the comb of the stag
foot, openwork buttstock. Two
screws secure the lock. A description in the inventory of the
French *Cabinet d'Armes* gives the
overall length of the firearm as 4
pieds 3 *pouces* (4 feet, 8 inches).
Courtesy of the State Hermitage
Museum, Leningrad.

This interior view of the Le
Bourgeoys flintlock depicts the
vertical sear with its full-cock and
half-cock notches; a distinguishing characteristic of the true flintlock. Courtesy of the Holland
Press Limited, London.

artist and *valet de chamber* to Henry IV and, in 1605, he was officially recognized as a royal *harquebuzier* (gunsmith).

On December 22, 1608, Marin le Bourgeoys was granted a *brevet de logement* at the then recently completed Louvre though he disdained the cosmopolitan atmosphere of Paris and the court, returning to provincial Lisieux where he devoted himself to his primary artistic endeavors and pursued his avocation as an art critic and dealer.

Jean le Bourgeoys (d. 1615), lesser known than Marin though a superbly skilled artisan in his own right, doubtlessly worked with Marin, for both their signatures are found on two similar firearms employing the earliest extant example of the true flintlock. The first lock is found on a splendidly executed firearm made for Louis XIII shortly after he assumed the French crown in 1610, and it was signed by Marin. The second lock graced an equally fine firearm dated 1615, and it was signed by Jean. Whether Jean or Marin invented the true flintlock independently or together cannot be determined, though the date of its introduction can be established as sometime between 1610 and 1615.

The relationship of the le Bourgeoys' flintlock to the wheellock, the snaphaunce, and the Italian flintlock is evident. The lockplate is reminiscent of the wheellock lockplate, though shorter, more narrow, and secured by two screws rather than three. The shape of the cock and the presence of the external cock buffer is characteristic of the Channel snaphaunce, while the L-shaped battery is identified with the Italian flintlock and, like that mechanism, all of the operating components are enclosed with the exception of the battery spring.

The le Bourgeoys' flintlock also incorporated the cock tumbler and vertical sear of the Italian flintlock though there was a radical innovation which transformed the French flintlock into the true flintlock: the half-cock tumbler notch for the sear. The French lock functioned like the Italian lock except for the half-cock. When the sear nose engaged the half-cock notch the cock was not permitted to fall despite trigger pressure, for tumbler movement was prevented by a short finger or pawl; thus the true flintlock could be carried "cocked and primed," i.e., ready for instant use by merely drawing the cock to the full-cock (firing) position. The tumbler pawl also kept the sear nose from engaging the half-cock notch after it was released from the full-cock notch by the trigger.

Like other ignition systems the French flintlock (*platine à silex*) was subsequently refined. The innovative cock shoulder buffer common to the Italian flintlock eliminated the external buffer by ca. 1635. By midcentury the cock became a separate entity, divorced from the shaft transversing the lockplate.

The square shaft head fit a corresponding hole in the cock body and it was secured by a (cock) screw, while the tumbler was attached to the shaft by a nut. The straight, snaphaunce cock was supplanted by the elegant, graceful gooseneck cock, and an internal bridle secured the sear and the tumbler.

Most of the early improvements associated with the French flintlock existed in the Italian lock, though Parisian gunsmiths initiated a trend to convex rather than flat cocks, lockplates, and sideplates ca. 1640; about the time the true flintlock began to be dispersed elsewhere in Europe. The true flintlock was ignored in Spain until the eighteenth century, for the efficient *patilla* and its variants were considered satisfactory.

Like other self-striking flintlocks the efficacy of the true flintlock was dependent upon the timing of the springs and a simple test was performed to determine if they were properly balanced: the weapon was fired with the lock inverted. If the powder fell from the priming pan prior to ignition the springs were incorrectly timed.

The true flintlock was not immediately adopted in France or elsewhere as the principal ignition system for military, sporting, or utilitarian firearms, because throughout the various stages of firearms evolution many radical innovations were slow to find acceptance as the result of technical problems, economic considerations, and traditional opposition to change.

Even after the widespread acceptance of the true flintlock ca. 1650 the matchlock remained the predominant ignition system in martial firearms, and that pragmatic decision was more an economic than technical problem or unreasonable opposition to change, because any extensive rearmament and retraining programs virtually drained national treasuries; a fact particularly evident in the seventeenth century because the evolution of the true flintlock was coeval with increasing domestic turmoil in Europe and the resurgence of colonial expansion in the New World.

Contrasting with the military viewpoint, public acceptance of the true flintlock in hunting and utilitarian firearms was much more rapid. In North America, however, the colonists willingly swept economic considerations aside because they needed the most reliable firearms available when confronting the perils of the wilderness.

European aristocracy also eagerly accepted the true flintlock because of its efficacy and the fact that it proved particularly suited to a challenging new form of wildfowl hunting which became popular late in the century: the sport of shooting birds in flight or, as it was known to the elite, pteryplegia.[17]

The true flintlock was heartily welcomed by those exceptionally skilled gunsmith-inventors seek-

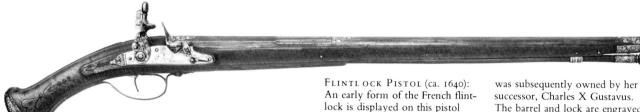

FLINTLOCK PISTOL (ca. 1640): An early form of the French flint-lock is displayed on this pistol made by Paris gunsmith P. Tomas for Queen Christina of Sweden who abdicated in 1654. It was subsequently owned by her successor, Charles X Gustavus. The barrel and lock are engraved and the grip has a heart and tulip motif. Courtesy of the *Liv-rustkammaren,* Stockholm.

ing new horizons in firearms development, for it readily lent itself to improvization and the improve-ment of designs previously considered impractical. Handguns especially benefitted from the introduc-tion of self-striking flintlocks because the compact mechanisms considerably reduced their size and weight.

The English Flintlock

The popularity of the snaphaunce in England during the final decades of the sixteenth century led gunsmiths there to seek improvements and they adopted some of the refinements found in the Italian flintlock. By ca. 1600 an improved English lock was developed, displaying the L-shaped battery and the dog safety, though retaining the lateral sear and the external cock buffer.[18]

By ca. 1620, shortly after the French flintlock appeared, a second, more sophisticated English lock emerged, and while still retaining the lateral sear it also incorporated a half-cock tumbler notch and a pawl; each working in conjunction with a secondary sear.

When the trigger was squeezed the primary (full-cock) sear nose was retracted from the cock foot and, as the cock fell forward under mainspring pres-sure on the tumbler, the tumbler pawl slid along a wedge-shaped ramp on the tumbler and forced the secondary sear to bypass the half-cock notch. The dog safety was often retained to supplement the half-cock. Neither English flintlock functioned as efficiently as the Italian flintlock or the true flintlock.

Both versions of the English flintlock were em-

ENGLISH FLINTLOCK (16th/17th Century): (1) Lockplate. (2) Bat-tery. (3) Priming pan. (4) Battery face. (5) Cock jaw screw. (6) Cock spur. (7) Cock jaws. (8) Sear bracket. (9) Sear heel. (10) Sear. (11) Cock shank. (12) Tumbler. (13) Mainspring, lower leaf. (14) Mainspring, upper leaf. Trigger pressure on (9) pivots (10), permitting (12) to move under tension from (13). Cock, attached to (12) by (11), strikes (4) to generate ignition spark as (2) pivots upward to re-veal priming powder in (3). Au-thor's sketch.

JACOBEAN FLINTLOCK (17th Century, ca. 1640): This fine pair of pistols depicts an early Jaco-bean flintlock. The 13-3/5-inch barrels are of .58 caliber. Note the dog safety and atypical battery spring. The lockplate of the pistol (top) is marked *WILLIAM WATSON FECIT* in script. Wat-son was a London gunsmith flourishing in the period 1630–1650. In 1632 his brother John, also a gunsmith, was ordered by Charles I "to search for and prove and mark all manner of hand-guns, great and small dags and pistols." British Crown Copy-right. Reproduced with permis-sion of the Controller of Her Britannic Majesty's Stationery Office.

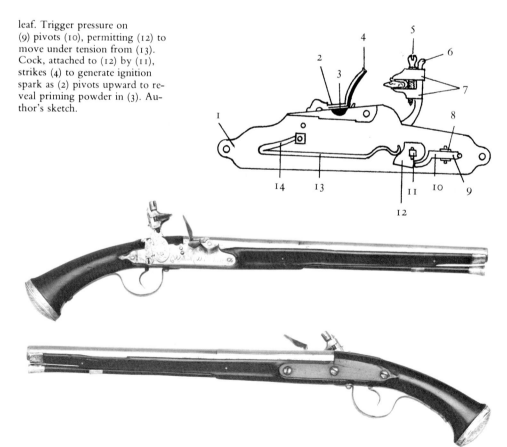

ployed during the reign of James I (1603-1625), successor to Elizabeth I and target of the Gunpowder Plot (1605), and they are often referred to as Jacobean locks, taking the name from the Latin form of James (*Jacobus*). Jacobean flintocks supplanted the snaphaunce in all but English martial firearms ca. 1635, though by midcentury they were almost entirely superseded in commercial firearms by the true flint-lock.[19] English martial firearms continued to use the matchlock and the snaphaunce until the end of the seventeenth century.

Gunspalls and Gunflints

Precisely when chert and flint were first utilized to produce ignition spark in firearms is obscure. Like the wheellock, the first self-striking gunlocks other than snapping matchlocks used marcasite, but with the proliferation of snapping locks ca. 1575 chert became popular because it was less inclined to fracture or crumble. Chert is identified by its glossy appearance and it was readily procured from glacial deposits.

Gunspalls were chipped from a suitable piece of chert with a small hammer and displayed thin, irregularly dressed bodies tapering to a sharp, central striking point.[20] Standard gunspalls emerged in France ca. 1650, characterized by a chipped body and a rounded heel abruptly tapering to the striking point, and thereafter most European gunspalls followed the French pattern.

The gunspall gradually began to be replaced by the gunflint ca. 1670 when the Neolithic method of flint knapping reemerged in Europe. Long blades of flint were struck from a large piece of flint by a flint striker (hammer), broken into manageable size, and then carefully knapped by controlling the pressure applied to the knapping tool when shaping the gunflint into its final form.

Flint quarrying and knapping were well established in France by 1675, the industry centered in the departments of Indre, Loire et Cher, and Yonne. A decade later English flint quarries were flourishing at Mindenhall, Savenham, Tuddenham, and Brandon; the latter presently the world-supplier of gunflints. Since prehistory flint knapping has remained a manual art and as a practical consideration during the flintlock era the flint industry was monopolized by governments to ensure adequate supplies at reasonable cost.

By 1675 gunflints could be readily distinguished as English or European by shape and color. The European gunflint, or Continental gunflint as it is

often termed, was derived from the gunspall design. The English gunflint displayed irregular, slanting sides, a square heel, and a tapered striking point extending from the bottom of the body rather than centered. European gunflints range in color from pearl grey to honey yellow and the English variety are dark grey or black. The French gunflint, superior to the English or other continental European varieties, dominated the world market until 1794 when the revolutionary government banned exports.

Contemporary sources indicate that two schools of thought early emerged concerning the best method of fixing the gunflint in the cock jaws to produce the most spark: placing the striking edge either up or down. Both methods had adherents and it was a common practice to invert the gunflint when it was apparent that the amount of spark began to diminish.

Whatever method was used the gunflint had to be properly adjusted and securely held in the cock jaws. A misaligned or improperly seated flint was easily broken when it struck the battery, causing misfires. A thin strip of lead or leather wrapped around the flint heel prior to inserting it in the cock jaws provided a secure grip and during the early eighteenth century flint caps emerged serving the same purpose, each thin, lead disc perforated to accommodate the cock jaw screw.

The chert gunspall was more brittle than the gunflint and delivered approximately 20 strikes before it had to be replaced, the central strike point precluding inversion. The gunflint delivered as many as 35 strikes and was readily inverted. For

GUNSPALLS & GUNFLINTS (16th/17th Century): First row, top and profile left to right. (1) European marcasite (iron pyrites) gunspall ca. 1510. (2) European chert gunspall ca. 1580. (3) French chert gunspall ca. 1620. Second row, top and profile left to right. (1) French gunflint ca. 1680. (2) English gunflint ca. 1685. (3) English gunflint ca. 1725. Bottom figure represents lead or leather strip wrapped around the heel of the gunspall or gunflint secured in the cock jaws. Author's sketch.

maximum efficacy the martial gunflint was usually replaced after about 20 strikes and during musket drill a wooden snapper was placed in the cock jaws, conserving flint and reducing battery face wear.

The English Influence

Gun-founding and gunsmithing languished in England until the final years of the fifteenth century when it gained some impetus under the direction of Henry VII (1457-1509). The English iron industry upon which the manufacturer of firearms and other ordnance depended was then centered in the Weald of Sussex in Ashdown Forest; and Henry, aware of the need for expertise, imported Flemish gun-founders and gunsmiths.

The infant armament industry was inherited by Henry VIII (1491-1547) who immediately grasped its significance and he was responsible for its enviable growth. When Henry ascended the throne in 1509 the venerable Tower of London was the single foundry capable of casting bronze cannon.[21] Like his father, Henry also imported gun-founders and in 1543 hired from Flanders Peter Baude (Bawd) and Peter van Collen.

During Henry's reign the few gunsmiths in the kingdom were known as armorers and, with minor exceptions, they were little more skilled than the blacksmith who also frequently made and repaired firearms. In 1537 William Hunt, possibly an emigré

Flemish gunsmith, purportedly made for Henry an ornate breech-loading wheellock saddle carbine.[22] The following year Hunt was appointed Keeper of the King's Handguns and Demi-Hawks.[23] Henry also owned a breech-loading arquebus and both firearms employed a loading chamber.[24]

Loaded with powder and ball, the cylindrical iron chamber was inserted in an innovative hinged-cover breech opening. The chamber displayed a vent and a small lug, the latter fitting a locking slot in the breech. The breech was loosely sealed by the hinged cover secured by a pin; the pin transversing the cover behind the loading chamber and resting in a detent at the base of the breech. A vent channel in the breech wall opposite the priming pan conveyed the ignition spark to the chamber.

Breech-loading firearms with separate loading chambers are depicted in the *Codex* 1390 (see p. 24) and were sketched in da Vinci's *Il Codice Atlantico;* thus originating at an early date, though whether they were merely conceptual or actually produced cannot be determined.[25] As far as it is known, the breech-loading firearms made for Henry VIII are the first English specimens.

Henry VIII violently opposed papal authority as much on principle as for his connubial convenience and in defiance he seized the Minories in 1539.[26] The Minories, a Carmelite convent established in 1293, was hastily transformed into a large arsenal and armory. Despite continuous though gradual growth (there were 37 armorers working there in 1590), the Minories did not produce firearms in sufficient quantity;[27] and in 1544 Henry purchased 1,500 matchlock arquebuses from Brescian gunsmiths.[28]

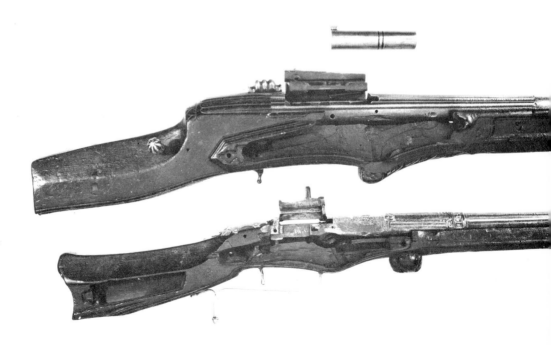

BREECH-LOADING FIREARMS (16th Century): These unique firearms were made for Henry VIII, the arquebus (top) ca. 1535 and the carbine in 1537. Both firearms have fluted breeches. The wheellock has been removed from the arquebus to illustrate the open breech and the projection on the metal charger (above) locked it in the breech. The arquebus has a 43½-inch barrel of .71 caliber. The carbine has a 26-inch barrel of .54 caliber and was converted from wheellock to match ignition. Note the accessory trap in the stock, possibly used for carrying the charger. The protrusion below the carbine breech is a palm rest. British Crown Copyright. Reproduced with permission of the Controller of Her Britannic Majesty's Stationery Office.

GUN SHIELD (16th Century): Made by English armorers during the reign of Henry VIII, this iron-covered target (shield) is a technological innovation which probably originated in Italy. Note the twisted, wrought iron barrel of the breech-loading matchlock pistol transversing the shield beneath the small aiming aperture. British Crown Copyright. Re- produced with permission of the Controller of Her Britannic Majesty's Stationery Office.

Rear view of the gun shield, details the breech of the match- lock pistol. British Crown Copy- right. Reproduced with permis- sion of the Controller of Her Britannic Majesty's Stationery Office.

English armorers were quick to adopt foreign innovations and in many instances improved them; an expedient early apparent in Spain and demon- strating minimum originality, though it was re- markably effective for keeping abreast of the most recent technological developments.

An outstanding example of "borrowed" tech- nology in sixteenth-century England is provided by the Italian gun shields purchased by Henry and faith- fully reproduced by indigenous artisans. The Italian gun shield also represents two radical innovations, for it combined defensive armor with a single-shot, breech-loading pistol; the only known matchlock pistols produced in Europe, though matchlock pistols were subsequently common in the Orient. In 1547, the year Henry died, a Tower of London inven- tory listed 40 gun shields.[29]

The English gun shield consisted of an eight- inch, .75 caliber, smoothbore matchlock pistol pro- truding through a wooden target (shield) 18 and one-half inches in diameter, plated with iron, and provided with an aiming aperture. In one variation the pistol barrel illustrates a discernable twist which was probably introduced as a means of strengthening the iron, though it could have been simply orna- mental.

Henry's shield pistols were provided with four iron loading chambers similar to those used in his wheellock breech-loaders and ". . . the system adopted for loading consists of a block hinged upon each side of the barrel: it is raised up for the insertion of a loaded thimble or . . . chamber. The match was affixed to a serpentin [sic] attached to a rod stapled to the interior of the shield, which was depressed by hand into the flash-pan upon the top [of the breech] to ignite the charge."[30]

The loading chambers employed in Henry's wheellock firearms and the shield pistols did not readily expand when the powder was ignited, conse- quently the powder gases escaped into the breech, reducing the efficacy; thus breech-loaders incorpor- ating the system were relegated to obscurity until resurrected by advanced technology.

Gaining the Tudor crown in 1547, Elizabeth I (1533-1603) did not neglect the armament industry so cherished by her illustrious father, nor did she ignore the challenge of domestic affairs and the potential of the New World. Elizabeth avidly studied the explorations and exploits of her captains and was particularly impressed by John Hawkins, first of the great English sea dogs and slave traders. In 1565 Hawkins assisted the Huguenots escaping from Fort Caroline (see p. 46) and brought her firsthand knowledge of La Florida.

VIRGINIA (17th Century): Capt. John Smith's map of Virginia illustrates the extent of his 1607-1609 explorations. The Spaniards discovered Chesapeake Bay 37 years prior to the English landing at Jamestown and founded a mission near present Williamsburg which was destroyed by the Native Americans in 1572. Courtesy of the Library of Congress.

Avoiding an open confrontation with Spain, Elizabeth covertly encouraged Francis Drake's excursions against the Spaniards and granted patents to Martin Frobisher and Humphrey Gilbert to establish colonies in North America. In 1583 Gilbert established in Newfoundland the first English colony in the New World though it subsequently failed. Determined to plant the Tudor standard beyond the Spanish sea, Elizabeth financed another attempt in 1584 promoted by her favorite, Walter Ralegh.

Ralegh's initial expedition explored the coast of what was Spanish Florida though he named the region Virginia to honor his patroness, the so-called Virgin Queen. In 1585 his second expedition, under the command of Sir Richard Grenville, brought one hundred and seven colonists to Roanoke Island (North Carolina). Leaving Ralph Lane to govern the settlement, Grenville sailed for England. Lane was forced to abandon the colony and on June 19, 1586,

he and the settlers departed for home with Francis Drake who had recently raided St. Augustine.

A second colony was started on Roanoke Island by John White in 1587 and he shortly thereafter sailed to England for additional supplies. His return delayed four years by war with Spain, White discovered all trace of the colony had vanished and with it neither Elizabeth nor Ralegh had realized their ambitions in North America.

What little knowledge of the firearms employed by the English in the so-called Lost Colony is provided by Gov. Ralph Lane's narrative, for he noted that in 1586 a Native American had been accidentally wounded by a wheellock *petronel,* then described as a firearm of carbine genre.[31] Lane also mentioned pistols which were probably wheellocks because no English reference to the snaphaunce appeared until 1588; thus he was the first to note the use of wheellock firearms in North America.[32]

Despite the failure of Elizabethan colonization efforts, England responded with renewed enthusiasm following the end of her protracted conflict with Spain in 1604. On April 10, 1606, James I chartered the London and Plymouth companies, granting each colonization and commercial rights in North America.

Commanded by Capt. Christopher Newport of the London Company, three ships sailed from England on December 20 with 144 adventurers bound for Virginia. They reached their goal May 13, 1607, disembarked the following day, and "set to worke about the fortification . . ." of what they called James Towne in deference to their sovereign.[33]

Fiery, forceful, and resourceful Capt. John Smith brought order out of chaos in the first lean years at Jamestown. Coerced by his critics and severely burned when his powder flask accidentally (?) ignited, Smith sailed for England late in 1609, reporting that the settlers had available "24 peeces of ordinances [cannon], 300 muskets, snaphaunces and fire lockes, shot powder and match sufficient . . ."[34]

The muskets mentioned by Smith were obviously matchlocks because there was "match sufficient," while the snaphaunces either incorporated the Channel region snaphaunce or the early form of the English flintlock; contemporary terminology often ignoring the distinction. The "fire lockes" used in the first permanent English settlement in North America were probably wheellock firearms, the term then commonly used to distinguish the wheellock from the matchlock, while the contention is supported by archaeological evidence recovered at the Jamestown site.[35]

On the first North American frontier defense was an imperative obligation for all European intruders. Spain provided professional soldiers to protect her settlements and can be credited with establishing the militia system in North America. The English colonists and other Europeans arriving in the seventeenth century immediately provided for defense by organizing quasi-military forces with

regular muster and drill periods and also erected stout wood and earthen fortifications which they copied from the Native Americans who had developed the system in the pre-Columbian era.

The entire male population able to bear arms was responsible for protecting Jamestown and a militia ordinance of 1611 required all to be furnished with a helmet, sword, light armor, and a snaphaunce, firelock, or pistol.[36] Sentries with matchlock firearms were advised to keep their match lighted at all times, and it was customary to stand guard with one or two musket balls kept in the mouth to facilitate loading in an emergency.

The Native Americans of the mighty Powhatan Confederacy early learned about firearms from the Virginia settlers and the tribes inhabiting coastal Maine apparently had some knowledge of matchlock firearms prior to 1607, for that year English explorer Ralegh Gilbert and a few of his crew nearly lost their lives as a result.[37]

As Gilbert and his men reached land in a small shallop to meet a group of Native Americans apparently eager to trade, one of his musketeers started to light his match from a firebrand when it was suddenly seized and thrown into the water by a Native American who apparently assumed the action to be hostile. Gilbert unhesitatingly ordered his musketeers to aim their useless weapons directly at the Native Americans and they fled in panic, unsure of the threat.

Self-striking flintlock firearms early supplanted matchlock firearms in the Virginia Colony and the flintlock emerged as the dominant ignition system in all but the Spanish dominions of North America at least 50 years before it found widespread military

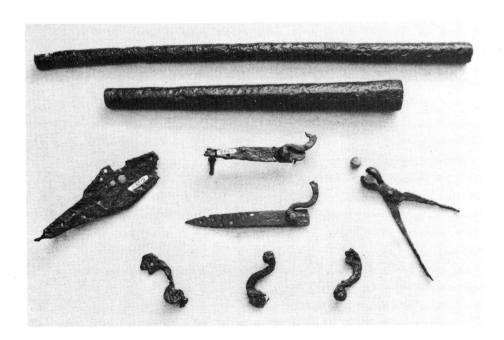

JAMESTOWN GUN FRAGMENTS (17th Century): Excavated by archaeologists at Jamestown, Va., these artifacts represent the firearms and accessories employed by the early English settlers. Top: Matchlock musket barrels. Center, from left: Fragmented wheellock lockplate, fragmented matchlocks, and single cavity bullet mould with musket ball. Bottom: Three matchlock serpentines. Courtesy of Jamestown Colonial National Historical Park, Jamestown, Va. Thomas L. Williams, photographer.

acceptance in Europe; the demand for flintlock firearms in the English colonies was predicated on desperate need.

The Virginia Colony census of 1624-1625 revealed six snaphaunces, 20 pounds of gunpowder,
and 180 pounds of lead and shot among the household effects of Gov. Sir Francis Wyatt, while at
Jamestown 92 firearms of various kinds were available.[38] An inventory of all the firearms and munitions dispersed among the 1,029 settlers disclosed
981 "peeces fixit" [flintlocks with combined battery
and pan cover] and snaphaunces, 55 pistols, six carbines, 1,129¾ pounds of gunpowder, 9,657 pounds
of shot, and only 47 matchlock firearms.[39]

Beyond the Spanish dominions all of the firearms, firearms components, gunpowder, match,
gunflints, shot, and bulk lead were imported prior to
ca. 1630; either brought to North America as personal possessions or held in common trust by civil
authorities. As a rule all firearms and munitions,
except personal arms and militia weapons kept at
home, were stored at a convenient armory or magazine and perpetually guarded as much against capture
or theft as fire.

In each settlement the armory and the magazine
were often specially constructed, usually as part of a
fortification, though frequently as separate entities
segregated from each other and adjacent structures to
prevent a holocaust and the simultaneous loss of
either the firearms or the gunpowder.

Throughout the colonial epoch and considerably thereafter the firearm, like the ax and the plow,
was a primary survival tool, for not only did it serve
as an individual and collective means of offense and
defense, but provided sustenance, protected crops
and livestock from predators, and preserved in the
individual sense a security however tenuous in
reality. Nor was the firearm ignored as a vital part of
commerce, legitimate or otherwise.

The London Company received a new charter
in 1609 and it was thereafter known as the Virginia
Company. English Separatists called Saints and now
referred to as Pilgrims had been for some time disenchanted with the accepted religious dogma of their
homeland and many lived in exile in Leiden,
Holland, to escape persecution, subsequently receiving permission from the Virginia Company to establish an independent colony in North America.

On September 6, 1620, a group of English and
Leiden Separatists numbering 108 including their
servants and assorted craftsmen sailed from Plymouth Harbor aboard the *Mayflower*. The frightening and difficult passage was further imperiled
when the child Francis Billington (ca. 1612-?) nearly
blew up the ship while playing with gunpowder
squibs (homemade firecrackers) near the powder
kegs stored aboard.[40] On November 11 O.S.* the

Mayflower anchored off New England. Two days
later 16 men went ashore at present Cape Cod "with
every man his musket, sword, and corselet, under ye
command of Captain Myles Standish."[41]

The practical Saints had armed themselves with
several matchlock muskets and a few flint-ignition
firearms of an unspecified kind, though considering
the date, the locks were either snaphaunce or
Jacobean.

Exploring near Wellfleet Bay on a bitter cold
December 8, Capt. Standish and his party had their
first clash with the Native Americans. Standish and a
companion, both armed with flintlock firearms, held
the "heathen selvages" at bay until the others recovered their matchlock muskets left in their shallop
beached nearby.[42] One warrior using a tree for cover
kept the Saints pinned down with a volley of arrows
and Standish, with a carefully aimed shot, cut the
bark above his head, showering him with splinters.
According to one of the Saints he "gave an extraordinary shrike, and away they went all of them."[43]

The Pilgrims shortly thereafter abandoned their
Cape Cod explorations and chose a site for a permanent settlement. In late December "New
Plimoth" began to take shape. A Common House
had been built, serving as a storeroom, hospital, and
magazine, while Standish had organized a militia and
mounted cannon on a wooden platform overlooking
the settlement.[44]

On January 14, 1621, the thatched Common
House roof was ignited by an errant spark and only
quick action prevented a tragedy, for kept among the
few patients were a number of primed muskets and
open barrels of gunpowder. Learning a valuable
lesson in the harsh realities of wilderness survival, the
Saints subsequently buried their gunpowder beneath
the Common House floor. To discourage curiosity,
the Pilgrims told the Native Americans that smallpox was buried there.[45] Smallpox spread by visiting
European fishermen had wreaked havoc among the
Massachusetts tribes just prior to the arrival of the
Pilgrims and thereafter the Native Americans gave
the Common House a wide berth.

The firearms employed at Jamestown and Plymouth exhibited little ornamentation because they
were primarily utilitarian and they were not standardized in the modern sense. The Saints evidently
considered the popular English long fowler a necessary and reliable firearm, for it was also used for
defense. The massive breech withstood the intensity

*The date given is from the Julian Calendar used in Protestant
countries after 1582 when the Gregorian Calendar had been
adopted by the Catholic countries. Britain adopted the Gregorian
Calendar in 1752. From 1582 to 1752 the so-called Historical Year
was used for practical purposes; beginning January 1 it employed
the O.S. (Old Style) Julian month-dates and the N.S. (New Style)
Gregorian year-dates.

of larger powder charges than used in the musket, resulting in greater range.

In 1621 Gervase Markham mentioned the flint-lock long fowler in *Hunger's Prevention, or the Whole Arte of Fowling by Water and Land,* vaguely describing it as having a barrel "five Foot and [a] half or six Foot long, with an indifferent Bore under Harquebus [size]. . . ."[46] Markham's ambiguity could be interpreted to mean that the long fowler was of approximately seventeen bore, i.e., about .65 caliber.

The Saints initially sustained themselves with an abundance of wildfowl and it was not surprising that Edward Winslow, former printer of Droitwich and twice governor of Plymouth, included the following advice in a tract designed to encourage other potential settlers.

Bring every man a musket or fowling piece. Let your piece be long in the barrell; and fear not the weight of it, for most of our shooting is from stands [blinds].[47]

Winslow might have added the counsel of Markham who suggested that for shooting birds on the wing ". . . pound your best sort of Powder, and let your Shot be well siz'd, and not too big; for then it scatters too much: And if too small it has not weight nor strength sufficient to do execution on a large Fowl. In Shooting observe always to Shoot with the Wind if possible, and rather behind the Fowl or side-ways, then full in their Faces; and observe you shelter your self behind a Hedge, Bank, Tree, or any thing else that may keep you from the sight of the Fowl. . . ."[48]

Despite exposure to the unrelenting natural elements, virulent disease, Native American raids, internal dissention, the Starving Time, and inescapable death, Jamestown and Plymouth flourished, inspiring other colonization efforts. The Massachusetts Bay Colony established in 1630 was the result of such inspired success and several years' planning by the Dorchester Company.

The New England Company, proprietors of the Massachusetts Bay settlement after the bankruptcy of the Dorchester Company, prepared an inventory of the items they believed essential for survival in distant New England, including 80 *bastard* muskets with snaphaunces and 48 inch barrels, six long fowling pieces six and ½ feet long with musket "boare" (12 bore); four long fowling pieces five and ½ feet long of "bastard muskett boare," ten full muskets with four foot barrels and rests; 90 bandoliers and bullet bags for the muskets and one pound of shot per bandolier; ten horn flasks for the fowling pieces, each with a one-pound powder capacity; and four barrels of powder "for small shot," i.e., firearms, and eight barrels "for the forte" (cannon powder).[49]

ENGLISH LONG FOWLER (17th Century): The venerable matchlock long fowler had evolved into flintlock form by ca. 1590. The specimen depicted is dated ca. 1620 and displays a Jacobean flintlock with a dog catch and a 61-inch barrel of .71 caliber. Courtesy of the Smithsonian Institution, Washington, D.C.

LONG FOWLER (17th Century): The silver-mounted English long fowler depicted has a 59½-inch barrel of .80 caliber and the length of the Jacobean flintlock is indicated by the position of the lock screws. The landed gentry among the Saints who established Plymouth Colony frequently owned such firearms and used them for hunting as well as defense. British Crown Copyright. Reproduced with permission of the Controller of Her Britannic Majesty's Stationery Office.

Some historians have declared that the bastard musket was the same caliber (12 bore) as the martial matchlock musket though provided with a shorter barrel. The Massachusetts Bay Colony inventory, however, reveals bastard muskets with snaphaunce locks and 48 inch barrels and full muskets with 48 inch barrels, indicating the same barrel length whether snaphaunce or matchlock. Mention is also made of fowling pieces with "musket boare" and "bastard muskett boare;" the latter a foot shorter in barrel length.

Bastard muskets were not provided with rests like the full musket, indicating that they were lighter and consequently shorter, while the reference to "musket boare" and "bastard muskett boare" is

ENGLISH MARTIAL MATCHLOCKS

Type	Barrel Length	Overall Length	Bore
Musket	4'	5' 2''	12
Caliver	3' 3''	4' 6''	17
Arquebus	2' 6''	3'	17
Carbine	2' 6''	3'	24

proof of a difference in caliber. It is probable that the bastard musket was shorter and of smaller bore size than the full musket, possibly akin to the martial *caliver* of the period.

The Massachusetts Bay Colony inventory reveals that English hunting and utilitarian firearms illustrated various characteristics and were known by several terms. Official records, however, disclose that by 1630 martial firearms were appreciably standardized regarding barrel length, overall length, and bore size as indicated in the Table.[50]

The obvious distinction between the martial arquebus and the carbine was bore size, and while the arquebus and the caliver had the same bore size the caliver was longer by 18 inches. The caliver, originating in France ca. 1550-1555, was classed between the musket and the arquebus ca. 1630, though about 40 years earlier it was comparable to the arquebus, for in 1588 Edmund York noted that the English caliver derived from the French *caliber* "which we use

MATCHLOCK MUSKET (ca. 1630): This specimen is typical of the English martial matchlock muskets employed in North America. The .82 caliber barrel is 48 inches long.

The close-up of the lock depicts the serpentine jaws with its thumbscrew for adjusting and securing the match, the finger piece for pivoting the priming pan cover to expose the priming pan, the fence attached to the vertical pan pivot, and the lockplate screws which enter the stock opposite the lock. The end of the front trigger guard screw can be seen protruding through the breech plug tang. Courtesy of the Royal Ontario Museum, Toronto.

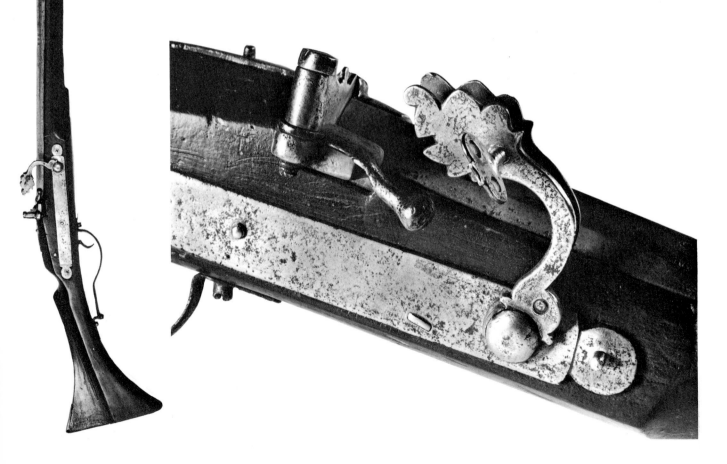

to call a Harquebuze [arquebus] a Calliver. . . .''[51]

Though firearms had been produced in England since the fourteenth century, gunsmithing did not attain independent status until the chaotic reign of Charles I (1625-1649) whose misfortune it was to rule during the sanguinary Puritan Revolution or Civil War (1642-1648) sparked by religious discord and sustained by Oliver Cromwell.

In England prior to 1600 few firearms were made outside London and the Minories. The majority of the London gunsmiths belonged to the Armourers' Company or the Blacksmiths' Company. Bound by those venerable guilds, gunsmiths were also regulated by the crown, and in 1631 the Royal Select Committee fixed prices for specific gunsmithing work (see Appendix II). Birmingham gunsmiths had attempted to organize an independent guild in 1634, though not until 1637 did London gunsmiths successfully break tradition, establishing the Worshipful Company of Gunmakers, subsequently known as the Gunmakers' Company.[52]

The French Influence

Significant progress was made in the French armament industry during the reign of Charles VII (1483-1498). Like other European powers with undeveloped or underdeveloped natural resources and few experienced craftsmen, France also imported cannon, gunpowder, firearms, gun-founders, gunsmiths, and raw materials from Germany, Italy, and the southern Low Countries. As A.N. Kennard notes, French gunsmithing was primarily influenced by Flemish and German masters until ca. 1550 when there was a proliferation of indigenous artisans.[53]

By 1560 a discernable domestic influence was evident in the matchlock arquebus which displayed a sharply curved buttstock with the firing lever gracefully arched to complement the stock configuration. Of a similar pattern, the French martial arquebus of the period accompanied Ribault and Laudonneiré to Spanish Florida. In addition to the sharply curved buttstock, the muzzle of the martial arquebus was distinctly swamped.

The French wheellock initially illustrated a distinct German character subsequently refined by Flemish influence though by ca. 1560 indigenous design innovations emerged; especially in the location of the mainspring and the wheel shank which were, unlike most other wheellocks, separate from the lockplate and fitted inside the stock.[54] The wheel was also larger and the stock consequently wider at that point to accommodate it.

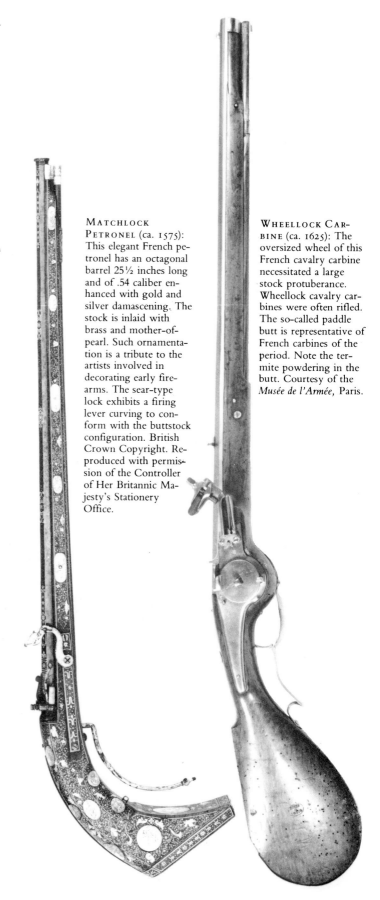

MATCHLOCK PETRONEL (ca. 1575): This elegant French petronel has an octagonal barrel 25½ inches long and of .54 caliber enhanced with gold and silver damascening. The stock is inlaid with brass and mother-of-pearl. Such ornamentation is a tribute to the artists involved in decorating early firearms. The sear-type lock exhibits a firing lever curving to conform with the buttstock configuration. British Crown Copyright. Reproduced with permission of the Controller of Her Britannic Majesty's Stationery Office.

WHEELLOCK CARBINE (ca. 1625): The oversized wheel of this French cavalry carbine necessitated a large stock protuberance. Wheellock cavalry carbines were often rifled. The so-called paddle butt is representative of French carbines of the period. Note the termite powdering in the butt. Courtesy of the Musée de l'Armée, Paris.

MATCHLOCK AR-QUEBUS (16th/17th Century): French colonists in *La Florida* and *Nouvelle France* were armed with matchlock arquebuses during the period 1562-1640. The arquebus weighed less and was of smaller caliber than the musket as indicated by this specimen depicted in A.M. Mallet, *Le Travaux de Mars, ou l'Art de la Guerre* (Amsterdam, 1696). Courtesy of the Library of Congress.

Paris emerged as the hub of sixteenth-century French gunsmithing and was never thereafter overshadowed, though there were several provincial artisans of outstanding merit, e.g., the Bourgeoys family dynasty. Like other major European powers, France had made several unsuccessful attempts to standardize the caliber and the bore diameter of martial firearms, yet not until late in the sixteenth century was a distinctive martial pattern matchlock musket adopted.

The most positive step toward interchangeable caliber in France was reported by Englishman Edmund York (see p. 86) who wrote ca. 1555 that the governor of Piedmont provided his entire regiment with arquebuses of the same caliber "of which Words of Calibre came first this unapt term . . . which is the Height [diameter] of the Bullet and not the Piece [firearm]."[55]

York, an astute military observer, further mentioned that "Before the battle of Montgunter [Moncontour, October 3, 1569] the Prynces of the Religion caused several thousand harquebuzes to be made all of one calibre, which was called '*harquebuze de calibre de Monsieur le Prince*' (arquebuses of the bore diameter designated by the prince)."[56]

The French *calibre* (caliber), possibly derived from the Arabic *q'alib* (a mould) or the Latin *qua libre* (of what weight?), used to identify the bore size of a firearm or the diameter of the ball was subsequently corrupted in England to calliver or caliver and by 1570 it described a kind of firearm, for that year armorer Thomas Rigges received £50 for making "100 calivers of old curriers, at 10 shillings each with

furnishings."[57] Parenthetically, it is not known what *curriers* were.

The massive, cumbrous matchlock musket was known in France by 1570, probably as a result of the Spanish war in the Netherlands, and a variation was adopted as a martial firearm in 1573 during the reign of Charles IX (1500-1574) through the influence of his Colonel General of Infantry, Philipe Strozzi.[58] Employing a barrel rest *(fourquine)*, the French musket weighed 16 to 20 pounds and fired a two-ounce ball effective at 200 yards. Despite the acceptance of the conventional trigger elsewhere in Europe, the French martial musket retained the lever trigger until it was supplanted by the flintlock musket in 1699.

Thwarted in the St. Lawrence region and in Spanish Florida during the sixteenth century, the main thrust of the seventeenth-century French colonial movement in North America was again focused in the north and was of economic rather than philosophic motivation. The French aristocracy, ever style-conscious and even then paying slavish obedience to *haut ton,* demanded fashionable furs from their *couturiers,* though an insatiable European market drained sources in Russia; thus inspiring numerous French commercial interests to invest in North American colonial ventures in an attempt to capture the lucrative trade.

Long before any European of record set foot in the New World the Native Americans had established a complex and widespread barter system of considerable economic stature with furs and hides serving as the basic commodity. The French were the first to try to capitalize on the Native American trade and in 1598 the Marquis de la Roche established a trading post on Sable Island east of Nova Scotia. His unsuccessful venture was followed in 1600 by Sieur de Pontgrave who had received a royal patent to exploit the fur trade. Pontgrave started a trading post on the St. Lawrence river at the mouth of the Sanguenay.

In 1603 Samuel de Champlain (1567?-1635), appointed pilot and navigator by Henry IV, explored the St. Lawrence with Pontgrave and returned in 1604 to start a trading post on St. Croix Island. The post was subsequently moved to Port Royal, Nova Scotia (Acadia), while in 1608 Champlain reestablished Quebec to serve as a base for further explorations in *Nouvelle France.*

Accompanied by friendly Algonquin, Huron, and Montagnais, Champlain penetrated the interior of New France and on July 29, 1609, at the south end of the lake now bearing his name, encountered approximately two hundred Iroquois (possibly Mohawks) who were the traditional enemies of his companions. Because it was nearing sundown the Iroquoian challengers postponed battle until the

A FRENCH/IROQUOIS CONFRONTATION (1609): Though the illustration is indistinct it is believed that Samuel de Champlain was armed with a wheellock arquebus during his celebrated skirmish with the Iroquois in 1609. Champlain (center) so alienated the Five Nations (Cayuga, Mohawk, Oneida, Onondaga, and Seneca) of the Iroquoian Confederation that they thereafter almost continuously opposed the French and their Native American allies. From the Sigmund Samuel Collection. Courtesy of the Royal Ontario Museum, Toronto.

following day and Champlain described his participation thusly:

I marched on until I was within thirty yards of the enemy, who . . . halted and gazed at me and I at them. When I saw them make a move to draw their bows . . ., I took aim with my arquebus and shot straight at one of the three chiefs, and with this shot two fell to the ground and one of their companions was wounded who died

thereof a little later. I had put four balls into my arquebus. . . ."[59]

Whether Champlain's arquebus was a wheellock or a matchlock cannot be ascertained, though using multiple-ball loads was then common in warfare and persisted beyond the colonial era, en-

FRENCH EXPLORATIONS Within the Present Limits of the United States (16th/18th Century). Courtesy of the National Park Service, Washington, D.C.

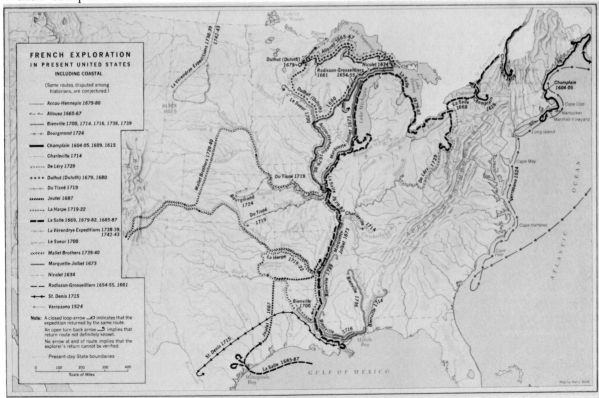

hancing the efficacy of smoothbore, single-shot firearms. A proper caliber ball backed by two or more pistol balls was a popular load and variations employing buckshot and pistol balls exclusively or in combination were used.

Champlain's lethal volley cost France dearly in the ensuing struggle for supremacy in North America, for thereafter the Five Nations comprising the powerful Iroquoian Confederacy (Cayuga, Mohawk, Oneida, Onondaga, and Seneca) displayed an implacable, nearly unremitting hatred of the French. The Iroquois subsequently became staunch friends of the English in an association contributing to the ultimate expulsion of the French as a dominant colonial power.

France initially failed to support early colonization efforts, responding to the needs of the settlers much the same as Spain had in the decaying Florida provinces, and neither were the French trading companies more solicitous. Many colonists returned to France rather than face the cruel winters, disease, famine, and the hostile Iroquois.

An indication of the kinds of firearms employed in New France is conveyed by an inventory of the goods procured to supply 80 colonists in 1619, though the intended expedition failed to materialize. The inventory included 40 matchlock muskets with slings, four wheellock firearms four to five feet long, 1,000 pounds of fine [serpentine] powder, and 6,000 pounds of bullet lead.[60]

On Wednesday, August 18, 1621, in a rare instance of sovereign support, Champlain received from Louis XIII "2 arquebuses with wheellocks, from five to six feet long; 2 others, with match locks of the same length; 523 lbs. of good match, and 187 more that was rotten."[61] In addition, there were two barrels of musket balls weighing 439 pounds.

Considering the precarious French position, the arms and munitions arriving from the mother country were pitifully few and the scarcity undoubtedly contributed to the relative ease by which Quebec fell to the English led by Capt. Louis Kirke on July 20, 1629. Kirke's party captured 14 muskets (one broken), one arquebus (possibly a snaphaunce), two large wheellock arquebuses six to seven feet long, two matchlock firearms of the same length, five to six thousand bullets, and 30 to 40 pounds of gunpowder; the latter certainly insufficient to sustain a prolonged defense.[62]

Like Spain and for identical reasons, France prohibited firearms distribution among the Native Americans; a stipulation clearly defined in Champlain's 1613 charter, and in 1620 he noted that the illegal commerce carried the death penalty. Despite the ultimate punishment, unscrupulous Frenchmen were raiding the St. Lawrence trading posts as early as 1617 and ". . . had given to the savages a large supply of firearms, with powder, lead and match—a most pernicious and mischievous thing. . . ."[63]

That passage clearly reveals that matchlock firearms were the first gunpowder weapons procured by the Native Americans in New France and, lacking contradictory evidence, it is evident that gunrunning in North America originated with the French. In 1640, five years after Champlain died, Governor General Charles Jacques Huault de Montmagny rescinded the ban to the extent that firearms could be legally traded to any Native American who had become a neophyte Christian, i.e., a French ally in less formal terms.[64]

The governor's action elicited an appreciative response from the trading companies and it was doubtlessly applauded by the Native Americans. The Jesuits, however, viewed his decision with ambivalence, for though proselyzation escalated so, too, did avarice and duplicity among the converts. And in New France the widespread distribution of firearms among the Native Americans would soon have a major cultural impact.

By ca. 1625 the matchlock arquebus and musket were predominant in New France, though wheellock firearms were more prevalent than in the Spanish, Dutch, or English colonies; not surprising when considering the then primitive state of wheellock development in England and Spain and its lack of popularity in the Netherlands. As yet the French displayed little interest in flintlock ignition. The snaphaunce had not been readily accepted in France and was therefore scarce in her American dominions and, in any event, the true flintlock superseded previous ignition systems in all but martial firearms prior to ca. 1650. The rapid acceptance of the flintlock in New France was coeval with its adoption in the English settlements; an event which would have far-reaching consequences in the Spanish dominions.

The Dutch Influence

By ca. 1550 the Netherlands emerged as the commercial crossroads of western Europe, the economy greatly stimulated by an extensive trade in cannon, firearms, munitions, and the raw materials needed for their manufacture. Comprised of seventeen relatively autonomous provinces under the hemogeny of Emperor Charles V, the Spanish influence was particularly strong in the southern Low Countries and continued to strengthen until the reign of Philip II. Philip's repressive rule antagonized the aristocracy and literally terrorized the industrious, enterprising lower estates.

Since early in the sixteenth century the Low Countries had actively supplied England, France, Portugal, Spain, and Sweden with much needed ordnance and those nations also employed a large number of Flemish gun-founders and gunsmiths because of their expertise.

Spain especially had purchased large quantities of ordnance from Flanders and by midcentury she was supplied from England as well; however, with Philip's involvement in the Low Countries many Protestant craftsmen refused to work in Spain or her dominions because they feared reprisals from the Inquisition tribunals established by Tomas de Torquemada in 1483 which then and thereafter perpetrated atrocities upon the apostates in the zealous pursuit of "heresy."[65] As conditions deteriorated Elizabeth I expressed her opposition in 1560, thereafter refusing to export weapons to Catholic countries.[66]

A 1566 Calvinist uprising in the Low Countries was met the following year with brutal retaliation and in 1568 revolution flamed across the Netherlands. Eight years later Spanish troops virtually destroyed thriving Antwerp, uniting opposition. The Dutch rebels (Beggars) controlled the vital sea lanes and seven northern provinces (Holland), while Spain occupied ten southern provinces (Flanders and present Luxembourg) where the major arms-making facilities were located, meanwhile revitalizing the royal gun foundry at Malines in 1574; an installation established in 1520 by Charles V.[67]

Severed from the southern provinces, Holland freely imported English and German ordnance and in 1581, under the banner of the United Provinces, Holland declared independence. It was then, under the exigencies of war, that the snaphaunce arrived in the Netherlands from Germany.

Prince Maurice of Nassau (1567-1625) initiated a widespread reorganization of the Dutch Republican Army during the period 1590-1600, instituting a system of relatively standardized martial firearms.[68] Amsterdam emerged as the principal arms-making center, counting among its inhabitants more gunsmiths than The Hague, Maastricht, and Utrecht combined.[69] The rapidly expanding Dutch armament industry was then dominated by St. Eloy's guild (gunsmiths) and St. Joseph's guild (carpenters); the former making barrels and locks, and the latter assembling those components to the stock.[70] The government and the guilds regulated the industry and established proofhouses.

Though firearms had been proved at Amsterdam during the late sixteenth century the first official Dutch proof regulations were defined at Dordrecht in 1603, followed by Amsterdam in 1604 and Utrecht in 1628.[71] The inspection and proving of firearms was supervised at the proofhouses by city

"A MUSKETEER with his Match-Lock, Bandileers and Rest," from Francis Grose, *Military Antiquities Respecting a History of the English Army and a Treatise on Ancient Armor* (London: S. Hooper, 1786). This illustration first appeared in Jacob de Gheyn, *Manual of Arms* (Amsterdam, 1608). Though the lock is obscured, the remainder of the musket is delineated. Note the flared butt, deep thumb rest at the stock wrist, trigger guard and breech flats. The powder chargers, bullet pouch, and powder flask are attached to the bandolier; the flask provided with an adjustable pour spout. The musketeer carries a fourquine (rest) with its wrist cord in his right hand, while in his left he holds the match lighted at each end. The sword was a standard infantry accouterment. Courtesy of the University of Toronto Library, Ontario.

MATCHLOCK MUSKET (17th Century): The Dutch matchlock musket depicted was made in 1611. The overall length of the musket is 64 inches and the 49-inch barrel is of .78 caliber. The muzzle of the octagonal barrel is slightly swamped and the walnut stock is elaborately inlaid with bone depicting a hunting motif. A detailed winged dragon bone inlay, head facing the butt, is mortised into the stock above the rectangular, brass lockplate decorated with a foliate design. The serpent was early used in the decorative scheme of Dutch firearms. Too elaborate for a martial musket, the firearm could have been made for a city guard or militia unit. Courtesy of the *Livrustkammaren*, Stockholm.

proofmasters *(stadsproefmeesters)* and was described by Amsterdam proofmaster Jan Lootsman on September 7, 1638:

> In proving barrels of muskets . . . nothing else is observed than that the ball and gunpowder are of the same weight and that the barrels are bored so truly that a ball of twelve in the pound [approximately .75 caliber] can run freely to the breechplug. . . ."[72]

Lootsman also described the bore gauge utilized by the city proofmasters as ". . . an iron ramrod at the end of which a sphere is fixed of the thickness [diameter] of a ball of twelve in the pound. These ramrods they put in the barrels to test them."[73]

The Dutch Republic adopted the Regulations of 1599 on February sixth, delineating the caliber, length, weight, and other specifications for firearms used by infantry, cavalry, militia, and city guards. The Regulations of 1599 were somewhat abridged by the Regulations of 1639 adopted October 22 of that year.[74]

The Dutch *lontslot* (matchlock) martial musket was initially patterned after the Spanish musket introduced in the Netherlands ca. 1565 though it had been substantially altered by the Regulations of 1599. The overall length of the Dutch musket was approximately 57 inches and the 48 inch barrel was of .78 caliber (ten bore) taking a ball measuring about .75 caliber (twelve bore); the windage necessary to facilitate loading. The musket weighed 14 pounds and used a *fourquine* for support. The rectangular lockplate was flat and displayed a pivotal priming pan cover. A match guide was mounted on the breech. The thick buttstock emulated the fishtail pattern and the wrist had a deep thumb notch, while a conventional rather than lever trigger was used.

The Dutch light infantry *caliber* (caliver) weighed approximately nine pounds and no *fourquine* was used. The 30 inch barrel was of .63 caliber taking a .57 caliber ball. The Regulations of 1599 specified that the wheellock was not acceptable for

the martial caliver and, as the snaphaunce is not mentioned relative to Dutch martial firearms, the caliver was a matchlock. A trend to lightweight martial firearms early in the seventeenth century saw the *caliber* replace the *lontslot* musket and take its name.

Substantially easier to handle on horseback than the cumbrous musket and less difficult to load than the musket or *caliber,* the wheellock carbine was adopted for Dutch cavalry. The cavalry carbine was attached by a lanyard and hook to the popular bandolier for convenience and it is believed the practice gave rise to the designation *bandelierroer.* The *bandelierroer* displayed a 30 inch barrel of .66 caliber taking a .64 caliber ball.

Dutch cavalry pistols were also wheellocks and the Regulations of 1599 specified a barrel length of 24 inches, though it was shortened to 20 inches by the Regulations of 1639. Cavalry pistols were of .54 caliber (thirty bore) and took a .52 caliber ball (thirty-three bore). Prior to ca. 1640 Dutch martial wheellocks illustrated a German influence and thereafter emulated the French design.[75]

Early seventeenth-century Dutch martial firearms were strictly utilitarian with little or no ornamentation, though a moulding delineated the breech from the barrel. Militia and city guard firearms followed the martial pattern though they were distinguished by modest to ostentatious ornamentation. Flat lockplates and sideplates were common until the convex French style came into vogue ca. 1660 and by 1675 most Dutch martial firearms incorporated true flintlock ignition.

Because the term *snap-haan* was used indiscriminately in the Netherlands to describe the snaphaunce and the true flintlock early in the seventeenth century, it is difficult to determine precisely the date when the true flintlock was introduced. Existing evidence indicates that the Dutch version of the true flintlock *(vuursteen)* emerged in the Aachen-Maastricht region ca. 1630–1640.[76] By ca. 1650 most Dutch sporting and utilitarian firearms employed the true flintlock.

The Dutch produced a wide variety of elegantly appointed firearms, the metal components exquisitely chased and engraved, and early in the seven-

WHEELLOCK PISTOL (17th Century): The Dutch martial *radslot-pistool* (wheellock pistol) depicted compared favorably with commercial specimens and was made by Utrecht gunsmith Jan Knoop ca. 1660. The .56 caliber barrel is 14½ inches long and the pistol weighs 5½ pounds with an overall length of 22½ inches. Courtesy of the *Tøjhusmuseet,* Copenhagen.

teenth century the serpent or so-called dragon emerged as a popular motif, probably arising as a result of Dutch commercial activity in the Orient. Stocks received equal artistic attention, displaying ornate carving and intricate inlay work of brass, bone, ivory, mother-of-pearl, precious gems and metals and other materials. Stocks were often made of exotic wood imported from the Dutch colonies in Africa and Asia; especially ebony which pleasantly contrasted with skillful silver inlays to produce lavish firearms of superb beauty.

The rapid growth of the Dutch armament industry after ca. 1600 can be ascribed to the earlier and protracted conflict with Spain which stimulated production and technology, and it is particularly exemplified by a substantial increase in the number of firearms produced for export. Denmark purchased 22,400 matchlock muskets at an average of six guilders each (about $14.40) from Amsterdam arms merchants during the period 1625-1627, while in 1630 Russia negotiated for 50,000 muskets.[77] A profitable trade also emerged in North Africa and along the Gold Coast where Arab slavers and Native Africans were introduced to the snaphaunce. Production was further stimulated by the demand for quasi-military firearms for the militia and city guards, as well as fowling pieces, rifles, and pistols for the commercial market in Europe and North America.

Once free from the long war with Spain, the Dutch quickly recognized the economic potential of a commercial empire abroad and much of the effort was directed to the New World. In 1602 the States-General (Parliament) chartered the Dutch East India Company, authorizing explorations in North America for a westward passage to the Orient (the elusive Northwest Passage subsequently sought without success by many European explorers) and the exploitation of trade opportunities with the Native Americans.

Henry Hudson (d. 1611) was familiar with the North American coast from his association with the Muscovy Company of London in 1607, and he was employed by the Dutch two years later. Hudson coasted Newfoundland and sailed as far south as Virginia, discovering in the interim the river bearing his name. Exploring the river in late 1609, Hudson and a small party went ashore seeking fresh water and game to replenish their supplies and they were soon engaged in a sharp encounter with the Native Americans. An unexpected shower extinguished their musket match, though they managed to return unharmed to the waiting *Halve Maen*.[78]

Hudson's expedition further stimulated Dutch interest and by 1610 several traders had visited the Hudson Valley and the Delaware Bay region. In 1613 Hendrick Christianson and Adriaen Block estab-

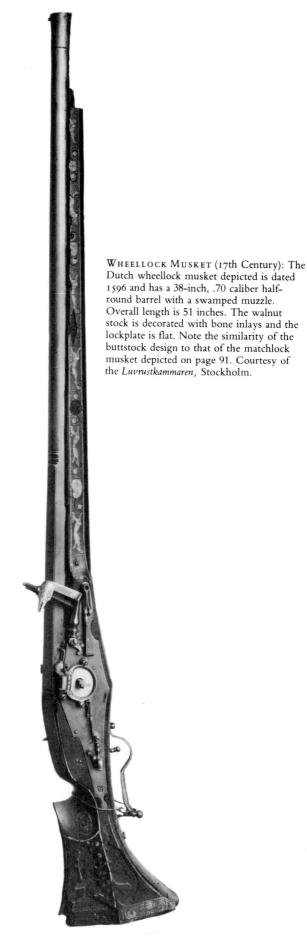

WHEELLOCK MUSKET (17th Century): The Dutch wheellock musket depicted is dated 1596 and has a 38-inch, .70 caliber half-round barrel with a swamped muzzle. Overall length is 51 inches. The walnut stock is decorated with bone inlays and the lockplate is flat. Note the similarity of the buttstock design to that of the matchlock musket depicted on page 91. Courtesy of the *Luvrustkammaren*, Stockholm.

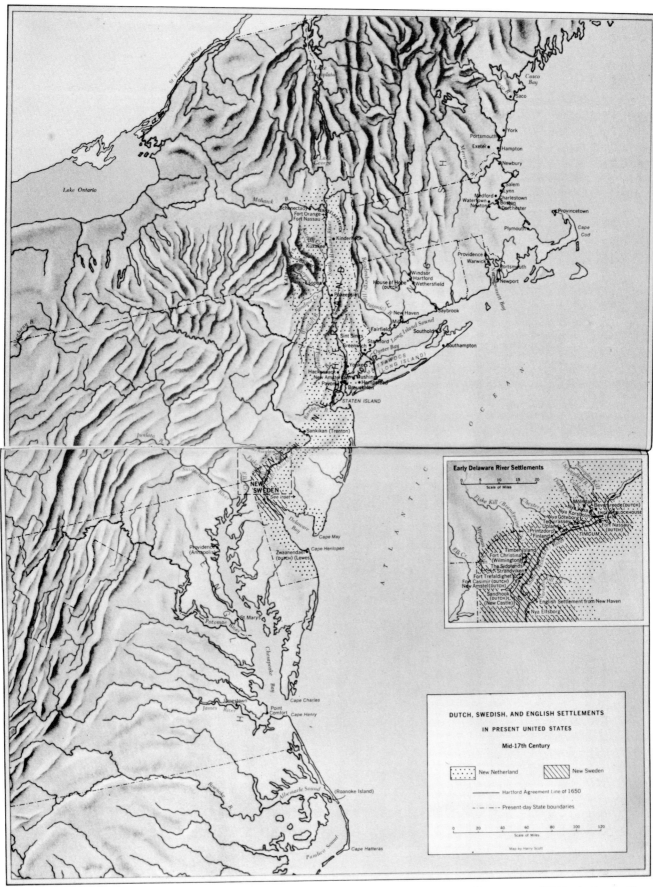

DUTCH, SWEDISH, AND ENGLISH SETTLEMENTS Within the Present Limits of the United States (17th Century): Courtesy of the National Park Service, Washington, D.C.

lished a small trading post on Manhattan Island, while a year later the New Netherland Company was chartered, granting Amsterdam merchants a three-year fur trade monopoly between the fortieth and forty-fifth parallels; a region extending from southern New Jersey to Maine's Passamaquoddy Bay. In 1614 Fort Nassau, later Fort Orange, was established at the present site of Albany, N.Y., and it served as headquarters for the Dutch trade in the Hudson Valley region even after the New Netherland settlements were absorbed by the English.

In 1621 the Dutch West India Company was formed with Peter Minuit (1580-1638) named director general. That same year war again erupted with Spain and not until 1624 were the first substantial Dutch settlements planted along the Hudson and the Delaware, while in 1626 Minuit established Nieuw Amsterdam on Manhattan Island.

Dutch settlers brought with them a variety of matchlock and snaphaunce firearms though wheellock firearms were a rarity, for as New Netherland officials noted "the people here are but little conversant with the use of the wheellock."[79] After ca. 1650 the true flintlock appeared in the Dutch settlements.

Eager Dutch traders plying the Hudson and its tributaries provided the Native Americans with matchlock firearms in 1614, and they can be considered the first Europeans in North America to legally engage in the arms trade.[80] The Dutch, unlike the Spanish and French, did not initially prohibit Native American firearms procurement though it was subsequently restricted and eventually banned under the penalty of death. The exorbitant profits generated by gun-running, however, provided incentive for risking the consequences.[81]

The aggressive, cannibalistic Mohawks of the Iroquoian Confederacy had received large numbers of matchlock firearms from the Dutch prior to 1630, soon turning them against their traditional Native American enemies as well as the French and the English. The early acquisition of firearms by the Mohawks and other Iroquoian tribes in the Hudson Valley foreshadowed a dark chain of circumstances which exerted a shattering impact on Native Americans and Europeans alike.

The Swedish Influence

Though firearms had been made in Sweden since the early fourteenth century the armament industry did not begin to flourish until the reign of Gustav Vasa I (1496-1560). Under his enlightened

leadership the mining industry blossomed and by 1570 exports of Swedish copper, iron, and tin rapidly increased, while in the interim he had imported German gun-founders and gunsmiths with several of the latter employed at the royal gun foundry in Arboga by 1556 (see p. 69).

Gustav's constructive influence in the mining and armament industries was negated by his inept successors, though revitalized when his grandson, Gustavus Adolphus (1594-1632), assumed the crown in 1611. His brilliant application of unorthodox tactics and technological innovations in warfare subsequently inspired the "modernization" of most European armies of consequence.

Between 1618 and 1648 Sweden, like most of continental Europe, was deeply embroiled in the horror of the Thirty Years' War exemplifying the Catholic-Protestant confrontation sparked a century earlier by the Reformation and bringing to seventeenth-century Europe an era of devastation and death.

During that termagant period Gustavus immeasureably improved the efficacy of his infantry by replacing the heavy matchlock musket and requisite *fourquine* with the lightweight wheellock musket and introducing the self-contained paper cartridge, each musketeer provided with a leather box slung across the shoulder on a strap and containing a dozen cartridges; thus accelerating firepower with an improved lock mechanism and eliminating the incon-

Landsknecht (16th/17th Century): The *Landsknecht* (land servants or servants of the lance) were mercenaries owing allegiance to elected leaders and fighting for the spoils of war. Their atrocities during the Thirty Years' War had no equal until the Nazis of World War II. From a woodcut by Sebald Beham (1498?-1549?) in A. Essenwein, *Quellen zur Geschichte der Feuerwaffen* (Leipzig, 1877), Author's sketch.

FLINTLOCK RIFLE (ca. 1650): This Swedish rifle displays an unusual form of stock ornamentation consisting of bone inlays and it is termed *Göinge-bössa*, taking the name from a region in southern Sweden where it originated. The lock has a swivelling steel. The 39-inch barrel has 8-groove rifling and overall length is 49 inches. The stock is birch. Though there is no conclusive proof Swedish rifles might have been used in New Sweden. *Skokloster Armoury*, Stockholm.

MATCHLOCK WALL GUN (ca. 1625): This massive deck or wall gun with its 34-inch, round, copper barrel was used on Swedish vessels and some specimens possibly saw service in New Sweden. Overall length is 46 inches. The wall gun has a conventional trigger and the front trigger guard screw also serves as the breech plug tang screw; a common feature of most matchlock firearms. Courtesy of the *Kungl. Armémuseum*, Stockholm.

SNAPHAUNCE MUSKET (ca. 1585): This Swedish musket depicts an early form of the Scandinavian snaphaunce. The .87 caliber, 57-inch barrel has a front and a rear sight. Courtesy of the *Livrustkammaren*, Stockholm.

venient and time-consuming chore of separately loading the powder and ball.[82]

Further, he increased the mobility of his infantry by removing the customary armor and escalated the volume of fire by converting two-thirds of his pikemen to musketeers arranged in six ranks rather than the usual mass formation; thus subsequently inspiring the development of linear tactics.

Despite his personal commitment to the war Gustavus displayed a keen interest in the prospect of a colonial empire in North America until his death at Lützen in 1632. His minor daughter Christina, though not assuming the throne until 1644, shared his interest and was guided by her regent and affluent Amsterdam merchant William Usselinx. In 1637, after five years of preparation, the New Sweden Company was formed.

Peter Minuit, former governor of New Netherland, offered his services to the Swedes and in December, 1637, sailed from Gothenberg with 50 prospective settlers. After a rough winter passage the *Grip* and the *Kalmar Kyckel* reached Delaware Bay in mid-March, 1638. Minuit purchased a large tract from the Native Americans along the river he had named Christina and also built a fort bearing her name; thus doubly honoring the future queen.

As far as it can be determined, no intact firearms survived the seventeen-year span of New Sweden, though some indication of the firearms employed there can be ascertained from representative specimens of the period presently reposing in Swedish and other museum collections.

Dated ca. 1625, a matchlock firearm in the *Kungl. Armemuseum* displays a thirty-four inch, round copper barrel of 1.6 caliber. Like other Swedish firearms of the period, the barrel is pin-fastened to the full-length walnut stock and illustrates the characteristic fishtail buttstock and deeply notched wrist. The uncommonly large bore diameter and copper barrel identifies the firearm as a wall or deck gun; copper resistant to salt water corrosion.

The large lockplate of the Swedish wall gun is reminiscent of the wheellock lockplate and the conventional rather than lever trigger has an extremely long guard with the front guard screw serving as the breech plug tang screw; a common feature during

that era. The forestock has a copper finial and a copper band serves as the ramrod guide. There are no sights, though a manual priming pan cover is provided. Although evidence is inconclusive, it is possible that matchlock muskets similar to the wall gun were used in New Sweden.

It is also likely that snaphaunce muskets served in New Sweden and they were probably akin to a late sixteenth-century specimen now in the *Livrustkammaren* collection. The octagonal, 57 inch barrel is of .87 caliber and displays a front and a rear sight. The pin-fastened forestock extends to the muzzle. The buttstock comb is straight and the butt flat rather than of the fishtail pattern, while the wooden ramrod is secured by two thimbles (pipes).

The lock is of the usual Scandinavian snaphaunce pattern with the lockplate emulating the wheellock. The priming pan has a disc-type fence and the long, flat mainspring is mounted externally with the forepart acting as the battery spring. The sharply pointed toe of the inverted, Z-shaped cock engages the lateral sear nose transversing the lockplate. The cock screw secures the mainspring bridle. The long, serrated cock jaws are common to the Swedish snaphaunce and other self-striking Scandinavian flintlocks. In the fired position the cock does not protrude above the lockplate and a curved finger piece extending from the upper cock jaw was a necessity rather than a convenience when cocking the firearm.

Though conclusive proof is unavailable it is also possible that Swedish flintlock muskets incorporating the combined, L-shaped pan cover and battery were used in North America. A typical specimen in the *Livrustkammaren* has an overall length of about 63 inches and the half-round, half-octagonal barrel is approximately 46 inches long and of .80 caliber, provided with a front and a rear sight.[83]

The full-length stock is pin-fastened to the barrel and the lockplate is of the wheellock pattern. Except for the ring surmounting the jaw screw, the cock is similar to the snaphaunce cock and a lateral sear is employed. The bridled, externally-mounted mainspring serves as the battery spring. The battery strike plate is an unique feature of the Swedish flint-lock and a radical innovation, doubling as a safety,

FLINTLOCK MUSKET (ca. 1640): This Swedish musket displays an early form of the Scandinavian flintlock and the cock is similar in design to that of the Swedish snaphaunce musket. The full-stocked barrel is 46 inches long and of .80 caliber. Overall length is 60 inches. The breech is marked L M and the underside of the butt is marked P I. Courtesy of the *Livrustkammaren*, Stockholm.

A close-up of the musket shows the lock characterized by the swivelling steel. The combined steel and pan cover was pivoted away from the flint; a safety feature. The lock is marked with a crown and the letters M I. The muskets incorporating this type lock were made in the Swedish Royal Armory at Jönköping. Courtesy of the Skokloster Armory, Stockholm.

FLINTLOCK SPORTING GUN (ca. 1650): Possibly a kind of firearm brought to New Sweden is this sporting gun displaying *Göinge-bössa* ornamentation and a 35-inch

barrel of .39 caliber. The lock has a swivelling steel and ornate mainspring bridle. Courtesy of the Skokloster Armory, Stockholm.

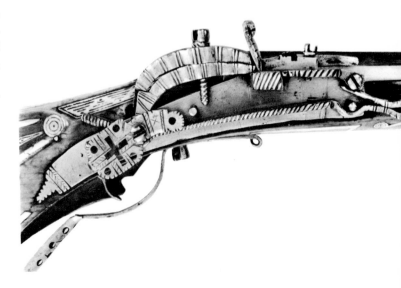

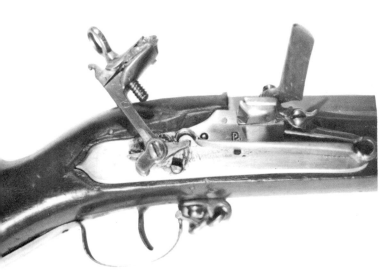

SNAPPING FLINTLOCK (17th Century): A close up of the Swedish martial musket lock in the cocked position depicts the pivotal steel. Note the similarity of the cock jaws and the cock jaw screw to the Spanish *patilla*. It is unlikely that Swedish muskets of this kind served in colonial America. Courtesy of the *Kungl. Armémuseum*, Stockholm.

seventeenth-century North America had not the debilitating Thirty Years' War deprived the nation of strong, cohesive leadership.

The Native American Influence

The war-like Caribs and the relatively placid Tainos of Arawakan stock initially bore the brunt of the European invasion as the Spaniards methodically invaded the West Indies. Shortly thereafter the Native Americans of Mexico, peninsular Florida, and the Gulf cultures felt the ruthless thrust of Toledo steel and the lethal firepower of the matchlock arquebus and musket.

Wherever the Spaniards trod in the Western Hemisphere they almost immediately alienated the Native Americans, for the realists involved in conquest rarely displayed the belated altruism expressed by the church and the crown; the former favoring proselization if possible, and the latter humane treatment if practicable. Those philosophical considerations, however, were frequently overridden by economic expediency.

During the early seventeenth century the Dutch cultivated an amicable relationship with the Native Americans though it soon wilted, and the initial English romance with them also died in the borning, for both the European powers succumbed to pernicious greed. Though the French were certainly not immune to avarice their relations with the Native Americans, excepting the mighty Iroquoian Confederacy, manifested a more tolerant attitude. Rather than intruding upon Native American culture, the scions of St. Denis largely accepted it and in many instances readily adopted the Native American lifestyle.

With minor exceptions the Native Americans totally rejected the alien Old World socio-economic philosophy rooted in land acquisition and exclusive ownership, while they quickly learned to distrust or ignore imperious European authority. Nevertheless, the Native Americans eagerly accepted the superior technology offered by the invaders and clearly recognized the economic advantages of firearms and the profusion of iron implements proffered by a host of venturesome traders penetrating the wilderness.

Providing the Native Americans with firearms and munitions soon emerged as a significant factor in the socio-economic structure of colonial America. Early demonstrating a political acumen of Michiavellian dimensions, the Native Americans rapidly learned to manipulate the invaders, often playing one against the other and frequently using transitory

for it could be swivelled aside. Accidental ignition was impossible when the strike plate was turned away from the cock.

A large number of flintlock muskets incorporating the swivel strike plate were produced at Jönköping and other Swedish armories prior to ca. 1650. An improved version of the flintlock was made for martial muskets after ca. 1670 and the cock and the sear were evidently adopted from the Spanish *patilla*; the cock readily identified by its short jaws and the jaw screw ring.

The true flintlock was not common in Sweden until the late seventeenth century though Parisian gunsmith P. Thomas executed an exquisite pair of flintlock pistols for future queen Christina ca. 1640 and they are currently in the *Livrustkammaren*.[84] The firearms of the aristocracy, however, were certainly not representative of the utilitarian firearms employed in New Sweden.

The Swedes, despite the brief span of their autonomous colony, entered into the Native American trade and sold firearms to the Munsee for protection from the marauding Mohawks.[85] They also formed an alliance with the powerful Susquehanna (Conestoga) and three Swedish soldiers trained 1,300 warriors in the use of firearms and orthodox European infantry tactics to counter increasingly persistent Iroquoian raids.[86]

The Swedish colonial experiment in North America collapsed in a practically bloodless coup in 1655, a year after Queen Christina abdicated in favor of her cousin Charles X (1622-1660), when New Sweden was absorbed by the militant Dutch who subsequently shared a similar fate. It is likely that the Swedish influence would have been much greater in

promises of peace, commerce, and military alliance to promote the procurement of firearms and other coveted trade goods. Neither were the Native Americans hesitant in bartering captives to achieve their purpose.

The mere possession of a firearm instantly elevated the social status of the Native American hunter-warrior to heretofore unfathomable heights and there was literally nothing he would not do to procure firearms of any kind. And once acquiring firearms, many of the sedentary and semi-sedentary tribes were transformed into aggressive nomads preying on their neighbors less fortunate in procuring them, as well as the Europeans who supplied them and who were usually better armed though initially fewer in number. The material cost of arming the Native Americans soon transcended the economic burden shouldered by the rival European powers, for on the first frontier the price was often paid in terror and blood in a maelstrom of savagery.

Old World Technological Innovation

The latter half of the sixteenth century and the advent of the seventeenth century ushered in a wide range of technological innovations in firearms evolution. While many of those developments were original, others were based on prior innovations rendered practical by interim technological achievements. The inventive proclivity of the European gunsmiths continued to flourish, inspired by necessity and nurtured by advancing technology.

No historic epoch is immune from the unscrupulous, and gunpowder, frequently in great demand and consequently expensive, was often deliberately adulterated by adding sand or sawdust, contaminated by using unrefined or improper ingredients, or offered for sale though rendered ineffectual by the chemical deterioration associated with age; those factors causing misfires or ignition failure which not only plagued military operations and those relying on firearms for self-defense, but the hunter facing dangerous game. As a result there emerged in the late sixteenth century an extremely valuable firearms innovation known as the powder tester.

Paul J. Wolf has pointed out that the first literary reference to the powder tester, or *eprouvette* as the French termed it, was mentioned by William Bourne, *Inventions and Devices very Necessary for all Generalles and Captaines* (London, 1587).[87] Though Bourne's work was published in England during the

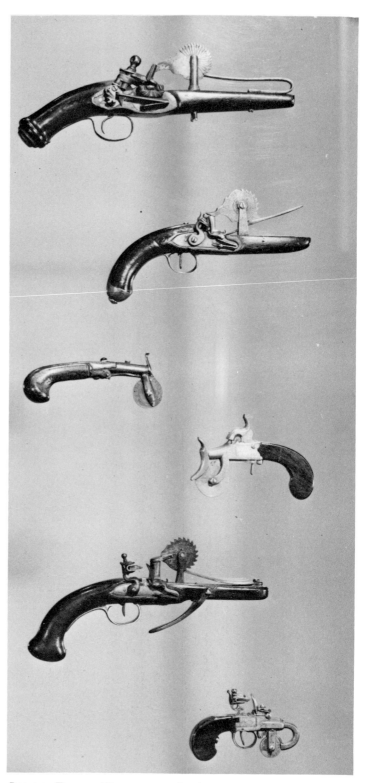

POWDER TESTERS *(Eprouvettes, 17th/19th Century)*: All of the *eprouvettes* depicted are of the disc (wheel) type; the top specimen displaying a Spanish *patilla*. The fourth specimen has a percussion lock (19th Century). Courtesy of the Eleutherian Mills Historical Library, Wilmington, Del.

late sixteenth century it cannot be assumed that the powder tester originated there, for many innovations were in use at various places years before receiving notoriety.

By ca. 1600 two kinds of powder testers appeared: the disc (wheel) type probably introduced before 1525, and the ratchet type emerging somewhat later, possibly in the Netherlands because it was popular there. Early powder testers used match ignition and were similar to and often combined with tinder lighters, while later specimens employed wheellock and flintlock ignition and were frequently mounted on a pistol style grip.

The wheel type powder tester displayed a spring-operated disc with notched edges, a number imprinted beneath each notch. The disc was also provided with an elongated cover. The cover projection rested atop a short, vertical spout-like chamber containing the test powder. The gas pressure exerted when the powder was ignited overcame the spring tension holding the cover and the disc violently rotated; the strength of the powder indicated by the numbered notch caught by a pawl. The ratchet type powder tester had a vertical scale with a sliding

weight, the weight covering the test powder spout. The explosive force of the powder elevated the weight which was caught by a ratchet on the numbered scale; the higher the number value the more potent the powder.

Initially appearing as a sporting accessory, an early French innovation was subsequently adopted as a martial weapon and significantly altered the concepts of orthodox European infantry tactics. By 1550 the famous Bayonne cutlery shops were producing a kind of dagger with a tapering, double-edged blade approximately ten inches to a foot long and a tapered wooden handle of almost the same length. The dagger soon became popular with military crossbowmen and alpine hunters who referred to it as a *bayonette,* the term later anglicized to bayonet.

The bayonet was at some undetermined time inserted in a sporting gun muzzle to serve like a lance, protecting the hunter if a wounded animal such as a bear or boar charged before he had reloaded; a common practice in France and Spain prior to ca. 1575. As far as it can be determined, the bayonet was first used in martial firearms by French troops serving in Flanders ca. 1642.[88] The tapered dagger handle was simply thrust into the bore, inspiring the modern appellation *plug bayonet.*

At the dawn of the seventeenth century most firearms incorporating multi-firing mechanisms were based on the venerable revolving cylinder principle consisting of a single barrel aligned with a manually rotated breech comprised of several chambers. William Drummond of Scotland, however, invented a multi-firing weapon in 1626 which employed 50 barrels arranged around a central axis.[89]

In the Drummond repeater each barrel was loaded with several charges à la roman candle and each charge was provided with a vent. A sliding matchlock successively positioned over each vent ignited the charges until all 50 barrels were expended. Drummond's multi-firing weapon was as cumbrous as it was difficult to load and the laborious reloading process negated any firepower advantage.

Of a more practical nature was the improved rifling engine devised by London gunsmith-inventor Arnold Rotispen in 1635.[90] Precisely how Rotispen improved the machine remains unknown, though it is possible that it was used to cut the lands and grooves in the distinctive breech-loading carbines and pistols appearing in England ca. 1625-1630.

Those radical single-shot firearms with rifled bores initially emerged on the Continent, possibly in Flanders, shortly after the turn of the century, though the breech design can be traced to that indefatigable master, da Vinci. It is doubtful, however, if firearms incorporating the design were made prior to the seventeenth century.[91]

PLUG BAYONETS (17th Century): (1) Spanish *cuchillo de monte,* a kind of martial plug bayonet used with the *escopeta* ca. 1680. (2) Another *cuchillo de monte,* the absence of the quillons could indicate an early type or a "homemade" product. (3) English plug bayonet ca. 1672. (4) Continental European plug bayonet ca. 1670; the quillons served as screwdrivers. (5) Continental European plug bayonet ca. 1685. (6) Continental European plug bayonet ca. 1680; the wide blade indicates it was fashioned from a broken sword, dagger, spontoon or other pole-type weapon. Author's sketch.

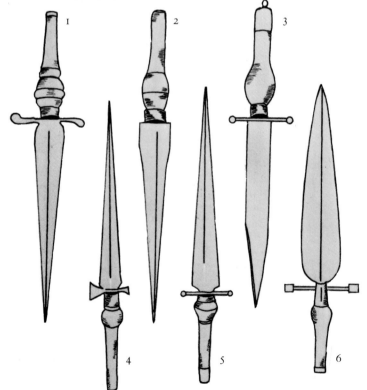

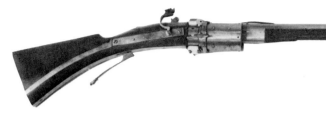

MATCHLOCK ARQUEBUS, Revolving Breech (17th Century, ca. 1620): The technological expertise and skilled craftsmanship attained by French gunsmiths is exemplified by this 5-shot, revolving cylinder, matchlock arquebus with a .55 caliber, 32½-inch barrel. Courtesy of the *Musée de l'Armée*, Paris.

While both pistols and carbines employing the innovative breech design were produced, it is believed that the former preceded the latter and came to be known as turn-off, screw-barrel, or cannon-barrel pistols, for the barrel readily unscrewed from the breech and the muzzle finial emulated the baluster moulding found on contemporaneous cannon barrels. The English version of the turn-off pistol was subsequently known as a Queen Anne pistol because of its popularity during her reign (1702-1714) and it remained so throughout the eighteenth century, influencing in the interim the design of a purely American pistol.

The turn-off pistol was loaded with the barrel in a vertical position. A spanner (wrench) engaging a barrel lug near the breech was used to unscrew the barrel, exposing a short, threaded breech pillar. The powder charge was loaded into the constricted breech chamber and the ball, slightly oversized, was seated atop the chamber mouth. The barrel was then replaced and secured by the spanner, forcing the ball firmly into the rifling. The pistol was then primed and fired in the conventional manner.

The constricted breech chamber, an innovation characterizing the fourteenth-century Tannenberg gun, generated the requisite force to overcome the inertia (weight) and friction of the tightly fitting ball, while the tight fit ensured positive obturation. Consequently the turn-off pistol was superbly accurate up to 50 yards (the maximum effective range of most

TURN-OFF PISTOLS (18th Century): The handsome pair of turn-off pistols depicted, made by London gunsmith H. Delaney (fl. 1690-1720), display the baluster muzzle finials common to early specimens. A serpent's head is incorporated into the foliate motif of the sideplate. The 7-1/16-inch barrels are of .64 caliber. Courtesy of the Smithsonian Institution, Washington, D.C.

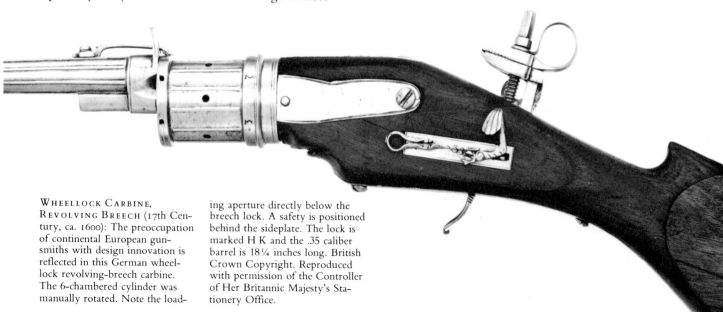

WHEELLOCK CARBINE, REVOLVING BREECH (17th Century, ca. 1600): The preoccupation of continental European gunsmiths with design innovation is reflected in this German wheellock revolving-breech carbine. The 6-chambered cylinder was manually rotated. Note the loading aperture directly below the breech lock. A safety is positioned behind the sideplate. The lock is marked H K and the .35 caliber barrel is 18¼ inches long. British Crown Copyright. Reproduced with permission of the Controller of Her Britannic Majesty's Stationery Office.

modern handguns) and readily penetrated the finest armor at half the distance; its single disadvantage being that it was considerably slower to load than the muzzle-loading pistols of the era.

The accuracy and range of the turn-off pistol was early attested to, though the tale could be apocryphal. In his *History of Staffordshire,* Robert Plot revealed that when Charles I halted his troops there on September 3, 1643, during the English Civil War, his nephew Price Rupert attempted to impress him with a marksmanship display. Rupert drew from a saddle holster one of a pair of turn-off pistols and shot at the weathercock on the steeple of St. Mary's church about 100 feet away. The weathercock spun violently, its head pierced. Charles scoffingly called it a lucky shot and to verify his skill Rupert fired with his second pistol, striking the weathercock's tail.

Early turn-off pistols displayed an abruptly curved wooden grip and various barrel lengths ranging from approximately two inches to 15 inches, while caliber fluctuated from .40 to .60. The design precluded a forestock and, unusual for rifled firearms, there were no sights. English specimens made prior to midcentury displayed Jacobean locks with or without the dog safety, though thereafter true flintlocks were prevalent, illustrating the convex lockplate, cock, and sideplate. The locks of cased pistols were often mounted on either side of the breech.

Dragoon (cavalry) versions of the turn-off pistol were usually provided with a short chain linking the barrel to the breech; an innovation preventing the loss of the barrel if inadvertently dropped when loading. Turn-off carbines were issued to a few troops of light dragoons. Difficult to load and more expensive because of precision construction and rifling, turn-off firearms never achieved the popularity of muzzle-loaders for either commercial or military use despite the advantages of accuracy, range, and penetration.

It is likely that English turn-off firearms were employed in North America, though as yet there is

no conclusive evidence substantiating the assumption. It is known, however, that a wide variety of firearms was brought to the English colonies during the English Civil War and the Great Puritan Migration of 1650.

Like the plug bayonet, paper cartridges, and the turn-off firearms, another sixteenth-century innovation which did not see widespread acceptance until the seventeenth century was the martial hand mortar, progenitor of the modern grenade launcher. The first hand mortars probably originated in Germany or Scandinavia ca. 1575 and they were similar to firearms though designed to hurl small explosive grenades farther than the limits of human capability.[92]

The first hand mortars are believed to have used wheellock ignition. The lock was attached to a stock conforming in length to the extremely short barrel with a heavy breech; the reinforced breech necessary to withstand the extra large powder charge required to propel the grenade or what was then termed a grenado. Integral with the muzzle was a cup-like receptacle into which the grenado was loaded.

The grenado was a hollow, cast-iron sphere filled with black powder and provided with a small, removeable plug for loading and securing the fuze (fast match); the fuze transversing the plug. The barrel was breech-chambered, increasing the propellant force needed to overcome the weight of the grenado. The introduction of hand mortars saw the emergence of grenadiers who continued to carry matchcord for lighting the fuze long after the matchlock had been rendered obsolete.

In early hand mortars which used a single propellant charge in the breech, the grenadier charged and primed the weapon, loaded the grenado and lighted its fuze, and then aimed and fired. The stock was normally placed against the ground or another solid object rather than the shoulder because of the extremely heavy recoil.

The hand mortar, like other firearms innovations, underwent a series of refinements over the years and flint-ignition locks were used prior to the turn of the century. The integral muzzle cup was

WHEELLOCK HAND MORTAR (GRENADE LAUNCHER, 16th Century, ca. 1580): This bronze-barreled German hand mortar has an overall length of 28 inches. The 2.06-inch diameter barrel is 10¾-inches long. The trigger has been placed a considerable distance from the lock and muzzle, probably to protect the grenadier from priming and powder flash. Courtesy of the Glasgow Art Gallery and Museum, Glasgow.

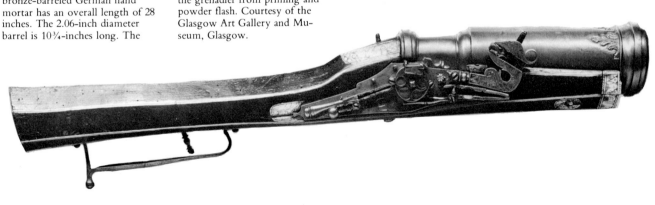

subsequently discarded for a detachable appendage; thus permitting the musket to be used as a mortar and also in the conventional manner.

A number of experimental hand mortars were tested by the English Board of Ordnance and in January, 1681, Thomas Swain was awarded £30 for a hand mortar he designed, though it subsequently failed to meet the criteria expected by the board.[93] Later that year "a new way of shooting Hand-granadoes out of small Morterpeeces" was introduced by English ordnanceman John Tinker.[94]

Tinker's hand mortar permitted the grenado to be fired independently or by the musket lock, for the grenade cup was incorporated into the buttstock of a conventional musket; the cup provided with a hinged cover doubling as the butt. There was also a folding rest, the yoke pinned to the forestock, and two grenadiers usually served the weapon.

If the grenado was to be fired independently the grenadier filled the butt cup with propellant powder and primed the integral cup pan, his companion steadying and aiming the weapon. The grenado was then placed in the cup, its fuze lighted, and the priming ignited. The priming flashed through the cup vent to the propellant which discharged the grenado.

Using the lock to fire the grenado was more complex. The grenadier first primed the lock pan and then filled a long tube extending through the buttstock from the base of the butt cup to the rear of the lock pan. When he put the grenado into the propellant-filled cup and lighted the fuze, his companion aimed and fired; the powder in the tube ignited by the lock and flashing upward to contact the propellant charge.

Whichever method was used to discharge the grenado there was one hazardous and obvious disadvantage: a misfire. If the propellant charge did not ignite after the grenado fuze was lighted the grenadiers and those around them were exposed to the possibility of an exploding grenado. In that event the grenadiers had three options: (1) quickly remove the grenado from the cup and throw it by hand, (2) immediately pull the fuze before it could ignite the explosive charge in the grenado, or (3) abandon the weapon and seek cover with unconstrained alacrity.

In 1685 the Board of Ordnance purchased fifty "Hand Morterpieces of Tinkers invencon" at £5/10s each and, for his innovative contribution to ordnance development, he was granted by the crown a quarterly stipend of £5. The following year the Board of Ordnance procured additional hand mortars differing substantially from Tinker's design.

Though no precise description is available, it is believed that the hand mortars were detachable rather than brazed or welded to the barrel or mounted at the butt, for ordnance brass founder

William Wightman cast a number of individual grenado cups at Moorfields in 1686, while the locks and the stocks were purchased from London gunsmiths James Peddel, John Hartwell, and Collins Groome.[95] The detachable cups were provided with a sleeve which slipped over the muzzle of a conventional musket.

Since the advent of breech-loading firearms late in the fifteenth century, European gunsmith-inventors sought to improve the systems exemplified by the revolving cylinder and the individual loading chamber; the latter employed in the Italian gun shield and Henry VIII's wheellock long arms. Not until the late sixteenth century, however, was a simple breech-loading system introduced and it was a radical departure from those then available.

Invented in 1593 by Freiherr von Sprinzenstein of Munich, the revolutionary breech-loading system employed an innovative screw plug.[96] The threaded plug transversed the upper surface of the breech and it was removed by a wrench (spanner) engaging a lug atop the plug; the method subsequently used in turn-off firearms.

With the plug removed and the muzzle elevated, the breech chamber was exposed for loading with powder and ball in that order. The ball was slightly larger than bore diameter which prevented it from rolling out of the barrel, while replacing and tightening the screw plug sealed the breech and provided positive obturation. Firearms employing the Sprinzenstein system and its subsequent variations were fired by a conventional ignition mechanism.

HAND MORTARS (18th Century): Left to right—Grenade cup mounted on musket barrel after the fashion of the socket bayonet, some provided with a spring-activated clasp. Grenade cup mounted on the stock with the hinged cover serving as the buttstock; the cup provided with a priming pan (not shown). Granado (grenade), exterior and interior view. The top and profile of the fuze plug are depicted below. Author's sketch.

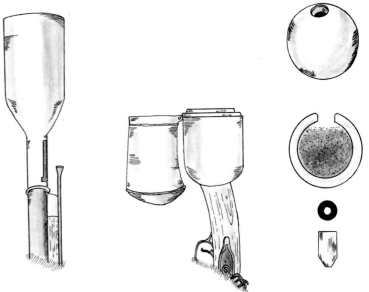

The initial advantage of the system was in eliminating the ramrod, for neither the powder nor the ball had to be tamped, and as improvements were made by others the loading procedure was greatly accelerated.

Emigré German gunsmith Kristofer Freirsblen (1565-1595?), known in Spain as Cristobal Frisleva, invented a similar screw breech system while working at Ricla in Aragón. In the Frisleva system, however, the upper surface of the screw plug was recessed to serve as the priming pan and it was also provided with a vent leading to the powder chamber.[97] Whether the Sprinzenstein system predated Frisleva's remains unclear.

The screw plug system was subsequently incorporated in either side or at the bottom of the breech and, in some instances, loading was the reverse of the Sprinzenstein or Frisleva systems, depending on whether the plug was positioned in front or to the rear of the powder chamber. The major disadvantage of the system was that after a few shots the plug

SCREW-PLUG BREECH (17th/ 18th Century): The von Sprinzenstein system was applied in various forms over the centuries and ca. 1710 Copenhagen master gunsmith Johann Merckel (fl. 1690-

1725) incorporated the screw-plug into the design engraved on the breech flat as depicted. Left: breech closed. Right: breech open. Courtesy of the *Tøjhusmuseet,* Copenhagen.

threads became clogged with powder fouling, making it extremely difficult to open or close the breech.

The problem was unresolved until the late seventeenth century when Danzig gunsmith Daniel Lagatz introduced an innovative screw plug which, rather than merely transversing the upper breech surface, passed completely through it and was provided with a convenient handle instead of a wrench; the handle also serving as the trigger guard. Not until the late eighteenth century, however, did the screw plug system express its full potential despite interim improvements.

The roman candle or superimposed charge method of loading and discharging firearms appearing in the late fifteenth century was also subjected to intensified experimentation early in the seventeenth century, and many of the ingenious innovations were described in detail by Italian gunsmith-inventor Captain Giuliano Bossi (1606-1679?) in his *Breve Tratato d'Alcune Inventione Che Sone State Futte Per Rinforzare Raddoppiare li Tiri Degli Archibugi—a Ruota* (Parigi, 1659).[98]

Bossi lived and worked for many years in Antwerp where he devised several innovative firearms and studied the designs of other European armsmakers, for Antwerp was the center of the renowned Flemish armament industry. Parenthetically, few English language texts are devoted to the evolution of the armament industry in Flanders despite the early reputation of Flemish masters and their myriad contributions to innovative firearms technology.

Bossi investigated and described several superimposed-charge firearms with similar systems, each incorporating pierced or grooved projectiles which permitted the passage of ignition flame either through or around them; thus permitting sequential loading, i.e., one charge behind the other.

An early, rather sophisticated firearm of the kind was loaded with several powder-filled balls and displayed a lock with two priming pans, one surmounting the other. The lower pan was served by a conventional vent leading to the powder chamber, while the upper pan was provided with a priming tube leading to a vent near the muzzle which ignited the charge behind the last ball loaded.

A solid ball was loaded first, separated by a thick wad from the powder charges and pierced balls sequentially loaded thereafter. The upper lock fired the powder in the priming tube and it ignited the charge behind the last ball loaded, the flash contacting the powder-filled hole of the following ball which ignited its charge and so on until all of the sequential loads were discharged in rapid succession. A unique feature was the reserve shot provided by the solid ball initially loaded and it was fired by the lower lock.

In 1631 Bossi invented a superimposed-charge firearm employing two barrels and two flintlocks,

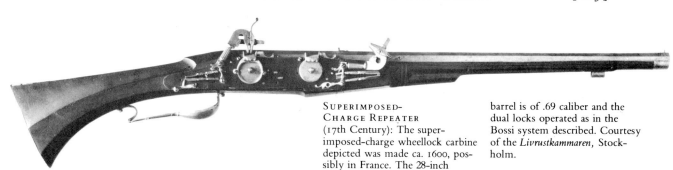

SUPERIMPOSED-
CHARGE REPEATER
(17th Century): The superimposed-charge wheellock carbine
depicted was made ca. 1600, possibly in France. The 28-inch

barrel is of .69 caliber and the
dual locks operated as in the
Bossi system described. Courtesy
of the *Livrustkammaren,* Stockholm.

one for each barrel. The system was thereafter used with as many as four barrels and locks. Though some superimposed-charge firearms employed match ignition, the flintlock was more effective, while the weight factor limited the number of barrels and locks.

Bossi also noted superimposed-charge firearms incorporating the sliding lock innovation earlier applied by William Drummond. The obvious disadvantage of the system was that the pan had to be primed for each shot, creating a delay not encountered with the priming tube system. In addition to the characteristic bulk of superimposed-charge firearms, their rapid-fire capability, as in the 1626 Drummond repeater, was negated by the tedious loading procedure, while their complexity rendered them inordinately expensive; those factors limiting popular acceptance.

An outstanding innovative superimposed-charge firearm is exemplified by a four-barreled wheellock pistol referred to by Eduard Wettendorfer who first encountered it in the Vienna Army Museum in 1940.[99] He subsequently recovered the pistol from the rubble of a bomb shelter looted in the 1945 liberation of the city during the final days of World War II.

Made by an unknown seventeenth-century gunsmith, the pistol had been described in 1870 as

firing all four barrels simultaneously. The four approximately .30 caliber barrels, each measuring ten and five-sixteenths inches, were skillfully brazed in a diamond-pattern and mounted in a pear wood grip. Each barrel had a breech plug of slightly different length.

Wettendorfer's examination of the pistol disclosed that each barrel, like the breech plugs, was correspondingly punch-marked for proper identification: barrel one (right) · , barrel two (left) ·· , barrel three (top) ∴ , and barrel four (bottom) ∷ . Barrel two was slightly longer than the others because its breech plug was shorter and barrels four, one, and three followed in that order.

He also discovered that barrel two had seven vents leading to barrel three and an equal number served barrel four, while a single vent communicated with barrel one. Barrel one had two vents: one at the breech for the priming pan and the other opposite the upper vent in barrel two. There were 17 vents in all, arranged so the pistol was capable of delivering 15 shots in sequence rather than merely four shots simultaneously as suggested in 1870.

Barrel one was loaded with a charge and single ball. Barrel two performed the function of a priming tube and was filled with a kind of flash powder consisting of equal measures of camphor, frankincense, rosin, turpentine, and varnish; two parts of

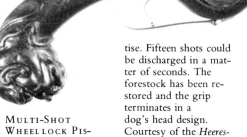

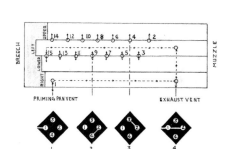

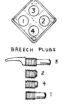

MULTI-SHOT
WHEELLOCK PIS-
TOL (17th Century):
The four-barreled, su-
perimposed charge
wheellock pistol de-
picted was made by an
unknown gunsmith
with outstanding exper-

tise. Fifteen shots could
be discharged in a mat-
ter of seconds. The
forestock has been re-
stored and the grip
terminates in a
dog's head design.
Courtesy of the *Heeres-
geschichtlichen Museum,*
Vienna.
Barrel, Breech, and
Firing Sequence Ar-
rangement: Interior
view of pistol barrels,
shaded area depicting

the breech. Dotted line
illustrates path of igni-
tion flash with arrows
indicating vents num-
bered 1 through 15.
The first barrel (bottom
right) incorporates the
priming pan vent and
the exhaust vent at the
muzzle. Extreme right:
Front view of barrels
showing position ar-
rangement and the cor-
responding breech
plugs. Bottom: Views
of muzzle showing vent
arrangements between

barrels. Author's
sketch, after *The Ameri-
can Rifleman.*

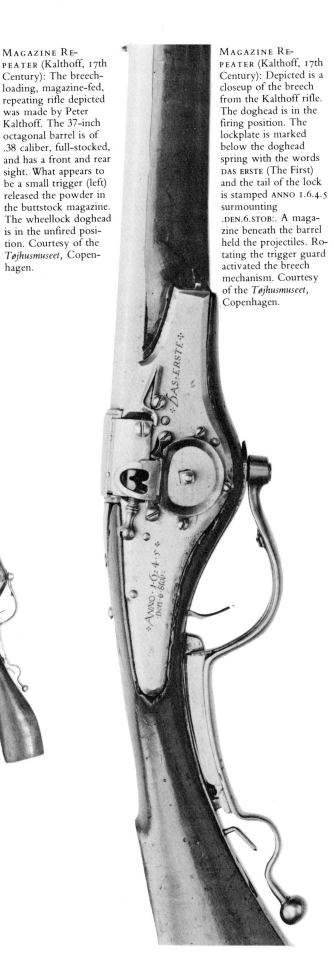

MAGAZINE RE-
PEATER (Kalthoff, 17th
Century): The breech-
loading, magazine-fed,
repeating rifle depicted
was made by Peter
Kalthoff. The 37-inch
octagonal barrel is of
.38 caliber, full-stocked,
and has a front and rear
sight. What appears to
be a small trigger (left)
released the powder in
the buttstock magazine.
The wheellock doghead
is in the unfired posi-
tion. Courtesy of the
Tøjhusmuseet, Copen-
hagen.

MAGAZINE RE-
PEATER (Kalthoff, 17th
Century): Depicted is a
closeup of the breech
from the Kalthoff rifle.
The doghead is in the
firing position. The
lockplate is marked
below the doghead
spring with the words
DAS ERSTE (The First)
and the tail of the lock
is stamped ANNO 1.6.4.5
surmounting
.DEN.6.STOB:. A maga-
zine beneath the barrel
held the projectiles. Ro-
tating the trigger guard
activated the breech
mechanism. Courtesy
of the *Tøjhusmuseet,*
Copenhagen.

saltpeter, three parts of Aqua Fortis (nitric acid) and
as much gunpowder and oil of saltpeter; and three
and a half parts of quick brimstone (sulphur). A thick
tow wad was tamped in the muzzle of barrel two to
prevent the escape of the flash powder. Barrels three
and four were carefully loaded, each with seven
powder charges and balls superimposed and aligned
with the corresponding vents in barrel two.

When the single load in barrel one was discharged the hot powder gases driving the ball passed
through the muzzle vent leading to barrel two and
ignited the flash powder. Acting like a fuze and
burning from muzzle to breech, the flash powder
alternately ignited each of the seven loads (fourteen
in all) remaining in barrels three and four; thus in
seconds the pistol discharged fifteen shots.

Though a magnificent testament to the creative
expertise of the gunsmith who conceived it and a
mirror reflecting the advanced state of seventeenth-
century technology, the multi-shot, rapid-firing
wheellock pistol described by Wettendorfer exhibited the same disadvantages as other firearms
incorporating the roman candle or superimposed-
charge system which generally precluded their procurement for martial or commercial use; yet rather
than discouraging innovation those firearms inspired
the development of more efficient repeaters, as exemplified by a number of breech-loading firearms
receiving the powder charge and ball from a radical
innovation now recognized as a tubular magazine.

The first breech-loading magazine firearm is
believed to have been invented by a thus far unidentified member of the famous Kalthoff gunsmithing
family, most of whom lived and worked beyond the
borders of their native Germany.[100] The first known
reference to the firearm and its apparent connection
with the Kalthoff family came in 1640 when Wilhelm
Kalthoff was granted a monopoly to produce it in
France, though whether he made any there or elsewhere remains moot and further details of his life are
obscure.

Peter Kalthoff, his relationship to Wilhelm unknown, was offered a similar arrangement to manufacture magazine repeaters by the Netherlands in
1641. Again, it is not known whether any were produced and Peter soon left the Netherlands, entering
the service of Duke Frederick of Denmark. In Denmark he made a wheellock version of the magazine
repeater in 1645 which is now preserved in the
Tøjhusmuseet, Copenhagen, and bears the inscription
Das Erste (the first).[101] A year later Peter produced a
flintlock version and each incorporated two tubular
magazines: one in the hollow buttstock holding the
powder and the other containing the projectiles
mounted beneath the barrel as in some modern firearms. The magazines had sufficient powder and ball
to deliver thirty consecutive shots.

In the basic Kalthoff design the trigger guard initiated the loading cycle, the front of the trigger bow integral with a vertical shank transversing the stock. Rotating the trigger guard pivoted the shank. The shank was connected to a carrier and to a box-like breech block moving laterally across the face of the breech. The breech block displayed three holes: one receiving the ball taken by the carrier from the tubular barrel magazine during the initial movement of the trigger guard, another serving as the chamber for the powder charge conveyed from the butt magazine by the carrier during the closing motion of the trigger guard, and the third delivering part of the powder charge from the carrier to the priming pan. Returning the trigger guard to its original position sealed the breech block with the barrel and the weapon was fired in the conventional manner.

Mathias Kalthoff, Peter's brother, joined him in Copenhagen and also made those ingenious magazine firearms, while Peter subsequently received a monopoly to make them in France. Another Kalthoff, Caspar, went to London ca. 1650 and was later joined by his son of the same name. They significantly improved the mechanism, introducing the innovative cylindrical breech which operated vertically rather than horizontally. The younger Caspar later worked in Moscow.

The Kalthoff monopolies in France and the Netherlands were apparently disregarded because other gunsmiths produced magazine repeaters of the same design or variations thereof, among them German master Heinrich Habrecht of Gottorp (fl. 1645) who made variants with full-or-quarter-cylinder breech locks, master Dutch gunsmith Harman Barne (1635-1660) who produced repeaters similar to those devised by Caspar Kalthoff in London, and Jan Flock of Utrecht (fl. 1650-1673).[102] Flock, formerly of Solingen, Germany, is thought to have worked with Barne before the latter went to London where he met the Kalthoffs and was subsequently employed by Prince Rupert prior to serving as royal gunsmith to Charles II.

Kalthoff magazine breech-loaders saw limited service as martial firearms and can be considered the first repeating firearms of any kind adopted by the military. A hundred Kalthoff magazine repeaters with rifled bores were issued to special marksmen of the Royal Danish Foot Guards during the siege of Copenhagen (1658-1659) in the Baltic War, and a

MAGAZINE REPEATER (Flock, 17th Century): Jan Flock of Utrecht produced the Kalthoff-type magazine repeater depicted ca. 1667. Overall length is 59 inches and the 48-inch, half-round barrel is of .52 caliber.

The close-up of the breech of the Flock magazine repeater de-

picts the craftsmanship and decorative motif of the lock. The cock and the lockplate are rounded. A grotesque mask adorns the tail of the lockplate and the remainder is covered with a hare-hunting scene. Note the relatively high position of the cock mounted on the lockplate. Courtesy of the *Livrustkammaren*, Stockholm.

number of them were later used in the second Anglo-Dutch conflict.[103]

The renowned Klett gunsmithing family of Suhl, Germany, also produced variations of the Kalthoff magazine repeaters. Johann Paul Klett left Suhl in 1634 and with his three sons Cornelius, Johann Paul II, and Sigmund, served the Prince Archbishop of Salzburg.[104] In 1652 Johann II and Sigmund conceived a variation of the Kalthoff design employing two vertical cylinder breech blocks, while a year later they received from Queen Christina of Sweden an order for a Kalthoff pattern carbine.[105]

The Kletts also produced remarkably innovative firearms of their own design as exemplified by the wheellock rifle made by Cornelius in 1653.[106] Only ten such rifles are known to exist and eight of them were fabricated by the Kletts, and what distinguishes them from other wheellock rifles is that they displayed two barrels, one sliding into the other; an innovation currently employed in some specialized firearms.

The larger or primary barrel is octagonal, measuring 26 and ¼ inches, and is of .75 caliber. The barrel weighs four pounds and has eight helical grooves with a right-hand twist making a single turn in the entire length. The insert or sub-caliber barrel weighs two pounds and two ounces, is 25 and ¾

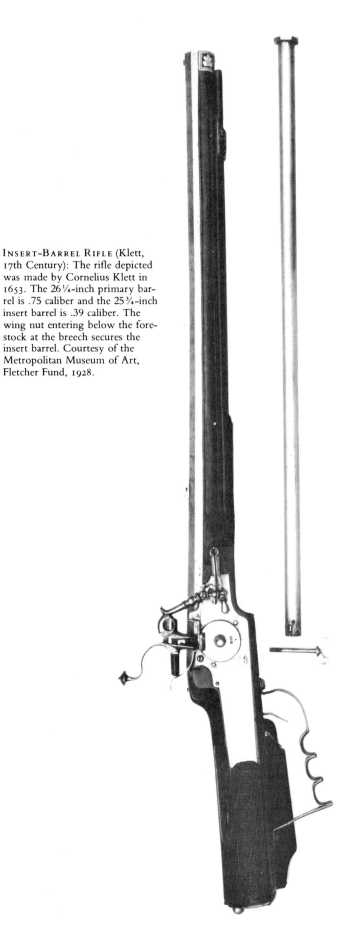

INSERT-BARREL RIFLE (Klett, 17th Century): The rifle depicted was made by Cornelius Klett in 1653. The 26¼-inch primary barrel is .75 caliber and the 25¾-inch insert barrel is .39 caliber. The wing nut entering below the forestock at the breech secures the insert barrel. Courtesy of the Metropolitan Museum of Art, Fletcher Fund, 1928.

inches long, and is .39 caliber with seven helical grooves of right-hand twist making three-quarters of a turn through the length.

The insert barrel is round and provided with an octagonal finial corresponding to the muzzle of the primary barrel. A small lug at the breech of the insert barrel serves to seat it properly in the large barrel and it is locked in position by a long, wing-head screw transversing it near the breech lug and engaging a corresponding hole in the base of the primary barrel. A brass, blade-type front sight is mounted on the primary barrel, while the rear sight consists of two leaves; the larger leaf sighted for the external barrel and the smaller leaf used for the insert barrel.

The innovative rifle was apparently designed for hunting large or small game with the insert barrel employed for the latter because of its smaller caliber. The wheellock is of conventional German pattern provided with a set-trigger. The pin-fastened forestock extends the entire barrel length and it is channeled for the wooden ramrod, while the typically blunt buttstock displays a buttplate. The trigger guard is distinguished by three finger supports behind the bow.

Cornelius Klett is also known to have produced a flintlock Kalthoff-pattern magazine repeater in 1653 and a four-barreled flintlock carbine. He subsequently made a revolving-breech wheellock firearm and a pair of double, revolving-barrel flintlock pistols for Prince Thun of Tetschen.[107] The pistols emulated the rotating-barrel design of what is known as turn-over or Wender system firearms.

The turn-over pistols made by Klett displayed superimposed (over-and-under) barrels manually rotated around the single lock on an axis pin extending from the breech plate. Each barrel was provided with a priming pan and battery for the lock and secured in firing position by a lockplate catch.

Where or when the first turn-over firearms were made cannot be precisely determined, though they probably originated in Flanders or France early in the seventeenth century; a matchlock arquebus of the type dated 1620 currently reposing in the *Musée de l'Armée,* Paris. Harman Barne and Jan Flock also made turn-over firearms, the latter designing an innovative mechanism which automatically cocked the lock and closed the priming pans when the barrels were rotated.[108]

All turn-over firearms were muzzle-loading and some with three barrels were produced. A few flintlock specimens appeared in North America at the beginning of the nineteenth century, while variations continued to be made in Europe until ca. 1850. Turn-over firearms were practical and efficient, their disadvantages only in the time expended for loading and those normally associated with the ignition mechanisms employed.

While the numerous mechanisms conceived to improve upon or to expand the spectrum of multi-shot and breech-loading repeaters distinctly illustrate the high level of technology apparent in seventeenth-century European firearms evolution, there was another significant achievement which supplemented previous barrel-making techniques and it is believed to have emerged ca. 1635.

Rather than the common longitudinal barrel seam the novel technique employed a helical (spiral) seam, i.e., the skelp was heated and hammered around the mandrel in a coil. While the barrel was being worked it was continuously bounced on the anvil to ensure the strength of the weld at the coils; the technique referred to as *jumping*. The helical method produced a lightweight barrel which came to be popular in fowling pieces as the century progressed and it was almost exclusively used for that purpose thereafter. Variations of the helical barrel-making technique subsequently emerged.

Helical barrels should not be confused with the Damascus or stub-twist barrels introduced to Europe ca. 1700 from the Syrian city of that name, for the so-called Damascus technique did not significantly influence European barrel-making until the nineteenth century and it is therefore beyond the scope of this study.

The Frontier Challenge

The second European invasion of North America was of far greater intensity than that initiated by Spain and more concerned with commerce and colonization than conquest or exploration. Slowly crossing the vast and frightening Atlantic in frail and crowded sailing ships with only limited protection from the elements or pirates and rival naval forces, few seventeenth-century Europeans could fully visualize the extent of the perils, privations, and extreme hardships they would be forced to endure in the stark, inhospitable wilderness of North America; and the dense, forboding forests were as much an adversary as the strange people and feral beasts inhabiting them.

Those determined, and adventurous Europeans, however we view them at present and whatever their motivation, managed to survive in the hostile environment and gradually established a foothold in the sprawling continent where their physical stamina and philosophical convictions were continuously tested and not found wanting. Theirs was a demanding life and, to preserve it, there was a continuing demand for firearms in the emerging colonies.

TURN-OVER (WENDER) SYSTEM FIREARM (17th Century): Attributed to an unknown Dutch gunsmith, this rotating-barreled pistol incorporates dual priming pans. The projection forward of the trigger guard is the catch which locks the barrels prior to firing. The 19-inch, .50 caliber barrels are characteristic of the period 1645-1665. Note the rugged construction of the flintlock cock and squared trigger guard. British Crown Copyright. Reproduced with permission of the Controller of Her Britannic Majesty's Stationery Office.

MATCHLOCK ARQUEBUS, ROTATING BARRELS (ca. 1600-1625): This French matchlock arquebus displays what has come to be called the Wender system, i.e., the superimposed barrels, mounted on a central axis, are hand-rotated into firing position. The 38¼-inch barrels are of .75 caliber. Note the exposed lock mechanism and skeletal stock; the latter common to French firearms of the period. Courtesy of the *Musée de l'Armèe*, Paris.

Notes

1. Dr. Arne Hoff, "Scandinavian Snap Lock," in *Encyclopedia of Firearms,* ed. Harold L. Peterson (New York, 1964), p. 285.
2. Howard L. Blackmore, *Guns and Rifles of the World* (New York, 1965), p. 28 n. 1 (hereafter cited as *Guns and Rifles*).
3. Ibid., n. 2.
4. Ibid., n. 6.
5. W.H.B. Smith and Joseph E. Smith, *The Book of Rifles* (Harrisburg, 1963), p. 21.
6. A.N. Kennard, *French Pistols and Sporting Guns* (London, 1972), p. 20.
7. J.B.Kist, J.P. Puype, W. Van Der Mark, and R.B.F. Van Der Sloot, *Dutch Muskets and Pistols* (York, Pa. 1974), p. 35.
8. Claude Blair, *Pistols of the World* (New York, 1968), p. 10.
9. James D. Lavin, *A History of Spanish Firearms* (New York, 1965), p. 158.
10. Ibid., p. 160.
11. Ibid., p. 158.
12. Ibid., pp. 170, 172; 181-182, 184, 231.
13. Ibid., p. 170.
14. Ibid., p. 164.
15. Ibid., p. 288.
16. Torsten Lenk, *The Flintlock, Its Origin and Development* (New York, 1965), pp. 29-31.
17. Ibid., p. 19. Lenk cites eighteenth-century historian G.F. Magne de Marolles who stated that shooting birds on the wing originated in Italy ca. 1510, giving as a source Cesare Solatio, *Excellenza della Caccia* (Rome, 1669).
18. Blackmore, p. 34.
19. Frederick Wilkinson, *British and American Flintlocks* (London, 1971), p. 18.
20. I have used the term gunspall to distinguish chert from flint. Gunspall as used by T.M. Hamilton, comp. "Indian Trade Guns," *The Missouri Archaeologist,* vol. 22 (1960), and *Early Indian Trade Guns: 1625-1775* (Lawton, 1968), corresponds to what is called a Clactonian spall by John Witthoft, "The History of Gunflints," *Pennsylvania Archaeologist,* vol. 36, nos. 1 and 2 (1966).
21. Carlo M. Cipolla, *Guns, Sails and Empires: Technological Innovation and the Early Phases of European Expansion 1400-1700* (New York, 1965), p. 37.
22. Smith and Smith, p. 19, refer to the carbine as made in Flanders and subsequently converted to match ignition or what could be termed retrogressive technology. Whether Henry VIII ordered the alteration remains unknown.
23. Ibid., p. 22. Demi-Hawks is apparently synonymous with demy-hakes (small arquebuses) as opposed to full-sized arquebuses (muskets?) or [w] hole-hakes.
24. Blackmore, p. 65.
25. Ibid., p. 64.
26. Smith and Smith, p. 13.
27. James Frith and Ronald Andrews, *Antique Pistol Collecting* (New York, 1960), pp. 61, 64.
28. Smith and Smith, p. 35.
29. Lewis Winant, *Firearms Curiosa* (New York, 1954), p. 12.
30. W.W. Greener, *The Gun and its Development* (New York, 1967), pp. 92-93.
31. Harold L. Peterson, *Arms and Armor in Colonial America 1526-1783* (New York, 1956), p. 24.
32. Ibid.
33. Edward M. Riley and Charles E. Hatch, Jr., *James Towne in the Words of Contemporaries* (Washington: National Park Service Source Book Series No. 5, 1955), p. 2.
34. Peterson, p. 320.
35. John L. Cotter and J. Paul Hudson, *New Discoveries at Jamestown* (Washington: National Park Service, 1957), p. 71.
36. Peterson, p. 321.
37. Ibid., pp. 20-21.
38. Riley and Hatch, p. 22.
39. Peterson, p. 321.
40. George F. Willison, *Saints and Strangers* (New York, 1945), p. 440.
41. Ibid., p. 148.
42. Ibid., p. 154.
43. Ibid.
44. Ibid., pp. 164-165.
45. Ibid., pp. 202-203.
46. Robert Held, *The Age of Firearms* (New York, 1957), p. 80.
47. Willison, p. 197.
48. Held, p. 80.
49. Peterson, p. 325.
50. Blackmore, p. 13.
51. Ibid.
52. Greener, p. 212.
53. Kennard, p. 3.
54. Ibid., p. 11.
55. Blackmore, p. 13.
56. Smith and Smith, p. 23.
57. Ibid.
58. Ibid., p. 22.
59. Samuel de Champlain, *The Works of Samuel de Champlain,* ed. H.P. Biggar, 6 vols. (Toronto, 1922), 2:97-100.
60. S. James Gooding, *The Canadian Gunsmiths 1608 to 1900* (West Hill, Ontario, 1962), p. 206.
61. Ibid.
62. Ibid., pp. 207-208.
63. Champlain, 5:13.
64. Gooding, p. 26.
65. Cipolla, p. 47.
66. Ibid.
67. Ibid., p. 34 n. 1.
68. Kist et al., p. 38.
69. Ibid., p. 35.
70. Ibid.
71. Ibid., p. 37.
72. Ibid.
73. Ibid.
74. Ibid., pp. 145-146.
75. Ibid., p. 35.
76. Ibid.
77. Ibid., p. 33.
78. Peterson, pp. 19-20.
79. Ibid., p. 48.
80. Frederick Webb Hodge, ed., *Handbook of American Indians North of Mexico,* 2 vols. (Washington, 1912), 1:922 (hereafter cited as *Bulletin 30*).
81. Carl P. Russell, *Guns on the Early Frontiers* (New York, 1957), p. 12.
82. Peterson, p. 65.
83. Letter to the author 5 September 1975 from Lena Rängstrom, Curator, *Skoklosters slott Styrelsen,* Stockholm, identified the musket described as a product of the seventeenth-century Swedish armory at Jönköping.
84. Lenk, pp. 58-59, gives an introductory date of ca. 1670.
85. *Bulletin 30,* 1:407.

86. Ibid., 2:656.

87. Paul J. Wolf, "Powder Tester," in *Encyclopedia of Firearms*, pp. 241-243.

88. R.A. Pickering, "The Plug Bayonet," *The Canadian Journal of Arms Collecting* (February 1972): 120.

89. Lt. Col. George M. Chinn, USMC, *The Machine Gun*, 3 vols. (Washington, 1951), 1:16.

90. Col. Robert Gardner, *Small Arms Makers* (New York, 1963), p. 312.

91. Geoffrey Boothroyd, *The Handgun* (New York, 1970), p. 17.

92. William Reid, "Grenade Launcher," in *Encyclopedia of Firearms*, p. 144.

93. Howard L. Blackmore, *British Military Firearms, 1650-1850* (London, 1961), p. 35.

94. Ibid.

95. Ibid.

96. Blackmore, *Guns and Rifles*, p. 60.

97. Ibid.; Lavin, p. 136.

98. Blackmore, *Guns and Rifles*, p. 77 gives the publication date of Bossi's treatise as 1625 which consequently dates the firearms he mentions prior to that year. In his excellent bibliography Merrill Lindsay, *One Hundred Great Guns* (New York, 1967), p. 316, renders the more realistic date as given in the text and a later (1679) edition.

99. Eduard Wettendorfer, "A Wheellock Automatic," *American Rifleman* (March 1954): 49.

100. Blackmore, p. 85.

101. Ibid.

102. Ibid.

103. Ibid., p. 86.

104. Steven V. Grancsay, "Cornel Klett, Hofbuchsenmacher," *Gun Digest* (Chicago, 1955): 50.

105. Blackmore, p. 86.

106. Grancsay, p. 47.

107. Ibid., p. 51.

108. Kist et al., p. 42.

THE FERTILE SEEDS of permanent colonization were firmly planted in North
America during the first half of the seventeenth century, and they sprouted into a
few widely scattered settlements until after midcentury when their strong roots began to spread
beyond the Atlantic littoral.

Invading a once exclusive Spanish domain, the
Dutch, English, French, and Swedes soon discovered
that the discontent clouding their former existence
had not been left behind, and although the wilderness
was a natural foe they lost no time cultivating
animosity among themselves and incurring the
wrath of the Native Americans. Yet despite those
formidable obstacles or, perhaps, because of them,
the colonists met the wilderness on its own terms and
recklessly pushed beyond the fringe of civilization
heedless of the consequences.

The Spanish Heritage

The desperate economic and military crises
confronting the Florida provinces in the wake of the
disaster befalling the Royal Armada in 1588 were
compounded in August, 1592, when lightning struck
the powder magazine at St. Augustine.[1] The loss was
of considerable magnitude, leaving Spanish Florida
virtually defenseless, and when in 1598 Philip III
(1578-1621) assumed the crown total collapse was
imminent.

In 1602 struggling St. Augustine recieved negligible support with the arrival of arms and munitions from the royal gun foundry in Havana, while
fervid pleas from colonial administrators and a determined populace managed to postpone the crown
decision to abandon the isolated settlement.

A major factor in preserving St. Augustine was
its vital role in protecting the heavily laden treasure

fleets sailing twice yearly from Caribbean ports with
the riches essential to Spain's economic survival; a
need so apparent once the English had established
Jamestown in 1607 that a royal gun foundry was
constructed at Seville in 1611 to serve exclusively the
Armadas y flotas de Indias (West Indies fleet) guarding
the treasure routes.[2]

The usual treasure fleet route from Havana
passed through the Straits of Florida and coasted the
peninsula to a point about 30 miles off St. Augustine
where the ships then tacked toward Spain. The
strong West Indies fleet shepherding the treasure
ships through waters increasingly infested with pirates and privateers could not protect them from the
violence of nature and many vessels and crews were
claimed by the deep.

A number of those ancient Spanish wrecks have
since yielded up their valuable treasure and equally
valuable artifacts. Among the tons of gold and silver
retrieved in 1971 from the Spanish galleon *Nuestra
Señora de Atocha,* sunk by a hurricane off Marquesas
Key in the Straits of Florida on September 6, 1622,
were numerous lead balls and 34 assorted matchlock
arquebuses and muskets; few more than half the
ship's complement of 60 firearms.[3]

Though no wheellock firearms were recovered
from the *Atocha* site they saw limited service in the
Spanish dominions prior to the seventeenth century.
Most experienced conquistadors, however, preferred the sturdy, inexpensive matchlock firearms as
indicated in 1596 when Pedro Ponce de León requested from Spain 500 arquebuses, 100 muskets,
and 60 *quintals* of match for his expedition to the
Indies.[4]

In 1597 Luís de Velasco, following in his father's
footsteps as viceroy of New Spain (1590-1595/
1607-1611), listed among his personal arms three
wheellock arquebuses *(arcabuces de rueda),* each with
its loading flask *(frasco),* priming flask *(frasquillo),*
bullet worm *(sacataco),* and bullet mould *(molde de
pelota).*[5] It is believed that Velasco's wheellocks were
included with the 19 matchlock and 19 wheellock

firearms taken by Juan de Oñate (1549?–1624) when his expedition left for New Mexico on January 26, 1598.[6]

The 1598 Oñate expedition established Santa Fé, and by 1608 the *presidio* settlers had substantially subdued the hostile Acoma nearby, subsequently developing huge *estancias* (ranches) and thereby inadvertently presented the Native Americans of the Basin, Plains, and Plateau cultures with an even more potent weapon than the firearm: the horse.

Lacking sufficient labor the Spaniards trained Native American *vaqueros* (cowboys) to handle livestock and many of them became adept at managing the vast number of horses required. The *vaqueros* deserted the *estancias* for various reasons, taking with them a few horses which they bartered with other Native Americans for provisions and trade goods. Stolen horses, combined with those lost or strayed, eventually contributed to the phenomenal growth of the huge mustang herds ranging free across the unlimited grasslands on either side of the Continental Divide.

Gradual assimilation of the horse into Native American culture profoundly influenced various

SPANISH SETTLEMENTS Within the Present Limits of the United States (16th/18th Century). Courtesy of the National Park Service, Washington, D.C.

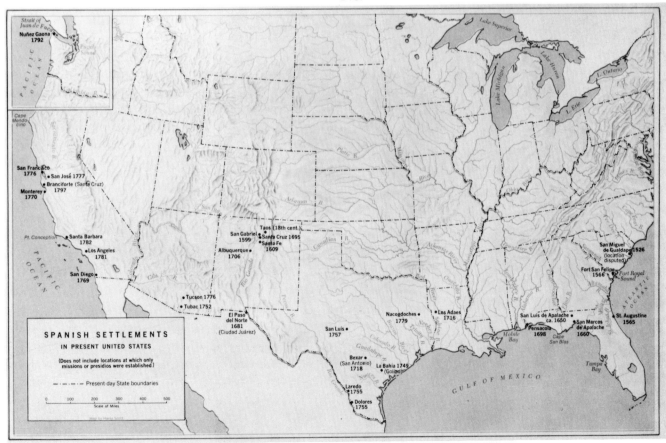

MATCHLOCK BARREL FRAGMENTS (17th Century): The barrel fragments depicted were all recovered from the sea at the wreck site of the Spanish galleon *Atocha*. Left: .80 caliber musket barrel damaged by oxidation (rust). Center: .62 caliber arquebus barrel. Right: Arquebus barrel with match guide intact, broken muzzle. The stock has been eaten away at the wrist by voracious teredoes (shipworms) though the lockplate mortise is clearly discernable. Courtesy of the Bureau of Archives, History and Records Management, Tallahassee, Fla.

LEAD PROJECTILES (17th Century): Recovered from the *Atocha* site, these lead projectiles show the effects of salt water corrosion though clearly depicting the mould sprue. Top: Musket balls. Center: Arquebus balls. Bottom: Shot, possibly used in the musket and arquebus to increase their efficacy; a common practice in the colonial period and thereafter. Courtesy of the Bureau of Archives, History and Records Management, Tallahassee, Fla.

socio-economic factors previously governing their lifestyle, for mastery of the horse gave them a beast of burden superior to the dog-wolf of prehistory, reduced the monumental labor performed by the woman, and provided a rapid transit system which increased mobility for hunting and warfare.

The horse, like the gun when introduced to the Native Americans of the Eastern Woodland culture, transformed many of the once sedentary and semi-sedentary tribes beyond the Mississippi River into a sizable nomadic population preying upon its less fortunate neighbors, while the mounted hunter-warrior subsequently emerged as a fighting force superior to any cavalry since fierce Mongol archers astride ponies from the Asian steppes swept a path of destruction and death across eastern Europe and Asia Minor in the thirteenth century.

Not until ca. 1750 did the horse become the dominant force in commerce and warfare among the Native Americans of the Basin, Plains, and Plateau cultures, and another century would pass before the horse would perform its most significant role when the last vestige of prehistoric culture in North America was all but destroyed by a vastly superior technology: the railroad, the telegraph, barbed wire, and a generous variety of breech-loading, single-shot and repeating firearms using self-contained metallic cartridges.

Open to speculation is whether Spain could have prevailed in the Great Southwest if the Native Americans there had procured large numbers of horses and firearms. Led by Po-pé, a Tewa shaman, the Pueblo Revolt of August 10, 1680, drove the Spaniards from New Mexico for 12 years, though the Native Americans lacked either of those advantages. The Spaniards initially withdrew to Santa Fé where, as Paul I. Wellman noted, "Every available weapon was issued, and men who were unaccustomed to firearms were instructed in handling them."[7]

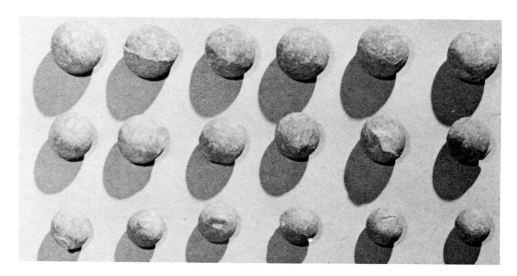

Spanish explorations in the Great Southwest brought the Native Americans a rudimentary knowledge of firearms, though procurement was strictly prohibited as in the Florida provinces. The few matchlock and wheellock firearms falling into their hands (usually as the spoils of war) were soon rendered useless because there were no repair facilities and bullets, matchcord, gunspalls, and powder could not be readily replenished; a situation prevailing until French traders penetrated beyond the Mississippi Valley early in the eighteenth century.

Though Spain's influence accelerated in the Great Southwest far removed from the Atlantic strand where the full, fatal impact of the European invasion fell, her dominions in *La Florida* declined. When in 1621 Philip IV (1605-1665) ascended the throne further English encroachments in Spanish America and the renewed Dutch conflict convinced him that St. Augustine was essential for defense and the forlorn settlement emerged as the focal point of the Spanish presence, supporting a few scattered military outposts and a weakening chain of missions from the Atlantic to the Gulf of Mexico.

When in 1653 crown officials inspected St. Augustine they were shocked to discover that in the armory of the rapidly decaying fort there were six matchlock arquebuses beyond redemption and all 178 matchlock muskets needed repairs, while the entire powder supply had been ruined by dampness and chemical deterioration. Again the "forgotten" Florida provinces could not muster an adequate defense.[8]

Conditions at St. Augustine aroused considerable alarm, for in 1653 the aggressive English had established settlements in the vicinity of present Edenton, N.C., and began pushing farther south, while pirate activity perceptibly increased, stimulated by the rich cargos traversing the Atlantic sea lanes.

On May 29, 1668, English pirate Robert Searles launched a vigorous night attack against St. Augustine. Several *arcubuceros* were slain when the pirates, armed with flintlock firearms, detected their glowing match. The incident graphically demonstrated the need for more effective firearms, prompting Gov. Francisco de la Guerra y de la Vega to order 50 *escopetas* from Vera Cruz.[9] He received only 24 in December, seven months later.[10]

Little is known of the 24 *escopetas* other than that they cost 22 *pesos* each, had an overall length of 50 inches, and were probably the first snapping flintlock firearms employed by the military in the Florida provinces. In October, 1671, 13 of the 24 *escopetas* were inventoried, listed as spare firearms.[11]

In probing Spanish or other armory inventory figures it should not be assumed that all available firearms were reflected therein because those in the hands of troops, i.e., issued to regular or militia forces, were not accounted for in armory reports. The 11 *escopetas* missing from the St. Augustine armory inventory of October, 1671, were issued to the garrison.

While a preponderance of matchlock firearms created no serious problem in Spain's military adventures in the Old World, Florida province administrators found it increasingly difficult to control the Native Americans and to defend crown settlements against the English and the French respectively active in the Carolinas and the Gulf region, for each had supplied their Native American allies with superior flintlock firearms and the commerce rapidly escalated.

Recognizing those threats Spain bolstered her sagging defenses at St. Augustine during the reign of Carlos II (1675-1700) whose mother, Mariana de Austria, assumed the regency upon the death of Philip IV in 1665. In 1672 construction began at St. Augustine on the impressive Castillo de San Marcos, the first masonry fortification in *La Florida,* though since 1565 nine wooden forts had protected the settlement.

In March, 1674, the St. Augustine garrison received from Spain 50 matchlock muskets and 100 matchlock arquebuses.[12] An inventory of the firearms in the Castillo armory on May 31, 1675, revealed 100 matchlock muskets and 30 matchlock arquebuses.[13] There was no mention of flintlock firearms either in the 1674 arms shipment or the 1675 inventory, indicating that if any were available they were issued.

By 1670 the English threat intensified with the founding on the Ashley River of a settlement which was subsequently relocated and came to be known as Charles Town (Charleston, South Carolina). It was from there that the English mounted the first of their continuing offensives against Spanish Florida when in 1680 the Santiago de Ocone mission on Jekyll Island was unsuccessfully attacked.

An armory inventory of March 2, 1680, revealed St. Augustine poorly prepared for defense, disclosing only 45 matchlock muskets available to replenish garrison arms or to supply the Guale outposts on Jekyll Island and Santa Catalina Island.[14] In May a worried Gov. Pablo de Hita Salazar informed the crown that "there are not two hundred firearms in the [Castillo] armory nor among the soldiers and natives [citizens]."[15]

Salazar's disturbing report apparently inspired action however belated, for in December an arms shipment arrived from Spain consisting of 100 matchlock arquebuses with their flasks and 100 matchlock muskets with their flasks and rests. Also, there were 75 *carabinas vizcaínas* [Biscayan carbines] with their flasks, slings, and springs; the latter possibly referring to extra mainsprings.[16]

The Biscayan carbines, as far as it is known, were the first martial wheellock firearms employed in the Florida provinces. Shorter than the matchlock arquebus and of a smaller though unspecified caliber, the wheellock firearms were issued to the *carabins* (cavalry), and it has been suggested that the word *carbine* derived from the Spanish term early in the century.

Ten of the Biscayan carbines were assigned to the garrison's mounted infantry, 16 were stored in the Castillo armory, and the remainder were declared unservicable because rust and metal fatigue had rendered their locks inoperable, while termites had riddled (powdered) the stocks.[17] Voracious termites also damaged or destroyed powder horns, wood flasks, gunpowder kegs, and other vital supplies, becoming such a problem early in the century that many *arcubuceros* began to carry their gunpowder in narrow-necked glass or ceramic *peruleras* (pitchers).[18]

In 1681 Santa Catalina was attacked by a mixed force of 300 Carolinians and Native Americans. Capt. Francisco de Fuentes offered a spirited defense with his five *arcubuceros* and forty "mission Indians." Desperate, he issued firearms to 16 of them though it was a futile gesture because many of them deserted when they were offered clothing, food, and flintlock firearms by the English. Fuentes was forced to surrender.[19]

Fuentes' decision to arm the Native Americans was obviously based on his crucial defensive posture and, as far as it can be determined, it is the first recorded instance when the stringent crown policy against Native American firearms procurement was deliberately abrogated. Gov. Salazar supported his action, for like previous administrators he recognized that arming the Native Americans would have greatly increased the defensive and offensive capability of the limited forces at his disposal.

Replacing Gov. Salazar, controversial and unorthodox Captain-General Juan Márquez Cabrera met the shortage of firearms with varying degrees of success by procuring them from other than official sources. In May, 1683, he purchased seven flintlock muskets from English trader John Grantland at eight *pesos* each, and on September 11 he bought 20 more at the same price from a New York trader.[20]

Earlier that year (April 24) an armory inventory at St. Augustine listed 102 matchlocks muskets, 73 forked rests, 57 carbines, and six flintlock *escopetas*.[21] In June another inventory disclosed 103 matchlock muskets, six matchlock arquebuses, 28 carbines, and one *escopeta*.[22] In 1684 eight *escopetas* were captured from English pirates during yet another raid on the increasingly beleaguered settlement.[23]

To preserve the nearly priceless flintlock firearms Cabrera explained that he distributed them and their "cartridge pouches . . . on [appropriate] occasions . . . and I collect them again and put them in wooden boxes because otherwise they would have been lost."[24]

Cabrera also recalled that in St. Augustine "It was a fixed custom . . . that when a soldier died, his wife or kinswoman felt they had a right to sell the arms, but I have taken away from them those that I have been able to locate. . . ." He further explained that "a few of these [women] used to sell the arms to crewmen of vessels calling at this port."[25]

Considering the irregular distribution of the *situado* it is little wonder that the penniless widows of the poorly paid soldiers resorted to selling their arms in order to survive, and neither is it peculiar that they were not especially fond of the governor; an opinion apparently shared by crown officials because Cabrera, like Salazar, supported arming the Native Americans and officially sanctioned it.

In a letter dated June 18, 1686, to Marcos Delgado of Apalachee province in northwest Florida, Cabrera instructed him to personally select "twelve soldiers . . . armed with their muskets or *carabinas* and also twenty Indians with firearms and twenty with bows and arrows . . ." for a reconnaisance into the Upper Creek country in Alabama where he suspected French encroachments; a suspicion subsequently confirmed.[26]

While keeping an eye on the French, Cabrera was equally alarmed by the threat of other English attacks, for of the 232 firearms issued to the two infantry companies at the Castillo de San Marcos in February, 1686, 228 were matchlocks and the remainder flintlocks.[27]

Despite the preponderance of inferior small arms at St. Augustine, in 1684 the Spaniards had raided and destroyed Stuart's Town, a Scottish settlement established near Port Royal, South Carolina, which was suspected of supplying the Cherokee, Creek, Yamassee, and other hostile border tribes with flintlock firearms.

When on April 13, 1687, Gov. Cabrera left *La Florida* because of continuing conflicts with the settlers and his superiors in Cuba and Spain, 13 flintlock *escopetas* were among his personal effects; possibly remnants of those he purchased with his own funds.[28] Though arbitrary and often dictatorial, Cabrera had been partially successful in strengthening the defensive posture of *La Florida*.

In the decade following Cabrera's administration Gov. Diego de Quiroga y Lozada, faced with many of the same problems, allowed defenses to deteriorate. A 1693 St. Augustine armory inventory disclosed 111 serviceable matchlock muskets and a pair of flintlock blunderbusses, while listed as unser-

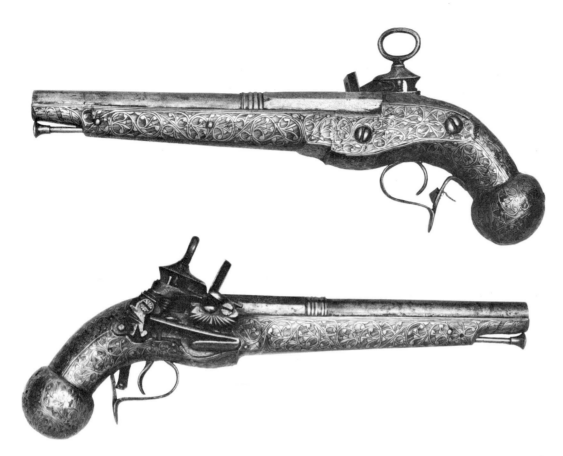

RIPOLL PISTOLS (17th Century, 1687): This elegantly embellished pair of Ripoll pistols with distinctive ball-butt grips have brass-covered stocks engraved with a foliate design. The *patilla* steel is marked VAL in a heart and the lock is signed Son De Aleix du Four. The 8⅞-inch barrels are .55 caliber and the overall length of the pistols is 12⅝-inches. Courtesy of the Metropolitan Museum of Art, Gift of Charles M. Schott, Jr., 1917.

viceable were 100 matchlock muskets, 16 matchlock arquebuses, nine wheellock *carabinas,* and nine flintlock *escopetas.*[29]

The final decade of the seventeenth century saw Spain increasingly preoccupied with foreign incursions and a 1694 report regarding the firearms intended for shipment to the proposed *presidio* of Pensacola, subsequently established in 1698 to discourage rival European encroachments in the Gulf region, revealed a much larger percentage of flintlock firearms, listing 300 matchlock muskets, 100 flintlock *escopetas,* 50 pairs of flintlock pistols, and 5,000 pounds of musket balls with half designated for the *escopetas* which suggests identical caliber.[30]

Though no description of the pistols was given in the Pensacola inventory they were probably cavalry pistols (being referred to as pairs) of the then popular Ripoll pattern. Ripoll gunsmiths early specialized in pistols, producing wheellock specimens in the late sixteenth century, though by ca. 1630 the *patilla* was preferred. Late seventeenth-century Ripoll pistols displayed the *patilla,* a ten to 12 inch barrel of about .60 caliber, and a distinctively flared grip with a flat butt.[31] Ripoll firearms of the period were usually chased and engraved and gunsmiths there produced a large number of blunderbusses.

The Spaniards maintained at least 40 missions in the Florida provinces by 1665. At San Joseph de Ocuya, identified in 1968 as one of 18 Franciscan

SPANISH *Patilla* COCK (17th Century): This lock fragment was recovered from a Spanish mission site on Fort George Island (Pensacola, Fla.) where in 1698 Andrés de Ariola built Fort San Carlos. Courtesy of the St. Augustine Historical Society, St. Augustine, Fla.

PISTOL STOCK (17th/18th Century): Recovered from the 1715 Spanish Plate fleet wreck off the Florida coast, this well preserved pistol stock is of a kind common to Spanish provincial pistols produced during the 17th and early 18th Century. Courtesy of the Bureau of Archives, History and Records Management, Tallahassee, Fla.

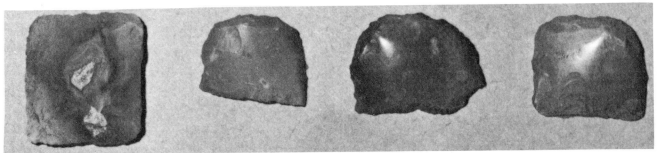

MISSION GUNFLINTS (17th Century): Found in the ruins of the Spanish mission *San Damian de Escambi* in Apalachee Province destroyed by James Moore during Queen Anne's War, these gunflints represent Native American and European craftsmanship. The English-style flint (left) was knapped from local flint by the mission Apalachees and the others are of continental European origin, possibly procured by the Spaniards from France as the rounded heel indicates. Courtesy of B. Calvin Jones, Bureau of Archives, History and Records Management, Tallahassee, Fla.

missions established in Apalachee between 1633 and 1683, archaeologists recovered two unidentified gun fragments, three lead balls ranging from .30 to .40 caliber, and five pistol-sized gunflints which were also used in carbines.[32]

The gunflints recovered from the Ocuya and other mission sites in *La Florida,* except those of known European origin, were made of indigenous mineral displaying Native American craftsmanship,

lending credence to the supposition that at least some of the 30,000 Native Americans gathered around the missions devoted some of their time to knapping gunflints either for the Spaniards or personal use; thus indicating that a home industry of sorts was established by the second half of the seventeenth century.

By ca. 1675 the martial matchlock firearms serving in *La Florida* since the sixteenth century gradually began to be replaced by superior flintlock firearms. Because of the economic, political, and religious discord engendered by the Thirty Years' War and the Second Dutch War (1665-1678), however, the military transition from match to flint ignition was much slower in Spain than elsewhere in Europe and, consequently, the practically orphaned Florida provinces received fewer flintlock firearms at a consid-

FRENCH POSTS and Settlements Within the Present Limits of the United States (17th/18th Century): Courtesy of the National Park Service, Washington, D.C.

erably later period than rival English and French colonies; a situation compromising Spanish sovereignty early in the eighteenth century and further aggravated by the refusal of the crown to arm the Native Americans.

As Spanish influence in *La Florida* continued to diminish there was an opposite reaction in the Great Southwest, despite gradually escalating Native American opposition and French penetrations across the broad Mississippi River; each exemplified by the threat to the San Francisco mission established in 1690 as Spain's eastern-most outpost in Texas which was sporadically attacked by Comanches supplied with French firearms.

The French Heritage

In 1625, during the reign of Louis XIII, Huguenot settlers were excluded from New France and the political administration of the vast territory was generally left to the discretion of the major trading companies, first among them *La Compagnie de la Nouvelle France* (The Company of New France) organized in 1627.

Prior to 1640 fewer than one thousand colonists had ventured to New France despite ambitious recruiting and most of them could not be considered settlers in the strict sense, for rather than establishing stable agricultural communities they worked for the *compagnie,* ranging the wilderness and trading with the Native Americans to earn the estimable sobriquet *courers de bois* (forest runners); predecessors of the equally peripatetic *voyageurs.*

Despite the menacing shadow of the Iroquois, the French pursued the fur trade with unconstrained dedication, assisted by the Huron and other Native Americans. Quebec, Montreal, and Trois Rivières (Three Rivers) emerged as the focal point of the burgeoning fur trade and as early as 1634 Jean Nicolet had traversed Lakes Ontario, Erie, Huron, and Michigan to explore the Wisconsin shore, thereby setting the stage for the succeeding acts in the dramatic expansion of New France. Louis XIII, however, did not live to see his North American dominions flourish, for he died in 1643 leaving a five-year-old son to assume the crown. And child-king Louis XIV (1638-1715) was destined to become the most powerful monarch in Europe.

By 1644 the *compagnie* had expanded its trading posts, though it was then competing with *Les Associes de la Conversion des Sauvages de la Nouvelle France* (The Society for the Conversion of the Native Americans of New France). It was also then that the

Armement et Posture d'un Mousquetaire qui Couche en Iouë (The Arms and Position of the Musketeer with his Accouterments, 17th Century): This plate from Louis De Gaya, *Traité des Armes, des Machines de Guerre* (A Treatise Concerning the Arms and Machines of War, Paris, 1678) depicts a 17th century French musketeer and his equipment, including a comparative illustration of a martial matchlock musket and flintlock fusil. The *Balles Ramées* (literally arbor ball) is similar to the bar shot used with cannon; the balls joined by a lead stem or cord to increase the efficacy of smoothbore firearms. Courtesy of the Eleutherian Mills Historical Library, Wilmington, Del.

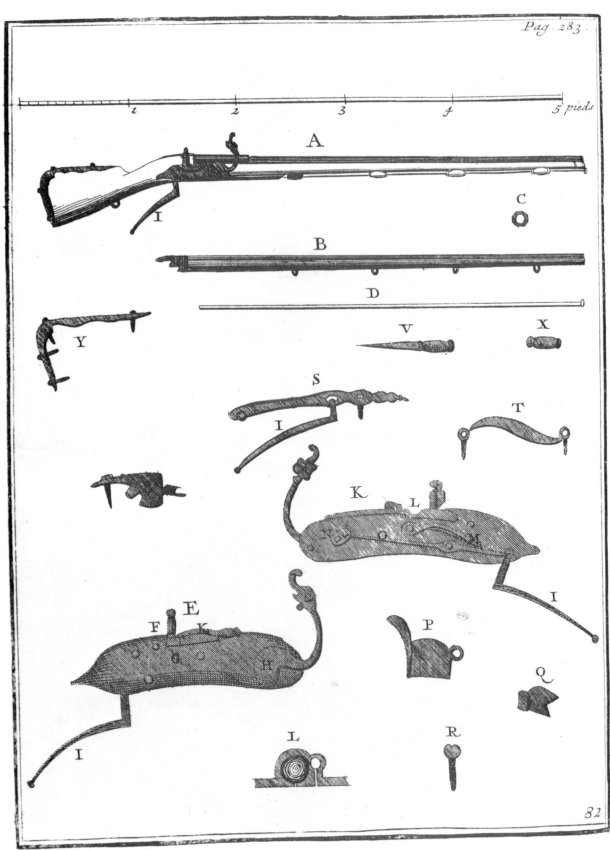

MATCHLOCK MUSKET (18th Century, 1702): This illustration from Saint-Remy, *Mémoires d'Artillerie* (Paris, 1702), depicts a French martial matchlock musket. (A) Assembled musket. (B) Barrel, delineating breech plug (detail, opposite the interior view of the lock) and barrel lugs. (C) Octagonal barrel (front view). (D) Wooden ramrod. (E) Lock, exterior. (F) Priming pan cover pivot. (G) Lockplate. (H) Serpentine. (I) Firing lever. (K) Lock, interior. (L) Priming pan (top view). (M) Sear spring. (N) Tumbler (Link). (O) Sear arm or bar. (P) Priming pan cover. (Q) Serpentine jaws (R) Jaw screw. (S) Trigger plate. (T) Sideplate (counterplate). (V) Plug bayonet. (X) Tompion (muzzle plug). (Y) Butt plate and long comb finial. Eleutherian Mills Historical Library.

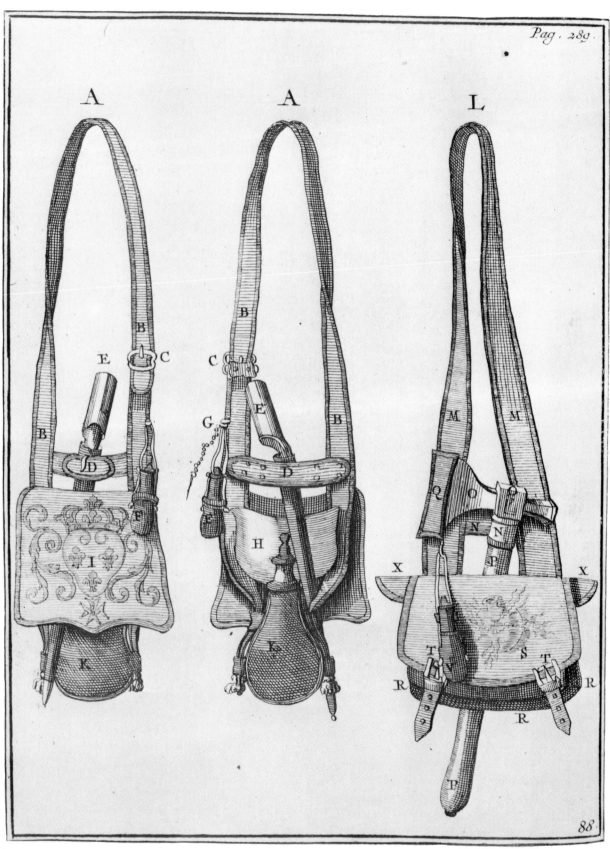

Pag. 289

88

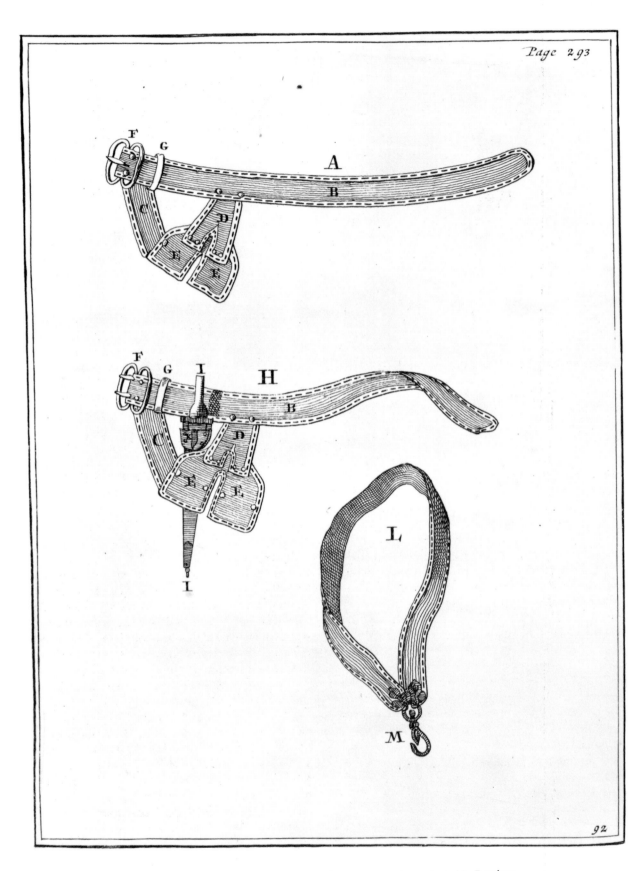

INFANTRY AND CALVARY AC- COUTERMENTS (17th/18th Century): These French accouterments illustrated in Saint-Remy (*Mémoires*) depict the cavalry sabre belt (A), the infantry sword belt (B) with plug bayonet, and a carbine shoulder sling (L) with snap–hook for the slide bar ring. Similar martial accouter- ments were adopted in Bourbon Spain. Courtesy of the Eleuthe- rian Mills Historical Library, Wilmington, Del.

hostile Iroquois, fired by the humiliation suffered at the hands of Champlain and jealously witnessing the preferential treatment accorded their ancestral Huron enemies, embarked on a path of savagery completely disrupting the lucrative fur trade. Abetted by the Dutch and the English who liberally supplied them with large quantities of flintlock firearms, the Iroquois ultimately destroyed the influence of the Huron and the Erie.

New France received little assistance from the mother country. Though the Peace of Westphalia had terminated the horrors of the Thirty Years' War in 1648, France remained embroiled in the Fronde* civil wars (1648-1653) and was also plunged into a conflict with Spain. Prospects brightened considerably in New France, however, when in 1653 the Iroquois suddenly initiated peace overtures.

Having dispersed the Huron, the Iroquois had hoped to replace them as the major influence in the fur trade and thereby procure more firearms for use in their protracted wars with their other Native American enemies. The Iroquois failed to realize their ambitions after three years of relative calm, and war clouds again gathered in 1656.

Though the true flintlock had supplanted previous ignition systems in New France by midcentury the military transition was more gradual there and in the mother country. In France, however, the flintlock found military acceptance more rapidly than in England or Spain, primarily through the influence exerted by Marshal Turenne and François Michel Le Tellier, Marquis de Louvois (1641-1691), who became minister of war in 1666.

Louvois had reorganized the French army by 1672 and as a result the martial matchlock musket was slowly phased out, replaced by the flintlock fusil adapted from the popular sporting gun which emerged in France ca. 1640. The martial fusil had been issued in limited numbers to small detachments guarding artillery parks and magazines as early as 1645, and those troops were subsequently known as fusiliers.[33] The flintlock fusil was suited to the purpose, for the ubiquitous glowing match of the martial musket constituted a distinct safety hazard in the proximity of large quantities of explosives and gunpowder.

In 1665 the Carignan-Salieres Regiment was the first to be fully armed with flintlock fusils.[34] Beginning in 1667, however, fusils were issued piecemeal to grenadier regiments, initially introduced at four or five per company, though entire companies had been armed with them by 1670.[35]

It was also in 1665 that Louis XIV established the royal arsenal of the Bastille as a central storage depot for arms and munitions produced for the military by independent contractors in Paris and the provinces; particularly provincial Saint-Étienne and Charleville.[36]

In 1515 Francis I had selected St. Étienne as the site for a royal manufactory and thereafter firearms were supplied to crown forces by that facility.[37] Flemish gunsmiths from Liège established the first armories at Charleville ca. 1620[38] and the excellent quality of the firearms produced there prompted Louvois to order all of them made after 1667 held in reserve for the king's forces.[39] Louis designated Charleville a royal manufactory in 1688.[40]

The massive martial matchlock musket employed in France during the first half of the seventeenth century was similar to other European specimens, though it was subsequently refined. A typical musket was described in 1697 by Pierre Surirez de Saint-Remy in *Memories d' Artillerie* two years before it was declared obsolete:

Standard muskets have a caliber of 20 lead balls per pound but use bullets somewhat smaller, 22 to 24, to the pound [windage], the Regulation ... caliber. This musket far outnumbers other arms because it is used by infantry for sieges and while in the trenches where firing is constant. According to *l'Ordinance du Roi* [King's Regulations], the barrel length is 3 feet 8 inches and the 5 foot long stock is walnut. Some muskets are better finished than others as certain Regiments are eager to have fine and correct arms with proofed barrels that are polished [bright finish], have the exact caliber, and are well [strongly] breeched. The range is 120 to 150 fathoms [240 to 300 yards].[41]

The typical French musket was approximately 60 and ½ inches long and it weighed 8 and ¾ pounds, nearly half that of earlier specimens. The octagonal breech extended 11 inches down the barrel, there were no sights, and the simple firing lever associated with the earliest form of the matchlock was retained, though conventional triggers with guards were incorporated in most martial matchlock muskets produced elsewhere in Europe.

Secured by two screws, the lockplate was flat, though in some later specimens it was shaped like the more sophisticated flintlock lockplate, and it measured 7 by one and ½ inches. The wooden ramrod was supported by two brass thimbles. There was no buttplate, sideplate, lower ramrod guide, or wrist escutcheon (thumbplate) on most muskets, though as St. Remy mentioned, some were more elaborately appointed than others. Because most French martial firearms were as yet contracted from independent *armuriers* (armorers) there were variations in dimensions and finish.

The hiatus in the Iroquois conflict saw the French continue to expand, penetrating the Great

---

*The civil conflict took its name from the ancient weapon initially wielded by the insurgents: the sling *(fronde)*.

Lakes region. In 1654-1655 Medard Chouart, Sieur des Groseilliers, and his brother-in-law Pierre Espirit Radisson, established a trading post in Wisconsin and in 1661 they explored Lake Superior and built Fort Radisson on the western shore.

In 1663 Louis XIV removed New France from trading company administration, and with the Iroquois threat again apparent in 1665 he dispatched Jean Talon, Count Frontenac, and Rene Robert Cavelier, Sieur de la Salle, with 1,000 troops to deal with them, including the Carignan-Salieres Regiment, the first French regiment dispatched to North America. A year later Gov. Frontenac had all but entirely defeated the Iroquois and an era of relative calm pervaded New France for nearly twenty years thereafter.

In 1672 Gov. Frontenac chose Louis Joliet and five others to seek a great river west of Lake Superior which had been reported by the Native Americans to *Père* Jacques Marquette at the Sainte Ignace mission on Michilimackinac Island. Contrary to the persistent legend, punctured by the diligent research of Franciscan Father Francis Borgia Steck, Marquette did not accompany Joliet's expedition which followed the Wisconsin River to sight the mighty "Missepi" on June 17, 1673.[42] Joliet's party subsequently descended the Mississippi River to the mouth of the Arkansas.

Inspired by Joliet's adventure and with Frontenac's approval, La Salle and his lieutenant, Henry de Tonty, mounted an expedition from the Illinois River in February, 1682, arriving at the mouth of the Mississippi on April 9. La Salle claimed the entire Mississippi Valley for the crown, naming the vast territory Louisiana for his sovereign.

In his association with the Native Americans encountered during the eventful journey, La Salle observed that "The savages take better care of us French than of their own children," amplifying his remark with the somewhat cynical comment, "From us only can they get guns."[43]

La Salle's initial incursion into the Gulf regions did little to ameliorate Spanish fears either in New Spain, *La Florida,* or the mother country, and his second expedition brought additional alarm. La Salle, however, was extremely unfortunate and his 1684 journey ended in disaster at Matagorda Bay on the Texas coast shortly after he built Fort St. Louis near the mouth of the Lavaca River. Disenchanted, La Salle and 17 companions started for the Illinois country and on March 19, 1687, he was treacherously murdered. Two years later the then deserted Fort St. Louis was burned by a Spanish expedition led by Capt. Alonso de León.

La Salle's explorations paved the way for further French efforts and a series of missions and settlements were established on the Mississippi River,

protected by a chain of forts few in number, sparcely garrisoned, and primarily used as trading posts to stimulate commerce with the Native Americans. Fort Prudhomme was founded in what is now western Tennessee in 1682 and four years later Henry Joutel established Arkansas Post with Henry de Tonty, La Salle's former lieutenant. Cahokia was settled in the Illinois country in 1698 and that same year the brothers Le Moyne, Pierre (Sieur d'Iberville) and Jean Baptiste (Sieur de Bienville), received a patent from Louis XIV to exploit the Native American trade in the Mississippi Delta region.

By 1686 the Iroquois had sufficiently recovered to once again confront the French and when King William's War began in 1689 they received support from the English. Gov. Frontenac retaliated with French-Native American raids in New York and New England, striking Schenectady in mid-January, 1690. Dutchman Peter Schuyler described the aftermath:

> No pen can write, and no tongue express, the cruelties . . . committed. The women bigg with Childe rip'd up, and the Children alive throwne into the flames, and their heads dashed against the Doors and windows."[44]

The European phase of the conflict saw Louis XIV embroiled with England, Spain, Holland, and Germany, while his dictatorial rule summed up in the arrogant *"L'etat c'est moi"* (I am the state) did nothing to endear him to a populace mired in poverty and torn by religious persecution. The evident socio-economic turmoil engendered rampant suspicion and in one instance it interfered with firearms evolution, for on August 21, 1688, French officials in Languedoc Province arrested a foreign traveler identifying himself as Abraham Soyer.

Among Soyer's belongings, as documents in the Montpelier archives attest, was a firearm of radical design in which crude cartridges were fed into the breech chamber from a magazine concealed in the buttstock.[45] No further description of what was apparently a remarkable and innovative breech-loading, magazine repeater was given, nor was Soyer's fate discussed beyond that he was ostensibly on his way to St. Étienne to have the firearm evaluated for possible government use.

The surname Soyer was of Hispanic origin, appearing in Spain as Solér, and Abraham Soyer was likely an antecedent of the famous Solér gunsmithing family prominent in Madrid during the eighteenth and nineteenth century (see p. 169). It is not known if Soyer invented the magazine repeater he took to France, though if it functioned as described and had been produced in large quantities for military use it is tempting to speculate upon what ambitious heights Louis XIV or his successors might have scaled.

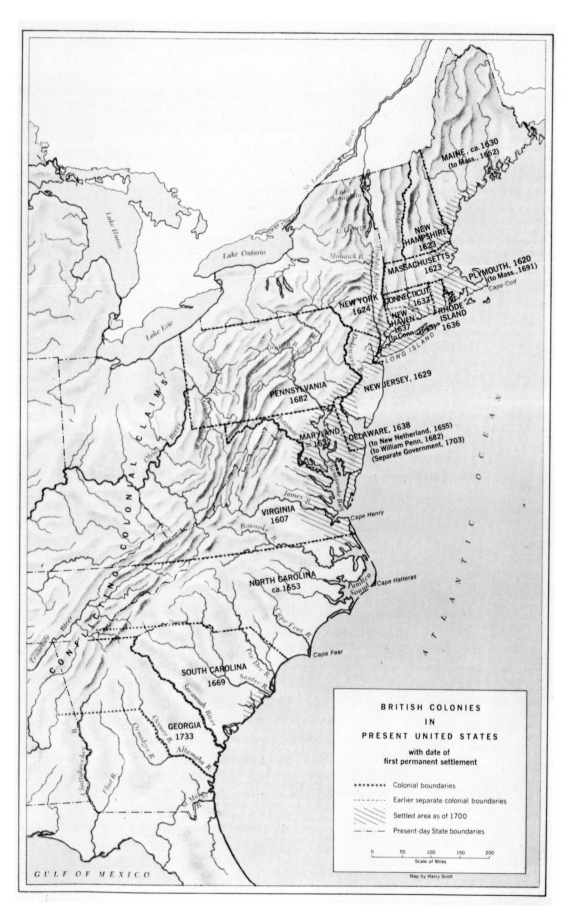

BRITISH COLONIES
Within the Present Limits of the United States (17th/18th Century). Courtesy of the National Park Service, Washington, D.C.

The pervasive, lasting impact of the English heritage in that part of North America which subsequently became the United States is perpetuated in our language, customs, social institutions, and technology. By 1630 there were an estimated 4,646 whites and negroes in the English colonies and the population swelled to more than 50,000 in the mid-century wake of the Great Puritan Migration.[46]

As the English colonies hesitantly began to expand, the settlers met increasing Native American resistance, internal dissent, inter-colony rivalry, and continuing incursions by Dutch, French, and Spanish interests, while in the mother country seethed burning economic and religious discord erupting into a civil war when in 1642 Oliver Cromwell's "roundheads" purged the island nation.

Most of the Native American opposition encountered during the colonial period and thereafter stemmed from economic avarice. The burgeoning seventeenth-century fur trade provided impetus for exploitation, though in many instances difficulties began when the Europeans intruded upon and took possession of what the Native Americans rightfully considered their prime hunting and agricultural land or meddled in their internal affairs.

In the English colonies those factors were greatly magnified by a condescending attitude manifested toward the "heathen selvages," an attitude sustained by the arrogant Anglo-Saxon assumption of racial and intellectual superiority. Nevertheless, because the Native Americans were the primary source for furs and pelts they were willingly tolerated and deftly exploited.

Though welcomed by the Native Americans, the lucrative commerce in firearms, gunpowder, gunflints, lead, and hard liquor was in most instances initially and mutually opposed by the national policy of the respective colonial enterprises. Continued economic rivalry among the European invaders, however, subsequently overwhelmed any moral opprobrium or cohesive resistance and the commerce flourished proportionately.

The first major demonstration of Native American opposition in the English colonies flamed on March 22, 1622, when the aggressive Pamunkey of the mighty Powhatan Confederacy, led by Opechananouch (1545?-1644), attacked Jamestown and its environs, killing 349 of Virginia's 1,250 settlers.

In the wake of the disaster the crown strengthened Virginia's defenses, sending 700 calivers, 300 matchlock arquebuses, 300 flintlock pistols, various kinds of light armor, and 400 longbows with 800 sheaves of arrows.[47] Virginia officials stored the bows in Bermuda, ostensibly to prevent the Native Americans from obtaining samples and reproducing them, for the powerful English longbow was emi-

nently superior to the Native American bow in range and penetration.

Though there is no evidence whether the English longbow was employed in North America, available records indicate that bows other than crossbows were brought to Spanish Florida and put up for sale at St. Augustine late in the sixteenth century (see p. 46). It is not known whether the Spaniards intended them for militia use or to be sold to the neighboring Timucua though the former is more likely.

The relatively tranquil New England frontier erupted in 1633 when the Pequot, a dissident Mohegan faction armed with Dutch and English matchlock firearms, retaliated against a dishonest Connecticut trader. A full scale conflict with the Pequot began in 1637. Capt. John Mason, commanding 90 Connecticut militia and nearly 500 allied Mohegan and Narragansett warriors, launched a surprise dawn attack against the palisaded Pequot town on the Mystic River, putting it to the torch and killing more than 600 men, women, and children. As Mason described it, the flames "did swiftly over-run the [Pequot] Fort . . . [while they] "lay pelting at us with their Arrows; and we repayed them with our small Shot. . . ."[48]

In 1638 Rhode Island, alarmed by the Pequot uprising and fearing additional raids, enacted militia regulations ordering "that every Inhabitant . . . shall be always provided of one muskett, one pound of powder, twenty bullets and two fademe* of match, with Sword and [musket] rest and Bandeliers, all completely furnished."[49]

A year later New Haven settlers were required to be "compleatly furnished with arms (viz), a muskett, a sworde, bandaleers, a rest, a pound of powder, 20 bullets fitted to their muskett, or 4 pounds of pistoll shott or swan shott at least."[50]

The Pequot slaughter, far out of proportion as punishment for their depredations, set the stage for a final war of extermination against the southern New England tribes later in the century and initiated a similar policy in Virginia after yet another Pamunkey attack in April, 1644, when 500 settlers were slain in a single day by warriors again led by the now aged Opechananouch.

The Virginia General Assembly ordered those marching against the Pamunkey to provide themselves with "4 lb. bullets (lead or pewter), 1 lb. powder, 1 good fixed gunne [flintlock with combined battery and pan cover] . . . , some defensive coat or armor and head piece sword or cutlass."[51] Opechananouch was eventually captured and unceremoniously shot, bringing a transitory peace to the Tidewater frontier.

---

*From fadme, meaning a fathom, i.e., about six feet.

At Plymouth Colony the Pilgrims especially disapproved of the often fatal consequences engendered by the commerce in firearms and "strong waters" between the Native Americans and profit-motivated Dutch, French, and English traders; particularly the larcenous band led by aristocratic opportunist Thomas Morton (?-1647?) of Mare Mount.

Nor was the nefarious trade condoned in the Massachusetts Bay Colony, for in 1631 Gov. Thomas Dudley complained that since 1623 English merchants and their dishonest factors "have furnished the Indians with guns, swords, powder and shott."[52] Thus shortly after gun-running began in the French colonies it emerged as one of the first and most profitable enterprises in English America.

Though Thomas Morton's "vilanies" were frequently overlooked by the Pilgrims, his continued infringements on their Native American commerce, particularly at Cushenoc (Augusta, Me.), brought him the dubious distinction of being the first English subject deported from colonial America. Morton's explusion in 1628 (he returned the following year) and subsequent complaints of gun-running prompted the crown to issue the following edict in 1641:

In trucking or trading with the Indians no man shall give them for any commodity of theirs, silver or gold, or any weapons of war, either guns or gunpowder, nor sword, nor any other Munition, which might come to be used against ourselves.[53]

The royal pronouncement was, of course, impossible to enforce in the vast wilderness, and even if the illegal commerce had been eliminated in the English colonies there remained eager Dutch and French traders willing to supply the Native Americans, and neither were the Dutch or French opposed to using other means to procure furs and hides.

In 1632 a French ship, under the guise of needing repairs, put in at the Pilgrim's Penobscot trading post and the crew quickly overpowered the few clerks and looted the post of several muskets, the gunpowder supply, and beaver pelts worth £500.[54] That same year the Pilgrim post at Sowams (Warren, Massachusetts), serving the Wampanoag, was threatened by the Narragansetts. Commanding the four-man garrison there, Capt. Myles Standish was acutely aware that Plymouth was short of gunpowder and sent a runner to Boston. When he returned with 30 pounds of the "black Stuffe," however, the Narragansett threat had evaporated, though there were repercussions.[55]

Gov. John Winthrop was severely censured for assisting Standish because gunpowder was also scarce in the Massachusetts Bay Colony. The incident further magnified the often acrimonious rivalry between the Pilgrims and the Puritans and it intensified during the English Civil War and the ensuing Commonwealth period.

Throughout the colonial era and considerably thereafter gunpowder was extremely scarce in North America and inordinately expensive because practically all of it was imported. In 1642 the Massachusetts Bay Colony attempted to produce saltpeter, ordering the settlers to start compost dumps with their accumulated waste because the decaying matter was a rich source of nitrate.[56] John Winthrop, Jr., the governor's son, was put in charge of the enterprise often cited as the beginning of the chemical industry in North America. The Swedish colony also felt the gunpowder shortage and in 1654 Gov. Johan Classon Rising commented that "if we could here establish powder mills it would bring us great profit."[57]

There is no evidence that other than small quantities of homemade gunpowder were produced in North America until 1666 when, financed by colonial officials, Richard Wooddey of Boston and Henry Russell of Ipswich established an experimental powder mill.[58] Nine years later another mill was started by the colony on the Neponset River at Milton. English powder-maker Walter Everenden of Kent was engaged to manage the works and, as one observer noted in 1676, the powder was equal to any made in England.[59] Everenden's son continued in the trade.

Everenden produced the only commercial gunpowder in seventeenth-century North America and despite that source, homemade gunpowder, and the quantities imported, there was never enough to supply the inordinate demand. Most colonists practiced strict conservation and were emulated by the Native Americans, for they never reached the stage of technological development permitting them to make gunpowder and they were entirely dependent on the frontier trader.

Gunpowder was often inadvertently saved, for the Puritan ethic found hunting and shooting on the Sabbath offensive, and those activities were proscribed in Virginia by Gov. Sir Thomas Dale in 1611[60] and suffered the same approbation in the Massachusetts Bay Colony somewhat later; the Massachusetts General Court enacting legislation against "unprofitable fowlers" wasting powder and shot on missed birds.[61]

In addition to hunting and defense there were other uses for gunpowder. The popular shooting match, practical from the standpoint of practice, was also an entertainment form. Colonists often used gunfire to scare birds and other wildlife away from their crops, while children were known to "sneak" a pinch or two of powder to make squibs.[62] Gunpowder also had medicinal use in treating man or beast, and it was frequently given as a purgative, ignited to cauterize a wound, and served as a poultice to cure the "itch."[63]

Lead, too, was in short supply in colonial America and equally costly because it was also imported. The negligible quantities smelted by the colonists from the small galena deposits shown to them by the Native Americans hardly met their needs. Like gunpowder manufacture, casting bullets was a common household enterprise and practiced by the Native Americans as well. Single and multiple-ball loads were common for hunting and customary in warfare, as militia regulations indicate.

With the scarcity of lead early apparent in the Massachusetts Bay Colony, musket balls often served as a convenient and legal exchange medium because a dearth of currency resulted in a brisk barter system. In Boston ca. 1630 each musket ball was worth a farthing (one-fourth of an English penny) though merchants were not required to accept more than a dozen per purchase.[64]

The colonies of Plymouth, Massachusetts Bay, Connecticut, and New Haven, despite mutual antagonism, eventually recognized the need for coöperation in defense and other affairs, forming in 1643 the United Colonies of New England. At Plymouth the General Court ordered that all able-bodied males possess a "muskett, either firelock or matchlock . . . Also match, pair of bandoliers or pouch for powder and bullets, a sword and belt, a worm, scowrer, a rest and a knapsack."[65]

The initially amicable relationship between the English and the Dutch began to deteriorate when in 1637 Wilhelm Kieft became director general of New Netherland. Kieft's tumultuous administration was characterized by internal dissention, Kieft's War (1643-1645) during which the Algonquin killed 2,000 Hudson Valley settlers and suffered as many losses, and a clash with Connecticut over arming the Mohegan and other tribes inhabiting the Anglo-Dutch borderlands.

Much of the frontier turmoil derived from Kieft's reprehensible scalp boundy and its subsequent employment by the English which led to outrageous abuse, for the unscrupulous indiscriminately murdered any Native American, children included, merely to collect the bounty. Scalping was not customary among the Native Americans of the Eastern Woodland culture before the European invasion; the usual practice being to take the entire head as a trophy of war.[66]

Deposed in 1646, Kieft was replaced by the energetic, equally despotic, peg-legged Petrus Stuyvesant. Though Stuyvesant placated the Algonquin and the Connecticut colonists, his dictatorial rule antagonized the New Netherlanders, while in 1655 he eliminated an imagined threat to the Dutch dominions by conquering New Sweden.

New Englanders readily traded with prospering New Netherland, though the Commonwealth was disinclined to applaude the thriving commerce because it directly contravened the Navigation Act of 1651 which, among other things, forbade transporting imported goods in other than English vessels. Repeated Dutch violations of the act and their refusal to allow the English to inspect cargos for suspected French contraband (England and France were then involved in an undeclared maritime conflict) provoked the first Anglo-Dutch War (1652-1654), and when in 1660 the amended Navigation Act was flouted, the war began anew.

Anticipating the English reaction, Stuyvesant reinforced New Amstel on the Delaware River. An inventory of the arms and munitions available at the fort included 40 snaphaunce firearms, 800 pounds of gunpowder, 600 pounds of bullets, 40 patrons, eight bullet moulds, and three iron ladles for pouring lead.[67]

During that period three Amsterdam gunsmiths made firearms for the Dutch settlements. Jacob Coutey (fl. 1661-1662) produced matchlock muskets, while Gerrit Schimmel (fl. 1660-1662) and Abraham Volckertsen (fl. 1658-1662) made snaphaunce firearms of an undetermined kind.[68] Whether those arms reached the Dutch settlements is unknown.

Cromwell, meanwhile, died in 1658 and the monarchy was restored with Charles II (1630-1685), the "Merry Monarch," assuming the throne. Charles raised an invasion force led by his brother James, Duke of York, and the English fleet arrived off Nieuw Amsterdam in August, 1664. Stuyvesant was forced to surrender New Netherland on the twenty-sixth because the Nieuw Amsterdam residents opposed to his harsh rule refused to fight. Renamed New York, the Dutch enclave was amicably absorbed into the English sphere and the Second Dutch War ended in 1668.

Charles, attempting to appease Parliament and his subjects, entered into the Triple Alliance with Holland and Sweden to block French designs on the Netherlands. He had, however, accepted financial assistance from France and in 1670 entered into the secret Treaty of Dover, renounced his Protestant faith, and joined Louis XIV against the Netherlands in 1672; thus initiating the Third Dutch War.

The Dutch recaptured New York in 1673, and pressure from Parliament forced Charles to repudiate his French alliance. The Treaty of Westminster concluded the conflict in 1674 and New York was restored to the English. Despite Charles' duplicity, the Lion and Unicorn emerged from the war in possession of a vast tract extending from coastal Maine to what became South Carolina; a wilderness

SAUGUS IRON WORKS (17th Century, 1646): One of the earliest and largest North American iron-making furnaces was located at Saugus, Mass., in 1646 and it was operated under the direction of the Undertakers for the Iron Works in New England. Courtesy of the American Iron and Steel Institute, Washington, D.C.

empire sporadically threatened by the French and the Spanish, though the Native Americans posed the greatest, most immediate impediment to colonial expansion.

Though seventeenth-century American economic development suffered in the wake of continuing European conflicts and increasing Native American retaliation, the enterprising colonists had managed to establish a firm techonomic foundation with the fur trade and expanded it with the iron industry. Like other manufactured products, iron was scarce and consequently expensive in colonial America prior to midcentury.

While iron ore was initially difficult to locate and extract, the other iron-making requisites were generously abundant. The immense forests provided an unlimited supply of wood for making charcoal and lime was extracted from the enormous quantities of shell lining the pristine coast and what was discarded by the Native Americans in their mounded refuse dumps.

The English pioneered the iron industry in North America when in 1609 the Jamestown settlers built a lime-slaking kiln and produced small quantities of bog iron. A decade later they constructed a large iron-making furnace at nearby Falling Creek. Before substantial production began, however, the furnace was demolished and the ironmasters and their families slain by the marauding Pamunkey.

IRON FURNACE BELLOWS (17th/18th Century): Huge bellows like the pair depicted forced air into the furnace, intensifying the heat required to liquify the ore. Cams on a shaft connected to a waterwheel contacted a short tang at the bellows top, compressing the diaphram. When the cams disengaged the rope attached to the pivoting counterbalance lever raised the diaphram. The small bellows used in the gunsmith's forge were similar though manually operated. Courtesy of the American Iron and Steel Institute, Washington, D.C.

IRON REDUCTION FURNACE
(17th/18th Century): Most of the
large iron furnaces in colonial
America emulated Old World
design and were built against the
side of a hill or as depicted above
to provide access to the top of the
tunnel or flue into which the ore,
charcoal, and lime were fed.
Gunsmiths frequently purchased
wrought iron directly from the
furnace. Courtesy of the American Iron and Steel Institute, Washington, D.C.

After the Falling Creek massacre the first mod-
estly successful colonial iron furnace was the Saugus
Iron Works located near Boston and organized between 1644 and 1646 by gunsmith Richard Leader
and John Winthrop, Jr., the enterprise financed in
part by the Massachusetts Bay Colony. A lack of
skilled ironmasters and quality ore closed the Saugus
furnace ca. 1675, though others were established
elsewhere, including the New Haven (Conn.) Furnace (1657) and the Shrewsbury (N.J.) Furnace
(1680). Only 1,500 tons of iron were produced in
English America prior to 1700,[69] and not until 1733
did iron-making begin in French America.[70]

Gunsmiths and other craftsmen relied on imported iron prior to the eighteenth century and in
colonial commerce iron was either identified as pig
iron, suitable for casting, or bar iron also known as
wrought iron and charcoal iron. Bar iron took its
name from its shape. Pig iron derived its name from
the trench-like ingot moulds scooped out of the
ground, for the molten iron was run from the
bloomery (furnace) via a trench connected to the
moulds; thus as the iron filled them they resembled
piglets nursing a sow.

The crude Jamestown furnace was similar to the
masonry kilns appearing in twelfth-century Europe.
The Falling Creek and the Saugus Iron Works, like
subsequent bloomeries, were more sophisticated,
emulating the construction of the contemporary
English furnace. The Saugus furnace was impressive,
made of stone and provided with a huge bellows. In
addition there was a casting house and forge, one or
two chaferies where the wrought iron bloom was

tilt-hammered, a rolling and a slitting mill, and ancillary buildings. Parenthetically, the primitive iron-
making kiln, like the charcoal kiln, was not
immediately rendered obsolete in North America
and remained a fixture in remote frontier settlements
for many years.

In the Saugus furnace and others the tunnel or
flue was built against the side of a hill because it was
serviced at the top; a wagon road providing access to
the tunnel mouth. Alternate layers of charcoal, iron
ore, and lime in that order were loaded into the
furnace and the charcoal was ignited; super-heated
by intense air blasts forced into the flue from a huge
bellows. The molten iron was collected from a sump
or run-off trench at the furnace base.

The discernable scarcity of suitable domestic
iron and steel combined with a paucity of gunsmiths
and the escalating demand for firearms from colonists and Native Americans alike, led to accelerated
growth in the English iron-and-gun-making industry while fostering a brisk commerce with the colonies in finished barrels, locks, and other
components.

By ca. 1675 a great deal of specialization
emerged in the European firearms industry. Arms
merchants contracted with gunsmiths who then
often sub-contracted with craftsmen specializing in
barrel forging, lock-making, and casting or forging
iron and brass components. Accessories and accouterments were procured in a like manner. Whatever
the enterprise it was generally confined to specific
areas within the community and largely undertaken
at home, i.e., what is termed a cottage or household
industry.

While gun-making was a thriving industry in
London by ca. 1650, firearms manufacture in Birmingham was a minor industry until 1683 when Sir
Richard Newdigate initiated a crown order for martial muskets and persuaded gunsmiths there to accept.[71] By 1690 Birmingham gunmakers were producing 200 military flintlock muskets per month,
much to the dismay of the London Gunmakers'
Company which had previously monopolized government contracts.[72]

The impetus gained in making martial firearms
convinced Birmingham gunsmiths to enter the
commercial market on a large scale, emphasizing the
export trade. As early as 1697 the commerce in firearms and firearms components imported from England and the Continent had grown to such proportions in English America that New York Colony
levied a tariff of six shillings for "every gun or gun-
baril with a lock" shipped up the Hudson River.[73]

An integral and lucrative part of early American
commerce, the importation of firearms, firearms
components, gunpowder, gunflints, lead, gunsmithing tools, gunscrews, and numerous other arti-

cles associated with the craft and the use of firearms transcended the colonial era and remained a vital economic factor during the early evolution of the United States firearms industry.

Frequently at odds, the United Colonies of New England managed to find common cause during King Philip's War or what with sufficient justification could be more appropriately termed the War of Puritan Perfidy (1675-1678). King Philip, also known among the English as Metacomet or Philip of Pokanoket, was the son of Ousamequin (Massasoit) to whom the Pilgrims owed so much.

Philip became chief of the Wampanoags in 1662 and, despite several disputes with the Puritans of Massachusetts Bay, maintained his friendship until 1675 when, following a specious confession accusing him of conspiring to war, colonial officials hanged two of his warriors and shot his son to death. Philip's vengeance knew no bounds, nor did the Puritan thirst for more blood. The United Colonies met the Wampanoags with 1,000 well-armed militia and in June the Killing Time began. Many of the other Native Americans blithely ignored Philip's call to arms, playing a waiting game with disastrous consequences.

The Narragansetts were the first to feel the treachery of the people they had befriended and had several times assisted in their wars with other Native Americans. On a freezing December 19—the Sabbath—the Narragansett camp in the Great Swamp near Kingston, R.I., was surprised by colonial forces. The Narragansetts lost nearly 1,000 men, women, and children, never recovering from the blow. Remnants of the nation, including some sympathetic Nipmuck warriors, joined Philip that spring and ravaged 52 of the 90 English settlements, completely destroying 12 of them.

In May, 1676 the militia killed Narragansett chief Canonchet and 120 warriors, while that summer Philip's fortunes continued to diminish. Learning from a Native American turncoat that the elusive Wampanoag chief had returned to his ancestral home near Mount Hope Neck, R.I., colonial forces now led by Benjamin Church mounted a dawn attack on August 12.

The disorganized Wampanoags and their few allies immediately scattered and Philip set off alone. He was ambushed by Caleb Cook and a "Christian Indian" named Alderman. Cook's musket misfired, though Alderman's shot found its mark and Philip "fell upon his face in the mud and water, with his gun under him."[74]

Native American resistance thereafter faltered, though desultory fighting continued until 1678. The United Colonies, embarking on a shameful episode of persecution and genocide unequalled in North America until the nineteenth-century, hanged or

ALDERMAN'S GUNLOCK (17th Century): This English (Jacobean) flintlock is from the firearm used by one of Benjamin Church's Native Americans to kill Wampanoag leader King Philip. Note the pivotal sear and extended trigger bar (rear) and the main-spring hook resting on the tumbler shoulder. The lock was secured by three screws and has a dog safety. Courtesy of the Massachusetts Historical Society, Boston. George M. Cushing, photographer.

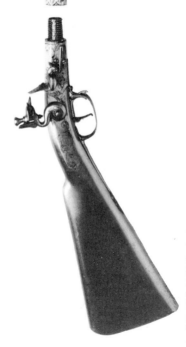

Turn-Off Rifle (17th Century): Turn-off firearms similar to the all-metal rifle depicted were popular in England and continental Europe for more than a century. Gunsmith Jan Cloeter of Gravenbroch, Prussia, made this specimen ca. 1680. Courtesy of the *Tøjhusmuseet*, Copenhagen.

MATCHLOCK MUSKETS (17th Century): These firearms illustrate the most advanced development of the English martial matchlock musket as used in the period 1675-1715. Both muskets have full-length, pin-fastened stocks with capped fore-ends. The 46-inch barrels of .75 caliber flare slightly at the muzzle. There are no sights and the forestock ferrule secures the wood ramrod. Note the similarity of the convex lock-plates to those of contemporary flintlock muskets. British Crown Copyright. Reproduced with permission of the Controller of Her Britannic Majesty's Stationery Office.

shot all male Wampanoags they had captured, sold most of the women and children into slavery, and thereafter inaugurated the reprehensible reservation system, i.e., prison camps by another name.

The War of Puritan Perfidy broke forever the power of the Native Americans in southern New England and the strength and solidarity gained by the United Colonies during the conflict brought to New England a fleeting measure of autonomy just as it had in Virginia in the wake of Bacon's Rebellion.

Nathaniel Bacon, Jr., came to Virginia in 1673, first establishing himself as a planter and second as an outspoken critic of Gov. William Berkeley. Bacon accused him of negligence in failing to halt Susquehanna depredations in the northern settlements, questioned his monopoly of the beaver trade, and protested his inequitable tax policy.

Failing to move the governor, Bacon and his followers took up arms against crown authority and attacked and burned Jamestown on September 19, 1676. Berkeley fled. The first American revolution withered after Bacon's suspiciously timely death in October; however, Gov. Berkeley was removed from office in 1677 and some reform measures were instituted.

Any semblance of independence retained by the New Englanders and the Virginians, interpreted by the crown as a potential threat, evaporated when in 1685 James II (1633-1701) ascended the throne; his repressive policies backed by the presence of royal troops in English America and the heavy hand of Sir Edmund Andros, appointed governor general of the Dominion of New England on June 3, 1686.

During the final quarter of the seventeenth century the firearms and accouterments employed in English America were somewhat improved in comparison to earlier specimens and several distinctive firearms had emerged, reflecting the earlier changes and transitions in firearms evolution occurring in the mother country.

Oliver Cromwell's Commonwealth Army had been disbanded following the Restoration in 1660,

and Charles II had been forced by Parliament to reduce the strength of the King's Militia which, upon his death in 1685, numbered fewer than 8,000 with at least 5,000 infantry still armed with the obsolescent matchlock musket.[75]

After ca. 1670 the majority of the martial firearms used in England were almost equally divided between matchlock and snaphaunce ignition; the former slightly predominant.[76] By 1678 only one English regiment, the North British Fusiliers, had been issued the light musket known as a fuzee or fusee which incorporated the true flintlock and was patterned after the French martial fusil, thus initiating the transition to true flintlock ignition which was not completed until the early eighteenth century.[77]

In 1679 Prince Rupert's Dragoons (heavy cavalry) were issued 68 snaphaunce muskets with slings and 12 flintlock fuzees.[78] Like the French, the English also armed their recently organized grenadier companies with flintlock fusils, and one company assigned to Sir Charles Wheeler's Regiment of Foot in 1679 was provided with 103 fusils with slings and an equal number of cartridge boxes with girdles (belts), grenade pouches, hatchets, and bayonets.[79]

By June, 1685, true flintlock ignition had become more prevalent in English martial firearms as noted in a request made by Lord Dartmouth, Master General of the Ordnance:

That ye 2300 Musquet Barrels last proved be forthwith stockt & lockt, that is all that are 3 foot or longer [in the barrel] to be stockt with Wallnuttree Stocks & ye locks to be Double Springes French Locks with Kings Cypher engraven. . . . All ye Barrels yt are shorter than 3 feet to be stockt with Beech—to have good Locks of ye old fashion."[80]

Though James II had managed to increase the strength of the King's Militia to nearly 32,000 only two regiments—the Royal Fusiliers and the Royal Welch Fusiliers—had been completely equipped with flintlock fusils when in 1689 James was deposed in favor of his Protestant son-in-law, William of Orange.[81]

Swept to the English throne by popular acclaim on April 11 in the liberal atmosphere generated by the Glorious Revolution, the Netherland prince became William III (1650-1702) and accepted the crown as joint sovereign with James' daughter, Mary, while England's involvement in the Grand Alliance against French incursions in the Netherlands spread to North America in the conflict known as King William's War (1689-1697).

Despite the introduction of true flintlock firearms to several units of the King's Militia after 1677, the martial musket contracts procured by Sir Richard Newdigate for Birmingham gunsmiths in 1689 distinctly specified snaphaunce locks. The Birmingham contracts also established the official length of the martial musket barrel and it was retained for nearly a century:

> . . . [the barrel] to be 3 feet 10 inches long with walnut tree and ash stocks and that one half of the said musquetts shall have flatte locks engraven, and the other half round locks and that all of them shall have brass pipes [thimbles] cast and brass heel [butt] plates and all the stocks varnished and to have six good thrids [threads] in the breech screws [plugs] and all the said gun stocks shall be well made and substantial and none of them glewed.[82]

After ca. 1660 the English commercial version of the French flintlock displayed the convex lockplate. By 1685 the lockplate developed a distinctive though slight bow-like configuration in the bottom profile—the so-called banana lockplate—with the rear of the plate tapering gracefully. The cock was also rounded and illustrated the elegant gooseneck design. Though the Birmingham musket contracts noted round and "flatte" locks, the Board of Ordnance adopted the flat lockplate and cock exclusively in the early eighteenth century.

The period 1675-1700 can be considered a transitional phase in English martial firearms evolution.

A survey of the English martial firearms utilized during the period 1687-1691, taken from "A Generall State of all the Ordnance etc.," lists no true flintlock firearms other than long carbines for light dragoons, i.e., those noted by Lord Dartmouth in 1685; thus indicating that the true flintlock had not yet superseded matchlock or snaphaunce firearms for military use.

The 1687-1691 ordnance survey notes that only seven basic English martial firearms were in use and seven variations were represented.[83] There were three kinds of matchlock muskets, three kinds of snaphaunce muskets, one designated for sea service; one heavy dragoon snaphaunce carbine, four kinds of light dragoon carbines, three snaphaunce and one flintlock; two kinds of English lock pistols, one for dragoons and the other for sea service; the naval blunderbuss, and the infantry musketoon; each of the latter barely distinguished from the other, though they would undergo substantial changes in the eighteenth century.

The martial musket in general service during the latter part of James' reign and in that of William and Mary displayed design features inherited from the matchlock of the Commonwealth era and employed either the matchlock or the snaphaunce, both secured by three screws. Some muskets, however, incorporated the Jacobean (English) lock, for it was a common practice to replace unserviceable matchlocks or snaphaunce locks with more efficient mechanisms, during a transition period.

The English infantry musket had no sideplate as yet. The 46 inch, 12 bore barrel had a front sight and the octagonal breech extended approximately 18 inches, giving the barrel a stepped appearance. All of the metal components except the brass buttplate

FLINTLOCK CARBINE (ca. 1690): This English carbine displays an innovative telescoping stock. The overall length of the .62 caliber carbine is 31⅛-inches with the butt extended; 24⅞-inches without. Barrel length is 16¾-inches and the carbine weighs 3 lbs. 6¼ ounces. Courtesy of the Glasgow Art Gallery and Museum, Glasgow, Scotland.

FLINTLOCK CARBINE (ca. 1685): London gunsmith R. Brooke made the English martial carbine depicted and also produced dual-ignition flintlock/matchlocks. The carbine has a .67 caliber, 31⅛-inch barrel flared at the muzzle. Note the heavy, octagonal breech and long rear trigger guard finial. Such firearms served during the Commonwealth and Restoration Periods. Courtesy of the Smithsonian Institution, Washington, D.C.

BOXLOCK PISTOL (17th Century): The boxlock design is represented by the elegant pair of pistols depicted which were produced by London gunsmith Richard Wilson (fl. 1660–1680). Note the centrally-hung cocks and fine, silver wire grip embellishment. The 6-inch barrels are .50 caliber. British Crown Copyright. Reproduced with permission of the Controller of Her Britannic Majesty's Stationery Office.

were wrought iron and either russeted (browned) or, like the walnut stock, painted black or varnished.

The lock was generally signed behind the cock, by the maker, while between the cock and the battery was the monarch's cypher denoting the reign: I or J R for James Rex (King) and W R for William Rex. The king's cypher was surmounted by a crown designating the Gunmakers' Company proof mark. (The letter I substituted for J in the English alphabet and it continued to be used in English-speaking nations until the nineteenth century.)

The full-length, pin-fastened forestock of the English martial musket was channeled to receive the wooden ramrod. The flared, fishtail stock was supplanted ca. 1670 by a butt with a flat heel and rounded belly (fish-belly) which was also evident in the contemporary English long fowler, indicating that the latter influenced the martial design. By ca. 1690 the buttstock began to emulate the French pattern with its relatively straight comb and belly; a more practical design.

During the reign of Queen Anne (1702–1714),* Queen Mary's sister, matchlock and snaphaunce muskets were entirely phased out of British line regiments, replaced by the so-called Queen Anne mus-

*During her reign England and Scotland were joined by mutual agreement under the 1707 Act of Union; thus creating Great Britain.

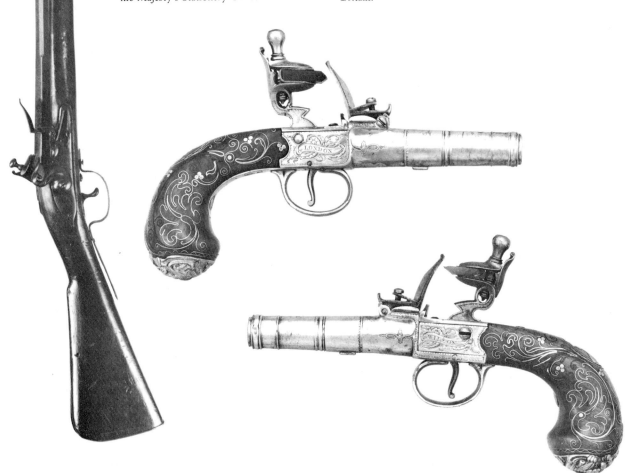

ket employing the true flintlock, though retaining the bore size and the barrel length of the former martial musket.[84] The weight of the Queen Anne musket was also reduced because the stock was somewhat shorter.

During the 1687-1691 ordnance survey period there was considerable confusion evident in the terminology applied to English martial firearms and the carbine was especially affected, known variously as a short gun, dragon, dragoon, musquettoone, extraord [i] nary bastard musquett, bastard carbine, short bastard snaphannce musquett, or a musquett for dragoons. The flintlock fusil, commonly referred to as a fusee or fuzee, was also termed a fuze or long carbine. Formerly used to describe the wheellock, the term firelock was then exclusively employed for flintlock firearms of any kind.

Carbine specifications were equally confusing. Early in the seventeenth century Gervase Markham (see p. 85) described dragons as "short peeces of 16 inches the Barrell, and full musquet bore with firelockes or snaphaunces."[85] By 1630 the carbine was of smaller caliber and longer in the barrel (see Table I). In 1668, however, Jonadab Holloway made 50 carbines with 33 inch barrels for the Yeomen of the Guard,[86] while the "ordnary" and "long" carbines mentioned in the 1687-1691 ordnance survey had 31 and 36 inch barrels respectively.

A number of short martial carbines appearing in 1685 were "all made full Carbine Bore ye full length of 2 ft. 7 ins. every Barrll and Coloured Blue with a Brydle Lock."[87] Later that year 400 carbines were made with "Double Brydle Locks according to ye pattern. . . ."[88] The presence of the battery and the tumbler bridle in the carbine lock was an innovation not generally seen in English martial firearms until ca. 1745-1750, though it was employed much earlier in commercial locks. Blued barrels were also infrequently found in martial firearms of the era, English or Continental.

The terms carbine and musketoon were frequently used synonymously in England, and though contemporary literature differs radically in some instances, the martial musketoon was usually described as similar to the carbine but always a smoothbore flintlock, while the carbine was often a wheellock prior to ca. 1625 and occasionally rifled. In the late seventeenth century the musketoon was often equated with the blunderbuss, adding to the confusion.

Carbines and musketoons displayed paddle-type buttstocks early in the century and some were provided with skeletal (open work) or telescoping extension stocks during the later years; each reducing weight which was a primary consideration in dragoon firearms. Because martial carbines and musketoons were generally horsemen's weapons they were provided with a convenient sling. The sling had a swivel at one end which clipped on a ring mounted in a slide bar opposite the lockplate; one end of the slide bar secured by a lockplate screw and the other a separate screw. The carbine and musketoon were slung from the shoulder barrel down, the muzzle resting in a leather cup attached to the saddle skirt.

English carbines and musketoons were usually smoothbores though turn-off specimens were almost always rifled. Caliber fluctuated between .50 and .65 and rifled specimens had a front and a rear sight; the latter of the adjustable leaf type. For dragoon use the carbine and musketoon were superior to the pistol in range and accuracy, particularly when rifled. Carbines and musketoons saw considerable use in English America and Nathaniel Bacon was armed with a carbine during the Jamestown attack in 1676.[89]

The smoothbore, muzzle-loading, single-shot flintlock pistols brought to English America ca. 1625 were massive, usually incorporating the snaphaunce or Jacobean lock. Few pistols had sights and the design, finish, and ornamentation were basically utilitarian. The typical English "horse" pistol employed during the Puritan Revolution and ensuing Commonwealth era (1642-1660) was approximately .60 caliber and barrel length fluctuated between 22 and 24 inches.

After ca. 1660 the English martial pistol was somewhat refined. During James II's reign the convex cock and lockplate were introduced and barrel length was reduced to about 15 inches. Brass grip caps were common and the wooden ramrod was secured by a single, fluted thimble. A plain iron trigger guard protected the slightly off-set trigger and the design can be noted in some carbine triggers, each dictated by the use of the vertical sear.

The pistol grip was usually walnut and displayed a pin-fastened forestock extending to the muzzle and channeled for the ramrod. By ca. 1670 the grip began to curve down from the breech plug tang, though retaining the flat heel of the wheellock dag. Shortly after 1700 the grip terminated with a bulbous pommel displaying an iron or brass cap with side straps. The capped pommel design is believed to have originated because the pistol was often used as a club when there was no time to reload.

After ca. 1660 most English pistols of commerical manufacture were provided with S-shaped sideplates and many of them displayed a belt hook attached there. Barrels were usually iron, though brass was also encountered and the musket lock used in earlier specimens was discarded for a smaller version which resulted in a lighter and therefore more compact handgun similar to those emerging on the Continent.

The small, popular, readily concealed pistol had

received ample notoriety in England as early as 1594, for on December 1 of that year Queen Elizabeth issued a proclamation against carrying "small Dags called Pocket Dags."[90] Even stronger measures were elicited from Parliament in 1612-1613, banning "the use, manufacture, or importation of pocket dags, or pistols, and commanding the surrender of all such."[91] Those early prohibitions were impossible to enforce, nor did they discourage the use of handguns by the criminal.

By ca. 1650 a few small English turn-off pistols incorporated the lock components between the lockplate and a plate integral with and positioned directly behind the breech. Pocket pistols with that innovation were further refined ca. 1685, the components and the cock situated between two integral breech plates with the cock said to be "centrally hung." The arrangement of the breech plates gave rise to the appellation box lock.[92]

The box lock was a technological innovation of major significance because it further reduced the bulk of the pocket pistol, whether of the common muzzle-loading variety or the breech-loading turn-off design. The centrally-hung cock was subsequently modified to prevent it from catching in the clothing when the pistol was quickly drawn. Box lock construction continued to be used in several kinds of firearms until the mid-nineteenth century.

Though no standard English martial pistol evolved in the seventeenth century the pistol-size lock was introduced ca. 1685 and the pistols were normally issued in pairs for dragoon use, with or without belt hooks. In its seventeenth-century form the saddle holster issued to dragoons displayed a protective flap and a brass muzzle cap with a drain to prevent the accumulation of water or débris which could impair the functioning of the lock. The holster was attached by thongs to a D-ring mounted on the saddle skirt, though there were variations; some holsters joined by a wide leather band and merely slung across the mount's withers and secured to the skirt rings.

English officers' pistols were generally purchased from an independent rather than martial contract gunsmith and consequently fluctuated widely in design and ornamentation; the later restricted only by the owner's imaginative taste and what he could afford. Officers' saddle holsters were frequently embellished as elaborately as the pistols they carried, displaying intricate embroidery on the cloth covers and silver rather than brass muzzle caps.

At some undetermined time in the seventeenth century there appeared a kind of pistol carrier similar to the baldric or hanger supporting the sword or cutlass. Slung across the chest, it supported as many as six pistols depending upon their size. The pistol carrier was especially favored by mariners and was

extremely popular with pirates. The phrase "pirate pistol" as used by some novelists can be disregarded, for those scavengers of the sea armed themselves with any available pistol rather than a special variety.

Most seventeenth-century pistols displayed trigger guards, though there is an exception exemplified by the innovative Scottish pistols emerging ca. 1590. Initially employing the snaphaunce, those extraordinary handguns were made in the major commercial centers of Scotland and the absence of trigger guards remained a hallmark even after true flintlock ignition was introduced ca. 1665.

In addition to exposed triggers Scottish pistols which for some unfathomable reason are now almost exclusively termed Highland pistols, though few if any were produced in that region, illustrate several other distinguishing features. Though very early pistols had wood grips, those produced after ca. 1625 were made entirely of brass or iron and all displayed a belt hook, while the grip design expressed a globular, heart, lemon, or ramshorn shape; the center usually incorporating a screw-in vent pick. The butt of the pick was often drilled so a lanyard could be attached. Most Scottish pistols displayed some form of ornamentation throughout, the more expensive specimens elaborately engraved and extensively inlaid with silver.

Charles E. Whitelaw has noted that the unusual design of the Scottish pistol survived for 250 years, much longer than other pistol designs.[93] In his illuminating study he has categorized Scottish pistols according to the ignition systems employed: Class I including the early (ca. 1598-1686) and the late (ca. 1647-1702) snaphaunce, and Class II the flintlock (ca. 1665-1820).[94] Though arbitrary of necessity, the dates clearly indicate a transition period during which one lock form was dominant though another had evolved and was used concomitantly, eventually replacing the former.

As a rule a wooden ramrod tipped with bone or brass accompanied Scottish pistols with wood grips and an iron ramrod served pistols of all-metal construction. Scottish pistols ranged in length from eight to 26 inches and a few had sights. In some early pistols the muzzle finial emulated the cannon-barrel pattern of the turn-off pistol, while others displayed a distinctively swamped (flared) muzzle. The exposed trigger was usually distinguished by a ball tip. Most of the metal components were engraved or chased; thus producing a practical as well as elegant sidearm.

Scottish pistols used snaphaunce ignition for a much longer period than other Scottish firearms or those produced elsewhere and the longevity was inspired by tradition rather than a lack of skill on the part of Scottish gunsmiths. Scottish gunsmiths became independent 50 years before English gun-

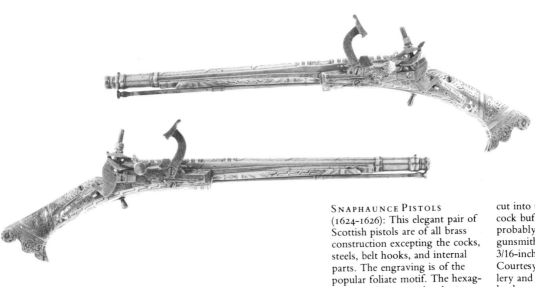

SNAPHAUNCE PISTOLS (1624-1626): This elegant pair of Scottish pistols are of all brass construction excepting the cocks, steels, belt hooks, and internal parts. The engraving is of the popular foliate motif. The hexagonal pan fences are dated 1624 and the barrels 1626. A rectangle cut into the lockplate below the cock buffer has the initials I.L, probably the mark of Dundee gunsmith James Low. The 11 3/16-inch barrels are of .35 caliber. Courtesy of the Glasgow Art Gallery and Museum, Glasgow, Scotland.

smiths, for after 1587 the gunsmithing craft was recognized as separate from the ancient Guild of Hammermen with which it had been formerly associated; the term hammermen synonymous with ironmasters and blacksmiths.[95] Until the early seventeenth century Scottish pistolsmiths were referred to as dag-makers.[96]

Numerous Scottish firearms were used in English America, for after ca. 1650 many Scots had immigrated to Boston and a large contingent settled Stuart's Town near Port Royal, South Carolina, where they were engaged in the Native American trade and were subsequently attacked by the Spaniards as a result. An even greater influx of Scottish settlers reached America early in the eighteenth century.

Of whatever origin pistols were extremely popular in North America during the seventeenth century and there was some distribution among the Native Americans. The smoothbore, muzzle-loading pistol was normally charged with a single lead ball though pistol shot approximating the size of present 00 (double 0) buckshot was commonly used because even at short range accuracy was notoriously poor.

Old World Technological Innovation

In colonial North America, as in Europe, firearms were frequently exposed to the natural elements and over the centuries several accouterments

SNAPHAUNCE PISTOLS (1634): This handsomely engraved pair of Scottish pistols are distinguished by their lemon butts with pierced vent picks. The overall length of the pistols is 16¾-inch and the barrels are dated 1634, while the lockplate bears the initials A G. Courtesy of the Anthropological Museum, University of Aberdeen, Aberdeen, Scotland.

were devised to protect them. Precisely when those accouterments were introduced remains conjectural, though most of them originated during the fifteenth century and thereafter served in the New World as well.

Particularly effective was the lock cover, for not only did it protect the components from the elements and thereby prevent oxidation (rust), but also served to keep the priming powder dry while leaving the firearm available for immediate use. The lock cover snugly fit the breech and was provided with a thong to secure it, while it was preserved and waterproofed with neatsfoot oil or saddle soap.

The lock cover was usually made by soaking a piece of leather until it was pliable and then moulding it around the lock and the breech; the leather retaining the moulded shape when it dried. In some instances, however, lock covers were made from an animal's knee joint which was naturally shaped to fit the cock as in the so-called calf-knee cover.

Another protective accouterment was the gun scabbard which was normally made from a single piece of leather folded over with the edges sewn or two pieces sewn together each leaving an opening sufficient to receive the entire firearm. When in the scabbard the firearm was completely protected, though not readily accessible. Scabbards were also preserved and waterproofed. Native Americans quickly adopted the lock cover and the scabbard, frequently expending considerable time and effort decorating the latter with pictographs and bead, feather, fringe, quill, and shell work.

Still another innovation was the tompion, a small wood plug which fit into the muzzle of a firearm to keep the bore free of water and débris. If ice, snow, dirt or other foreign matter remained in the bore when the weapon was fired it usually resulted in a bulged or ruptured barrel because the obstruction blocked the passage of the load. The load was forced against the obstruction and the powerful propellant gases rapidly expanding behind it exerted inordinate pressure against each when seeking to escape, either greatly distending or shattering the barrel at that point. While the tompion served a useful purpose it presented the same hazard as an obstruction if not removed from the muzzle prior to firing.

Shortly after the helical barrel-making technique was introduced (see p. 109) European gunsmiths discovered that overlapping the edges of the barrel skelp when hammer-forging it produced a much stronger lognitudinal seam and that innovation was followed by an improved method of bore polishing or lapping (see p. 30). The technique consisted of plugging the bore with clay approximately an inch from the muzzle, inserting and centering a rod of less than bore diameter in the muzzle to that

point, and then casting a lead slug around it. When the lead solidified the rod was rapidly pushed back and forth with the movement of the tight slug polishing the bore.

With the introduction of more sophisticated barrel-making techniques the venerable barrel band was resurrected, though it would not entirely replace the barrel lug and pin until the nineteenth century. Precisely where barrel bands originated remains obscure though they were used with fourteenth-century hand cannon.

Seventeenth-century barrel bands were initially flat, cast of brass or iron, and as many as three were slipped over the muzzle and forestock binding the latter to the barrel by friction. By midcentury rounded barrel bands appeared, secured either by friction or an L-shaped spring clip with a pin and shoulder. The pin was set in a hole drilled into the forestock and a mortise received the spring clip. The barrel band was forced over the clip shoulder which was pressed into the mortise, and when the band cleared the clip shoulder it sprang out to catch the leading edge of the band, securing it by spring tension.

In the decade following the devastating Thirty Years' War most European armies of consequence followed the example of Sweden's late king, Gustavus Adolphus, and adopted paper cartridges. Paper cartridges were employed in the English colonies of North America by 1650 and saw widespread use by 1675, and they were doubtlessly used in Spanish Florida by 1683, for Gov. Cabrera then referred to cartridge pouches being distributed with flintlock *escopetas* (see p. 116). Cartridges might have been utilized in New France with the arrival of the Carignan-Salieres Regiment in 1665 though there is no direct evidence.

Paper cartridges did not supersede the powder flask or the powder horn employed in colonial America since the fifteenth century, for each continued to serve a populace long accustomed to their use for hunting and militia duty and they were equally popular among the Native Americans who duplicated powder horns and made flasks from birch bark, tortoise shell, and other materials.

The leather cartridge box conveniently attached to the infantry belt or shoulder strap was introduced in colonial America with the appearance of paper cartridges. The cartridge box was known in New Sweden by 1654, for Gov. Rising then described "bags of leather with three or four compartments, in which one could place cartridges; these are many times better in the woods than bandoliers."[97] In New Netherland the Dutch retained the bandolier for use with matchlock firearms and preferred the patron as a cavalry accouterment, while cartridge boxes were used with flintlock firearms.

CONTROL AND GUNSMITHS' MARKS (17th/18th Century): (1) Amsterdam (Holland) city control mark ca. 1600 used exclusively on the barrels of martial firearms. (2) Copenhagen (Denmark) city control mark ca. 1611-1620 found on the barrel; C surmounted by a crown denoted royal cypher of Kings named Christian. (3 & 4) London (England) city control marks ca. 1655. (5) London city control mark ca. 1685. (6) Munich (Germany) city control mark ca. 1600 represented cleric giving a blessing. (7) Worshipful Company of Gunmakers (London) proof mark of 1637; G P stood for Gunmakers' Proof. (8) London proof mark ca. 1637; V meant viewed. (9) Swedish proof mark found on gunlock ca. 1625. (10 & 11) Charleville (France) city control marks ca. 1690. (12) St. Étienne (France) city control mark used on martial locks ca. 1690. (13) Liège (Belgium [Flanders]) city control mark ca. 1685, representing a tower. (14) Vienna (Austria) city control mark of 1661. (15) Mark of gunsmith Claudio Beretta ca. 1580-1640 (Gardone, It., founder of current Beretta firm). (16) Mark of master gunsmith Peter Kalthoff of Flensburg and Copenhagen ca. 1641-1672. (17) Mark of London gunsmith William Truelock ca. 1655-1685. (18) Mark of London gunsmith I. (J) Parr ca. 1677-1710. (19) Mark of London gunsmith Joseph Stace ca. 1680. (20) Mark of master gunsmith Nicolas Bis, Madrid. (21) Mark of master gunsmith Simon Marquart, son of Siegmund Marquart (Simon the Elder), appointed royal gunsmith to Philip III of Spain in 1620. (22) Mark of gunsmith Juan Belen, appointed royal *arcubucero* to Carlos II of Spain 1680-1691; he taught Nicolas Bis, Alonso Martínez, and Luis Santos. (23) Mark of master gunsmith Diego Esquivel of Madrid ca. 1694-1732. Author's sketch, not to scale.

As far as it can be determined, the first reference to the hand mortar in seventeenth-century America appeared during King William's War when in 1694 the Maryland Colony Council ordered from the Tower of London "Ten hand Mortars . . . with one hundred hand Granadoes . . . and fuzes [fast match] with proper Wadding and directions how to Use them."[98]

Though no precise description of the hand mortars is given, they were probably of the kind invented by John Tinker (see p. 103). The Maryland Council authorized £ 250 to pay for the mortars in addition to six powder testers and suitable grenadier arms including "slung fusees [fusils] Sanguined [browned] or otherwise fited the best way to keep them from Rust & Bayonets fit for the Bore of those fusees with large Cartouch boxes to hold betwixt two or three dozn of carthrages."[99]

The Maryland Council also instructed Tower officials "to Send good hatchets," and requested that the cartridge boxes should be designed to "goe upon one belt and the Hatchet & Bayonet in two hangers upon the Same belt . . . and pouches to carry the Granadoes in."[100]

As the Maryland Colony records indicate, the plug bayonet was known in the English colonies by 1694 though it had long before transcended its initial use as a sporting accessory when in 1642 it was employed as a martial weapon by the French. English troops had been issued plug bayonets in 1662,[101] and they were first made for the Board of Ordnance in 1672.[102]

The plug bayonet was not immediately popular in English America, for hatchets and knives were preferred by colonial militia when campaigning against the Native Americans. Militia regulations usually specified the cutlass or the sword as auxiliary weapons, while various kinds of pole arms remained popular in colonial America until the eighteenth century.

Of all the seventeenth-century technological innovations contributing to European firearms evolution the most significant were the martial flintlock musket, paper cartridges, and the bayonet, for they emerged as the backbone of infantry tactics and became the mainstay of the eighteenth-century weapons system.

The adaptation of the sporting bayonet for military use was the most important innovation, however, because it rapidly emerged as the decisive factor in determining the outcome of the volatile infantry confrontation. The bayonet, as Fletcher Pratt pointed out, "made pikemen unnecessary and furnished musketeers with a weapon both for driving home an attack and for defense against cavalry, enormously simplifying the minor tactics of infantry."[103]

As a martial weapon the plug bayonet had several disadvantages. Inserted in the muzzle it rendered the weapon useless except as a pole arm or bludgeon because it could not be instantaneously fired. If the tapered handle did not fit the bore snugly, the bayonet readily fell out or was jerked from the muzzle when any attempt was made to remove it from an adversary; if it fit the bore too tight it was extremely difficult to extricate.

Numerous attempts were made to circumvent the limitations of the plug bayonet, including a dual, ring-type attachment appearing ca. 1678. The most successful improvement, however, emerged in 1687 when the renowned French military engineer Sebastien Le Prestre de Vauban (1633-1707) devised the socket bayonet.[104]

The socket bayonet had a sleeve (socket) forged to an elbow integral with the tapered, triangular blade made for stabbing rather than slashing, and it did not interfere with firing because the blade was offset from the muzzle by the elbow. The socket slipped over the muzzle and had an L-shaped locking slot which engaged a lug usually welded to the upper barrel surface about two inches from the muzzle though the lug position varied.

Vauban's sturdy, innovative socket bayonet was adopted by France in 1688 and shortly thereafter appeared in English ranks, while by 1700 it was common in most European armies.[105] The socket bayonet remained a practical, effective martial weapon for nearly two centuries. Early in the eighteenth century the socket was often provided with a locking ring in addition to the lug slot, otherwise the socket bayonet was little altered except for minor changes in the length and blade design.

The fusils mentioned in the 1694 Maryland Colony order for grenadier arms were doubtlessly similar to those issued to the North British Fusiliers in 1678. Martial fusils were initially provided with plug bayonets and subsequently used the socket bayonet, while they quickly found acceptance in the ranks because of their light weight and superiority to matchlock and snaphaunce firearms. The martial fusil reached French America with the Carignan-Salieres Regiment in 1665 and appeared in the English colonies almost 20 years later.

Even before the turn of the century the potential of the martial fusil was observed by colonists, wilderness traders, and Native Americans alike who preferred it to the heavier musket for several reasons; its popular appeal inspiring European gunsmiths to manufacture it for the commercial market. Called a *fuke* in frontier parlance, the commercial fusil varied considerably in barrel length, caliber, weight and other design characteristics owing to where it was made though typical English specimens displayed

31 inch barrels of .66 caliber (sixteen bore) and weighed seven to seven and one-half pounds.

The short, lightweight fusil was easier to carry and handle in the dense forests of North America and, being of smaller caliber, proportionately increased the number of shots available in relation to the quantities of powder and lead required for the heavier, large-bore musket. Only 12 balls were cast from a pound of lead for the English musket whereas 16 were cast for the fusil, and the smaller and consequently lighter ball required less powder; those factors significantly reducing the cost and the weight of the ammunition and both were prime considerations for travelling and hunting in the wilderness far from trading posts or other sources of supply. By 1700 the flintlock fusil had become an important article of commerce in colonial America and its influence rapidly escalated thereafter; especially in the fur trade.

Though rifling had emerged at an early period in firearms evolution it only gradually exerted its influence and by ca. 1650 two successful rifling systems appeared. The most common rifling system emulated the wide, flat lands and grooves initially introduced, though it fluctuated considerably; the width of the land equal to or nearly twice that of the groove, the groove depth varying in accordance with the idiosyncrasy of the riflesmith or his patron, and the number of grooves also determined by that criteria, though usually ranging from 7 to 10. A nineteenth-century variant currently used is known as the Enfield system of rifling.[106]

Less evident, though popular in France during the seventeenth century, was a rifling system incorporating 20 to 50 lands and grooves of equal width and depth, triangular in cross-section, and known as the polygroove system, predecessor of the so-called microgroove rifling evident in some modern firearms. The twist or pitch used in each of those innovative rifling systems ranged from almost one turn in 48 inches to one in 70 or more inches, though the former was typical. Of the two systems the flat-groove remained popular throughout Europe and it was applied to a variety of firearms.

Throughout the various stages of firearms evolution the design and construction of martial firearms was almost totally divergent from sporting and utilitarian firearms, for each was developed for specific purposes rarely compatible in practical application, though there were a few notable exceptions.

Whether long arms or handguns, martial firearms were usually heavy, cumbrous weapons designed for durability and dependability. Conversely, sporting and utilitarian firearms were comparably reliable yet often less rugged and they frequently displayed an elegance coupled with innovative design and construction techniques because they were

1   2   3

RIFLING (17th/18th Century): Left to right. (1) Polygroove (antecedent of current microgroove) rifling consisting of 20 to 50 lands and grooves of equal width, triangular in cross-section; a system used in France and the Netherlands. (2) Popular *Jäeger* rifling system of the late 17th Century employed 7 to 10 semi-circular grooves and originated in Germany. (3) German flat groove system preceded the semi-circular and polygroove systems and continued to be used; also found in the American rifle and American pistol. Author's sketch, exaggerated.

either made to order for affluent patrons or exhibited the inventiveness of the master gunsmith.

Among the seventeenth-century sporting and utilitarian weapons transcending the traditional and technological barriers to be employed by the military were the bayonet, turn-off firearms, the blunderbuss, the rifle, including some breech-loading magazine repeaters, and the versatile fusil which had the unusual distinction of first appearing as a fowling piece ca. 1640, then a light-weight martial firearm ca. 1645, and finally as a utilitarian frontier firearm ca. 1665. Significantly, the fusil continued to serve in all those forms for two centuries and remained a frontier firearm even into the twentieth century.

Of Flemish or Dutch origin the blunderbuss initially appeared in matchlock form ca. 1580, yet saw its greatest period of development in the seventeenth century.[107] By ca. 1620 the blunderbuss employed wheellock and snaphaunce ignition and emerged in England and on the Continent as a true flintlock ca. 1645. In Germany and Holland the weapon was known respectively as a *Dunderbüchse* or *Donderbus* (thunder gun); those terms subsequently anglicized to blunderbuss.

A defensive weapon fluctuating considerably in design, the blunderbuss served in the Old and New World in either a military or utilitarian capacity; its versatility making it difficult to determine which role emerged first. The blunderbuss was extremely popular with coachmen protecting their passengers from dangerous highwaymen and equally so with merchant mariners defending their lives, cargos, and ships from marauding pirates, while it was also the lethal tool of the amateur or professional assassin.

The blunderbuss was subjected to the vagaries of the natural elements and the ravages of the sea and, consequently, it early displayed brass, bronze, or copper barrels in addition to iron; the non-ferrous barrels less susceptible to rust and salt corrosion. By ca. 1600 the blunderbuss began to assume the charac-

BLUNDERBUSS (17th Century): The coaching blunderbuss depicted has a 26-inch brass barrel of 1.5 caliber and an overall length of 38½ inches. The covex lockplate is marked CRIPS, a London gunsmith active ca. 1685-1715. British Crown Copyright. Reproduced with permission of the Controller of Her Britannic Majesty's Stationery Office.

BLUNDERBUSS (18th Century): Displaying a spring-activated bayonet folded back along the barrel, the blunderbuss depicted was made ca. 1780. The barrel and furniture are brass and the stock walnut. Muzzle diameter is 1-3/16 inches and the barrel measures 14½ inches. Courtesy of the Metropolitan Museum of Art, Gift of George D. Pratt, 1925.

teristics of the martial musket rather than the wall or deck gun it initially favored, and its muzzle was either distinguished by a discernable flare or an elliptical shape. Exaggerated in the blunderbuss, the swamped or flared barrel was not unique, for matchlock arquebuses, muskets, and other firearms dating from the sixteenth century illustrate the design.

By ca. 1650 the blunderbuss barrel and stock had been considerably shortened, typical specimens displaying an overall length of 36 inches with barrels ranging between 14 and 26 inches. There were, however, considerable variations in those dimensions just as there were in bore diameter which fluctuated from one and one-eighth inches to two and one-half inches. The diameter of flared or elliptical barrels also varied, some funnel-shaped muzzles measuring up to six inches and some elliptical muzzles measuring as little as one and one-fourth by two and one-half inches. In some instances the flared or elliptical muzzle section was brazed or welded to the barrel which was separately forged.

Shortly after midcentury the blunderbuss was often fitted with a spring-activated bayonet as much as 12 inches long and provided with a positive catch to lock it in position. The bayonet was mounted atop or under the barrel and when not in use the blade folded back along the barrel.

By ca. 1675 the blunderbuss was recognized in English military circles as "very fit for doing great execution in a crowd, to make good a narrow passage, door of a house, stair-case; or in boarding a ship."[108] It was not a surprising assessment, for the customary load consisted of 20 pistol shot or buckshot backed by 120 grains of black powder; a lethal combination at the short range for which the blunderbuss was designed.

There is no doubt that the blunderbuss had emerged as a martial firearm in England prior to 1685, for in 1684 it was mentioned in "An Account of Allowance of Ordnance, etc. to H.M. Shipps." Ships of the line bearing 100 cannon were issued ten blunderbusses, eight were supplied to 90-gun ships, and five were allotted to ships carrying 70 and 80 cannon.[109]

It has been suggested that the abnormally wide, gaping muzzle of the blunderbuss gave its user a distinct psychological advantage though most anyone staring into the black maw of any firearm would respond with considerable anxiety and fear. The practical advantage of the swamped or elliptical barrel, however, was that it remedied loading difficulties on a violently jouncing coach or aboard the swaying deck or in the wind-ripped rigging of a fighting ship, because it served as a funnel for powder and shot.

Contrary to the persistent fallacy and as previously noted the blunderbuss was loaded with a measured powder charge and quantity of shot rather than an agglomeration of stones, nails, or scrap iron, because if such objects lodged in the bore there was an excellent chance that both blunderbuss and user would be blasted into oblivion by the explosive force of the propellant gases trapped in the barrel.

According to seventeenth-century ballistics theory, based more on conjecture than scientific investigation, the swamped or elliptical blunderbuss muzzle spread the shot in a wide pattern, mowing down anything in its path. Tests conducted in 1955 dispel that venerable hypothesis, demonstrating that the shape of the muzzle had no relationship to the performance of the shot, for once it passed true bore diameter it dispersed at a given rate with the pattern spreading wider the farther it travelled.[110]

Admirably suited to its varied tasks, the blunderbuss in its time can be compared to the legendary sawed-off shotgun popularized by lawmen and desperados of the nineteenth and twentieth century, though the latter is a much more efficient instrument.

The blunderbuss is surrounded by as much pervasive historical myth as the log cabin, fixed in the minds of generations of Americans as the creation of eighteenth-century Appalachian pioneers braving the perils of the frontier, and while it is true that many of them built log cabins they were introduced in North America by Swedish colonists in 1638. Likewise, the blunderbuss until recently has been described in much of our literature as the dependable, ubiquitous companion of the indomitable Pilgrim who effectively used it to put meat on the trestle table and fear into the heart of anyone so bold as to seriously challenge the sanctified Anglo-Saxon hearth.

While a number of English Separatists had lived in exile in Holland prior to their New World adventure, the blunderbuss had not then emerged there or in England in sufficient numbers to be plentiful nor in the form by which it is presently recognized; and if the Pilgrims knew of the blunderbuss there is no reason to believe that they would have preferred a strictly defensive firearm to more practical firearms which could be used for hunting as well as defense.

No archival or archaeological evidence has yet surfaced to show that the blunderbuss was known or popular in New England prior to the eighteenth century. What is believed to be the first reference to the blunderbuss in North America is found in a 1678 Maryland Colony inventory listing one in a total of 791 firearms, while a 1693 St. Augustine inventory revealed a pair of flintlock blunderbusses (see p. 116).[111]

Seventeenth-century European technological innovation was basically stimulated by necessity and the increasingly important role performed by the emerging scientific societies, for they encouraged

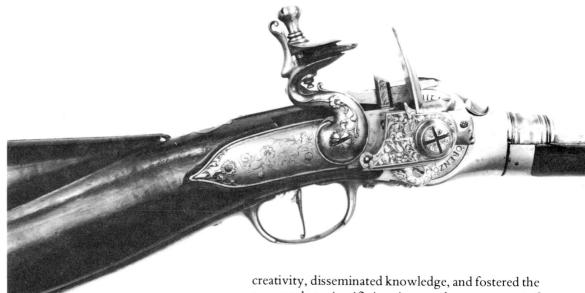

MAGAZINE BREECH-LOADER (17th Century): Turning a lever located opposite the lock operated the breech of the Michele Lorenzoni repeater depicted, delivering the powder charge and the ball from individual buttstock magazines. This flintlock specimen was made ca. 1690 and the .52 caliber barrel is 35½-inches long.

The close-up of the Lorenzoni breechloader delineates the maker's name engraved in the circular breech. Note the delicate scroll and foliate engraving on the lock and breech plate. Such firearms reflect the advanced technological design capabilities and craftsmanship exemplified by 17th Century European gunsmiths. Courtesy of the *Tøjhusmuseet*, Copenhagen.

creativity, disseminated knowledge, and fostered the concept that scientific inquiry was the cornerstone of future technological expansion. In England the Royal Society was founded in 1662, and four years later the *Académie Royale des Sciences* (Royal Academy of Sciences) was established in France.

That firearms technology had certainly progressed during the seventeenth century is represented not only by the evidence thus far presented, but by the radical theoretical concept advanced by one Palmer and recorded in the "Transactions of the Royal Society, 1663-1664." Whether Palmer originated the imaginative concept is moot, though he described a firearm able "to shoot as fast as it could be and yet be stopped at pleasure, and wherein the motion of the fire and bullet within was made to charge the piece with powder and bullet, to prime it, and to pull back the cock."[112]

Palmer thereby set forth the idea that the energy generated by the ignition of the powder charge could be harnessed to operate a firearm mechanism; a revolutionary hypothesis resurrected in the late nineteenth century and exemplified by the various gas-or-recoil-operated automatic and semi-automatic firearms then emerging and currently evident.

Though technology had certainly progressed to the point where the theory introduced by Palmer could have been applied, it was regarded by skeptics as simply impossible, and that negative attitude was a major factor in suppressing the exploitation of advanced weapons systems, as well as progress in contiguous and unrelated fields of technology, for negativism consistently engendered extreme reluctance on the part of government, industry, and individuals to risk substantial capital in the development of innovative technology.[113]

During the latter half of the seventeenth century a number of improvements were seen in firearms earlier developed and the trend toward improvement seldom faltered thereafter despite many obstacles. Bologenese master gunsmith Giacomo Berselli, active in Rome ca. 1660-1672, improved the Kalthoff breech-loader with an innovative magazine.[114] In the Berselli design and subsequent variations both magazines were located in the buttstock. With the muzzle pointed down, the ammunition was gravity-fed into a vertically-mounted, circular breech rotated by a handle opposite the lock; the breech provided with a shallow recess for the ball and a deeper one for the powder.

Turning the handle rearward activated a cam which closed the priming pan as it was simultaneously primed from a small reservoir integral with the battery and also operated an arm positioning the cock at half-cock. Returning the handle picked up a ball from the butt magazine, deposited it in the shallow breech recess, and carried it to the concave barrel face; the ball slightly oversized to prevent it from fully entering.

The action of the handle also drew the breech to the powder magazine and the charge was deposited in the deep breech recess serving as the chamber. It was then aligned with the ball in the barrel face. The priming and loading cycles were completed when the handle was returned to its original position, and the firearm was discharged in the conventional fashion.

Berselli's design was also applied to pistols, and on March 3, 1664, London gunsmith Abraham Hill patented a similar breech-loader "for small shott, carrying seven or eight charges of the same in the stocke of the gun."[115] The Berselli design is also attributed to Florentine gunsmith Michele Lorenzoni (fl. 1684-1733) who served as royal gunmaker to Kurfurst Johann Georg III of Saxony.[116]

Firearms closely related to the Berselli system were produced in London by the obviously talented though enigmatic gunsmith John Cookson (fl. 1686-1700).[117] Bartolomeo Cotel (fl. 1660-1740) also made magazine repeaters similar to those devised by Berselli and Lorenzoni, while design variations continued to be produced until the early nineteenth century.[118]

The first example of a pivotal breech firearm was probably invented by London gunsmith John Bicknell (fl. 1660-1680), personal gunmaker to Charles II.[119] In the Bicknell design the chamber was separate from the barrel. The rear of the chamber was attached to an extremely long lever serving as the trigger guard which, when pressed down and forward, withdrew and elevated the chamber for loading. A simple mechanism, its primary disadvantage was improper obturation because the pivotal chamber was merely butt-joined to the barrel. Prolonged use loosened the juncture and the powder gases escaped, not only presenting a danger to the shooter but reducing the velocity and therfore the range and striking energy of the ball.

Enter again Abraham Hill who was granted another patent in 1664 for "a new Way of making of a gun or pistoll, the breech whereof rises upon a hinge by a contrivance of a motion from under it, by which it is alsoe let downe againe & bolted fast by one and the same motion."[120] Hill was certainly an enterprising if not an exceptionally skilled gunsmith, for in the same year he patented a flintlock repeater of Berselli's design he received another for a flintlock breech-loader suspiciously similar to Bicknell's design; doubtlessly aware that he was protected by law if challenged.

Mainz gunsmith Peter Duringer (fl. 1680-1685) also produced a pivotal-breech firearm, though the design was a radical departure from Bicknell's.[121] In the Duringer system the powder chamber was hinged to the rear of the breech. The breech was joined to the barrel by an innovative screw thread arrangement; the threads interrupted to facilitate unlocking the breech which was accomplished by pulling forward on the barrel while sharply twisting the breech. The hinged chamber was simutaneously pivoted upward, the powder and the ball loaded in that order.

Unless contrary evidence is forthcoming, Duringer can be credited with inventing the interrupted screw thread; a technological concept revived in the nineteenth century and currently applied in industry as well as in the breech design of most modern forms of artillery, including the so-called recoilless rifle developed in World War II and currently in use.

Duringer's breech-loader featured several other design innovations which had previously appeared, including the folding bayonet hinged to the barrel, a combined matchlock and flintlock, and an open buttstock handgrip at the comb which was used when opening the breech.

The desire to improve firearms was also amply demonstrated in the quest for more powerful explosive concoctions and the search produced positive results not immediately appreciated. While there had been no radical change in gunpowder since the introduction of the corning process early in the fifteenth century, improved manufacturing techniques during the late seventeenth century produced a propellant suitable for loading, priming, and cartridge-making, thus eliminating the inconvenience of carrying a priming flask and a loading flask except among riflemen who continued to use coarse-grained powder for loading more from tradition than any rational scientific principle.

Giuliano Bossi, noted for his investigations into the history of superimposed-charge firearms and the innovations he produced, also experimented with black powder, adding to the simple ingredients an agglomeration of antimony, *aqua fortis,* mercury, oil

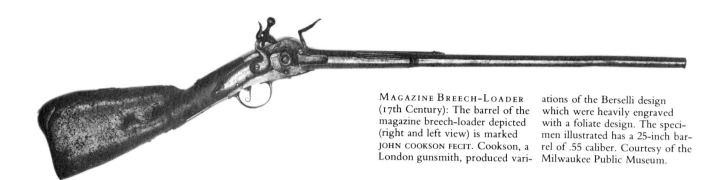

MAGAZINE BREECH-LOADER (17th Century): The barrel of the magazine breech-loader depicted (right and left view) is marked JOHN COOKSON FECIT. Cookson, a London gunsmith, produced variations of the Berselli design which were heavily engraved with a foliate design. The specimen illustrated has a 25-inch barrel of .55 caliber. Courtesy of the Milwaukee Public Museum.

MAGAZINE BREECH-LOADER (17th Century): This left side view of the Cookson breech depicts the loading handle with its grotesque mask engraving and the magazine gate is open. Powder was loaded in the round, upper opening and ball in the lower; each gravity-fed into the breech when the loading handle was rotated. Courtesy of the Milwaukee Public Museum.

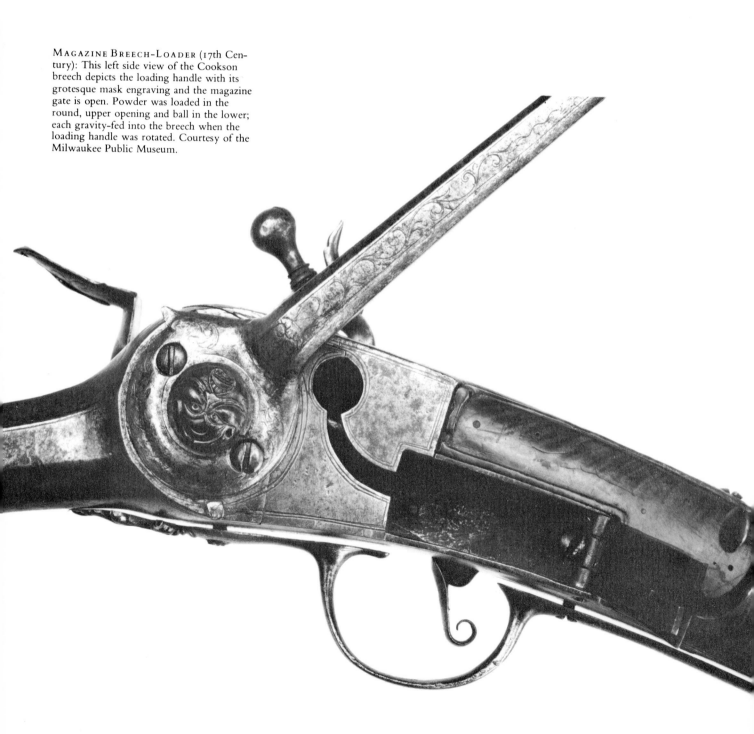

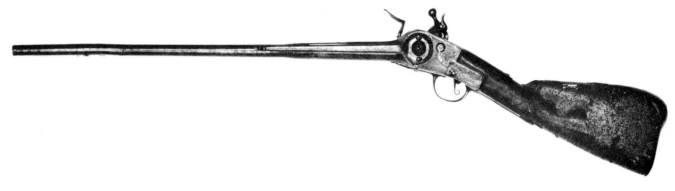

PIVOTAL CHAMBER BREECH-LOADER (17th Century): The breech-loading mechanism depicted was invented by John Bicknell ca. 1660. Depressing the trigger guard raised the pivotal breech for loading. The original firearm, in the Tower of London, displays a 49-inch barrel of .64 caliber. The trigger guard catch is located beneath the stock wrist. Author's sketch.

of tartar, powdered gold, and sal ammoniac (ammonium salts) to make what in 1659 he appropriately described as "The Fart of the Devil."[122]

Though Bossi's flatulent formulae failed to fortify gunpowder, he is believed to have inadvertently discovered fulminate of gold or what Samuel Pepys recorded in his *Diary* on November 11, 1663, as *arum fulminans;* a concoction he described as producing "a blow like a musquett." Shortly thereafter Johann Kunckel, a German seeking to improve gunpowder, apparently stumbled upon a method for making fulminate of mercury.[123]

In 1664 the Royal Society of London conducted a number of experiments comparing fulminating compounds to gunpowder, discovering that they were distinctly more volatile. Often shattering test weapons, fulminates displayed a high sensitivity to friction, heat, and shock with the susceptibility to the latter so great that detonation was readily accomplished by a sharp blow. Thus fulminates emerged as radically innovative chemical explosives ignited by spark as well as a percussive blow.

As fulminate experiments diminished in England because of the unstable characteristics of the explosive compounds, the pace accelerated in France. Parisian chemist and pharmacist Nicolas Lemery (1645-1715) probed the properties of various fulminates, though he was forced to flee to England in 1683, a victim of his Calvinist beliefs. Converting to Catholicism three years later he returned to Paris where from 1712 to 1714 the Royal Academy of Sciences fostered his work.[124]

After ca. 1650 the inordinate demand for firearms was largely responsible for the rapid evolution of improved manufacturing techniques and the gradual emergence of European gunsmithing from a predominantly cottage or household craft to a viable, increasingly specialized industry concentrated in a separate shop or what could be termed a factory. Innovative manufacturing techniques were particu-

larly evident in the Netherlands armament industry where in Amsterdam and Utrecht triphammers were operated by horse-driven machinery to make barrel skelps shortly after midcentury.[125]

Netherland gunsmiths had also devised hardening techniques for such critical lock components as the mainspring, battery spring, cock, battery, and sear; the process similar to cementation (see p. 17) and considered to be an early manifestation of case-hardening.[126] The parts to be treated were placed in a clay crucible containing salt, vinegar, soot, oxhoof, ramshorn, and ground glass though the ingredients often varied. The crucible was then fired at a high and precise temperature for a predetermined time, permitting the parts to absorb the mixture; thus they were less inclined to break under the stress factors produced in normal operation.

The most revolutionary seventeenth-century technological innovation applied to firearms, however, was an optical scientific instrument with the ability to magnify objects at various distances: the telescope.

Though the invention of the telescope is usually attributed to the Dutchman Hans Lippershey of Middleburg in 1608 it is believed to have first appeared in England or Italy somewhat earlier.[127] Popularized in scientific circles by the gifted astronomer, mathematician, and physicist Galileo (1564-1642) who also delved into the rudimentary science of ballistics, the telescope was the progenitor of the versatile microscope, and prior to the end of the century it was suggested for use as a sight for firearms.

The telescope early suffered from two flaws: (1) body construction, and (2) lens manufacture. Improvement in body construction came ca. 1640 when the lenses were incorporated in wooden tubes with coarse threads turned on a mandrel lathe, though not until John Dolland (1706-1761) of London perfected the thin, soldered sheet brass tube was it possible to make the telescope body in any practical length or diameter.[128]

The lenses used as the eyepieces and the objectives in the telescope early came from Murano, then the glass-making center of Italy. The lenses were initially moulded into concave glass discs which were ground and polished on crude mirror-polishing lathes. In 1646 Ippolito Francini (?-1653), a Florentine lens grinder employed by the Medici family, devised a superior lathe incorporating a horizontal hand crank which, via a belt arrangement, turned a vertical spindle supporting a concave grinding and polishing head.[129]

Francini's lathe was improved by Eustachio Divini (1620-1695) of Rome who also introduced an innovative lens grinding technique.[130] It was Guiseppi Campani (1635-1715) of Rome, however,

who radically improved the technique ca. 1660-1664 when he invented a lathe which ground and polished lenses directly from flat glass discs rather than the moulded concave discs previously used, and Campani's lenses were vastly superior to any made otherwise for many years.[131]

With the proliferation of telescopes employing superior lenses it was not long before telescopic sights appeared. What might be the first description of a telescopic sight is found in Francesco de Lana's 1684 manuscript *Magister Naturae et Artis*. Conclusive proof, however, came in 1702 when Johannes Zahn of Nuremberg recorded in his *Oculus Artificialis Teledioptricus* a telescopic sight with four concave lenses interposed by a plain glass disc with an aiming dot engraved in the center; an innovation currently evident.[132]

No less a personage than Frederick the Great, King of Prussia, recorded in his diary for 1737 that he used a rifle mounted with a telescopic sight at a shooting match; his believed to be the first documented use of an optical sight and, significantly, it was on a rifle.[133] Rifles, because of their accuracy and greater range, were ideally suited for telescopic sights. The use of telescopic sights in the seventeenth and eighteenth century was rare and they were generally regarded as scientific curiosities rather than practical shooting accessories until the mid-nineteenth century.

Blade-type front sights made of brass had become popular by ca. 1675, though silver blades were prominent on elegant sporting firearms. Blade sights were often mounted on the barrel band in martial firearms, but in some instances the bayonet lug was used as an aiming reference, because as yet smoothbore martial firearms were pointed rather than aimed.

In German and Scandinavian martial firearms the most common method of drawing the shooter's attention was a narrow groove cut into the surface of the breech plug tang, while some sporting firearms employed a pointed or oval ridge integral with or brazed to the breech. A peep sight variant emerged for rifles in the Netherlands, consisting of a vertical plate dovetailed into the breech and laterally adjusted for windage by a screw. The plate had a round aperture, and finer sighting was achieved by mounting a thin sheet of metal with a smaller hole over the aperture.

In France ca. 1680 some pistols and fowling pieces were provided with front sights, though rear sights were conspicuously absent. Instead, the eye was drawn to the front sight by a flat rib nearly extending the entire barrel length; an innovation which became popular on many fine English sporting guns during the early nineteenth century and it is currently evident on a variety of firearms. If any sight

LENS-GRINDING LATHE (17th Century, ca. 1665): This crude though improved version of the early lens-grinding lathe was devised by Florentine artisan Ip-

polito Francini who made lenses for Galileo. The concept of using optical sights for firearms originated in the late 17th Century. Author's sketch.

was found on late seventeenth-century Spanish fowling pieces it was a front sight.

There appeared in Prussia ca. 1698 another though as yet obscure military innovation which distinctly enhanced the stolid musketeer's ability to deliver an even more devastating fusillade, for it was then that aggressive Leopold I (1676-1747), Prince of Anhalt-Dessau, issued flexible wrought iron rather than wooden ramrods to his infantry and concomitantly modified the tedious loading drill. The iron ramrod, combined with fewer loading movements, gave Leopold's infantry a decisive advantage because they could deliver four shots to every three discharged by their adversaries; an advantage apparent for 50 years and materially contributing to Leopold's victory at Mollwitz in 1730.[134]

Anticipated by Martin Merz ca. 1475 (see p. 26), the use of the iron ramrod virtually eliminated the problem of broken wooden ramrods plaguing generations of foot soldiers. The widespread acceptance of the iron ramrod and linear tactics in the eighteenth century, coupled with the use of the socket bayonet and paper cartridges, inordinately increased the efficacy of the infantryman and the customary slaughter characterizing warfare escalated to even greater proportions.

The First American Gunsmiths

The influence of the gunsmith and the production of firearms on nearly every aspect of colonial endeavor in North America cannot be overstated, and that pervasive influence continuously escalated following the colonial era; yet gun-making has been one of the most neglected fields of study in the broad development of the remarkable techonomic system currently prevailing in the United States.

Among the many Europeans arriving in sixteenth-and-seventeenth-century North America were a cadre of able, industrious craftsmen initiating a technological legacy deeply rooted in the Old World and continuing to flourish, contributing immensely to the rapid growth of the New World. From armorer to wheelwright those enterprising and highly skilled artisans established the foundation for our presently preeminent techonomic culture.

Of all the creative craftsmen identified with colonial America the gunsmith can be considered foremost among them, for he frequently labored with the most basic hand tools under the most primitive conditions to fashion or repair a complex and inordinately vital commodity needed for survival in a pristine and generally hostile environment.

Though the Spaniards had established arms-making facilities in Cuba and Mexico during the late sixteenth century and thereafter, they were primarily devoted to casting cannon. The few firearms made or repaired were martial matchlocks and, consequently, the skills of the gun-founder, military armorer, blacksmith, and Native Americans recruited for the work cannot be equated with those of the gunsmith proper. Unfortunately, available translations of documents pertaining to that early phase of Spanish imperialism in North America are mute concerning the gunsmithing craft.

Like their Spanish predecessors the Dutch, English, French, and Swedes arriving in North America initially relied on military armorers and blacksmiths to make and repair firearms or other weapons, and during that climactic period skilled technicians were few and widely scattered, while in many instances the names and the activities of those artisans have been lost to history.

As far as it can be determined there were no gunsmiths or arms-making facilities in the English colonies prior to 1630 or in Dutch America before 1646, nor do available records indicate that the Swedes participated in any gun-making activity. In New France, however, at least two gunsmiths were active before 1625.

Antoine Natel, a *serrurier* (lock-maker), repaired firearms for Champlain's 1608 expedition and died in November of the year.[135] And in his journals Champlain also referred to an unidentified *serrurier* working in Quebec in 1620.[136] Unless other data are unearthed Natel can be considered the first gunsmith active in North America.

It is possible that English blacksmith James Read repaired firearms at Jamestown in 1607 though no concrete evidence supports that contention.[137] Nor can it be ascertained if firearms were repaired by Moses Fletcher of Sandwich, the first Pilgrim blacksmith.[138] It is known, however, that the Plymouth Company hired London armorer William Pitt who arrived on the *Fortune* in November, 1621; yet there is no record of his activities and he either died or left Plymouth Colony prior to 1627.[139]

Available documentation indicates that Eltweed Pomeroy of Devonshire was the first English gunsmith established in North America.[140] In 1630 Pomeroy founded a gunsmithery and family gunsmithing dynasty at Dorchester, Massachusetts Bay Colony, and he was active there until 1635 when he moved to Windsor, later Connecticut Colony. Pomeroy returned to Dorchester in 1670 and died there a year later. His sons Eldad and Medad were also gunsmiths as were most Pomeroy males thereafter. The Pomeroy gunsmithing dynasty, one of several to emerge in and transcend the colonial era, produced an unbroken line of gun-makers flourishing for 219 years, terminating in 1849 with the death of Lemuel Pomeroy, Jr., at Pittsfield, Mass.

English gunsmiths Bennet and Packson made and repaired firearms on Kent Island in 1631, a year before the Maryland Colony was officially chartered.[141] And in 1632 Richard Waters founded a gunsmithery at Salem, Massachusetts Bay Colony.[142] Thomas Nash served as town and colony armorer at New Haven in 1640.[143]

James Phips started a gunsmithery on the Kennebec River to handle the growing Native American trade for the Pilgrims in 1643 and he was active there until 1663.[144] His son William, one of 26 children born of the same mother, subsequently found a fortune in sunken Spanish treasure, served in King William's War, secured a knighthood, and became royal governor of Massachusetts in 1692.

By 1650 Boston could boast three gunsmiths of record: William Davies,[145] Herman Garret,[146] and Richard Leader, one of the principles of the Saugus Iron Works.[147] Covert Barent was active as a gunsmith in Nieuw Amsterdam from 1646 to 1650,[148] while Francis Soleil began a gunsmithery there in 1655.[149]

At least 19 armorers, gunsmiths, and lockmakers were active in *Nouvelle France* prior to 1660, some arriving as independent settlers and the majority as *armurier-engagés,* contracting to serve *La Compagnie* or *Les Associes* for two years or more.[150] Curiously, the term *harquebusier* (gunsmith) rarely appears in French colonial records; rather the gunsmith was called an *armurier* (armorer) or *armurier-engagé* (contract armorer). It is possible that the distinction between the *harquebusier* and the *armurier* was made because the latter was a journeyman gunsmith who had not earned the title *harquebusier.*

Armurier Geoffroy Robert contracted with the *compagnie* for two years' service at Fort La Tour (New Brunswick) on March 31, 1642.[151] Two *armurier-engagés,* Jean Bousquet[152] and Abraham Mussy,[153] came to New France that same year; the former paid 120 *livres* per year for three years and the latter 100 *livres* per year for two years.

Armorer Anthonie LeBouesme arrived at Montreal in April, 1644, contracting to work three years for the *associes.*[154] In 1646 Barthelemy Chasteau[155] and Jean Lamaison[156] came to Acadia (Nova Scotia) and settled at Port Royal, hired as gunsmiths by fur trader Emanuel Le Borne; each receiving 160 *livres* per year for two years and they were guaranteed return passage to France.

The gunsmiths of New France often emulated the *coureurs de bois,* living and working among the Huron, Erie, and other friendly Native Americans; a somewhat perilous lifestyle because the Iroquois generally despised the French and their Native American allies.

On May 30, 1649, a now anonymous *serrurier* was captured by the Iroquois during a journey to Montreal.[157] His unknown fate probably paralleled the slow, exceedingly painful torture and death suffered by other captives and exemplified by gunsmith Jean Poisson. Poisson arrived in New France ca. 1647 and was active at Trois Rivières in 1650. Taken in 1652, his last known communication included the names of his fellow prisoners and was crudely etched with charcoal on a discarded Iroquois shield, concluding with the terse comment, "I have as yet lost only a Fingernail."[158]

The number of gunsmiths active in colonial America gradually increased after 1650 though probably fewer than 100 had arrived prior to 1700; those scattered from New France to the Carolinas in English America. And while the apprentice system originating in the Old World was retained, the guild system failed to take root because the few colonial gunsmiths were initially dispersed, of varied ethnic background, and often of opposing political and religious views.

At least one attempt was made to establish a gunsmithing guild and it occurred in New France. It failed, however, because of a schism among the members. Founded in 1676 by Pierre Gadois, Rene Fezeret, Jean Bousquet, Oliver Quesnel, and Simon Quillory, *La Corporation des Armuriers à Montreal* (The Montreal Armorers' Company) was either disbanded by mutual consent in 1681 or shortly thereafter withered from apathy.[159] A few gunsmithing associations were formed in eighteenth-century North America though they cannot be considered guilds in that they were oriented socially rather than technologically.

The conditions responsible for the absence of a guild system in colonial America also prevented the adoption of a comprehensive proof system for firearms and the European colonies never became self-sufficient in firearms manufacture. All firearms imported by the various colonial enterprises were inspected and proved by the affiliated mother country prior to shipment. Though proof regulations were established in the English colonies during the eighteenth century there was no standard system, for each colony promulgated regulations which varied considerably; thus throughout the colonial epoch the quality of the firearms made in North America was entirely dependent upon the skill and the integrity of the individual gunsmith.

The first gunsmiths arriving in North America had been taught as apprentices at the bench and the forge of Old World masters, and not only did gunsmiths bring with them their esoteric technical skills, whether exemplary or barely adequate, but the various hand tools and the few machines representing their craft.

John and Thomas Matson[160] started a gunsmithery at Boston in 1655 and Enoch Bolton was active at nearby Charlestown between 1660 and 1665.[161] John Browne served as New Jersey Colony armorer from 1664 to 1691,[162] while in 1670 Alexander Toulson established a gunsmithery at St. Mary's, Maryland Colony.[163] That same year Alexander and William Waldren were gunsmithing at Boston[164] and in 1671 John Odlin started a shop there.[165]

Richard Brooks,[166] Thomas Ricks,[167] and Nathaniel Sherman[168] were also gunsmithing in Boston between 1675 and 1695, while from 1697 to 1747 Theophilus Munson practiced the craft at New Haven, Connecticut Colony.[169] Gunsmith Ephraim Kempton[170] worked at Boston and Salem during the 1680-1685 period and, though the majority of the gunsmiths in English America were active in New England, New York, and East and West (New) Jersey, a handful established themselves in the southern colonies.

Gunsmiths John Hawkins[171] and John Jones[172] worked in Charles Town, Carolina Colony, from ca. 1685 to 1700, while Huguenot gunsmith Anthony Boureau started a gunsmithery there ca. 1695, his name mentioned the following March 10 in conjunction with "An act for the making Aliens free of this part of the Province, and for granting liberty of Conscience to all Protestants."[173]

The Native American Trade

It is perhaps ironic that two French explorers and fur traders were instrumental in encouraging foreign competition with *La Compagnie* and *Les As-socies*. Medard Chouart and Pierre Radisson (see p. 124), after failing to interest French entrepreneurs, contacted London merchants with a proposal to establish a series of trading posts far to the north of the principal French posts scattered along the St. Lawrence from the Atlantic to the Great Lakes. As a result Charles II, on May 2, 1670, granted a royal charter to "The Governor and Company of Adventurers of England Trading into Hudson's Bay;" thus formally establishing the Hudson's Bay Company.

Like the earlier French trading enterprises the Hudson's Bay Company engaged contract gunsmiths whose work primarily consisted of repairing the firearms traded to the Native Americans. Among the first company gunsmiths were Samuel Oakes,[174] Thomas Coleman,[175] and James Blaymire.[176] Oakes spent five years (1675-1680) at Albany Fort (Chechichewan) on James Bay, the company's first factory, before he was recalled to London at the company's request to make pattern trade fusils. He returned to Albany Fort under a two-year contract in 1683. Coleman worked at Albany Fort between 1680 and 1692, then joining Blaymire at the company factory on the Nelson River at Fort (now Port) Nelson. Blaymire served at Fort Nelson from 1682 to 1685.

At least five other gunsmiths of record were engaged by the Hudson's Bay Company in North America between 1675 and 1700, while in the French provinces as many as 50 gunsmiths were active during that period; the majority working in Province Quebec and New Brunswick.[177]

European rivalry continuously escalated in seventeenth-century North America, giving the Native Americans an increasingly wider knowledge of firearms and, understandably, they were willing to go to any length to procure firearms of any kind heedless of the consequences. The profitable fur

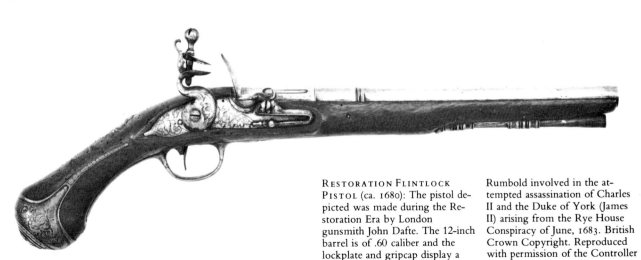

RESTORATION FLINTLOCK PISTOL (ca. 1680): The pistol depicted was made during the Restoration Era by London gunsmith John Dafte. The 12-inch barrel is of .60 caliber and the lockplate and gripcap display a foliate motif combined with grotesque figures. Dafte supplied arms to Whig extremist Richard Rumbold involved in the attempted assassination of Charles II and the Duke of York (James II) arising from the Rye House Conspiracy of June, 1683. British Crown Copyright. Reproduced with permission of the Controller of Her Britannic Majesty's Stationery Office.

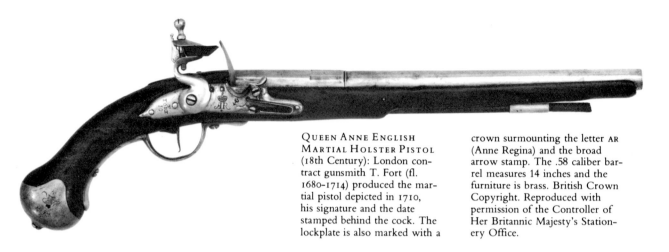

QUEEN ANNE ENGLISH
MARTIAL HOLSTER PISTOL
(18th Century): London contract gunsmith T. Fort (fl.
1680-1714) produced the martial pistol depicted in 1710,
his signature and the date
stamped behind the cock. The
lockplate is also marked with a
crown surmounting the letter AR
(Anne Regina) and the broad
arrow stamp. The .58 caliber barrel measures 14 inches and the
furniture is brass. British Crown
Copyright. Reproduced with
permission of the Controller of
Her Britannic Majesty's Stationery Office.

trade animated the commerce in firearms and related
commodities except in the Spanish dominions and
eager Dutch, English, French, and Swedish traders
sponsored by various European merchants roamed
the wilderness practically unmolested even during
hostilities, for they were recognized by the Native
Americans as the primary and often the only source
of firearms, gunpowder, and lead.

In addition the Native Americans procured firearms from settlers they plundered or killed, militia
and regular troops killed or wounded in battle, and
the many victims of the internecine power struggles
between the various nations and even among the
many tribal divisions representing their culture. The
number of firearms acquired, however, was insignificant when compared to what was initially supplied
by the frontier trader, and even that was subsequently surpassed by the enormous quantities
overtly or surreptitiously provided by the military
forces of the rival European powers.

Whatever the motives encouraging the firearms
trade, the Native Americans generally employed
firearms to their own advantage. In 1614 the
Mohawks quickly turned their Dutch muskets
against rival Delawares; particularly the Munsee inhabiting southern New York and northern Pennsylvania and New Jersey. The Mohawk ranged far from
their villages in the New York valley of that name,
reaching into the Hudson's Bay region and the
Schoharie watershed melding into the Susquehanna
River.

The Iroquoian nations in eastern New York and
Pennsylvania had received at least 400 matchlock
muskets from Dutch and English traders by 1634[178]
and, in the following quarter-century, they had ruth-
lessly driven the Erie and the Huron across the upper
Mississippi and had all but destroyed the French fur
trade. That the harried Huron were able to partially
resist the Iroquoian onslaught was because they had
received assistance from the Susquehanna in 1647
(see p. 98).

Extremely vulnerable to those aggressive Native Americans who had early procured firearms,
many of the less favored nations were soon driven
from their ancestral dominions into land occupied by
other nations and were there decimated further or
forced to adopt an alien culture in what was often an
entirely different environment; an involuntary and
monumentally tragic migration which began ca.
1635 and continued almost without interruption
until the late nineteenth century.

From 1630 to 1644 the Susquehanna of southeastern Pennsylvania and northern Maryland, then
engaged in a series of wars with the Patuxent, Pis-
cataway, and Yaomaco, caused Maryland colonists
so much grief that Gov. Cecilius Calvert proclaimed
them "public enemies" in 1642. The Susquehanna
were then living on a high mountain where "they
have a fort or square building, surrounded by
palisades, in which they reside . . . [and] have guns,
and small cannon, with which they shoot and defend
themselves, and take when they go to war."[179]

By 1663 the Susquehanna apparently had their
fill of war and ceded most of their ancestral land to
the English. On July 28, as part of that concession,
the Maryland Colony Council gave them two barrels of gunpowder, 200 pounds of lead, and a small
cannon which they subsequently employed against
marauding Cayuga and Seneca.[180]

The French supplied the Cree with flintlock
firearms ca. 1675 and they soon conquered or dispersed most of their neighbors in the Hudson's Bay
region and began ca. 1680 to harass the English at
Fort Nelson and Albany Fort. The closely affiliated
Chippewa (Ojibwa) employed French fusils to drive
their ancestral Fox enemies into Illinois and the Sioux
from the western Great Lakes into interior Wisconsin and then Minnesota, enabling the French to reës-
tablish their trading post near present La Pointe,
Wisconsin.

Because the Native Americans early displayed a
naiveté quickly lost and were willing to pay almost

any price to procure firearms and munitions they were often flagrantly exploited in the fur trade and other transactions. In 1664 the Reverend John Woodbridge of Newbury, Massachusetts Bay Colony, relocated in East Jersey and there purchased from three Lenape the vast Elizabethtown tract for a miserly "20 fathom of trayden [trading] cloth, 2 cotes [coats], 2 Gunnes, 2 Kettles, 10 barrels of Lead, 20 handful of Powder, 400 fathom of white Wampom or two hundred fathoms of Black wampum."[181]

The Native Americans of the Eastern Woodland culture were initially provided with obsolete or obsolescent matchlock arquebuses and muskets, though when the fur trade gained impetus ca. 1640 they demanded and received more sophisticated flintlock firearms. After ca. 1650 the English provided them with muskets using snaphaunce or Jacobean flintlock ignition and French traders offered true flintlock firearms. The Dutch, more amenable to Native American demands, designed a flintlock fusil especially for the trade ca. 1660.

The early Dutch trade fusil was characterized by a 50 to 63½ inch barrel with a 19 to 24 inch octagonal breech section. Caliber fluctuated between .62 and .68. The barrel was pin-fastened to the full-length stock and was provided with an open, v-notch, iron or brass rear sight and a post-type front sight. A triangular sheet brass buttplate was secured to the stock by nails rather than screws, and a wooden ramrod was used exclusively.

The Dutch trade fusil lockplate emulated the wheellock pattern representative of most early European flintlocks. There was no sideplate and the lock screws were supported instead by small brass washers distinguished by four lobes. The most striking features of the Dutch fusil, however, were the brass or iron trigger guard with its extremely long rear final which was retained for at least 60 years,[182] and the dragon or serpent sideplate which supplanted the lobed washers ca. 1675.

Because Dutch traders in the Rensselaerswyck region along the upper Hudson River were initially exempt from the States-General law forbidding the sale of firearms to the Native Americans they reaped exorbitant profits. Flintlock trade fusils sold for as much as 20 beaver pelts, while gunpowder brought the equivalent in beaver of 12 guilders a pound, i.e., about $4.00 U.S. ca. 1950.[183]

Since ca. 1650 the States-General had attempted to regulate the Native American trade, fixing prices and issuing permits. Those measures, however, were unsuccessful because they were nearly impossible to enforce in the wilderness. Under the aegis of the States-General trade fusils were priced at six guilders, pistols sold for four, and gunpowder cost six stivers per pound.[184]

Liège gunsmiths developed a trade fusil similar to the Dutch pattern and sold large quantities to European merchants for resale in the American colonies at greatly inflated prices; especially in relation to their relatively poor quality. The practice was not confined to Flemish gunmakers nor to the firearms industry.

No trade fusils with discernable English attributes have been thus far encountered by archaeologists examining early seventeenth-century trading post sites or contemporary Native American habitat, inviting the premise that prior to midcentury the English did not manufacture firearms expressly designed for the fur trade or produced very few of a pattern failing to survive the ravages of time. The English apparently relied on an abundance of obsolete or obsolescent martial firearms or purchased trade fusils from foreign sources early in the century, and it is not likely that an indigenous fusil design appeared until after 1670 when the Hudson's Bay Company entered the competitive fur trade.

An English firearm of the period 1625-1650, excavated at a Native American site in New York, displays a full-round, 49½ inch wrought iron barrel of about .59 caliber with a breech diameter of 1¼ inches. The lock is of the Jacobean pattern incorporating the dog catch and L-shaped battery.[185] While barrel length does not preclude identification as a martial musket, the caliber and the lock indicate that it is a commercial firearm, possibly a long fowler.

Of particular interest, as T.M. Hamilton notes, is that the cock of the firearm described holds a Dutch gunspall similar to the French pattern of the period, pointing out that Dutch spalls have been found in English and French firearms recovered from sites ranging from the St. Lawrence-Great Lakes region to the lower Susquehanna Valley in southern Pennsylvania; thus testifying to the widespread Dutch influence in the Native American trade.[186]

The Native American trade was of paramount economic significance in the seventeenth-century English colonies and literally and figuratively took three directions. Plymouth and Boston were the focal points of the New England trade early in the century and the English influence spread into the upper Hudson Valley and Pennsylvania after the Dutch defeat in 1665. After 1670 the Hudson's Bay Company dominated the far north trade and gradually expanded westward, while Charleston merchants directed the southern trade after ca. 1690. The Hudson's Bay Company, however, profoundly contributed to the escalating English influence among the Native Americans, for it was responsible for the development of the English trade fusil.

On March 4, 1671, less than a year after the

Hudson's Bay Company received its charter, the governor (company president) requested "That Mr. Bailey . . . treat with such persons as he thinks fit . . . for supplying 200 fowleing pieces . . . first bringing patterns of the guns to be bought unto the next committee [meeting]."[187]

The company apparently considered the preference of the Native Americans when selecting the lightweight fowling piece as a pattern for the trade fusil and it was a significant factor in gaining their confidence and respect. Mr. Bailey, doubtlessly a business agent, evidently acquitted his duty. By 1680, however, other fusil patterns apparently had been selected, for Samuel Oakes was then sent from Albany Fort to London to make "3 pattens of the 3 sorts of guns which are fit for the country."[188]

On June 21, 1680, Oakes was paid £210 for 100 trade fusils, his employer obviously satisfied with the work, for in 1683 he returned to Hudson's Bay. In 1685, after a French-inspired Cree raid destroyed a company factory on the upper bay, Oakes left for London where he resumed gunsmithing though it is not known whether he remained in company service.

The fusil patterns selected by the company in 1680 were distinguished by their barrel length: short (48 inches), medium (54 inches), and long (60 inches). As J.P. Tyrell noted, "the longest gun must be bartered for 12 beaver skins. A medium-length gun cost ten beaver, and a short gun eight beaver."[189]

Though the barrel length of the fusil was explicit there was no precise caliber and shot rather than solid ball was more frequently used. S. James Gooding mentions eight shot sizes available at company factories as of December, 1683, purchased from London purveyor John Lyons: Bristow, Calliver bore, Dutch, East India Bore, Mould goose, Pistoll bore, Plover, and Drop No. 1.[190]

Using beaver pelts as a standard the Hudson's Bay Company set the value of fusils, gunpowder, gunflints, and lead at its scattered wilderness factories in 1689, following the prevailing Dutch rates, for the Dutch remained active in the fur trade even after New Netherland had been absorbed into the English sphere. At the time Dutch traders charged two pelts for a fusil and one purchased eight pounds of gunpowder, while 40 pounds of lead sold for the same.[191]

The contemporary French trade fusil sold for five plews, equal to 30 *livres* ($6.00 U.S. ca. 1950), and four pelts bought eight pounds of gunpowder, while three purchased 40 pounds of lead.[192] Though French fusils were generally more expensive than Dutch or English, rates frequently fluctuated among the competitors and even between non-competitive factories owing to supply and demand, tariffs, transportation costs determined by the distance of the factories from ports-of-entry, and the quality of the pelts. Oddly enough the Dutch disregarded pelt quality as a trade criterion.

By ca. 1680 the French trade fusil had developed certain characteristics distinguishing it from earlier specimens, supporting the contention that the French had then initiated the manufacture of fusils rather than relying on Dutch or Flemish imports. French trade fusils enjoyed widespread distribution by 1700, as indicated by specimens recovered from archaeological sites ranging from northern Canada into western Alabama via the Great Lakes and the Mississippi Valley.

TRADE FUSIL FLINTLOCK (ca. 1680): Excavated from a Yuchi gravesite in Alabama, this lock is from a French trade fusil and has no tumbler or frizzen bridle. French trade fusils were widely distributed in the Mississippi Valley region during the late 17th Century and thereafter. Courtesy of the Museum of the Great Plains, Lawton, Okla.

(17th/18th Century): Top. Brass serpent sideplate found on Dutch, English, and French trade fusils ca. 1675 and thereafter. Second row, from left. Variants of the so-called Chevrolet design found on the trigger bow of French trade fusils after ca. 1720. Third row, from left. 1 & 2 are variations of the snowflake design found on the wrist escutcheon (thumbplate) and buttplate finial of English trade fusils ca. 1730- 1760. 3 & 4 are respectively the potted plant mark found on the buttplate finials and front trigger guard finials of French trade fusils ca. 1685-1730 and the bow and quiver with club mark featured on the buttplate finials of French trade fusils ca. 1730-1760. Bottom. Mark of London gunsmith Thomas Henshaw (fl. 1740) found on trigger bows of English trade fusil fragments unearthed at Fort Frederica, Ga. Author's sketch, not to scale.

Prior to ca. 1675 there was no standardization apparent in the design of the trade fusils produced in Europe and the affluent proprietors of the various fur companies placed little emphasis on quality. With increasing competition late in the century, however, quality was somewhat improved though standardization was minimal; primarily reflected in the decorative motif of the furniture (mountings).

Studies undertaken by Hamilton reveal that the French trade fusil of the late seventeenth century was made in two grades: poor and standard. There is however, a possible third grade which Hamilton describes as above average, comparable in quality to the popular European sporting fusil.[193] Consequently it is difficult to determine whether the "above average" fusil was made for the general trade or specially purchased to be given to certain Native American leaders to induce them to deal exclusively with the French.

The typical French trade fusil distributed from ca. 1680 to ca. 1730 incorporated the true flintlock. The .50 to .69 caliber wrought iron barrel ranged from approximately 36 to 53 inches and displayed an octagonal breech of almost ten inches. The full-length stock was pin-fastened to the barrel and had a relatively straight comb and belly. Like most of the furniture the buttplate was iron, secured by two or three screws, and had a long upper finial extending into the comb. The finial was lightly engraved with what Hamilton has described as a potted plant design.[194]

A bead-type front sight was usually provided and in some fusils the v-notch rear sight was forged integral with the breech. The bottom of the trigger guard bow was also lightly engraved, illustrating what is now termed a Chevrolet design because it is similar to the popular trademark employed for years by the Chevrolet Division of General Motors Corporation.[195]

The fusil lock had no tumbler or battery bridle, was secured by two screws, and displayed a rounded gooseneck cock and lockplate. The rear of the lockplate terminated in a rather sharp point and had a slight bow-like configuration at the bottom profile. The sideplate was usually cast-brass with a foliated, pierced design. The French fusil, like the Dutch and English, displayed numerous design variations throughout the century.

That the Native Americans came to recognize quality fusils is attested to by Baron de Lahontan who in 1685 noted a Huron warrior bitterly complaining that "The French give us fusees that burst and lame us."[196] Though there were extenuating circumstances in some instances it was often a legitimate complaint, for unscrupulous arms merchants sold poor quality fusils to equally unethical trading companies.

French trading companies apparently ignored Native American complaints or found them unjustified, for as Carl P. Russell has indicated there was little subsequent improvement in the average French fusil, pointing out that as late as 1795 the Spanish proprietors of the Upper Missouri Company received similar complaints about the French fusils they traded to the Omaha on the Platte River in Nebraska.[197]

Initially unaware of the consequences, the Native Americans frequently loaded their firearms with small stones or bits of metal scrap when lead was scarce; a dangerous practice and probably one reason for the continuing complaints about fusils "that burst and lame us." Improper loading or poor quality firearms, however, were not always the cause for bulged or shattered barrels because they often ruptured when subjected to extreme cold for prolonged periods; freezing often altering the molecular structure of the wrought iron.

As far as it can be determined there is no seventeenth-century precedent for the previous statement, however, it is supported by an entry in the diary of nineteenth-century frontier artist Rudolph Frederick Kurz who in 1851 reported that hunters "very often [were] wounded on the face and hands by the bursting gun barrels, which, especially when the weather is extremely cold are shattered as easily as glass."[198] Kurz was referring to Native American and frontier buffalo hunters; the former still using flintlock trade fusils.

The various trading companies dealing with the Native Americans, except the Hudson's Bay Company, purchased fusils from arms merchants who dealt with independent gunsmiths under short term contracts which were subsequently renewed or extended if production was maintained. The method employed by the Hudson's Bay Company in procuring firearms differed from that used by its competitors and remained virtually unchanged from ca. 1675 to 1875.[199]

The number of fusils made for the Hudson's Bay Company was determined by a committee and based on projections of factory requirements for the forthcoming year; a determination which also regulated the number of contract gunsmiths employed. The number of London gunsmiths under company contract varied, reaching as many as 40 in peak years, and the company also hired arms inspectors who viewed all contract firearms for serviceability.[200]

Between 1675 and 1775 the company bought an average of 480 fusils annually, though the figure occasionally reached 1,000 and included some pistols.[201] Additional firearms were procured for the use of factory personnel and the crews of the many ships carrying the company flag; a commercial innovation reducing transportation costs and enabling the company to remain competitive despite sporadic price wars and other common cutthroat business tactics currently evident.

Once viewed by the company inspectors the trade fusils were sent to company warehouses and crated for shipment. The weather at Hudson's Bay, especially the condition of the ice pack, determined when the fusils could be shipped and when they were made. Most purchase orders were placed in December so the fusils arrived at the warehouses in late April or early May in time to reach the factories after the late summer thaw in August.[202]

Independent traders competing with the established trading companies frequently charged for their goods as much as the commerce would bear. Though exploitation undoubtedly existed, the cost of the fusil and other trade goods was dictated by competition and, in some instances, legislation; consequently there is no reason or trustworthy evidence supporting the persistent legend that Native Americans were required to provide beaver plews equal in height to the full length of a fusil in order to procure one.[203]

Few Native Americans were gullible enough to pay an outrageous price much less barter furs equal to the height of a fusil, for they often shortened the barrel for easier handling and to reduce its weight, and none of those practices was necessary when dealing with the Hudson's Bay Company because they were offered fusils with three barrel lengths.

Most of the Native Americans remaining in New England and those of the Hudson Valley were dissatisfied with the obsolete or obsolescent firearms offered them by English traders late in the seventeenth century. In 1693 Gov. Benjamin Fletcher of New York Colony, known among the Iroquois as Great White Arrow, attempted to present a number of their chiefs with heavy flintlock muskets; relics of King Philip's War. They indignantly refused the gift. Fletcher, aware of the possible consequences, hurriedly requested of the Committee of Trade in London "200 light fuzees for a present from their Majesties to the Five Nations of Indians; they will not carry the heavy firelocks . . . being accustomed to light, small fuzees in their hunting."[204]

Among the goods distributed in 1694 to the "Mohaques, Onedes, Onodages, Cayouges, and Senekes within the River Indian at Albany . . . [were] 50 guns as the Traders have from Liege, the barrel of 4½ foot long which used to cost at Amsterdam about eight stivers the foot, and the lock with all that belongs to its [sic] use to cost there twelve stivers."[205] Whether the fusils referred to were purchased from Flemish makers or produced by London or Birmingham makers after the Flemish pattern remains unknown.

As European rivalry continued unabated in colonial America the procurement of firearms and munitions was less difficult for the Native Americans, though adequate supplies of powder and lead remained a paramount concern. The Native Americans recovered bullets and shot from the game or enemies they killed when it was feasible, commonly reduced powder charges, and frequently split their bullets in half; neither of the latter measures conducive to accuracy, range, or striking energy, and probably accounting for the undeservedly poor reputations they acquired as marksmen.

All Native Americans were not poor shots. Even during the early colonial period a number of them were noted for their keen shooting ability. Thomas Morton, painted as that "petie-fogger of Furnefell's Inne" by Gov. William Bradford of Plymouth Colony, taught many of his Native American cohorts how to shoot, and their skill generously contributed to his larder, profitable fur trade, and possibly to a number of his devious schemes.[206]

Once the Native Americans had procured firearms they, like the colonists, faced maintenance and repair problems, although they normally ignored the former. The Narragansetts had made limited progress in learning to repair firearms by 1675 and during King Philip's War and subsequent conflicts Native American forges were prime military objectives.[207]

Surviving trade fusils with several inches crudely hacked from the barrel indicate that rudimentary metal work was accomplished at Native American forges and they mended cracked or broken gunstocks with animal or vegetable glue used in conjunction with wet rawhide strips which, when dried, shrunk to make an effective repair.

The majority of the Native Americans on amicable terms with the colonists relied on the skills of the frontier blacksmith, gunsmith, or military armorer when and where available. The French were especially accommodating early in the seventeenth century, providing gun repair service in Native American villages, and the Dutch and English offered the service at their trading posts. As the fur trade continued to escalate profitably, colonial civil and military officials did their utmost to provide firearms and repair service either as a means of retaining or gaining a customarily transient allegiance.

When a firearm was beyond repair most Native Americans traded for another, utilizing the metal components of the discarded weapon for various purposes. Long arms were commonly stripped (cannibalized) of useful parts which replaced broken components in other firearms when possible. Butt-plates, sideplates, heel caps, and trigger guards were often used to make hide scrapers, knives, awls, or other utilitarian implements, as well as ornaments for personal adornment.

Native Americans generally expended considerable time and effort on personal adornment and decorating their possessions. Firearms were no exception. The most common seventeenth-century embellishment was stock carving or painting, usually consisting of crudely executed animistic pictographs, though an especially favored totem compatible with their pantheistic religious philosophy was often attached to the weapon.

The pervasive impact of firearms on Native American culture beyond the Spanish dominions began early in the seventeenth century and continuously accelerated thereafter, its external effect primarily demonstrated by warfare with all its detrimental attributes. The internal effect, however, can be in one aspect compared to the English when during the reign of Henry VIII the populace abandoned the longbow and the crossbow for the less efficient firearm and archery was quickly rendered moribund. Native American dependence on firearms rather than bows is no more graphically or earlier exemplified than by the Iroquois who approached their French adversaries in 1641 begging for firearms without regard to their customary pride, pleading that they needed them to live.[208]

Toward the end of the seventeenth century the Native Americans of the Eastern Woodland and Gulf cultures had amassed a considerable number of firearms ranging in variety and efficacy from the obsolete matchlock arquebus to the compact, lightweight, flintlock trade fusil. Virginians trading with the Cherokee in the Carolinas noted a few Spanish flintlock firearms among them as early as 1673.[209] Spain not being involved in the Native American trade at the time, those firearms were probably recovered from shipwreck sites or bartered or taken from the Creeks, Catawba, Yamasee, and others who often raided the Florida provinces.

Reliable estimates indicate that at least a half million Native Americans inhabited the English and the French colonies during the late seventeenth century. The percentage of the population receiving firearms, however, is necessarily speculative owing to a dearth of surviving records and the often clandestine nature of the firearms trade. In any event it is known that from 1670 to 1689 the Hudson's Bay Company alone distributed at least 10,100 trade fusils and 100 pairs of pistols, i.e., 10,300 individual firearms in a 19-year base period.[210]

The fur industry provided an extremely lucrative market of nearly unlimited potential for firearms, munitions, and other trade goods produced in the Old and New World; a diverse market further expanding in the coming century as the rival European powers extended their boundaries by exploration and force of arms. While the economic impact of the Native American trade in colonial America cannot be adequately assessed, it is known that the value of the furs exported to the mother country from the English colonies alone had reached £16,280 by 1700 (see APPENDIX III).

The Native American trade touched practically every aspect of European culture and one indication of its powerful techonomic impact is exemplified by the fact that the manufacture of trade fusils in England rivalled martial firearms production even in wartime. In colonial America the geopolitical implications of the Native American trade alone were staggering, for unlike the gold and glory inexorably drawing the Spaniards to the New World in the sixteenth century, it was in the seventeenth century that the fur trade initially provided the impetus to push beyond the docile realm of civilization in search of unknown horizons.

The religio-political overtones responsible for seating Protestant William of Orange on the English throne during the Glorious Revolution were also evident in the ensuing War of the Grand Alliance; that part of the conflict spilling over into colonial America known as King William's War. The determined English attempt to conquer New France failed however, degenerating into a series of bloody border raids in which the Native American allies of the respective combatants proved extremely effective. In 1697 the Treaty of Ryswick terminated the war and neither England nor France achieved positive results; the American colonies returning to *status quo ante bellum*.

With the advent of the eighteenth century colonial America was again thrust into a series of sanguinary conflicts as raw wounds were once more torn open among the rival European powers. As ever, the Native Americans were swept up in the violent epicenter of that vortex and the role of the firearm continuously escalated. It was the beginning of a turbulent epoch destined to alter forever the fate of many nations and decide the future of an infant republic.

Notes

1. Paul E. Hoffman and Eugene Lyon, "Accounts of the *Real Hacienda*, Florida, 1565 to 1602," *Florida Historical Quarterly* (July 1969): 66 (hereafter cited as *FHQ*).

2. Carlo M. Cipolla, *Guns, Sails and Empires: Technological Innovation and the Early Phases of European Expansion 1400-1700* (New York, 1965), p. 33n.

3. Eugene Lyon, Ph.D., "The Trouble With Treasure," *National Geographic* (June 1976): 808.

4. James D. Lavin, *A History of Spanish Firearms* (New York, 1965), p. 47.

5. Harold L. Peterson, *Arms and Armor in Colonial America 1526-1783* (New York, 1956), pp. 25, 319-320 (hereafter cited as *Arms and Armor*).

6. Ibid.

7. Paul I. Wellman, *Glory, God and Gold: A Narrative History*, ed. Lewis Gannett (New York: Doubleday & Company, Inc., 1954), p. 101.

8. Verne E. Chatelain, *The Defenses of Spanish Florida, 1565 to 1763* (Washington, 1941), p. 56.

9. North Carolina Spanish Records Collection, Department of Archives and History, Raleigh (hereafter cited as *NC*), *Archivo General de Indias*, Seville (hereafter cited as *AGI*), 58-2-2/14, Viceroy Marquess de Mancera of *Nueva España* to the crown, Mexico, April 20, 1669, 89 fols., fol. 27.

10. Stetson Collection, P.K. Yonge Library of Florida History, University of Florida, Gainesville (hereafter cited as *SC*), *AGI* 58-2-2/15, Mancera to the crown, October 28, 1669, 35 ff., p. 14. For the references cited in *NC* and *SC* the author is indebted to Luis R. Arana, Chief Park Historian, National Park Service, Castillo de San Marcos-Fort Matanzas National Monuments, St. Augustine, Fla.

11. *SC, AGI* 58-2-2/24, Gov. Manuel de Cendoya of Florida to the crown, St. Augustine, October 31, 1671, 4 ff., p. 4.

12. *NC, AGI* 54-5-11/11, Gov. Nicolas Ponce de León of Florida to the crown, St. Augustine, May 6, 1674, 2 ff., p. 1.

13. *SC, AGI* 32-4-29/35/2, Gov. Pablo de Hita Salazar of Florida to the crown, St. Augustine, June 15, 1675, 51 ff., p. 37.

14. *SC, AGI* 54-5-/55, Salazar to the crown, March 6, 1680, 7 ff., p. 2.

15. Chatelain, p. 160, n. 23.

16. *NC, AGI* 54-15-11/71, Royal officials of Florida to the crown, St. Augustine, December 12, 1680, p. 7ff.

17. *SC, AGI* 58-2-2/38, p. 12.

18. Albert Manucy, *Artillery Through the Ages* (Washington: National Park Service Interpretive Series History No. 3, 1949), p. 25.

19. Robert Allen Matter, "Missions In the Defense of Spanish Florida," *FHQ* (July 1975): 31.

20. *SC, AGI* 58-2-2/38, pp. 2, 8; *NC, AGI* 54-5-11/111, Gov. Juan Márquez Cabrera to the crown, St. Augustine, October 8, 1683, 51 ff., p. 44.

21. *NC, AGI* 58-1-26/79, Cabrera to the crown, June 28, 1683, 21 ff., p. 8.

22. Ibid., pp. 17-18.

23. *SC, AGI* 58-2-2/38, p. 8.

24. Ibid., p. 2.

25. Ibid., 22 ff., p. 1.

26. Mark F. Boyd, "The Expedition of Marcos Delgado from Apalachee to the Upper Creek Country in 1686," *FHQ* (January 1937): 9-11.

27. *SC, AGI* 58-2-2/38, p. 22.

28. Luis R. Arana, "The Day Governor Cabrera Left Florida," *FHQ* (July 1961): 154.

29. *SC, AGI* 54-5-13/60, Royal officials of Florida to the crown, St. Augustine, December 22, 1693, 9 ff., p. 7.

30. *SC, AGI* 61-6-21/38, Count of Montellano to Don Juan de la Rea, Sevilla, June 15, 1694, 11 ff., p. 6.

31. Lavin, pp. 218-237 *passim* gives a more detailed history of Ripoll.

32. B. Calvin Jones, "A Semi-Subterranean Structure at Mission San Joseph de Ocuya, Jefferson County, Florida," (Tallahassee: Bureau of Historic Sites and Properties Bulletin No. 3, 1973): 39-43.

33. A[nthony]. D. Darling, "A Late 17th Century French Military Matchlock Musket," *The Canadian Journal of Arms Collecting,* (May 1971): 39.

34. Ibid.

35. Ibid.

36. Clement Bosson, "Saint Étienne," in *Encyclopedia of Firearms,* ed. Harold L. Peterson (New York, 1964), p. 268.

37. Ibid.

38. Bosson, "Charleville," in *Encyclopedia of Firearms,* p. 82.

39. Ibid.

40. Bosson, "Saint Étienne," p. 268.

41. Darling, p. 47.

42. Francis Borgia Steck, *Marquette Legends* (New York, 1960), p. 102.

43. Carl P. Russell, *Guns on the Early Frontiers* (New York, 1957), p. 19n.

44. Francis Parkman, *Count Frontenac and New France under Louis XIV* (Boston, 1888), p. 15.

45. Lt. Col. George M. Chinn, USMC, *The Machine Gun,* 6 vols. (Washington, 1951) 1:17.

46. U.S. Bureau of Census, *Historical Statistics of the United States* (Washington, 1961), Series Z 1-19, p. 756 (hereafter cited as *H S*).

47. Peterson, *Arms and Armor,* p. 322.

48. Charles Orr, *History of the Pequot War* (Cleveland, 1897), pp. 25-29; 36-40.

49. Peterson, p. 326.

50. Ibid.

51. Ibid., p. 327.

52. Russell, p. 40n.

53. Ibid., p. 42n.

54. George F. Willison, *Saints and Strangers* (New York, 1945), p. 295.

55. Ibid., p. 296.

56. Norman B. Wilkinson, *Explosives in History, The Story of Black Powder* (Chicago: Rand McNally & Company, 1966): 9.

57. Ibid., p. 10. As Wilkinson notes, Rising's remark was somewhat prophetic, for Wilmington, Del., became the site of the famous Du Pont powder mills early in the nineteenth century.

58. Russell, pp. 222-223.

59. Wilkinson, p. 10.

60. John C. Miller, *The First Frontier: Life in Colonial America* (New York, 1966), p. 88.

61. Ibid., p. 55.

62. William E. Woodward, *The Way Our People Lived* (New York, 1965), p. 50.

63. Eliot Wigginton, ed., *The Foxfire Book* (New York, 1972), p. 241.

64. Woodward, p. 21.

65. Peterson, p. 327.

66. Frederick Webb Hodge, ed., *Handbook of American Indians North of Mexico,* 2 vols. (Washington, 1912), 2:482 (hereafter cited as *Bulletin 30*).

67. Peterson, p. 327.

68. Col. Robert Gardner, *Small Arms Makers* (New York, 1963) pp. 249, 314, 326.

69. *H S,* Series Z 131-222; General Note, Table I, p. 746.

70. S. James Gooding, *The Canadian Gunsmiths 1608 to 1900* (West Hill, Ontario, 1962), p. 42 (hereafter cited as *Canadian Gunsmiths*).

71. W.W. Greener, *The Gun and its Development* (New York, 1967), p. 212.

72. Ibid., p. 214.

73. Dr. J.H. Mayer, "Flintlocks of the Iroquois, 1620-1687," (Rochester: Research Records No. 6, Rochester Museum of Arts and Sciences, 1943): 55.

74. Willison, p. 399.

75. Robert Held, *The Age of Firearms* (New York, 1957), p. 105.

76. Howard L. Blackmore, *British Military Firearms 1650-1850* (London, 1961), p. 32.

77. Held, p. 105.

78. Blackmore, pp. 32, 35.

79. Ibid., p. 35.

80. Ibid., p. 36.

81. Held, p. 105.

82. Clive Harris, *History of the Birmingham Gun-Barrel Proof House* (Birmingham, 1946), p. 10.

83. Blackmore, p. 37.

84. Ibid., p. 38.

85. Ibid., p. 32.

86. Ibid.

87. Ibid., p. 36.

88. Ibid.

89. Edward M. Riley and Charles E. Hatch, Jr., "James Towne in the Words of Contemporaries," (Washington: National Park Service Source Book Series No. 5, 1955): 29.

90. Claude Blair, *Pistols of the World* (New York, 1968), p. 17.

91. Ibid.

92. Ibid.

93. Herbert J. Jackson and Charles E. Whitelaw, *European Hand Firearms* (London, 1923), reprint edn., n. d., p. 59.

94. Ibid., pp. 60-66.

95. Ibid., p. 83.

96. Ibid., p. 84.

97. Peterson, *Arms and Armor,* p. 65.

98. Ibid., p. 328.

99. Ibid., pp. 328-329.

100. Ibid.

101. R.A. Pickering, "The Plug Bayonet," *The Canadian Journal of Arms Collecting* (November 1972): 121.

102. Ibid.

103. Fletcher Pratt, *The Battles That Changed History* (New York, 1956), p. 199.

104. Harold L. Peterson, "The Bayonet," in *Encyclopedia of Firearms,* p. 55.

105. Ibid.

106. Named for a rifling method developed at the Royal Small Arms Factory, Enfield Lock, Middlesex, England, established in 1804.

107. J.B. Kist et al, *Dutch Muskets and Pistols* (York, Pa., 1974), p. 34.

108. Harold L. Peterson, "Blunderbuss," in *Encyclopedia of Firearms,* p. 58.

109. Blackmore, p. 32.

110. Harold L. Peterson, "Did it Work?", *American Rifleman* (February 1955): 20-23.

111. Peterson, *Arms and Armor,* p. 41.

112. Chinn, 1:17.

113. W. Paul Strassman, *Risk and Technological Innovation: American Manufacturing Methods during the Nineteenth Century* (Ithaca, 1959) thoroughly discusses the myriad ramifications of risk factors involved in technological development, many of them applicable to the seventeenth- and eighteenth-century American and European firearms industry.

114. Blackmore, *Guns and Rifles of the World* (New York, 1965), p. 86.

115. Gardner, p. 272.

116. Blackmore, p. 86; Gardner, p. 286.

117. Blackmore, p. 87; Gardner, p. 249.

118. Blackmore, p. 86; Gardner, p. 249.

119. Blackmore, p. 62.

120. Gardner, p. 249.

121. Blackmore, p. 62.

122. Ibid., p. 45.

123. Ibid.

124. Ibid.

125. Kist, p. 36.

126. Ibid., p. 40.

127. Silvio A. Bedini and Derek J. De Solla Price, "Instrumentation," in *Technology in Western Civilization,* ed. Melvin Kranzeberg and Carroll W. Pursell, Jr., 2 vols. (New York and London 1967) 1:172-182.

128. Ibid., p. 175.

129. Ibid., pp. 173-174.

130. Ibid., p. 174.

131. Ibid.

132. Dr. Arne Hoff, "Sights," in *Encyclopedia of Firearms,* p. 299.

133. Ibid.

134. W.H.B. Smith and Joseph E. Smith, *The Book of Rifles* (Harrisburg, 1963), p. 16; Pratt, pp. 206-207, 209.

135. Gooding, pp. 2, 140.

136. Ibid., p. 2.

137. Letter to the author 13 November 1972 from J. Paul Hudson, Museum Curator, Colonial National Historical Park, Jamestown, Va., "Only one blacksmith was mentioned by name—James Read—who . . . arrived at Jamestown May 13, 1607. No record is available which informs us how long he lived in Virginia."

138. Willison, p. 439.

139. Ibid., p. 445. Pitt was not a Separatist and not until 1637 were London gunsmiths independent from the venerable Armourers' or Blacksmiths' Company.

140. A. Merwyn Carey, *American Firearms Makers* (New York, 1953), p. 96; Gardner, p. 152.

141. Carey, pp. 9, 92; Gardner, p. 145.

142. Carey, p. 130; Gardner, p. 204.

143. Carey, p. 84.

144. Carey, p. 95; Gardner, p. 151.

145. Carey, p. 27.

146. Carey, p. 43; Gardner, p. 71.

147. Carey, p. 69; Gardner, p. 113.

148. Carey, p. 6; Gardner, p. 12.

149. Carey, p. 115; Gardner, p. 183.

150. Gooding, p. 3.

151. Ibid., p. 156.

152. Ibid., pp. 5, 68-69.

153. Ibid., pp. 5, 136.
154. Ibid., p. 123.
155. Ibid., p. 78.
156. Ibid., p. 122.
157. Ibid., p. 4.
158. Ibid., pp. 4-5; 149-150.
159. Ibid., pp. 211-214.
160. Carey, p. 75; Gardner, p. 178.
161. Carey, p. 11; Gardner, p. 172.
162. Gardner, p. 27.
163. Carey, p. 123; Gardner, p. 195.
164. Carey, p. 129; Gardner, p. 201.
165. Carey, p. 90; Gardner, p. 143.
166. Carey, p. 13.
167. Carey, p. 104; Gardner, p. 162.
168. Carey, p. 112; Gardner, p. 176.
169. Carey, pp. 82, 143; Gardner, p. 138.
170. Carey, p. 64; Gardner, p. 106.
171. Carey, p. 53.
172. Carey, p. 62; Henry J. Kauffman, *Early American Gunsmiths 1650-1850* (New York, 1952). p. 56.
173. Kauffman, p. 11.
174. Gooding, p. 143.
175. Ibid., p. 80.
176. Ibid., p. 67.
177. S. James Gooding, "Gunmakers to the Hudson's Bay Co.," *The Canadian Journal of Arms Collecting* (February 1973): 20 (hereafter cited as "Gunmakers").
178. *Bulletin 30*, 1:588.
179. Ibid., 2:656.
180. Ibid., 2:654.
181. Earl Schenck Miers, *Where the Raritan Flows* (New Brunswick, N.J.: Rutgers University Press, 1964): 9.
182. T.M. Hamilton, *Early Indian Trade Guns: 1625-1775* (Lawton: Contributions of the Museum of the Great Plains, Number 3, 1968): 23.

183. Russell, p. 12.
184. Ibid., p. 13.
185. Hamilton, p. 21.
186. Ibid.
187. Harold L. Innis, *The Fur Trade in Canada* (New Haven, 1930), p. 127.
188. Gooding, *Canadian Gunsmiths,* p. 143.
189. Charles J. Keim, "Beaver Pelts and Trade Muskets," *American Rifleman* (February 1958): 27.
190. Gooding, p. 29.
191. Russell, pp. 13-14.
192. Ibid.
193. Hamilton, p. 7.
194. Ibid., p. 3.
195. Ibid., p. 13.
196. Baron de Lahontan, *New Voyages to North-America,* ed. Reuben Gold Thwaites (Chicago, 1905), p. 93.
197. Russell, p. 19, n. 25.
198. Charles E. Hanson, Jr., "The Indian Trade Fusil," *Gun Digest* (Chicago, 1959): 128.
199. Gooding, "Gunmakers," p. 19.
200. Ibid., pp. 20-21.
201. Ibid., p. 19.
202. Ibid., p. 21.
203. Keim, p. 27.
204. Russell, p. 14.
205. Ibid.
206. Willison, p. 278.
207. William Brandon, *The American Heritage Book of Indians* (New York, 1961), p. 173.
208. Gooding, *Canadian Gunsmiths,* p. 27.
209. Brandon, p. 214.
210. Gooding, p. 8.

THE THEME OF THE EUROPEAN presence in eighteenth-century North America was militant expansion primarily influenced by the strong economic growth of the fur trade, radical advances in science and technology, and an unexpected shift in the European balance of power. Providing counterpoint, however, was the evident dissatisfaction manifest toward the mother country in the English colonies and the seemingly perpetual confrontations with the Native Americans on the frontier.

The fiery dawn of that epoch saw Spain emerging from a heretofore lethargic posture in the fermenting southeast and continuing to expand in the Great Southwest; both movements given direction and impetus by zealous Philip V (1683-1746), grandson of powerful Louis XIV and in 1701 the first Bourbon to occupy the Spanish throne. That convenient albeit clouded alliance of France and Spain was violently opposed by England during the War of Spanish Succession known in North America as Queen Anne's War (1701-1714).

The Gallic influence in Spain flourished throughout Philip's progressive reign, was perpetuated by Ferdinand VI (1713-1759), and endured when the dynamic Carlos of Bourbon (Charles III, 1716-1788) became king in 1759; his reign distinguished by a series of political machinations climaxed in 1779 when Spain joined France in rendering assistance to the beleaguered English colonists struggling for independence from the imperious crown.

Throughout most of his impressive 73-year reign the immense power and prestige of Louis XIV exerted a profound and shattering impact on European affairs and also spanned the surging Atlantic. Under Louis' aegis the French in North America, preoccupied with the lucrative fur trade, advanced beyond the shimmering Great Lakes and embarked upon the mighty network of rivers serving as broad superhighways penetrating the wilderness heartland of the continent. Though *le Roi Soleil* died in 1715,

succeeded by his great grandson Louis XV (1710-1774), he had guided France to the zenith of her power and distinctly expanded her horizons in the Western Hemisphere.

After ca. 1675 the English began to exert mounting pressure toward the beckoning Appalachians and intruded in *La Florida* as well as *Nouvelle France,* meanwhile continuing to actively cultivate a profitable commerce with the Native Americans. In 1691 Plymouth Colony was absorbed by her avowed rival, the Massachusetts Bay Colony, and the Carolina Colony was divided into North and South, though Charleston remained the center of English activity in the vast southeast.

The population of English America, estimated at 250,888 in 1700, swelled to 359,763 in the following decade, expanded by a steady influx of indentured laborers, black slaves, and displaced Palatine German, Irish, Scottish, and Swiss settlers; thus further nurturing a polyglot culture earlier diversified by the Dutch, French Huguenots, and Swedes, while among them all was a continuing miscengenation also extending to the Native Americans.[1]

King William's death in 1701 saw Anne (1665-1714) placed at the helm of the realm and the beginning of the American phase of the War of Spanish Succession. The Treaty of Utrecht terminated the conflict in 1713 with what now could be called Great Britain (see p. 134) receiving the most beneficial terms, though the flammable issues remained unresolved. During the war Britain's principal asset in opposing the seemingly invincible French was the formidable John Churchill, 1st Duke of Marlborough (1650-1722), who had permanently destroyed Louis' designs on the Netherlands.

During the balance of the eighteenth century Britain was the province of the alien Hanoverian sovereigns: Georges I, II, and III. With the ascension of George I (1660-1727) in 1714 the German influence in English affairs was strongly felt on the Continent and in British America. The War of Jenkins' Ear (1739-1743), followed by the even more de-

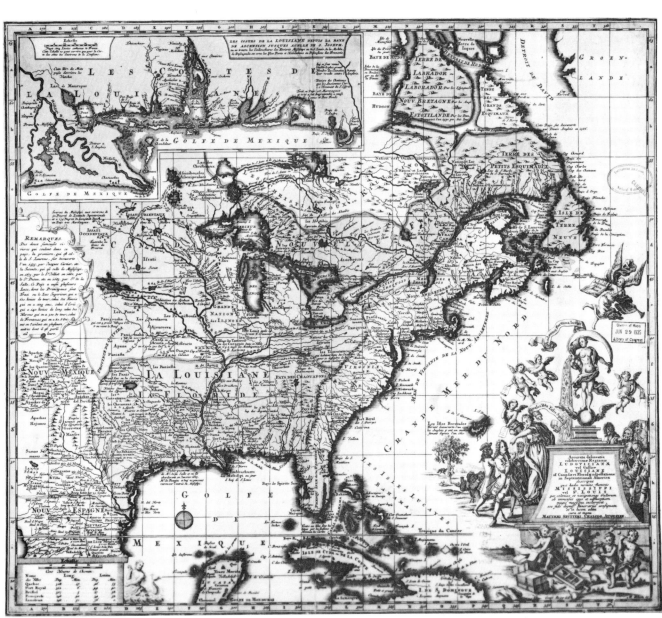

NORTH AMERICA (1734): Cartographer Matthew Seutter's 1734 map of North America delineates the English colonies, *Nouvelle France* (New France), *La Louisiane* (Louisiana territory), *La Floride* (Spanish Florida), *Nouv Espagne* (New Spain), and *Nouv Mexique* (New Mexico territory). Inset (upper left) defines the Gulf coast from the Mississippi delta to the Florida panhandle. Courtesy of the Library of Congress.

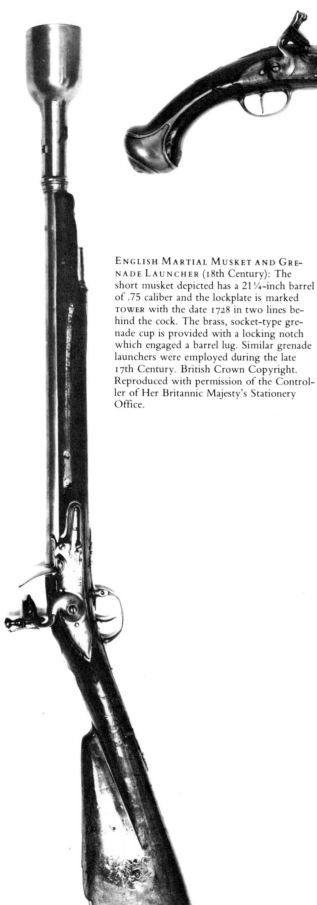

HOLSTER PISTOL (ca. 1720): Of a kind popular during King George's War, the English martial pistol depicted has a .62 caliber, 14¼-inch barrel; the barrel somewhat longer than exemplified in later pistols. This specimen was made by London gunsmith I. (J) Clarkson (fl. 1680-1740). Courtesy of the Smithsonian Institution, Washington, D.C.

ENGLISH MARTIAL MUSKET AND GRENADE LAUNCHER (18th Century): The short musket depicted has a 21¼-inch barrel of .75 caliber and the lockplate is marked TOWER with the date 1728 in two lines behind the cock. The brass, socket-type grenade cup is provided with a locking notch which engaged a barrel lug. Similar grenade launchers were employed during the late 17th Century. British Crown Copyright. Reproduced with permission of the Controller of Her Britannic Majesty's Stationery Office.

bilitating War of Austrian Succession (1744-1748), punctuated the pervasive animosity displayed toward Britain by France and Spain during the reign of George II (1727-1760); the latter conflict referred to in North America as King George's War.

Those sanguinary confrontations were also indecisive and, as ever, the colonial frontier had erupted with terrifying war cries as the European antagonists continued to exploit their Native American allies. Anglo-French relations further polarized and reached a climax shortly after midcentury, plunging both nations as well as Spain into the fiery crucible of an unwanted conflict inaugurated in North America, though destined to become the first truly global war and the final contest between Britain and France in the protracted struggle for ascendancy in the Western Hemisphere: The French and Indian War (1754-1763) or, as it was known in Europe, The Seven Years' War (1756-1763).

The conflagration spread from the Ohio Valley to continental Europe with bitter campaigns fought in India and on the high seas, eventually involving Austria and Spain as French allies. Supporting the Hanoverian cause was Portugal and, in 1756, the Prussian Iron King, Frederick the Great (1712-1786). Former prime minister William Pitt the Elder, reluctantly recalled to Parliament by George II in 1757, vigorously prosecuted the conflict with positive results.

Linear Tactics

Spawned by Gustavus Adolphus early in the seventeenth century linear tactics gradually supplanted the cumbrous *en masse* infantry formations previously characterizing orthodox European warfare. Subsequently improved and introduced in France by the estimable Marshal Henri de La Tour d'Auvergné de Turenne (1611-1675), linear tactics were used to advantage in the Dutch War (1672-1679) wherein the effectiveness of the flintlock musket was greatly enhanced by the innovative plug bayonet. Not until after 1700, however, with the widespread acceptance of paper cartridges and the

Pl. 1.

BAYONET DRILL (18th
Century): This plate
depicts French bayonet
drill insofar as affixing
the socket bayonet to
the infantry musket
(Figs. 1 to 9) and the
manner of presenting
the infantry sword for
inspection (Figs. 10 to
13). From Diderot and
D'Alembert, *L'Encyc-
lopédie, ou Dictionnaire
Raisonné des Sciences, des
Arts et des Mètiers* (Paris,
1770), *Recueil de
Planches Sur Les Sciences
et Les Arts,* Vol. I, Plate
I, p. 225: *Art Militaire,
Exercice* (The Military
Art, Exercise). Cour-
tesy of the Eleutherian
Mills Historical Li-
brary, Wilmington,
Del.

Art Militaire, Exercice.

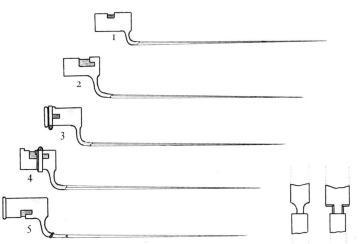

SOCKET BAYONETS (18th Century): Top to bottom. (1) M1717 French - Blade length 14½ inches, Socket length 2¾ inches, single mounting and locking slot. (2) M1746 French - Blade length 14 inches, Socket length 2¾ inches, double and parallel mounting and locking slots. (3) M1763 French - Blade length 14 3/16 inches, Socket length 2¾ inches, single mounting and locking slot with reinforcing ring and locking band. (4) M1777 French - Blade length 14 3/16 inches, Socket length 2¾ inches, single mounting and locking slot with reinforcing rings for the socket and locking band. (5) British Long Land and Short Land - Blade length 16¾ inches, Socket length 4 inches, double and parallel mounting and locking slots with reinforcing socket ring. Figures (right) depict the shape of the elbow connecting the socket with the blade. The rounded French elbow has a curved shoulder at the base of the blade. Author's sketch.

socket bayonet, did linear tactics drastically influence the efficacy of the foot soldier.

With linear tactics the principal criteria were rate of fire rather than accuracy and the decisive momentum of the savage bayonet charge. The infantry formation was predicated on the employment of two or three compressed ranks (another in reserve if manpower was available) concentrating the greatest amount of continuous firepower against an adversary.

The musket was pointed rather than aimed and fired in unison on command. At a point 50 yards or less from the enemy as dictated by the notoriously inaccurate smoothbore musket, the order to fire was executed and the shoulder-to-shoulder ranks reloaded and fired by volley to deliver as many as three fusillades if time and distance from the enemy permitted before all were swallowed up in a vicious melee of stabbing bayonets and clubbed muskets amid the horrible, deafening screams and curses of the wounded and the dying.

Despite the 20-odd precise movements prescribed for loading and firing the flintlock musket by most eighteenth-century drill, Thomas Simes reported shortly after midcentury that even the lowliest British recruit was not "to be dismissed from the drill, till he is so expert with his firelock, as to load and fire fifteen times in three minutes and three quarters,"[2] i.e., he was expected to deliver one shot every fifteen seconds; a criterion exceeded only by the Prussian infantryman (see p. 149).

Considering the state of eighteenth-century martial musket development, the ammunition used, and variations in the quality of musket drill, it is extremely doubtful if the rate of fire mentioned by Simes was attained or sustained by most infantry, for parade ground performance is seldom reflected in the heat of battle. Presupposing peak efficiency under fire (a dubious supposition at best), it can be estimated that 500 troops could deliver 500 shots every 15 seconds, i.e., approximately 7,500 rounds every three and ¾ minutes.

Even if not sustained at peak efficiency such withering fusillades, combined with thrusting bayonets, resulted in extremely high casualties suffered by the adversaries, though infection continued to account for more fatalities than those caused by instantly lethal hits or the formidable bayonet.

That vulnerable flesh stood up to such murderous, point-blank fire and the prospect of cold, cruel steel to unmercifully follow is difficult to comprehend in this nuclear age; that it stood with such sustained regularity is something more than astonishing and can be attributed to abject fear; fear not of the enemy, but of the punishment inflicted by a military system traditionally indifferent to human suffering and preserved by an iron discipline maintained by the stigma of cowardice and the awesome authority manifest in the lash, gallows, and firing squad.

The Spanish Frontier

Flowing from the resplendent court of young Philip V the French influence was evident in most aspects of Spanish life. The army was revamped along lines previously suggested by Marshall Turenne, and in 1703 Spain somewhat belatedly discarded the obsolescent matchlock *mosquete,* adopting a flintlock musket with the socket bayonet; the term *mosquete* also abandoned for the Gallic-sounding *fusile* (fusil).[3]

Like the martial flintlock muskets of the British and the French, the Spanish *fusile* did not immediately emerge as a standard pattern, and, prior to 1728, it incorporated a *patilla* identified only by its lateral sear, for the mechanism externally resembled the French flintlock. What can be called the Franco-Iberian flintlock, produced exclusively in Madrid in commercial and martial patterns, was termed a *llave a la moda* to distinguish it from the *patilla* proper, while the true flintlock was referred to as a *llave a la francesa.*[4]

Significantly, the transition from match to flint

ignition in Spanish martial firearms was not immediately apparent in *La Florida*. The English-inspired Native American raids on missions and military outposts characterizing the late seventeenth century escalated during Queen Anne's War, distinctly demonstrating the superiority of flint ignition to match.

In May, 1702, an English-led Creek foray destroyed Mission Santa Fé de Toloco. The raiders, armed with flintlock firearms, were pursued by a Spanish-Apalachee punitive expedition 800 strong and mostly armed with matchlock muskets. Almost half of the Spaniards and Apalachees were annihilated, ambushed on the Flint River in southern Georgia.

The situation further deteriorated when in October aggressive Gov. James Moore launched from Charleston a concentrated but futile assault against St. Augustine. Most of the 500 Carolina militia and their 300 Native American allies had flintlock firearms. Approximately 25 percent of Gov. Jose de Zuñiga y Cerda's infantry were armed with matchlock muskets, at least 37 percent had matchlock arquebuses, and the remainder were pikemen.[5]

The siege of St. Augustine was lifted at the end of the year when reinforcements arrived from Cuba. The English, however, had practically levelled the settlement, though they failed to capture the imposing Castillo de San Marcos; and at no time in its long history was it taken by force of arms, though it subsequently changed hands on several occasions.

Moore was replaced as governor of South Carolina Colony yet he was even more determined to drive the Spaniards out of *La Florida*. In January, 1704, he initiated a series of raids against Apalachee Province with 50 Carolina volunteers and 1,000 Native Americans, primarily Creeks. On April 16 Moore proudly boasted to the Lords Proprietors of South Carolina Colony that he had "killed, and taken as slaves 325 men, and have taken [as] slaves 4,000 women and children. . . . All . . . with the loss of 4 whites and 15 Indians."[6]

Moore's singularly bloody campaigns directed against predominantly peaceful agrarian Native Americans were a nearly fatal blow, for Apalachee Province supplied most of the foodstuffs needed to sustain St. Augustine. In 1705 Spanish officials reported to the crown that the English in general and Moore in particular had destroyed 32 Apalachee villages and at least five missions.

Replacing Gov. Zuñiga in 1706, Gov. Francisco de Córcoles y Martínez bitterly complained to the viceroy of New Spain that *La Florida* "will be lost, not by enemy attack, but by the delays in provisioning the presidio."[7] His appraisal was not without foundation, for at that time Spanish territory in the southeast extended no farther than the range of the most powerful cannon at the Castillo de San Marcos.

MATCHLOCK MUSKET REST (17th Century): Two-pronged, iron musket fork excavated in 1968 from the ruins of the Spanish mission *San Damian de Escambi* destroyed by English and Creek raiders during Queen Anne's War. Courtesy of the Bureau of Historic Sites and Properties, Tallahassee, Fla.

Patilla (17th/18th Century): This partially intact Spanish *patilla* suffered fire damage when the English and their Creek allies burned the mission *San Juan de Aspalaga* early in the 18th Century. The flint has been removed from the cock jaws. Note the mainspring bridle attached to the cock. Courtesy of the Bureau of Historic Sites and Properties, Tallahassee, Fla.

The number of flintlock firearms at St. Augustine visibly increased in 1706, brought about by a retaliatory Spanish-French assault on Charleston that year which terminated without victory. A Castillo armory inventory of April 28 revealed 170 serviceable and 37 unserviceable matchlock muskets, 130 forked musket rests, 25 serviceable and 41 unserviceable matchlock arquebuses; 125 serviceable flintlock *escopetas,* 13 *escopetas* with missing locks and damaged stocks, eight serviceable *trabucos de chispa* (blunderbusses: five with iron barrels and three with bronze), and 248 serviceable *fusiles de mecha.*[8]

The *fusile de mecha* is an enigma among Spanish firearms and would seem to be a contradiction in terms because after Spain adopted the martial *fusile* in 1703 *fusile* exclusively referred to flintlock long arms. *Mecha* (match), however, had been long used to identify matchlock firearms. It is extremely unlikely that *fusile de mecha* was synonymous with *escopeta,* for the latter had employed flint ignition since ca. 1660. There is, however, the strong possibility that *fusile de mecha* described an innovative, transitional martial firearm incorporating match and flint ignition.

Dual ignition lock mechanisms were early known in Germany (see p. 69) and sporadically appeared elsewhere in Europe thereafter. A match/flint lock was produced by Italian gunsmith Montecucoli (d. 1681), while London gunsmith R. Brooke (fl. 1660-1688) made a similar lock bearing the cypher of James II. The Brooke lock is presumed to predate the dual ignition lock invented by French military engineer Vauban in 1688.[9]

It is not inconceivable that firearms employing Vauban's match/flint lock were available in Spanish Florida, for they could have been used by French troops during the cooperative Charleston attack in 1706 and subsequently stored at the Castillo. Considering the Bourbon influence, it is possible that dual ignition French firearms were delivered in an arms trade agreement responding to the demand for firearms in Spanish Florida, nor is it beyond reason that the Vauban lock was made in Spain for military use on a limited, experimental basis prior to the acceptance of the martial flintlock *fusile* in 1703. Such firearms, thereafter considered obsolescent, were nevertheless serviceable and could have been sent to *La Florida* to meet the inordinate demand arising in the wake of English aggression. The foregoing hypotheses, however, are not supported by valid evidence and, consequently, the *fusile de mecha* remains an enigma.

After King William's War the Florida provinces became a refuge for blacks fleeing involuntary servitude in the English colonies and they were joined by large numbers of Native Americans. As early as 1695 Lower Creek bands from present Alabama and Georgia began to drift into the Apalachee region as a result of an internal schism. By ca. 1700 some of the Lower Creeks had broken their traditional blood ties and came to be called by their former brethen *Istisimanole,* meaning runaway or separatist in Muskhogean dialect and subsequently anglicized to Seminole.

Conversely, many of the Apalachees thoroughly decimated by the Carolinians, Creeks, and roving Seminoles abandoned their ancestral land when they realized the Spaniards could not protect them. Turning to their former English foe who now offered land, firearms, and other trade goods, most of the Apalachees moved to Georgia and by 1709 they had established a thriving commerce in horses and deer skins with Charleston traders. A few Apalachee bands moved into western Alabama and traded with the French in the vicinity of present Mobile.

Though England and Spain clashed again during Queen Anne's War a rather curious and lucrative commerce emerged between English traders at Charleston and Gov. Córcoles' second-in-command, Sergeant Major Juan de Ayala y Escobar. Ayala procured from the enemy flour, rice, hardtack, beef, and other edibles to feed the starving defenders of St. Augustine. His motives, however, were not entirely altruistic for he personally profited from the covert transactions. His threatened arrest by the governor on June 19, 1712, nearly resulted in a mutiny, for the Spaniards had been reduced to eating cats, dogs, and horses.[10]

Eighteenth-century Spanish arms-making, despite an increasing French influence, retained much of its national flavor which continued to reflect its early Teutonic and Neapolitan heritage. Unlike most European nations of consequence, however, Spain had developed no adequate commercial proof system, nor were gunsmithing guilds organized as a practical, self-regulating alternative.

The lack of regulation apparently had no effect on the quality of Spanish firearms, for after ca. 1685 Iberian gunsmiths came to be recognized as the finest barrel-makers in Europe and maintained the position until ca. 1750. The evident and enviable popularity of Spanish barrels can be measured by the inordinate demand and the extraordinary number counterfeited.

Spanish gunsmiths of less renown frequently marked their barrels with the distinctive gold-filled *punzon* (signature mark) of famous Spanish masters, nor was the practice unknown elsewhere in Europe where even the most capable gunsmiths used spurious Spanish markings. Of all the Spanish gunsmiths whose marks were counterfeited, Diego Esquivel (1695-1732) was apparently the most famous and popular, for his *punzon* continued to be found on barrels made at least 20 years after his death.[11]

What is known of Esquivel and most other Spanish gunsmiths of the period 1685-1795 was brought to light by Isidro Solér (1740?-1825), royal *arcubucero* (gunsmith) to monarchs Carlos III, Carlos IV, and Fernando VII, and it is preserved in his 86-page *Compendio Historico de los Arcabuceros de Madrid* (An Historical Summary of the Gunsmiths of Madrid [Madrid: 1795]).[12]

As Solér said, the outstanding and deserved reputation of Spanish gun barrels evolved from manufacturing techniques devised by an emigré gunsmith, the great German master known in Spain as Nicólas Bamproyssem y Bis (?-1726). Induced to come to Spain in 1688 by Carlos II, Bis entered royal service ca. 1691 and was appointed royal gunsmith to Philip V in February, 1701, remaining in that position until his death.[13]

Bis painstakingly experimented with various barrel-making methods and concluded that while the traditional forging techniques were sound, the problem of poor quality barrels could be traced to inferior iron. Solér disclosed the "secret" of Bis' discovery in his *Compendio:*

Until the beginning of this century, the method of forging barrels from new iron was maintained . . . and how in spite of all precautions taken in seeking and selecting the best, many barrels failed at the time of their proof. The famous Nicolas Bis . . ., realizing that this loss sprang rather from the poor quality of the material than from the manner of working it, strove to correct it at its very origin.

Having verified through repeated trials, that the iron of Biscayan horseshoes [*herraduras*] was the most ductile of all Europe, and therefore should be the best suited to the construction of barrels, of any employed until that time, considering the brittleness and inequality of the new [iron], the prime defect from which they suffered, he selected a lot of the said horseshoes after they had been well beaten on the feet of horses, and forging a barrel from them, not only achieved that it result as pure and solid as he wished, but also that it resist, with no effect whatever, all tests to which it was submitted: delighted with this important discovery, he publicized it, and although the ignorant or envious maligned him because of the innovation he introduced, he discreetly ignored them all, remaining constant to his project.

Adopted from that time [ca. 1715] on in Madrid, the practice of forging with horseshoes was done in the following manner: There are chosen for each ordinary barrel, two arrobas [fifty pounds] of the best [horseshoes], and these

are divided into five parts; the first should weigh fourteen pounds, twelve the second, and the three remaining, eight each; thus divided, the first group is taken . . . and placing it in the forge, it is beaten and joined until it is shaped in the form of a spade; but in order to interrupt and cross the grain of the iron, it is notched with the Cutter some three fingers from the end, and doubling this part over the other, it is heated intensely; which operation is repeated three or four times, heating always in the same manner until the piece shaped like a spade, remains transformed into a brick: it is necessary to take great care to shake the piece each time it is folded, in order to knock off the . . . dross that forms whenever it is heated; for if any should remain within the fold at the time it is joined or welded, the barrel could result disastrously: shaped in the form of a brick, it is doubled while hot, overlapping the edges, that is, placing one over the other, and placing within the hollow a mandrel . . . of iron tightly fitting, with which it is made into a small tube . . ., and the same with those remaining [piles of horseshoes]; all being disposed in this manner, the barrel is begun by taking the first piece . . . which weighed fourteen pounds . . . which should be that of the breech, and placing it in the forge, it is fastened to an old barrel in order to manipulate it: after this, the second [piece] is widened at the end in the manner of a funnel, and is joined to the first, as are successively the three remaining, according to the length [of the barrel] desired: it should be understood that each cylinder . . ., in order to be perfect, should be given at least thirty-two heatings, and in this manner the barrel will come from the forge with its final shape and octagonal section [breech], and weighing five pounds more or less, for it rarely reaches six, considering that, in order to achieve the solidity and strength that is needed, the fire should consume the forty-four pounds lacking to complete the two arrobas that were gathered to begin the operation: after it is finished . . . come the drilling [boring] and rifling, and then the filing, with which it is reduced to the weight desired by the person who ordered it, for some like them very light, and others do not; and as this is not essential, the Artificer should concede on this point to the gratification of the buyer.

This is the secret that the Gunsmiths of Madrid have discovered, and preserved it, in order to achieve, that none of the many barrels that have been proved in competition with theirs, have exceeded them in range and resistance; and the reason why the persons who use them and know this inestimable advantage,

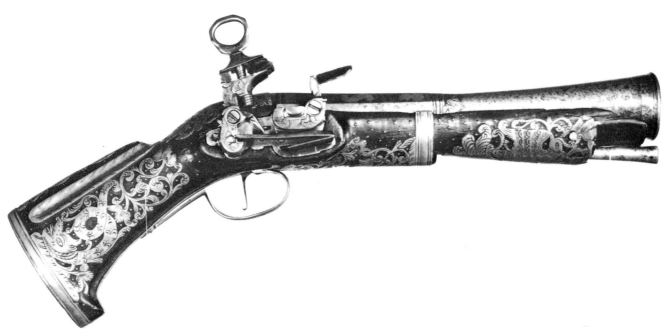

BLUNDERBUSS *Pistola* (18th Century): This pistol typifies a style made by Ripoll gunsmiths in Catalonia for the export trade ca. 1750. Silver or brass ferrules at the butt and forestock and the engraved brass overlay are characteristic. Wood or iron ramrods were provided, mounted in the forestock without thimbles. The *patilla* is well made and the grip is typical of the Catalan design with the flat, pronounced toe. This pistol weighs 2 lbs. 8 ounces with an overall length of 15⅜ inches. The 8⅞-inch barrel measures 1⅜ inches at the muzzle. The lock measures 3 × 1 inch. An iron belt hook is provided. Courtesy of the Arizona State Museum. Helga Teiwes, photographer.

prefer them to all the rest; such is the confidence that has produced the reputation founded upon the experience of almost one century.[14]

Initially met with derision, Bis' innovative barrel-making technique soon came to be embraced with a fervor bordering religious fanaticism, and barrels made by the Bis method came to be known as and marked *de callos de herraduras* (the ends of horseshoes), though subsequently shortened to *de herraduras*. Alonso Martínez, Bis' contemporary, went so far as to forge barrels from horseshoe nails *(clavos de herraduras)*; an innovation Solér explained as "something no one has imitated . . . because of the extreme cost and tedious labor."[15]

As Lavin points out Solér, in referring to the Bis technique, mentioned rifling only in relation to its sequence in barrel-making rather than to the widespread use of rifled firearms in Spain.[16] The rifle *(arquebuz rayado)* had been known in Spain prior to 1580, and in *The Art of Shooting and Horsemanship* of 1644 Espinar noted greased patches as well as a Madrid riflesmith. The rifle, however, never became popular in Spain and no significant domestic rifle-making industry was developed there before the nineteenth century.

The end of Queen Anne's War saw the Florida provinces again free to trade with Britain. Philip, however, was increasingly provoked by French intrusions upon Spanish sovereignty in the Gulf regions. He refrained from demonstrating his displeasure during his grandfather's reign, though after Louis XIV died in 1715 the rift ruptured when Philippe II, Duc d'Orleans, emerged as regent for young Louis XV. The festering boil was pricked when Gov. Bienville attacked and captured Fort San Carlos at Pensacola in 1719. When in 1723 Louis XV reached his majority, Philippe's irritating influence was removed and the wound healed with Fort San Carlos restored to Spain by treaty.

As a result of Spain's 1728 military reorganization the martial *fusile* incorporated two significant changes: (1) the Franco-Iberian lock *(llave a la moda)* was replaced by the French flintlock *(llave a la francesa),* and (2) bore diameter was standardized at .75 caliber using a .69 caliber ball.[17] The 1728 regulations also specified that dragoons, officers and enlisted, carry the flintlock infantry *fusile* though carbines and pistols were subsequently employed by mounted troops. While a slight German character was reflected in furniture design, the French influence on Spanish martial firearms was unmistakable thereafter.

By ca. 1730 a flintlock cavalry *pistola* was introduced and the French influence was distinctly evident, for the lock was the *llave a la francesa* and the grip displayed a rounded pommel with a heavy brass cap and side straps unlike the earlier Ripoll design. Caliber and bore diameter were the same as the *fusile;* thus simplifying logistics because the ball was interchangeable. Interchangeable caliber for the musket and the *escopeta* was intimated in 1694 if not previously established (see p. 117).

The cavalry *pistola* had an overall length of approximately 19 inches and it weighed almost two and ¾ pounds. Barrel length was 11 and ¾ inches and the breech was octagonal. There were no sights. Furniture was brass and the pinned forestock extended almost to the muzzle, while the wooden ramrod was secured by a single thimble and a guide. The gooseneck cock and the lockplate were flat, though the edges were beveled (chamfered) and an external screw held the lower leaf of the battery spring. The brass sideplate was also flat, secured by the two lock screws.

Introduced with the *pistola* was a flintlock cavalry *carabina* featuring a pinned forearm, French buttstock, and a *llave a la moda*. The barrel was approximately 34 inches long, tapering to round from the octagonal breech. Caliber was interchangeable with the *fusile* and the *pistola*. The carbine weighed six and ½ pounds and had an overall length of approximately 48 and ½ inches. Furniture was brass and a front sight was provided. The socket bayonet lug was located under the barrel almost two inches from the muzzle. Most carbines displayed a sling with a slide bar and ring though some had belt hooks, while they were slung muzzle up with the buttstock secured in a leather boot suspended from the saddle skirt; opposite of the English method.

In eighteenth-century Spain the martial blunderbuss *(trabuco* or *trabuco de chispa)* was also known as a carbine-blunderbuss. The *trabuco* weighed almost six pounds and had an overall length of approximately 38 inches. Furniture and barrels were usually brass though there were exceptions. Bore diameter fluctuated from one to one and ⅓ inches and the octagonal/round barrel was almost 23 inches long, pin-fastened to the full-length forestock. After ca. 1728 banded barrels emerged. From the time of its introduction the *trabuco* muzzle illustrated a distinctive flare.

Patterned after the *trabuco* was the massive martial *arcabuz de gancho* (deck or wall gun). Primarily a defensive firearm it exhibited a bore diameter of one to three inches and a swamped (flared) muzzle. The round barrel was made of brass, bronze, or iron, measuring between 32 and 34 inches. Most specimens weighed approximately 25 pounds and had an overall length of almost 45 inches.

A *patilla* or one of its variants was initially used with the *arcabuz de gancho,* though by midcentury they had been supplanted by the *llave a la moda* or the *llave a la francesa;* each slightly larger than the standard *fusile* lock. There were no sights and in most instances the furniture was brass. The full-length stock was of the matchlock musket pattern though more massive and it was provided with a swivel mount permitting a free (360°) traverse. Like the *trabuco* the *arcabuz de gancho* used a single ball, shot, or a combination of the two.

Though the French influence was evident in

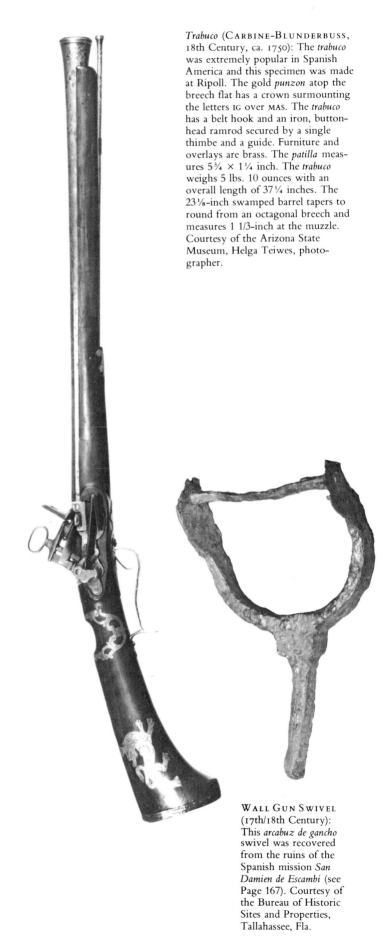

Trabuco (CARBINE-BLUNDERBUSS, 18th Century, ca. 1750): The *trabuco* was extremely popular in Spanish America and this specimen was made at Ripoll. The gold *punzon* atop the breech flat has a crown surmounting the letters IG over MAS. The *trabuco* has a belt hook and an iron, button-head ramrod secured by a single thimbe and a guide. Furniture and overlays are brass. The *patilla* measures 5¾ × 1¼ inch. The *trabuco* weighs 5 lbs. 10 ounces with an overall length of 37¼ inches. The 23⅛-inch swamped barrel tapers to round from an octagonal breech and measures 1 1/3-inch at the muzzle. Courtesy of the Arizona State Museum, Helga Teiwes, photographer.

WALL GUN SWIVEL (17th/18th Century): This *arcabuz de gancho* swivel was recovered from the ruins of the Spanish mission *San Damien de Escambi* (see Page 167). Courtesy of the Bureau of Historic Sites and Properties, Tallahassee, Fla.

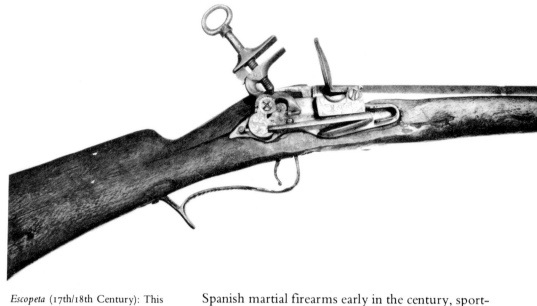

Escopeta (17th/18th Century): This light flint-ignition musket is typical of those employed by the militia in Spanish America. The 33½-inch, .60 caliber barrel is secured to the stock by two friction bands. Note the pronounced Catalan stock toe. Overall length is 46½ inches and the furniture is a mixture of iron and brass though the standard half-buttplate is usually iron. Militia *escopetas* saw hard service on the frontier and many display crude repairs. Courtesy of the Museum of New Mexico, Santa Fe.

The martial *escopeta* employed a *patilla* (*miquelet lock*). Note the mainspring and steel bridles. The close-up of the lock from the *escopeta,* left, depicts the cock in the full-cock position restrained by the rectangular nose of the primary sear transversing the lockplate. Courtesy of the Museum of New Mexico, Santa Fe.

Spanish martial firearms early in the century, sporting and utilitarian firearms retained much of their original character prior to ca. 1750 and it is exemplified in the Catalan buttstock with its slightly drooping comb and pronounced toe; features readily recognized in many of the firearms reaching Spanish America early in the century; particularly militia arms.

Spain, like other European nations involved in the New World, often provided her colonial militia with obsolescent martial firearms and the Catalan rather than the straight, French-pattern buttstock is evident on the many flintlock *escopetas* serving in America after ca. 1680. Damaged stocks replaced by colonial gunsmiths retained the Catalan style until late in the eighteenth century.

Coupled with the demand for lightweight sporting firearms with strong barrels, the aesthetic sensitivity of the justifiably proud Spanish barrelmakers preferring simplicity eliminated the traditional barrel lugs early in the century. The stock (*caja*) was secured to the barrel (*cañon*) by flat bands held by tension; an innovation emerging in English martial firearms ca. 1685.

By 1730 the barrel band (*abrazadera*) was found on most Spanish sporting and martial firearms though by midcentury, as elsewhere in Europe, the tension springs were discarded when it was discovered that friction was sufficient to secure the bands. In Spanish martial firearms the front sight (*punto*) continued to be mounted on the barrel, though elsewhere in Europe it was usually mounted on the barrel band, while the rear sight (*miro*) was incorporated with the rear barrel band. Barrel bands were common on Spanish fowling pieces, though sights were not usually found.

When early in the eighteenth century extended trigger guard finials and tangs (*guardamontes*) and trigger plates (*planchas del guardamonte*) became fashionable on most Spanish firearms, the breech plug tang screw (*tornillo de recamara*) was shortened and repositioned, entering the tang from above because separate screws were used to secure trigger guard finials and tangs; an innovation evident in most other European firearms by ca. 1685.

The flintlock infantry *fusile* employed in Spanish Florida from ca. 1739 to ca. 1755 was similar in most respects to the pattern introduced in 1728, displaying a full-length Catalan or French stock attached to the barrel by three bands; the front band of the split-ring type secured by spring clips. The *fusile* weighed approximately eight and ½ pounds and had an overall length of 59 inches.

The .69 caliber barrel was 43 inches long, tapering to round from the octagonal breech. The bayonet lug was located atop the barrel near the muzzle. The wooden ramrod was secured by the three barrel bands rather than thimbles; the ramrod guide integral with the front (split-ring) band. Furniture was brass and the rear trigger guard finial was extremely long, held by two screws, and emulated the German pattern. The buttplate was secured by two screws, while the three lock screws held the wide, flat sideplate. The *llave a la francesa* was also flat and chamfered. The cock jaw screw was of the large ring-type associated with the earlier *patilla*.

Identification and proof markings vary considerably in location with Spanish martial firearms. The maker's signature is usually found on the lockplate behind the cock. A letter designating the royal arsenal or other place of manufacture is normally displayed between the cock and the battery, surmounted by a crown or fleur-de-lis denoting government property. After ca. 1750 the breech was marked with an inspector's initials in addition to the proof mark; the latter generally expressed by the letters E X. Letters are also found on the sideplate, buttplate, barrel bands, and trigger guard, indicating the mark of an inspector, maker, or arsenal. All markings were stamped.[19]

By ca. 1730 the martial *escopeta* differed from earlier specimens, primarily in the dimensions of the components and furniture design. The *escopeta,* referred to in English as a scuppet or escuppet and now termed an escopette, weighed approximately seven pounds and had an overall length of 54 inches. The full-length Catalan stock was secured to the barrel by two rather than three bands which held the wooden ramrod. Furniture was brass and a front sight was provided. An L-shaped, brass heel cap rather than a full buttplate was common, secured by a screw transversing the long comb finial and another through the cap.

Not until the late seventeenth century was the sideplate (*chapilla*) found on most Spanish firearms and it approximated the size of the lockplate (*plantilla* or *platina*) which ranged from five to six and ½ inches long by one and ¼ to one and ⅜ inches wide.

By 1750 Spanish gunsmiths had also adopted the gold vent bushing (*grano*) employed in the most expensive and elegant European sporting firearms somewhat earlier. Gold, it had been found, successfully resisted the corrosive effects of powder fouling, and platinum was subsequently used.

While Charleston traders had quickly taken advantage of the desperate economic situation in Spanish Florida following Queen Anne's War, increasing pressure on the provinces was applied when in 1733 James Edward Oglethorpe established the Georgia Colony and three years later built Fort Frederica on St. Simon's Island to serve and to protect British commerce.

Charleston merchants reaped enormous profits from the Florida trade with contraband goods, smuggling firearms and munitions to the Seminoles, runaway slaves, and even the American-born (*crillo*) populace; thus precipitating another devastating frontier conflict. In 1739 Spanish revenue agents arrested contraband trader Robert Jenkins, confiscated his ship, and as the penalty for smuggling they lopped off his ear as a lesson to others so inclined. Jenkins subsequently presented his pickled ear to Parliament and the incident served as a *casus belli* in the seemingly endless struggle between Britain and Spain.

The military transition to flintlock firearms was apparently completed in Spanish Florida either shortly before or during the War of Jenkins' Ear (1739-1743), for on September 12, 1740, there were 400 flintlock *fusiles* available at St. Augustine: 150 *fusiles* with their socket bayonets were stored in the Castillo armory, 49 were issued to the local militia company, 41 to the three infantry companies comprising the garrison, 60 to the eight infantry companies reinforcing the *presidio,* 20 to the free negroes in the settlement, and 80 to the convicts confined to the Castillo.[18]

Though arming prisoners might appear to have been a drastic move, Gov. Manuel de Montiano had little choice if St. Augustine was to be properly defended. Oglethorpe twice assaulted *La Florida* and failed, the first attempt directed at St. Augustine. Spain responded by erecting Fort Matanzas in 1743 to shield the vulnerable southern approach to the Castillo and attacked Fort Frederica in an equally futile attempt to retaliate. The War of Jenkins' Ear merged into King George's War which terminated in 1748.

The *escopeta* displayed a *patilla* or one of its variants, secured by two screws, and some specimens were provided with sideplates prior to 1700. The front and the rear trigger guard finials were each secured by a screw and the trigger bow terminated with a finger rest. A decorative annulus often separated the octagonal breech from the remainder of the

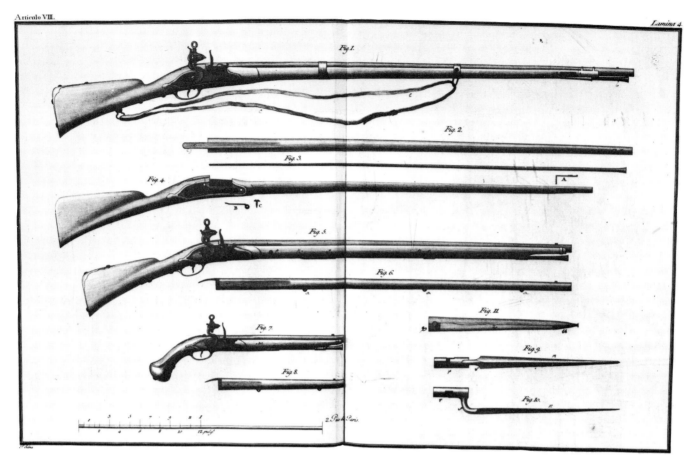

SPANISH MARTIAL FIREARMS (18th Century): From Tomas de Morla, *Tratado de Artilleria para el uso de la Academia de Caballeros Cadetes del Real Colegio Militar de Segovia* (Madrid, 1803), 6 vols. (1) M1752 musket *(fusile)* with sling *(porta fusile)*. (2) Musket barrel (top view). (3) Iron ramrod. (4) Musket stock with barrel band retaining spring (a). (5) M1752 carbine *(carabina)*. (6) Carbine barrel. (7) M1752 cavalry pistol *(pistola)*. (8) Pistol barrel. (9) Socket bayonet (top view). (10) Socket bayonet (side view). (11) Bayonet scabbard. Courtesy of the Arizona Historical Society.

round barrel. The plug bayonet was used exclusively prior to 1703.

The barrel length of the *escopeta* ranged from 34 and ½ inches to 39 inches, and while caliber fluctuated in earlier specimens it was standardized at .69 in 1728. The martial *escopeta* was extremely popular among colonial militia, for it was similar to the lightweight fowling piece and known by the same designation.

With the flammable conditions characterizing the eighteenth-century Anglo-Spanish frontier and increasing French intrusions into the Gulf regions and beyond the Mississippi River, Spain reluctantly altered the traditional ban on Native American firearms procurement. Precisely when the policy change commenced remains moot, though it is believed to have occurred ca. 1740, and while it was condoned there is no evidence that the crown officially recognized it until 1754 with the advent of the French and Indian War.

In 1744 the Spaniards established a trading post in Apalachee Province, hoping to lure the Apalachees back to their homeland and to placate marauding Creeks, Seminoles, Yamasees, and equally hostile renegade bands displaced by the devastating Native American wars in the Carolinas.

Comparing Spanish trade goods to what they had received from the British the Apalachees disgustedly exclaimed, "King of Spain no good. English goods [sic], give much, much. . . ."[20] It was a common Native American complaint, for Spain could not compete with the British and the French long established in the frontier trade and strongly supported by a growing industrialization.

Despite overwhelming competition Spain nevertheless entered the Native American trade in *La Florida* as well as New Spain shortly after midcentury and the commerce continued in the Florida provinces until the early nineteenth century when she no longer exercised any influence within the continental limits of the United States.

Spain initially offered obsolete or obsolescent martial firearms to the Native Americans in her fading dominions and at no time were trade fusils produced by the Spaniards. When the political climate was amenable, however, Spain purchased fusils from Britain, France, Flanders, and Holland.[21]

In 1752 Spain again reorganized her armed forces. The martial *fusile* adopted in 1703 and altered

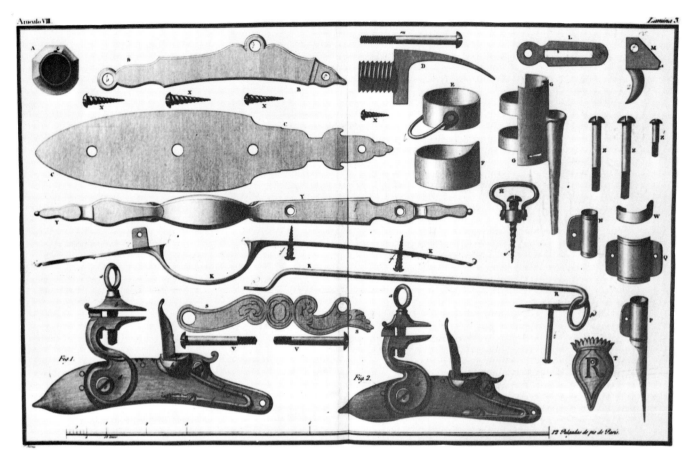

in accordance with the 1728 ordnance regulations was essentially a transitional flintlock firearm and not until May 24, 1752, was it formally recognized as the standard infantry pattern *fusile*.[22] The M1752 infantry *fusile* retained most of the characteristics found in its predecessor. The most significant innovation, however, was introduced in 1755 during the reign of Ferdinand (Fernando) VI when the iron ramrod *(baqueta)* was adopted; long after the transition had been made in France.[23] The M1752 *fusile* remained in general issue with only minor alterations until 1791 when a new pattern was introduced.[24]

Like the infantry *fusile* the Spanish cavalry *pistola* was not officially adopted until 1752 and it also retained the characteristics of the 1728 pattern. Some martial pistols were provided with belt hooks, though the majority were carried in saddle holsters. Like elsewhere in Europe, Spanish officers customarily purchased their handguns from independent gunsmiths and they were elegantly embellished, though an officers' *pistola* was also adopted in 1752, retaining the caliber, exhibiting slimmer lines and a better finish, and a barrel and a lock of superior quality than the enlisted version. Both M1752 *pistolas* carried an iron ramrod after 1755, secured under the forestock by a single barrel band and one thimble *(canutillo* or *portabaquetero)*.

The M1752 Spanish cavalry carbine generally followed the pattern of the 1728 carbine, though it

SPANISH MARTIAL FIREARMS COMPONENTS (18th Century, 1752): From Morla. (A) Barrel (front view) illustrating the muzzle and breech flats' and the front sight. (B) Sideplate, musket. (C) Buttplate with heel finial. (D) Breech plug with tang. (E) Sling swivel (front). (F) Barrel band: iron - *de hierro,* brass - *de laton.* (G) Ramrod guide (front). (H) Sling swivel (rear). (K) Trigger guard with finials, tang, and screws. (L) Trigger plate. (M) Trigger. (N) Ramrod thimble. (P) Ramrod guide (rear). (Q) Fore-end cap, pistol. (R) Carbine ring (slide) bar. (S) Sideplate, pistol. (T) Thumbplate. (V) Lockplate screws. (W) Fore-end band for pistol barrel. (X) Buttplate screws. (Y) Trigger guard, bottom view. (Z) Lockplate screws for musket. (m) Breech plug tang screw. Fig. 1, M1752 musket lock, exterior. Fig. 2, M1752 pistol lock, exterior. Courtesy of the Arizona Historical Society.

was provided with a *llave a la francesa* and two barrel bands, while it was also made in .65 caliber for light cavalry. The wooden ramrod was discarded for the iron ramrod after 1755. The .69 and .65 caliber carbines carried socket bayonets and had the usual sling arrangement. With the exception of the M1752 .65 caliber carbine, all Spanish martial firearms were of identical caliber (see Appendix V).

With the adoption of martial flintlock firearms in Spain after 1703 there were refinements and changes in the various accouterments and accessories, usually reflecting the French influence, though expressing Spanish character. Just as the bandolier had been supplanted by paper cartridges, the venerable match case, except for grenadier use, gradually disappeared with the adoption of the flintlock.

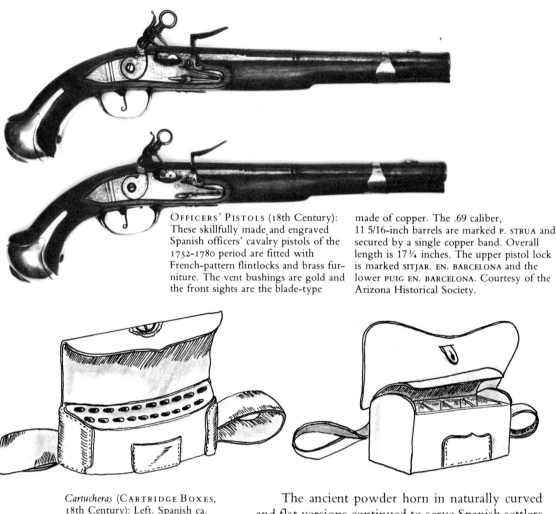

OFFICERS' PISTOLS (18th Century): These skillfully made and engraved Spanish officers' cavalry pistols of the 1752-1780 period are fitted with French-pattern flintlocks and brass furniture. The vent bushings are gold and the front sights are the blade-type made of copper. The .69 caliber, 11 5/16-inch barrels are marked P. STRUA and secured by a single copper band. Overall length is 17¾ inches. The upper pistol lock is marked SITJAR. EN. BARCELONA and the lower PUIG EN. BARCELONA. Courtesy of the Arizona Historical Society.

Cartucheras (CARTRIDGE BOXES, 18th Century): Left. Spanish ca. 1770 had leather-covered wood block holding 20 to 21 cartridges though earlier specimens (ca. 1735) carried 9 to 10. The Royal crest is embossed on the leather cover. Right. Spanish ca. 1760-1770. Infantry cartridge box with tin liner had four compartments. An inner flap also protected the cartridges and the leather tongue on the outer cover fit over a brass stud beneath the box. The small pouches at the front are believed to have been for flints. Author's sketch.

Arcabuz de Gancho (WALL/DECK GUN, 18th Century): The *Arcabuz de Gancho* was an important defensive firearm in Spanish America. This specimen, an enlarged form of the blunderbuss, weighs 25 pounds with an overall length of 43⅞-inches. The 26½-inch barrel is secured by a single brass band pierced for a swivel mount. The flared muzzle measures three inches and the oversized *patilla* 6⅝ × 2⅛-inch. Courtesy of the Arizona Historical Society.

The ancient powder horn in naturally curved and flat versions continued to serve Spanish settlers throughout the eighteenth century, while ca. 1750 there emerged a penchant for ornamental horns aristically embellished with relief carving which was not generally found elsewhere in North America.

While ceramic or glass powder flasks remained popular with Spanish colonial militia, regular troops were issued a triangular, cloth-covered, and iron-bound *estuche* (flask) displaying a long pour spout with a spring closure designed to dispense a single charge, a belt hook, and four shoulder belt keepers. By ca. 1730 the *estuche* declined in popularity with the widespread military use of paper cartridges.

The leather cartridge pouch *(balsa de cartucho)* of the late seventeenth century remained in use among colonial militia long after the leather cartridge box *(cartuchera)* was introduced for military service ca. 1728. The 1728 regulations specified that the royal coat of arms be embossed on the *cartuchera* cover flap. The *cartuchera,* like most European specimens, was a leather-covered wooden block containing 18 to 20 holes into which the paper cartridges were inserted to prevent damage and provide some protection from the elements; the block often curved to fit the conformation of the body.

Shortly after 1752 an improved *cartuchera* was introduced consisting of a tin liner divided into four compartments and covered with leather. An interior

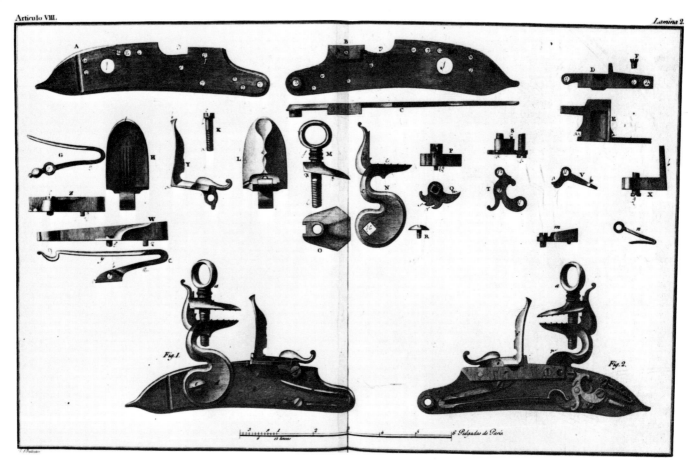

flap was provided in addition to the cover, giving more protection from the elements. The cartridges were horizontally packed in the compartments and at the front of the box there was a small pouch believed to have been used for carrying spare gunflints. The early *cartuchera* was carried on the waist belt *(correa)* or the shoulder belt *(cinturón)* and the later box was suspended from the shoulder belt; the fashion dictated by military punctilio.

Also carried like the *estuche* and the *cartuchera* was the socket bayonet *(bayoneta)* and it was provided with a brass-throated and brass-tipped leather scabbard *(vaina)* with either a belt hook or stud for attaching it to the belt. Early eighteenth-century *escopetas* used the plug bayonet *(cuchíllo de mónte)* because they had no bayonet lug. The plug bayonet also doubled as a fighting knife and, in addition, Spanish militia carried hatchets *(acuilas)* like their British and French counterparts.

Spanish cleaning implements like the priming wire (vent pick) and the bullet worm were similar to conventional European design though the popular *eslabón* was distinctive.[25] The *eslabón* was a combination tool, i.e., it performed several functions related to the care of firearms. The *eslabón* incorporated a T-shaped hammer head and a three-inch handle terminating in a screwdriver blade, while some specimens also displayed a vent pick. The hammer face was striated like the *patilla* battery and was primarily

SPANISH MI752 FLINTLOCK *(Llave a la Francesa)* and Components (18th Century): From Morla. (A) Disassembled lockplate *(plantilla)*, exterior. (B) Disassembled lockplate, interior. (C) Disassembled lockplate, top. (D) Priming pan *(cazoleta)*, interior. (E) Priming pan, top. (F) Priming pan screw. (G) Steel spring *(muelle de rastrillo)*. (H) Steel *(rastrillo)*. (K) Steel screw. (L) Steel, rear view. (M) Cock jaw screw *(tornillo pedrero)* with upper cock jaw *(quijada)*. (N) Cock *(gatillo)*. (O) Lower cock jaw. (P) Tumbler *(muez)*, top. (Q) Tumbler, side. (R) Cock screw. (S) Sear bridle *(brida)*, top. (T) Sear bridle, side. (V) Sear *(calzo)*, side. (W) Mainspring *(muelle grande* or *muelle real)*, top and side view. (X) Sear, top. (Y) Steel, side. (m) Sear spring *(muelle de fiador)*, top. (n) Sear spring, side. Fig. 1, Assembled lock, exterior. Fig. 2, Assembled lock, interior. Courtesy of the Arizona Historical Society.

used for striking fire, though it also doubled for flint knapping. The screwdriver blade was obviously used for disassembling and assembling the firearm and its components.

After the successful Pueblo Revolt of 1680 12 years elapsed before the Spaniards reconquered New Mexico and again began to expand in the Great Southwest. In 1723 colonial officials resurrected the ancient Taos Fair, for the settlement reemerged as the focal point of the annual trade rendezvous attended by a host of Basin, Plains, and Plateau tribes which had gathered there centuries before the European invasion.

Though early regaining New Mexico, Spanish attempts to establish permanent settlements in Texas were all but defeated by the fierce Cuartelejo

Apaches and the hostile Comanches abundantly supplied with tough mustangs and French trade fusils. San Antonio de Bexar was founded in 1718 yet 31 years elapsed before frontier conditions permitted starting the settlement of La Bahía (Goliad).

In 1752 Tubac was established in southern Arizona, while shortly thereafter Spanish interest shifted to beckoning California initially explored by Juan Rodriquez Cabrillo in 1542. The shift was instituted because Spain required a more convenient supply base for her growing Philipine involvement, and also the crown noticed with consternation a substantial increase in the activities of Russian fur interests moving steadily southward from the Aleutians.

The Spaniards began the swift conquest of the Pacific strand with a combined land-sea expedition mounted from Baja California in 1769 which founded a settlement on the shores of San Diego Bay. By 1770 the Monterey *presidio* was established and, the following year, the settlement and the Mission San Gabriel were started near present Los Angeles.

The struggling though determined California colonists were at first dependent upon inadequate supplies irregularly delivered from New Spain by sea, a tenuous link at best. In 1774, during the reign of Carlos III, Juan Bautista de Anza mounted an expedition from Tubac which opened the first overland route to San Gabriel. He proceeded from there in 1775 with a number of settlers bound for San Francisco Bay, oblivious to the portentous events then transpiring in British America little more than 3,000 miles eastward.

The French Frontier

In the wake of seventeenth-century pathfinders Joliet and LaSalle came the brothers Le Moyne who had in 1700 established Fort de la Boulaye about 40 miles below the future site of New Orleans to prevent Spanish penetrations and English incursions in the Mississippi Valley and Gulf regions. Jean Baptiste Le Moyne, Sieur de Bienville, was appointed governor of Louisiana in 1701, and the following year he founded Fort Louis de la Mobile in what Philip V considered Spanish territory. That and the permanent establishment of Mobile in 1710 perceptibly widened the acrimonious gap between the House of Anjou and the House of Orléans (see p. 170).

Louis XIV actively supported colonial aspirations in Louisiana, though a treasury seriously depleted by his unfortunate military escapades forced him to seek private funding for his Gulf region adventures; thus in 1712 he assigned monopolistic trade and colonization rights to financier Sieur Pierre Crozat (1665-1740).

Under Crozat's direction Gov. Bienville mounted several exploratory expeditions and carried on a considerable commerce with the Native Americans which early transcended the Mississippi River and spread to the Great Plains. Between 1712 and 1717 Étienne Veniard de Bourgmond traded with the Arapaho, Osage, and Pawnee in the Missouri country, while in 1717 Louis Juchereau de St. Denis began a trading post on the Red River, naming it Fort St. Jean Baptiste de Nachitoches.

In 1716 Gov. Bienville founded Fort Rosalie at what became Natchez, Miss., and a year later established Fort Toulouse on the Alabama River north of present Montgomery. Fort Rosalie quickly emerged as a key military outpost and commercial center, subsequently becoming a bone of contention among the British, Spanish, Native Americans, and ultimately the United States.

Crozat removed tactful Gov. Bienville and replaced him with Antoine de la Mothe Cadillac in an effort to stimulate profits. Cadillac, however, promptly antagonized colonists, traders, and Native Americans alike with his dictatorial policies and the rift widened when he demanded outrageously inflated prices for firearms and other essential trade goods while simultaneously slashing the exchange rate for prime pelts. Discouraged, Crozat recalled Cadillac in 1717 and assigned his trade concessions and colonization rights to the Company of the West.

New Orleans began in 1718 as a small settlement named for the regent of France and the following year Bienville's successful assault on Fort San Carlos at Pensacola transpired, highlighting the Franco-Iberian conflict. During that tremulous period Claude Charles de Tisné traded with the Native Americans in the Missouri country and penetrated to the North Platte with Bourgmond, while Bernard de la Harpe dealt with the Apache and the Comanche at the confluence of the Arkansas and Canadian Rivers in present Oklahoma.

In 1723 Bourgmond established Fort Orléans on the upper Missouri River, though it was abandoned in 1728. The western-most French trading post in the vast Trans-Mississippi region by 1725 was Ferdinandino, situated on the Arkansas River near the present Kansas-Oklahoma border not far from the terminus of Coronado's 1541 penetration.

Vincennes (Ind.) was founded on the Wabash River in 1702 and, a year later, Kaskaskia was started on the Mississippi River in Illinois country. Fort Beauharnois was established on the St. Croix River in 1727, while in 1744 Fort Cavagnial became an important trading post on the Missouri River in northern Kansas. The French also reached far beyond

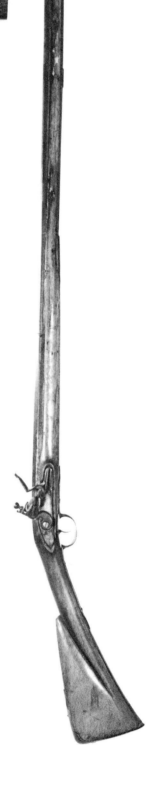

the Lake Superior region, founding Fort L'Huillier (Mankato, Minn.) in 1700, followed in 1716 by Fort La Baye (Green Bay, Wisc.).

The Company of the West, a privately financed venture, exploited Crozat's former concessions and unfortunately became ensnarled in the financial manipulations of Scottish land speculator John Law who in 1716 founded the French national banking system. After reaping enormous profits Law's shaky enterprise collapsed in 1720, puncturing the so-called Mississippi Bubble and wiping out thousands of large and small investors, while the settlers in *La Louisiane* were stranded without assistance or sustenance.

In 1731 the Company of the Indies absorbed the liabilities of the distressed Company of the West and promptly went bankrupt. Despite land speculation schemes and bankrupt colonial enterprises *La Louisiane* continued to expand and even prosper as the French settlers were joined by other Europeans contributing to the polyglot nature of that richly endowed wilderness.

One of the most important Trans-Mississippi French settlements was Sainte Genevieve (Mo.), directly across the river from Kaskaskia. Saint Genevieve was founded in 1732 to exploit the nearby galena deposits discovered in 1715. Most of the lead smelted from the galena mined by slaves and experienced Germans imported for the purpose supplied the French frontier with bullets, while large quantities of lead were shipped to various posts in the Great Lakes region and also New Orleans for transport to France.

While French traders had established a lucrative commerce with the Native Americans west of the Mississippi River, none had been so daring as the brothers Paul and Pierre Mallet. In 1739 they left the Illinois country with a pack train of trade goods and subsequently reached Santa Fé. The Spaniards were

TRADE FUSIL (17th/18th Century): The French trade fusil depicted was made ca. 1740 and its characteristics differ little from late 17th Century specimens. The octagonal breech extends nine inches, separated from the remainder of the round barrel by an annulus. The .55 caliber barrel is 48 inches long and the full-length stock is pin-fastened. There is no rear sight. Note the deep groove extending from the stock comb.

The close-up of the lock from the French trade fusil somewhat indistinctly illustrates the club, bow, and quiver engraving on the lockplate behind the cock. There is no battery bridle. Courtesy of the Museum of the Fur Trade, Chadron, Nebraska.

as much astonished as alarmed by their arrival, the former in recognition of the great hazards involved in such a long overland journey, and the latter because they realized that their once remote settlements in the Great Southwest were now exposed to eastern encroachment.

At the time the Mallet brothers were carving out trade routes followed a century later by United States frontiersmen, other French explorers founded Fort La Reine on the Assiniboine River in Manitoba. In 1737 Gaultier de Varennes, Sieru de la Vérendrye, obtained from Louis XV a monopoly on the northwestern fur trade to finance yet another expedition seeking the fabled Northwest Passage dreamed of by Henry Hudson and his contemporaries a century earlier.

Using Fort La Reine as a base between 1738 and 1742, de la Vérendrye and his sons Francois and Louis-Joseph explored the upper Missouri River and traded with the Mandan more than 30 years before Meriwether Lewis and William Clark were born. Though failing to discover a northwest passage the de la Vérendrye expeditions penetrated Dakota country and came within sight of the Black Hills in 1743.

In the lower Mississippi Valley the French actively courted amicable relations with the Native Americans and early counted the Caddo and the Choctaw as allies. The Natchez, however, violently opposed the French and destroyed Fort Rosalie in 1716. The French returned in force, and though an indecisive battle was fought in 1722, they virtually exterminated the Natchez in 1729 despite the latter's interim alliance with the Chickasaw.

Of all the Native Americans opposing the French in *La Louisiane* the Chickasaw were the fiercest in battle and were also feared by most other Native Americans encountering them. An Iroquois war party wandered into Chickasaw territory in 1732 and was annihilated, while four years later they struck and defeated a greatly superior French force at Amalahta (Ala.). Aided by the Choctaw the French retaliated in 1739-1740 and were again mauled. Significantly, the Chickasaw fought most of those engagements without the benefit of firearms, for they had then received but few from British traders.

Though early affiliated with the French and assisting them against the Natchez and the Chickasaw, the Choctaw allowed the relationship to deteriorate and by ca. 1750 they preferred to deal with the British who provided them with firearms, gunpowder, and other desireable trade goods at reduced prices.[26] And the cutthroat competition characterizing the frontier trade was as literal as figurative.

Commensurate with French expansion on the American frontier was trade fusil production, yet despite a rapidly growing market the eighteenth-century French trade fusil was not materially improved in quality or design when compared to earlier specimens though there were exceptions, and there is sufficient evidence to suggest an early military involvement in the manufacture and distribution of trade fusils and other firearms among the Native Americans.

T.M. Hamilton has noted a distinctive group of French trade fusils produced during the 1730-1760 period which enjoyed widespread distribution from the lower Mississippi Valley to the upper Great Lakes.[27] The fusils displayed a sophisticated form of engraving consisting of leaf scrolls, animals, flowers, bows and arrows, quivers, sunbursts, and refined expressions of the potted plant and Chevrolet design (see p. 155).

Those engraved motifs appeared on the buttplate, trigger bow, and flat brass sideplate of one group of trade fusils exhibiting superior craftsmanship and Hamilton has traced the origin of the engravings to the period 1710-1720, for similar motifs are found in pattern sheets then signed by le Conardel, a master French gunsmith and engraver of St. Lô, Normandy, and they were thereafter copied by others.[28]

Though less represented elsewhere in Europe, pattern books were common in France after ca. 1650, and most of them were produced by Parisian engravers to illustrate the myriad and intricate forms of etching devised to complement firearms components ranging from the smallest screw head to the entire barrel and lock. Pattern book sheets served to assist the gunsmith's patron in choosing a suitable decorative motif and in some instances they retain the only known examples of innovative lock designs and the work of outstanding engravers.

TRADE FUSIL LOCK (18th Century): The English trade fusil lock depicted has the serpent sideplate attached. The smooth surface and the loop near the tail of the serpent identifies the lock as from the period ca. 1720-1740. The lock was recovered from a Mohawk grave in New York. Courtesy of the Museum of the Fur Trade, Chadron, Nebraska.

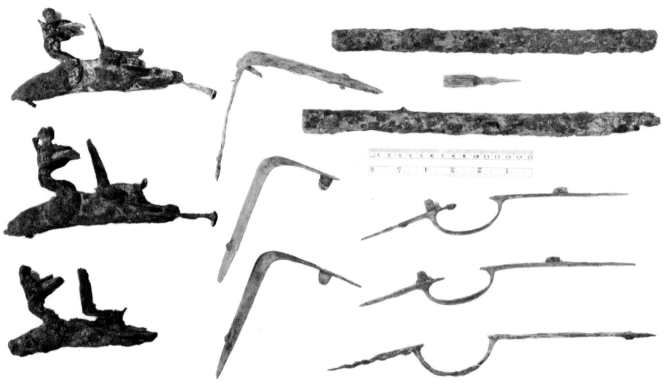

In addition to the le Conardel-pattern engraving those trade fusils noted by Hamilton are marked in some instances with a crown surmounting an R though the crowns differ somewhat. The crowned R mark is found on the buttplate toe and Hamilton suggests that it represents the acceptance mark of the national armories at St. Étienne and Maubeuge.[29]

Hamilton's hypothesis is consistent with the marking found on another group of French trade fusils he has identified, fragments of which have been recovered from Native American sites in Alabama, Missouri, Oklahoma, and Texas.[30] The buttplate finial on those fusils is marked on the underside with the letters A•R X, identified as the mark of Monsieur Desjardins who seved as the manager of the Maubeuge Armory from 1718 until his death in 1755.[31] The mark, as Hamilton notes, is the same as that found on French musketoons produced ca. 1733-1734.[32]

The appearance of French armory marks on two distinct groups of trade fusils found at such diverse locations is of more than minor significance, for it indicates strongly that France (a) supplied the Native Americans with martial firearms prior to the Seven Years' War (1756-1763), (b) produced trade fusils at government armories on a limited scale, (c) sold as surplus obsolete, obsolescent, or over-stocked martial firearms components to trade fusil makers, (d) released obsolete or obsolescent martial firearms for distribution to the Native Americans, (e) subsidized commercial trade fusil production, and (f) engaged in a combination of the preceding or as yet unexplored contributing factors.

TRADE FUSIL COMPONENTS (17th/18th Century): All of the French trade fusil components depicted are made of iron and were excavated in 1934 from a Native American gravesite found on the left bank of the Mississippi River near the Louisiana-Mississippi border; a site known as Angola and mentioned by LaSalle and de Tonty in 1682. The flint-ignition locks (left) are of the period 1680-1730 as are the buttplates (center) and trigger guards (bottom right). The barrel fragments (upper right) range in caliber from .56 to .69 and had an original length of about 47 inches. The ramrod tailpipe (guide) seen between the barrels is formed from a single piece of folded iron. Courtesy of Louisiana State University, Baton Rouge.

Hamilton ventures the theory that the fusils marked A•R X were originally French officers' fusils made on special order and utilizing some excess musketoon parts, and that they reached the Native Americans by a series of circumstances now unknown; an hypothesis consistent with the aforementioned (c) and (d). The fusils bearing the crowned R mark and mentioned by Hamilton are also consistent with (c) and (d) though they could also represent (a), (b), (e), or (f).

Though the flintlock had been employed in some French martial firearms since ca. 1645, they remained transitional firearms because no standard patterns had been adopted. An ordnance directive issued January 4, 1717, however, outlined the specifications for a standard martial flintlock musket and established a national system of martial firearms manufacture and procurement.[33]

French martial firearms were shortly thereafter fabricated at designated royal armories under government supervision although there was one exception, viz exigent wartime demands during which martial firearms were contracted from independent

FRENCH MILITARY MUSKETS: 1717-1777

Model	Caliber	Barrel Length	Overall Length
1717	.69	46.0″	62.5″
1728	″	″	″
1746 (irod ramrod)	″	″	62.0″
1754	″	″	″
1763	″	44.5″	60.0″
1766	″	″	″
1768	″	″	59.0″
1770	″	″	″
1771	″	″	60.0″
1773	″	″	″
1774	″	″	″
1777 (Infantry)	″	″	″
1777 (Artillery)	″	36.0″	51.5″
1777 (Dragoon)	″	42.5″	57.5″
1777 (Navy)	″	44.5″	″

makers because government facilities could not meet production requirements.

A management and inspection system was also early established, for on May 12, 1717, the Duc d'Maine, supreme commander of the *Corps de Artillerie* (Artillery Corps), was ordered by the crown to appoint certain artillery officers "upright, intelligent and alert, for the permanent superintending of the manufacture of arms for the King at Maubeuge, Charleville and Saint-Etienne."[34]

In most eighteenth-century European armies the artillery corps was responsible for managing all ordnance functions including the manufacture, procurement, and distribution of small arms; a role unrelinquished until the late nineteenth century when firearms technology reached such complex proportions that artillery and small arms became separate entities administered by an Ordnance Department or Bureau of Ordnance.

While Charleville and St. Étienne had been designated royal arms manufactories prior to the eighteenth century, Maubeuge did not receive that distinction until 1704 though the city had been engaged in making firearms since the late sixteenth century when it had been a Flemish principality.[35]

The January 4 ordnance directive standardized the caliber of the French flintlock infantry musket at .69, barrel length at 46 inches, and overall length at 62 and ½ inches, while shortly thereafter production began on what is known as the M1717 infantry musket.[36] Between 1717 and 1777 the French martial musket underwent 15 model changes, most of them minor, and there were slight component variations owing to the manufacturing techniques employed at the royal arms manufactories.

All French martial muskets were provided with the socket bayonet and the sturdier iron ramrod was introduced in 1746.[37] Caliber .69, adopted by Spain in 1728, was retained throughout the period 1717-1777. In 1777 three musket models were made in addition to the infantry pattern: artillery, dragoon (cavalry), and navy.

The M1717 musket is distinguished by its round barrel flattened on the upper surface to within five inches of the muzzle. There are no sights and the bayonet lug is positioned atop the rounded part of the muzzle. The barrel is secured to the stock by four pins and a single band situated near the middle; the breech end held by the breech plug tang screw.

All M1717 furniture is iron and the wooden ramrod is retained by three thimbles. The upper sling swivel is attached to the left side of the single barrel band and the lower swivel is secured to a ring set into the stock behind the sideplate. The full buttplate displays a long finial extending into the stock comb where it is held by a short post integral with the finial. The gooseneck cock is flat like the lockplate and the sideplate and the jaw screw is slotted for the combination tool blade. The iron priming pan is chamfered and provided with a fence, while an atypical vertical bridle extends from the battery screw to the battery spring screw.

With the appearance of the M1728 musket came a series of minor design refinements thereafter continuing throughout the evolutionary period. Three barrel bands were substituted for the barrel lug and pin arrangement previously used, each band secured by a flat tension spring. The split-ring upper band has an integral ramrod guide. A conventional lock bridle extending between the priming pan and the battery screw supplanted the M1717 vertical bridle.

The external battery bridle was eliminated with the introduction of the M1746 musket and the iron, button-head ramrod was adopted. The barrel has eight long flats at the breech and the stock is ½ inch shorter. The three barrel bands were retained, the upper and center band held by friction and the lower band by a tension spring.

The M1754 musket was adopted shortly after the start of the French and Indian War. The sling swivels were relocated beneath the barrel, the front swivel attached to the center band and the rear swivel mounted just forward of the trigger guard. The conventional battery bridle was reintroduced. The demands of the French and Indian War precluded any musket model changes until 1763.

With the introduction of the M1763 musket the breech displayed a flat on either side like the M1717. The barrel, however, was shortened one and ½ inches. A brass, blade-type front sight and a ramrod retaining spring were added to the upper barrel band and the sling swivels were oval rather than round at

M1717 FRENCH IN-
FANTRY MUSKET
(18th Century): An
Ordnance directive is-
sued January 4, 1717,
established specif-
ications for the first official French martial
flintlock musket, stand-
ardizing caliber at .69,
barrel length at 46
inches, and overall
length at 62½ inches.
Courtesy of the *Musée
de l'Armée*, Paris.

M1746 FRENCH IN-
FANTRY MUSKET
(18th Century): The
M1746 musket was
shortened ½ inch and it
was the first to employ
an iron rather than
wood ramrod. The ex-
ternal steel bridle was
eliminated and the
lockplate was flat rather
than convex to simplify
manufacture. Courtesy
of the *Musée de l'Armée*,
Paris.

M1754 FRENCH IN-
FANTRY MUSKET
(18th Century):
Adopted at the outset
of the French and In-
dian War, the M1754
musket emulated the
specifications of its predecessor with only
minor changes. A
French officers' fusil
was adopted in 1754,
retaining the regulation
infantry caliber though
it was shorter, lighter,
and more elegantly
finished. Courtesy of
the *Musée de l'Armée*,
Paris.

M1763 FRENCH IN-
FANTRY MUSKET
(18th Century): With
the introduction of the
M1763 the barrel was
shortened 1½ inches,
the brass, blade-type
front sight and the
ramrod retaining spring
were incorporated into
the upper barrel band
and the sturdier,
throat-hole cock was
introduced. Courtesy of
the *Musée de l'Armée*,
Paris.

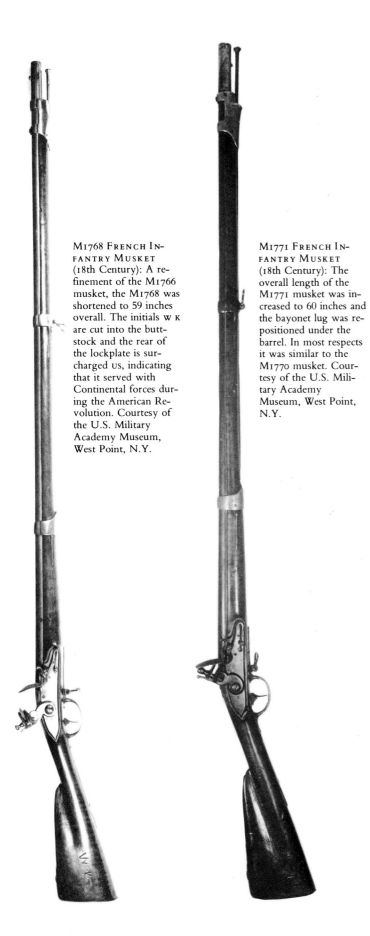

M1768 FRENCH IN-FANTRY MUSKET (18th Century): A re-finement of the M1766 musket, the M1768 was shortened to 59 inches overall. The initials W K are cut into the butt-stock and the rear of the lockplate is sur-charged US, indicating that it served with Continental forces dur-ing the American Re-volution. Courtesy of the U.S. Military Academy Museum, West Point, N.Y.

M1771 FRENCH IN-FANTRY MUSKET (18th Century): The overall length of the M1771 musket was in-creased to 60 inches and the bayonet lug was re-positioned under the barrel. In most respects it was similar to the M1770 musket. Cour-tesy of the U.S. Mili-tary Academy Museum, West Point, N.Y.

the ends. The buttplate finial is considerably shorter and the iron ramrod exhibits a trumpet-shaped head. A stronger, innovative cock was introduced (now known as a throat-hole cock because of its design) and eliminated the graceful gooseneck cock. The jaw screw is pierced rather than slotted.

The M1766 musket is somewhat lighter than prior specimens because the stock was perceptibly slimmed and the barrel reduced in weight though retaining its length. The button-head ramrod was reintroduced and the ramrod retaining spring was attached to the bottom of the barrel rather than the upper band. The M1768 musket closely resembles the M1766 except that the trigger guard of the former is separate from the trigger plate, overall length had been reduced to 59 inches, and the ramrod retaining spring and the lock mechanism were slightly reduced in size.

With the introduction of the M1770 musket the barrel bands were thicker and the ramrod retaining spring was relocated at the lower barrel band, while for some unfathomable reason the rounded (convex) cock and lockplate were resurrected. The M1771 musket saw the return of the heavy barrel and overall length was increased to 60 inches, while the bayonet lug was attached to the underside of the upper barrel band.

The singular distinction between the M1771 and the M1773 musket was that the ramrod retaining spring was again attached to the underside of the barrel. The M1774 musket displays three changes. The ramrod retaining spring was once more located on the lower barrel band, the ramrod exhibits a pear-shaped rather than button head, and the typically rounded pan cover tang is flat.

There were numerous design changes and alterations in the dimensions of the components with the adoption of the four M1777 musket patterns. The M1777 infantry musket incorporates a convex, throat-hole cock and the pan cover tang is again rounded. A brass priming pan was introduced to resist the corrosive effect of powder residue and the saline erosion encountered at sea. The pan fence was eliminated by angling the pan forward, away from the eyes. The barrel has five short breech flats and a tenon was added for the upper barrel band retaining screw. The center band is also secured by a screw though the lower band is spring-held. The front sight and the ramrod retaining spring are attached to the upper barrel band.

The M1777 artillery musket is similar to the infantry model though the barrel is shorter and, ex-cepting the sling swivels, all furniture is brass. The M1777 dragoon musket displays a 42 and ½ inch barrel and the furniture is also brass except the unusual split-ring center barrel band of iron. The M1777 navy musket duplicates the infantry pattern

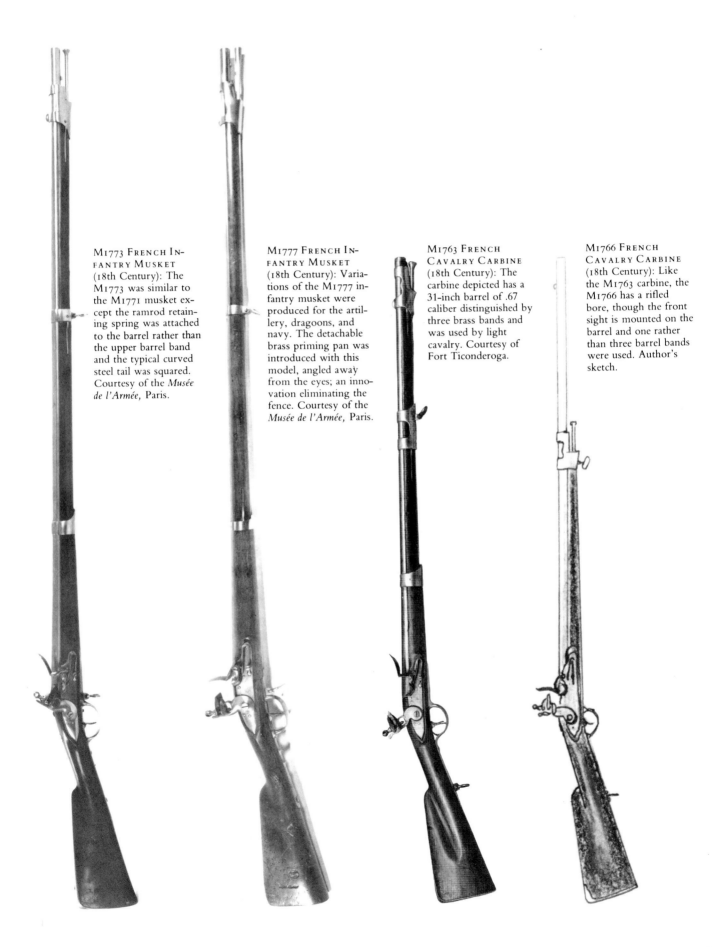

M1773 FRENCH IN-
FANTRY MUSKET
(18th Century): The
M1773 was similar to
the M1771 musket ex-
cept the ramrod retain-
ing spring was attached
to the barrel rather than
the upper barrel band
and the typical curved
steel tail was squared.
Courtesy of the *Musée
de l'Armée,* Paris.

M1777 FRENCH IN-
FANTRY MUSKET
(18th Century): Varia-
tions of the M1777 in-
fantry musket were
produced for the artil-
lery, dragoons, and
navy. The detachable
brass priming pan was
introduced with this
model, angled away
from the eyes; an inno-
vation eliminating the
fence. Courtesy of the
Musée de l'Armée, Paris.

M1763 FRENCH
CAVALRY CARBINE
(18th Century): The
carbine depicted has a
31-inch barrel of .67
caliber distinguished by
three brass bands and
was used by light
cavalry. Courtesy of
Fort Ticonderoga.

M1766 FRENCH
CAVALRY CARBINE
(18th Century): Like
the M1763 carbine, the
M1766 has a rifled
bore, though the front
sight is mounted on the
barrel and one rather
than three barrel bands
were used. Author's
sketch.

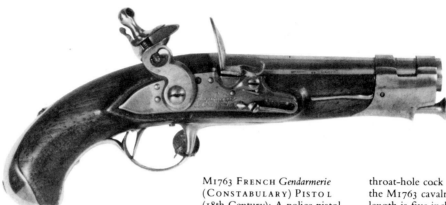

M1763 FRENCH *Gendarmerie* (CONSTABULARY) PISTOL (18th Century): A police pistol, this specimen made at Charleville displays a flat lockplate and the throat-hole cock characterizing the M1763 cavalry pistol. Barrel length is five inches, caliber .59. Courtesy of the *Musée de l'Armée,* Paris.

M1777 FRENCH CAVALRY (DRAGOON) CARBINE (18th Century): The M1777 carbine displayed a 33-inch smoothbore barrel with a bayonet lug. Unlike light cavalry, the heavy cavalry (dragoons) fought dismounted. Courtesy of Fort Ticonderoga.

though all the furniture is brass, while the overall length is two and ½ inches shorter.

French martial muskets, though subjected as they were to various and seemingly whimsical design changes, generally weighed between eight and nine and ½ pounds. All stocks were walnut though in some instances there was no fore-end cap. The exigencies of wartime production were primarily responsible for the changes in dimension and design.

In 1754 France adopted a standard officers' fusil and it thereafter followed the pattern changes of the infantry musket. The officers' fusil, however, was somewhat lighter than the infantry musket and more attention was lavished on the final finish, while the lock and the trigger bow were generally engraved. Officers' fusils and infantry muskets were of the same caliber.

Curiously, not until 1763 did France make any concerted attempt to standardize the martial carbine, musketoon, or pistol.[38] Prior to that year specifications for those firearms were left to the discretion of the various corps commanders except that the carbine and pistol caliber was designated at .67; thus French martial firearms did not have the flexibility of interchangeable caliber as exemplified in Spanish martial firearms.

The French martial musketoon produced in 1733-1734 (see p. 181) was not a standard cavalry firearm and was supplanted in 1763 when the carbine was standardized. The M1763 carbine displays a 31 inch, round iron barrel secured to the stock by three brass bands and the forestock extends to the muzzle. The upper barrel band incorporates the blade-type front sight and the ramrod guide. The upper sling swivel is integral with the distinctive split-ring center barrel band, while the lower swivel was attached to the stock belly.

The M1763 carbine has a dual sling arrangement, for an iron slide bar and ring is also provided, permitting the carbine to be readily carried by mounted or dismounted cavalry. The front of the

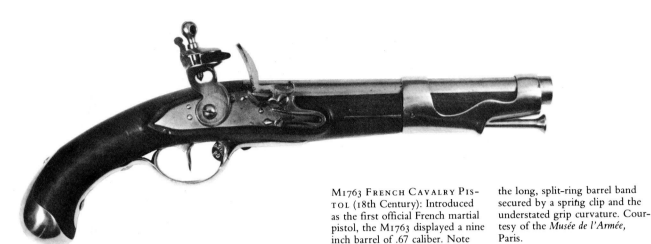

M1763 FRENCH CAVALRY PISTOL (18th Century): Introduced as the first official French martial pistol, the M1763 displayed a nine inch barrel of .67 caliber. Note the long, split-ring barrel band secured by a spring clip and the understated grip curvature. Courtesy of the *Musée de l'Armée*, Paris.

slide bar was attached to the rear barrel band and the opposite end was secured by the front sideplate screw. Excepting the sling swivels and the slide bar and ring, all furniture is brass. The iron ramrod displays a trumpet-shaped head and the lock is the same as the standard M1763 musket lock.

The M1766 carbine illustrates features similar to the M1763 except that the blade-type front sight is affixed to the barrel. Significantly, both the 1763 and 1766 model carbines were rifled and the lands and grooves terminated approximately eight inches from the muzzle; thus making it easier to load when mounted because the ball could be dropped into the smooth part of the bore without resistance and then rammed into the rifling.

The M1777 carbine was longer and heavier than the M1766, displaying a round, iron barrel of approximately 33 inches and measuring almost 46 inches overall. Two rather than three bands were used to secure the barrel because the forestock was shortened to within 14 inches of the muzzle, providing clearance for the socket bayonet. The upper barrel band is secured by a flat tension spring and carries the front sight and the ramrod guide. The lower band secures the front sling swivel and the rear

sling swivel is attached to the stock belly. The M1777 carbine is also provided with a dual sling arrangement.

The presence of a bayonet lug approximately one and ½ inches from the muzzle on the underside of the smoothbore barrel testifies that the M1777 carbine was designed for dragoon (heavy cavalry) use and it could be termed a musketoon inasmuch as dragoons fought afoot and the bayonet and rapidity in loading were requisites.

Though flintlock martial pistols had been employed in France since ca. 1650 and reference has been made to a flintlock cavalry pistol introduced in 1733, there is no conclusive evidence that a standard pistol pattern was adopted before 1763, for no French pistols had official military markings prior to that date.[39] The national firearms system instituted in 1717 made no provision for pistol manufacture though there was an exception in those procured for the *Maison du Roi* (Royal Household).[40]

By 1700 the flintlock pistols employed by the Royal Household Light Cavalry were privately purchased from independent gunsmiths because there were no established standards. In 1714, however, the Duc d'Chaulnes purchased 230 pairs of pistols each

M1777 FRENCH CAVALRY PISTOL (18th Century): Innovative design renders the M1777 pistol a radical departure from contemporary martial handguns, featuring a brass priming pan and lock housing. Of 14 bore (.69) with a barrel length of 7½ inches, it was used by French land and naval forces and was the pattern for the first U.S. martial pistol. Courtesy of the *Musée de l'Armée*, Paris.

marked with three fleurs-de-lis and they were distributed without obligation among the Royal
Household Light Cavalry.[41] Six years later Louis
XV's *carabinier* (carbine) regiment was similarly provided with "the best pistols available of 15 *pouces*
[inches] overall length."[42]

In 1763 France adopted a cavalry pistol and a
constabulary pistol.[43] The M1763 constabulary
(*gendarmerie*) pistol has a round, five-inch barrel of
.59 caliber and is similar to the M1763 cavalry pistol
in other respects. The M1763 cavalry pistol displays a
nine and ½ inch barrel of .67 caliber. The convex
lockplate and throat-hole cock are identical to the
M1763 musket lock. A single, split-ring band at the
muzzle secures the barrel to the stock and there were
no sights. Furniture is iron and an iron, button-head
ramrod is provided. The walnut grip is somewhat
elongated in comparison to later French martial
pistols and the pommel butt displays a heavy iron
cap. Contrary to the popular notion there were no
M1763 navy pistols per se; rather the M1763 cavalry
pistol provided with brass furniture was used for sea
service.

In 1776 a compact, innovative martial pistol
with a distinctive design was adopted and production began the following year. The M1777 French
martial pistol was a radical departure from other
contemporary and conventional martial and utilitarian pistols. The seven and ½ inch, round iron
barrel of .67 caliber tapered toward the muzzle and
there were no sights.

The salient design innovation of the M1777
martial pistol is the brass breech casing wherein the
barrel is mounted and it also serves as a receptacle for
the iron, button-head ramrod. The conventional
throat-hole cock, battery, and lockplate are iron
though the priming pan is brass, cast integral with
the breech casing. An atypical, inverted battery
spring is positioned beneath the pan. There is no
forestock and the sharply curved walnut grip has a
brass cap connected to the breech plug tang by an
iron grip strap secured by a screw.

Some M1777 French martial pistols were provided with belt hooks and were issued for sea service,
though like the M1763, there was no distinct navy
model. The M1777 pistol was affectionately known
among French soldiers and seamen as a pistol *à la
Mandrin,* apparently because it had been popularized
by a notorious French smuggler with that pseud-
onym.[44]

The Seven Years' War ravaged the French national treasury and strained the production capacity
of the royal arms manufactories and the crown was
forced to purchase firearms from independent contractors and foreign merchants; the latter generally
supplying inferior weapons. After hostilities ceased
the martial musket was altered at an average two-

year interval until the introduction of the M1777.
Thereafter the flintlock remained the ignition agent
in various kinds of French martial firearms until
supplanted by the percussion ignition system in
1840.[45]

Old World Technological Innovation

The seventeenth-century European armament
industry had heavily relied on the technical skills of
the experienced, individual gunsmith though late in
the century there had arisen from necessity a large
cadre of craftsmen specializing in specific gunsmithing work, e.g., barrel borers, forgers, and straighteners; breechers, lock-makers, and stock-makers;
furniture forgers and casters, filers, parts hardeners
and polishers; browners and bluers, woodcarvers,
and engravers; bayonet forgers, sight fitters, screw-
and-pin makers, bullet mould makers, and parts as-
semblers.

By 1725 commercial gunsmithing had so diversified throughout Europe that there had emerged
specialists achieving outstanding reputations as pistolsmiths, riflesmiths, and makers of quality fowling
pieces. The specialization or diversity of craftsmanship associated with gunmaking continuously expanded thereafter, fostering a broad division of labor
in the commercial and martial armament industry,
while each had grown to the extent that gunmaking
was no longer an exclusive household enterprise because the demand for firearms created a need for
larger facilities or what could be unequivocally
termed factories, producing therein all the components of a firearm.

The casual relationship between science and
technology existing throughout the centuries of firearms evolution became more direct and clearly
defined during the eighteenth century and thereafter
proliferated; an association gradually perceived by
progressive European nations and the principal
reason why those nations progressed. And it was
during the early eighteenth century that the growing
alliance of science and technology began to be
applied to the military infrastructure with more significant results.

Most European powers fully recognized the
need to develop adequate and reliable facilities to
produce firearms, gunpowder, and the other habiliments of war and to provide the essential technical
skills and resources to support those facilities, reaching into related fields like chemistry and metallurgy.
While the need was perceived, however, it was often
difficult to implement and attain, for not only was

there a paucity of skilled technicians and available financing, but many of the supportive industries were neither consolidated nor competently and rationally utilized.

The advent of the eighteenth century certainly did nothing to diminish the inventive proclivity of the gunmakers; rather it provided a stimuli in conjunction with the relationship between science and technology, and while many previous firearms systems were improved there were original innovations of sufficient magnitude to influence profoundly the European and American armament industries; the latter in most instances belatedly emulating the former.

Among those irrepressible dreamers and inveterate mechanicians who significantly contributed to eighteenth-century firearms evolution was French engineer Isaac de la Chaumette (fl. 1695-1725). In 1700 he designed a pair of innovative saddle or horse pistols which could be readily converted into a carbine, i.e., *pistolets d'arcon dont on peut faire une carabine*.[46] Those unique flintlock handguns were provided with a screw plug system similar to that earlier devised by von Sprinzenstein (see p. 103) although its application by de la Chaumette was not originally involved with breech loading.

One pistol of the pair had a hollow stock and a vertical screw plug which did not penetrate the upper breech surface, though it was connected to the trigger guard. The other pistol displayed a rear sight and was identical to the first except that the stock was solid, there was no screw plug, and the muzzle was threaded. The latter pistol barrel was inserted into the hollow stock of the former and the muzzle was screwed into the threaded breech. When the breech screw was lowered by turning the trigger guard, it cleared the bore of the first pistol to pass the shot fired from the second.

De la Chaumette's pistol-carbine was somewhat impractical, though he recognized the potential of the screw plug and in 1704 he applied it to a breech-loading firearm with two significant innovations: (1) the plug fully penetrated the breech surface, and (2) an integral rim prevented the plug from being removed when the breech was opened.

The chamber was revealed by merely unscrewing the trigger guard two or three turns and, with the muzzle down, the ball was dropped in the opening, followed by the powder charge; the ball cast slightly oversized to prevent it from rolling through the bore. Rotating the trigger guard in the opposite direction sealed the breech, the churning screw threads disposing of any excess powder. The vent was located slightly forward of the breech opening and a conventional flintlock was used.

De la Chaumette's design was superior to previous screw breech systems because the trigger guard, connected to the plug, gave sufficient leverage in most instances to force the breech open even if the threads were clogged with powder residue. Though de la Chaumette was anticipated in the design of the screw transversing the breech by Danzig gunsmith Daniel Lagatz (see p. 104) late in the seventeenth century, it is doubtful if the Frenchman was aware of that innovation, while Lagatz used it for isolating the breech from the buttstock magazine of a flintlock breech-loader he had devised rather than as a system for opening and closing the breech.[47]

As Peterson has noted, de la Chaumette's 1704 system might have been the prototype for the breech-loading carbines issued to a French dragoon regiment in 1723.[48] By 1705, de la Chaumette had produced two variations, the first similar to his 1704 design except that the screw entered the side of the breech, and the second employing a spring-loaded trigger guard which supported a conical, pull-drop plug; spring tension securing the plug. Neither design was as successful as the 1704 system.

Because of his Huguenot affiliation de la Chaumette was forced to flee to London and in 1721 he received from George I a patent for a "cannon, fusil and pistol which being charged by the breech through the barrel, is cooled by charging it and cleaned by firing it, and carries twice as far as those commonly in use, and requires but half the quantity of powder."[49] The British patent evidently applied to his 1704 system, while the efficacy of the half-charge was enhanced by the resistance provided by the oversized ball and the positive obturation of the tight screw breech.

The famous Kalthoff gunsmiths (see p. 107) also experimented with screw-plug breech-loaders as did Copenhagen gunsmith Johan Merckel who in 1706 devised one using a separate handle rather than the integral trigger guard to open the breech. French master gunsmith Bidet—de la Chaumette's contemporary and also exiled in London because of religious persecution—improved the screw-plug system with an innovative, quick-turn thread which dropped the vertical screw with a single turn of the trigger guard,[50] while he subsequently made a lavishly embellished breech-loader for George I.

De la Chaumette's screw breech system was highly touted by the brilliant French marshal Hermann Maurice, Comte de Saxe, in *Mes Rêveries* (Paris, 1757) where he suggested that it be used in a carbine of his own invention which he termed an *amusette*, i.e., a light field piece or large wall gun also known as an *arquebus à croc*.[51] Parisian gunsmith Brion (fl. 1734-1739) made several sporting guns using the de la Chaumette system, though it was a Scot serving in the British Army who brought de la Chaumette's innovative design to ultimate perfection in 1776.

BREECH-LOADING PISTOLS/
CARBINE (18th Century, ca.
1701): De la Chaumette's version
of the screw-plug breech system
was applied to a unique pair of
pistols which could be converted
into a carbine. Top. View of the
rear pistol barrel which screwed
into the breech of the front pistol.
Turning the trigger guard permitted the breech plug to be lowered, thus providing clearance for
the ball from the rear pistol. Author's sketch.

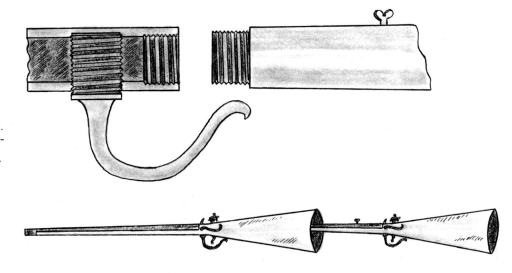

BREECH-LOADING MUSKET
(ca. 1704): This illustration from
Diderot's *Encyclopèdie* depicts in
Fig. 3 the De La Chaumette
breech system as applied to a
musket. Courtesy of the University of South Florida Library,
Special Collections.

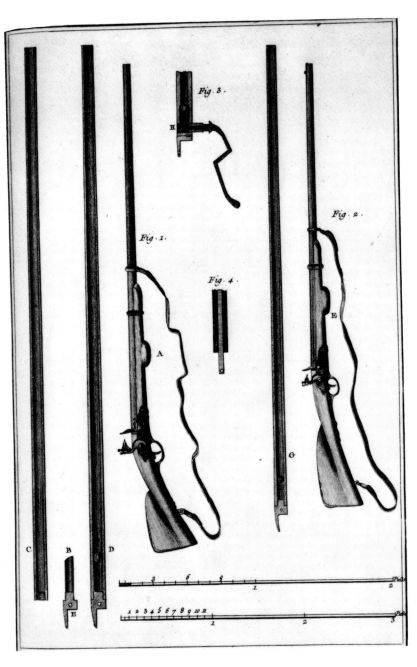

In 1736 a breech-loader based on two previous systems was commissioned by Don Nicolás de Olivares from Madrid gunsmith José Cano (?-1751), a former student of Spanish master Juan Fernández.[52] Cano's design incorporated the separate loading chamber (see p. 80) in conjunction with a break-open breech action; the former innovation appearing in the sixteenth century and the latter in the seventeenth century. Cano's breech action, however, employed a hinge, and the breech dropped open in the manner of some modern shotguns rather than pivoting upward or to the side, while the separate chamber was combined with a battery, priming pan, and vent.

The Cano breech-loader was provided with a dozen loading chambers which were charged with the powder and projectile and inserted in the breech; a vertical projection at the rear of the chamber permitting rapid extraction. The weapon was fired with a conventional flintlock minus the battery which was attached to the separate chamber.

When Don Nicolás died his son presented the firearm to Philip V who returned it to Cano for refurbishing. Cano completely refinished the firearm at a cost of 27,000 *reales;* a considerable though not outrageous sum, for he altered the lock, restocked it after the French fashion, and embellished it with the king's coat of arms, gold inlay, and 12 diamonds.[53]

The seventeenth-century pivotal breech system was for many years ignored by serious firearms inventors because gas leakage caused by improper obturation had rendered it impractical. The system, however, was resurrected in 1770 by Milan gunsmith Giuseppe Crespi (fl. 1765-1790).[54] In 1772 Crespi went to Vienna and induced the Austrians to adopt rifle and carbine versions as martial firearms. He then supervised their manufacture at the renowned Ferlach Arsenal in 1775.

In 1788, 30 Crespi-system carbines with spear-like bayonets were made by London master gunsmith Durs Egg (fl. 1770-1834) for the Master of the Ordnance. The Crespi carbine was rejected as a British martial firearm because the specter of improper obturation still haunted the mechanism despite an improved breech design and it was subsequently abandoned in Austria for the same reason.[55] Significantly, the Crespi breech-loader was the first to be adopted as a martial firearm on a large scale by any nation.

An increasing preoccupation with wildfowling among the aristocracy and affluent middle class in eighteenth-century Europe saw a number of technological innovations emerge in the evolution of the fowling piece. By ca. 1730 the heavy, long-barreled, full-stocked sporting fusil of the previous century had been somewhat refined and in Britain a trend toward more elegantly appointed sporting firearms was initiated.

By 1715 most fowling pieces had become shorter in the barrel, the length reduced from as much as six feet to four. Forestocks were shortened commensurately and, consequently, the fowling piece emerged as a more manageable, lightweight firearm and the addition of a battery bridle improved the efficacy of the flintlock because it reduced friction and wear on the battery screw; thus accelerating the snapping action of the cock to ensure almost instantaneous ignition.

Several attempts would be made during the century to improve the range and killing power of the fowling piece. One of the first and most significant improvements is attributed to Stanislaus Paczelt of Prague (fl. 1730-1738) and it is possibly the precursor of the modern shotgun choke.[56] Paczelt also experimented with the so-called concealed flintlock.

Although there is no conclusive evidence, Paczelt apparently theorized that if the fowling piece bore was constricted or choked a few inches from the muzzle the powder gases would exert more pressure there and the shot would be compressed; thus while the velocity of the load was increased it would also spread in a dense, even pattern after leaving the bore and be more effective at a greater distance. Not until the nineteenth century, however, would the concept prove feasible.

To circumvent misfires caused by damp or wet priming powder and to reduce or eliminate the flash and voluminous powder smoke produced by ignition, several unknown seventeenth-century gunsmiths had introduced the enclosed or concealed flintlock. In most instances a metal box surrounded the lock and it was cocked either by an exposed lever or a false lock mounted on the box; the external cock connected to the internal cock by a shank. Both methods were cumbrous and ineffectual, for while the priming pan was covered it was not entirely waterproofed, the powder smoke escaped, and priming flash scorched the stock and built up excessive carbon deposits in the lock and around the battery.

A partial solution was found ca. 1660 by Danish gunsmith Mathias Kalthoff (fl. 1652-1665).[57] Kalthoff's concealed lock incorporated a cock driven by a flat spring which slid along the breech atop the lockplate to strike a horizontal battery covering the pan. Though Kalthoff reduced the bulk of the mechanism the attendant problems were unresolved.

In 1738 Paczelt devised a concealed flintlock of superior design wherein a secondary trigger, located behind the primary trigger, was used to cock the mechanism. When the primary trigger was squeezed a powerful coil spring propelled the sliding cock forward, the flint striking a hinged, pivotal battery flush with the breech. There was no priming pan or vent, for when the battery was struck it directly exposed the powder in the chamber.[58]

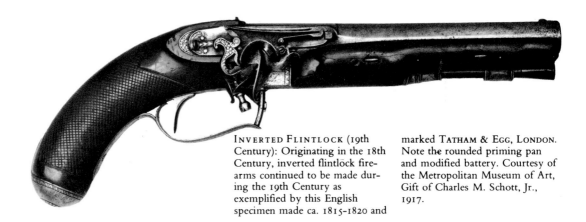

INVERTED FLINTLOCK (19th Century): Originating in the 18th Century, inverted flintlock firearms continued to be made during the 19th Century as exemplified by this English specimen made ca. 1815-1820 and marked TATHAM & EGG, LONDON. Note the rounded priming pan and modified battery. Courtesy of the Metropolitan Museum of Art, Gift of Charles M. Schott, Jr., 1917.

CONCEALED FLINTLOCK (18th Century): The Paczelt concealed flintlock depicted was made in 1783 and illustrates the steel raised for loading and priming. The first trigger was used to cock the sliding lock concealed behind the breech. British Crown Copyright. Reproduced with permission of the Controller of Her Britannic Majesty's Stationery Office.

Variations of the Kalthoff and Paczelt designs were subsequently introduced, some incorporating a chimney-like flue to redirect ignition flash and the resultant powder smoke. A double-barreled firearm employing concealed locks was made in Germany ca. 1740. Firearms with concealed locks never became popular, for despite improvements those innovations failed to adequately accomplish their avowed purpose.

There also appeared in Europe ca. 1750 a number of firearms in which the conventional, side-mounted flintlock was inverted or, in some instances, the lock was situated beneath the breech with the cock centrally-hung. The inverted lock provided an unobstructed sighting plane and shielded the priming pan from the elements. Efficacy, however, relied on a lock delivering extremely fast ignition, otherwise the powder fell from the priming pan. That firearms with inverted flintlocks worked at all is a tribute to the lock-maker who exhibited great skill in timing the springs (see p. 72).

Introduced ca. 1745-1750 the false breech was possibly an English innovation which made it easier and faster to assemble or disassemble the barrel from the stock and it was initially employed in fowling pieces. The false breech was a metal plate with an integrally-forged tang extending from one side and a slot (detent) with a crossbar incised in the other.

The false breech was installed on the stock where the rear of the breech plug was seated, the tang mortised into the upper stock wrist and secured by a screw. The breech plug was modified, incorporating a hook-like lug at its base; the lug engaging the crossbar in the false breech plate detent. The tang screw prevented any lateral breech plate movement.

Subsequent variations of the false breech incorporated a spike instead of the tang, the spike merely driven into the stock, or a screw-like projection turned into the wood. The false breech eliminated the breech plug tang and screw which made removing the barrel less difficult once the barrel bands or barrel lug pins had been removed.

An improved breech plug was also introduced around midcentury.[59] With that innovation the vent channel in the barrel wall was aligned with an L-shaped channel in the breech plug. A slightly wider channel was drilled in the center of the breech plug, directly in line with the L-shaped channel, and served as the powder chamber. The powder chamber was smaller than bore diameter and the ball was seated against its concave face. Known as chamber-breeching, the concept was in theory and design similar to breech-chambering as displayed in the fourteenth-century Tannenberg gun (see p. 8).

Prior to the advent of chamber-breeching the flash from the priming powder entered the chamber directly through the vent channel, igniting the charge at that point, and while it was sufficient to effect combustion there was always a considerable amount of powder which failed to ignite, leaving a residue and obviously reducing the efficacy of the firearm.

With chamber-breeching the flash from the priming powder traveled a short distance through the breech channel and made a turn before reaching the powder charge. The charge in the chamber, however, was ignited in the center rather than at the side and practically all of the powder was consumed; thus leaving less residue while the ball flew farther and faster with greater striking energy.

Because of chamber-breeching the firearm was turned on its side after priming the pan and struck sharply with the palm of the hand near the lock to make certain that sufficient priming filled the long, L-shaped breech channel; a slight inconvenience. The primary disadvantage of chamber-breeching, however, was that the priming flash was forced to travel farther to reach the powder chamber, creating a discernable lapse of as much as a half-second from the time the flint struck the battery until the firearm was discharged.

Though the perceptible ignition lag was no real problem when firing at stationary objects, it was disconcerting when shooting at objects in motion like flying fowl or running animals. The lapse made it extremely difficult for the shooter to judge the proper lead, i.e., the distance ahead at which the firearm was aimed and fired to allow for the speed, direction, and range of the moving target under various shooting conditions and in relation to the velocity and wind factors effecting the projectile or projectiles. A positive solution to the ignition lag problem was found late in the century by the celebrated London gunsmith and inventor Henry Nock.

While the fowling piece had undergone several refinements the previous method of shot-making continued in Europe, though the French had established the enterprise on a large scale with expanded facilities in Paris ca. 1750. In 1769, however, English

CHAMBER-BREECHING (ca. 1750): The innovative breech design depicted is similar to that used in the 14th Century Tannenberg gun. The powder charge is ignited in the center via a long, L-shaped vent. In chamber-breeched firearms the breech was often turned to the side and the lock tapped with the palm to make certain the priming powder filled the long vent channel. Author's sketch.

plumbing engineer William Watts of Bristol revolutionized shot-making with a technological innovation producing huge quantities of nearly perfect spherical shot in various sizes both faster and more economically.[60]

Watts accomplished his purpose by erecting a tall, frame structure now generally referred to as a shot tower which increased the distance the molten lead traveled from the perforated trencher to the water-filled tub as noted in Prince Rupert's description of shot-making (see p. 64), for at the top of the tower Watts installed the melting furnace and trenchers. Passing through the trenchers or shot pans the molten lead fell to a large tank below and the air-hardened pellets were cushioned by the water to preserve their spherical form.

Though shot towers shortly thereafter were made of masonry as well as wood, the shot-making equipment did not realize substantial improvement until the nineteenth century, while not until the twentieth century was it discovered that the long drop to the water rather than the impact determined the spherical form of the lead pellets.[61] The shot towers currently used are merely improved versions of Watts' innovation.

The widespread use of shot towers resulted in the greater distribution of less expensive shot and there was a larger selection of shot sizes available. Shot-moulding, however, was not eliminated, for the individual continued to make shot when the need arose. While the demand for shot escalated in eighteenth-century Europe, marketing potential was even greater in North America with the burgeoning fur trade.

Just prior to midcentury there was introduced a French barrel-making technique which shortly thereafter became extremely popular with the many gunsmiths producing quality fowling pieces and it was no less well received by their affluent patrons enamored of bird hunting. The innovative technique, known as *canon à ruban* (ribbon barrel) or *canon tordu* (twist barrel), combined the helical and the longitudinal barrel seam and it was described by G.F. Magne de Marolles, *La Chasse au Fusil* (Paris, 1788):

With a strip of much less thickness than is required for an ordinary barrel, a tube is formed as though a barrel were to be made. On this *chemise* is rolled a strip three or four lines in thickness, an inch broad, and chamfered to a point on each side. The whole is put into the fire and heated a few inches at a time. This strip is called the *ruban* [ribbon]. To roll it round the *chemise* they use a pair of tongs, of which one beak is flat and short and the other rounded and very long. This long arm serves first to turn and press the strip of metal on the *chemise*. It is worthy of note that the twist-barrel is not made all in one piece like other barrels, owing to the difficulty of rolling a piece sufficiently long to form a barrel of the usual length—that is to say, about 3 feet. It is made in three pieces, which are afterward welded together. Five feet of *ruban* are required for each foot of barrel. When the *ruban* is thus spirally turned the whole length of the *chemise,* and made to overlap, edge to edge, they give [it] a few heats to forge the whole together, as in an ordinary barrel. The barrel is at once passed to the boring shop, and bored until the lining, or *chemise,* is for the most part taken out by the boring bits, and there remains little but the strip with which it is covered. One cannot deny that the barrel made in this manner possesses a strength superior to that of the ordinary barrels, insomuch as it has not, so to say, a weld, or at any rate the weld is almost transversal, and in this way better placed to resist the force of the explosion than if it were straight along, or even if it were spiral, as in the barrels which are simply twisted tubes.[62]

Canon à ruban barrels should not be confused with Damascus barrels as the foring technique differed considerably, nor should they be mistaken for twist barrels in which the barrel was simply reheated after the longitudinal seam was welded and then twisted upon itself; a technique thought to strengthen the fiber of the iron. Twist barrels were known since the early sixteenth century as exemplified in the pistol barrels made for the Italian gun shields purchased by Henry VIII.

Also fashionable in France and Spain at the time the *canon à ruban* technique was introduced was the saddle-type rear sight generally employed with sporting firearms. Resembling its namesake when viewed in profile, the saddle-type rear sight was attached to the barrel by a thin, flat band more fragile than the common barrel band.

With the eighteenth-century escalation of militant colonialism and maritime exploration flintlock firearms were known and used even in the most remote regions of the globe as witnessed by Capt. James Cook's expeditions to the frigid polar extremes and the steaming Pacific isles during the period 1768-1779. Cook and his successors exposed the uninhibited and unspoiled people of those vast areas to the rampant exploitation and degredation characterizing western European culture and also introduced them to firearms and other technological innovations.

As a result of global expansion numerous kinds of flintlock firearms were devised to suit a variety of needs, ranging in size from the diminutive pocket pistol to the cumbrous rampart piece and the heavy, four-bore elephant gun employed by the avaricious spoilers of Africa and Asia. The elephant, however, was by no means the largest mammal to fall prey to flintlock firearms; the distinction reserved for the remarkably intelligent leviathan of the deep: the whale.

In 1820 Capt. William Scoresby of the British South Sea Company described the introduction of flintlock firearms to the whaling industry in his "Account of the Arctic Regions, with a History and Description of the Northern Whale-Fishery," noting that:

The harpoon-gun . . . is well calculated to facilitate the capture of whales, . . . particularly in calm clear weather, when the fish [sic] are apt to take the alarm whenever the boats approach within fifteen or twenty yards of them. The harpoon-gun was invented in . . . 1731 and used . . . by some individuals with success. Being, however, difficult and somewhat dangerous in its application, it was laid aside for many years.[63]

Like many technological innovations in firearms evolution the flintlock harpoon gun was not immediately accepted, nor was it because it was "difficult and somewhat dangerous in its application," for eighteenth-century harpooners clung tenaciously to their cherished traditions. When their prejudice was momentarily abandoned in 1733, however, one ship employing a flintlock harpoon gun took two of the three whales harvested.

Convinced that the harpoon gun was practical, the Society of Arts in London offered 20 guineas to any inventor interested in submitting an improved design and also encouraged its use by paying harpooners an equal premium for any whale taken. The society's initial offer was apparently heeded, for according to Scoresby "In 1771 or 1772 a new one [harpoon gun] was produced . . . which differed so materially from the instrument before in use that it was received as an original invention."[64]

Capt. Scoresby did not describe that doubtlessly

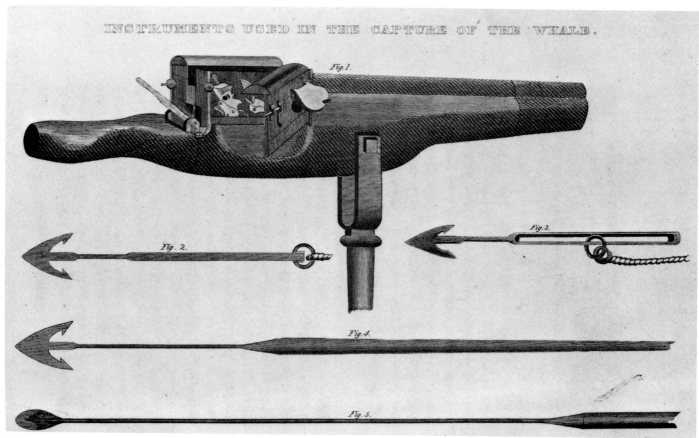

INSTRUMENTS USED IN THE CAPTURE OF THE WHALE.

innovative harpoon gun and not until the early nineteenth century was the reluctance of the harpooners to use it partially conquered.

With the dawn of the eighteenth century further improvements were seen in the development of the mandrel lathe, the most significant devised by Charles Plumier, La Lievre, and Gideon Duval. Plumier's innovative mandrel lathe, depicted in his *L'art de Tourner en Perfection* (Lyons, 1701), was capable of working wood and metal though utilizing special cutting tools for the latter.[65]

La Lievre introduced an improved mandrel lathe prior to midcentury, adding a rudimentary sine bar working in conjunction with the spindle which, for the first time, permitted the lathe to originate a screw thread.[66] La Lievre's accomplishment would have a monumental impact on machine-tool evolution and the sine bar was refined ca. 1763 by Gideon Duval. With the possible exception of turning gun screws, the mandrel lathe was not otherwise engaged in eighteenth-century firearms manufacture.

While it is not in the purview of this study to dwell upon machines and tools not directly associated with firearms manufacture, it is necessary occasionally to investigate the impact of firearms technology on other technological accomplishments. The steam engine, destined to supplant the power sources by which for centuries all machinery and machines were driven, is a graphic illustration, for two innovative machine tools associated with

FLINTLOCK WHALING (HARPOON) GUN (18th Century): As far as it can be determined the flintlock harpoon gun was first used in 1731. Note the enclosed lock mechanism; an attempt to protect the lock from salt water corrosion and keep the priming powder dry. Courtesy of the Library of Congress.

gunmaking were directly involved with steam engine evolution: (1) the barrel boring mill, and (2) the milling (planing) machine.

Intimated in Classical antiquity when it was discovered that the vapor from heated water could be used as a power source, the steam engine was initially patented in 1698 by Englishman Thomas Savery (1650?–1715).[67] Savery did not live to see the fruits of his unique contribution to technology feed a world becoming gradually more dependent upon machines to perform manual labor, though his efforts inspired others; first among them Devonshire ironmaster Thomas Newcomen (1663–1729) who devised a superior atmospheric steam engine. Like the Savery engine, Newcomen's invention was used as a pump, successfully draining a coal mine near Birmingham in 1712.[68]

By 1735 Newcomen's steam engine was in general use for pumping mines throughout Europe, while in North America the first Newcomen engine was constructed by an immigrant Cornwall mechanician and in 1753 it was employed to drain a New Jersey Colony copper mine.[69] Newcomen's engine was adapted to fill reservoirs and to operate municipal water systems like the great Marley Water Works installed near Paris.

MANDREL LATHE
(18th Century): This
model represents the
mandrel lathe invented
by P. Charles Le
Plumier and illustrated
in his *L'art de Tourner
en Perfection* (Lyon,
1701). Though incapa-
ble of originating a
screw thread, Plumier
noted that it could be
used for metal-working
with special cutting
tools. Courtesy of the
Smithsonian Institution.

The pump barrels made for the steam engine
operating the innovative Marley system were shaped
by a milling machine employed in 1751 at the French
national armory in Maubeuge to cut the breech flats
on musket barrels. The invention of the milling machine is generally attributed to Nicolas Forq.[70]

Whether the innovative milling machine was
used at Maubeuge and other French armories prior
to 1750 cannot be ascertained, though in its early
form it was mounted in a wooden frame and provided with a horizontal iron carriage serving as a
fixture for the laterally-rotating cutter. The carriage
slowly moved over the workpiece, carrying the
cutter with it, and a vertical adjustment permitted the
cutter to be raised or lowered; thus the operator
could regulate the depth of the cut.

Milling machines of the Forq design were employed in the French national armories prior to 1770,
while an apparent variation emerged in Britain
before 1783, for that year the *Transactions of the Society of Arts* mentioned a devise for "planing cast
iron," though no details concerning its origin, construction, or operation are known.[71]

Thomas Newcomen apparently initiated the
concept of boring steam engine cylinders by machine
in an attempt to achieve conformity and to provide
sufficient obturation to prevent the steam from escaping around the piston head so the engine would
perform with maximum efficacy; the problem early
faced by gunsmiths attempting to prevent powder
gases from escaping around the projectile. Precision
boring, however, was not then imperative because
Newcomen's engines were relatively unsophisti-
cated.

That Newcomen accomplished his goal was the
result of technological innovations which had
emerged in the Netherlands. By 1700 the Netherlands was more advanced in heavy ordnance manufacture than other European nations and often recruited experienced gun-founders from elsewhere
on the Continent.[72] Employed in the state gun
foundry at The Hague in 1715 was a Swiss inventor
known to history as Maritz, and in 1713 he had
devised a mill designed for boring cannon barrels.[73]

In the Maritz mill the cannon barrel was supported by and secured in a vertical, wooden frame.

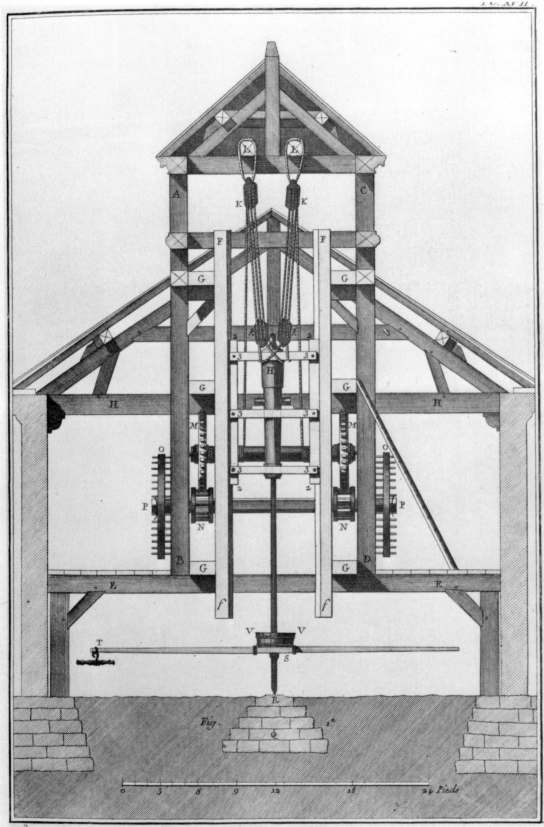

Fonte des Canons.

Elevation de l'Alézoir pour Forer et Alézer les Pieces.

VERTICAL CANNON-BORING MILL (18th Century): This French cannon-boring mill was probably copied from Dutch mills appearing early in the 18th Century. Note the gear and pulley system which lowered the cannon into the boring bit attached to the vertical shaft which was turned by animal energy as the single-tree on the turnstile suggests (T & V). From Diderot and D'Alembert, *L'encyclopédie, Recueil de Planches Sur Les Sciences et Les Arts,* Vol. V, plate XVII. Courtesy of the Eleutherian Mills Historical Library, Wilmington, Del.

CYLINDER-BORING MILL (18th Century, 1770): The cylinder-boring mill depicted is a model of the machine tool designed by John Smeaton for boring steam engine pistons. The cutaway in the cylinder mounted on a wheeled carriage exposes the circular cutter. Courtesy of the Science Museum, London.

The barrel was lowered to a long boring rod by a complex system of gears and pulleys. The vertical boring rod with its large cutting bit was slowly rotated by animal power and smoothed the rough interior of the cast barrel rather than boring through it.

Netherland gun-founder Andrew Schalch installed a boring mill similar to the Maritz design in the royal arsenal at Woolwich, England, ca. 1715.[74] A mill of like pattern was constructed in 1723 at the extensive Coalbrookdale Iron Works, and shortly thereafter Newcomen adapted it to bore his steam engine cylinders.[75]

Collaborating with Swiss gun-founder Jacob Ziegler, Dutchman Jan Verbruggen invented a cannon-boring mill operated by water power ca. 1758.[76] The mill design, however, differed radically from the Maritz concept, for the cannon barrel was mounted horizontally and a system of gears rotated it around a boring rod fed into the bore by a gear-and-pulley arrangement.

Scottish instrument maker James Watt (1736-1819) of the University of Glasgow had repaired a teaching model of the Newcomen engine and it so impressed him that he spent two years studying it and his investigation revealed a number of shortcomings. Watt's attempts to rectify the deficiencies of the Newcomen design resulted in an entirely new concept and in 1769 he received a patent for an improved steam engine.[77]

The most difficult problem confronting Watt was accurately boring the piston cylinder. English civil engineer John Smeaton (1724-1792) who had also taken an interest in Newcomen's engine par-

tially solved Watt's dilemma with an improved cylinder-boring mill in 1770.[78] Smeaton's cylinder-boring mill operated horizontally, though the technique was opposite of the Verbruggen cannon-boring mill, for the piston cylinder was secured in a wheeled carriage, fed into the rotating bit by a gear-and-pulley arrangement, and bored completely through.

Despite an improved technique Smeaton's mill incorporated the singular disadvantage of the boring rod being supported at one end only, thereby precluding a precision cut. Not until April, 1775 was a satisfactory solution to Watt's problem of improper obturation found when John Wilkinson (1728-1808) invented a boring mill of such accuracy that a cylinder 50 inches in diameter could be drilled to a tolerance of 1/1000 of an inch throughout its length.[79] Built at the Bersham Iron Works, Wilkinson's mill emulated the horizontal Verbruggen design and incorporated the wheeled carriage introduced by Smeaton, though it was more condusive to accurate boring because the water-powered boring rod was rigidly supported at either end.

Wilkinson's precision cylinder-boring mill greatly enhanced the efficacy of the steam engine and, like the cannon-boring mills preceding it, it was a true machine tool. The ancestry of the cylinder-boring mill and the cannon-boring mill, however, can be traced to the small, manually-operated barrel boring and rifling engines emerging in late fifteenth-century Germany (see p. 29). Wilkinson's mill specifically displayed a mechanical affinity with the venerable rifling engine, for the boring rod was supported at each end.

CYLINDER-BORING MILL (1775): The model depicted illustrates the features of the steam engine cylinder-boring mill devised by John Wilkinson. Note the dual boring arrangement. The levers atop the waterwheel (center) regulated the speed of the boring rods which are supported at each end, producing a more accurate cut than Smeaton's 1770 mill. Cannon-boring and cylinder-boring mills can trace their ancestry to the venerable boring and rifling engines devised in 15th Century Germany. Courtesy of the Science Museum, London.

The proliferation and widespread dissemination of scientific and technical knowledge early in the eighteenth century sparked a cataclysmic upheaval in applied technology. Many of the tasks previously and laboriously performed by hand were gradually assimilated by ingenious devices conceived to relieve the burden of the craftsman by reproducing identical or nearly the same manual functions by mechanical means; reproducing them efficiently, rapidly, and consequently more economically. Those factors ignited a concept which flamed into the so-called Industrial Revolution during the final quarter of the century.

While the innovative technology contributed by other Europeans involved in the eighteenth-century armament industry cannot be discounted or dismissed, the French displayed a remarkable propensity for technological innovation which extended into the realm of advanced manufacturing concepts and techniques, consequently elevating their commercial and martial arms-making technology above that of most nations.

However insignificant in the beginning, the immediate and long term effects of science and technology on the eighteenth-century European armament industry are incalculable. From the manufacturing techniques pioneered in the French national armories prior to midcentury were resurrected the revolutionary concepts of mass production and interchangeable components intimated in Classical antiquity; concepts which would subsequently engender a plethora of socio-economic changes.

In Great Britain the Royal Society ambitiously attempted to collate a compendium of scientific and technological data pertaining to all significant crafts and sponsored Ephraim Chambers (?-1740) whose two-volume *Dictionary of Arts and Sciences* appeared in 1728. Following in the footsteps of the Royal Society was the French *Académie Royale des Sciences*.

The *académie* commissioned a series of illustrative plates depicting most eighteenth-century crafts, and in 1750 sought to correlate them with a comprehensive text. The following year the *académie* influenced the release from prison of the eminent philosopher and political activist Denis Diderot (1713-1784). During the succeeding 21 years and in association with Jean La Rond d'Alembert (1717?-1783), Diderot assiduously labored to produce the prodigious *L'encyclopédie, ou Dictionnaire Raisonné des Sciences, des Arts et des Métiers* (The Encyclopedia, or Analytical Dictionary of the Sciences, and the Arts and Crafts).

The masterful *L'encyclopédie* initially consisted of 28 volumes and in 1776-1777 it was supplemented with six additional volumes and further broadened by two volumes of tables in 1780; a herculean effort greatly overshadowing Chambers' 1728 exposition and it remains an undisputed classic in the literature of science and technology. *L'encyclopédie* was published in several editions, each with slight variations in the title and the illustrative plates.

Much of what is presently known about the eighteenth-century French gunmaking and gunpowder industry is preserved in *L'encyclopédie;* particularly the accomplishments achieved in the development of innovative machine tools and in the radical manufacturing techniques employed at the national armories and powder mills, while also represented with unstinting devotion to detail are the hand tools and equipment associated with those activities.

The illustrations from *L'encyclopédie* reproduced here are from volumes *i* and *vi* of the eleven-volume pictorial supplement, *Recueil de Planches Sur Les Sciences et Les Arts* (The Collection of Plates Pertaining to the Sciences and the Arts), accompanying the 1770 edition of *L'encyclopédie*.

(The page numbers, identification letters, and figure numbers referring to the 1770 edition plates cited are set in brackets.)

Plates *i* through *vi* of volume *i* pertain to the *Arquebusier* (Gunsmith) and have been selected to identify the hand tools, instruments, gauges, and machines used for firearms manufacture in the French national armories and by independent gunsmiths. Many of the hand tools depicted were commonly used during the fourteenth century and most of them, incorporating only minor design changes in the interim, are currently employed by gunsmiths throughout the globe. The plates also illustrate the basic components of a contemporary French pistol and sporting fusil.

From the part of volume *i* pertaining to *Minéralogie* (Mineralogy) are plates *ii*, *iii*, *iv*, *vii*, and *ix* concerned with the mining and refining of *salpêtre* (saltpeter), and plates *iv*, *ix*, *xii*, *xiv*, and *xvii* relating to the manufacture of black powder *(poudre)* as regulated by the *Régie des Poudres* (Gunpowder Bureau).

It is probable that the *Machine à Forer et à Alezar les Canons de Fusil* (Machine for Boring and Reaming Gun Barrels) depicted in volume *i*, plate *i* [pp. 218-219] was used in the various national armories prior to midcentury. Whether the design was French or influenced by machines previously developed in the Netherlands cannot be determined.

Plate *i* is a perspective view of the boring and reaming machine, its complexity exceeded only by its prodigious size. A water wheel provided sufficient power for the spoked wheel [D] connected by rope belts to four barrel-boring and reaming spindles [G, H, M, and O]. The boring and reaming bits [P and I] attached to the spindles slowly rotated, their speed regulated by reduction gears operated by [D] and a breaking system [V].

The rough-forged barrel blanks, i.e., barrels prior to boring and reaming, were secured in the boring vises [S] situated in the pits [Q]. The pits had stairs [R] so the attendants could supervise the boring and reaming operations. The boring bits were cooled and lubricated by water from the tank [A] flowing along a trough system [C and CC]. The water was discharged from the pits by a drainage system not depicted.

Some chroniclers of technology and not a few firearms historians have indicated that the tedious boring and reaming operations were performed with the barrel blanks completely submerged. It would have been extremely difficult for the attendants, however, to stand in water-filled pits while feeding the barrels into the rotating bits, occasionally changing the bits, and clearing away the metal chips removed by the bits.[80]

The upper part of plate *ii* [p. 220] illustrates a *Machine à Caneler les Canons de Fusil* (Machine for Grinding and Shaping the Gun Barrels), i.e., a milling machine (see p. 62). The workman [fig. 1] is shaping and finishing the barrel clamped in the grinding guide; the technique tapering the barrel to its proper dimensions and cutting the breech flats. An apprentice [fig. 2] is cranking the drive wheel providing the power to operate the milling machine; the drive wheel and pulley arrangement initially introduced during the late sixteenth century. The lower part of plate *ii* details the complex milling machine design [fig. 3] and also illustrates the barrel clamping device [fig. 4] which is more fully delineated in plate *iii* [p. 221, figs. 5-20].

Plate *iv* [p. 222] of volume *i* displays the numerous hand tools, gauges, and measuring instruments employed by the gunsmith during that epoch. Curiously, the numerals designating the figures begin at the right of the plate. The English nomenclature, as indicated, is followed by the French in parentheses.

Plate IV: arquebusier

Fig. 1 Wood auger *(foret en bois.)*
Fig. 2 Pointed awl *(broche pointue).*
Fig. 3 Rat-tail rasp, wood handle *(queue de rat en bois).*
Fig. 4 Spring compass *(compas en ressort).*
Fig. 5 Multi-sided (barrel) reamer *(broche à pans).*
Fig. 6 Marking gauge *(trusquin).*
Fig. 7 Metal-marking slate *(pierre sanguine).*
Fig. 8 Chisel *(ciseau).*
Fig. 9 Cleaning rod *(lavoir).*
Fig. 10 Scraper *(gratoir)*, to remove powder fouling from bore.
Fig. 11 Stock template *(calibre).*
Fig. 12 Carbine barrel *(canon carabiné).*
    1) Barrel cross-section *(le canon coupé en deux sur la longueur).*
    2) Breech plug *(la culasse).*
Fig. 13 Components separated from the barrel *(canon brisé).*
    1) Barrel *(le canon).*
    2) Breech (plug) or breech block *(la culasse).*

Machine à Forer et à Alezer les Canons de Fusil. (18th Century): From Diderot, *L'encyclopédie, ou Dictionnaire Raisonné des Sciences, des Arts et des Métiers* (Paris, 1770), *Recueil de Planches Sur Les Sciences et Les Arts*, Vol. 1, Plate 1 (hereafter cited as *Recueil de Planches*). Courtesy of the Eleutherian Mills Historical Library, Wilmington, Del.

Pl. II

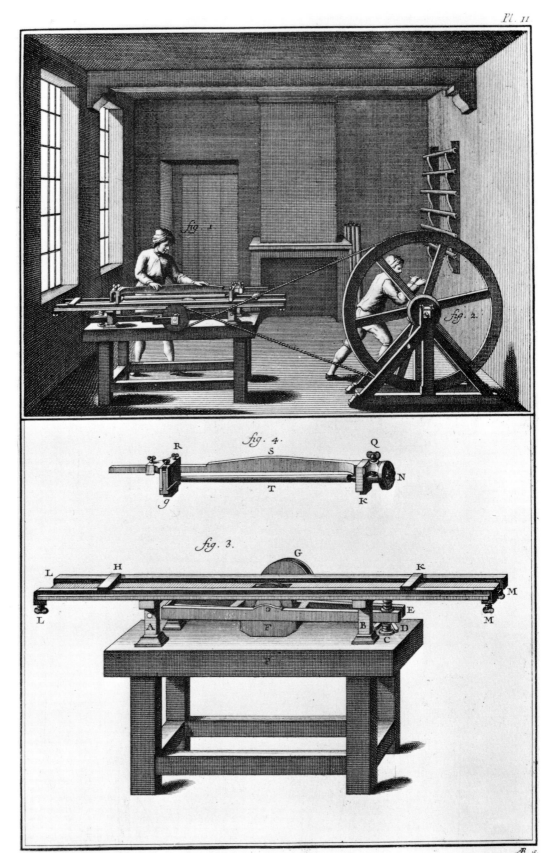

Machine à Caneler les Canons de Fusil (18th Century): *Recueil de Planches,* Vol. I, Plate II. Courtesy of the Eleutherian Mills Historical Library, Wilmington, Del.

Arquebusier,
Machine à Caneler les Canons de Fusil.

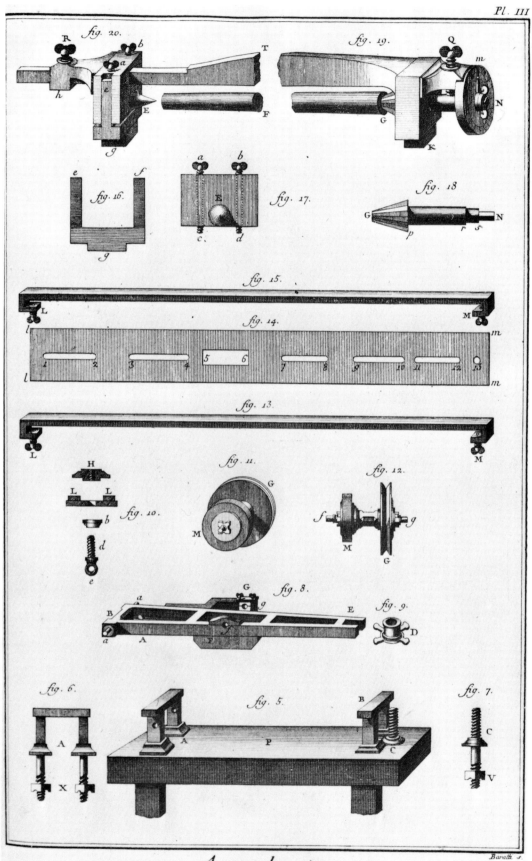

Pl. III

Barath. s.

Arquebusier,

Dévelopements de la Machine à Caneler.

Dévelopements de la Machine à Caneler (18th Century): *Recueil de Planches,* Vol. 1, Plate III. Courtesy of the Eleutherian Mills Historical Library, Wilmington, Del.

Arquebusier (18th Century): *Recueil de Planches,* Vol. I, Plate IV. Courtesy of the Eleutherian Mills Historical Library, Wilmington, Del.

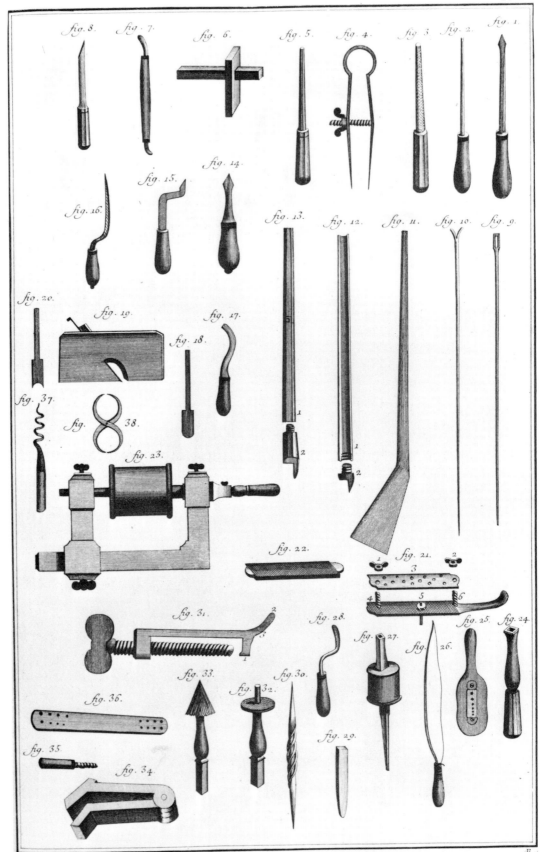

Arquebusier.

Pl. V.

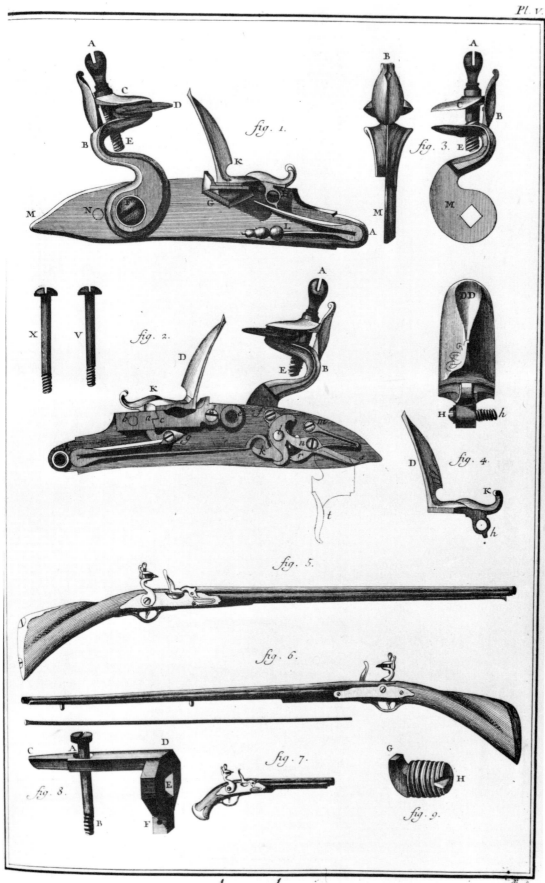

Arquebusier (18th Century): *Recueil de Planches,* Vol. 1, Plate v. Courtesy of the Eleutherian Mills Historical Library, Wilmington, Del.

Arquebusier

Pl. VI.

Arquebusier (18th Century): *Recueil de Planches,* Vol. I, Plate VI. Courtesy of the Eleutherian Mills Historical Library, Wilmington, Del.

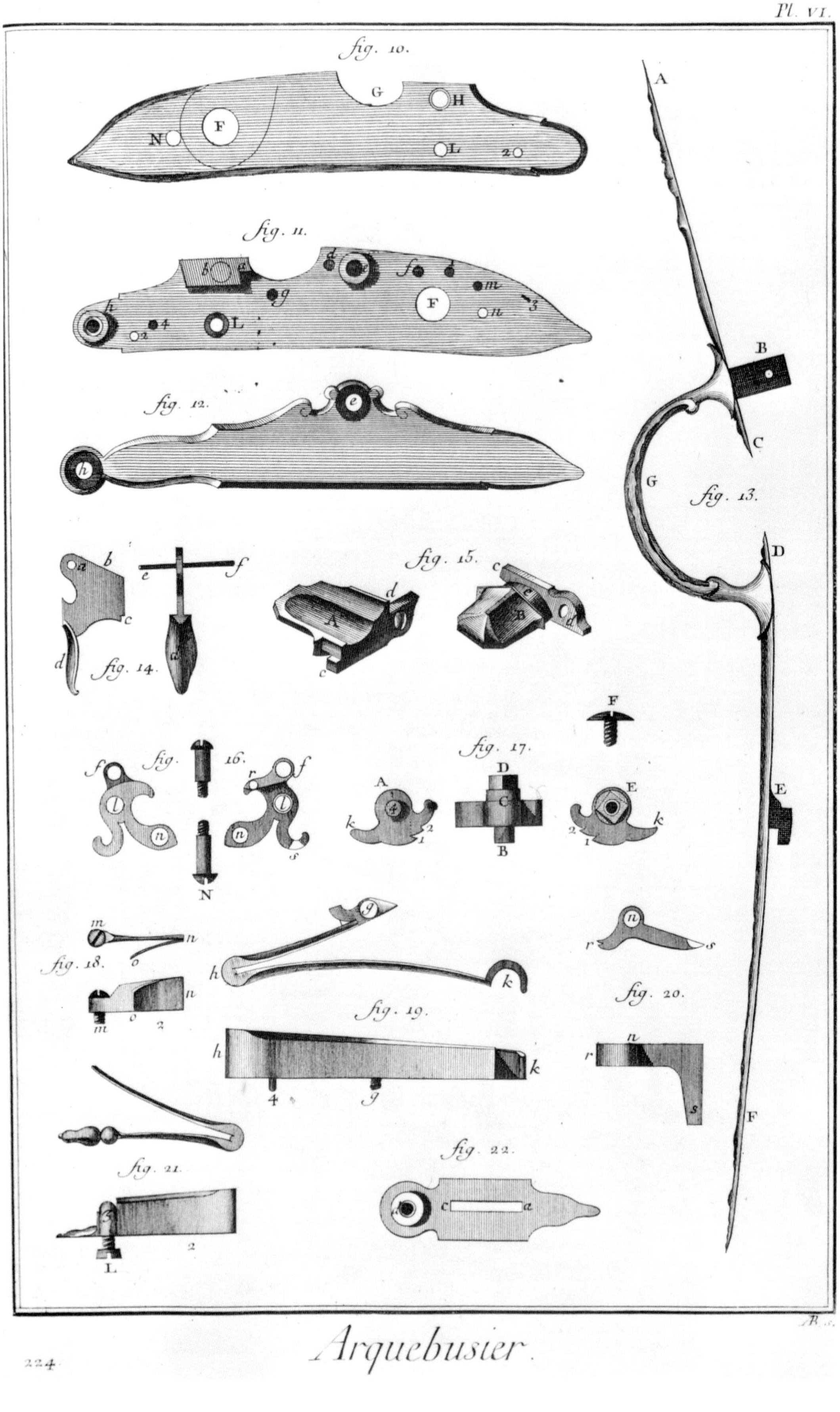

Arquebusier.

Plate *v* [p. 223] of volume *i* illustrates the exterior [fig. 1] and the interior [fig. 2] of the French flintlock *(platine à silex)* ca. 1750, including the cock *(corps du chien)* [fig. 3], the battery *(batterie)* [fig. 4], and the lockplate screws *(vis de platine)* [x and v]. Also represented is the right [fig. 5] and the left [fig. 6] sides of a contemporary flintlock fowling piece *(fusil)* and a common pistol *(pistolet)* [fig. 7], the false breech *(culasse fausse,* see p. 192) with its tang [fig. 8], and the breech plug *(culasse)* with its hook *(arque)* [fig. 9, G]. Also depicted [fig. 1] are the flint *(silex)* [D], the top jaw *(mâchoire)* [C], the top jaw screw *(grande vis du chien)* [A], and the cock spur *(ergot de corps du chien)* [B].

The views of the cock [fig. 3] clearly delineate the shoulder [M] arresting its forward movement when striking the upper edge of the lockplate *(corps de la platine)* [fig. 2, N]. The rear view of the battery [fig. 4] shows the inverted, tear-shaped depression and the ridge [DD] designed to deflect water from the priming pan *(bassinet)* [fig. 1, G], i.e., a waterproof pan *(bassinet imperméable)* which was not entirely effective in preventing rain or snow from entering the pan though it is characteristic of most expensive locks.

The most significant technological innovation depicted in plate *v* is the false breech [fig. 8] with its detent [E] which receives the distinctive breech plug hook [fig. 9, G]. Note also the clearance notch [H] for the vent channel cut into the breech plug threads. In this example the false breech is held in the stock by a lug [F] and a screw [A] passing through the short breech tang *(talon de la culasse)* [C and D].

The identification figures in plate *v*, volume *i*, continue in plate *vi*, depicting the disassembled (stripped) flintlock mechanism. The exterior [fig. 10] and the interior [fig. 11] of the stripped lockplate are shown with the sideplate or counterplate *(contre-platine)* [fig. 12]. The lockplate cutaway [G] is for the priming pan, while the holes and recesses in the lockplate and the counterplate correspond to the figures and letters designated on the disassembled lock components.

The combined trigger guard *(garde de détente)* and finials [fig. 13] are shown with the method of attaching them to the stock *(monture de fusil)*; the rear finial [A and C] secured by a pin transversing the stock and the stud [B], and the front finial [D and F] lug [E] engaging a slot [c and a] in the trigger plate *(pièce de détente)* [fig. 22]. The trigger *(détente)* is represented [fig. 14] with the trigger pin *(cheville de détente)* [e and f].

Figure 15 illustrates the top [A] and the bottom [B] of the priming pan with the hole [d] for the pan screw, while Figure 16 depicts the tumbler bridle *(bride de noix)* and the bridle screw *(vis à bride)*. The tumbler *(noix)* is illustrated in Figure 17 which also shows the square shoulder [E] which engages the corresponding recess in the cock body; the tumbler shoulder secured therein by the cock screw [F]. Figure 18 is the sear spring *(ressort de gâchette)* accompanied by the sear spring screw [m] which fits the recess in the lockplate correspondingly marked.

The mainspring *(grand ressort)* [fig. 19] has a hook [k] at one end which rests against the tumbler nose [k]. The mainspring pins [4 and g] fit correspondingly marked recesses in the lockplate. The sear *(gâchette)* [fig. 20] also depicts the sear nose [r] which engages the tumbler notches [1 and 2] at full cock and half cock, and the sear heel [s] upon which the flat, angled surface [b] of the trigger bears. Figure 21 depicts the battery spring *(ressort de batterie)* and the battery/pan cover screw *(vis de batterie)* [L].

Of all the martial firearms produced in the eighteenth-century it would be no exaggeration to state that those made in the French national armories under constant supervision and inspection were of superior workmanship and design, nor would it be remiss to consider the French national armories as factories in the modern sense despite the absence of an assembly line, for the firearms components were produced in sequence and eventually reached an assembly point. By ca. 1775-1780 even some of the lock components were initially rough-machined and then filed, polished, and fitted by artisans specializing in the work.

Using the methods described and depicted in the plates the French national armories produced large quantities of martial firearms. The M1717 French flintlock infantry musket and the models introduced thereafter were generally slimmer, lighter, more reliable, and of smaller caliber than rival European muskets and they also shot farther with less powder; the latter another result of innovative French technology.

By 1700 British, Dutch, and French gunpowder were considered superior to any produced elsewhere and large quantities were exported to colonial America. The ratio of saltpeter, sulphur, and charcoal used in the manufacture of martial black powder in Britain was officially standardized by 1718 at 75:10:15.[81] In France at that time martial gunpowder was formulated by the *Régie des Poudres* as 75:12½:12½.

France procured saltpeter from natural deposits located in her southern departments though, like Britain, most of it was imported from her colonies in India; a source denied following the Seven Years' War when Britain gained full control of the economy in India through the venerable East India Company established there in 1600. Though there was some domestic production, France imported most of her sulphur *(soufre)* from Sicily, while her vast forests provided adequate supplies of wood for making charcoal (charbon de bois).

L'encyclopédie graphically depicts black powder manufacture in France and the illustrations from the part of volume vi concerned with Minéralogie define the process from the extraction and refining of saltpeter and sulphur to the hand tools, techniques, and machines employed. Significantly, France regarded gunpowder manufacture with utmost concern and in 1776 named as director of the Régie des Poudres the renowned scientist Antoine Laurent Lavoisier (1743-1794). Known as the Father of Modern Chemistry, Lavoisier devised innovative refining methods which consequently elevated the quality of French gunpowder to the best in the world.

Plate ii [p. 216] of volume vi represents the hand tools used to gather and initially separate the obvious impurities found in natural saltpeter: pick [fig. 1] and shovel [fig. 2] for digging, maul [fig. 3] for breaking large lumps, scoop [fig. 4] for the initial sifting; sieve [fig. 5] for sifting and removing débris [D] from the saltpeter [I], and the baskets [fig. 6] to carry it to a collection point where it was packed and shipped to the huge government refinery and laboratory at Essonnes for distribution after processing.

The Plan et Profil de la Chaudiere et de son Fourneau (Plan and Perspective View of the Copper Refining Kettle and its Furnace) depicted in plate iii [p. 217] shows the first stage in the refining process. The raw saltpeter was dumped into the copper kettle [A], mixed with water, and boiled from ten to twelve hours. The saltpeter liquified as it boiled, and while some of the débris floated to the surface of the kettle most of it sank. The impurities were periodically dipped out, skimmed off, and ladled into the wooden tubs [B] provided for the purpose.

The upper part of plate vii [p. 223], L'Opération de puiser la Cuitte de celle d'enlever le Sel (The Boiling, Skimming, and Removing of the Salts), illustrates a workman [fig. 1] pouring the dross or sludge into large wooden tubs, while a companion [fig. 2] skims and disposes of the other impurities.

The lower part of plate vii depicts the various implements employed, including a hook [fig. 1] with a wooden handle [d] for manipulating the dross basket [X]; a fork [fig. 2] for maneuvering the shallow copper drying pans [fig. 7 and fig. 8]; a paddle [fig. 3] for stirring the liquified saltpeter; a ladle [fig. 4] for dipping and pouring the saltpeter into small casks; a perforated skimmer [fig. 5] for removing and straining the floating débris; and a yoke [fig. 6] for carrying the casks of molten saltpeter to the crystallization bed.

As the liquified saltpeter cooled in the crystallization bed it was constantly raked until crystals were formed by evaporation. After crystallization the granules were thoroughly washed to flush out any remaining impurities and then the crystals were dried. The ladles and skimmers depicted in plate vii are also shown in plate iv [p. 218, figs. 1-4].

In addition plate iv details the copper drying kettles [figs. 6 and 9] with their woven reed covers [figs. 7 and 8]. The drying flue [fig. 5] conveyed the hot air tapped from the refining furnace to the drying room to expedite the process [fig. 9]. The hot air was permitted to circulate freely around the pans by elevating them on wooden wedges [A and B].

Plate ix [p. 225] illustrates the washing vat [fig. 1] used during crystallization in the Laboratoire (laboratory) and the saltpeter cakes [fig. 2] prior to drying. After drying [fig. 3] the saltpeter cakes were stored [fig. 4] in readiness for preparation into gunpowder.

The sublimation or purification of sulphur was less complex than refining saltpeter; little changed from the fourteenth-century method though the equipment was more sophisticated and considerably larger. The sulphur was mixed with water and placed in a covered vat provided with a flue extending from the vat cover to a sealed condensing chamber. Heated to an extremely high temperature the sulphur vaporized and passed through the flue into the cooler condensing chamber where it immediately liquified, leaving any impurities in the vat. The liquid sulphur was then drained from the condensing chamber into drying and hardening pans and when solidified it was stored until needed.

Charcoal, the third gunpowder ingredient, was still prepared by the venerable kiln method and pulverized as it had been during the early fifteenth century.

The technological innovations evident in the French gunpowder industry are also represented in L'encyclopédie, the plates in the Minéralogie supplement showing the hand tools, machines, and the other equipment devised to mass-produce quality black powder, while the industry was stringently supervised by the Régie des Poudres.

Throughout the centuries the first stage in the preparation of gunpowder was pulverizing the refined ingredients. In France ca. 1750 the charcoal and the sulphur were usually pulverized together in proper proportion prior to adding the requisite amount of saltpeter; the method not only accelerating the process but making it safe, for if the ingredients were blended simultaneously there was the possibility that static electricity would ignite them, precipitating a holocaust. The traditional though more refined tumbling process was used for pulverizing charcoal and in glazing the powder granules.

The upper part of plate iv [p. 231], volume vi, concerned with the Fabrique de la Poudre à Canon (The Manufacture of Gunpowder) illustrates a Vue per-

Pl. II

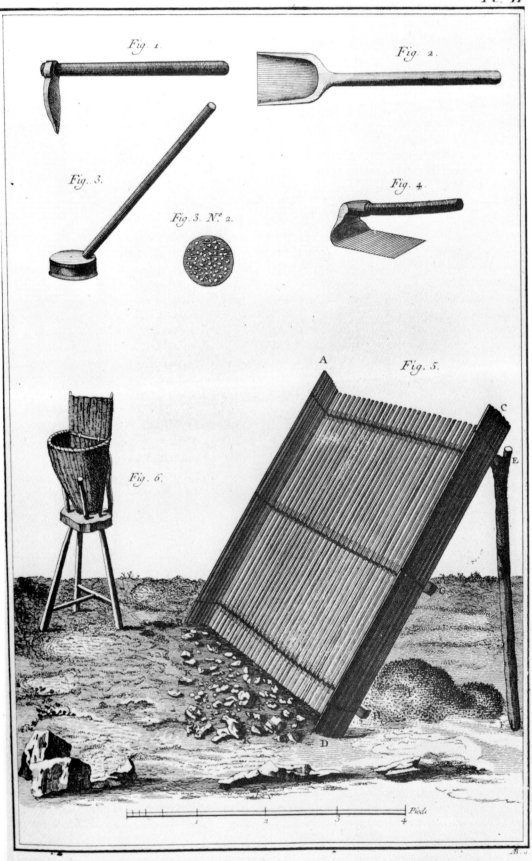

Minéralogie, Extraction
du Salpêtre, Préparation
des Plâtres &c. (18th
Century): Recueil de
Planches, Vol. VI, Plate
II. Courtesy of the
Eleutherian Mills His-
torical Library, Wil-
mington, Del.

Minéralogie, Extraction du Salpêtre. Préparation des Plâtres &c.

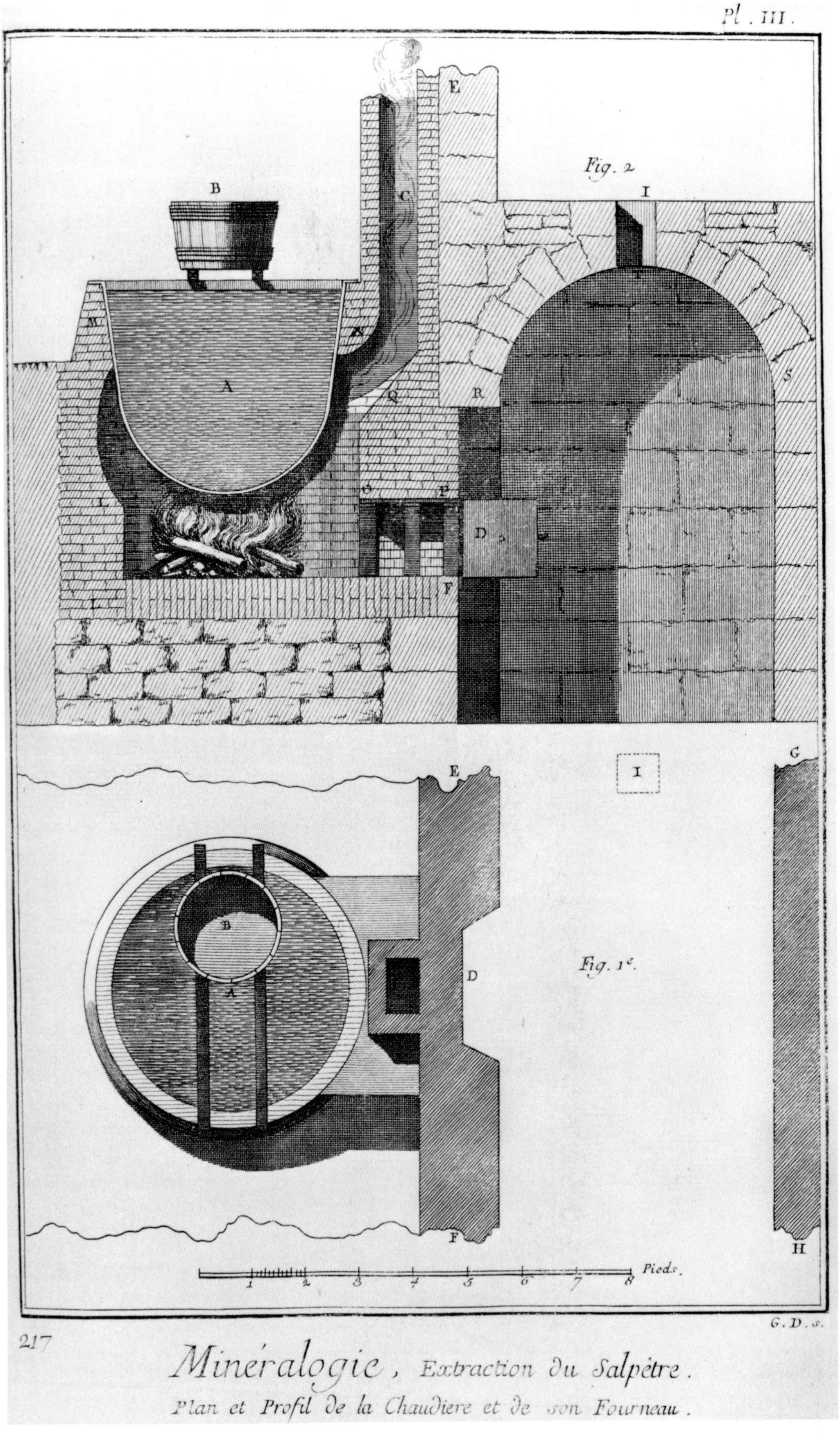

Pl. III.

Fig. 2

Fig. 1.ᵉ

Minéralogie, Extraction du Salpêtre, Plan et Profil de la Chaudiere et de son Fourneau (18th Century): *Recueil de Planches,* Vol. VI, Plate III. Courtesy of the Eleutherian Mills Historical Library, Wilmington, Del.

Pieds.

1   2   3   4   5   6   7   8

217

G. D. s.

Minéralogie, Extraction du Salpêtre.
Plan et Profil de la Chaudiere et de son Fourneau.

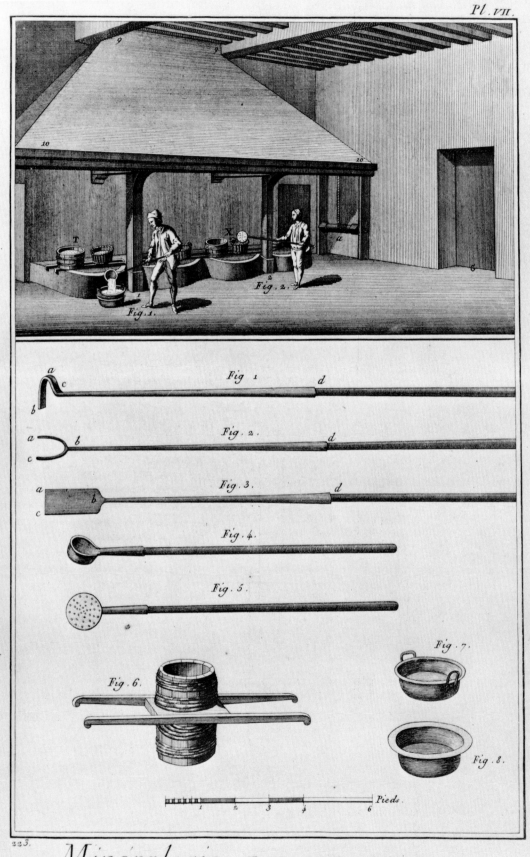

Pl. VII.

Fig. 1
Fig. 2.
Fig. 1.

Fig. 1
Fig. 2.
Fig. 3.
Fig. 4.
Fig. 5.
Fig. 6.
Fig. 7.
Fig. 8.

Pieds.

225

Minéralogie, Raffinage du Salpêtre.
L'Opération de puiser la Cuitte et celle d'enlever le Sel.

Minéralogie, Raffinage du Salpêtre, L'Operation de puiser la Cuitte et celle d'enlever le Sel (18th Century): *Recueil de Planches,* Vol. VI, Plate VII. Courtesy of the Eleutherian Mills Historical Library, Wilmington, Del.

Minéralogie, Extraction du Salpêtre. Outils de la Chaudiere et Bassins &c. (18th Century): *Recueil de Planches,* Vol. VI, Plate IV. Courtesy of the Eleutherian Mills Historical Library, Wilmington, Del.

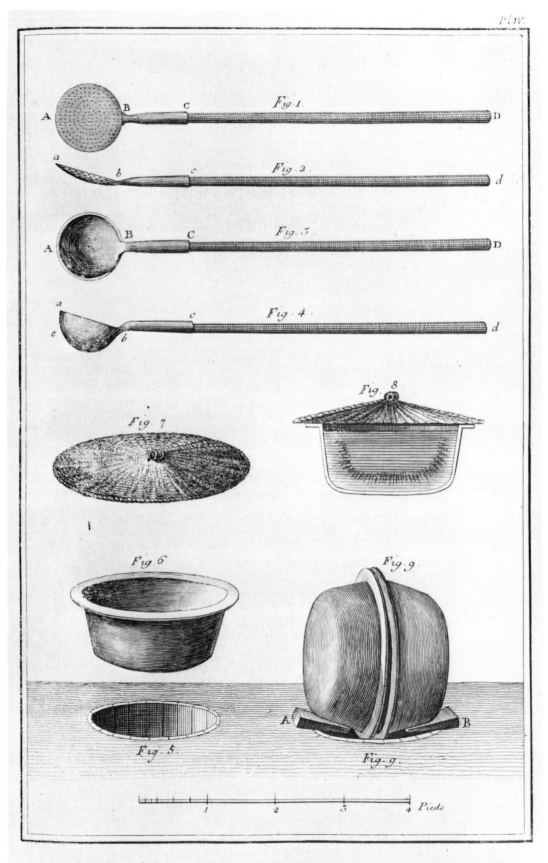

Minéralogie, Raffinage du Salpêtre. Fragments du Laboratoire où on met Cristalliser la Cuitte, de Celui où on met egouter les Bassins, et du Sèchoir (18th Century): *Recueil de Planches*, Vol. VI, Plate IX. Courtesy of the Eleutherian Mills Historical Library, Wilmington, Del.

Minéralogie, Raffinage du Salpètre. Fragments du Laboratoire où on met Cristalliser la Cuitte, de Celui où on met egouter les Bassins, et du Sèchoir.

Minéralogie, Fabrique de la Poudre à Canon. Vue perspective de l'intérieur du Moulin à Pilons (18th Century): *Recueil de Planches,* Vol. VI, Plate IV. Courtesy of the Eleutherian Mills Historical Library, Wilmington, Del.

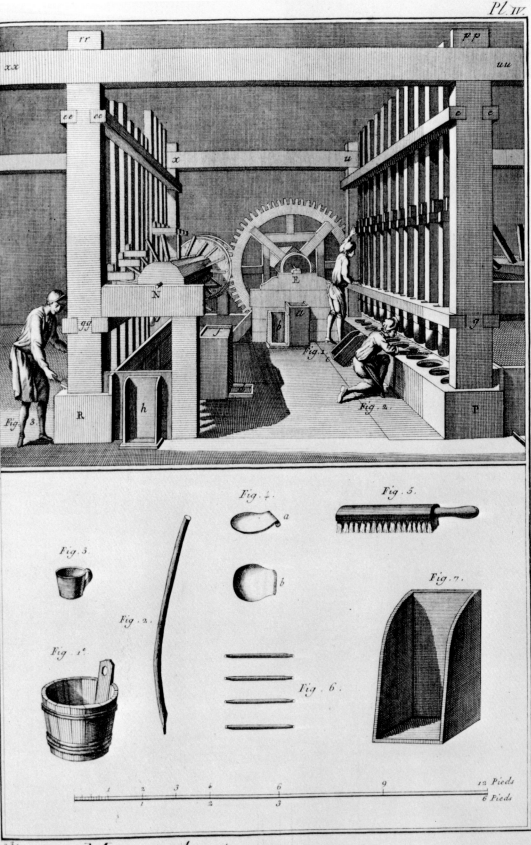

Minéralogie, Fabrique de la Poudre a Canon.

Vue perspective de l'intérieur du Moulin à Pilons.

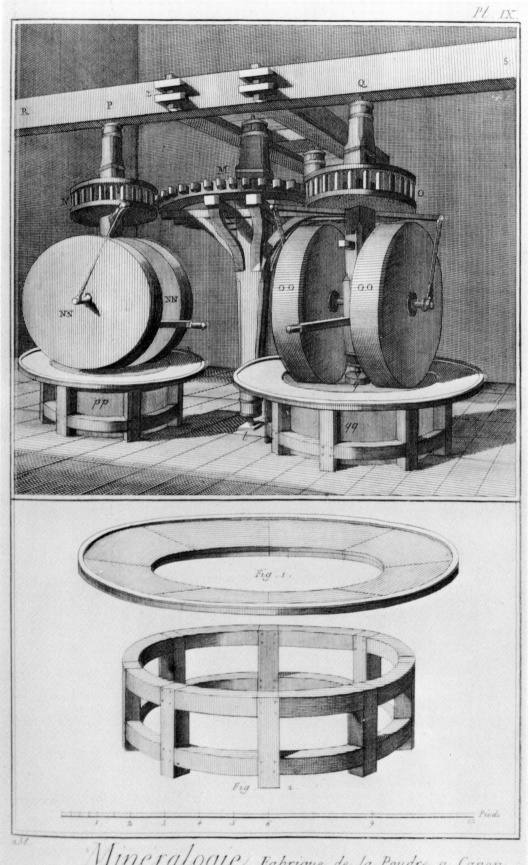

Minéralogie, Fabrique de la Poudre à Canon. Vue perspective de l'intérieur du Moulin à Meules roulantes (18th Century): *Recueil de Planches,* Vol. VI, Plate IX. Courtesy of the Eleutherian Mills Historical Library, Wilmington, Del.

spective de l'interieur du Moulin à Pilons (A Perspective View of the Interior of a Stamping Mill). The stamping mills constructed by the French early in the eighteenth century were much larger and more sophisticated than the mill depicted by Furtenbach and they were operated by water power rather than a hand crank.

The gunpowder ingredients were combined and mixed with water at the stamping mill and a workman [fig. 3] scooped the viscous paste into a series of shallow depressions (mortars) situated along the length of a huge beam [R and P] serving as part of the mill base and securely anchored to the building floor. The moist powder was then pounded for ten to 12 hours by a series of vertical shafts fitted with heavy, bronze heads (pestles) corresponding to the mortars.

The pestle shafts were raised and dropped in rapid succession by the camming action of a series of short spokes mounted on a horizontal, fluted cylinder [N] driven by a large gear [E] powered by a water wheel. During the lengthy stamping process an attendant [fig. 2] continuously moistened the powder to keep it from drying because the friction heat generated by the pestles might possibly ignite it with disastrous consequences.

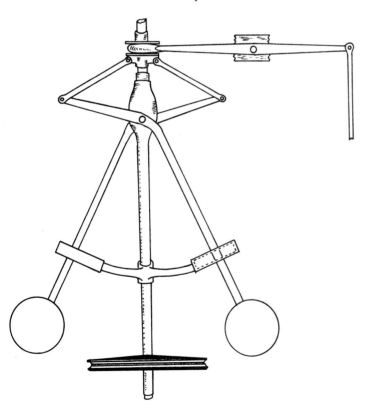

FLY-BALL GOVERNOR (15th/ 19th Century): Originally employed to regulate the speed of the huge grinding wheels in grist mills, the fly-ball governor was subsequently used to regulate the rolling mill wheels in the powder-making process and the pressure valve invented by James Watt to regulate the speed of the piston in steam engines. Author's sketch.

The lower part of plate *iv* depicts the stamping mill attendant's implements, including a bucket [fig. 1] and a cup [fig. 3] for the water used to moisten the powder; a stir stick [fig. 2] for blending the water and the powder; bronze or copper scrapers for cleaning the pestles and gathering the powder paste from the mortars [fig. 4, a and b]; a brush [fig. 5] for recovering dry powder which was immediately recycled; positioning pins [fig. 6] for adjusting the level of the pestle shafts to regulate the length of their stroke; and a large, scoop-like box for collecting the mealy powder paste once the stamping process had been completed.

By ca. 1775-1780 the stamping mill gradually began to be replaced by a machine which more rapidly and thoroughly blended the ingredients: the incorporating (rolling) mill. Depicted in plate *ix* [p. 238], volume *vi,* the rolling mill was also water-powered; a rotating shaft driving a system of horizontal gears [M, N, and O] which turned a pair of shafts [L and H] each provided with an axle. Each axle was connected to a huge stone roller [NN and OO] weighing several tons. In some instances the rollers were subsequently made of wood and faced with iron or bronze.

Simultaneously turning and rotating in a circular pattern via the gear-shaft arrangement, the heavy rollers crushed the moist powder between them and against the surface of a large stone anvil [pp and gg] surrounded by a slanted wooden trough [fig. 1] mounted on a wood frame [fig. 2] and inclined toward the rollers. As in stamping the powder was continuously moistened and a plough-like device constantly churned the mixture as a team of attendants recycled it beneath the rollers from the troughs slanted for the purpose.

Rather than a radical innovation the incorporating mill was adapted from the grist mill employing mechanical principles known for centuries throughout Europe. The speed of the rollers and the distance between them was regulated by the venerable flyball governor commonly used in the grist mill and subsequently applied to the steam engine by Watt. ca. 1785 to control the speed of the innovative reciprocal arm adapted to driving a pulley wheel.

The fly-ball governor was a scissor-like device with two moveable arms, each provided with a weighted ball, pivoting from a vertical shaft. A spindle mounted on the shaft was driven by a pulley connected by a belt to the central mill shaft. As the speed of the mill shaft increased the velocity of the powder rollers it also accelerated the spindle, thrusting the ball-arms farther outward. The scissor-like action of the arms drew downward a pivotal lever sliding on the spindle shaft. Drawn down at one end, the lever was consequently raised at the other which was connected to a breaking system via a long rod.

The breaking system was attached to a gear arrangement and, working in conjunction with the fly-ball governor, it determined the speed of the rollers and the distance between them; the distance diminishing as the velocity of the rollers increased.

The quality of the gunpowder was dependent upon the purity of the ingredients and the time expended in the stamping or rolling mill. Martial gunpowder was rolled in ten to 12 hours though the best sporting powder demanded at least 18 hours, and following the rolling operation the still moist, mealy powder was sent to the press.

The gunpowder press was similar to the familiar cider press or printing press in design and operation and it formed the moist powder into what is referred to as press cake. Under pressure from the press a considerable amount of moisture was removed from the powder and it was then taken to a drying or curing room. There the press cake was covered with cheesecloth and stored in racks conveniently spaced for proper air circulation. Once dried the press cake was ground into smaller pieces by a series of sharp zinc rollers; zinc being less susceptible to nitrate corrosion and less inclined to produce hazardous sparks because it is non-ferrous.

The large granules broken from the press cake were again reduced in size as depicted in plate *xi* [p. 240], *L'Opération de Grainer la Poudre et Plan d'un quart du Grainoir* (The Graining Process and a Plan of the Granulating Room). The grainers [fig. 1-4] shown at the graining stations in the upper part of the plate sifted the cake granules through large, round sieves to achieve the desired granulation; the size of the powder grains determined by the number of perforations per inch in the sieve face.

Sieves with 14 to 16 holes per inch were used for graining cannon powder, 16 to 24 holes per inch for musket powder, and 24 to 26 holes per inch for rifle or sporting fusil powder. The wooden graining discs illustrated in the lower part of the plate were placed in the sieves and rapidly rotated, forcing the powder through the perforations into the collection bin below the graining station. The grained powder was then scooped into a tub [F] and put in casks or barrels [A to E].

Plate *xii* [p. 241] delineates the grainer's implements, showing the sieves and the action of the graining discs [figs. 1 and 2], the graining discs [figs. 3 and 4], and the sieve perforations [figs. 5 and 6]. The sieves were supported by and manually rotated against the wooden brace [fig. 7] secured by a v-notched series of blocks [a and b] attached to the sides of the collection bin [fig. 8]. A wood powder scoop [fig. 9] is also illustrated.

The lower part of plate *xiv* [p. 244] depicts an early method of drying the powder grains consisting of a simple, cloth-covered table on which they were scattered and periodically spread by a wooden graining rake [figs. 1 and 2]. The graining rake, as noticable in most of the tools and machines used in gunpowder manufacture, was made of wood to prevent dangerous sparks and non-ferrous metals were also employed where practicable.

The upper section of plate *xiv* illustrates a drying house. The house covered the drying table [C and D], protecting the powder grains from inclement weather. Open construction permitted free air circulation and indirect solar heat reached the powder through the slanted facade [A and B]. Once properly dried the powder was again sifted to remove broken particles and dust; the residue then recycled.

Military powder was then packed in barrels, casks, or kegs and stored until needed though in some instances sporting fusil powder was glazed. Prior to 1800 only small quantities of gunpowder were glazed, the only demand coming from aristocratic sportsmen who preferred it for hunting. While more expensive, glazed powder was also superior to unglazed powder, for the process coated the grains with graphite; a lubricant which not only made it easier to pour, but greatly reduced hygroscopicity and powder fouling encrustations.

The upper part of plate *xvii* [p. 249] represents a profile of the typical late eighteenth-century French glazing mill [fig. 4] and the lower part depicts a glazing and tumbling barrel [fig. 5] and the collection bin [T]. The end of the barrel [fig. 6] shows the opening for the shaft with which it rotated. The mill illustrated was operated by an undershot water wheel [B] which turned a long shaft and gear [F]. The shaft gear simultaneously transmitted the power to additional gears also mounted on rotating shafts. Each of those shafts transversed a pair of glazing and tumbling barrels [o and p, q and r] revolving above a series of collection bins [t and u].

The gunpowder intended for glazing was placed in the barrels and powdered graphite was added, coating the grains in an operation lasting twelve hours or more. After glazing the powder was once more sifted to remove accumulated particles and dust which was then recycled. In some instances unglazed powder was tumbled for a short time to round off the imperfect grains.

The innovative machines and manufacturing techniques incorporated in the infrastructure of the eighteenth-century French national armories and powder mills subsequently exerted a profound influence on the American armament industry though the immediate effect was to stimulate the genius of Gen. Jean Baptiste Vaquette de Gribeauval (1715-1789), commander of the *Corps de Artillerie*.

In 1765 Gribeauval devised a successful system for manufacturing standardized cannon carriage components.[82] As far as it can be determined he can

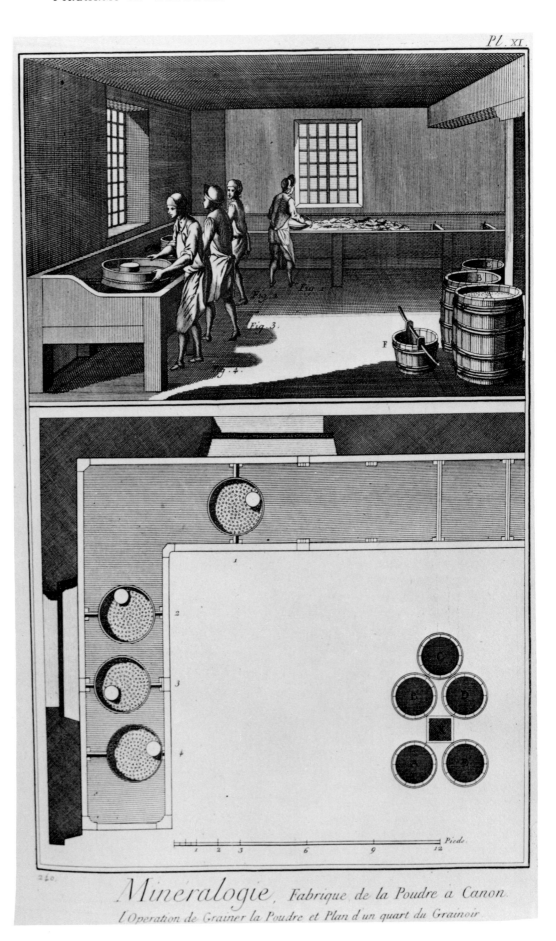

Minéralogie, Fabrique de la Poudre à Canon. l'Opération de Grainer la Poudre et Plan d'un quart du Grainoir (18th Century): *Recueil de Planches,* Vol. VI, Plate XI. Courtesy of the Eleutherian Mills Historical Library, Wilmington, Del.

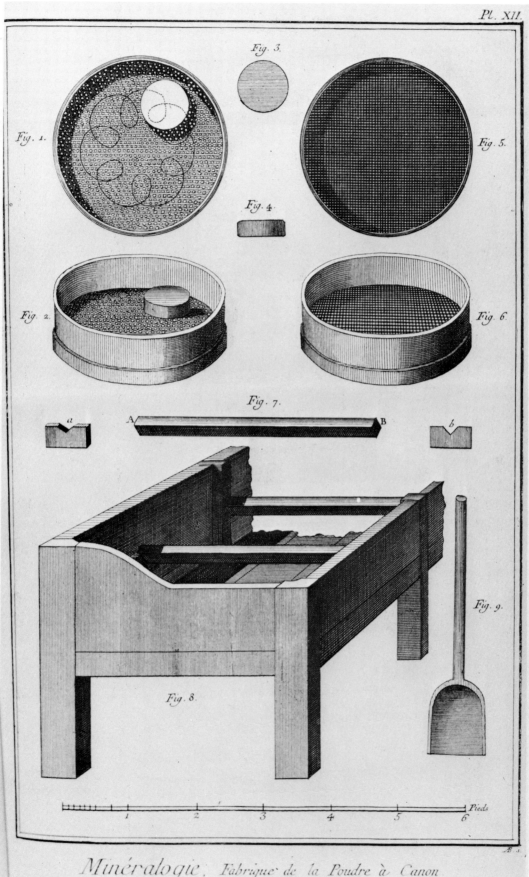

Minéralogie, Fabrique de la Poudre à Canon. Dé-velopements du Grainoir &c. (18th Century): *Recueil de Planches,* Vol. VI, Plate XII. Courtesy of the Eleutherian Mills Historical Library, Wilmington, Del.

Minéralogie, Fabrique de la Poudre à Canon. Profil de l'Essorage et dévelopements du Sèchoir (18th Century): Recueil de Planches, Vol. VI, Plate XIV. Courtesy of the Eleutherian Mills Historical Library, Wilmington, Del.

PL. XIV

Fig. 1.

Fig. 2.

Minéralogie, Fabrique de la Poudre à Canon.
Profil de l'Essorage et developements du Sèchoir.

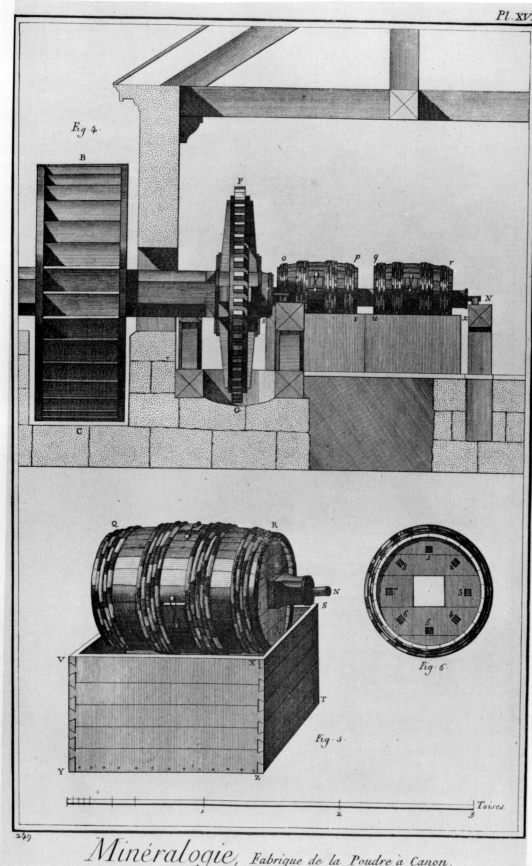

Minéralogie, Fabrique de la Poudre à Canon. Elévation et dévelopements du Lissoir (18th Century): *Recueil de Planches,* Vol. VI, Plate XVII. Courtesy of the Eleutherian Mills Historical Library, Wilmington, Del.

Minéralogie, Fabrique de la Poudre à Canon.
Elevation et dévelopements du Lissoir.

be credited with resurrecting from Classical antiquity the revolutionary concept of interchangeable parts introduced by Hero of Alexandria (see p. 32). By that time technology had certainly progressed to the stage where interchangeability was a feasible manufacturing concept. Gribeauval's contribution, however, was not immediately grasped by his contemporaries in France or elsewhere and not until 20 years later would the radical technique be introduced in firearms manufacture; an event of monumental socio-economic impact.

Notes

1. U.S. Bureau of Census, *Historical Statistics of the United States* (Washington, 1961), Series Z 1-19, p. 756.
2. Thomas Simes, *The Military Medley* (London, 1768), p. 23.
3. Francisco Barado y Front, *Museo Militar: Historia de Ejército Español; Armas, Uniformes, Sistemas de Combate, Instituciones Organizacion del Mismo*, 3 vols. (Barcelona, 1889), 3:543.
4. James D. Lavin, *A History of Spanish Firearms* (New York, 1965), p. 184.
5. Charles W. Arnade, *The Siege of St. Augustine in 1702* (Gainesville: University of Florida Press and the St. Augustine Historical Society, 1959): 39.
6. Robert Allen Matter, "Missions in the Defense of Spanish Florida," *Florida Historical Quarterly* (July 1975): 33 (hereafter cited as *FHQ*).
7. William R. Gillaspie, "The Threatened St. Augustine Mutiny," *FHQ* (October 1968): 153.
8. North Carolina Spanish Records Collection, Department of Archives and History, Raleigh, *Archivo General de Indias*, Seville (hereafter cited as *AGI*), 58-1-27/89, Gov. Francisco de Córcoles y Martínez of Florida to the crown, St. Augustine, May 3, 1706, 66 ff., pp. 3-4.
9. Col. Robert Gardner, *Small Arms Makers* (New York, 1962), p. 241.
10. Gillaspie, p. 153.
11. Lavin, p. 139.
12. Ibid., p. 118.
13. Ibid., p. 96.
14. Ibid., pp. 195-196, n. 17.
15. Ibid., p. 195, n. 15.
16. Ibid., pp. 67-68, 206.
17. Sidney B. Brinckerhoff and Pierce A. Chamberlain, *Spanish Military Weapons in Colonial America, 1700-1821* (Harrisburg, 1972), p. 28.
18. Stetson Collection, P.K. Yonge Library of Florida History, University of Florida, Gainesville, *AGI* 58-1-32/23, Governor and Royal officials to the crown, St. Augustine, September 25, 1740, 41 ff., pp. 10-11.
19. Brinckerhoff and Chamberlain, p. 30.
20. James W. Covington, "Migration Into Florida of the Seminoles, 1700-1820," *FHQ* (April 1968): 345.
21. T.M. Hamilton, *Early Indian Trade Guns: 1625-1775* (Lawton: Contributions of the Museum of the Great Plains, Number 3, 1968): 2.
22. Brinckerhoff and Chamberlain, p. 28.
23. Ibid.
24. Ibid., p. 31.
25. Lavin, pp. 212-213.
26. Frederick Webb Hodge, ed., *Handbook of American Indians North of Mexico*, 2 vols. (Washington, 1912), 1:288.
27. Hamilton, p. 13.
28. Ibid.; Torsten Lenk, *The Flintlock: Its Origin and Development* (New York, 1965), p. 153.
29. Hamilton, p. 13.
30. Ibid.
31. Ibid., p. 14.
32. Ibid.
33. Harold L. Peterson, *Arms and Armor in Colonial America, 1526-1783* (New York, 1956), p. 172 (hereafter cited as *Arms and Armor*).
34. Clement Bosson, "Saint-Etienne," in *Encyclopedia of Firearms*, Harold L. Peterson, ed. (New York, 1964), p. 268.
35. Bosson, "Maubeuge," in *Encyclopedia of Firearms*, p. 217.
36. Peterson, *Arms and Armor*, p. 171.
37. Richard K. Sprague, "Early French Muskets in America," *American Rifleman* (January 1958): 21.
38. Peterson, p. 176.
39. Raymond Caranta, "A History of French Handguns," *Gun Digest* (Chicago, 1969): 6n.
40. Ibid., p. 6.
41. Ibid.
42. Ibid.
43. Ibid.
44. Ibid.
45. Herschel C. Logan, *Cartridges* (Harrisburg, 1959), p. 4.
46. Howard L. Blackmore, *Guns and Rifles of the World* (New York, 1965), p. 60n.
47. Ibid.
48. Harold L. Peterson, "Breechloaders," in *Encyclopedia of Firearms*, p. 62.
49. Gardner, p. 278.
50. Blackmore, p. 62.
51. John C. McMurray, "Amusette," in *Encyclopedia of Firearms*, p. 25.
52. Lavin, p. 99.
53. Ibid.
54. Blackmore, p. 86.
55. Gardner, p. 272.
56. Merrill Lindsay, *One Hundred Great Guns* (New York, 1967), p. 185.
57. Blackmore, p. 42.
58. Ibid.; Lindsay, p. 102.
59. Robert Held, *The Age of Firearms* (New York, 1957), p. 137.
60. James E. Serven, "The Shotgun," *Gun Digest* (Chicago, 1963): 8.
61. *The Winchester-Western Ammunition Handbook* (New York: Pocket Books, Inc., 1964), pp. 4-5.
62. A.N. Kennard, *French Pistols and Sporting Guns* (London, 1972), p. 43; W.W. Greener, *The Gun and its Development* (New York, 1967), p. 218.
63. Donald Baird, "The Flintlock Whaling Gun," *The Canadian Journal of Arms Collecting* (August, 1968): 84.
64. Ibid.
65. Silvio A. Bedini and Derek J. De Solla Price, "Instrumentation," in *Technology in Western Civilization*, Melvin Kranzeberg and Carroll W. Pursell, Jr., ed., 2 vols. (New York and London, 1967), 1:183.
66. W. Steeds, *A History of Machine Tools* (Oxford, 1969), p. 2.
67. Eugene S. Ferguson, "The Steam Engine Before 1830," in *Technology in Western Civilization*, 1:246-247.
68. Ibid., 248-249.
69. Ibid. The date 1755 is given in Robert L. Breeden, ed., *Those Inventive Americans* (Washington, 1971), p. 18.
70. Steeds, p. 24.
71. Ibid.
72. Ibid., p. 5.
73. Ibid.
74. Ibid.
75. Ibid., p. 6.
76. Ibid.
77. Ferguson, 1:251.
78. Steeds, p. 8.
79. Ferguson, 1:272.
80. Bernard Lecuyer, "The Arquebusier: 1765," *The Canadian Journal of Arms Collecting* (May 1964): 43.
81. James R. Partington, "Gunpowder," in *Encyclopedia of Firearms*, p. 147.
82. Mitchell Wilson, *American Science and Invention* (New York, 1960), p. 82.

DOG LOCK PISTOL (17th Century): This English flintlock pistol typifies those employed in English America from ca. 1607 to 1725. Note the straight butt design identified with the wheellock dag and the dog safety. This pistol was owned by the Rev. John Williams (1644-1729) of Deerfield, Massachusetts Bay Colony. Courtesy of the Longmeadow (Mass.) Historical Society.

THE EIGHTEENTH CENTURY was a crucial, decisive epoch in the turbulent and relatively brief history of British and French America, and neither of those rival European powers struggling for ascendancy fulfilled their colonial aspirations.

The early years of the century saw the English colonies emerge as a strong if not entirely cohesive enclave with a rapidly growing populace continuing to broaden its territorial acquisitions and enlarge its narrow techonomic foundation. The French colonies also continued to expand and challenged Britain's prerogatives with disastrous consequences, while both colonial powers battled the vast wilderness and lived under the seemingly eternal shadow of anxiety cast by the restive Native Americans.

On January 7, 1699, the Massachusetts Bay Colony concluded a treaty with the hostile Abenaki which temporarily halted depredations in northern New England, and on August 4, 1701, the French at Montreal at last appeased the Iroquoian Confederation; thus freeing themselves from retaliation as they intensified their struggle against the British.

With Iroquoian neutrality the French menace precipitated additional defensive measures in New England and in 1702 the Massachusetts Bay Colony decreed that every available male be armed and accoutered with "a well fixt Firelock [flintlock] Musket of Musket or Bastard Musket boare; the barrell not less than three foot and a half long, or other good Fire Arms, to the Satisfaction of the Commission Officers of the [militia] Company, a Snapsack [knapsack], a Coller with Twelve Bandeleers [i.e., a bandolier with a dozen powder containers] or Cortouch box, one Pound of good Powder, twenty Bullets fit for his Gun, and twelve Flints, a good Sword or Cutlash [cutlass], a Worm and Priming-wire fit for his gun. . . ."[1]

The mutual antagonism between Britain and France during Queen Anne's War was amplified by their respective Native American allies, and one of the most infamous acts of the conflict was the raid on Deerfield, Mass. On the frigid night of February 28-29, 1704, 50 French troops and 200 Native Americans commanded by Maj. Hertel de Rouville surprised the sleeping frontier village of 300 souls. The Deerfield Massacre left in its terrifying wake 50 dead and 111 captives were forced to march to New France in the dread face of winter.

Among the few relics surviving the nightmarish attack is an English martial flintlock pistol once the property of Reverend John Williams (1664-1729), a Harvard graduate ordained in 1688 and minister of the Deerfield Church. As tradition has it he attempted to shoot one of the Native American raiders but the pistol misfired. Williams, his son Stephen, and daughter Eunice survived the frigid, 300-mile march through the wilderness. His wife and youngest child, failing to keep pace, were murdered on the desolate trail.

The Williams pistol displays a dog safety and has an overall length of 23 inches.[2] The .58 caliber, 15¼ inch barrel tapers to round from an octagonal breech. The forestock extends to the muzzle and there are no sights. Furniture is iron though a brass ferrule (band) surrounds the grip base and another secures the pinned forestock, also serving as a ramrod guide; the wood ramrod now missing. The pistol is typical of many reaching the English colonies during the late seventeenth century and it is similar to those popular during the English Civil War (1642-1649), though the barrel is shorter.

In the southern colonies Jamestown meanwhile had gone into eclipse after Bacon's Rebellion and it was devastated by another fire in 1698. The following year Williamsburg, established in 1633 as a military outpost to protect Jamestown, became Virginia's capital. Though the danger to Virginia and the Carolinas from Spanish Florida was more imagined than real at the beginning of the eighteenth century, the threat was magnified as a result of Gov. Moore's unsuccessful 1702 attack on St. Augustine.

Anticipating a violent Spanish reaction which was slow to materialize, the crown that year approved shipping to Williamsburg 1,000 snaptice muskets, 400 carbines, 400 pair of holster pistols, 1,000 cartridge boxes, 400 carbine slings with swivels, and 1,000 infantry and 400 cavalry swords with waist and shoulder belts for each.[3] The snaptice muskets referred to were probably snaphaunces, however, snaptice and firelock were often used interchangeably in relation to flintlock firearms because the term flintlock was not then employed in the English idiom.

Meeting at Williamsburg in 1705 the Virginia General Assembly revised former militia regulations, ordering "Every foot soldier to have a firelock, musket or fusee [fusil], a sword and cartouch box and six chargers of powder, to have 2 lbs powder and 8 lbs shot at home and to bring that, too, when required. horsemen to have a case [pair] of pistols, sword, double cartouch box [patron?] and 12 chargers of powder. Carbine with belt and swivel at home."[4]

The proximity of Charleston to Spanish Florida prompted additional defensive measures there in 1686 and the Acts of the Assembly provided for a "store of powder . . . and a Powder Receiver."[5] Powder receivers were appointed to four-year terms by the Carolina Assembly Commons House and the office was apparently retained until shortly after the French and Indian War.

The five known powder receivers appointed between 1693 and 1763 were William Bradley (1693), Richard Bellinger (1698), Thomas Heyward (1699-1700), Miles Brewton (1717-1759), and Jacob Motte, Jr. (1760-1764). A number of powder receivers like Brewton succeeded themselves and others were appointed to fill unexpired vacancies as indicated by the duration of Bellinger's and Heyward's terms.[6]

In 1703 additional and extensive fortifications were constructed at Charleston and kept in what is believed to be the first masonry powder magazine built in the English colonies were the "powder, armes, and other stores and habilaments of war."[7] The magazine was completed in time to serve during the French-Spanish assault of 1706.

The demands on the Charleston magazine escalated during the invidious Tuscarora War (1711-1713) which flamed through the Carolinas as a result of the harsh treatment the Native Americans received from English and Palatine German settlers, and the magazine was refurbished at the outset of the Catawba War (1714-1715) which started when the Carolinians reneged on a promise of less expensive firearms and other trade goods if the Catawba would join them against the Tuscarora.

The completely renovated Charleston magazine met the demands arising from the sanguinary Yamasee War (1715-1716). Incited by the Spaniards

CHARLESTON POW-
DER MAGAZINE (18th
Century, 1703): Sir
Nathaniel Johnson,
Royal Governor of
South Carolina, was
ordered by an Act of
the General Assembly
to construct a brick
powder magazine
within Charleston's de-
fenses in 1703. The
original magazine
measured 30 by 18 feet.
Charleston merchants
stored powder in the
magazine in 1719 and it
served until ca. 1780.
Courtesy of the South
Carolina Historical So-
ciety, Charleston.

and in league with other coastal tribes aware of the Tuscarora and Catawba disasters, the hostiles slaughtered settlers and traders from the Cape Fear (N.C.) River southward, though they later shared a similar fate.

Virginia Gov. Alexander Spotswood, inspired by the Native Americans wars in the Carolinas, recognized the need for a larger magazine at Williamsburg and recommended that a "good substantial house of brick" be built for the purpose and he designed an unique octagonal magazine which was erected in 1715.[8] The Williamsburg magazine, like the earlier Charleston facility, still stands as a monument reflecting the urgency of that distant era.

British Martial Firearms

While various kinds of snapping flintlock firearms had early supplanted matchlock firearms in British America, match ignition remained prevalent in martial firearms until late in the seventeenth century when increasingly large numbers of flintlocks appeared, e.g., a 1676 arms shipment to Virginia consisted of 300 matchlock and 200 flintlock muskets; thus illustrating a substantial increase in the ratio of the latter to the former.[9] Not until Queen Anne's reign, however, would the matchlock musket be rendered obsolete (see p. 134).

The rapid growth of the English firearms industry early in the eighteenth century, partially predicated on the expanding colonial market, instigated several reforms in martial firearms procurement. Initiated in 1715 the ordnance reform movement had the salubrious effect of discouraging graft in the military establishment, reducing production costs, and providing an adequate arms inventory for wartime emergency.

It was also during the ordnance reform movement that a standard pattern British flintlock infantry musket was introduced. Officially termed the Long Land Service Musket, it was subsequently dubbed the Brown Bess by generations of British soldiers and it purportedly evolved from a design submitted to the Board of Ordnance by the aged, enfeebled John Churchill, Duke of Marlborough, shortly after his reinstatement as captain general of the British Army in 1715.

The Long Land Service Musket was an improved version of the Queen Anne musket, and from the time when it was initially manufactured ca. 1718 it paralleled the evolution of the M1717 French infantry musket, though it was not distinguished by model year, while few of the refinements subsequently introduced significantly improved its efficacy. Col. George Hanger, a veteran eighteenth-century British officer, astutely observed that:

> "A soldier's musket, if not exceedingly ill-bored . . . will strike . . . a man at eighty yards; it may even at 100; but a soldier must be very unfortunate indeed who shall be wounded . . . at 150 yards, provided his antagonist aims at him. . . . I do maintain . . . that no man was ever killed at 200 yards, by a common soldier's musket, by the person who aimed at him."[10]

Frequently referred to as the first model Brown Bess, the Long Land Service Musket incorporated the true flintlock. The lockplate, rounded like the gooseneck cock, was approximately seven inches long and displayed the so-called banana profile, while it was secured to the stock by two screws entering via the convex sideplate. Relief carving around the lock mortise in the stock was characteristic.

British musket lock markings varied considerably throughout the evolutionary period. The tail of the Long Land Service Musket lock was initially engraved with the contractor's signature and the year date, or the date with the word TOWER denoting the official proofhouse. In some variations only the last two digits of the year date were used and in others the tail of the lock was engraved with a regimental rack number or a company number instead of the date.

A crown surmounting the royal cypher G R (George Rex) was used throughout the Georgian period, engraved on the lockplate between the cock and the priming pan. The broad arrow mark signifying crown property was engraved directly below the pan, the head of the arrow pointing to the cock.

The round, gradually tapering .75 caliber wrought iron barrel of the Long Land Service Musket was 46 inches long, displaying a bayonet lug two inches from the muzzle which was used as a pointing reference in the manner of a front sight. Furniture was iron though brass was introduced in 1725 and it entirely supplanted iron by 1728. Existing inventories of iron furniture were not completely expended until 1736. The walnut stock was stained or painted black and the pinned forestock extended to within four inches of the muzzle to provide clearance for the bayonet socket. The buttplate was attached by two screws and a long heel finial with a short post inletted into the comb.

The Long Land Service Musket was originally provided with a wood ramrod though the iron ramrod was in use by 1724; much later than it was introduced in Prussia (1698) and somewhat earlier than in France (1746) and Spain (1755). Between 1730 and 1740, however, the wood ramrod was resurrected, though by midcentury most service muskets were again equipped with iron, while in some regiments the wood ramrod was retained until 1776.[11] Three thimbles and a guide secured the ramrod. Muskets supplied with iron ramrods were altered by adding a spring in the front guide to prevent rattling.

By ca. 1745 the Long Land Service Musket was provided with a stronger cast-brass trigger guard and a trumpet-mouthed upper ramrod guide, while the curved bottom profile of the lockplate and its mortise were eliminated, thereby simplifying manufacture and reducing cost. The efficacy of the lock was improved ca. 1754 with the addition of a battery bridle. Though the tumbler bridle had been early introduced, not until 1755 did the double-bridle lock become a standard feature on British martial firearms despite its appearance on some dragoon carbines ca. 1685 (see p. 135).[12]

The practice of including the musket contractor's signature and the date on the tail of the lock was abandoned in 1764, replaced by the word TOWER.[13] The readily identified bulbous protrusion on the forestock immediately ahead of the lock, dictated by the design and location of the rear ramrod guide (tailpipe), gradually disappeared from British martial pattern muskets ca. 1770.

In England the heavy dragoons traditionally fought dismounted like infantry and had been issued muskets rather than the carbines or musketoons used by the light dragoons. By ca. 1722 heavy dragoons were issued Long Land Service Muskets of standard caliber though the barrels were shortened to 42 inches.

The heavy dragoon musket, subsequently influencing the design of the Short Land Service Musket, had no forestock cap and it was initially provided with a brass-tipped wood ramrod, while the lock was marked like the regulation infantry musket. Under Marlborough's influence the role of the heavy dragoons gradually merged with that of the light dragoons and the metamorphosis was completed shortly after 1745 when the Duke of Cumberland, son of George II, assumed command of the British Army. Thereafter the heavy dragoons were issued carbines or musketoons.

The introduction of the Short Land Service Musket ca. 1750 distinctly influenced the development of the Sea Service Musket and the Marine or Militia Musket, both appearing in 1755. The Short Land Service Musket, also known as the second model Brown Bess, adopted the 42 inch barrel of the heavy dragoon musket. Many Long Land Service Muskets excessively worn or damaged near the muzzle were converted to Short Land Service Muskets by shortening the barrels four inches; a common modification in British America during the protracted French and Indian War.

For some unaccountable reason Britain neglected the development of suitable naval firearms despite the fact that the Royal Navy ranked as the senior service and was primarily responsible for the emergence of the island nation as an estimable world power. The Royal Navy had customarily employed British infantry muskets and in some instances foreign muskets, many of them inferior. By 1755, however, the distinctive Sea Service Musket appeared.

The Sea Service Musket retained the caliber and other features of the Short Land Service Musket, though it was also produced with convex and flat locks. A flat sideplate was standard. The flat lock incorporated a slotted and pierced top jaw screw, an extended top jaw encompassing the cock spur, a pointed battery spring extension on the pan cover, though there was no battery bridle, and a less expensive, sturdier throat-hole cock; characteristics unchanged for a quarter-century.

Sea Service Muskets used wood ramrods exclusively, possibly to eliminate surplus quantities after the iron ramrod was adopted for land pattern muskets or to circumvent the problem of iron ramrods corroding and sticking in the guides and thimbles when subjected to prolonged salt exposure. Some Sea Service Muskets displayed barrels approximately ten inches shorter than land patterns, making them easier to handle when used in the rigging.

The Sea Service Musket was also provided with a socket bayonet. The pin-fastened walnut stock was painted or stained black and the flat buttplate had an extremely short heel finial. There were no sling swivels because it was customary to lock the muskets in racks or chests until needed; a traditional practice designed to discourage mutiny by preventing ready access to shipboard firearms.

George II, recognizing the need to bolster fleet operations in the early stage of the French and Indian War, recommissioned the Royal Marines in 1755 and they were initially provided with Short Land Service Muskets. The passage of the Militia Act in 1757 was designed to provide British domestic militia with firearms in the event France invaded the mother country. Those actions resulted in the introduction of the Marine or Militia Musket.

The Marine or Militia Musket was similar to the Short Land Service Musket in most respects though characterized by minor furniture design alterations. Less attention to quality craftsmanship was given to the Marine or Militia Musket during the war years, though an improved version appeared ca. 1763 and it remained in service until production ceased in 1775.

The financial burden of the French and Indian War resulted in rising production costs for martial firearms and that fact, combined with the revelation from extensive tests that muskets with 42 inch barrels performed as well ballistically as those with 46 inch barrels, prompted the Board of Ordnance to

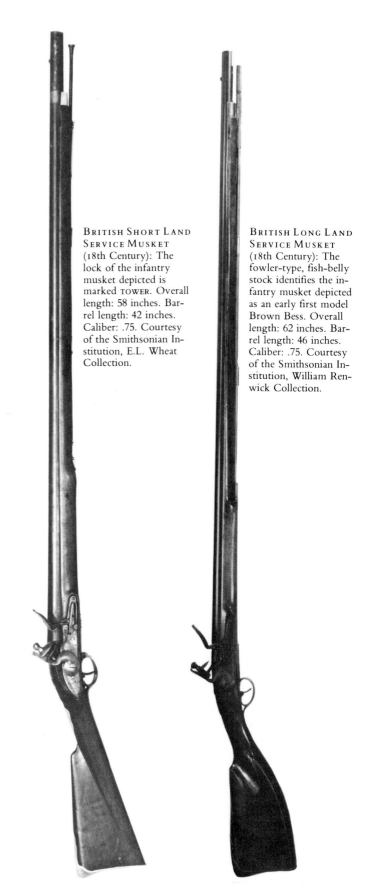

BRITISH SHORT LAND SERVICE MUSKET (18th Century): The lock of the infantry musket depicted is marked TOWER. Overall length: 58 inches. Barrel length: 42 inches. Caliber: .75. Courtesy of the Smithsonian Institution, E.L. Wheat Collection.

BRITISH LONG LAND SERVICE MUSKET (18th Century): The fowler-type, fish-belly stock identifies the infantry musket depicted as an early first model Brown Bess. Overall length: 62 inches. Barrel length: 46 inches. Caliber: .75. Courtesy of the Smithsonian Institution, William Renwick Collection.

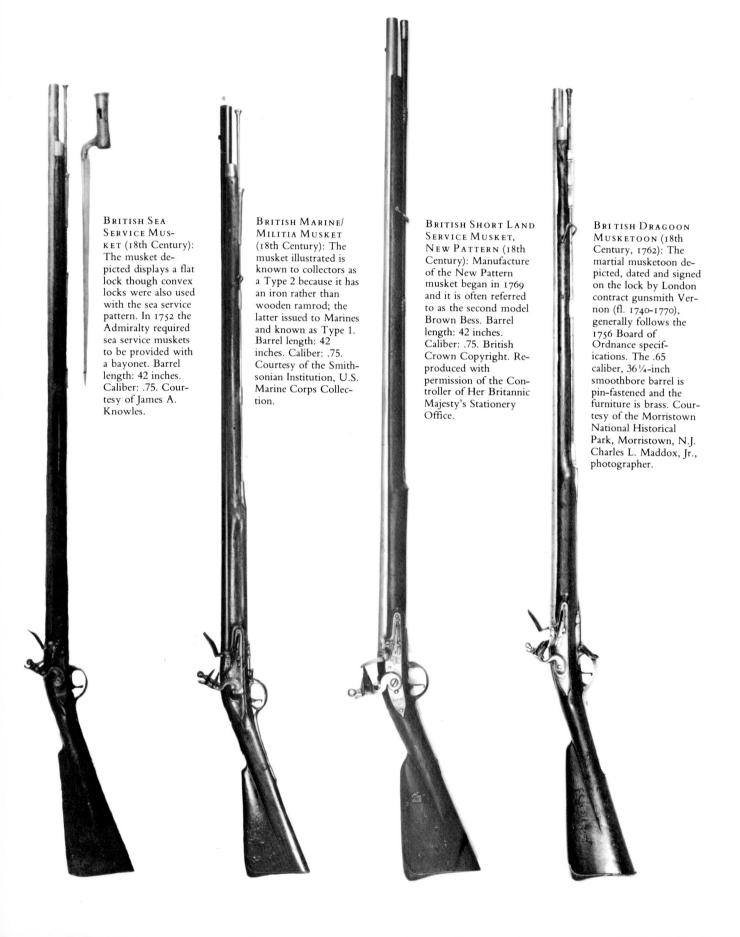

BRITISH SEA SERVICE MUSKET (18th Century): The musket depicted displays a flat lock though convex locks were also used with the sea service pattern. In 1752 the Admiralty required sea service muskets to be provided with a bayonet. Barrel length: 42 inches. Caliber: .75. Courtesy of James A. Knowles.

BRITISH MARINE/MILITIA MUSKET (18th Century): The musket illustrated is known to collectors as a Type 2 because it has an iron rather than wooden ramrod; the latter issued to Marines and known as Type 1. Barrel length: 42 inches. Caliber: .75. Courtesy of the Smithsonian Institution, U.S. Marine Corps Collection.

BRITISH SHORT LAND SERVICE MUSKET, NEW PATTERN (18th Century): Manufacture of the New Pattern musket began in 1769 and it is often referred to as the second model Brown Bess. Barrel length: 42 inches. Caliber: .75. British Crown Copyright. Reproduced with permission of the Controller of Her Britannic Majesty's Stationery Office.

BRITISH DRAGOON MUSKETOON (18th Century, 1762): The martial musketoon depicted, dated and signed on the lock by London contract gunsmith Vernon (fl. 1740-1770), generally follows the 1756 Board of Ordnance specifications. The .65 caliber, 36¼-inch smoothbore barrel is pin-fastened and the furniture is brass. Courtesy of the Morristown National Historical Park, Morristown, N.J. Charles L. Maddox, Jr., photographer.

adopt a new pattern musket on June 11, 1768.[14]

The Short Land Service Musket, New Pattern, retained the caliber, barrel length, and basic features of the Short Land Service Musket and became standard for infantry, marines, and domestic militia in 1775. The New Pattern musket served British forces throughout the American Revolution (1775-1783), though as a result of wartime exigency it was supplemented by existing stores of obsolete and obsolescent martial firearms.

Like earlier British muskets the New Pattern also underwent minor changes over the years and by ca.1790 four variations had emerged; the locks of the latter stamped with the proper markings rather than engraved. The average Short Land Service Musket, New Pattern, weighed ten pounds and six ounces without a sling or bayonet; those appendages adding about two pounds (see APPENDIX VI).

The iron components of British martial firearms were generally russeted, lending credence to the supposition that the browned finish inspired part of the popular appellation used in reference to the infantry musket: Brown Bess. Some firearms historians, however, attribute the designation to the color of the walnut stock before it was either painted or stained black. Also contentious is the term Bess. Some historians have asserted that Bess alluded to Queen Elizabeth I; an hypothesis which is unlikely because she died more than a century before the Long Land Service Musket was adopted, while other ascribe it to a popular pet name and common corruption of Elizabeth, i.e., Bess. The circumstances surrounding the origin of Brown Bess remain conjectural and not until 1785 did it appear in print, though it was used much earlier in oral idiom.[15]

Eighteenth-century British dragoons (cavalry) were issued several kinds of carbines and there were light infantry and artillery models as well, varying only slightly in design. Early in the century most carbines were patterned after the Long Land Service Musket and later specimens were similar to the Short Land Service Musket, New Pattern. Prior to mid-century carbines were oftened shortened versions of infantry muskets; their barrels reduced to 36 inches.

As a rule the carbine was shorter, lighter, and of smaller caliber than the service musket; frequently corresponding to pistol caliber (.65). Eighteenth-century carbines retained the slide bar and ring for the shoulder belt as well as sling swivels. Furniture was brass and the iron components were blued or browned. The pin-fastened walnut stock was finished like the musket stock, while the locks were marked after the prevailing manner.

The typical British light cavalry carbine of the 1735-1750 period weighed approximately seven pounds and 12 ounces and had an overall length of 57

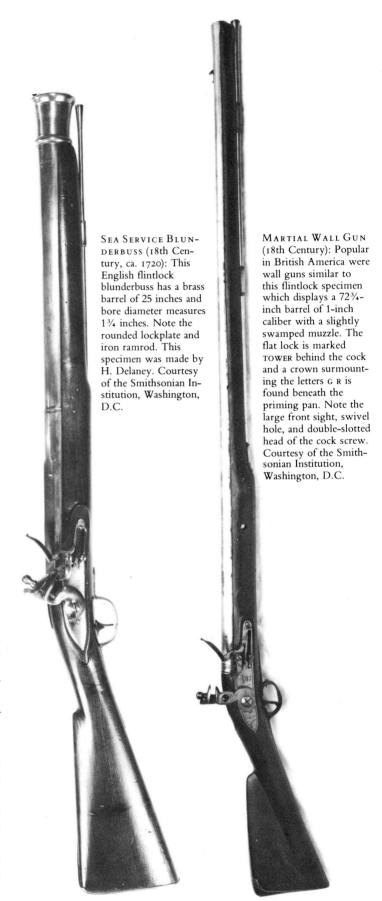

SEA SERVICE BLUNDERBUSS (18th Century, ca. 1720): This English flintlock blunderbuss has a brass barrel of 25 inches and bore diameter measures 1¾ inches. Note the rounded lockplate and iron ramrod. This specimen was made by H. Delaney. Courtesy of the Smithsonian Institution, Washington, D.C.

MARTIAL WALL GUN (18th Century): Popular in British America were wall guns similar to this flintlock specimen which displays a 72¾-inch barrel of 1-inch caliber with a slightly swamped muzzle. The flat lock is marked TOWER behind the cock and a crown surmounting the letters G R is found beneath the priming pan. Note the large front sight, swivel hole, and double-slotted head of the cock screw. Courtesy of the Smithsonian Institution, Washington, D.C.

inches with a 42 inch barrel of .65 caliber displaying a 17-inch socket bayonet. Light cavalry (dragoon) carbine specifications adopted by the Board of Ordnance on April 17, 1756, called for slightly swamped (flared) 36 inch barrles of .65 caliber; the flare assisting in loading while mounted. The overall length of the light cavalry carbine was 51½ inches and it weighed seven pounds and ten ounces without the 17-inch socket bayonet.

Adopted in 1773, Elliott's carbine weighed approximately seven pounds with an overall length of 43½ inches and it had a .65 caliber, 28 inch barrel taking a 13-inch socket bayonet. The artillery carbine weighed the same as the light cavalry model, was provided with a 13-inch socket bayonet, and it had a 37 inch barrel of .65 caliber, while the overall length was 52 inches.

Like the French the British also adopted an officers' fusil and in the Warrants of 1768-1769 either officers' fusils or carbines were specified for grenadier sergeants. Typical officers' fusils had pinned walnut stocks, weighed about seven pounds, and displayed barrels ranging in length from 34 to 40 inches, while caliber fluctuated between .65 and .70. Officers' fusils were usually more ornate and superior in quality to the service musket and carbine, while in many instances they were purchased from independent gunsmiths and the finish and ornamentation was governed only by what the officer could afford.

Blunderbusses continued to be used by the Royal Navy and several variations had appeared by 1750, most of them weighing ten to 12 pounds and displaying distinctly swamped brass barrels of .90 to .98 caliber. Barrel length ranged between 22 and 24 inches and musket locks were employed. The British Army also employed the blunderbuss and its somewhat larger manifestation: the wall or deck gun. Those massive, smoothbore firearms were more portable than light cannon and similar to the French *amusette* (see p. 189), while they were used aboard ship and to defend various kinds of fortifications. In British America the wall or deck gun was often mounted on small, shallow-draught boats for riverine warfare. Typical British specimens weighed approximately 25 pounds with an overall length of 70 to 73 inches. Barrel length fluctuated between 52 and 54 inches and caliber ranged from .98 to one inch.

At about the time the Long Land Service Musket was introduced the British adopted a horse or dragoon pistol displaying a round, pin-fastened, 12-inch barrel of .65 caliber; the same as the carbine. Furniture was brass and the convex lockplate and sideplate resembled that of the musket. The wood ramrod was secured to the walnut stock with a single thimble and it was brass-capped like the bulbous pommel grip. There were no sights. The lock was marked after musket fashion and barrels displayed Birmingham or London proofmarks and the broad arrow property stamp.[16] Sea Service pistols were identical except that a belt hook was provided.

In 1760, during the French and Indian War, the Board of Ordnance adopted new pattern martial pistols which were shorter and more durable, displaying round, nine-inch barrels of .65 caliber and retaining pin-fastened stocks, though some of the brass furniture was redesigned or eliminated. There were no sights and the lockplate, cock, and sideplate were flat. A belt hook was provided for sea service models. In 1762 a light dragoon and sea service pistol was introduced, each retaining the nine-inch barrel though reduced to .56 caliber, while the navy model had a belt hook.

The various Highland (Scottish) regiments serving in the British Army were the only units in which all enlisted personnel were issued pistols. Highland regiment pistols emulated the pattern of the typical, all-metal construction Scottish pistol and generally employed the true flintlock after ca. 1702, though preserving its other distinguishing characteristics (see p. 136). Officers' pistols were made of iron, often heavily chased and inlaid with silver. Enlisted versions had brass stocks with iron barrels and were equipped with belt hooks. Iron ramrods were used in either version.

Highland regiment pistols made before 1758 were marked H R (Highland Regiment) and thereafter R H R (Royal Highland Regiment). Prior to ca. 1762 the pistols were exclusively made in Scotland though thereafter Birmingham and London also emerged as production centers. Typical specimens of the period displayed round barrels seven to eight inches long of .55 to .57 caliber.

Subtle design variations and diverse ornamentation characterized Scottish pistols throughout their evolutionary period, whether commerical or martial patterns. Many Scottish pistols appeared in British America, particularly with the influx of Scottish settlers arriving in the acrimonious wake of the disastrous Jacobite defeat at Culloden Moor on April 27, 1746, and with the Highland regiments serving in the French and Indian War and the subsequent American Revolution.

Prior to 1689 and the Newdigate contracts London gunsmiths produced all British martial firearms, supplying under contract the complete stand, i.e., the firearm including the ramrod and the socket bayonet. In some instances London contractors could not satisfy their government obligation because they were unable to produce sufficient quantities of barrels and locks.

When exigent wartime or other demands severely strained the production capacity of the London contractors the crown was often forced to pay a

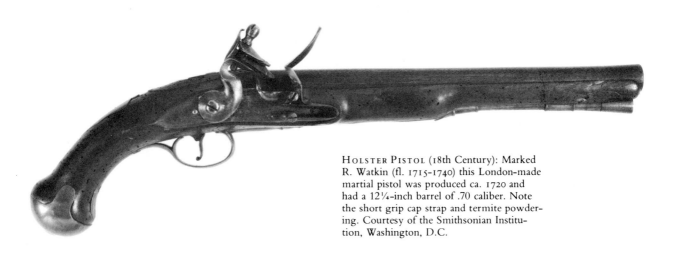

HOLSTER PISTOL (18th Century): Marked R. Watkin (fl. 1715-1740) this London-made martial pistol was produced ca. 1720 and had a 12¼-inch barrel of .70 caliber. Note the short grip cap strap and termite powdering. Courtesy of the Smithsonian Institution, Washington, D.C.

HOLSTER PISTOL (18th Century, 1743): The sylistic variations between this martial pistol made by Grice in 1743 and the Watkin pistol of ca. 1720 are not readily discernable. Both have wood ramrods secured by a single thimble and a guide, the forestocks are pin-fastened, and the trigger guards are bridged (arched) at the rear. The Grice pistol, however, has longer grip straps and the caliber has been reduced to .60, while the maker's name and date are stamped behind the lock rather than beneath the pan. The Grice pistol also has the crowned G R and the crown and broad arrow stamp (below pan) denoting government ownership. Courtesy of the Smithsonian Institution.

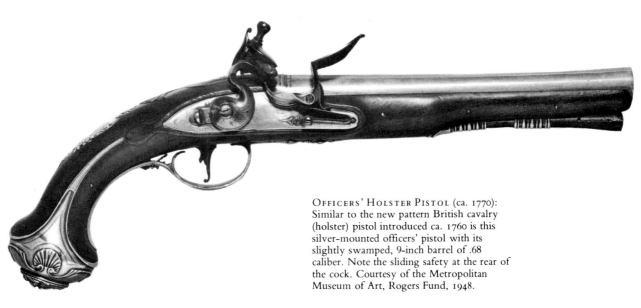

OFFICERS' HOLSTER PISTOL (ca. 1770): Similar to the new pattern British cavalry (holster) pistol introduced ca. 1760 is this silver-mounted officers' pistol with its slightly swamped, 9-inch barrel of .68 caliber. Note the sliding safety at the rear of the cock. Courtesy of the Metropolitan Museum of Art, Rogers Fund, 1948.

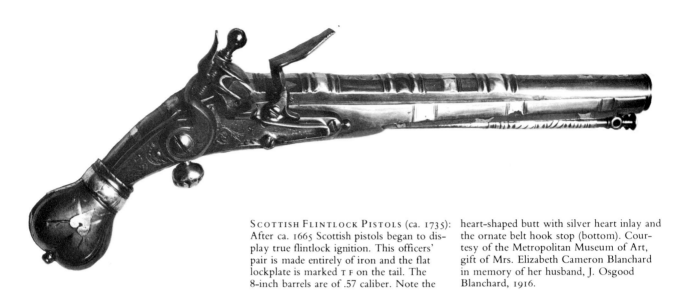

SCOTTISH FLINTLOCK PISTOLS (ca. 1735): After ca. 1665 Scottish pistols began to display true flintlock ignition. This officers' pair is made entirely of iron and the flat lockplate is marked T F on the tail. The 8-inch barrels are of .57 caliber. Note the heart-shaped butt with silver heart inlay and the ornate belt hook stop (bottom). Courtesy of the Metropolitan Museum of Art, gift of Mrs. Elizabeth Cameron Blanchard in memory of her husband, J. Osgood Blanchard, 1916.

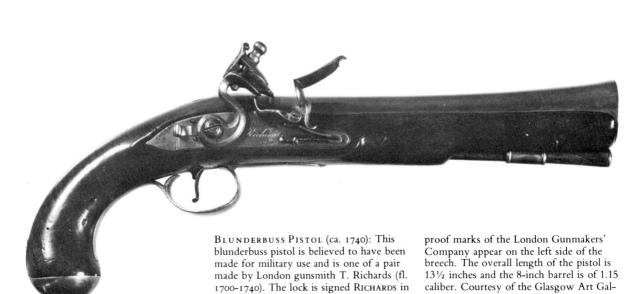

BLUNDERBUSS PISTOL (ca. 1740): This blunderbuss pistol is believed to have been made for military use and is one of a pair made by London gunsmith T. Richards (fl. 1700-1740). The lock is signed RICHARDS in script beneath the pan and the view and proof marks of the London Gunmakers' Company appear on the left side of the breech. The overall length of the pistol is 13½ inches and the 8-inch barrel is of 1.15 caliber. Courtesy of the Glasgow Art Gallery and Museum, Scotland.

premium to gunsmiths engaged under emergency contracts and contractors and sub-contractors were also covered by an overtime work allowance. In addition the shortfall in production often forced the crown to purchase from abroad generally inferior firearms at highly inflated prices; consequently there was considerable financial manipulation which further escalated costs, contractors frequently approached or declared bankruptcy because the crown in some instances deferred payment, and worse there were severe shortages of firearms and firearms components at crucial times.

Graft and peculation in martial firearms procurement was not confined to contractors or subcontractors, for under the traditional purchase system the regimental colonel who often as not bought his commission also assumed command of the regiment's finances. Muskets issued to the regiment were often returned to the crown at full cash value and the colonel purchased less expensive and usually inferior muskets elsewhere, pocketing the difference.[17]

The nefarious and widespread practice was eliminated in 1722, however, when the Board of Ordnance required replacement muskets to be inspected by "Proper Officers of the Ordnance" prior to purchase, and that the muskets be fabricated under certain specifications; the latter requirement giving rise to the term "sealed pattern musket."[18] The contract gunsmith was loaned a musket of proper specifications with the official wax seal of the Board of Ordnance affixed and the sealed pattern musket was to be used as a production pattern.[19]

In 1715, shortly before the Long Land Service Musket was adopted, the venerable purchase system of martial firearms procurement was dissolved and supplanted by the ordnance system. London contractors monopolizing the business could no longer claim that a lack of materials or skilled labor created the shortfall in martial firearms and, in any event, those reasons were not always valid, for many of them were more profitably engaged in making firearms for commercial interests.

The ordnance system effectively curtailed shortages of martial firearms and their components, for they were purchased in advance rather than as needed with the quantity based upon projections of future requirements; a practice similar to that successfully employed by the Hudson's Bay Company.

Aware since the 1689 Newdigate contracts that Birmingham gunmakers were capable of fabricating large quantities of firearms and components, the Board of Ordnance began to rely upon them for the requisite barrels, locks, and furniture. Barrels were proved prior to finishing and brass and iron furniture were generally bought by the pound, i.e., by weight rather than piece. Viewed by ordnance inspectors,

those components were stored in the Tower of London Armouries until needed, much like the finished firearms kept in reserve there during the Seven Years' War (see Appendix VI).

Advanced purchases provided an adequate supply of firearms and their components, thereby eliminating the high rates charged for emergency and overtime production because when needed the parts were distributed to the London contractors traditionally responsible for stocking and final assembly.

The ordnance system also decentralized martial firearms procurement and stimulated standardization, while virtually ending foreign purchases and substantially reducing some of the unsavory aspects of political corruption because London gunsmiths and their agents no longer dominated contract negotiations. Production costs also diminished because martial firearms components were often purchased at lower prices when demands were slack and assembled during inflationary periods created by wartime conditions.

The ordnance system was also beneficial to the London and Birmingham contractors, for advanced purchasing created a continuing demand which meant substantial if not full employment, while crown payment was more prompt; the latter also improving the relationship between the firearms industry and the crown.

In addition to crown contracts Birmingham and London gunsmiths also made large numbers of trade fusils for the Hudson's Bay Company with London contractors often purchasing components from Birmingham makers, and equally substantial quantities of quasi-martial firearms for the East India Company which maintained a private military force. East India Company and Hudson's Bay Company contracts frequently surpassed in number and profit those granted by the Board of Ordnance and London gunsmiths were inclined to favor commercial rather than crown contracts, for payment was prompt and quality standards were usually less rigid; thus economics frequently served as the foundation for military-industrial coöperation rather than patriotism, whether firearms or other products were involved.

The productivity of Birmingham and London gunsmiths contracting to make firearms for the Board of Ordnance and the East India Company has been detailed by Howard L. Blackmore. Referring to London contractors John Hirst (fl. 1718-1770) and Richard Waller (fl. 1715-1772), Blackmore notes that during the Seven Years' War (1756-1763) Waller and a staff of 40 produced 263,000 new martial musket stocks and repaired 18,000. Hirst, working with Waller and employing at least 34 filers and fitters, assembled 298,720 martial muskets, turning out 60,000 annually in 1759 and 1760.[20] Those impressive figures represent stocks and finished muskets only, for the locks and furniture were made by Birmingham craftsmen dominated by the gunsmithing facilities of John and Thomas Ketland (fl. 1745-1800).

Blackmore also mentions that between 1768 and 1769 proofmasters at the Ordnance Proof House on the Tower wharf passed 95,558 barrels produced by Gunmakers' Company artisans for the East India Company alone.[21] The remarkable productivity achieved by Birmingham and London gunsmiths during that period reflects the high level of technology attained by the British armament industry despite the fact that it was much less mechanized than the French armament industry.

During the 1775-1785 period brass furniture for the average land pattern musket weighed 28½ ounces and it was purchased at one shilling (s) and two pence (d) per pound. Brass components like forestock caps and long and short ramrod thimbles were purchased by piece at 2d, 6d, and 1½ d respectively. Iron parts were also bought separately, including triggers at 7s per hundred, sights at 8s per hundred, sling swivels at 2½d per pair; ramrod tail-pipe springs at 2d each, woodscrews at 4s per 100, breech and side nails (breech plug tang and lockplate screws) at 1s/6d per 100; carbine ribs (slide bars) at 1s/2d each, slide bar rings at 1½d, bolts at 3s per 100, and belt hooks at 9s each.

Musket ramrods were purchased from subcontractors at 1s/3d each for iron, while those for carbines were 1s. Wood musket ramrods were 11s per 1,000 and those for pistols were 4s/6d per 100. Socket bayonets were bought according to length: 13-inch at 1s/7d each and 17-inch at 2s/10d each. Bayonet scabbards were 8½d each. Musket and carbine slings were respectively 1s/4d and 1s/3d each, and the combined priming pan brush and vent pick cost 2d.

As of 1785 a complete Short Land Service Musket, New Pattern, cost £ 1/3s/3½d, while a Sea Service Musket was purchased at £ 1/4s/8d; each stand including 3d for proving the barrel and 1d for fitting the bayonet. Musket flints were purchased at 14s per 1,000, while carbine and pistol flints were sold at 10s per 1,000.[22] The rates paid to British martial contract gunsmiths for making and fitting various musket components can be found in APPENDIX VI.

Eighteenth-century British martial accouterments were suspended from shoulder or waist belts. The leather cartridge box with its wood insert had a greater capacity than French or Spanish boxes, usually carrying as many as 30 paper cartridges and weighing from five to six pounds when filled.[23] The cover was normally embossed with a crown surmounting the letters G R (George Rex). The box hung at the right side when slung from a shoulder belt and it was carried on the front of the waist belt, secured by two loops nailed to the wood liner.

The British cartridge-making method was described by Timothy Pickering, Jr. (1745-1829), *An Easy Plan of Discipline for a Militia* (Salem, 1775); the first American military manual.[24] The lead ball was put in the hollowed-out end of a forming stick conforming to ball diameter. Heavily textured cartridge paper was then wrapped around the stick, slightly protruding beyond the ball. The excess paper was tied and the stick minus the ball was withdrawn, leaving a tube. A single powder charge plus a sufficient amount for priming was poured into the tube and the end was simply twisted closed.

The French, usually more inclined to accept practical innovations, were slow to adopt paper cartridges despite the urging of Louis XIV who had recommended their use in 1702.[25] A 1738 ordnance directive described how the cartridges were to be made, though not until ca. 1745 were they generally employed among French forces.

CARTRIDGE BOX (ca. 1775): This British infantry cartridge box has a wood liner and the embossed crown and G R denoting government ownership. Note the simple stud arrangement for latching the cover. Courtesy of the Morristown National Historical Park, Morristown, N.J.

In the French cartridge-making technique the paper was rolled around the forming stick which had a flat end and the slightly protruding paper was folded against the stick and pasted. The stick was withdrawn and the ball with an adequate powder charge for loading and priming was then poured into the tube; the end of the paper simply folded or twisted. The method was more difficult and time-consuming and the cartridges more fragile than British because paste rather than string was used.

In addition to a bore scower, priming wire, and bullet worm, British soldiers were issued a combination tool described by Pickering as consisting of "three blades, each of which is fitted to turn a screw . . . [and] united at a common center."[26] Though the tool was adequate for firearms disassembly and assembly, Pickering designed a superior, innovative tool similar to the Spanish *eslabón* and incorporating in a single unit a vent pick, two screwdriver blades, and a hammer.

Pickering's combination tool was four inches long, shaped like a small letter *t* with the left arm of the crossbar removed, and provided with a leather case which he suggested to be used as a handle. The bottom curve of the spine served as a vent pick, while the upper tip and the right arm were screwdrivers. The spine was approximately ¼ inch thick and was used for chipping a sharp edge on a fractured flint, driving in pins, and other utilitarian purposes. It is not known if any of the Pickering-design combination tools were made.

The grenade launcher (hand mortar) continued to be used by eighteenth-century British grenadiers, though the Tinker buttstock model (see p. 103) had been generally supplanted by the socket type which was attached to the muzzle like the bayonet; a spring clip securing it. Early in the century an extremely short version of the grenade launcher was developed for dragoons, mounted on the front saddle bow, and it is likely that it was experimental rather than standard issue.

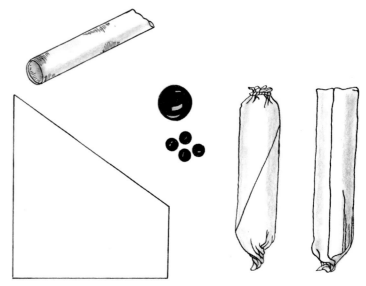

PAPER CARTRIDGES (18th Century): Top. British cartridge forming stick with concave head. Left to right. Cartridge paper measuring 6 × 5½ × 2 inches; round ball and buckshot, a popular load commonly called buck and ball; British cartridge with tied end; and French cartridge with pasted end. Author's sketch.

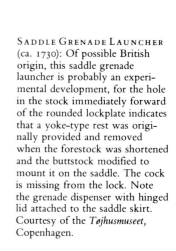

SADDLE GRENADE LAUNCHER (ca. 1730): Of possible British origin, this saddle grenade launcher is probably an experimental development, for the hole in the stock immediately forward of the rounded lockplate indicates that a yoke-type rest was originally provided and removed when the forestock was shortened and the buttstock modified to mount it on the saddle. The cock is missing from the lock. Note the grenade dispenser with hinged lid attached to the saddle skirt. Courtesy of the *Tøjhusmuseet*, Copenhagen.

PUCKLE REVOLVING BREECH
GUN (ca. 1715): Though differing
in some aspects from the patent
drawing, this view of the Puckle
gun illustrates the adjustable rear
sight and hooded vent. Note the
sliding priming pan covers of the
breech chambers, the yoke and
elevating bar arrangement, and
the stabilizing chains on the
tripod legs. British Crown
Copyright. Reproduced with
permission of the Controller of
Her Britannic Majesty's Stationery Office.

PUCKLE REVOLVING BREECH GUN
(18th Century): The original patent drawing of the Puckle gun depicted
illustrates its salient features: 1 - Barrel, 2 - Breech, 3 - Magazine
spindle, 4 - Magazine and integral locking crank, 5 - Trunnion
yoke, 6 - Elevation bar, 7 - Pintle, 8 - Elevation bar mounting
plate, 9 - Tripod leg, 10 - Tripod leg retention chains,
11 - Tripod leg braces, 12 - Pintle socket, 13 - Square
(cubed) shot (multiple), 14 - Square shot (single), 15 -
Magazine base depicting ratchet, 16 - Magazine
(square bullet type), 17 - Magazine (round
bullet type), 18 - Round loading chamber,
19 - Square loading chamber, 20 - Square
bullet, 21 - Bullet mould. British Crown
Copyright. Reproduced with permission
of the Controller of Her Britannic
Majesty's Stationery Office.

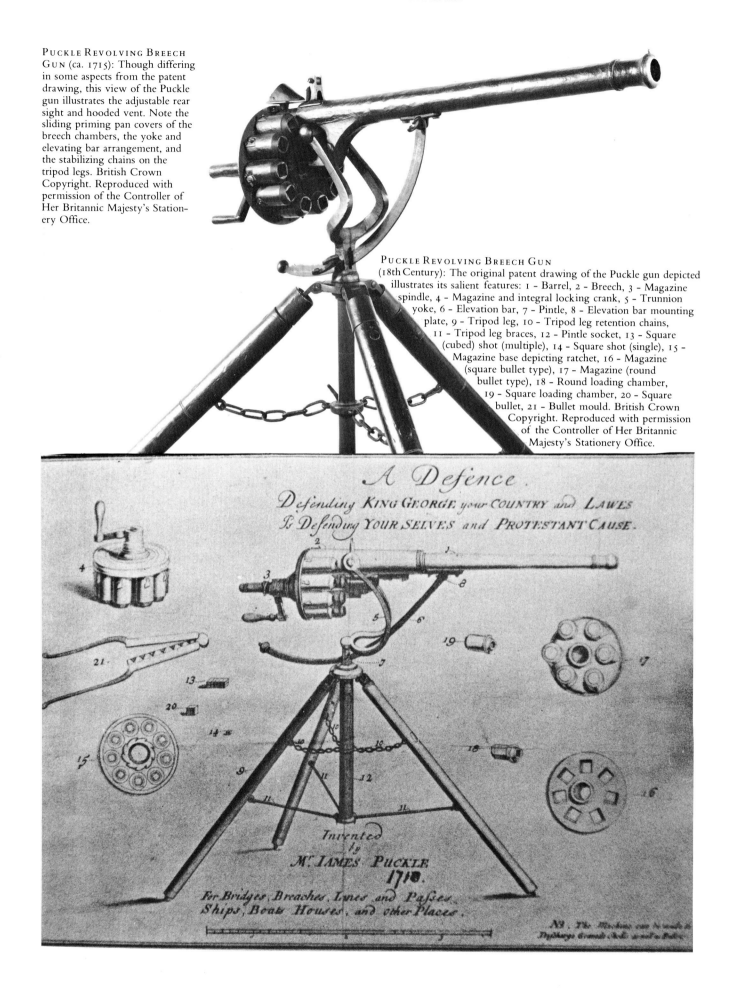

Coeval with the introduction of the Long Land Service Musket there appeared in Britain a mechanical device which was, as its inventor James Puckle of Sussex declared, "a portable gun or machine that discharges so often and so many bullets, and [can] be so quickly loaded as renders it next to impossible to carry any ship by boarding."[27]

On May 15, 1718, Puckle received royal patent No. 418 for his peculiar firearm he further described as designed to protect "Bridges, Breaches, Lines and Passes, Ships, Boats, Houses and other Places." He also averred that "The Machine can be made to Discharge Granado [explosive] Shells as well as Bullets."[28]

A refined application of the venerable revolving cylinder, breech-loading concept, Puckle's novel weapon incorporated a number of technological innovations subsequently resurrected and, in a limited sense, it can be considered the first practical machine gun. The Puckle gun initially employed match ignition, though a flintlock version appeared ca. 1720, the lock in either system situated atop the breech.

A single, smoothbore barrel was mounted on an adjustable tripod by a pintle attached to a U-shaped yoke securing the breech trunnions; the pintle locked in position or permitted to rotate 360° in the tripod head. Passing through the pintle was a curved bar attached to the barrel; the bar adjustable for elevating or depressing the barrel. The tripod and elevating systems are currently reflected in automatic and semi-automatic weapons design.

Extending from beneath the heavy breech was the barrel axis pin, the revolving breech plates sliding over it. Matchlock guns used six-chambered breech plates and the flintlock models had nine-chambered plates; each of the plate chambers provided with a round or square loading chamber containing the powder and projectile. Each breech plate had a shank to which the operating handle or crank was attached.

Each breech plate chamber was tapered to fit the concave breech mouth and had a manually-operated, sliding cover corresponding to the ignition vent in the loading chamber. When the handle was cranked the breech plate rotated and each tapered chamber was successively and positively locked in the breech to ensure obturation. The obvious disadvantages of the Puckle gun were manifest in the ignition system wherein the mechanism had to be cocked for each shot and in the chambers which had to be uncovered individually to permit ignition.

Puckle's "machine gun" was demonstrated at the Royal Artillery Proving Ground at Woolwich in November, 1717. Though impressive, its performance failed to interest the Board of Ordnance and dashed Puckle's hope for a military contract which was usually a lucrative proposition. Puckle, however, was neither the first nor would he be the last

inventor to see his dream perish, shattered by men of little imagination and even less perspicacity.

Undaunted, Puckle then established a stock company to finance the manufacture of brass and iron guns and several public trials were held. The *London Journal,* covering a 1722 exhibition taking place in a heavy downpour, enthusiastically reported that despite the rain the weapon discharged 63 shots in seven minutes; an amazing nine rounds per minute which at the time was nothing short of phenomenal.

However astounding the performance, only a few Puckle guns were sold, some to individual military commanders using their own or regimental funds. A pair of Puckle guns taken to the West Indies with the Duke of Montagu's 1727 expedition were never used and, as far as it is known, no data has been unearthed regarding the performance of the gun under combat conditions. Puckle's company folded shortly thereafter, possibly because few had confidence in a weapon touted by its inventor as designed to employ round bullets against Christians and square ones for infidels.

Old World Technological Innovation

Deforestation had reached a crucial state in eighteenth-century Britain, for agricultural expansion, the increasing use of wood in construction, and the nearly insatiable demands for charcoal by the iron-making and armament industry all contributed to the scarcity of the basic fuel.

The quest for a substitute fuel in the iron industry was partially successful when in 1709 Abraham Darby, Sr., of the large Coalbrookdale Iron Works in Shropshire discovered that coal, first converted to coke by pre-cooking and previously used to smelt copper and lead, could be employed for iron-making because it generated extremely high temperatures.

Darby's utilization of coke produced an inferior grade of wrought iron not immediately accepted by British gunsmiths, although there was limited application outside the firearms industry which subsequently led to the widespread use of fossil fuels in Britain much earlier than elsewhere in the Old and New World.

Though bituminous (soft) coal was discovered in the Illinois country by Joliet in 1673 and first mined in the Richmond Basin of Virginia in 1750, charcoal remained the basic fuel for gunmaking and iron-making in British America where there was an abundant wood supply. Coal, however, was employed by some patriot gunsmiths during the American Revolution.

Iron-making rapidly expanded in British America during the eighteenth century with the discovery of large ore deposits in New Jersey, Pennsylvania, and Virginia. So valuable was the iron industry to the colonial economy that settlements near ore-bearing sites offered ironmasters and blacksmiths free land and homes if they promised to work in the region at least seven years.

Prior to 1750 the most active iron-making operation in British America was the Cornwall Furnace on Furnace Creek near the Cornwall Ore Mines in Lebanon County, Pa.[29] In 1732 the Penn proprietors granted Joseph Turner 9,669 acres covering the Cornwall site and he later assigned the land to William Allen. Allen sold it to Peter Grubb of Cornwall, England, for £135 in 1737; one of the most profitable investments made in British America, for two feet below the surface Grubb found a virtually unlimited supply of iron ore (see APPENDIX VII).

In 1742 Grubb built the Cornwall Furnace and bought two contiguous tracts of 142½ acres. From 1732 when the first ore was dug at the Cornwall Ore Mines until 1973 when they were closed after 241 years of continuous operation they produced in excess of 105 million tons of iron in addition to large quantities of copper, gold, iron pyrites, and silver.

The next significant iron-making operation in size and longevity was the Roxborough (Berkshire)

Furnace established in Heidelberg Township, Berks County, Pa., in 1755. The Roxborough Furnace, subsequently known as the Reading Furnace and then the Robesonia Furnace, remained active until ca.1913.[30]

A resurgence of Virginia iron-making began when in 1727 the Fredericksville Furnace and the Germanna Furnace were established in Spottsylvania County.[31] Five years later the Rappahannock Furnace was started on the river of the name above Fredericksburg and at the same time the Massaponax Furnace was built on the river below the settlement.[32] The third most important Virginia furnace was the Accokeek Furnace, known also as England's Iron Mines Furnace, established 12 miles from Fredericksburg ca. 1748.[33] The Accokeek Furnace shipped 410 tons of pig iron to Britain in 1750 (see APPENDIX VIII).

While there was no improvement in early eighteenth-century wrought iron, the quality of the blister steel produced in Britain was vastly upgraded ca. 1740 by Doncaster watchmaker Benjamin Huntsman (1704-1776).[34] Living near the famed cutlery center of Sheffield where most British steel was made, Huntsman was chagrined to find that the quality and the uniformity of the steel he purchased for making watch springs left much to be desired.

In his search for a uniform, high quality steel

IRON-MAKING COMMUNITY (ca. 1770): Entire communities often called plantations were frequently involved in iron-making. At least 1,200 men, women, and children were associated with the manufacture of iron at the Hopewell (Pa.) Iron Plantation depicted. At the outset of the American Revolution such plantations were producing 1/6th of the world's iron, much of it used for firearms manufacture. Courtesy of the American Iron and Steel Institute, Washington, D.C.

Huntsman employed a number of technological innovations previously used in making iron and glass. His blast furnace, constructed of a superior sandstone with excellent heat-retaining properties, incorporated the tall tunnel or flue earlier devised which had improved the draught. For fuel he chose coke, previously pioneered by Darby, which burned hotter than charcoal; particularly with an intensified furnace draught.

Huntsman's melting crucibles, similar to those used by Sheffield glass-makers, were made from the best local clay and he carefully packed them with the requisite amount of charcoal, specially selected Swedish wrought iron cut into small pieces, and a borax flux which amalgamated the other ingredients. The crucibles were subjected to a temperature of more than 1000° F for several days.

Huntsman thereby produced a high-carbon steel of superior quality which could be uniformly tempered and it remained unsurpassed until the nineteenth century. Despite his efforts to keep the process a secret his competitors discovered the technique and shortly after he died 11 steel refineries were operating in Sheffield and the "secret" spread elsewhere; thus giving the gunsmith a steel more suitable for lock springs and the world in general a metal of sufficient strength and durability to use as the cutting edge in the bits of common hand tools and those employed in the novel machine tools then coming to the fore.

The burgeoning eighteenth-century British American iron industry gave the colonists a heavy industry with a large income potential, for both cast-iron and wrought iron were used to make a variety of utilitarian products not the least of which were firearms components. The startling success of the industry, however, engendered what the crown saw as a serious problem with ramifications which nullified economic considerations.

The proliferation of forges and furnaces presaged the development of a viable British American armament industry which the crown considered inimical to the security of the empire and, consequently, Parliament passed the infamous Iron Act of 1750. The Iron Act was nothing less than a flagrant attempt to minimize the expansion of a potentially dangerous war machine and it came as one of the first in a long series of legislative barriers nurturing colonial resentment.

Not only did the Iron Act give crown administrators the power to impose heavy fines and other penalties upon the colonies circumventing its provisions, but permitted them to limit the future construction and operation of mines, forges, furnaces, foundries, rolling mills, and slitting mills as well as determine the number and kinds of products made.

While those restrictions and repressive powers certainly curtailed colonial commerce, the Iron Act

IRON PRODUCTION: BRITISH AMERICA AND THE WORLD, 1700-1790

Year	British America	World
1700	1500[1]	100,000[2]
1750	10,000	150,000
1775	30,000	210,000
1790[3]	38,000	325,000

[1]In tons.
[2]Estimated, including pig iron, bar iron, and cast iron ware made at furnaces.
[3]Includes U.S. production after 1783.

created additional antagonism by permitting bar iron and pig iron from British America to enter the mother country duty free though the colonists were required to pay a burdensome tariff on imported iron and iron products.

Despite the oppressive Iron Act production increased in British America. In 1750 approximately 10,000 tons of iron were produced, yet by 1775 the figure trebled, as noted in the Table.[35] Significantly, iron production sharply increased after the Iron Act was implemented and it has been estimated that at least 82 charcoal furnaces and 175 forges were operating in British America at the outset of the Revolutionary War; the former making a total of 24,600 tons of pig iron and 26,250 tons of wrought iron annually.[36]

While some colonial furnaces and forges operated clandestinely, a substantial number continued production with the connivance of British officials either financially involved in the industry or accepting bribes for not interfering; a too common practice among present government regulatory agencies. It cannot be ignored, however, that the French and Indian War in 1754 stimulated the manufacture of military hardware vital to British defense and that the colonial armament industry relied on a vigorous iron industry; thus in contravening the Iron Act the colonists materially contributed to Britain's victory and kept alive an industry essential to the patriot cause in the coming conflict with the crown.

The Growth of the Colonial Gunsmithing Craft

Despite the rapid proliferation of gunsmiths in colonial America at the beginning of the eighteenth century, the colonists were still obliged to look to the mother country for adequate supplies of firearms, gunpowder, and related ordnance material and in British America they remained dependent until the War of Independence.

Gunsmiths substantially contributed to the burgeoning techonomic and geographic expansion of North America, for many of them were since the seventeenth century established on the hostile fringe of civilization and catered to the needs of the Native American as well as the settler, frontier trader, and those otherwise disposed toward wilderness living, like the long hunter of British America and his counterpart in French America, the *coureur de bois*. Like most colonial craftsmen the gunsmith was a respected community member and many of them became important civil and military leaders.

The number of gunsmiths active in North America dramatically escalated with the inordinate population explosion during the first quarter of the eighteenth century. While a per capita ratio cannot be ascertained, fewer gunsmiths established themselves in New France than in British America, and the latter saw a substantial increase in German, Swiss, Irish, and Scottish gunsmiths seeking surcease from the political and religious persecution still rampant in the Old World. It was also early in the century that the continental European gunsmiths in British America began to assert a significant impact on technology and introduced the first major technological innovation in American firearms evolution.

The colonial American gunsmith, like his European counterpart, perpetuated his skills through the apprentice system originating with the Old World guilds. In British America the apprentice gunsmith was often as not the gunsmith's son or a related family member, another gunsmith's son when the two were mutually incompatible, an orphan, an illegitimate child, or a suitable bondman. The bondman was either an indentured servant held in involuntary servitude for a period of four to seven years, or a redemptioner volunteering his labor for a like period to pay for his passage to the colonies. Black slaves also became adept at the gunsmithing craft, exposed to and trained in the work by their owner-masters without benefit of apprentice status.

Apprenticeships were generally initiated between the ages of 12 and 14 in British America with the term and conditions governed by statute; some colonies requiring a minimum seven-year indenture which included provisions clearly defining the role of the master and the apprentice. Apprentice statutes were based on earlier English law and varied considerably from colony to colony. In addition to teaching the apprentice his trade, the master gunsmith was required to provide him with food, clothing, shelter, and a small stipend in some instances.[37] The agreement was usually torn in half at the start of the term, the apprentice given the gunsmith's half when the term was satisfactorily completed which acknowledged and certified his expertise.

The apprentice was obliged to work for the master throughout the term, often performing menial chores in addition to learning the craft. The apprentice's life was virtually dominated by his tutor; an aspect of the system occasionally lending itself to abuse. While the master obviously benefitted from all the services rendered by the apprentice, society also received its reward, for the apprentice had been taught a trade vital to the community and, upon entering the professional mainstream, the apprentice's social status and standard of living were at once enhanced proportionate to his contribution to society.

A 1708 Virginia law governing indentures specifically mentioned that the master, upon completion of the bondman's term, would give him a felt hat, two suits of clothes, 12 bushels of corn meal, 50 acres of land, and a firearm worth 20 shillings.[38] Whether apprentice gunsmiths in Virginia then received similar benefits cannot be corroborated because few apprentice gunsmith agreements have survived that early epoch to demonstrate a comprehensible comparison.

As fragmentary records indicate, the apprentice gunsmith completing his term in the Pennsylvania Colony was normally provided with a suit, some acerage or a small cash settlement, and a set of gunsmithing tools which he had made during his term. There were, of course, innumerable variations in what satisfied the stipulations of the agreement. In addition the former apprentice gunsmith customarily took with him an example of his work to illustrate his proficiency in the craft.

Once free of his obligation the apprentice was then able to begin his career often as a journeyman gunsmith for as long as three years because he either sought additional experience or desired to specialize in making certain kinds of firearms, or because he depended on an income prior to establishing his own shop. Apprentices often remained associated with their masters, either working for wages or as a partner in the business, and they frequently married within their peer group; thus in some instances creating family gunsmithing dynasties, e.g. the Pomeroys of Massachusetts Bay Colony.

From the beginning one indelible characteristic of colonial American society was mobility and that freedom of movement was omniverous. As the frontier expanded the gunsmith often preceded the settler. Like his contemporaries he normally built his home with or without assistance from his neighbors, frequently hunted and planted a crop for sustenance and to supplement his income, married young and raised a family, and often as not moved on to new horizons when the mood struck.

The typcial seventeenth-century North American gunsmithery was a small, one room, single story structure built of wood, fieldstone, brick, or a combination of those materials and it frequently appeared as an addition to the gunsmith's home rather than a separate entity.[39] The shop floor was usually earthen, though brick and fieldstone came to be used, while the roof was generally steep to shed rain and snow and often shingled with slate rather than shakes (wood shingles) as a fire prevention measure though slate was more expensive. There were, of course, variations in the choice of architecture and construction materials.

Like in many early colonial structures the windows of the gunsmithery were few, small, and without panes because glass was scarce and therefore expensive. Stout wood shutters provided protection from the natural elements and on the frontier loopholes were usually added for defense. The shop was generally served by a single door which could be barred or bolted from the inside. Lighting was minimal because of the few windows and supplemented by the forge glow, tallow candles, or oil lamps. Though the early colonial gunsmithery was of generally sound construction, it emerged as a cramped, poorly illuminated and ventilated structure almost unbearably hot in summer and the opposite in winter.

During the early colonial period the bellows-operated, brick or fieldstone forge was often as not separate from the gunsmithery, though it was covered for protection from the elements. Gun-smitheries with interior forges incorporated a chimney for draught and exhaust. The bellows generated sufficient oxygen to intensify the heat of the charcoal fire which also warmed the work area in winter.

The work area of the gunsmithery doubled as a retail outlet and it was large enough to accommodate a long, sturdy workbench or two and sufficient space for the gunsmith's forge, anvil, vise, and hand tools. Until ca. 1750 gunsmithing in colonial America was primarily an individual, household enterprise with the work force consisting of the gunsmith and, depending on his economic situation, an apprentice, journeyman, or partner.

With the advent of the eighteenth century somewhat larger gunsmitheries emerged, and while most gunsmithing was performed with hand tools a number of crank-or-treadle operated barrel boring engines and grinding wheels were employed. By ca. 1725 some of the larger gunsmitheries used water power to drive those basic machine tools.

The gunsmith of the early colonial period generally relied on imported barrels and locks; particularly the latter because procuring suitable steel for spring-making remained problematical. Prior to ca. 1770 colonial gunsmiths fashioned lock springs from scrapped bayonets, swords, or other edged weapons and implements made of quality crucible steel.[40] Steel was extremely scarce in colonial America and

GUNSMITHING OR BLACKSMITHING FORGE (17th/18th Century): During the early colonial period in North America the forge was often separate from the gunsmith's shop. The bellows was operated by vigorously pumping the pole-like lever. Early forges were often made of fieldstone. Note the grooved barrel anvil and the quenching tub. Author's sketch.

imported at great expense, while Huntsman's superior steel was virtually unobtainable until after the American Revolution.

In the seventeenth century most of the colonial gunsmith's time and effort were devoted to repairing rather than making firearms, and what firearms that were produced were assembled from imported components. Stock-making, however, was fundamental because firearms frequently saw rough service and the stock was the weaker of the three basic components. Damaged stocks were often replaced with those made from domestic wood like hard maple, American walnut, cherry, or other suitable varieties.

Because the early colonial gunsmith was isolated from the expanding mainstream of European culture he was not immediately aware of the latest technological developments in firearms manufacture nor did he always benefit from the emerging specialization in barrel and lock-making. Neither did he have convenient access to the complex commercial system supplying the essentials of his craft, for the time and the hazards involved in crossing the Atlantic precluded rapid communication and transportation, while on the frontier the wagon and pack animal link was often tenuous because of weather conditions and warfare.

Bereft of the many European technological and commercial advantages, the colonial gunsmith became singularly adept in the use of hand tools and improvization; that latter aspect of American craftsmanship the foundation upon which was built that intangible quality currently referred to as Yankee ingenuity. The colonial American gunsmith, by virtue of his isolation and the primitive conditions under which he lived and worked, was forced by circumstances to become a self-reliant and truly individualistic craftsman and the latter trait was often reflected in the innovative firearms he produced.

The evolution of the various hand tools and machine tools employed by the gunsmith was the gradual product of centuries of technological innovation. The colonial American gunsmith, despite his reliance on imported components, often made the entire firearm himself because in some instances he was unable to procure the essential parts, and from earliest times the most important hand tool used by the gunsmith was the file, for it was the basic and most versatile implement for shaping and removing the hardest of metals.

The early gunsmith developed an expertise with the file unchallenged by the modern metalsmith, for there were then no sophisticated machine tools to perform the intricate work, and he possessed an assortment of files unknown to the modern craftsman. The file was employed in virtually all phases of gunmaking though the lock components received the most attention. An indication of the various kinds of files used by the colonial gunsmith is found in a 1739 inventory of the hand tools needed to equip a Hudson's Bay Company gunsmithery and it included at least one each of those listed in the Table.[41]

Like his European counterpart the colonial gunsmith early relied on the simple bow drill for boring the vent in the breech and drilling screw and pin holes in wood and metal. Also used for boring wood were plain awls, the quill and the twist gimlet, and "burn" awls and augers; the points of the latter fired red-hot and pressed or twisted into the wood.

By ca. 1675, however, the innovative brace or bitstock appeared as a boring tool, its body usually made of naturally-shaped, seasoned hardwood. The elbow (handgrip) freely rotated around a button-head palm rest though the chuck and the bit were stationary; the bit secured in the chuck by a lead collar. Iron bitstocks emerged ca. 1720, utilizing

EIGHTEENTH-CENTURY GUNSMITHING FILES

Large band	Large flat bastard	Small round smooth
Large ruff (rough)	Large flat bastard, hand	Feather edge
Large half-round	Small half-round	Flat hand ruff
Large round edge	Small round edge	Half-round 9″ smooth
Large 3-square	Small 3-square	Smooth 4″ burr
Large 3-square ruff	Small round	Flat bastard
Large hand ruff	Small 3-square ruff	Smooth bastard
Large half-round ruff	Small half-round ruff	3-square [as] sorted
Large round edge ruff	Small round edge ruff	Half-round, round edge
Large flat smooth	Small half-round bastard	Flat

AUGERS, AWLS, AND GIMLETS (15th/18th Century): Left to right (1) Small burn auger. (2) Small twist gimlet. (3) Large burn awl. (4) Quill gimlet. (5) Small reaming awl. Author's sketch.

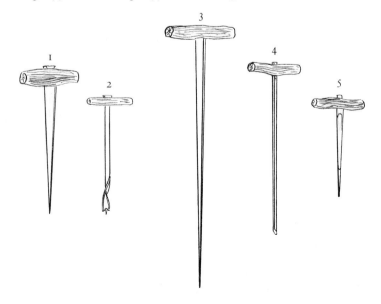

interchangeable bits held in the stationary chuck by a wedge or lock screw.[42] The bits had wedge-shaped butts which corresponded to the chuck recess and the steel cutting edge was forged integral with the helical bit body; the steel folded into the wrought iron in a method also used in making knife and axe blades.

The colonial American gunsmith early made woodscrews and gunscrews with thread-cutting dies or the judicious use of files and subsequently purchased them from European makers specializing in gunsmithing supplies. Furniture was also made or purchased. Barrel lug pins and lock pins were hand-made from wire imported for the purpose.

A straight tap of the proper size was used to cut the female threads in the breech end of the barrel and a corresponding die cut the male threads for the breech plug. The gunsmith also employed an assortment of taps for threading bored through or blind holes in the various firearms components.

When installing a fixed (non-adjustable) sight the gunsmith used soft solder, a mixture of lead and tin, to fuse it to the iron barrel and fluxed the solder with a compound of beeswax. borax, and iron filings; the sharp nose of the soldering iron merely heated in the forge. Solder was also used for filling holes and mounting priming pans, barrel ribs, and ramrod pipes and guides.

To fill a misaligned hole in a lock or other component the gunsmith plugged one side of the hole with clay or putty, filled the cavity with solder, and filed off the excess. Blind holes obviously were not plugged before filling. Spelter or hard solder, a mixture of copper and zinc, was unknown prior to 1746 for it was then that zinc was first isolated by Andreas Sigismund Marggraf (1709-1782).[43]

The many small firearms components like the priming pan, cock, tumbler, sear, and furniture were usually cast in moulds of sand, iron, hardwood, sandstone, and soapstone; the latter two readily hollowed out to the desired shape of the object. Sandstone and soapstone were also used for making single-and multiple-cavity bullet moulds. Cast components were finished by filing, grinding, and polishing.

The thin, sheet brass used by the gunsmith for making butt caps, forestock caps, ramrod thimbles and guides, thumbplates (signature plates), escutcheons, trigger plates, and other furniture or ornamentation was either cut to shape with shears or formed by a swedge, i.e., a mould-like implement made of hardwood or metal in a single or two-piece unit and used in conjunction with hammering.

The single swedge was male or female, the male displaying a raised pattern of the object and the female an incised pattern. The gunsmith simply hammered the sheet brass in or around the pattern to form the design. In using a two-piece, male-female

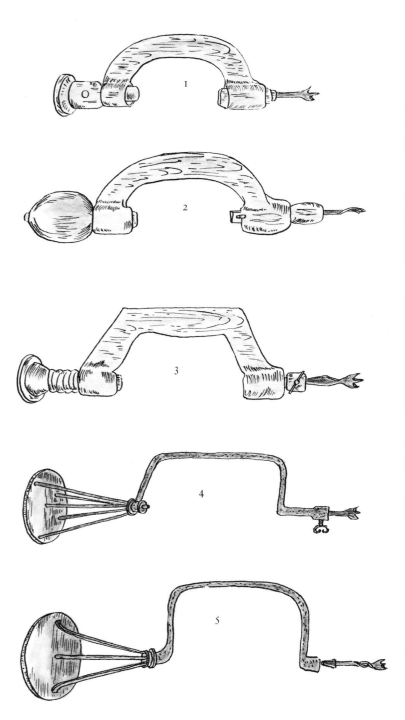

BITSTOCKS (BRACES, 17th/18th Century): Top to bottom. (1) All wood New England bitstock with steel-tipped iron bit held by lead cuff ca. 1690-1725. (2) All wood New England Pumpkin handle brace with bit held by lead cuff and wedge ca. 1730. (3) All wood Pennsylvania brace with bit held by turn screw ca. 1765. (4) All metal (wrought iron) New England brace with bit held by turn screw ca. 1720. (5) Wrought iron brace with bit held in chuck by wedged-shaped butt ca. 1775. Author's sketch, various sources.

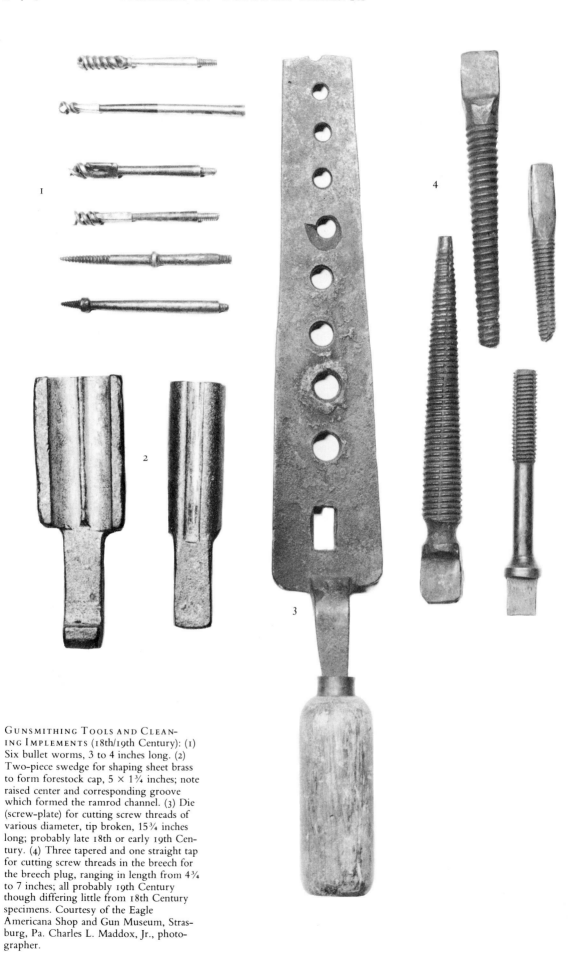

GUNSMITHING TOOLS AND CLEAN-
ING IMPLEMENTS (18th/19th Century): (1)
Six bullet worms, 3 to 4 inches long. (2)
Two-piece swedge for shaping sheet brass
to form forestock cap, 5 × 1¾ inches; note
raised center and corresponding groove
which formed the ramrod channel. (3) Die
(screw-plate) for cutting screw threads of
various diameter, tip broken, 15¾ inches
long; probably late 18th or early 19th Century. (4) Three tapered and one straight tap
for cutting screw threads in the breech for
the breech plug, ranging in length from 4¾
to 7 inches; all probably 19th Century
though differing little from 18th Century
specimens. Courtesy of the Eagle
Americana Shop and Gun Museum, Strasburg, Pa. Charles L. Maddox, Jr., photographer.

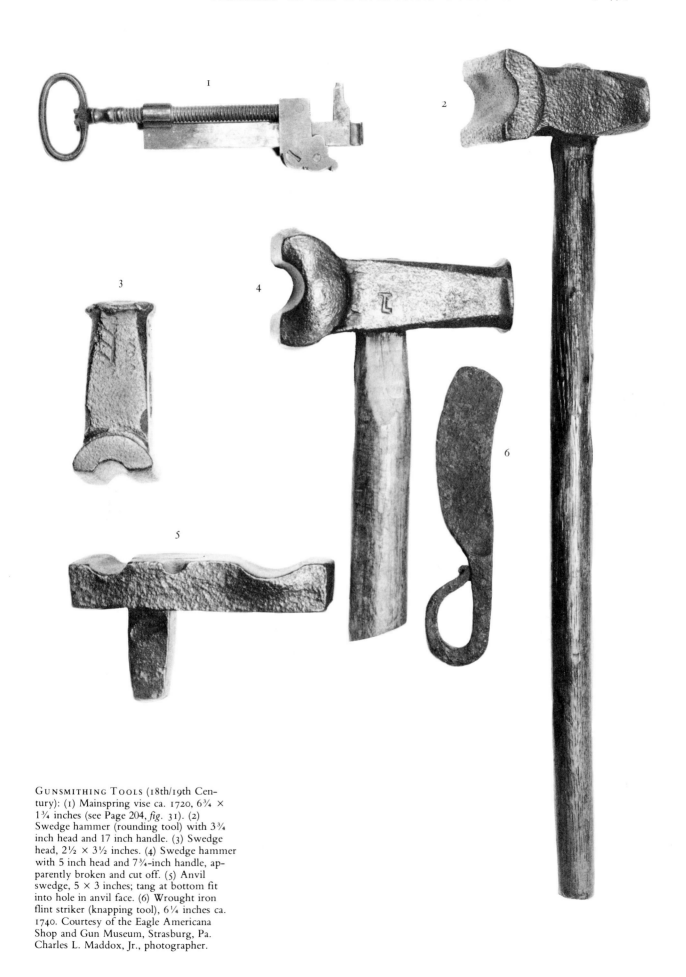

GUNSMITHING TOOLS (18th/19th Century): (1) Mainspring vise ca. 1720, 6¾ × 1¾ inches (see Page 204, *fig.* 31). (2) Swedge hammer (rounding tool) with 3¾ inch head and 17 inch handle. (3) Swedge head, 2½ × 3½ inches. (4) Swedge hammer with 5 inch head and 7¾-inch handle, apparently broken and cut off. (5) Anvil swedge, 5 × 3 inches; tang at bottom fit into hole in anvil face. (6) Wrought iron flint striker (knapping tool), 6¼ inches ca. 1740. Courtesy of the Eagle Americana Shop and Gun Museum, Strasburg, Pa. Charles L. Maddox, Jr., photographer.

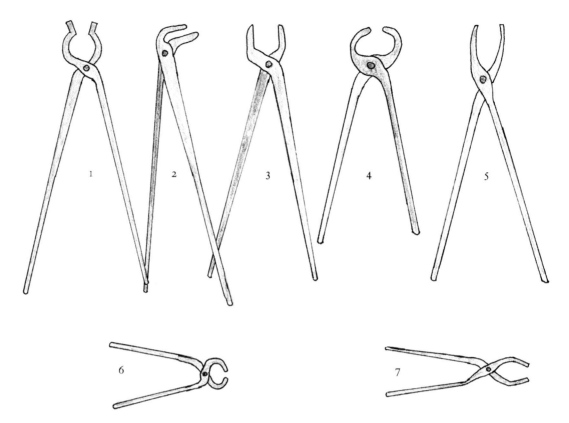

IRON-WORKING TONGS (16th/19th Century): A variety of tongs were used by the blacksmith and the gunsmith for working hot metal from the forge. These specimens (from left) depict only a few: (1) Hammer tongs. (2) Offset barrel skelp tongs. (3) Flat bit tongs. (4) Large pincers. (5) Hammer tongs. (6) Small pincers. (7) Small hammer tongs. Author's sketch.

swedge the thin brass was inserted between them and the object was formed by hammering.

The sheet brass and sheet silver customarily used for inlay work was hammered cold rather than heated in the forge because each was thin and consequently malleable. The gunsmith also employed numerous kinds of swedges to shape wrought iron taken from the forge. Hammer swedges, as the term implies, resembled hammers and were employed in a like manner.

Hammer swedges, known also as rounding tools, were often used for shaping the barrel of a firearm and strengthening the longitudinal or helical seam. The barrel section selected was heated in the forge and placed in the desired anvil groove and repeatedly struck with the rounding swedge, its head provided with a groove of corresponding diameter.

The colonial American gunsmith also utilized several kinds of brass, copper, lead, and iron hammers and a variety of wood and leather mallets; the hammers distinguished by weight and the face and peen design. Forging hammers were provided with flat, iron heads and a sharp peen for notching or creasing the iron when it was desired to fold it. Hammers with non-ferrous metal heads were ordinarily used on finished iron work as in barrel-straightening when it was desirable to strike the surface without marring it; the non-ferrous metal being softer. Brass and silver were worked with leather or wood mallets for the same reason.

An equally varied assortment of tongs were also employed by the gunsmith for grasping and bending the charcoal-fired iron as it was worked on the anvil. Tongs are readily identified by the jaw (bit) design and include the flat bit, crook bit, hammer bit, round bit, square bit, and barrel-forging bit as noted in making helical or *canon à ruban* barrels (see p. 194).

The colonial American gunsmith made many of his tools and occasionally purchased them from a blacksmith specializing in tool-making. Gunsmiths were usually adept at blacksmithing, though blacksmiths were seldom qualified gunsmiths despite making minor, emergency gun repairs when possible. On the frontier and particularly when dealing with the Native Americans, gunsmiths frequently doubled as blacksmiths.

In addition to the hand tools previously mentioned the gunsmith used various kinds of hacksaws, screwdrivers, pliers, punches and drifts for removing straight or tapered pins, templates (jigs) for aligning screw or pin holes in the lockplate and sideplate, and several measuring instruments including rulers, calipers, squares, and bore gauges.

In addition to the gunsmith's expertise as a metalsmith he was also an adept wood-worker and used a variety of hand tools for making gunstocks and pistol grips. In fashioning a stock or grip the colonial American gunsmith often as not felled the tree, choosing a suitable hardwood like maple or walnut though occasionally selecting other deciduous varieties such as cherry, beech, and apple. The eighteenth-century gunsmith was more discerning

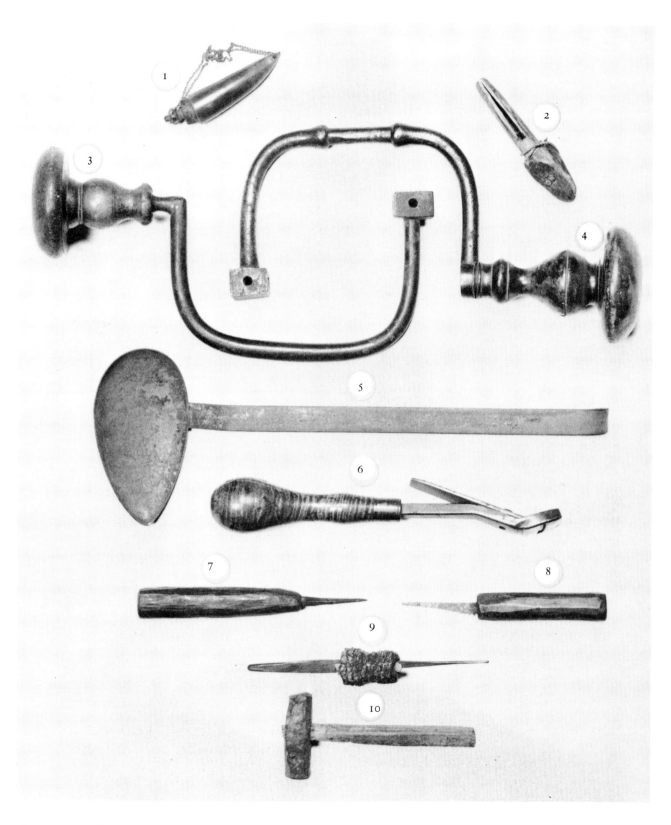

GUNSMITHING TOOLS AND FRONTIERSMAN'S ACCOUTERMENTS (18th/19th Century): (1) 18th Century small grease horn (3¼ inches); similar horns carried salt. (2) 19th Century hand-carved barrel tompion (3¾ inches). (3) Hand auger, 19th Century (9½ inches). (4) Hand auger, 19th Century (10 inches). (5) Iron ladle for pouring lead to cast bullets (length: 12¾ inches, bowl: 4½ inches); possibly 18th Century. (6) 19th Century stock inletting tool for grooving forestock to fit barrel, 8¾ inches. (7) 18th Century awl/scriber, hand-wrought, 5½ inches. (8) 18th Century saw, hand-wrought, 5⅛ inches. (9) 18th Century drift, hand-wrought, 6 inches. (10) 18th Century small, wrought-iron hammer, hand-wrought, head: 2 inches, handle: 4¾ inches. Courtesy of the Mercer Museum, Bucks County Historical Society, Doylestown, Pa. Charles L. Maddox, Jr., photographer.

TARGET BLOCK, STOCK
BLANK AND POWDER
PESTLE (18th/19th Century): A
section of hardwood stump
mounted on three tree-limb legs
was used by gunsmiths as a back-
stop and target block for testing
firearms. The walnut stock blank
(right) measures 31¾ × 2 inches
and was probably cut for use as
the stock of a fowling piece or
half-stocked rifle. The heavy
wood pestle was used for crushing charcoal to make black powder and it measures 21½ inches
long with a head circumference of
18½ inches; it should not be confused with the similar froe club
used in shingle-making and rail-
splitting. Courtesy of the Mercer
Museum, Bucks County Historical Society, Doylestown, Pa.
Charles L. Maddox, Jr., photographer.

STOCKMAKER'S TOOLS (18th/
19th Century): Though of 19th
Century origin, the tools depicted
were little changed from those
employed by 18th Century
stockmakers. From left: Barrel
bedding (routing) plane (17 × 3
× 2½ inches). Forestock (rounding) plane (11 × 2¼ × 2 inches).
Each plane made a ¾-inch cut.
The spokeshave (overall length:
11 inches) was used for shaping
the sides of the buttstock. Courtesy of the Eagle Americana Shop
and Gun Museum, Strasburg, Pa.
Charles L. Maddox, Jr., photographer.

than his seventeenth-century antecedent, often preferring stump or crotch wood because it usually produced a beautifully-figured grain which was esthetically appealing while also complementing the finish of the metal components.

Slightly oversized blanks corresponding to the general shape of the stock or grip were sawed out of the green wood and naturally dried (seasoned) in the open air, protected from direct sunlight and precipitation to prevent splitting or warping. Blanks were also artificially seasoned by "cooking" them in a kiln for several weeks during which the dry heat slowly drew out most of the moisture in the wood fiber.

Selecting a properly seasoned stock or grip blank the gunsmith marked a rough design on the surface as a guide to shaping the butt and inletting the forestock to receive the components, furniture, and inlays. At this point all the requisite holes were bored and any carving was performed though inlay work and carving were not generally evident on firearms made in colonial America prior to the eighteenth century.

Preparing the wood, as in making the barrel and the lock, consumed a great deal of time and effort, for the components were all painstakingly fitted to the stock or grip by hand. Shaping and mortising were accomplished with a host of woodworking tools including rasps, chisels, gouges, awls, augers, draw knives (snitzels as they were known among the so-called Pennsylvania-Dutch), planes, pocket knives, various grades of sandpaper, and a selection of polishers usually fashioned from bone. The previously cited 1739 Hudson's Bay Company inventory mentions five kinds of wood rasps: (1) Large, fine, half-round, (2) Small, fine, half-round, (3) Small, half-round, (4) Small, coarse, and (5) Coarse.

After the blank was rough-shaped the gunsmith or stock-maker began refining its features. The comb and the belly of the buttstock was smoothly rounded by a hollow (rounding) plane and a similar plane was employed for shaping the forestock after the ramrod channel, if any, was inletted; the latter also accomplished with a plane. The forestock interior where the barrel was bedded was roughed out with several kinds of gouges and chisels, including the common firmer or forming chisel and the so-called slick which was pushed through the wood rather than struck with a mallet. Chisel cuts were usually dressed (finished) with a sharp knife.

The barrel bed was further smoothed with a rounding (bedding) plane and the gunsmith then incised the barrel lug recesses though the step was eliminated in banded barrels. To ensure a perfect fit between the barrel and the forestock the gunsmith chalked the underside of the barrel or blackened it with soot, carefully fitting it to the mortise. When the barrel was removed from the bed the "highs,"

i.e., where the wood needed to be relieved for a proper fit, were clearly discernable as were the lows. The method was also used in fitting the lock and other metal components to the stock though by ca. 1750 a color pigment was substituted for chalk and soot. The pigment, known as Prussian blue (ferric ferrocyanide), was introduced in 1704 by a Berlin chemist.[44]

The curved sides of the buttstock were worked with the snitzel and a refined version of the spokeshave, while the gunsmith also designed and made special cutting tools for inlay work and relief carving. Significantly, not until ca. 1750 did stock-making become a more specialized and independent craft in colonial America.

Once the blank had been properly shaped, mortised, and incised with the decorative carving added, the wood was carefully and thoroughly sanded with successively finer grades of sandpaper. Between each sanding the gunsmith slightly dampened the wood, bringing to the surface any stray fibers which were subsequently removed until the surface was completely smooth.

While the stocks and grips of martial firearms were usually painted or stained black, the latter frequently made of soot, beeswax, and raw linseed oil derived from flax seed, commercial or utilitarian stocks and grips were treated with boiled linseed oil which inhibited dry rot and prevented moisture from entering the wood so it would not warp or crack; the oil boiled so it would rapidly penetrate the wood fiber.

Linseed oil was repeatedly hand-rubbed into the wood, the friction generating heat which opened the grain; consequently the fibers swelled somewhat and the gunsmith then smoothed them with a slicker in a process call boning, i.e., the surface was polished by forcefully rubbing it with a piece of bone or slicker as it was termed. While any kind of hard bone could be used, the wing bone of the wild turkey was preferred by many craftsmen because of its natural curvature and the fact that there was then an abundant supply. Though the practice was rare in colonial America, a few gunsmiths shellacked or varnished the stock after it had been treated with linseed oil though the usual method was to polish the stock to a high lustre with beeswax.

Throughout the colonial era in North America and considerably thereafter the most popular and enduring method of finishing the iron components of a firearm was browning (russeting). The gunsmith used several chemical mixtures to achieve what he considered an adequate finish, usually developing a browning solution which he preferred and which was often perpetuated among his gunmaking descendants; many formulae currently surviving like the one recorded in the Table.[45]

The browning mixture was stored in a tightly sealed jar or bottle and permitted to cure in a warm place for at least a week so the ingredients thoroughly amalgamated. The gunsmith then prepared the iron components for the browning process. The barrel vent was plugged and the bore heavily greased, while the muzzle and the breech were sealed with hardwood dowels sufficiently long to facilitate handling.

The barrel and other metal components were then meticulously cleaned by scouring them with emery powder to remove any oil, grease, perspiration, or old finish. After scouring a coat of powdered chalk, plaster of Paris, or whiting was applied to

A COMMON BROWNING FORMULA

Quantity	Ingredient
1 quart	Rain water
½ ounce	Nitric acid
½ ounce	Spirits of niter
1 dram	Spirits of wine
1 dram	Tincture of steel
2 drams	Blue stone

absorb any residual oils, for they contaminated the raw iron and produced a dark stain which ruined the appearance of the finish when the process was completed. Without then or thereafter touching the metal with the bare hands, the components were wiped clean with a lint-free cloth.

The gunsmith applied the browning solution with a soft linen rag, stroking it on evenly in a single direction and making certain that it did not run. The components were then put in a warm, dark place with the barrel standing upright on the muzzle plug

GUNSMITHING TOOLS (18th/ 19th Century): Leg vise (left), bolted to the heavy workbench, has a barrel section clamped in the jaws. Note the longitudinal seam. The vise is early 19th Century though the design originated in the late 18th Century. Small barrel anvil (9 × 4 × 7 inches), often called a Buffalo head on the frontier, has concaved sides for making ladles and the surface has five grooves for maintaining the shape of the barrel as it was hammer welded by the gunsmith. A pair of tapered mandrels rest against the anvil (left, 21½ inches; right, 19½ inches). Courtesy of the Pennsylvania Farm Museum of Landis Valley. Charles L. Maddox, Jr., photographer.

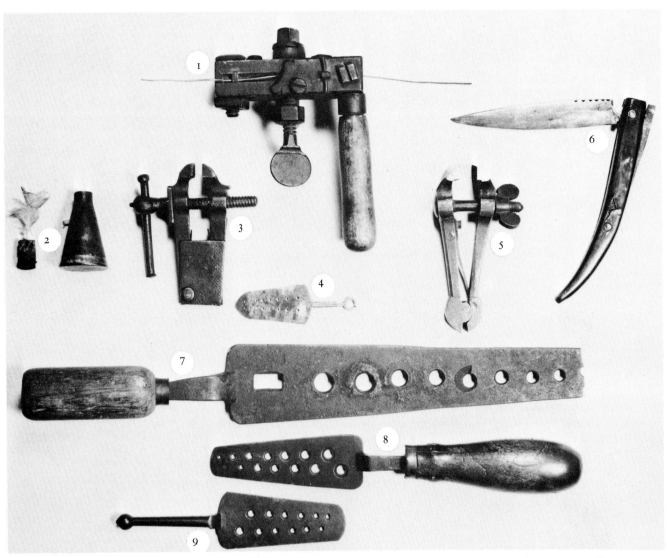

and they remained there for a minimum of 12 hours; longer if the temperature dropped below 60 degrees Fahrenheit, for the process was much more rapid when the iron was warm rather than excessively hot or cold.

The acid reaction from the browning solution produced artificial oxidation (rust) on the components and a corrosive blue-green scale also appeared. The rust and the scale were removed with a fine, mild steel bristle brush passed over the components in smooth, longitudinal strokes. This scratching or carding was repeated thrice daily (usually morning, noon, and night) for at least two days because the finish became darker the longer the components were scratched.

When the desired russet color appeared the parts were again scratched and then flushed with boiling water which halted the corrosive action of the solution. The boiling water rapidly evaporated, the heat drying the metal, and the components were again lightly scratched. After the final scratching the gunsmith applied a light coat of boiled linseed oil, wiping

GUNSMITHING TOOLS (18th/ 19th Century): (1) Wire drawing tool for inlay wire of brass or silver, late 18th or early 19th Century (4¼ × 1¼ inches). (2) Tin oil can with cork stopper and feather applicator, ca. 1790–1800 (2 × 1½ inches). (3) Mainspring vise, ca. 1795–1815 (4½ inches). (4) Bolt thread die ca. 1800 or earlier (3½ inches). (5) Mainspring vise ca. 1800–1840 (4½ inches).

(6) Hand-made clasp knife ca. 1815 used for cutting patch material and other utilitarian purposes. (7) Bolt thread die with broken tip ca. 1840–1850 (15¾ inches). (8) Bolt thread die ca. 1850 (10½ inches). (9) Bolt thread die ca. 1840 (6 inches). Courtesy of the Eagle Americana Shop and Gun Museum, Strasburg, Pa. Charles L. Maddox, Jr., photographer.

away the excess, and the components were allowed to stand for a few days to harden the finish which ranged from a pleasing light red-brown to a deep, rich chocolate.

One of the most important tools used by the colonial American gunsmith was the vise and it had either iron jaws or wood jaws faced with iron and it was mounted on his workbench. In most instances the jaws were covered with brass plates to prevent damage to the finished surface of the work. Late in the eighteenth-century a free-standing vise constructed entirely of iron and mounted on the shop

BULLET-MAKING IMPLEMENTS (18th/19th Century): (1) Single cavity bullet mould, cal. .34, ca. 1830-1840 (6 inches). (2) Rare multiple cavity soapstone bullet mould, cal. .67 and .34 with birdshot, measuring 7¾ × ⅝ × ¾ inches; one half of mould depicted. (3) Multiple cavity soapstone bullet mould, cal. .32, .30, buckshot and birdshot. Both

halves measuring 7 × 1 × ¾; one half marked SHENANDOAH, sunburst engraved on the other. Both moulds date ca. 1825 though similar moulds were used much earlier in colonial America. (4) Lead ladle with pouring spout and wood handle ca. 1840. (5) Cherry, cal. 1.75 for making bullet moulds for large wall guns. (6) Lead-

melting pot, 4 × 4 inches. (7) Cherry, cal. .68 with cal .68 bullet mould ca. 1850. (8) Cherry, cal. .65, ca. 1840; cherry, cal. .45 ca. 1845. Courtesy of the Eagle Americana Shop and Gun Museum, Strasburg, Pa. Charles L. Maddox, Jr., photographer.

floor was introduced though it never entirely replaced the bench vise.

Several kinds of small hand vises were also used by the gunsmith for holding or clamping small components; among them the practical mainspring vise which compressed the powerful mainspring leaves; thus making it easier to assemble or disassemble the lock or to replace a broken spring. The hard use to which martial firearms were subjected often resulted in broken mainsprings and regular army and militia sergeants normally carried a supply of springs and a mainspring vise for use in the field.

While most of the hand tools described are commonly encountered in the present machinists' and carpenters' trades, and while in most instances their functions are readily recognized or self-explanatory, the gunsmith's cherry is an exception and it is currently found among the tools of the accomplished gunsmith.

Precisely when the gunsmith's cherry emerged remains conjectural though it was known during the seventeenth century. The cherry was made of steel, its round head and short shank suggesting the fruit with its stem attached for which it was named. The versatile cherry was used for drilling the cup in brass or iron priming pans, chamfering the muzzle, and making bullet mould cavities. The head of the cherry, provided with a series of sharp cutting edges, corresponded to the desired caliber of the lead ball or the circumference of the priming pan and the shank was clamped in the chuck of the brace when it was used.

The majority of the German and Swiss gunsmiths early arriving in eighteenth-century British America settled among their kind in the Susquehanna Valley of southeastern Pennsylvania. A few of them also settled in the Dutch-German communities of East and West Jersey or ventured farther south to the Moravian settlements of Virginia and North Carolina.

The displaced Irish and Scots chose equally varied locations, many of them settling in Boston though the majority preferred the Penn proprietorship or the Carolinas; several of them there establishing themselves in the frontier trade and subsequently exerting a profound influence among the Native Americans which extended well into the nineteenth century.

In 1700 German gunsmith Christian Durr started a shop in the small frontier settlement of Lancaster, Pa.[46] A decade later Swiss gunsmith Martin Meylin (also Maylin or Mylin, 1670-1749) established a gunsmithery in Lampeter Township, Lencaster County, Pa.[47] In 1719, on what came to be known as Meylin's Run, he purportedly built what was possibly the first water-powered barrel boring mill in North America.[48]

In 1701 a John Cookson (1686-1762), possibly related to the London gunsmith of the same name, started a gunsmithery in Boston and enlisted in the Ancient & Honorable Artillery Company where from 1722 to 1726 he was company clerk.[49] In 1727 he was engaged in general gunsmithing and in cleaning and repairing firearms for the colony.

While there is a chronological distinction between the two Cooksons the London inventor of breech-loading firearms remains an enigma and his relationship, if any, with his Boston namesake has yet to be established. There is, however, a positive link between them, for on April 12, 1756, the *Boston Gazette* carried this announcement:

Made by John Cookson and to be sold at his house in Boston: a handy gun of 9 pounds and a half weight; having a place convenient to hold nine charges and nine primings; the said gun will fire 9 times distinctly, as quick or slow as you please, with one turn with the handle of the said gun, it doth charge the gun with powder and bullet; and doth both prime and shut the pan, and cock the gun. All of these motions are performed immediately at once, by one turn of the said handle. Note, there is nothing put into the muzzle of the gun as we charge other guns.[50]

John Pim, another emigrant London gunsmith, established himself on Boston's Anne Street ca. 1720.[51] Like Cookson he experimented with repeating firearms and in 1722 reputedly invented an 11-shot flintlock breechloader though no other description of the firearm has survived.

There is also a six-shot, .52 caliber snaphaunce revolver bearing the engraved inscription "J. Pim of Bostonne, fecit" on the sideplate. Whether Pim invented the pistol or whether it was imported and marked with his name remains unknown, though if the former it can be considered the first revolver of record produced in North America. Pim, however, did not originate the design, for similar pistols were made in England at least 20 years earlier, while a revolving cylinder snaphaunce carbine was produced ca. 1655 by London gunsmith John Dafte (fl. 1640-1685).

Neither John Cookson of Boston nor John Pim apparently attempted to patent their purported inventions and, as far as it can be determined, there were no firearms patented in colonial America, though patents had been granted since the seventeenth century. In 1641 the Massachusetts Bay Colony issued the first American patent to Samuel Wilson for a salt-making process, and in 1646 Joseph Jenkes is believed to have been granted the first patent for a machine which made scythe blades.

The patent or exclusive right to the use of an invention originated ca. 700 B.C. with the Achaeans

COMMEMORATIVE MARKER
(Current): This impressive
marker, bearing an image of what
is commonly known as a Kentucky rifle and the date 1719 with
the surname MEYLIN, is dedicated
to Swiss gunsmith Martin Meylin
(Maylin or Mylin) who arrived in
the Pennsylvania Colony in 1710.
The marker is adjacent to what is
purported to be Meylin's
gunsmithery at Eshelman Mill
Road and Long Rifle Road in
West Lampeter Township, Lancaster County, Pa. Photographed
by the author, September, 1974.

mouth), Me., in 1722.[55] Eltweed Pomeroy survived
his son Eldad who died at Boston in 1662,[56] though
his other son Medad was an active gunsmith at
Northampton until his death on December 30,
1716.[57] Medad's son Ebenezer carried on the family
gunsmithing tradition.[58]

Richard Gregory started a Boston gunsmithery
in 1730[59] and in the southern colonies the Huguenot
gunsmith Gideon Fancheraud was active at Charleston in 1708.[60] Seven years later John Brush established a gunsmithery at Williamsburg, Va.,[61] while
John Young served as Maryland Colony armorer in
1728.[62]

Several of the gunsmiths immigrating to British
America from the alpine regions of southern Germany and northern Switzerland specialized in making rifles, among them Martin Meylin (see p. 255)
and J. Metzger who in 1728 established himself in
Lancaster, Pa.[63] Riflesmith Philip Lefever also
started a Lancaster gunsmithery in 1731[64] and Jacob
Dechard settled in bustling Philadelphia a year later,
moving to Lancaster in 1753.[65]

In 1730 gunsmith James Geddy was active at
Williamsburg, Va., and on July 8, 1737, the *Virginia
Gazette* established the year before noted that he had
for sale "a great Choice of Guns and Fowling-Pieces,
of several Sorts and Sizes, true bored, which he will
warrant to be good; and will sell them as cheap as
they are usually sold in *England*."*

Geddy also made "several Sorts of wrought
Brasswork, and cast small bells." David Geddy en-
tered the family gunsmithing craft upon the death of
*Italics original.

of Sybaris.[52] The first use of the term patent is believed to have appeared early in the fourteenth century when Edward II of England (1284-1327) issued
"Letters of Patent." The Council of Venice granted
similar privileges in 1474 and thereafter the practice
rapidly spread throughout Europe.

In addition to Cookson and Pim, John Gerrish[53]
and John Wood[54] were active gunsmiths in Boston
between 1710 and 1725, while Ebenezer Nutting
established a gunsmithery at Falmouth (Ports-

GUNSMITHERY (18th Century,
ca. 1719): This rectangular,
single-story fieldstone building
with shingled roof is said to have
been one of the earliest built in
West Lampeter Township, Lancaster Co., Pa., and is supposedly
the gunsmithery of Martin
Meylin, one of the first European
riflesmiths to settle the region and
reputedly a pioneer in the development of the American rifle.
The small, heavily shuttered win-
dow and gun port (left) proclaim
the turbulent nature of the 18th
Century Pennsylvania frontier.
Photographed by the author, September, 1974.

his father in 1744 and enlisted the aid of his brother William as an apprentice. Geddy's estate subsequently prosecuted a claim of £21/8/4 against the colony for cleaning "Seven Hundred Arms in the [Williamsburg] Magazine."[66]

Benjamin Massey established a gunsmithery on Tradd Street, Charleston, S.C., ca. 1730[67] and shortly thereafter Philip Massey was engaged in the trade on Kings Street.[68] Another Massey, Joseph, was an active Charleston gunsmith from ca. 1732 until 1736 when he died following "a lingering Sickness."[69] Joseph had served as a Charleston militia captain and engraved and printed the first South Carolina Colony currency. The three Masseys were probably related.

Philip Massey died in 1739 and of particular significance is the following advertisement appearing from August eighteenth to twenty-fifth in the *South Carolina Gazette*:

All Persons that have any demands on the estate of Philip Massey . . . , are desired to bring their Accounts as soon as possible. . . . Also belonging to the said Estate and to be sold, a Negro Man and boy both which can work at the Gunsmith's Trade. . . .[70]

The impressive role of the black craftsman in colonial America has been seldom expressed and until recently the performance of the black in the evolution of North American culture has been generally ignored. Prior to and after the establishment of the United States many blacks, slave and free, were members of the militia and a number of them were blacksmiths; several noted for their expertise in casting and forging farm and mill equipment as well as the artistic, ornamental iron work gracing homes, businesses, and public buildings; much of it still evident.

Blacks were also skilled gunsmiths when circumstances permitted, for while they were denied apprenticeship benefits they were taught by their masters as were the anonymous man and boy of the

SNAPHAUNCE REVOLVER (17th/18th Century): The .52 caliber revolver depicted was made ca. 1720 and is marked J. PIM OF BOSTONNE FECIT in script on the lockplate. Each chamber of the hand-rotated cyclinder has a sliding pan cover. The revolver is similar to those produced by London gunsmith John Dafte (fl. 1640-1685) who also made carbines. Courtesy of the Winchester Museum, Olin Industries, New Haven, Conn.

previously mentioned Massey estate, or the slave Prince owned by Charleston gunsmith John Milnor. When Milnor died in 1749 Prince became the property of Milnor's son who was also bequeathed "my Smiths pair of Bellows, an Anvil & Vice."[71]

The role of the black gunsmith in America, like that of his white counterpart, was a continuing portrayal and not merely an isolated performance in the cultural mainstream, and the many innovative technological contributions made by black craftsmen in North America alone is a rich field ripe for further investigation and exposure.

German riflesmith Adam Deterer established himself at New Hanover, N.C., in 1740,[72] while that same year gunsmith William Moll settled in Allentown, Pa., where his descendants continued in the trade until 1883.[73] Henry Albrecht (also Albright),[74] John Fraser,[75] Peter Hench,[76] and Mathias Roessor all were active gunsmiths in or near Lancaster, Pa.; Roessor arriving in New York City from Rotterdam on September 1, 1736, and moving to Pennsylvania four years later.[77]

Mathias Roessor, whose name underwent numerous alterations in colonial records like many other immigrants, was also known as Rosser, Reasor, Roesor, Resor, and Reeser to note but few. Roessor was a rifle-maker and he established a gunsmithing dynasty active until the late nineteenth century, while several of his apprentices achieved outstanding reputations and also created family gunsmithing dynasties.

On January 26, 1771, Mathias Roessor died, leaving his shop in the care of his brother Peter who remained an active gunsmith until ca. 1782.[78] Peter's son William then entered the trade.[79] An inventory of Mathias' assets included the hand tools and other paraphernalia representative of the eighteenth-century colonial American gunsmithing craft as noted in the Table.[80]

The four "ramer bits" mentioned in the Roessor inventory were used to bore or ream out the powder chamber in the breech plug, while the "britchen tools" were the taps and dies employed for threading the breech and the breech plug. Also listed in the inventory were assorted punches, wheel bearing bits and floats for the boring and rifling engines, pieces of iron, stock blanks, various forging and stock-making tools, "boaring" (boring) rods, casting tools and sand for casting brass and iron components; spelter, block tin (tin in ingot form), needsfoot (neatsfoot) oil for preserving leather, and several firearms parts including a new gunlock, six double "trickers" (possibly set-triggers), a smooth rifle (probably an unrifled barrel or a smoothbore firearm of rifle pattern though used for shot), a half-finished gun, several half-finished pistols and barrels, and four old guns.

William Henry, protege of riflesmith Mathias Roessor, became one of the most celebrated rifle-makers and prominent citizens of British America.[81] He was born in Chester County, Pa., May 19, 1729, of John and Elizabeth Henry (nee De Venny) who had come from Scotland in 1722. At age fifteen, shortly after his father died, Henry was apprenticed to Roessor and completed his indenture in five rather than the customary seven years. In 1749 he established a gunsmithery at Lancaster where in January,

THE 1771 ROESSOR INVENTORY

1 ax	1 small screw plate
1 hatchet	1 tumbler tool
1 beck [bick] iron	1 stock drill
1 polishing leath [er]	1 rifling engine
1 barrel anvil	1 boaring [boring] mill
1 saw	1 compass saw
1 pair, large stillyards	1 square
1 pair, bullet moulds	12 smooth files
1 powder proof [eprouvette]	1 grindstone and frame
2 bellows	1 barrel [bore] gauge
2 saw frames	2 small hacks [hacksaws]
2 rasps	2 vise claps [jaw plates]
2 pair, old shears	2 draw knives
2 spring hooks	2 pair, nippers
2 soddern [soldering] irons	2 casting picks
3 saw plates	3 vise wedges
5 pair, tongs	4 ramer [reamer] bits
6 pair, plyers [pliers]	6 [mainspring] vises
7 pair, compasses	8 bench hammers
9 planes	20 cherrys
12 large screw plates [dies]	12 britchen [breeching] tools

1755, he married Ann Wood who gave him three sons: William Jr., John Joseph, and Abraham.

In the spring of 1755 Henry left a thriving gunsmithery to join Gen. Edward Braddock's mixed force of British regulars, frontier militia, and Native Americans as an armorer; thus initiating a life of public service characterized by devotion and integrity. He returned with Braddock's bloodied survivors of the ill-fated Fort Duquesne campaign which was the first estimable battle of the devastating French and Indian War, resuming his trade and entering a partnership with a merchant known only as Simon to furnish firearms for the lucrative Native American trade.

Undaunted by his first military experience, Henry again served as an armorer in 1758 with Gen. John Forbes' command which successfully assaulted Fort Duquesne to halt the French penetration into the Ohio Valley. A year later Henry dissolved his partnership with Simon and visited England where he met James Watt and was thoroughly impressed with his steam engines. He returned to Lancaster in 1761 and gradually expanded his gunsmithing business.

William Henry's life and that of his descendants was woven into the closely knit fabric of frontier American history, and though he died on December 15, 1786, the family remained active in gunmaking until 1891 with the retirement of Granville Henry (1835-1912).[82]

Another colorful figure whose life was also enmeshed in the dramatic cross-currents of frontier history was John Fraser, a Scot who first settled in Lancaster and in 1750 established a trading post (station as they were then called) at Venango, a Seneca village at what is now Franklin, Pa.[83]

Like the celebrated frontier trader George Croghan and the veteran North Carolina trader and scout Christopher Gist, Fraser was among the first to warn the Pennsylvania Council of Celeron de Bienville's 1749 invasion of the fur-rich Ohio Valley which set the stage for the volatile French and Indian War. In 1753 Fraser was first among the frontier traders to be driven out of western Pennsylvania by Philip de Joncaire who preceded de Bienville in an attempt to convince the Native Americans under British influence to join the French. After that encounter Fraser reestablished his station and gunsmithery at the confluence of the Monongahela River and Turtle Creek, not far from Gist's station on Chesnut Ridge.

Fraser's occupation as a gunsmith has been challenged by some historians and the question will probably never be satisfactorily resolved; yet there is evidence to indicate that he was engaged in the craft. Edward Shippen (1729-1806) whose daughter Peggy subsequently married Benedict Arnold was a partner

WILLIAM HENRY,
SR., GUNSMITH (18th
Century, 1729-1786):
Of Scottish ancestry,
William Henry was the
first of a family guns-
mithing dynasty
flourishing in Pennsyl-
vania for nearly two
centuries. Courtesy of
the Historical Society
of Pennsylvania,
Philadelphia.

in the profitable frontier trading firms of (James) Logan & Shippen and Shippen & (Thomas) Lawrence.

Shippen was Fraser's contemporary, either personally acquainted or aware of his frontier enterprises. In a letter discussing whether the advancing French had a fort at Cussewago (they did not) in western Pennsylvania, Shippen wrote that "Weningo [Venango] is the name of an Indian Town on [the] Ohio, where Mr. Freser [Fraser] has had a Gunsmiths Shop for many years."[84] The tone of the letter suggests that Shippen apparently thought of Fraser as more a gunsmith than a frontier trader. It is possible that Fraser owned the gunsmithery and em-

ployed a gunsmith if not actually trained in the craft himself though if the assumption is correct, there is no record of a gunsmith hired by Fraser which has thus far surfaced.

Yet another celebrated colonial American gunsmith was Hugh Orr born in Renfrewshire, Scotland, January 13, 1717. In 1737 Orr established himself at Easton, Mass., and moved to Bridgewater a year later.[85] He operated a scythe and ax works there and has been credited with employing the first trip-hammer used in New England though the distinction is reserved for the Saugus Iron Works established nearly a century earlier.

Orr subsequently turned to musket manufacture and as far as it can be determined he made the first public contract firearms in North America when in 1748 he fabricated 500 muskets for the Massachusetts militia. Orr, like William Henry, was also involved in politics, science, and technology, while in 1753 he invented a machine for dressing the flax seed used to make linseed oil.

Though Hugh Orr did not introduce the triphammer to New England he is thought to be the first to use it for making scythe and ax blades at his Bridgewater factory and it was probably of the improved design emerging in Europe ca. 1680. The refined triphammer employed a separate wooden arm extending above the hammer beam which interrupted its upward movement to provide some resistance and resilience, while the hammer beam was provided with an innovative iron collar to prevent excessive wear when struck at that point by the operating cams (see p. 17). The resilience of the innovative arm communicated additional energy to the hammer beam which consequently delivered a more powerful blow to the object worked on the anvil.

The Jäeger Rifle

Most of the German and Swiss immigrants arriving in British America early in the eighteenth century settled among their predecessors in the proprietorship established by William Penn in 1681, for they preferred the familiarity of the stable agricultural communities ranging along the Susquehanna Valley in what is now southeastern Pennsylvania.

And those Germanic immigrants brought with them a firearm unknown to North America though it had been popular for more than a century with the alpine hunter or *jäeger* of their homeland; a rifled firearm so closely associated and long identified with the hunter that it was known as a *jäeger* rifle. As with any displaced cultural entity the Germans and Swiss were accompanied by their craftsmen who brought with them the tools of their trade and the gunsmith was no exception; thus the means to make rifles arrived with those who made them.

The *jäeger* rifle is a direct ancestor of the first European rifles. By ca. 1580 gunsmiths in the mountainous region of southern Germany and northern Switzerland had developed the wheellock prototype of the *jäeger* rifle; the first specimens incorporating the sophisticated skills of the guild artisans combined with the needs expressed by the alpine hunter.

The character of the *jäeger* rifle was determined by several factors: (1) the nature of the game pursued as exemplified by the dangerous bear and the fleet-footed chamois, (2) the rugged terrain which limited prolonged stalking and dictated shooting at the elusive prey in excess of 200 yards, and (3) the radical changes in wind velocity created by rapidly fluctuat-

TRIPHAMMER (ca. 1750): This profile view of the improved triphammer illustrates the spring beam arrangement (P, M and L). The large, water-powered wheel (Z) rotated the shaft (S) fitted with wood gear pegs (R) which operated in conjunction with the gear pegs on the beam wheel (Q). The pegs engaged the teeth (Fig. 9, X) connected by a yoke (Fig. 10, Y) to the spring beam by Fig. 9, V. A stiff steel spring (K, N) provided the spring beam with sufficient resistance and resilience to impart more strength to the blow from the hammer head (Fig. 11, X and Y); the spring beam pivoting at M and the hammer beam at H. The mechanism is mounted in a wood frame (O). From Diderot, *L'encyclopédie, Recueil de Planches*, Vol. VII, Plate XIII. Courtesy of the Eleutherian Mills Historical Library, Wilmington, Del.

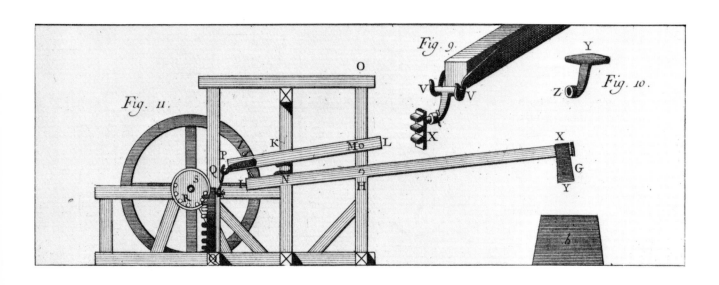

ing air currents swirling around the peaks and valleys which had a profound influence on the trajectory (flight path) of the projectile.

Those conditions spawned a short, light-weight firearm easily carried slung across the shoulder when climbing, a rifled bore to assure accuracy beyond 200 yards, and a heavy lead ball backed by a large powder charge to buck the capricous air currents and provide sufficient kinetic energy to either kill instantly or at least seriously incapacitate the prey. The latter was an extremely important factor, for while the prey was often shot at moderate to long range the hunter frequently had to negotiate a circuitous, hazardous route of far greater distance to reach it, and tracking a slightly wounded, enraged animal under those conditions was equally perilous.

Thus was born the *jäeger* rifle and by ca. 1665 it had completed the transition to flint ignition and had undergone several design alterations. A more substantial trigger guard had been added because of the rough terrain, set-triggers were more prevalent, and the buttstock was also more massive to withstand the rigors of climbing. It can be said without exaggeration that at the end of the seventeenth century the *jäeger* rifle was the most accurate firearm ever produced; a fact which was not ignored by a small cadre of military tacticians though their suggestion that it be adopted as a martial firearm went unheeded; lost in the traditional roar of musketry.

The eighteenth-century *jäeger* rifle was a rugged, dependable flintlock firearm weighing approximately 7½ to 8 pounds though there were exceptions ranging to 22 pounds.[86] The normally octagonal barrel was characterized by a heavy breech to withstand the force of the large powder charge. The barrel also tapered slightly toward the muzzle where there was a perceptible swamped effect. The swamped barrel, however, all but disappeared from the *jäeger* rifle by the end of the century.

The average length of the *jäeger* rifle barrel was 28 to 33 inches though exceptions fluctuated from 18 inches to 36 inches. The bore was rifled with seven semi-circular grooves though atypcial bores had as few as four and as many as eight grooves, while straight-grooved rifling was not unknown. In *jäeger* rifles of the 1665–1700 period the grooves were comparatively deep in relation to later specimens. Caliber averaged around .58 and fluctuated between .52 and .65.

The front and the rear sight of the *jäeger* rifle were dovetailed into the barrel flat. The blade-type front sight was usually made of brass or iron though silver was used with more vermiculated specimens. The rear sight was iron, consisting of a flat, v-notch bar though it often had two leaves, both pivoting and laying flat when not in use to minimize damage or misalignment.

Jäeger RIFLE (ca. 1690): This alpine hunting rifle has a 26-inch, .60 caliber, octagonal barrel rifled with seven grooves. Overall length is 41 inches. The full-length, pin-fastened, walnut stock displays light scroll carving, a raised moulding around the lock mortise terminating in a so-called beaver tail, a sliding wooden trap cover, and a full buttplate with a long comb finial. In addition to the dual-leaf, adjustable rear sight mounted on the breech, there is an adjustable tang sight at the stock wrist. Note the slightly swamped muzzle, rear sling swivel, and set trigger with the short adjustment screw in front of the primary trigger. The large trigger guard with deep finger rest incorporates a front sling swivel mount (swivel missing). Courtesy of the U.S. Military Academy Museum, West Point, N.Y.

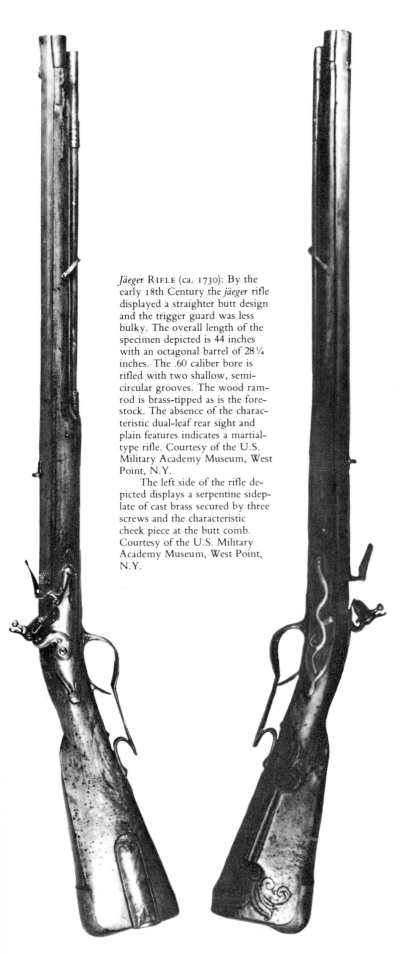

Jäeger RIFLE (ca. 1730): By the early 18th Century the *jäeger* rifle displayed a straighter butt design and the trigger guard was less bulky. The overall length of the specimen depicted is 44 inches with an octagonal barrel of 28¼ inches. The .60 caliber bore is rifled with two shallow, semi-circular grooves. The wood ramrod is brass-tipped as is the forestock. The absence of the characteristic dual-leaf rear sight and plain features indicates a martial-type rifle. Courtesy of the U.S. Military Academy Museum, West Point, N.Y.

The left side of the rifle depicted displays a serpentine sideplate of cast brass secured by three screws and the characteristic cheek piece at the butt comb. Courtesy of the U.S. Military Academy Museum, West Point, N.Y.

The iron components of the *jäeger* rifle were commonly blued or browned though occasionally left bright. While the flint ignition mechanism was not distinctive it was skillfully made and reliable. Set-triggers were common, often incorporating as many as six stages, and many *jäeger* rifles had gold vent bushings. Furniture was usually brass though iron-mounted specimens are infrequently encountered.

All *jäeger* hunting rifles were provided with leather slings which were exclusively employed for carrying rather than assisting with aiming as with some modern rifles, and the majority of the *jäeger* rifles featured a front sling swivel only; the tail of the sling attached to a large button-like projection located beneath the buttstock to the rear of the trigger guard.

Jäeger rifle stocks were full-length, usually made of walnut, and the forestock was capped with horn though bone and brass are encountered. The flat butt was provided with a full buttplate. The right side of the buttstock displayed a rectangular recess known in Europe as a trap which was used to store extra flints, cleaning implements, or other small accessories. The trap had a sliding cover usually made of wood though brass covers were characteristic of some *jäeger* rifles made in Bavaria.

The *jäeger* rifle butt trap was not used for greased loading patches as in some other European rifles though patches were employed by most alpine hunters, and neither was the trap an innovation peculiar to the *jäeger* rifle, for traps with sliding wood covers had appeared on German matchlock arquebuses as early as 1607, while a matchlock musket now in the *Musée de l' Armée* was made in France for Cardinal Richelieu ca. 1625 and it also displays that innovation.

Most *jäeger* rifles, however, plain, featured some form of relief carving on the buttstock and around the lock mortise. Many specimens also displayed a cheek piece on the left side of the stock adjacent to the comb against which the cheek was pressed when firing. As with any handmade product the quality of the *jäeger* rifle also varied though most of them displayed excellent to outstanding craftsmanship.

A *jäeger* rifle with an iron ramrod was a rarity because when loading the tight-fitting ball it could damage the rifling or distort the soft lead; either possibility inimical to accuracy. The wooden ramrod normally used was tipped with the same materials as the forestock and it was usually secured by two thimbles and a guide.

Two methods of loading the *jäeger* rifle ball evolved, each achieving adequate results and unswerving adherents. With the most common method a slightly undersized ball was wrapped in a greased linen patch and merely rammed home; a fast

technique employed in central European rifled firearms since ca. 1590. Slower and less popular, the
alternative was to use a slightly oversized ball and
drive it four to six inches down the bore with a
hardwood bullet starter struck by a small mallet and
then use the wood ramrod to seat it at the chamber
mouth. Adherents of the latter technique averred
that the ball was more accurate because it gripped the
rifling tighter though its detractors had discovered
that the ball was distorted when struck by the starter;
thus rendering it less accurate.

Whichever loading technique was employed the
jäeger rifle was extremely accurate at the range for
which it was designed; especially so in the hands of
an experienced hunter adept at judging distance and
wind velocity. Experiments conducted in 1953 at
50 and 100 yards between an average *jäeger* rifle of ca.
1730, a quality wheellock rifle of earlier vintage, and
a new, mass-produced .30-30 lever action carbine
proved the *jäeger* rifle more accurate.[87]

Though various kinds of muzzle- and breech-
loading rifles had been used for military purposes
since the early seventeenth century none had been
officially adopted. The *jäeger* rifle, however, began to
emerge as a martial firearm around the time it first
appeared in British America.

Norwegian ski troops were issued *jäeger*-pattern
rifles in 1711 and shortly thereafter many European
sovereigns armed their elite bodyguard units with
similar firearms.[88] First in the Germanic states and
then elsewhere on the Continent light infantry were
equipped with *jäeger*-pattern rifles and redesignated
as *jäeger* companies, while prior to 1750 many of
those units had expanded to battalion strength.

Jäeger or light infantry companies began to send
out riflemen to scout the forefront of the infantry
advance, and while seeking the enemy they also prevented the advance from blundering into enemy
lines or detachments performing the same function.
It was usually the *jäeger* rifleman who initially contacted the enemy, engaging his pickets in a prelude to
battle which came to be known as a skirmish; the
term subsequently used to describe the leading element of the advance as skirmishers. And it was in
wilderness North America during the French and
Indian War that the skirmisher's role significantly
escalated, for an integral factor of Native American
warfare was the ambuscade.

Thus during the eighteenth century the rifle,
one of the first major technological innovations in
firearms evolution, gradually began to exert a profound influence in hunting and warfare, and it was
the *jäeger* rifle which emerged to dominate the evolution of the American rifle.

The American Rifle

Unlike the German and Swiss immigrants who
established themselves among the stolid agricultural
communities flourishing on the eighteenth-century
Pennsylvania frontier, the individualistic Scottish
and Irish emigrants fleeing an imperious English
authority and Anglican theocracy possessed a
fiercely combative, self-reliant character ideally
suited to a remote wilderness existence.

That hardy, determined Anglo-Saxon and Celtic stock produced a restless and explosive breed of
skilled woodsman dressed in buckskin and homespun; fearless, often reckless men tough as boiled
leather and as cunning as the wolf; men stalking the
dense forests as silently as the tawny panther and
challenging all of the dangerous elements spawned
by a hostile environment, Native Americans included.

They were the frontiersmen, the men who conquered the wilderness, and they took their women
and children with them as they moved ever westward to penetrate deep into the unknown regions of
Appalachia to explore and conquer the seemingly
limitless horizon. By 1748 they had established
Draper's Meadow as the first settlement west of the
verdant Allegheny Mountains.

Arising among the frontier people was a special
breed of woodsman; a solitary venturer known as the
long hunter. The long hunter lived off his wits and
the bounty of the land, frequently roving the inhospitable wilderness for months and even years—hence
the name—before returning temporarily to an isolated settlement; there only to barter furs and hides
for firearms, lead, gunpowder and the other requisites of frontier survival.

And as a condition of survival the long hunter
rapidly learned the customs and manners of the Native American who had roamed the pristine land
millennia before his arrival, and he quickly became
accustomed to and as skillfully employed the unorthodox tactics of wilderness warfare.

Though forswearing the amenities of civilization the long hunter by accident or design became the
eyes and ears of the frontier, often serving as the first
line of defense, emissary to the Native Americans,
guide for the settler and trader, scout for the military
(spies as they were then known), and surveyor for
the land speculator.

Of the many prowling the wilderness only a few
long hunters and a handful of other frontiersmen left
their indelible mark on history, earning reputations
both enviable and reprehensible to enter the dispas-

sionate pages of archival record and the fanciful realm of folklore. Many of their names and deeds appear here though many more do not, while others have never received the recognition they deserve or deserve the recognition they received; the former exemplified by erudite Dr. Thomas Walker who crossed the Blue Ridge Mountains in 1750 to discover the dark and bloody ground of Kentucky and penetrate the Appalachian barrier by discovering Cumberland Gap; gateway to the Tennessee country and beyond.

A constant source of anxiety on the expanding frontier was the abundance of hostile Native Americans in contrast to the nearly perpetual dearth of gunpowder. Moderate quantities of gunpowder were regularly used by the settlers for hunting; yet a single, sustained hostile attack on an isolated frontier settlement saw more gunpowder expended in an hour than was used otherwise in a year.

The long hunter especially, because of the singular nature of his frontier excursions, early grasped the need for a practical, reliable firearm designed for self-defense and suited for hunting the large and medium-sized game inhabiting the densely forrested terrain of Appalachia; an accurate, lightweight firearm capable of quick, clean kills at distances beyond the effective range of the common musket or fowling piece first carried into the wilderness; a firearm using a minimum of gunpowder and lead to achieve maximum performance, for those vital commodities were often difficult to procure and equally burdensome to carry during his protracted and perilous sojourns beyond the knife-edge of civilization.

By 1725 the prototype for such a distinctive frontier firearm was available in British America, the product of several centuries of cumulative European technology, and a fortuitous amalgam of circumstances created it, for while it was conceived by the peripatetic Scottish and Irish frontiersman, it was born in the fiery crucible of the frontier gunsmith's forge dominated by the German and Swiss riflesmiths of the Pennsylvania Colony. And it is for those obvious reasons that the innovative frontier firearm is here referred to as the American rifle.

An extensive body of literature exists concerning the legendary American rifle, and of all the firearms produced in North America during and after the colonial epoch it remains subjected to numerous misconceptions and has been long the object of controversy among firearms historians and aficionados.

The American rifle, simply called a rifle or rifle gun by early eighteenth-century frontiersmen, is now popularly and universally known as the Kentucky rifle, while purists prefer to call it the Pennsylvania rifle, and those who recognize its origin and where it received its enviable reputation have dubbed it the Pennsylvania-Kentucky rifle.

Late in the eighteenth century it came to be referred to as the long rifle, for it was then that specimens with extremely long barrels emerged. Nor would one be remiss in applying the sobriquet frontier rifle because it served there for more than six score years. Regardless of what it is called, the American rifle remains a monument to those who made and used it, and it stands alone as the first major technological innovation produced in North America.

The late Joe Kindig, Jr., in his masterful *Thoughts on the Kentucky Rifle in its Golden Age* said that the term Kentucky rifle was unknown prior to the nineteenth century, pointing out that in 1815 it initially appeared in the lyrics of the then popular, rousing ballad *The Hunters of Kentucky,* subtitled "The Battle of New Orleans" to commemorate the celebrated American victory over the British there during the War of 1812.[89]

Though Kindig's research is unimpeachable concerning the use of the term Kentucky rifle in print, it does not account for oral tradition. Significantly, the battle of New Orleans remains a classic example of the rifle versus the smoothbore musket, although the preeminence of the former was actually predicated more on British blunder than American weapons superiority.

Of all the various places the American rifle came to be produced, Pennsylvania riflesmiths were responsible for its development and made more than gunsmiths located elsewhere, and in essence the American rifle was sired by the *jäeger* rifle familiar to the riflesmiths of southeastern Pennsylvania; specifically those active in and around Lancaster during the first quarter of the eighteenth century.

The American rifle in flintlock form saw three somewhat arbitrary stages of development: (1) ca. 1725-1750, (2) ca. 1750-1780, and (3) ca. 1780-1825. During the first evolutionary period the American rifle was gradually transformed from the *jäeger* rifle into the readily identifiable form it assumed during the second period, and during the third period it entered what Kindig so aptly described as the "Golden Age."

Though the origin of the American rifle has been ascribed to Swiss riflesmith Martin Meylin of Lancaster County, Pa., there is no concrete evidence supporting the contention. There is also sufficient reason to suspect the 1728 date marked on an American rifle signed J. METZGER which is purported to be the first positively identified specimen (see p. 256), for American rifles of the early transitional period are not customarily signed or marked.

The American rifle of the first evolutionary period was distinctly transitional and the numerous character variations persisted thereafter; consequently there is no such thing as a typical American rifle. The first specimens strongly resembled the *jäeger* rifle, exhibiting octagonal, wrought iron barrels of .50 to .52 caliber ranging in length from 36 to 40 inches. The overall length of the rifles fluctuated between 52 and 55 inches, and they weighed approximately eight and ½ to nine pounds though there are exceptions. Furniture was almost exclusively brass and the stocks were made of walnut or maple, exceptions again noted.

Throughout the evolutionary periods discussed the American rifle usually displayed helical (spiral) rifling with seven flat, relatively deep and square-shouldered grooves equal or nearly equal in width to the lands. There are, however, exceptions to the number of lands and grooves and the pitch (twist).[90] Some rifles had as few as five and as many as eight grooves, while the normally right-hand twist variously described as little as one turn in 36 inches to as much as one turn in 48 inches. Infrequently used was straight-groove (parallel) rifling and in most instances it was comparably accurate.

In its early form the American rifle displayed a full-length forestock which, depending upon barrel length, was attached by three or four lug pins often unevenly spaced. The stock comb was rather straight and the butt was slightly curved to fit the shoulder, while the buttplate conformed and had an extremely long heel finial or tang.

American rifles made prior to ca. 1735 usually had no butt trap or a trap of *jäeger* design with a sliding wood cover. The rifles made in the southern colonies before midcentury either had no trap or a coverless, often shallow and rounded trap. The stocks of early rifles were neither carved nor displayed any inlay work though a raised border surrounding the lock mortise was customary. By midcentury some rifles began to exhibit moderately deep, C-scroll carving extending from the comb.

During the early evolutionary period the American rifle lock was usually imported, either from Britain or Germany with the latter inclined to display light engraving. Some Pennsylvania riflesmiths made locks, though imported specimens were preferred because they were of better quality; the colonial craftsman lacking suitable steel to make the springs. The pan was normally provided with a fence and the lockplate and the gooseneck cock were flat, illustrating a chamfered edge. Single or double-bridle locks were used, and while set-triggers were found they were not then common.

The sights of the American rifle were less sophisticated than those of the *jäeger* rifle. The front sight, usually of the blade-type, was either soldered or dovetailed into the barrel flat an inch or so from the muzzle and it was brass or iron, though during the second evolutionary period silver was also used. The rear sight base was dovetailed into the breech flat

AMERICAN RIFLE (ca. 1750–1760): This unsigned Pennsylvania-Kentucky rifle of the first evolutionary period has a .54 caliber barrel of 44 inches. The full-length stock is pin-fastened and the forestock is brass-capped. The wood ramrod is secured by two thimbles and a guide. Note the flat lockplate, simple carving at the comb, and sliding wooden patchbox. Courtesy of the Smithsonian Institution, Washington, D.C.

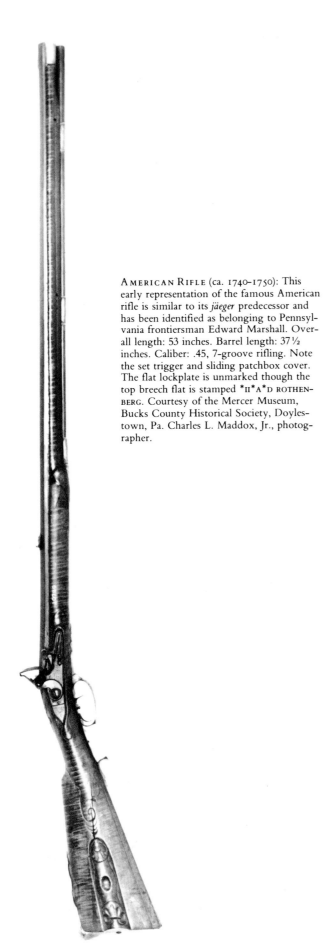

AMERICAN RIFLE (ca. 1740-1750): This early representation of the famous American rifle is similar to its *jäeger* predecessor and has been identified as belonging to Pennsylvania frontiersman Edward Marshall. Overall length: 53 inches. Barrel length: 37½ inches. Caliber: .45, 7-groove rifling. Note the set trigger and sliding patchbox cover. The flat lockplate is unmarked though the top breech flat is stamped *II*A*D ROTHENBERG. Courtesy of the Mercer Museum, Bucks County Historical Society, Doylestown, Pa. Charles L. Maddox, Jr., photographer.

and provided with a v-notch crossbar. Transitional rifles occasionally displayed the leaf-type *jäeger* rear sight.

An early example of a transitional American rifle closely resembling the *jäeger* rifle can be seen in the Mercer Museum, Doylestown, Pa. (Accession No. 10780), and it has been identified as once the property of Pennsylvania frontiersman Edward Marshall and purportedly accompanied him on the famous, so-called Walking Purchase.

On August 25, 1737, the Penn proprietors negotiated with the Native Americans of the region for as much land as a man could walk across from the west branch of Neshamony Creek to the Delaware River in a day and a half. Marshall and two companions started from Wrightstown (Bucks County) on September 19. Though his comrades failed to complete the gruelling trek, Marshall covered approximately 75 miles in the time allotted and it is obvious from the distance involved that he set a non-stop pace much faster than a walk. Marshall and his family perished during a Native American attack shortly after the outset of the French and Indian War, and theirs was a cruel fate shared by many on the blood-soaked frontier.

The Marshall rifle has several curious characteristics which readily lend themselves to considerable speculation about its history and also illustrate the complexities involved in determining the authenticity and the identification of early firearms, and whether Marshall took the rifle on his walk as tradition has it cannot be precisely ascertained.

The Marshall rifle has an overall length of 53 inches and the seven-groove, caliber .45 octagonal barrel is 37½ inches long. The front sight is of the knife-blade pattern and the rear sight has a v-notch crossbar. All the furniture is brass and the wood ramrod is secured by two thimbles and a guide. The lock is flat and chamfered, displaying a slightly curved bottom profile and light engraving. The top jaw and the jaw screw are missing from the gooseneck cock and the pan has a fence. The oval trigger guard is rather long and provided with a finger grip extension; the length of the trigger bow necessary to accommodate the set-trigger adjusting screw situated in front of the trigger.

In addition to the set-trigger the most outstanding feature of the Marshall rifle is the full-length, brass-trimmed, tiger-striped mapel stock secured by three pins and incorporating a rectangular buttstock trap with a sliding wood cover; the surface incised with a thumb recess in the center and what can be described as exaggerated fleurs-de-lis carved at each end of the thumb recess. A simple C-scroll is cut into the buttstock, trailed by crescents of diminishing size, and there is some relief carving around the lock mortise. The buttplate exhibits an extremely long heel finial.

The appealing tiger-striped graining of the Marshall rifle stock is also found on other American rifles and it is artificial rather than natural, the design artistically produced by deftly staining in the contrasting dark grain lines with soot or lightly charring the wood surface with a candle or lamp flame before applying the final finish. Artificial graining was a sixteenth-century European cabinet-making innovation and it was subsequently applied to gunstocks and musical instruments; the esthetically-pleasing result currently employed, though the design is achieved by more refined techniques.

The Marshall rifle stock emulates the *jäeger* pattern and the set-trigger lock is also compatible, though it bears no date, signature, or other significant characteristics which identify its origin or date other than that it is similar to many imported flint-ignition mechanisms. There is the possibility that the lock is German; an assumption barely supported by the absence of any markings and that it is equipped with a set-trigger.

While barrel length is comparable to *jäeger* barrels of the early eighteenth century the .45 caliber bore of the Marshall rifle is substantially smaller in comparison to the *jäeger* or contemporary American rifles. Caliber, however, is not an infallible guide in dating or otherwise identifying firearms; especially the American rifle, for throughout its evolutionary period there was considerable latitude because the riflesmith deferred to the demands of his patron, while barrels were often rebored or replaced.

The Marshall rifle barrel is marked on the top breech flat with the stamped inscription *II*A*D ROTHENBERG. Rothenberg presumably made the barrel, though as yet his background remains blank, therefore it is not known whether he was a riflesmith or a barrel-maker or even if he was active in Pennsylvania or Europe, and neither can it be determined what significance is conveyed by the snowflake design or the roman numerals other than the snowflake design was ornamental and also found on English trade fusils of the period ca. 1725-1770. (see p. 155).

The anomalies apparent in the Marshall rifle are consistent with the character of transitional American rifles and those produced thereafter, for they were all subject to the idiosyncrasies of the riflesmith and his discerning frontier patron, while there were introduced practical innovations like the patchbox exclusively designed as a receptacle for the greased loading patches.

By ca. 1735 Pennsylvania riflesmiths introduced the distinctive patchbox which early distinguished the American rifle from its *jäeger* predecessor; a technological innovation also recognized as a genu-ine form of American folk art. The artistic significance of the patchbox rests upon the unique design and ornamentation of the cover and its sideplates which can be used to date the rifle and identify its maker.

The patchbox was a rectangular recess cut into the right side of the buttstock, one end usually flush with the buttplate Early patchboxes displayed simple brass covers hinged at the upper end. The patchbox head, i.e., where the cover hinge was attached, was normally secured to the stock by three brass screws though an equal number of brass brads were occasionally used. The cover was also provided with a riveted spring latch. Iron patchbox covers, heads, and sideplates are rarely encountered.

Early patchbox covers and heads were often devoid of ornamentation, though after ca. 1740 a variety of sharply engraved motifs emerged and the cover was also provided with sideplates which were also incised and attached by screws or brads. After ca. 1750 there was a great deal of ornamentation lavished on the patchbox and a variety of flora and fauna designs emerged; especially on the head and sideplates which were in some instances perforated to expose the stock; the darker finish pleasantly contrasting with the bright brass. The subject of American rifle patchboxes is probed extensively by Roy F. Chandler, *Kentucky Rifle Patchboxes and Barrel Marks* (Camp Hill, Pa., 1972).

The octagonal barrel design of the American rifle was derived from the *jäeger* rifle and retained throughout the eighteenth century, the flats early shaped by filing and subsequently made with water-powered grinding wheels of hard, abrasive stone. As the century progressed so, too, did barrel length, and as barrel length increased the caliber diminished.

In the second evolutionary period American rifles displayed barrels fluctuating between 42 and 45 inches and caliber ranged from .40 to .45, while during the third period 48 inch barrels were not uncommon and at the start of the nineteenth century caliber was reduced to between .32 and .38. Martin Frey of York, Pa., made an American rifle ca. 1799-1800 with a 54 and one half inch barrel.[91]

Ballistically, the long barrel of the American rifle was no more effective than the shorter *jäeger* rifle barrel, a conclusion early drawn by German and Swiss riflesmiths or they would have made *jäeger* rifles with longer barrels. Since the seventeenth century, however, there grew a persistent though fallacious assumption among some European and colonial American gunsmiths and their patrons that all of the powder charge was consumed in a long barrel, thereby imparting greater velocity and range; an assumption responsible for the extraordinary barrel length associated with the long fowler and most martial muskets.

It is probable that many eighteenth-century Pennsylvania riflesmiths made long barrels to please their English, Irish, and Scottish patrons familiar with long-barreled firearms. While the long barrel did nothing to improve the ballistics efficacy of the American rifle it did have two advantages: (1) the sight radius, i.e., the distance between the rear sight and the front sight was increased, permitting the rifleman to draw a finer bead (sight picture) on his intended target, and (2) the balance or feel of the rifle was enhanced, thereby improving its handling qualities. As American rifle barrels became longer the appellation long rifle appeared and, disregarding efficacy, the long rifle continues to evoke a pleasurable response though whether the frontiersman was concerned with its esthetic appeal remains moot.

To determine the proper powder charge for the American rifle the time-consuming trial-and-error method was used, employing either the ancient practice of covering the ball with powder or the seventeenth-century European mathematical ratio of three grains weight of powder for each seven grains weight of the ball; each giving practically the same measure and performance.

The riflesmith fired the rifle with the muzzle extending over a smooth, white surface like a bleached cloth or even snow and any unburned powder residue staining it indicated that combustion was incomplete. The powder charge was thereafter successively reduced as much as possible without diminishing the accuracy or the range of the ball until the proper powder charge was found. The riflesmith then made a charger of sufficient capacity to hold the powder for the particular rifle because even if the same amount of powder and the same caliber ball were used each rifle performed (shot) differently.

The American rifle was provided with a flexible, straight-grained hickory ramrod exhibiting very little taper and it was occasionally spiral-striped for decorative purposes as in graining a stock, while in some instances it was tipped with soft brass which also secured a threaded iron sleeve designed to hold the scower or bullet worm.

The volatile nature of the frontier frequently presented situations during which rapid loading was the decisive factor in determining whether the frontiersman, his family, his neighbors, or his companions lived or died; consequently the patched ball was used in the American rifle and the flat rifling was designed for it. Greased patches and flat rifling permitted the American rifle to be loaded more expeditiously than using the bullet starter and mallet method preferred by some European alpine hunters using the bare ball which was also employed in firearms with polygroove rifling.

Though linen was preferred for bullet patches, other kinds of cloth and even thin leather was used if necessary, while in an emergency a bare ball was loaded. The patch assumed various forms as dictated by the rifleman's preference, including triangular, star, cross (using two thin strips of material), and irregular shapes though the round or square patch were the most popular. Patches were usually lubricated with bear, hog, or goose fat collectively referred to as grease, while beeswax was occasionally employed and also lubricated the ramrod. Even saliva was used when there were no alternatives. The lubricated patches were kept in the patchbox, ready for instant use.

English and German flintlock mechanisms were commonly used with the American rifle and by ca. 1750 set-triggers were more prevalent than early in the century. In 1774, however, as war between Britain and her American colonies threatened, George III convinced Parliament to place an embargo on all firearms and firearms components; consequently the shortage of locks stimulated domestic production, though procuring suitable spring steel remained a problem and American-made locks were inferior to imported specimens.

Though iron was occasionally used the furniture of the American rifle was primarily brass. On early rifles the sideplate was usually a simple rectangle secured by the two lock screws. During the second evolutionary period the brass sideplate terminated in a point rather than a square shoulder, while the sides were often decoratively notched and there was some light, C-scroll engraving. The third evolutionary period saw the sideplate ends rounded and a hump appeared along the upper profile, serving as an escutcheon for a third screw as in some musket sideplates.

During the second evolutionary period the American rifle buttstock began to change from the relatively straight *jäeger* rifle design, dropping perceptibly at the comb, and by the turn of the century it became extremely pronounced. There was also a commensurate and discernable curvature in the butt which was relatively deep; the buttplate conforming. The long buttplate heel final of the first evolutionary period gradually diminished during the second period though in the third period it was again extended but less pronounced.

By the beginning of the third evolutionary period the sharp shoulder (nose) at the stock comb had been somewhat rounded, exhibiting what has come to be called a roman nose; a characteristic of American rifles originating in Berks County, Pa., though not thereafter limited to that region because the innovative design accompanied the riflesmith as he followed the expanding frontier.[92]

Cheek pieces became more popular during the

third evolutionary period and there was a discernable increase in the amount of relief carving which was normally confined to the left side of the buttstock because the patchbox head and sideplates on the right side were substantially wider and longer, often extending to the stock wrist. The relief carving was generally of a flowing, refined C-scroll pattern.

The forestock, extending the entire barrel length, was provided with a swedge-formed, brass cap often secured by a screw entering from below. Throughout the evolutionary periods the cast-brass trigger guard displayed a short front tang, a narrow bow, and an arched bridge at the rear of the bow which terminated with a curved finger rest. By ca. 1750 most American rifles incorporated a brass or silver signature plate (thumbplate) mortised into the upper surface of the stock wrist and it was often engraved with the owner's initials in script.

Stock inlays were an exception in the early part of the first evolutionary period, though some American rifles had two or three, usually confined to the forestock. During the second period the rifle was more lavishly embellished, while in the third period the inlay work became garish and utterly ostentatious and widely varied in location, design, and choice of materials as indicated by the taste of the gunsmith's patron.

Stock inlays were usually made of brass or coin silver, i.e., silver melted from coins, though on the frontier specie was often difficult to procure. Late in the century German silver, comprised of copper, nickel, and zinc was used; nickel isolated in 1751 by Swedish chemist Baron Axel Frederic Cronstedt. Though designs varied the most popular inlays were five-six-and eight pointed stars, lozenges, crescent moons, numerous kinds of so-called Pennsylvania Dutch hex symbols, and several representations of the fish; the ancient symbol of Christianity. After the birth of the infant United States of America eagle designs became extremely popular.

Most American rifles were early distinguished by plain stocks of walnut or hard maple illustrating an almost complete disregard for the grain of the wood. After midcentury more care was taken in choosing stock blanks expressing an esthetically appealing grain and beautifully figured bird's eye and fiddle-back maple were used in addition to burled cherry, apple, and beech. Maple blanks were selected from trees growing on the slope of a hill because the wood displayed a hard, dense grain compared to maples in lower regions where the wood was soft from absorbing too much water and had a propensity to split or warp.

Late in the third evolutionary period the American rifle displayed a rudimentary form of checkering at the stock wrist, although it was an uncommon feature. Checkering appears to have been an English

AMERICAN RIFLE (18th Century, ca. 1780): This outstanding example of the frontier riflesmith's craft was made by Henry Albright (fl. 1772-1816). Born in Lititz, Pa., Albright worked in Nazareth (Lancaster Co.) until ca. 1796 when he moved to Chambersburg. Shortly after 1800 he moved to Gnadenhutten, Ohio, returning to Nazareth ca. 1816. Courtesy of the Metropolitan Museum of Art, N.Y., N.Y., gift of Winfrid Wood, 1956.

AMERICAN RIFLE (ca. 1790): Made by Pennsylvania riflesmith G. Weiker ca. 1790, this third evolutionary period American rifle is unusual in that it displays a sliding wooden patchbox cover. Overall length: 56½ inches. Barrel length: 43 inches. Caliber: .48. Note the pronounced stock curvature. The moulded lock cover is a rarity, few surviving the vicissitudes of time. The hand-sewn bullet block contains 7 patched balls. Courtesy of the Eagle Americana Shop and Gun Museum, Strasburg, Pa. Charles L. Maddox, Jr., photographer.

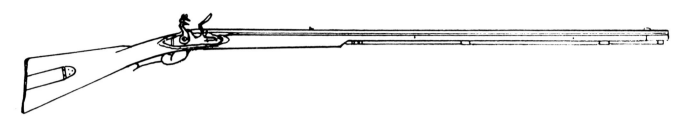

AMERICAN RIFLE (18th Century): The buttstock configuration and simple, straight patchbox cover without sideplates identifies the American rifle depicted as made between 1760 and 1775.

American rifles of the second transitional period were generally devoid of ornamentation and brass furniture was almost exclusively used. Author's sketch.

innovation emerging ca. 1770. A form of checkering can be seen on a Dutch flintlock musket made ca. 1640 though it was executed as part of the overall decorative motif rather than confined to the stock wrist. It is probable that checkering was merely decorative in its initial application and subsequently found practical because it furnished a non-slip surface at the stock wrist.

Most of the checkering found on late eighteenth-century American rifles was diagonally carved with wide, deep, intersecting lines and it was confined to the stock wrist. Early in the nineteenth century checkering became more refined, the lines cut finer and closer and producing smaller lozenges of greater appeal. The v-shaped tools used to incise the lines also brought a sharp point to the lozenge surface.

The American rifle literally and figuratively grew up with the ever-expanding frontier, whether serving as a tool for survival or a source of entertainment; the latter an integral part of frontier culture like the folk dance and folk ballad. The shooting match of the Appalachian frontier was a rifleman's event either planned or spontaneous and the frontiersman took as much pride in his marksmanship as the riflesmith exhibited in making the rifle.

The simple sighting arrangement of the American rifle made no provision for elevation or windage, i.e., the rear sight could not be adjusted to either compensate for the distance of an object or the wind velocity effecting the yaw of the bullet to the right or left during flight. Winds from the front and the rear had little adverse influence on the spinning ball. The frontiersman consequently learned to become an excellent judge of distance and wind velocity when firing at a stationary or moving target, relying on instinct and rapid mental calculation to compensate for those variables; a phenomenon which perhaps appropriately became known as Kentucky windage.

To ensure the accuracy of the rifle the riflesmith aligned the sights with the bore, i.e., it was boresighted. Removing the breech plug and securing the barrel in a vise or other stationary fixture, the rifle-

smith looked through the bore at a target or mark fixed at a known distance; the mark precisely aligned with the center of the bore. Without moving the barrel he then painstakingly aligned the sights with the mark; thus the sights and the bore corresponded to the aiming point or mark.

Because one person does not usually see an object in precisely the same way as another, and while eyesight varied between individuals, the riflesmith finished making the necessary sight adjustments with the partron shooting the rifle; compensating for the variables by moving the rear sight to the right or left and increasing or decreasing the height of the front sight until his patron was satisfied that the rifle was on the mark.

The frontier rifle match was shot for fun or profit between two or more contestants firing at a target approximately 60 to 80 paces distant, i.e., around 150 to 200 feet using the standard 30-inch pace as a guide. Competitive matches and game were shot at approximately the same distance and only occasionally did the frontiersman have an opportunity for long-range shooting, for the dense forest limited his field of vision.

The mark or target was often merely a cross (X) drawn on a tree or other suitable object with charcoal or chalk; the rifleman whose ball struck nearest the intersecting lines considered the winner. If a prize was at stake it was usually presented in "kind" rather than specie, e.g., the winner received something of value in lieu of coin which was rarely plentiful on the frontier. Prizes ranged from livestock to a few pounds of gunpowder or firearms and knives especially made for the event. In some instances special matches were arranged between riflemen of outstanding marksmanship skill, though the shoot was usually a community affair, either event guaranteed to draw considerable spectator interest.

Popular on the frontier were beef and turkey shoots. In the beef shoot the contestant initially shot for a quarter-section of the animal on the hoof and, if an excellent shot, he stood to win the entire beef. In the turkey shoot only a head shot was considered a legitimate win. The turkey shoot remains a popular entertainment medium promoted by shooting clubs and civic organizations to raise funds for charitable or other projects, though paper targets and shotguns are currently employed rather than rifles and a live turkey.

Competition was keen on the frontier, especially in prize matches, and the target was frequently moved farther from the firing line to test the skill of the riflemen not eliminated during the first few relays; thus increasing the air of expectancy and the competitive spirit among the participants and the spectators who had their favorites and wagered on them enthusiastically with or without the incentive of homemade hard cider or other invigorating spirits.

While the shooting match was an entertainment form it also served to perfect the marksmanship skill of the frontiersman whose life and that of others often depended upon his loading dexterity and the precision of his aim. Nor did the frontiersman always rely on his rifle, for in the wilderness he lived under the immutable law of calculated risk and frequently relied on his woods lore and fleetness of foot in the face of overwhelming odds, deciding like the Native American that on occasion the better part of valor was, indeed, discretion.

The American rifle was neither as infallible nor as unerringly accurate as the many myths concerning it have indicated, though it shot as straight as the riflesmith could bore and sight it and the rifleman could aim it under the conditions and at the range for which it was intended. The smaller caliber ball with its light powder charge had a flat trajectory compared to the large-bore *jäeger* rifle with its heavy

BORING AND RIFLING ENGINES (18th/19th Century): These bench-type boring and rifling engines are typical of those used by American gunsmiths and they are similar to those brought from Europe in the early 18th Century. The specimens depicted are mounted on a single wall bracket and rotate on pegs (left); thus pivoting around for convenience or set out of the way when not in use. The boring engine (background) measures 106½ inches long and 35 inches high with a boring cylinder of 60 inches; it is unmarked and was used for boring and straight rifling. The rifling engine (foreground) has the same measurements though the rifling cylinder has helical grooves and the bench is marked W. KINDELL. Note the indexing plates forward of the guide handles and the barrels (left) clamped to the bench. Courtesy of the Pennsylvania Farm Museum of Landis Valley, Lancaster, Pa. Charles L. Maddox, Jr., photographer.

charge; yet one disadvantage of the smaller ball was that it was easily deflected by strong winds or thick underbrush.

The frontier rifleman experienced in determining elevation and windage could hit what he was aiming at in excess of 200 yards when shooting conditions were favorable; yet the American rifle was not really designed for long-range shooting. Consequently and contrary to the popular fallacy, the American rifle had no super powers, though it was adequate for the role it performed on the frontier, while no better proof of its performance is found than that there is a United States of America.

While the frontier riflesmith and other colonial American gunsmiths were largely dependent on imported firearms components, it was shortly after midcentury that specialization also emerged in British America and, significantly, it was on the frontier where in the Pennsylvania Colony a number of boring mills and barrel forges were established as the demand for rifles dramatically escalated. And it was also in the Pennsylvania Colony that the triphammer was first used to make barrel blanks.

It is known that Bridgewater gunmaker Hugh Orr employed a triphammer for making scythe and axe blades prior to midcentury (see p.259), however, there is no conclusive evidence supporting the contention that he used it for forging the barrels of the 500 muskets he produced in 1748, or that triphammers were employed for that purpose either in Massachusetts or elsewhere in New England before 1755.

As far as it can be determined, the first large scale manufacture of barrel blanks by triphammer began in North America in 1755 on Wyomissing Creek south of Reading, Pa., between Gouglersville and the Schuykill River.[93] Wyomissing Creek early received the appellation *Schmutz Deich* (dirty ditch) because its racing waters were heavily polluted by charcoal and iron tailings from the forges and boring mills using the rapid fall of the creek as a power source.[94] The last barrel forging and boring mill in the region ceased operations in 1906.

As the Wyomissing mills proliferated shortly after midcentury the mass production of pre-forged and pre-bored barrels suitable for rifling was greatly accelerated. While not completely abandoning the traditional hand-forging technique, Pennsylvania riflesmiths began to purchase ready-made blanks at a price more reasonable than making them from scratch and the only immediate concerns were the labor and time involved in rifling.

The time saved in using pre-forged and pre-bored barrels permitted Pennsylvania riflesmiths in the Wyomissing Creek vicinity to make more rifles at a faster rate and enhanced their capacity to supply the inordinate demand spawned by the expanding frontier. And in the years preceding the American Revolution triphammer forges and boring mills were established elsewhere in the Pennsylvania Colony.

The majority of the gunsmiths active in eighteenth-century North America were located in the British colonies with the largest concentrations in Massachusetts and Pennsylvania; the Lancaster region emerging as the center of rifle-making and at no other place in North America was there such a concentration of craftsmen specializing in the manufacture of a specific kind of firearm.

Rifle-making, however, was not entirely confined to the Lancaster area, and it gradually spread to other Pennsylvania counties as the century progressed; principally Bucks, York, Cumberland, Berks, and Northampton prior to 1755 and Bedford, Dauphin, Northumberland, and Westmorland before the American Revolution. In neighboring Maryland the craft early emerged in the border communities of Emmitsburg, Frederick, and Cumberland.

By ca. 1760, during the latter part of the French and Indian War, rifle-making began on a limited scale in Virginia, the Carolinas, and possibly northern Georgia. Likewise, a few riflesmiths were established in New York and the Hampshire grants a decade or so before the War of Independence. It was not until the war began, however, that the American rifle was known in the eastern settlements.

The technology represented in European firearms manufacture since the closing decades of the seventeenth century distinctly influenced the development of the colonial American firearms industry and rifle-making in particular, for it was during the latter half of the eighteenth century that boring mills and triphammer forges were established in Pennsylvania and New England though they had been introduced in the French national armories by 1725 and even earlier in the Netherlands. In England, however, most barrels were hand-forged until the late eighteenth century; gunmakers there apparently preferring traditional methods.

Though an outgrowth of three centuries of European firearms evolution the American rifle emerged as a profound example of technological specialization because it was created to fulfill the specific needs of the colonial American frontier, while it also can be considered a major technological contribution to firearms evolution because, in one form or another, it continuously served on the frontier for more than a century and a half in what was an explosive epoch of unlimited geographic expansion punctuated by seemingly endless warfare, and during that period it distinctly influenced the evolution of other American sporting, trade, and martial firearms.

The American Pistol

Most of the firearms made in British America were similar to those produced in the mother country and pistols were no exception; emigrant gunsmiths obviously familiar with the various patterns. On the Pennsylvania frontier, however, there emerged ca. 1755 an unique pistol designed and made in the Lancaster region.

The first readily identified frontier pistols appeared ca. 1735 and reflected some of the characteristics of the popular turn-off or so-called Queen Anne pistol; particularly in the shape of the barrel which retained the cannon-barrel muzzle finial and had no sights.[95] The resemblance ended there, however, for the barrel was exclusively smoothbore and did not turn off (unscrew), while a conventional rather than box lock was used with the atypical pommel grip provided with a cap and side straps. The maple or walnut forestock was pin-fastened and caliber ranged between .50 and .65.

Shortly before midcentury frontier pistols displayed fully octagonal or half-round barrels of .45 and .50 caliber ranging in length between ten and 11½ inches; the octagonal breech extending approximately 1/3 of the length. Some bores were rifled.

The grip assumed what is now termed a bird's head configuration curving sharply inward toward the trigger guard and there was no butt cap. The wood ramrod was secured by a thimble and a guide. Furniture was generally brass.

By ca. 1755 the frontier pistol had been further transformed, strongly resembling the American rifle and emerging as the prototype for those appearing thereafter. Though the bird's head grip was retained, most pistols had fully octagonal, rifled barrels provided with sights and ranging from seven and ½ to nine and ½ inches long, while caliber fluctuated between .40 and .45. Furniture was brass and there was some silver inlay work. Although there are exceptions, most pistols had an overall length of 14 to 15 inches and weighed approximately 30 ounces.

The American pistol appeared in mature form by 1775 and often reflected the workmanship of several craftsmen. Following the War of Independence caliber was further reduced to between .36 and .40 and there was a propensity toward more lavish ornamentation and silver furniture. Significantly, the

AMERICAN PISTOLS (18th Century): The unmarked pistols depicted are typical of those produced by frontier gunsmiths ca. 1740. The half-round, full-stocked barrels are brass with no rifling and are .47 caliber measuring 7½ inches. Overall length s 13¾- inches and the furniture is also brass. There are no sights and the lockplate screws (bottom pistol) are secured by brass washers rather than a sideplate. Note the tulip motif displayed on the lockplate. Courtesy of the Huntington Galleries, Huntington, W. Va.

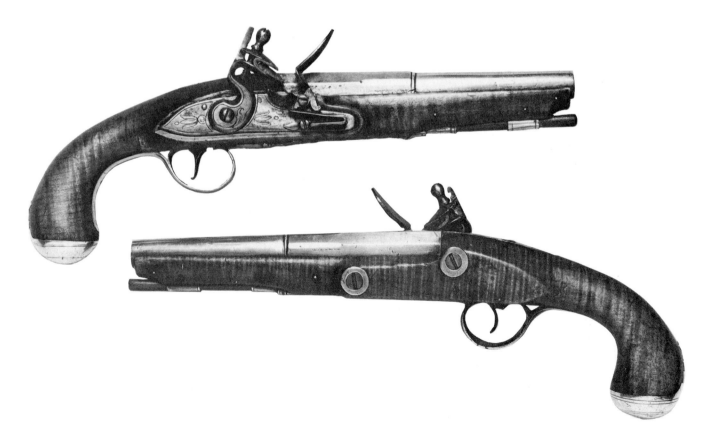

AMERICAN PISTOL (18th Century): The pistol depicted is representative of the late 18th Century frontier type. The 8-inch, octagonal barrel has a front and a rear sight and it is rifled with seven grooves, measuring .50 caliber from groove to groove. The overall length of the pistol is 13½ inches and the full-length, pin-fastened stock has 12 silver inlays. The lock is marked J BISHOP WARRENTED in two lines beneath the pan; possibly referring to a Philadelphia pistolsmith of the name flourishing ca. 1780-1790. Courtesy of the Huntington Galleries, Huntington, W. Va.

American pistol was superior to other contemporary pistols in design and craftsmanship, while its resemblance to the American rifle inspired the current appellations Kentucky pistol or silver-mounted Kentucky pistol.[96]

The American silver-mounted pistol in flintlock form is presently considered a rare and highly prized collector's item and it is also an innovative contribution to American technology. By ca. 1850, however, those elegant frontier pistols passed from the historical scene, victims of the technology they had helped spawn.

Frontier Accouterments

The colonial American frontiersman's home was the hostile, uncompromising wilderness and he accordingly accoutered himself with the requisites of survival. His rifle gun was his constant companion and often his only true "friend," and he occasionally gave it a name just as he would a dog or horse. The celebrated Kentucky woodsman Daniel Boone "christened" his rifle "Ol' Ticklicker" and other frontiersmen employed names such as "Deer Killer," "Old Sure Fire," and "Indian Lament."[97]

Because the frontiersman depended upon his rifle for survival he frequently lavished more atten-

tion on it than himself, and like other firearms emerging throughout the centuries the American rifle required various accessories for its proper maintenance, preservation, and performance.

The frontier rifleman carried a large horn for the coarse powder used for loading and a small horn for the fine, fast-burning priming powder, each suspended from the shoulder by a leather thong. A thong or a brass or iron chain supported the vent pick and a small bristle brush for cleaning the priming pan, screw heads, the lock, and other places where dirt usually accumulated. The bullet worm and scower were also common accessories and the greased loading patch also lubricated the bore, minimized leading, and reduced fouling accumulations.

The acute necessity for rapid loading was directly responsible for the introduction of the bullet block or loading block, as it was often termed; an innovative frontier accessory purely American in origin and usually carried on a thong suspended from the neck. Made of soft wood or several layers of leather sewn together, the bullet block had a number of holes slightly smaller than the diameter of the patched rifle balls forced into them.

While it is not known when the bullet block first appeared it materially assisted the rifleman by reducing the time and movements involved in groping for a ball in the bullet pouch, retrieving a greased patch from the patchbox, seating the patched ball in the muzzle with the sprue trim facing down as was customary, and then finally ramming the ball down the bore. The block with its prepared ball was simply held over the muzzle, the ball quickly seated a few inches down the bore with the ramrod. The ramrod was rapidly withdrawn, freeing the block, and the ball was rammed home.

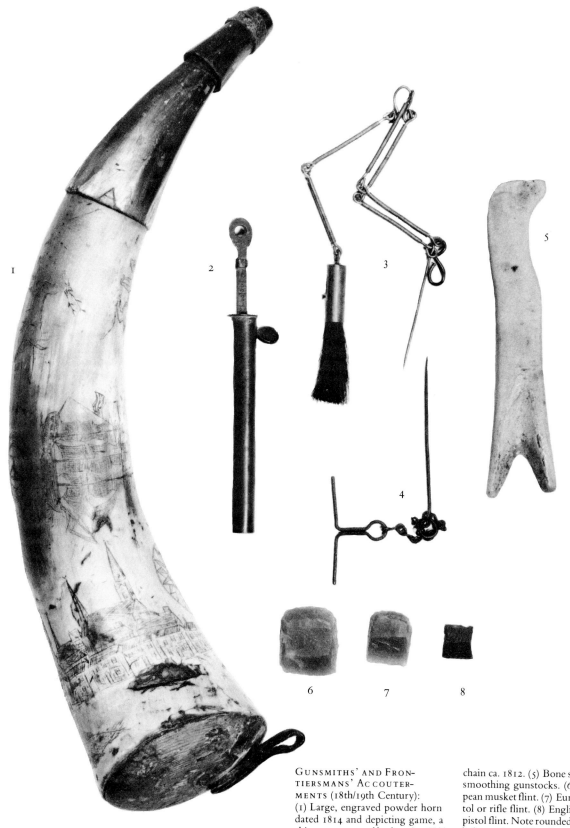

GUNSMITHS' AND FRON-
TIERSMANS' ACCOUTER-
MENTS (18th/19th Century):
(1) Large, engraved powder horn
dated 1814 and depicting game, a
ship, compass, and harbor site, 15½
inches. (2) Adjustable brass powder
measure and charger combined ca.
1830, 5 inches. (3) Vent pick, iron
with brass chain and pan brush ca.
1840. (4) Vent pick, iron with iron
chain ca. 1812. (5) Bone scraper for
smoothing gunstocks. (6) European musket flint. (7) European pistol or rifle flint. (8) English pocket
pistol flint. Note rounded edges and
lighter color of Continental flints as
contrasted to dark English flint
with square heel. Courtesy of the
Eagle Americana Shop and Gun
Museum, Strasburg, Pa. Charles L.
Maddox, Jr., photographer.

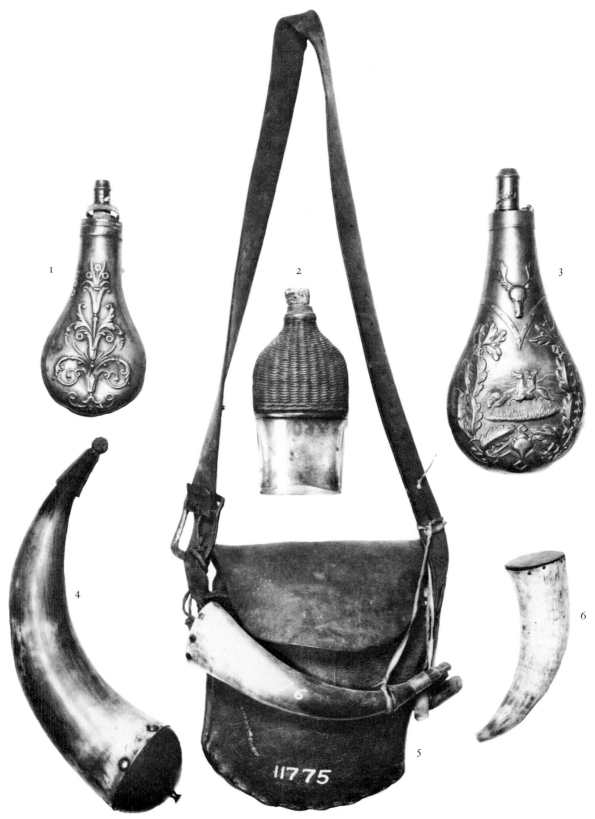

FRONTIERSMANS' ACCOUTERMENTS (18th/19th Century): (1) Imported English (Birmingham) foliate design brass powder flask with adjustable pour spout, ca. 1790–1800. (2) Woven wicker-covered bottle used for powder or shot flask, cork stopper, ca. 1790–1800. (3) American Flask & Cap Company nickel-plated Indian and Buffalo motif powder flask, 19th Century. (4) Large powder horn, ca. 1785–1810. (5) Frontiersman's possible sack with two small horn chargers and powder horn. (6) Small powder horn, possibly a rifleman's priming horn or a pistol horn. Courtesy of the Mercer Museum, Bucks County Historical Society, Doylestown, Pa. Charles L. Maddox, Jr., photographer.

An experienced rifleman, using the bullet block and ramrod in conjunction with the loading and priming horns, could fire two shots in the time expended by a musketeer firing three shots using the iron ramrod and paper cartridges; a major factor preventing the acceptance of rifles as martial firearms for many years. In emergency situations such as in the close-quarters fighting characterizing most frontier warfare, the rifleman loaded a bare ball and carried a number of bullets in his mouth to expedite the process.

The frontiersman occasionally thrust a pair of pistols into his wide leather belt, though he preferred the rifle; pistols and their accessories adding to the weight he carried and practically useless beyond point-blank range unless they were rifled. Equally deadly at that distance were the frontiersman's sheath knife and hatchet; the latter known as a tomahawk in some regions.

The sheath knife and hatchet also served for a variety of utilitarian purposes including the construction of the frontiersman's customary albeit temporary lean-to shelter. Clasp knives were also carried and equally versatile, used among other things for trimming patch material. Judicious and frequent honing with a whetstone kept the frontiersman's edged weapons extremely sharp.

Though the frontiersman frequently cut patch material with his clasp knife he also used a handmade cutter, its head conforming to the desired shape of the patch. Patch lubricant was carried in a small horn known as a grease horn and it was similar to the frontiersman' salt horn; the former often mistakenly identified as the latter.

A common accouterment in colonial America was the venerable knapsack or what the frontiersman called his possible bag or possible sack, for in it he carried anything he thought he could "possibly" use for wilderness survival. The ordinary knapsack used by the settler when hunting or called to militia duty was made of leather or heavy sail cloth. The frontiersman's possible bag was frequently made by his Native American wife of doeskin or the pelts of other animals skillfully sewn and often lavishly decorated with a variety of bead, feather, fringe, quill, and shell work; an artistic accouterment not unlike the clothing he wore.

Crammed into that commodious pouch were those items the frontiersman considered essential for survival, including patch material, a worm and scower, candles, his lock cover and scabbard when not in use; extra bullets or bullet lead, gunflints, additional powder, a bullet mould, and a small melting pot and ladle; fishing line and hooks, needle and thread, salt, dry tinder for starting fires, a whetstone, leather thongs for snares and other utilitarian purposes; tobacco and a pipe, dried meat (jerky), pemmican (the survival food originated by the Native Americans), and a host of other serviceable items.

One of the most important accouterments in colonial America was the powder horn and it was simultaneously utilitarian and decorative, ranking with the patchbox cover of the American rifle as a form of folk art which occasionally provides and preserves valuable historical data. As James E. Serven has pointed out, the powder horn has begun to receive from historians the interest it deserves.[98] Rufus A. Grider (1817-1900) pioneered the study of American powder horns in the late nineteenth century, compiling hundreds of sketches which are currently preserved in the archives of the New York Historical Society and the New York State Museum.

The first powder horns were made in fourteenth-century Europe and cow or ox horns were preferred because they were of sufficient size to carry a large amount of gunpowder, while they also curved to fit the conformation of the human body. In North America the first powder horns were made by the Spaniards in the sixteenth century (see p. 43); some specimens emulating the flat European pattern.

It is likely that the Spaniards in the Great Southwest used the horns of the American bison (buffalo) for carrying powder, while along the Atlantic strand they and other Europeans utilized the horns of the smaller woodlands bison; a species hunted to extinction by both colonists and Native Americans prior to the eighteenth century.

Once a horn of suitable size and configuration was procured it was boiled until the cartilaginous interior fiber became soft. Exercising a great deal of care to prevent puncturing the outer surface, the fiber was removed with a knife or other sharp instrument until only a white, translucent shell remained. The horn was scraped and smoothed until a uniform thickness of approximately 1/16 inch was achieved. The exterior was then polished with a mixture of oil and pumice. The stark whiteness from boiling the horn was diminished by dying it with saffron root or onion skins which gave it a yellow to amber color; thus making it less conspicuous in woodlands warfare.

In some instances, after the horn was hollowed out and before it lost its pliability from the boiling process, it was moulded around a wooden form with rounded edges and flat sides and then clamped in a press. When the horn dried it retained the shape of the form and emerged as a flat horn.

Once the exterior and interior of the horn had been prepared a portion of the pointed end was removed and often made into a powder charger. A hole was then drilled into the tip of the horn and the edges tapered to fit the mouth of the charger or the muzzle of a firearm, the tip serving as a pour spout. Some horns were fitted with brass pour spouts capable of

MAP HORN (18th Century): This outstanding example of a map horn was made in British America ca. 1750 and illustrates the Royal coat of arms (center) inscribed HONI SOIT QUI MAL Y PENSE and the significant landmarks on the Hudson River-Lake Champlain route from New York Colony to New France, including Fort Edward and Fort George. Like many horns, this specimen has an adjustable, brass pour spout of a kind frequently imported. British Crown Copyright. Reproduced with permission of the Controller of Her Britannic Majesty's Stationery Office.

throwing a predetermined powder charge. The spout neck was generally left larger than the tapering horn body and served as a ferrule for the shoulder thong. In some instances, however, the spout edges were scalloped and a metal ferrule used for attaching the thong. Early powder horns used a small wood plug for a tip stopper.

A round wood plug was made for the large end of the horn and it was secured by hardwood pegs, brass tacks, or brass brads and frequently waterproofed with beeswax. The large plug was provided with a knob or separate ferrule for the carrying thong. Medium capacity horns were made for pistols and somewhat smaller horns for the priming powder, and much smaller horns were used for grease and salt.

Early powder horns were usually plain and strictly utilitarian, marked not at all or merely with the name or initials of the owner crudely incised so they could be identified by the powder master whose duty was to fill them when the militia was activated. With the advent of the eighteenth century a variety of methods were used to identify and decorate the American powder horn. Horns were often trimmed with brass and silver wire and the ferrules were made of the same material, while end plugs and stoppers were frequently carved and made of bone, ivory, ebony, and other exotic wood.

Though imported European powder flasks and horns were common in colonial America since the seventeenth century, the manufacture of powder horns became an independent craft in the British possessions by ca.1740 and continued thereafter; a profitable enterprise and especially for those engaged in the Native American trade.

As far as it can be determined the emergence of the engraved powder horn in colonial America was coincidental with the protracted French and Indian War when the frontiersman resurrected an art form common to many prehistoric cultures, including Native American, and identified as scrimshaw, i.e., carving designs in horn, bone, ivory, shell, and other natural substances.

Working with engraving tools no more sophisticated than a sharp knife or a needle embedded in a stick, the horn etcher patiently and carefully engraved the surface with whatever his creative fancy nurtured. While most horns were incised relief carving was also employed though it was rarely encountered beyond the Spanish dominions in North America and even there it was uncommon.[99]

A martial theme dominated incised powder horns in British America, characterized by patriotic overtones often combined with a geographic motif as exemplified in the so-called map horn, i.e., a horn displaying a map of a particular region which frequently delineated prominent landmarks and topographical features like frontier forts, settlements, trading posts, trails, and Native American villages to note but few.

In some instances map horns have become invaluable sources of historical data, introducing information previously unknown, and at times confirming or disputing prevalent hypotheses. A map horn, even if not dated, can be often identified as to when it was made by what is or is not etched on its surface, and in addition to the map it frequently incorporated a quotation or popular contemporary slogan often rendered in Latin or verse.

Powder horns without maps also displayed mottos and prior to the American Revolution a popular subject for the horn engraver in the British colonies was the royal coat of arms bearing the inscription HONI SOIT MAL Y PENSE (Shamed be he who thinks evil of it) and DIEU ET MON DROIT (God and my right). In some instances horn-makers signed their work.

The flammable events leading to the American Revolution reflected the temper of the times in engraved horns displaying sentiments like: I POWDER WITH MY BROTHER BALL WILL SMITE THE BRITISH ONE AND ALL, or the variant I POUDRE AND MY BROTHRE BALL NOBEL LIKE TO LEVIL ALL; the latter appearing on a horn signed by Lt. Obediah Lansing, 4th Albany (N.Y.) Militia.[100]

In addition there were horns bearing the legend TEN DOLLARS BOUNTY ON WOLVES & PANTHERS AND BRITISH LIONS, and the philosophic MAY THE BLOSSOM OF LIBERTY NEVER FAIL AND THE KING AND TIRANTS NEVER PREVAIL. In many instances the spelling was more phonetic than accurate but the meaning was certainly clear. There were, of course, innumerable variations in the design of the carving and the content of the phrases.

Once the design, inscription, or both were etched into the horn the maker usually gave it more definition by blackening the lines with soot, charcoal, gunpowder mixed with oil or water to make a paste, and occasionally tobacco juice or that from wild berries. The horn etcher whose artistic ability was superior was often asked to engrave horns for others less talented and it is probable that a few good

engravers turned what was usually a leisure activity into a thriving business.

While colonial militiamen were generally admonished by regulations to keep a supply of powder and a serviceable powder horn on hand, they relied on the powder master to fill their horns or flasks when campaigning, and the role of the powder master as well as the military armorer has been almost totally ignored by historians, despite its significance during the colonial period and thereafter.

Wagons were generally used to transport the heavy powder kegs to the camp or other central location though in inaccessible terrain pack horses and mules or the militiamen themselves carried the powder, while before and during battle the powder master filled each militiaman's horn or flask directly from the kegs. The men occasionally formed a line at the powder wagon, though in most instances one or two men collected the horns and flasks from the unit and helped fill them.

Because many militiamen employed their personal firearms for active service there was a great deal of caliber variation which frequently presented problems in supplying the proper ammunition. Prepared paper cartridges were not always readily available, and neither were cartridges distributed to riflemen who invariably used the patched ball. During rest periods militia and regular troops frequently used the time to make cartridges and the powder master issued musket, carbine, and pistol balls of various caliber as well as shot, cartridge paper, twine, and the requisite forming stick in addition to the proper size bullet moulds when required.

Gunflints were often dressed during a lull and also distributed by the powder master in a ratio of one per 20 cartridges, though in that regard militia regulations fluctuated greatly from colony to colony. In British America gunflints were generally imported in half-casks of 2,000 to 4,000 weighing 65 to 75 pounds and flint knappers were paid by the thousand; the rate regulated by the government which gained control of the industry during the seventeenth century.[101]

As previously noted, militia sergeants customarily carried a mainspring vise and a supply of

SCISSOR MOULD (18th Century): Scissor moulds with long jaws were often called alligator moulds. This specimen cast 39 buckshot on one side of the jaw and 44 BB shot on the other. Few moulds had wood handles prior to the 19th Century. Courtesy of the Mercer Museum, Bucks County Historical Society, Doylestown, Pa. Charles L. Maddox, Jr., photographer.

mainsprings for musket locks; a practical consideration inasmuch as militia units were infrequently provided with armorers. The militia armorer was generally a gunsmith serving one of the settlements from which the militia was drawn, e.g. William Henry of Lancaster who accompanied the Pennsylvania Militia in Gen. Braddock's command. Armorers repaired damaged firearms in the field when possible, i.e., what is now termed first echelon repair. Firearms beyond first echelon repair were collected and sent to the one or more gunsmiths serving the colony as designated public armorers.

In addition to the frontiersman's other paraphernalia he frequently carried a talisman often exemplified by a fox-or-'coonskin cap, a rabbit's foot, or perhaps a necklace of bear claws or teeth. In the Pennsylvania Colony the talisman was known as a powwow and purported to ensure a successful hunt or otherwise bestow good fortune upon the bearer.

One form of the frontier powwow can be traced to Classical antiquity and it was brought to British America by the large number of Germans arriving early in the eighteenth century.[102] The powwow was kept in the knapsack, possible sack, or the rifle patchbox. It was usually a small piece of paper inscribed in two lines, the Latin text separated by three symbolic crosses and an equal number of stars possibly representing the Trinity:

Ut nemo in sese tentat descendere, nemo!
Sed praecendenti spectatur mantica tergo.

There are several variations of those lines from the fourth satire of Aulus Persius Flaccus written during Nero's reign (A.D. 37-86). A liberal translation reveals the quotation as a parable, suggesting a more profound philosophic comment, "No one looks deeply into himself, but does see the pack [burden] on the back of the one who walks before."

The strong belief in and reliance on the powwow in the German communities of southeastern Pennsylvania was also reflected in occult incantations or spells which supposedly transformed the rifle into a firearm that never failed for whatever purpose it was used; a so-called *"Freischutz,"* literally a "free rifle," though translated with a deeper connotation meaning a rifle with a guardian angel or free spirit. Another common regional tenet was manifest by the following:

Load a gun with a bullet, cast on a crossroad on Christmas Eve, and it will hit the mark or bring down the game without fail.[103]

The frontiersman's superstitions regarding firearms is related to his familiarity with them as tools for survival; a familiarity which also extended to his wife and children, including the pre-adolescent who, if not actually using firearms to defend their wilderness enclave, loaded and primed for those who were.

The preoccupation and familiarity with firearms in colonial America bred a common, firearms-related parlance sprinkled with expressive phrases which in many instances originated in the Old World much earlier and currently survive, though they are frequently unrecognized as initially related to firearms, e.g. the phrase "lock, stock, and barrel" which is an obvious reference to the three major firearms components and now carries a different meaning.

The venerable expression "to go off half-cocked" is presently euphemistic, referring to one who reacts quickly without considering the consequences of his action, though it once referred to the accidental discharge of a firearm caused by a defective sear or worn half-cock tumbler notch. Derived from the extremely light pull as dictated by the set-trigger is the phrase "hair-trigger temper," while "cocked and primed" once meant just that rather than its present connotation of eager or ready.

Another common expression, "flash in the pan," has emerged to describe a passing fad or fancy rather than a misfire resulting from a clogged vent or damp priming powder which merely produced a harmless puff of smoke readily dissolved in the atmosphere; thus as firearms distinctly influenced our techonomic heritage they also inspired many of the oral traditions associated with our cultural heritage and those remain preserved in our language.

The Native American Trade

The eighteenth-century Native American trade was a commercial enterprise fraught with political and socio-economic overtones of unfathomable depth and it was deeply enmeshed with the expanding European and American firearms industry. There was, however, a significant delineation between the Native American trade in the French and Spanish dominions as compared to the British, for by midcentury a burgeoning firearms industry had been established in British America and it had an enormous growth potential which made itself known in the final quarter of the century and thereafter proliferated.

In British America the growth of the Native American trade was not only predicated on demand, for there was a cadre of aggressive, determined frontier traders and mercantile enterprises either individually or collectively active in seeking out lucrative markets and the influence exerted by the royal commissioners of Indian Affairs was also significant. Favorable too was the geographic position of the

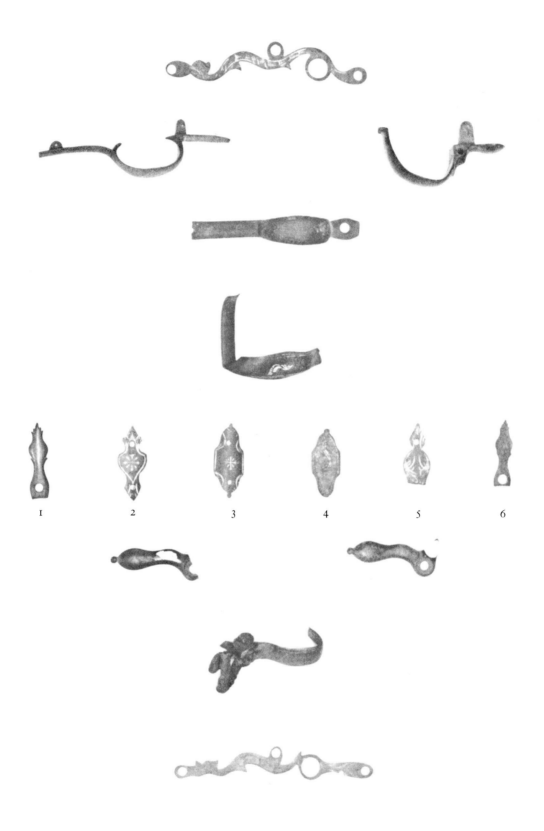

TRADE FUSIL AND MUSKET COMPONENTS (ca. 1735): The English trade fusil and musket components depicted are all from Fort Frederica, St. Simons' Island, Ga., and its environs, site of a Kelsall & Spaulding trading station. Top: cast-brass engraved serpent sideplate. First row: Trade fusil trigger guard (left), martial musket trigger guard (right). Note lugs for pin-fastening to the stock. Second row: Trade fusil trigger guard (top view) stamped with mark of London gunsmith Thomas Henshaw (fl. 1690-1740). Center: Bent trigger guard and finial, engraved. Fourth row (from left): (1&6) Front trigger guard finials, (2 to 4) Thumbplates with engraved snowflake design, and (5) Thumbplate with foliate design. Fifth row: Fragmented musket sideplates. Sixth row: Musket trigger guard fragment with sling swivel. Bottom: Cast-brass engraved serpent sideplate from trade fusil. Courtesy of Fort Frederica National Monument, St. Simons' Island, Ga.

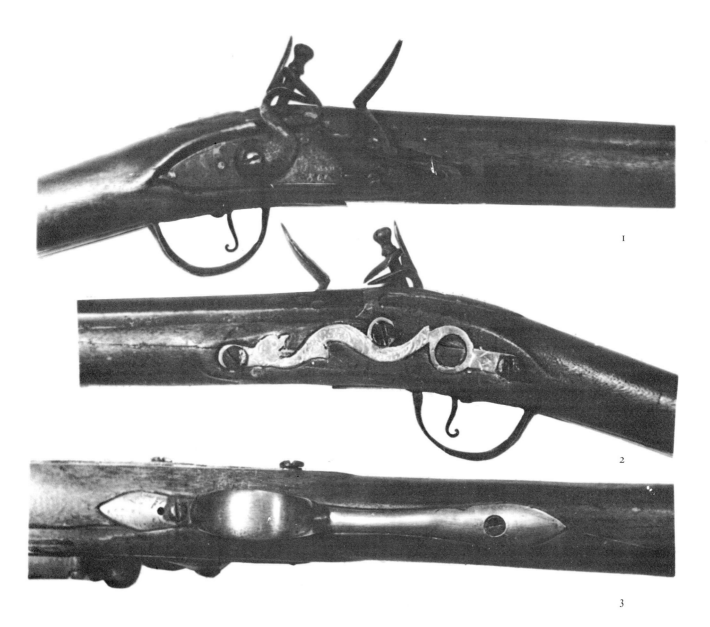

1

2

3

TRADE FUSIL (18th Century): The furniture and other components of this Native American trade fusil identifies it as made in England ca. 1750. The lock is marked KETLAND & CO., noted Birmingham armsmakers, and the barrel is stamped with the initials I H, possibly those of London gunsmith Joseph Heylin (fl. 1745-1760). Overall length: 63⅛ inches. Barrel length: 47⅝ inches. Caliber: .68. Note the lack of a rear sight (1); an iron front sight was provided. The typical serpent sideplate (2) is secured by three screws and the serpent head faces rearward. The long rear trigger guard finial (3) typifies trade fusils of the 1740-1780 period as does the short buttplate finial (4) held by an integral post. Courtesy of the Museum of the Great Plains, Lawton, Oklahoma.

4

colonies, for in the middle Atlantic and southern regions the predominantly east-west river network afforded ready access to the interior.

By ca.1750 the British traders had established a nearly unshakable rapport among the Native Americans despite French and Spanish competition because they offered them firearms, gunpowder, and other trade goods cheaper than the French and superior in quality to the Spanish. When competition was especially keen British traders often resorted to economic warfare by cutting prices, even among themselves, to the extent of suffering a temporary loss, and neither did they hesitate to employ violence when other methods failed; an expedient also embraced by their competitors and not unknown among themselves.

Like the French the British had recognized the Native American need for firearms repair in the seventeenth century and continued to provide the service thereafter. As early as 1730 the Upper Creeks asked Georgia traders for free firearms repair.[104] Archaeological evidence confirms that from 1736 to 1743 English trade fusils were repaired at and distributed from Fort Frederica on St. Simon's Island, Georgia.[105]

In 1747 the Pennsylvania Colony, at the behest of the influential Oneida chief Shikellamy, erected a forge and gunsmithery at Shamokin and provided a gunsmith who also served as a blacksmith.[106] Frontier traders also employed gunsmiths at their scattered wilderness stations and firearms repair was usually requested by the various Native American nations negotiating treaty provisions during the eighteenth century and thereafter.

Prior to ca. 1730 the English trade fusil was distinctive only insofar as it could be identified as made expressly for the Native American trade, for it remained essentially similar to the three patterns adopted by the Hudson's Bay Company. The prominent fish-belly stock found on some early trade fusils had disappeared by ca. 1725, supplanted by the popular, so-called handrail butt of martial design displaying a straight belly and comb.

The butt was provided with a full, brass buttplate with a short heel tang, secured by a single screw

and a tang post mortised into the comb. The forestock extended to the muzzle and after ca. 1725 a thumbplate was found at the stock wrist bearing an engraved snowflake design. Furniture was iron or brass with the latter predominant and the ramrod was wood, secured by a single thimble.

The flintlock mechanism was flat and strictly utilitarian, displaying a straight cock spur rather than the curved style which emerged ca. 1730. Some early locks retained the dog catch appearing on trade fusils early in the seventeenth century. During the period 1700-1730 both the lock and the barrel displayed British proof marks and the initials of the maker; the practice continuing thereafter.

An English trade fusil recovered from a Yuchi village on the Alabama side of the Chattahoochee River is stamped on the barrel flat behind the rear sight with London proof marks known to have been introduced in 1702 and the initials R W, the mark of London gunsmith Richard Wilson (fl. 1700-1760) whose family for more than a century produced trade fusils, many of them contracted by the Hudson's Bay Company.[107]

After ca. 1730 there were substantial changes made in the English trade fusil and a distinctive pattern emerged. Most barrels fluctuated between 31 ½ and 48 inches in length, caliber ranged from approximately .56 to .58, and the octagonal breech extended around nine to ten inches, measuring at least an inch across the flats, while the remainder of the barrel was round and tapered toward the muzzle. Sights were usually iron, forged integral with the barrel; the front sight of the post type and the rear sight, if any, incorporating a v-notch crossbar or a split post, i.e., the post was merely separated by a file cut. Variations with brass sights are uncommon.

A distinguishing feature of the eighteenth-century English trade fusil serving as a readily identified characteristic until the late nineteenth century was the brass sideplate shaped like a serpent or dragon. The distinctive sideplate also appeared on Hudson's Bay Company fusils ca. 1675, i.e., around five years after the company was chartered.[108] Similar sideplates have been found on three trade fusils which T.M. Hamilton has tentatively identified as

TRADE FUSIL CAST-BRASS SERPENT SIDEPLATE (18th Century): Obverse view of serpent sideplate found on Native American trade fusils since ca. 1675. Note the rough casting. Courtesy of the Museum of the Great Plains, Lawton, Oklahoma.

DUTCH MUSKET (17th Century): The Dutch flintlock musket depicted was made ca. 1640 and the buttstock and the lock amply demonstrate the serpent motif. The chased lockplate is completely covered with a winged dragon, the head extending beneath the pan. Dutch gunmakers introduced the serpent motif in trade fusils and it was copied by other European gunsmiths engaged in the fur trade, while many Native Americans refused to barter for trade fusils without the design. Courtesy of the *Livrustkammaren*, Stockholm.

eighteenth-century French and they were recovered from an Osage village in Vernon County, Mo.; each plate illustrating a design variant.[109]

The origin of the serpent or dragon sideplate remians obscure. Hudson's Bay Company records are mute on the subject and the prevalent theory at present is that the design was a Dutch innovation introduced ca. 1640, for trade fusils and other firearms produced in the Netherlands during the seventeenth century incorporated the serpent motif in the design of the cock, the lockplate, and the stock.

A matchlock musket made in Amsterdam ca. 1611 and now in the *Livrustkammaren* (No. 11673) displays a wealth of bone inlay featuring a highly stylized, winged dragon or serpent mortised into the stock directly above the lock. Also in the *Livrustkammaren* is a Dutch flintlock musket in which the design is incorporated in the cock and the ornately carved stock, while the entire lockplate is cast in the form of a winged serpent or dragon.

After ca. 1650 Netherlands arms merchants sold large quantities of trade fusils to the British and the French and continued to do so even after those nations introduced and produced patterns of their own. That in itself, however, is insufficient to explain why the dragon or serpent sideplate design was accepted and reproduced by the British and possibly the French. Significantly, the serpent design was extremely popular with the Native Americans from the time of its introduction, and even before the eighteenth century many of them refused to trade for fusils which did not feature it; that a plausible if not absolute explanation why the design continued to be employed.

Precisely why the serpent sideplate design evoked such a response from the Native Americans, however, remains uncertain, though it is possible that it was eagerly accepted because the serpent was a powerful and highly esteemed totem in their pantheistic religious philosophy and served as the guardian diety of certain gens (clans) within the tribes; the most prominent in addition to the snake being the bear, deer, turtle, and wolf clans.

The serpent design therefore represented a diety and symbolized the omnipotence sought by the Native American hunter-warrior, while the fusil itself was a personification of that supernatural power. Though the hypothesis is somewhat oversimplified perhaps, the frontier trader was ever sensitive to the moods and the desires of the Native American and, shrewdly perceiving a preference, saw that the serpent sideplate was retained; much like a distinctive trademark presently identifies a product.

As initially seen on some Hudson's Bay Company trade fusils the cast-brass serpent sideplate was convex, featuring two holes for the lockplate screws and at least three others for tacks or brads. There was no discernable head though the sideplate body resembled a coiled snake, and there was no engraving or other decorative marks.[110]

A more distinctive serpent design emerged ca. 1720, also of cast-brass but with a flat surface incised with a scroll design. There were three screw holes and no additional perforations. The serpent's head, usually though not always facing rearward because it was designed to show the head facing in either direction, was clearly defined to illustrate the fangs, tongue, and eyes, while the body described a completed coil near the tail.[111]

By ca. 1750 there were variations of the serpent sideplate which displayed a head and body with a distinctive scaly appearance; the scaly effect either cast integrally or stippled, i.e., the scaly effect was made by striking the soft brass with a rounded, punch-like instrument. The serpent sideplate remained characteristic of the English trade fusil until production ceased ca. 1875 and the design was adopted by American trade fusil makers during the late eighteenth century though trade fusil manufacture terminated in the United States with the advent of the Civil War.

At the beginning of the eighteenth century the Hudson's Bay Company continued to represent British influence in French America and Gooding's estimable research has revealed 21 London gunsmiths producing company trade fusils during that era. At least two of them, Charles Kiplin (fl. 1729-1735) and Thomas Williams (fl. 1735-1738), died and left the operation of their gunsmitheries to their widows. It is likely that Hester Kiplin and Ann Williams were administratively engaged in the business rather than active gunsmiths, though the latter possibility is not unreasonable.[112]

Also provided by Gooding are the names of 30 gunsmiths actively employed as armorers for the Hudson's Bay Company prior to 1775, most of them working in the company factories at York Fort, Prince of Wales Fort, Albany Fort, and Moose Fort, or at Rupert's House or Severn House.[113] James Lyner worked at Albany Fort from 1698 to 1722, while John Fleming was active as an armorer and a blacksmith at Moose River from 1757 to 1767. Ed Wall served on the Churchill River between 1741 and 1746, while from 1756 to 1760 armorer Nathan Brown was active at York Fort and Rupert's House.

In eighteenth-century British America the Native American trade was a lucrative enterprise that neither the crown nor the colonists were willing to relinquish and it served as a *casus belli* for the French and Indian War. The value of the furs and pelts exported to England in 1700 reached £16,280 (see APPENDIX III). The Hudson's Bay Company alone accounted for £2,360 or nearly as much as the £2,430 for the furs shipped from all of New England, while those sent from New York Colony were more than double the value (£4,960) of the furs sent by the Hudson's Bay Company and New England combined. Accounting for the balance in 1700 were furs from Newfoundland, Pennsylvania, East and West Jersey, Delaware, Maryland, Virginia, and the Carolinas. By 1740 the total value of the furs and pelts reaching Britain from her American colonies was £25,196, a significant economic gain.

While the profits from the fur trade were certainly welcomed, Britain reaped other benefits from her Native American commerce as exemplified when at Lancaster, Pa., in 1744 she managed a coup of unprecedented geopolitical impact, for the Iroquoian Confederacy then ceded to the crown most of the land it controlled in the Ohio Valley north of the river of that name. The transaction netted the Iroquois the goods delineated in the Table, most of which was conspicuous in any frontier trading station.[114]

The shrewd Iroquois considered the trade goods a bargain because they had carefully assessed the competition between the British and the French and correctly concluded that the former were more powerful; thus by cultivating the British they recognized an opportunity to procure more British firearms in the future which they could use to maintain control in the Ohio country, expand their intact dominions elsewhere, and make life miserable for

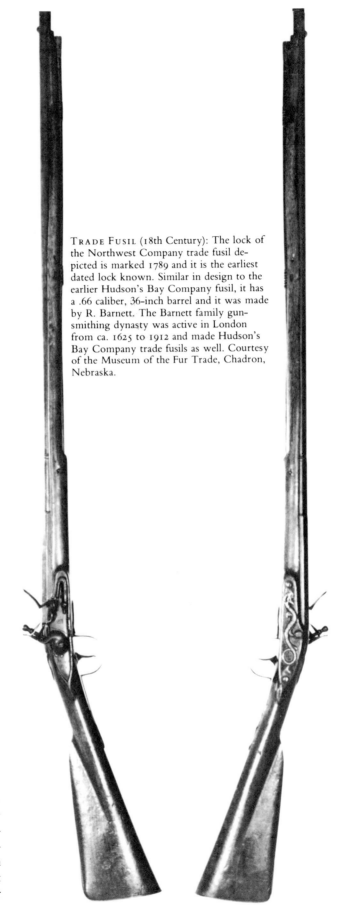

TRADE FUSIL (18th Century): The lock of the Northwest Company trade fusil depicted is marked 1789 and it is the earliest dated lock known. Similar in design to the earlier Hudson's Bay Company fusil, it has a .66 caliber, 36-inch barrel and it was made by R. Barnett. The Barnett family gunsmithing dynasty was active in London from ca. 1625 to 1912 and made Hudson's Bay Company trade fusils as well. Courtesy of the Museum of the Fur Trade, Chadron, Nebraska.

BRITISH TRADE GOODS PROCURED BY THE IROQUOIS:
1744

2000 needles	200 yds. half-thick [cloth]	100 hoes
1000 gunflints	200 lbs. tobacco	60 kettles
1000 tobacco pipes	120 combs	40 hats
600 lbs. lead	100 diffil [duffle] coats	40 pr. stockings
500 lbs. gunpowder	100 hatchets	25 gal. rum
500 knives	100 blankets	24 mirrors
500 awl blades	100 shirts	24 doz. gartering
60 stroud [coarse cloth] match coats	100 tobacco tongs	10 tin pots
45 firearms*	100 pr. scissors	2 lb. vermillion dye

*Unidentified, probably trade fusils

their ancestral enemies or anyone else they chose, including their benefactors. The Iroquois had cunningly maneuvered themselves into a situation paralleled in the present century as many less favored nations align themselves with the world powers.

While the Hudson's Bay fuke and other trade fusils were in great demand, especially prized by the Native Americans was the American rifle. Many a long hunter and isolated frontier settler were murdered merely to procure a rifle because its ability to deliver a lethal ball at a great distance early earned the respect of the hunter-warrior if not his unrequited awe, and rifles subsequently became valuable items of frontier commerce.

Precisely when the trade rifle was introduced in colonial America remains debatable, though manufacture and distribution never approached the trade fusil. Because the American rifle was popular on the frontier some firearms historians have assumed that it was the prototype for the trade rifle and that trade rifles were made exclusively in British America prior to the Revolutionary War.

While the American rifle doubtlessly influenced the design of the trade rifle in the British colonies there is no valid evidence indicating that either were the only rifles employed in North America prior to 1750. The *jäeger* rifle was employed in the German settlements at the beginning of the century and the French certainly recognized that rifles were well suited for use on the frontier and rifle manufacture was not unknown in France; yet there is a dearth of information concerning the use of the rifle in New France and it is a subject worthy of more comprehensive investigation.

As far as it is known the earliest reference to the use of rifles by the Native Americans is the statement made by French frontiersman and trader Auguste Chouteau which was reported by John G. W. Dillin: "In 1736 the Chickasaws were not only armed with rifles but were generally good shots."[115] Though Chouteau did not qualify or amplify his remark it has led a number of historians to assume that the Chicka-

saws were armed with large numbers of rifles at an early date.

Of Muskhogean stock the Chickasaw lived in the vicinity of the confluence of the Tombigbee and Yazoo rivers in northern Mississippi where they were found by DeSoto in 1540 and called *Chicazas*. Inhabiting what France and Spain each considered part of their colonial domain, the Chickasaw early developed an aversion to both and established trade relations with Charleston merchants ca. 1725 (see p. 180).

Though it is likely that Chouteau knew of rifles, it is not known whether his knowledge of their use among the Chickasaw was heresay or derived from personal experience. It is doubtful, however, if he had encountered a *jäeger* rifle or its American offspring in Chickasaw country by 1736, and neither is it probable that the Chickasaw had procured either, for the American rifle had then barely entered its first evolutionary period and few were produced, while those transitional firearms as well as the *jäeger* rifle were generally limited to the Pennsylvania frontier which was far removed from Chickasaw country.

It is possible that the Chickasaw had procured a rifle or two from Charleston traders by 1736 and that they might have been early specimens of the American rifle or even the *jäeger* rifle. There is also, however, the alternative that Carolina traders had procured European rifles of a pattern now unknown. If the Chickasaw did indeed have rifles in 1736 only a few were available, while then even trade fusil distribution among them was less than generous.

While it is known that Lancaster riflesmith William Henry produced firearms for the Native American trade prior to 1759 there is nothing to indicate whether they were rifles or smoothbore fusils, and by that time the American rifle had not yet made its influence felt to any appreciable extent on the frontier though as the French and Indian War progressed it was more frequently encountered.

The Treaty of Aix-la-Chapelle (October 18, 1748) terminated King George's War and just prior to that declaration the Virginia Council granted the recently organized Loyal Land Company 800,000 acres in the western part of the colony; a dispensation ripe for exploitation and settlement. Many were eager to take advantage of the opportunity and not all of them were British subjects.

Céleron de Bienville took exception to Britain's interest in the pristine Ohio country, leaving his Lake Erie base in 1749 to reassert a previous French claim by erecting a chain of forts extending along the broad Ohio River; thus challenging Britain's economic and geographical prerogatives there. George II added fuel to the combustible situation when on May 19, 1749, he granted 500,000 acres on the upper Ohio to the newly chartered Ohio Company.

In 1750 Virginia officials heeded the advice of frontier traders George Croghan and John Fraser, sending Christopher Gist to explore the fur-rich Ohio country and report on suspected French incursions. Gist traversed the Loyal Land Company grant instead of the Ohio Company land and returned the following year only to be sent out again by the militant, newly appointed Virginia governor, Robert Dinwiddie.

Gist, accompanied by frontiersman Thomas Cresap, blazed a direct trail from the Potomac River to Cresap's Station at Will's Creek and on nearby Chesnut Ridge he established a storehouse for the Ohio Company, shortly thereafter negotiating trade concessions with the powerful Shawnee, Delaware, and Miami at Logstown; a large village where Croghan had earlier started a station and located about 18 miles below the strategic Forks of the Ohio, i.e., present Pittsburgh, Pa., at the confluence of the Allegheny and Monongahela.

Dinwiddie and Bienville, meanwhile, had been instructed by their respective governments not to provoke a conflict, for it was not intended by either to ignite another war which would invite the inevitable Native American onslaught and expose the frontier to yet more terror and bloodshed. Dinwiddie accordingly sought a tactful emissary who could ask the French to leave the disputed territory without antagonizing them. Selected for the mission was 21-year-old Virginia planter, surveyor, and militia officer George Washington.

With Gist as his guide Washington left Williamsburg in the bitter winter of 1753, hesitated momentarily at the Forks of the Ohio and chose the site for a proposed Virginia fort, and reached the French at Fort Le Boeuf in mid-December. On the sixteenth Washington headed back with the negative French response, crossing the frigid mountains, despite an attempted ambush to arrive at Williamsburg a month to the day later.

Dinwiddie was furious, calling for armed intervention and the support of the Pennsylvania Colony. Though Pennsylvania hesitated to act without official sanction from London, the Ohio Company quickly dispatched a party to build a fort at the site Washington had selected.

In April, 1754, Washington as a recently promoted Virginia Militia lieutenant colonel retraced his winter sojourn with two companies of raw recruits, building a road as he went. Arriving at Will's Creek he learned that the French had captured the unfinished Ohio Company fort at the Forks of the Ohio and named it Duquesne.

Pierre de Contrecoeur, commanding the French, had been appraised of Washington's movements by his Native American spies and sent Ensign Villiers de Jumonville with a mixed party of 34 French and Native Americans to intercept the Virginians, ostensibly with the admonition to refrain from hostile action but to advise them to leave.

Jumonville's approach was detected by Washington's scouts when less than a days' march away. Washington, aware of the value of surprise though unaware of Jumonville's intent, nevertheless made a forced night march in a driving rain and struck the unsuspecting French as the first gray streaks of dawn crept across the Allegheny Mountains.

The two forces collided on May 28, 1754.

Jumonville and several of his men were killed and the others were with a single exception taken prisoner. Washington's casualties were extremely light in his first military victory: one killed and one wounded in a deliberate sneak attack on an outnumbered force with no declaration of war in a territory not only claimed by Britain and France but also disputed between Connecticut, Maryland, Pennsylvania, and Virginia.

Thus in the wilderness of what is now western Pennsylvania did Virginia Militia without express orders draw first blood in what shortly thereafter erupted into an international conflagration to alter forever the face of the globe and ultimately give Britain nearly complete mastery over the fate of North America.

The triumphant Virginians resumed their road building in June and an incensed Contrecoeur, seeking vengeance, dispatched none other than Jumonville's brother, Coulon de Villiers, to destroy them. Washington, learning from his scouts that he was outnumbered, rapidly withdrew to Great Meadows between Laurel and Allegheny Ridge and hastily erected what he appropriately called Fort Necessity. There the rain-soaked Virginians, short of rations and the majority sickened and drunk from a rum ration downed on empty stomachs, capitulated after a befuddled defense during which one in five was killed or wounded.

Considering the circumstances, Villiers was more than lenient and allowed the survivors to withdraw the following day. For Washington it was an ignominious defeat after his initial though treacherous success and he would well remember the date: July 4, 1754.

John Fraser participated in the Fort Necessity debacle and lost a considerable number of personal belongings including a "Complete set of Armourer's tools."[116] In addition the French captured "7 rifled guns" valued at £ six each and "5 smooth guns, 2 cases neat pistols and furniture, 4 dozen pipe tomahawks, 2 dozen bridle gun locks, 6 dozen plain gun locks, 5 ct. [hundredweight] gunpowder, 5 ct. bar lead."[117] There is no description of the captured rifles and it has been assumed that they were made by Lancaster riflesmiths.

Marching against Fort Duquesne little more than a year later Gen. Edward Braddock's redcoat regulars, supported by colonial militia and a contingent of Native American scouts, followed Washington's wilderness road and the now militia colonel was Braddock's second-in-command. On July 9, 1755, seven miles from his objective, Braddock fell into the deadly jaws of a French ambush.

Assisted by Native Americans, though commanding a French force of inferior strength, Capt. Daniel Hyacinth de Beaujeu skillfully directed the ambuscade and the confused British wilted under the assault which seemed to come from all directions. A mortally wounded Braddock died in the retreat which degenerated into a rout despite Washington's desperate effort to regroup.

The Fort Necessity battle proved conclusively that the American rifle early served in wilderness warfare and the Braddock disaster confirmed that rifles of a now unknown description were used by the French or their Native American allies, for Braddock's men reported receiving rifle fire from Beaujeu's forces.[118] Whether rifles had been issued to the French regulars and their Native American allies and whether they were French rifles remains conjectural, for there is the possibility that the Native Americans had procured them from Fraser's Station and others overrun in the 1749 French penetration of the Ohio country, the 1754 Fort Necessity battle, or yet unrevealed sources.

Braddock's successor, Gen. John Forbes, also slashed a road through the wilderness from the British supply base at Carlisle, Pa., and on November 25, 1758, he captured Fort Duquesne and renamed it Fort Pitt in deference to Britain's capable Secretary of State for the Southern Department, William Pitt the Elder. Forbes' victory, coupled with Gen. James Wolfe's successful assault against the resolute Louis Joseph de Montcalm on the Plains of Abraham at Quebec in September, 1759, was the turning point of the French and Indian War, though the conflict dragged on for little more than another three years.

While the British were fully occupied with the French threat in the north the southern colonies were shattered in October, 1759, by the Cherokee War which technically terminated in 1761, though it continued sporadically until 1794; the Cherokees defending their ancestral dominions from an aggressive frontier people contravening official policy rather than the British per se, and with few exceptions the Cherokees subsequently joined the British during the American Revolution. Thus, as frequently happened, the frontier was engulfed in a war within a war.

As a result of French activity in the Ohio Valley in 1749 and thereafter the value of the furs and pelts exported to Britain in 1750 declined to £2,379 less than the 1740 figure, while in 1760 the value dropped to £19,985; a balance nearly on par with the £19,377 total for 1720. Despite the decline in the fur trade Britain's rapport with the Native Americans, particularly the Iroquois, steadily improved under the energetic and tactful leadership of Sir William Johnson, Superintendent of Indian Affairs of the Northern Department from 1755 to 1774.

Johnson, even more influential than George Croghan, reported that in the 1760's trade fusils sold for 30 shillings each in New York Colony currency, while a pound of gunpowder cost three shillings, a doeskin, or its weight in beaver pelts. Lead brought sixpence a pound or three small bars for a doeskin or a small beaver plew. A muskrat pelt purchased six gunflints. Johnson also mentioned that British martial muskets were then produced in London for approximately 24 shillings.

On February 10, 1763, the Treaty of Paris concluded the enervating and protracted French and Indian War and Britain emerged as a virtually unrivalled world power: her mastery of the seas was unchallenged, her army was fortified by numbers and confidence, her position in India was solidified, her relations with her American colonies were briefly cemented, and her commercial prospects distinctly improved as a result of her enormous territorial acquisitions.

In the aftermath of victory Braddock's Road, as Washington's rough track came to be called, and Forbes' Road guided a resolute and ever-growing stream of settlers from the tidewater communities to the broad expanse of the Ohio country as well as the Valley of Virginia, while in the ensuing quarter-century a veritable torrent of frontier people poured through Cumberland Gap first penetrated by Dr. Thomas Walker in 1750. There were, however, two disturbing events which temporarily stemmed the accelerating tide of the frontier movement.

In the immediate wake of the French and Indian War the frontier was plunged into another bloodbath by Pontiac's Conspiracy. The powerful Ottawa chief not only attempted to drive the British out of the Ohio country, but completely out of North America with support garnered from other Native American dissidents. After three years of death and destruction the plan miscarried and the threat was terminated with the Treaty of Oswego in July, 1766.

Meanwhile, on October 7, 1763, Britain established the controversial Proclamation Line, an imaginary boundary extending from the Atlantic Ocean just north of what was formerly Spanish Florida to the Appalachian barrier and then following the mountain chain northward beyond New England to the St. Lawrence; thus separating the established British possessions from those newly created by territorial acquisition: Quebec, East Florida, and West Florida.

While the Proclamation Line was ostensibly an altruistic manifestation of British diplomacy reputedly designed to keep the frontier settlers from invading Native American land, it was actually motivated by economic avarice. The Board of Trade and the crown as represented by George III since 1760 each recognized the political demarcation as a means to control the vital commerce with the Native Americans living beyond it; a conclusion also ascertained by the French and the Spanish who both encouraged it and by the frontier people and colonial merchants who as readily despised it.

Land speculators were deprived of the vast profits they envisioned, merchants and traders suffered the same loss and felt restrained by crown license, and the frontier people were denied access to land which they believed that they had earned and deserved after suffering through yet another frontier war because the crown was aware that peaceful relations with the Native Americans ensured a profitable commerce and could be maintained only if access was restricted.

Though retaining a foothold in Louisiana, Spain had lost Florida to the British in exchange for the vital port of Havana and Britain had promptly divided the Florida provinces with St. Augustine serving as the capital of East Florida, while the seat of government in West Florida was Pensacola; each provided with a governor appointed by the crown.

In 1762 France, under the dissolute reign of Louis XV and pressured on all fronts, was forced to cede New Orleans and her remaining Louisiana territory to Spain as compensation for her assistance during the conflict. The broad Mississippi Valley, however, remained predominantly French by virtue of the settlers who continued to reside there. In the north the French provinces were incorporated under British rule as Quebec and, significantly, competition with the Hudson's Bay Company was eliminated; thus the company was permitted to expand freely.

Neither Spain nor the French settlers in *La Louisiane* desired further Native American conflicts and the Proclamation Line provided a supposedly inviolable boundary separating British settlers from Native American territory. In theory Spain was given an almost unlimited opportunity to pursue Native American commerce; an aspect of the Proclamation Line which the French saw as a weak link in Britain's armor and one open to exploitation with or without Spanish assistance.

There was, however, an imponderable equation which confounded the British and destroyed French and Spanish calculations as well, for they all had failed to take into account the variable compounded

in the determined nature of the frontier people who openly defied the crown, disregarded the Native Americans, and flouted the Spanish borderlands by breaching the offensive paper barrier.

With Britain now in charge of a generous amount of North America and most of her difficulties with the Native Americans either suspended or suppressed, the commerce in furs and pelts dramatically escalated. In 1765 the total value of those commodities shipped to Britain reached £49,293; an increase of £29,308 over the total for 1760. Of that formidable increase Canada and the Hudson's Bay Company contributed £34, 282.

In 1763, meanwhile, Roger Kelsall and James Spaulding established at Sunbury, Ga., a mercantile empire soon rivalling that of the old-line, independent Charleston traders John Leslie, Thomas Forbes, and William Panton.[119] Panton acquired an interest in Kelsall & Spaulding and subsequently joined Leslie, forming Panton, Leslie & Company.

By 1774 Spaulding was operating from St. Simon's Island and had started two trading stations in East Florida on the St. Johns River around 50 miles apart: one at Astor and the other at Palatka. He later opened a third station in the Alachua country and a fourth at Talahasochte on the Suwannee River in West Florida.[120]

Another consequence of the French and Indian War was that a number of astute British officers serving on the frontier had noted with interest the efficacy of the American rifle and sent a few to Britain for evaluation. The Board of Ordnance was impressed with the accuracy and range of the rifle though its slow rate of fire as compared to the infantry musket convinced them it was unacceptable as a martial firearm.[121]

Significantly, while the Treaty of Paris terminated the war and momentarily halted the posturing of armies larger and more formidable than ever before engaged in North America, the frontier people continued to suffer the unrelenting terror of unconstrained Native American confrontations for another 30-odd years as they attempted to wrest an empire from beyond the despised Proclamation Line, and elsewhere British subjects were troubled by the increasingly totalitarian attitude expressed toward them by the mother country and the economic stranglehold which curtailed colonial commerce and industry.

Thus an irreparable schism was created in the years between 1763 and 1775 when the Lion and Unicorn again came to be challenged by force of arms when a small but determined body of dissident colonists unleashed a cataclysm ultimately shattering the strong chain binding them to the mother country on the anvil of economic and ideological rebellion.

Notes

1. Harold L. Peterson, *Arms and Armor in Colonial America, 1526-1783* (New York, 1956), p. 329 (hereafter cited as *Arms and Armor*).

2. George J. Heckman, President, The Longmeadown (Mass.) Historical Society, supplied the author with a photograph and description of the pistol.

3. Peterson, pp. 329-330.

4. Ibid., p. 330.

5. Ellen Parker, comp. and ed., *Historical Sketch of the Old Powder Magazine, Charleston, South Carolina* (Charleston, 1924 and 1930), p. 5.

6. Ibid.

7. Ibid., p. 6.

8. Colonial Williamsburg, *Colonial Williamsburg Official Guidebook* (Williamsburg, 1968), p. 34 (hereafter cited as *Williamsburg Guidebook*).

9. Howard L. Blackmore, *British Military Firearms 1650-1850* (London, 1961), p. 32.

10. Anthony D. Darling, *Red Coat and Brown Bess* (Ottawa: Museum Restoration Service, Historical Arms Series No. 12, 1970), p. 11.

11. Ibid., p. 21.

12. Ibid., p. 25, n. 11.

13. Ibid., p. 19.

14. Ibid., p. 36.

15. Ibid., p. 15.

16. Birmingham gunmakers Thomas Galton (fl. 1750-1785) and John and Thomas Ketland (fl. 1750-1800) established private proof marks ca. 1750 which came to be used on British contract firearms. The early Ketland mark consisting of a crown over crossed scepters was developed into the official Birmingham Proof House mark and it was used until 1904. The customary proof load ca. 1715 was a single ball and double powder charge. Parliament authorized the Birmingham Proof House by the Act of [July 31] 1813 and operations began on March 16, 1814. A. Baron Engelhardt, "The Story of European Proof Marks," *The Gun Digest* (Chicago, 1954): 160.

17. Darling, pp. 17, 19.

18. Ibid., p. 19.

19. Ibid., p. 24, n. 8.

20. Blackmore, p. 57.

21. Ibid.

22. Ibid., p. 278.

23. Peterson, p. 237.

24. Ibid., p. 235, n. 10.

25. Ibid., p. 231.

26. Ibid., p. 242.

27. Lt. Col. George M. Chinn, USMC, *The Machine Gun,* 3 vols (Washington, 1951), 1:18; also Dudley Pope, *Guns* (London, 1965), pp. 123-129.

28. Chinn, 1:18.

29. "Cornwall," *Steel Labor* (Pittsburgh), January, 1973, p. 10.

30. Scott Graham Williamson, *The American Craftsman* (New York, 1940), p. 204.

31. Ibid.

32. Ibid.

33. Ibid.

34. Cyril Stanley Smith, "Metallurgy—Seventeenth and Eighteenth Centuries," in *Technology in Western Civilization,* Melvin Kranzeburg and Carroll W. Pursell, Jr., ed., 2 vols (New York and London, 1967), 1:161-162.

35. U.S. Census Bureau, *Historical Statistics of the United States (Washington,* 1961), Series Z 131-222. General Note, Table I, p. 746.

36. Ibid.

37. Research in the field of apprentice gunsmiths in colonial America has been seriously neglected though pioneered by Henry J. Kauffman, *The Pennsylvania-Kentucky Rifle* (Harrisburg, 1960), pp. 141-152. Kauffman's investigation, however, is regional, confined to southeastern Pennsylvania, yet it has opened a fascinating area deserving broader study.

38. William E. Woodward, *The Way Our People Lived* (New York, 1965), p. 67.

39. The student and historian again must rely on Kauffman, *The Pennsylvania-Kentucky Rifle,* pp. 152-160, whose research is basic though regional.

40. Robert B. Gordon, "Early Gunsmiths Metals," *American Rifleman* (December, 1959): 32.

41. S. James Gooding, *The Canadian Gunsmiths 1608 to 1900* (West Hill, Ontario, 1962), pp. 32-33 (hereafter cited as *Canadian Gunsmiths*).

42. There are several excellent sources dealing with eighteenth- and nineteenth-century hand tools and the location of tool collections including Brooke Hindle, *Technology in Early America* (Chapel Hill; The University of North Carolina Press, 1966); Eric Sloane, *A Museum of Early American Tools* (New York: Ballentine Books, Inc., 1964); Alexander Farnham, *Tool Collectors Handbook* (Stockton, N.J.: the author, 1972); Elmer L. Smith and Mel Horst, *Early Tools and Equipment* (Lebanon, Pa.: Applied Arts Publishers, 1973); and Vernon S. Gunnion and Carroll J. Hopf. ed., *The Blacksmith, Artisan Within the Early Community* (Harrisburg: Pennsylvania Historical and Museum Commission, 1972). Additional material appears in various issues of *Foxfire* magazine produced by the student body and faculty at Rabun Gap-Nacoochee School, Rabun Gap, Ga., and a series of books based on that publication.

43. Col. Chester Mueller, USA (ret.) and John Olson, *Small Arms Lexicon and Concise Encyclopedia* (South Hackensack, N.J., 1968), p. 235.

44. Ibid.

45. Ned H. Roberts, *The Muzzle-Loading Cap Lock Rifle* (New York, 1940), pp. 260-262.

46. A. Merwyn Carey, *American Firearms Makers* (New York, 1953), p. 31.

47. Col. Robert Gardner, *Small Arms Makers* (New York, 1962), p. 138; Carey, pp. 78, 143.

48. Gardner, p. 138.

49. Carey, pp. 23, 143; Gardner, pp. 42-43.

50. Gardner, p. 43; Henry J. Kauffman, *Early American Gunsmiths 1650-1850* (New York, 1952), p. 20 (hereafter cited as *Early Gunsmiths*).

51. Kauffman, p. 75; Gardner, p. 152, and Carey, p. 95.

52. Hank Wieand Bowman, *Famous Guns From the Smithsonian Collection* (Greenwich, Conn.: Fawcett Publications, Inc., No. 624, 1966), p. 7.

53. Carey, p. 44; Gardner, p. 73.

54. Carey, p. 70.

55. Carey, p. 88; Gardner, p. 143.

56. Carey, p. 96; Gardner, p. 152.

57. Carey, p. 96; Gardner, p. 153.

58. Carey, p. 96; Gardner, p. 152.

59. Carey, p. 46; Gardner, p. 78.

60. Kauffman, p. 29.
61. Carey, p. 14.
62. Carey, p. 138; Gardner, p. 217.
63. Carey, p. 78; Gardner, p. 131.
64. Carey, p. 69; Gardner, p. 115.
65. Carey, p. 27.
66. Carey, p. 43; Gardner, p. 72; Kauffman, p. 34, and *Williamsburg Guidebook,* pp. 42-45.
67. Carey, p. 75; Kauffman, p. 64.
68. Carey, p. 75; Kauffman, p. 65.
69. Kauffman, p. 64.
70. Ibid., p. 65.
71. Ibid., p. 67.
72. Carey, p. 29. Gardner, p. 52, states that Deterer was employed by William Henry, Sr., to work on public arms in 1777-1778.
73. Carey, p. 80; Gardner, p. 134, and Kauffman, p. 68.
74. Carey, p. 1; Gardner, pp. 2-3, and Kauffman, p. 1.
75. Carey, p. 40; Gardner, p. 68.
76. Carey, p. 53.
77. Carey, pp. 105-106; Gardner, p. 164, and Kauffman, p. 79.
78. Carey, p. 103; Gardner, p. 160, and Kauffman, p. 78.
79. Carey, p. 106.
80. Henry J. Kauffman, *The Pennsylvania-Kentucky Rifle* (Harrisburg, 1960), p. 147 (hereafter cited as *Rifle*).
81. Carey, p. 54; Gardner, p. 90; Kauffman, *Early Gunsmiths,* p. 49, and Kauffman, *Rifle,* pp. 256-264, citing Francis Jordan, Jr., *The Life of William Henry* (n.p., 1910).
82. Gardner, p. 89.
83. Frederick Webb Hodge, ed., *Handbook of American Indians North of Mexico,* 2 vols (Washington, 1912), 2:880 (hereafter cited as *Bulletin 30*).
84. Ibid.
85. Carey, p. 90; Gardner, p. 144; also James Grant Wilson and John Fiske, ed., *Appleton's Cyclopaedia of American Biography,* 6 vols (New York, 1888), 4:592.
86. Bluford W. Muir, "The Father of the Kentucky Rifle," *American Rifleman* (Centennial ed., January, 1971): 30; also Robert Held, *The Age of Firearms* (New York, 1957), pp. 138-149.
87. Muir, p. 76.
88. Ibid., p. 30.
89. Joe Kindig, Jr., *Thoughts on the Kentucky Rifle in its Golden Age* (New York, 1961), p. 26.
90. Henry Kinzer Landis and George Diller Landis, "Lancaster Rifles," *The Pennsylvania German Folklore Society* (Lancaster, 1942), vol. 7, pp. 136-137.
91. Kindig, p. 329.
92. Kauffman, *Rifle,* p. 167.
93. Landis, pp. 117-119.
94. Ibid.
95. Charles Edward Chapel, *Guns of the Old West* (New York, 1961), pp. 23-27.
96. John S. du Mont, "American Silver-Mounted Kentucky Pistols," *American Rifleman* (August, 1962): 20-21.
97. Norman B. Wilkinson, "The Pennsylvania Rifle," (Harrisburg: Pennsylvania Historical and Museum Commission, Historic Pennsylvania Leaflet No. 4, 1970): 3.
98. James E. Serven, "Powder Horns With A Message," *American Rifleman* (December, 1960): 34.
99. Landis, pp. 140-142, Plate *d,* depicts a horn with relief carving probably made in Pennsylvania ca. 1780-1800. An early eighteenth century natural horn and a late eighteenth century flat horn, both with relief carving and used in New Spain, are illustrated in Sidney B. Brinckerhoff and Pierce A. Chamberlain, *Spanish Military Weapons in Colonial America 1700-1821* (Harrisburg, 1972), pp. 66-67.
100. Chester A. Jordan, "Powder Horn Recalls Bicentennial History," *The Gun Report* (June, 1975); 12. There are two excellent studies devoted to powder horns: Steven V. Grancsay, *American Engraved Powder Horns* (New York, 1945), and the late Ray Riling's masterful *The Powder Flask Book* (New York, 1956).
101. Carl P. Russell, *Guns on the Early Frontiers* (New York, 1957), pp. 236-237.
102. Landis, pp. 146-148.
103. Wilkinson, p. 4.
104. William Brandon, *The American Heritage Book of Indians* (New York, 1961), p. 217.
105. T.M. Hamilton, *Early Indian Trade Guns: 1625-1775* (Lawton: Contributions of the Museum of the Great Plains, Number 3, 1968): 27, 31.
106. *Bulletin 30,* 2:549.
107. Hamilton, pp. 19, 21, 33.
108. S. James Gooding, "Gunmakers to the Hudson's Bay Company," *The Canadian Journal of Arms Collecting* (February, 1973): 21.
109. Hamilton, p. 27.
110. Gooding, p. 21.
111. Ibid.
112. Ibid., p. 20.
113. Gooding, *Canadian Gunsmiths,* pp. 72, 94, 126, 177 passim.
114. Dale Van Every, *Forth to the Wilderness* (New York, 1962), p. 55.
115. John G.W. Dillin, *The Kentucky Rifle* (Washington, 1924), p. 89; also Russell, p. 103. Chouteau was one of the founders of St. Louis, Mo.
116. Kauffman, *Rifle,* p. 234.
117. Ibid.
118. Stanley Pargellis, ed., *Military Affairs in North America,* 1748-1756 (New York, 1936), p. 115. Pargellis also notes (p. 486) that in 1754 Braddock's ordnance stores included a thousand flintlock muskets with wood rather than iron ramrods and no pan bridle, and another thousand Dutch flintlock muskets with wood ramrods; all intended for Shirley's (50th) and Pepperrell's (51st) Regiment of colonial recruits.
119. Thelma Peters, "The Loyalist Migration from East Florida to the Bahama Islands," *Florida Historical Quarterly* (October, 1961): 123 (hereafter cited as *FHQ*).
120. J.A. Brown, "Panton, Leslie and Company, Indian Traders of Pensacola and St. Augustine," *FHQ* (July, 1959): 329.
121. Kindig, pp. 27, 30.

BOSTON MASSACRE (18th Century, March 5, 1770): Paul Revere's engraving of the Boston Massacre added fuel to an already combustible situation as British Americans chafed under the repressive economic yoke of Parliament and the crown. Courtesy of the New York Historical Society, New York City.

WITH THE CONCLUSION of the French and Indian War on February 10, 1763, the awesome political, military, and economic strength accrued by Great Britain was unreservedly recognized and warily respected by her rivals. There remained, however, conspicuous problems with her vast dominions sheltered beyond the broad Atlantic dominated by the Royal Navy.

While the political administration of British America fell largely to Parliament, economic policy settled upon the First Lord of Trade in the person of Charles Townshend. With a seemingly planned precision abetted by George III and Parliament, Townshend and his successors managed to disrupt completely colonial commerce and deliberately alienate the Americans with a series of oppressive statutes thoroughly trampling what little remained of individual freedom and colonial autonomy; thus creating an atmosphere which conjured forth the rebellious spirit of Nathaniel Bacon from the mouldering dust of the previous century.

The enormous cost of prosecuting the recent war and preserving a defensive posture in British America thereafter continued to be an exorbitant burden which Britain expected the colonies to share and accordingly imposed heavy taxes. The British reaped more protests than taxes and there were also difficulties involved in occupying the former French and Spanish possessions; the restive Native Americans were by no means subdued; and the frontier people began to chafe under tidewater rule and the restrictions imposed on westward expansion by the Proclamation Line.

While many Americans, particularly craftsmen and merchants, openly defied British policy they did not represent the majority. In North Carolina, however, the frontier people unified against tidewater rule stepped beyond the bounds of simple protest in 1768 and took up arms in the War of Regulation. That confrontation was crushed by Royal Governor William Tryon at the Battle of Alamance Creek on May 16, 1771.

There were, however, other flammable incidents.

Generations of solid New England merchants regarded circumventing customs duties as a sacred obligation and it had become a tradition, carried to the extreme by volatile Bostonian John Hancock. On June 10, 1768, Hancock's sloop *Liberty* with its smuggled cargo of Madeira wine was seized. Waterfront riots ensued, customs agents were obtrusively harassed, and on August 1 Hancock and other Boston merchants vowed not to import British goods; a tactic emulated by some Virginians the following year.

Further discontent was nurtured in Massachusetts and it exploded with the rattle of British musketry in Boston on March 5, 1770, shortly after the mantle of prime minister was assumed in London by Lord Frederick North, 2nd Earl of Guilford. News of the Boston Massacre spread like a pox and throughout the colonies there were outraged protests. Indignant Sam Adams made the most of the British blunder and the tragic incident was graphically exploited in a broadside engraved by an ardent member of the Sons of Liberty and one of Boston's finest silversmiths, Paul Revere. Shortly thereafter the first Committee of Safety was organized at Boston.[1]

The now throbbing pulse of American defiance quickened with other incidents. On June 10, 1772, Rhode Islanders taunted the crown when Providence merchant John Brown and several others discovered the British revenue cutter *Gaspée* grounded on a sandbar in Narragansett Bay near Namquit Point. That night as they prepared to board the vessel participant Ephraim Bowen later recalled:

> About 9 o'clock, I took my father's gun and my powder horn and bullets and went to Mr. Sabin's, and found the southeast room full of people, where I loaded my gun, and all remained there till about 10 o'clock, some casting bullets in the kitchen, and others making arrangements for departure, when orders were given to . . . embark.[2]

The Rhode Islanders boarded the *Gaspée,* forced

the crew and captain ashore, confiscated the firearms and gunpowder, and burned the ship to the water-line.

In May, 1773, Lord North attempted to stave off the financial difficulties of the East India Company by placing a three penny tax on imported tea, and Bostonians were further inflamed when Royal Governor Thomas Hutchinson assigned his two sons as managers of the tea monopoly. Disguised as Native Americans, they retaliated on December 16 with the now famous Boston Tea Party subsequently emulated in New York City, Philadelphia, and far away Charleston, S.C.

George III did nothing to ameliorate the explosive situation and ignited another fuze in March, 1774, with the reprehensible Boston Port Act; the first of the so-called Intolerable Acts designed to curb colonial opposition by imposing economic sanctions. As of June 1 Boston's thriving port would be closed to all commerce.

Britain's economic warfare infuriated rather than intimidated the Bostonians and created additional animosity elsewhere. On May 12 the Massachusetts Committee of Correspondence recommended to the other colonies that all trade be suspended with the mother country, effective December 1.

On May 13, 1774, Gen. Thomas Gage arrived in Boston, relieving Gov. Hutchinson, and shortly thereafter four redcoat regiments landed to enforce the Port Act. George III took still another repressive step and nullified the colony's royal charter on the 20th with the Massachusetts Government Act. Four days later the Virginia House of Burgesses was dissolved by Royal Governor John Murray, Earl of Dunmore.

The irate Burgesses met the next day at Ralegh Tavern in Williamsburg and adopted a resolution calling for an intercolonial congress. On June 17 Massachusetts elected delegates to attend the conclave scheduled to begin at Philadelphia on September 5. Once fragmentary, American resistance to imperious British authority was measurably solidified.

As the portentous events transpiring in the seething tidewater settlements drew toward their inevitable conclusion, the frontier people faced the stark terror of Pontiac's Conspiracy and the apathy of crown administrators blithely ignoring their demands for protection from the Native Americans who were justified in considering them intruders under the Proclamation Line agreement.

The Illinois French under British rule founded St. Louis in 1764 and continued to conduct a lucrative Native American trade, though between 1765 and 1766 the French in Nova Scotia (Acadia) were mercilessly uprooted and sent to Louisiana. On March 5, 1766, Don Antonio de Ulloa arrived to become the first Spanish governor of the former French enclave,

his administration largely ineffectual, and the British retained access to New Orleans and the Mississippi River.

Like the Ottawa, the Cherokee recognized the futility of continued hostility toward the crown and ceded most of their land in Virginia and the Carolinas with a treaty concluded at Hard Labor, S.C., on October 14, 1768, while the calculating Iroquoian Confederation relinquished to the British the dominion they controlled between the Ohio and Tennessee rivers with the second Treaty of Fort Stanwix (Oswego, N.Y.), November 5, 1768.

The Iroquois cecession saw Pennsylvania-born Daniel Boone of the Moravian settlement at Bethabara, N.C., exploring the Kentucky wilderness in 1769 and Virginia emigrants establish the Watauga settlement in what is now eastern Tennessee. In June of that year British and American land speculators founded the Vandalia Company, petitioning the Board of Trade in London to purchase 2,400,000 acres in western Virginia and eastern Kentucky.

By 1770 the white and black population of British America had reached an estimated 2,148,076 compared to the 11,935 represented a century earlier.[3] Though most Americans inhabited the coastal settlements, arbitrary and capricious British rule was for many an incentive to move west despite the perils of the frontier.

The character of Spanish Florida gradually changed with the British occupation and the Lion and Unicorn gained only three settlements of consequence: St. Augustine in East Florida with a population of around 3,200 and Pensacola and Mobile in West Florida with a combined populace of approximately 450; two-thirds of them inhabiting Pensacola.

During the 18-month transition to British rule the frontier erupted with several Native American attacks and the majority of the Spaniards decided to abandon La Florida rather than live under British domination. Many of them withdrew to Cuba and the other Spanish possessions in the West Indies, a substantial number relocated in New Spain, and some returned to the mother country.

Throughout the refractory 20-year British occupation, as it had been during the latter part of the first Spanish period, blacks far outnumbered whites in the Florida provinces; most of them slaves who had fled the British colonies and the majority gathered in and around Fort Mosa located approximately three miles north of St. Augustine.

Fearing British reprisals or a return to slavery numerous blacks chose to leave with the Spaniards and they were joined by segments of loyal Apalachees and Yamasees. The British quickly moved to forstall additional problems with the remaining Native Americans, predominantly Creeks and

Seminoles, and attempted to restore their confidence with generous trade concessions negotiated by John Stuart, Superintendent of Indian Affairs for the Southern Department from 1761 to 1779.

Royal officials in *La Florida* soon discovered what their predecessors had early learned and they were equally powerless to cope with it. The subtropical climate proved excessively debilitating and created ideal conditions for the propagation of virulent fevers. Lethal maladies felled private and general and master and slave alike, and while pestilence was rampant in St. Augustine it was pandemic in Pensacola and Mobile.

The pernicious and peculiar institution of slavery was abolished by Great Britain in 1772 yet it remained an integral part of the socio-economic infrastructure in her American colonies, though by no means was it confined to blacks, for after ca. 1650 at least half of the whites arriving in the colonies were subject to some form of bondage either as indentured servants, redemptioners, or apprentices; the latter slavery of a kind because in many instances there was unbridled exploitation.

Though slavery was never abolished in British America, some consideration was given to releasing the blacks remaining in or brought to East and West Florida; particularly in view of their vital economic role and active participation in the defense of the crown dominions, for whether free or slave many of them served in the provincial militia. Consequently the East Florida Slave Code was more liberal than elsewhere and slaves could testify in court, while with written permission from their owners they were allowed to travel and to hunt with and otherwise carry firearms in peacetime.[4]

By 1774 conditions in the tidewater settlements and on the frontier had created an economic and political rupture between Britain and her contumacious child, and while it was not yet complete it was favored by a large number of adherents embracing each strata of society from the "leather aprons" (craftsmen) to the "silk stockings" (professional men). And as American defiance escalated so too did George III attempt to discourage, suppress, or eliminate it.

In Boston on September 1, 1774, four days before Continental Congress convened at Philadelphia, Gen. Gage sent a detachment of regulars to confiscate the two cannon and the gunpowder stored at nearby Charlestown.[5] Shortly thereafter other troops were dispatched to Marshfield, Jamaica Plains, and Salem with similar intentions; the British fearing a planned uprising when the delegates met.[6]

Acting on the king's order in October, Parliament approved a strict embargo on all firearms, firearms components, gunpowder, lead, gunflints, and other war matériel destined for British America; a

move deliberately designed to limit the capacity of the radical Whig element to resist the crown by force of arms.[7] The reaction to the embargo was the immediate acceleration of the infant American armament industry.

On the frontier, meanwhile, Col. Richard Henderson organized the Transylvania Company on August 27, 1774 attracting disgruntled North Carolinians to the recently opened Kentucky wilderness where earlier James and Samuel Harrod of Pennsylvania established Harrodsburg, the first permanent settlement.

In Virginia that summer the northwest settlements were terrorized by Cornstalk's hostile Shawnee. Lord Dunmore was eventually persuaded to take action and Col. Andrew Lewis' mostly untried volunteer frontiersmen, in the desperate Battle of Point Pleasant, shattered the powerful Shawnee at the mouth of the Great Kanawha on October 10, 1774, in what is now referred to as Lord Dunmore's War.

In Philadelphia four days later Continental Congress drafted a Declaration of Rights and Grievances and it was followed on October 20 by a resolution to suspend all commerce with Great Britain on December 1 as suggested by the Massachusetts delegation. Congress adjourned on the 26th after adopting a proposal to reconvene if necessary on May 10, 1775.

On December 14-15, 1774, as relations with Britain steadily deteriorated, aggrieved New Hampshire citizens led by John Sullivan overran the surprised redcoats in Fort William and Mary at New Castle, the entrance to Portsmouth harbor, and confiscated 100 barrels of gunpowder and a large number of martial firearms.[8]

The British and the Americans were distinctly aware of the paramount significance of gunpowder in the event of hostilities. As far as it can be determined, however, there were no powder mills operating in British America on the eve of overt rebellion.[9] The seventeenth-century powder mill established in Massachusetts by Walter Everenden had ceased production ca. 1750. In 1753, however, his son Benjamin started a second mill at Canton, Mass., and operated it until his death in 1766 whereupon his son Abijah continued to run it until ca. 1770 when it was closed.[10]

American privateers and smugglers operating off the coast seized firearms and gunpowder from British merchant ships prior to the outbreak of hostilities.[11] Like the *Gaspée* affair and the Fort William and Mary raid, those measures did little to increase the amount of gunpowder available to the radicals, though they succeeded in further antagonizing the British. The scarcity of gunpowder was so pronounced in Pennsylvania at the end of 1774 that to conserve it Gov. John Penn banned the firing of cannon salutes, small arms, and fireworks in celebrating the New Year.

On March 10, 1775, as tension grew in the tidewater communities, Henderson's Transylvania Company hired Daniel Boone and 30 axemen to cut a road from the Cumberland trace to the Kentucky River—the Wilderness Road—and on the 17th Boone and Henderson negotiated the Treaty of Sycamore Shoals, purchasing from the Cherokees for $10,000 in trade goods 20 million acres between the Cumberland and Kentucky rivers.

As restless spring slowly mounted its assault against the harsh New England winter the shifting winds of change stirred Massachusetts with an aura of expectancy. Despite Lord North's Conciliatory Resolution attempting to appease the Americans, passed by a worried House of Commons on February 27, 1775, Britain's tattered relationship with the colonies continued to disintegrate and Parliament hastened the process with the New England Restraining Act on March 30.

Tottering on the brink of rebellion the 13 American colonies were almost totally unprepared for war. The trenchant oratory of Sam Adams and the tempestuous Virginian, Patrick Henry, had fallen mostly on deaf ears, for despite the intolerable restrictions imposed by Britain on American commerce, industry, and personal liberty at least ⅓ of the colonists remained loyal to the crown and an equal number were uncommitted; a fact little altered throughout the coming conflict.

Not until February 1, 1775, had direct action been taken to ensure adequate supplies of arms and munitions when, meeting at Cambridge, the 2nd Provincial Congress of Massachusetts placed the colony on emergency war footing and revitalized local Committees of Safety; each empowered to mobilize the militia and to confiscate British military stores. Similar committees or councils were organized in the other colonies, some of them after hostilities commenced.

Eighteenth-century British America was basically agrarian, dependent on a brisk commerce with the mother country for manufactured goods. Parliament and the crown had deliberately conspired to preserve that dependence as exemplified by the Iron Act of 1750, thereby limiting technological growth and confining colonial manufacture to widely dispersed household enterprises. The ironmaster, gunsmith, blacksmith, and whitesmith remained the foundation of colonial industry, while the backbone of defense was the militia.

From the beginning, militia service in British America was mandatory and few exceptions were granted. Each colony was responsible for enforcing militia statutes which regulated the frequency of muster and the degree of training. Militia regulations also required each member to supply his own firearm, ammunition, and accouterments, though in wartime they were usually augmented by the colony and the mother country; one of the reasons for the maintenance of armories and magazines.

In the decade following the French and Indian War civilization began to weigh heavily on the eastern settlements and the militia there had not been subjected to any strenuous campaigning. Though there were exceptions like in Massachusetts and Virginia where strong radical sentiment flourished, many tidewater militia units had degenerated into clannish community organizations. Discipline, as it was known to British regulars, had become virtually extinct and muster call served as a social gathering marked more by convivial gossip over generous quantities of grog than the hard, routine work characterizing infantry tactics and musket drill.

Nevertheless, as war clouds ominously gathered, innumerable local militia companies were revitalized, regularly drilled, and their equipment refurbished. The Provincial Congress of Massachusetts went so far as to create special companies, consisting primarily of men under 25, where every fourth man was ordered to be ready for action "at a minute's notice." Minutemen as those young stalwarts came to be known, were the first line of defense, supported by companies of the middle-aged, while the elderly were to be used as home guards.

Unlike most Europeans and despite the lackluster quality of their foot drill, British Americans of whatever occupation were familiar with firearms, for from childhood they had been taught the proper method of handling them whether for amusement, hunting, personal protection, or militia duty. And it was the citizen-soldier, adequately trained or not, who would bear the greatest burden in the demanding struggle to come, for not only was it a war for independence, but also a tragic civil war involving Whig (patriot) and Tory (loyalist) alike; a conflict frequently breaking even the most binding family ties.

With the dawn of April 18, 1775, Bostonians awoke to yet another day of British rule, though before noon a strong rumor began to drift through the narrow, cobbled streets and by midafternoon it reached Hatter's Square and the shop of a gunsmith known only to history as Jasper.[12] Whether Jasper was the first to warn Dr. Joseph Warren cannot be ascertained, though the latter learned that Gen. Gage secretly intended to send a strong British detachment to Concord to confiscate or destroy all of the firearms and other accouterments of war stockpiled there by the dissidents.

Late in the evening a lookout posted in the

steeple of Old North Church flashed a lantern signal revealing the redcoat movement. Dr. Warren of the Committee of Safety dispatched post rider William Dawes and silversmith Paul Revere to arouse the countryside, sparking a cataclysmic upheaval which remains indelibly engraved upon the face of the globe.

In the chill and early hours of April 19, 1775, 700 British troops commanded by corpulent Lt. Col. Francis Smith began their unhesitating march toward a date with destiny at Concord. Leading the hand-picked van of 400 regulars was Maj. John Pitcairn of the Royal Marines.

The 38 minutemen of the Lexington Alarm, commanded by Capt. John Parker, were the first to meet the British and stood ready, blocking the Concord Road. From his position in the militia center Pvt. Sylvanus Wood recalled a British officer who ". . . swung his sword and said, 'Lay down your arms, you damned rebels, or you will all be dead men! Fire!' "

"Some guns were fired by the British at us . . .," Wood continued, "but no person was killed or hurt, [the guns] being probably charged only with powder. Just at this time, Captain Parker ordered every man to take care of himself. The company immediately dispersed, and while . . . dispersing . . ., the British fired and killed some of our men."

"There was," as Wood remembered, "not a gun fired by any of Captain Parker's company within my knowledge. . . ."[13]

Four militiamen fell with the second British volley and Maj. Pitcairn was furious. A subordinate had shouted the order to fire and his own cease fire order was ignored, for as Lt. John Barker of the King's Own (4th) Regiment reported, "The men were so wild they could hear no orders."[14]

Eight militiamen had been killed and ten were wounded. A redcoat received a minor leg wound and Maj. Pitcairn's favorite mount had been twice grazed by musket balls. As the sulphurous powder smoke drifted slowly away on the damp morning air the British regrouped and marched confidently and briskly toward Concord.

Wood, emerging unscathed from the brief encounter, then recalled that he returned to the Lexington Common ". . . and found Robert [Munroe] and Jonas Parker [Capt. Parker's cousin] lying dead . . . near the Bedford Road, and others dead and wounded. I assisted in carrying the dead into the meetinghouse. I then proceeded toward Concord with my gun. . . ."[15]

Pvt. Wood was not alone.

Nervously fingering their flintlock muskets, grim-visaged militia from Acton, Carlisle, Chelmsford, Lincoln, and elsewhere in the aroused Massachusetts countryside converged on Concord and assembled under Col. James Barrett on the heights beyond North Bridge—"the rude bridge that arched the flood."

As the British entered Concord and began searching for rebel supplies, Capt. Lawrence Parsons of the 10th Regiment advanced to North Bridge with seven companies of light infantry to keep an eye on the militia forming on the heights. Leaving two companies at the bridge to guard his rear, Parsons marched with the remainder toward Col. Barrett's farm where Gen. Gage suspected most of the patriot supplies had been concealed.

The militiamen on the heights suddenly detected smoke arising from the town. *The British were burning Concord!* It was then around half-past nine of that electrifying April morning and time for a bold decision. Col. Barrett ordered part of his command forward to protect the town. Crusty Maj. John Buttrick asked Capt. Isaac Davis of Acton if he would be afraid to lead the advance. "No, I am not," Davis coolly replied. "And there isn't a man in my company that is."[16]

The militia stood ready. For most of them this would be their baptism of fire and what next transpired was recorded by one of David Brown's Concord Minutemen, Corporal Amos Barrett:

. . . We then warnt Loded. we wair all orded to Load and had stricked [strict] order not to fire till they fird firs, then to fire as fast as we could. We then marched on. . . . Capt Davis had got, I Be leave, within 15 Rods of the B [ritish?] when they fird 3 gons one after the other. I see the Balls strike in the River on the Right of me. as soon as they fird them, they fird on us. their [musket] balls whisled well. we then was all orded to fire. . . . it is Straing [strange] that their warnt no more kild but they fird to high. . . . we soon Drove them from the Bridge.[17]

The thunderous rebel fusillade saw three redcoats killed and four privates and four officers wounded. The now blooded and bloodied Americans had fared no better. Several were wounded and two were killed, one of them Acton gunsmith Capt. Isaac Davis, the first patriot officer to fall in the War of Independence.[18]

Unlike the Lexington Alarm the rebels at Concord had not faltered. Stunned momentarily, the British suddenly broke and dashed across the bridge for the dubious safety offered by Smith's main body despoiling the town. Rather than mounting a decisive assault on the rebel position, Smith ordered a withdrawal which degenerated into a march of despair as described by Lt. Barker:

. . . we were fired on from all sides, but mostly from the rear, where people had hid themselves in houses till we passed and then fired. The country was an amazing strong one, full of hills, woods, stone walls, etc., which the rebels did not fail to take advantage of, for they were all lined with people who kept an incessant fire upon us, as we did too upon them, but not with the same advantage, for they were so concealed there was hardly any seeing them. In this way, we marched . . . miles, their numbers increasing . . ., while ours was reducing by deaths, wounds, and fatigue; and we were totally surrounded with such an incessant fire as it's impossible to conceive; our ammunition was likely near expended.[19]

The wrath of the Americans flanking the catastrophic British retreat to Boston was unfettered, and neither was outrage confined to men, for an anonymous letter writer disclosed that ". . . even women had firelocks. One was seen to fire a blunderbuss between her father and husband from their windows."[20]

Thus on a convulsive April morning in an aroused Massachusetts countryside the United States of America was conceived in a raw act of violence and gestation was immediate, for that same tumultuous day the once strong umbilicus binding mother England to her lusty offspring was crudely severed, as an infant nation came to be born of blood and fire in the white-hot crucible of revolution.

Significantly, the American Revolution was nearly precipitated in Virginia on the night of April 20-21, for in Williamsburg Gov. Dunmore had ordered the Royal Marines to remove the colony gunpowder supply from the magazine. As in Massachusetts the plan was discovered and the militia called to arms. Patrick Henry and other indignant Virginians angrily demanded either the gunpowder or prompt payment for it.

Lord Dunmore, evading the true issue, declared that he had acted to prevent a "slave insurrection," though he placated the irate populace by making immediate restitution for the powder. Grumbling militiamen disbanded, only to be quickly mustered once more on April 30 when the *Virginia Gazette* boldly announced:

THE SWORD IS NOW DRAWN

The shocking events at Lexington and Concord where embattled Massachusetts farmers ". . . fired the shot heard round the world . . ." created innumerable, nearly insurmountable obstacles for Whig and Tory alike; not the least difficult an insatiable demand for firearms and the other habiliments of war. As news of the tempest in Massachusetts spread, rebels in the other colonies concentrated on seizing British stores, protecting their own negligible supplies, enlisting recruits, and manning long abandoned fortifications.

Before the end of April a rag-tag American "army" surrounded Boston and Generals Artemus Ward, William Heath, and Dr. Joseph Warren established headquarters at nearby Cambridge. Amid the confusion of an army in the making was Benedict Arnold, an aggressive Connecticut militia captain with a decisive plan which had also occurred to New Hampshire rebel Ethan Allen. They proposed to capture Fort Ticonderoga, a vital link in the British defense of the Hudson Valley situated at the juncture of Lake George and Lake Champlain to protect the vulnerable passage to Canada. Arnold, accompanied by Allen and his Green Mountain boys, took the fort on May 10.

That same day in Philadelphia the 2nd Continental Congress met. Many of the delegates were veterans of the savage wilderness campaigns during and after the French and Indian War and they were convinced of the value of the American rifle in warfare. On June 14 they voted to raise ten rifle companies for the fledgling Continental Army: six from Pennsylvania and two each from Maryland and Virginia. The next day they appointed Virginia militia colonel George Washington as commander-in-chief of the Continental Army.

Washington arrived at Cambridge on July 3, nearly 21 years to the day since he had marched out of Fort Necessity in bitter defeat, and began the monumental task of creating a formidable fighting force from factious and fragmented militia and volunteers; most of them wanting for weapons, accouterments, uniforms, food, shelter, confidence, experience and, most of all, cohesive leadership.

With the advent of the American Revolution the British offered freedom to any black slave who entered the king's service and many seized the opportunity, joining Col. Thomas Brown's East Florida Rangers and Lord Dunmore's Ethiopian Regiment; the latter formed in November, 1775. By 1779 1/7 of the East Florida Rangers were blacks.[21] Crown officials were well aware that blacks constituted a major manpower source in the colonies, for one in every six Americans was a black held in bondage, i.e., nearly 500,000.

Though there were some black freedmen in British America the majority were slaves like Crispus Attucks who died in the snowy street with a British musket ball lodged in his belly during the infamous Boston Massacre. While many slaves were employed in the northern colonies, most of them worked on the southern plantations. On June 25, 1776, 11 slaves fled Sabine Hall, the Virginia plantation of Col. Landon Carter, and he indignantly assumed that they had planned to join Dunmore ". . .

for they got privately into Beale's room . . . and took out my son's gun and one I had there."[22]

The poignant question of free or enslaved blacks serving in the Continental Army was a sensitive socio-economic and political issue, noticeably embarrassing to an infant nation struggling for freedom. Congress could not, in the eyes of the world, justify using slaves in the defense of liberty and therefore ruled that blacks would not be acceptable in patriot ranks.

The free blacks already serving at Cambridge and elsewhere, as Washington noted, were ". . . very much dissatisfied with being discarded."[23] He consequently championed their cause and Congress partly acquiesced, declaring that only freemen could serve. All of the colonies except Georgia and South Carolina subsequently provided for black enlistments whether free or slave, compensated owners for their loss, and gave the slaves ". . . their freedom with their muskets . . ." as mulatto soldier-statesman Alexander Hamilton and others had so often and volubly advocated.[24]

Gunpowder: The Imperative Ingredient

The patriots had managed to stockpile a meager 80,000 pounds of gunpowder prior to the conflict and the shortage was particularly acute in the Provincial Army surrounding Boston.[25] Aware that a lack of powder precluded an immediate American attack, Gen. Gage decided to strengthen his position by fortifying Dorchester Heights and the Charlestown peninsula; that latter neck of land dominated by Bunker Hill.

Forewarned of British intentions American forces moved across Charlestown Neck on the night of June 16, 1775, with orders to dig in on Bunker Hill. The patriots inexplicably miscalculated and occupied Breed's Hill, a less imposing eminence, and it was there in the heat of the following day that the savage and bloody engagement known as the Battle of Bunker Hill was fought.

The gunpowder seized by now Col. John Sullivan at Fort William and Mary in December, 1774, was used by the Americans in the maelstrom of Breed's Hill, though it failed to sustain their efforts and the British carried the day in a decidedly Pyrrhic victory. Among the 226 redcoat dead of the 2,250 engaged was Maj. John Pitcairn. All 12 of Gen. Sir William Howe's staff and 80 other British officers were wounded in addition to 1,054 enlisted. Of the approximately 1,500 Americans involved, radical leader Dr. Joseph Warren and 139 others were slain and 271 were wounded.

Though outnumbered at Breed's Hill the principal reasons for the American defeat were a dearth of artillery, bayonets, and gunpowder; the latter reducing the patriot cartridge supply. The scarcity of cartridges, however, was partially responsible for the high British casualty rate because the rebels made every shot count, heeding the sage admonition attributed to flinty old Isreal Putnam of Connecticut who cried, "Hold fire! Wait until you can see the whites of their eyes. Then up—and tear out their bellies! Shoot at their belts, God damn 'em!"[26] Interestingly, the center of the crossed shoulder belts (X) carrying the eighteenth-century soldier's accouterments provided a conspicuous target.

The fact that American losses were light compared to those of the British can be partially attributed to the steep ascent and the solid rebel entrenchments at Breed's Hill, though it cannot be ignored that even among thoroughly trained British regulars there was a propensity to fire too high when shooting uphill; a shortcoming detected at Concord by Cpl. Barrett (see p. 297).

In the wake of Breed's Hill as the New England summer waned the harried commander-in-chief brought a semblance of order to the infant Continental Army, and while the Americans now outnumbered the British blockaded at Boston two to one there was neither sufficient artillery nor powder to oust them, forcing the usually optimistic Washington to admit, "Our situation in the article of powder is much more alarming than I had the most distinct idea of."[27]

Though many volunteers joined patriot ranks without arms or accouterments, others brought their personal firearms and equipment and some of the colonies approved bonuses for the latter, e.g., Connecticut Colony paid £3 to Pvt. Joseph Plum Martin for his ". . . gun, bayonet, cartouche box, and blanket."[28]

The Boston stalemate continued as summer slipped into autumn and autumn bowed to winter. The crucial lack of artillery and gunpowder denied Washington a victory, yet a solution was proposed by a corpulent, 25-year-old former Boston bookseller who had planned and supervised the extensive field fortifications surrounding the British enclave, Col. Henry Knox (1750-1806).

In 1768 Knox at 18 held a Boston Militia commission and found military life agreeable. He was also an avid sportsman, though during a hunt on Noddle's Island in 1773 he lost two fingers of his left hand when the breech of his fowling piece shattered.[29] Always the maverick, Knox embraced the patriot cause and married Lucy Flucker, the daughter of a staunch Tory. He and Lucy fled Boston in the

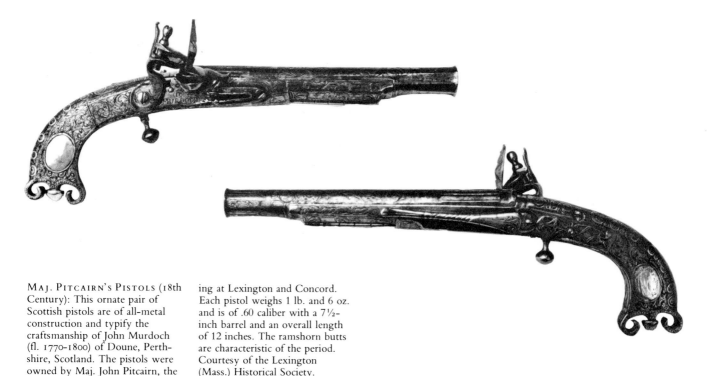

MAJ. PITCAIRN'S PISTOLS (18th Century): This ornate pair of Scottish pistols are of all-metal construction and typify the craftsmanship of John Murdoch (fl. 1770-1800) of Doune, Perthshire, Scotland. The pistols were owned by Maj. John Pitcairn, the British Marine officer command-ing at Lexington and Concord. Each pistol weighs 1 lb. and 6 oz. and is of .60 caliber with a 7½-inch barrel and an overall length of 12 inches. The ramshorn butts are characteristic of the period. Courtesy of the Lexington (Mass.) Historical Society.

confused aftermath of Concord and his courage at Breed's Hill earned him the rank of colonel in the Continental Army; his profession having given him access to the most advanced martial literature of the era which he had discussed with the many British officers visiting his shop.

In early November, 1775, Knox devised a wild scheme to remove the heavy ordnance from Fort Ticonderoga to rectify the lack at Boston. With winter in the offing Washington's staff ridiculed the idea, though its boldness instinctively appealed to the general. Knox salvaged 55 cannon, howitzers, and mortars from the 78 pieces available at Fort Ticonderoga and secured in addition several tons of shot, 2,300 pounds of bullet lead, and 30,000 gunflints.[30]

Loading the vital ordnance on leaky scows, Knox floated it 33 miles down the ice-choked Hudson on the first leg of an incredible 300-mile journey of almost unbearable hardship. Knox considered winter an ally, for he planned to use sleds to transport the big guns. The vagaries of the elements, however, nearly thwarted his tactics because an unexpected thaw rendered the sleds useless. The frontier people of New York and New England came to his rescue with teamsters, wagons, horses, and oxen.

Alternating between sleds and wagons, Knox and his weary, half-frozen, nearly starved men threatened, cursed, cajoled, and nursed the vital cargo through the treacherous wilderness. One cannon was irretrievably lost when crossing the Mohawk River on thin ice though his "noble train of artillery" literally slid across the formidable Berkshires in the dead of winter to reach Westfield, Mass., on January 14, 1776.

A wildly cheering army greeted Knox when he reached Cambridge four days later and he was elated by the news that an American warship had captured the British supply ship *Nancy,* her hold filled with tons of gunpowder.[31] A grateful Washington appointed him chief of artillery and ordnance and it was subsequently approved by Congress with the rank of brigadier general.

In December, 1775, as Knox battled hostile climate and terrain and the patriot assault on Quebec under Gen. Richard Montgomery failed miserably in the cruel Canadian winter, the French agent Bonvouloir covertly approached Congress with an offer to supply unlimited quantities of gunpowder and the equivalent in saltpeter and sulphur. The proposal was apparently the result of earlier efforts pursued by wily Benjamin Franklin, heading a secret committee with £6000 at its disposal, who had contacted French and Netherland officials sympathetic to the rebel cause.

France and the Netherlands were willing conspirators and Spain, with her evident Bourbon tie to France, was equally interested in the clandestine gunpowder traffic, for not only did they stand to reap a handsome profit from the venture, but also saw the American Revolution as a potent threat to Britain's awesome power; a threat that they hoped would weaken her global influence.

Connecticut radical Silas Deane was appointed a confidential agent to France on March 3, 1776, and he conferred secretly with Louis XVI's foreign minister, Charles Gravier, Comte de Vergennes. Vergennes enlisted the aid of Pierre Caron de Beaumarchais, a worldly financier and playwright, to act as an intermediary with Spain through Charles III's foreign minister, Grimaldi.

In May, 1776, the covert American-French-Spanish coalition organized Roderique Hortalez et Cie., a dummy corporation capitalized at one million French *livres,* to channel firearms, gunpowder, and other vital war matériel to the Dutch, French, and Spanish possessions in the West Indies or, in some instances, directly to Spanish Louisiana.[32] The usual practice, however, was to transfer the precious cargos to American blockade runners calling at West Indies ports. Either option was hazardous and grew more perilous as the British strengthened their blockade of patriot ports.

From 1776 to 1779 France and the Netherlands supplied American forces with an estimated 1,500,000 pounds of gunpowder and sufficient ingredients to make another 700,000 pounds.[33] The bulk of the powder and ingredients was contributed by France via the *Régie des Poudres* directed by Lavoisier who was then manufacturing the finest gunpowder in the world.

Dutch, French, and Spanish agents also purchased unknown quantities of gunpowder and its ingredients from other European sources. The Dutch, like the French, shipped firearms and gunpowder to West Indies ports, though most of their traffic was centered at St. Eustatius.

Continental Congress early acted to establish an army, though not until November did it create the complementary maritime forces. On the 10th the delegates "Resolved that two Battalions of Marines be raised . . .," while on the 28th they adopted rules for the regulation of the Continental Navy and on December 22 confirmed as commander-in-chief with the rank of admiral the volatile Rhode Island sea captain and brigadier general of militia, Esek Hopkins.

Fiercely independent, Admiral Hopkins promptly disregarded orders and in February, 1776, sailed directly for the Bahamas to take the war to the enemy with the seven small ships, including his own armed sloop *Providence,* then comprising the entire American fleet. On March 3 Hopkins struck New Providence on Nassau, disembarking 234 marines and 50 sailors in what was the first American amphibious assault on foreign soil.

The landing party attacked Fort Montague and Fort Nassau protecting the harbor, capturing 88 cannon, 15 mortars, 24 casks of gunpowder, and large quantities of shot. The bloodless encounter gave the patriots their first significant maritime victory and made a valuable contribution to the seriously depleted arms chest, for Hopkins also engaged and captured at sea five British ships.

The day before Hopkins had struck New Providence, Washington's artillery opened fire on Boston.

ANTOINE LAURENT LAVOISIER (18th Century): Known as the Father of Modern Chemistry, Lavoisier was appointed director of the *Regié des Poudres* in 1776 and through his experiments with gunpowder he explained combustion as the amalgamation of a burning substance with a part of air that he termed oxygen. In 1790 he was a member of the commission responsible for establishing a uniform system of weights and measures. Courtesy of the *Bibliothèque Nationale,* Paris.

Gen. Howe prudently decided to abandon the city. Evacuation was completed on March 17 and, in addition to their own supplies, the British took with them the 500 Massachusetts militia muskets made by Hugh Orr in 1748.[34]

Despite the vivid exploits of Knox, Hopkins, and others, as well as the promises of foreign agents as yet entirely fulfilled, it was apparent that a domestic gunpowder industry was needed to sustain the war effort. Printing presses throughout the colonies worked overtime, making and distributing broadsides and pamphlets with explicit instructions for manufacturing gunpowder and locating and preparing the ingredients.

Henry Wisner, a New York congressional delegate who later built a powder mill in his native Ulster County, published his 38 page *Essays Upon the Making of Salt-Petre and Gunpowder*, while most colonies either built or financed the construction of powder mills and frequently converted to the task existing grist mills.[35]

Many patriot communities operated charcoal kilns and artificial niter beds, collecting human urine and taking it to a place with dry, sandy soil where it was dumped and eventually leached out small quantities of saltpeter. Barns, stables, chicken coops, dovecotes, and tobacco houses were stripped of droppings and even the earth under compost heaps was processed to recover saltpeter, while also searched were attics, caves, church steeples, lofts, and other bird rookeries. Small amounts of sulphur were recovered from the earth surrounding sulphurous springs and the water was distilled in the quest for that vital commodity.

Early in 1775 Pennsylvania established a Committee for Erecting Powder Mills and subsequently emerged as the center of American gunpowder production, making more than the remaining colonies combined.[36] One of the first to supply the patriots with gunpowder was Oswell (Oswall) Eve who in 1775 started a mill in Philadelphia.[37] Using saltpeter and sulphur supplied by the colony and charcoal locally produced, Eve was paid eight cents a pound for finished powder.

In the Philadelphia area, particularly around Frankfort, there were many swift streams suited to the operation of the water-driven mill machinery and by the end of 1775 at least five powder mills were established in the vicinity and another was built in Dauphin County. Most of the Pennsylvania powder-makers were German immigrants who ". . . knew the art as well as the old women knew how to make soft soap."[38]

Massachusetts decided to revitalize the idle Everenden powder mill in 1775 and the Committee of Safety sent Paul Revere to observe Eve's mill and to ". . . obtain an exact plan of the best constructed powder mill, the quantity of powder that may be made in one day . . ., the expense of the . . . mill, and whether a skilled powdermaker can be obtained."[39]

Early in 1776 Congress authorized the construction of the Continental Powder Mill on French Creek in Chester County, Pa., thereby establishing powder-making on a national level as it was in

France, though not nearly as sophisticated or widespread.[40] The mill was shattered by an explosion shortly after operations began, though it was rebuilt and production continued until September, 1777, when the proximity of the British then engaging Washington at Brandywine forced it to close.

By the end of 1776 American powder mills were operating in every colony except Delaware and Georgia, including one on the Tennessee River. An estimated 200,000 pounds of gunpowder had been made by 1780[41] and, though it was a paltry contribution in light of the exigent demand, it nevertheless illustrated the extensive technological expertise existing in America, and it can be considered an industrial triumph in the face of nearly insurmountable obstacles.

American gunpowder production never reached the point where it could sustain the war effort; an effort doomed to failure from the beginning without generous foreign financial support and military intervention. The mills were beset with disruptive and destructive explosions, escalating inflation, shortages of labor and raw materials, mechanical malfunctions, profiteering and peculation, shut-downs precipitated by British and Tory activity, and the harsh reality of capture as happened on September 26, 1777, when Charles Cornwallis' redcoats entered Philadelphia.

Oswell Eve, like many patriot powder-makers receiving a fixed price for their product, was equally plagued by inflation and to preserve his small profit he began to cut corners. Increasing complaints from field commanders about the poor quality of Eve's powder reached Congress and on June 7, 1776, a committee was appointed to investigate.[42]

On August 28 the committee suggested that state-appointed inspectors should be assigned to the mills with orders to mark all acceptable gunpowder with the letters U S A to denote quality.[43] The probe, however, failed to establish Eve's culpability in the matter of the adulterated gunpowder and he continued to operate until late 1778 when, branded a traitor for collaborating with the British, his property was confiscated and sold.[44]

The ubiquitous gunpowder shortage plaguing Continental forces in the eastern war theatre was doubly evident on the western and southern frontier where virtually every settlement was vulnerable to the British-inspired Native Americans raiding from their almost inaccessible wilderness villages and equally remote British forts.

Though veteran Native American agent Sir William Johnson had died in 1774, British influence among the Iroquois and other nations was preserved by his son and nephew as well as his protege, the Mohawk Pine-tree chief Thayendanegea also known as Joseph Brant. Excepting the neutral Oneida and

JOSEPH BRANT, Mohawk name THAYENDANEGEA (18th Century, 1742-1807): This full-length portrait (opposite) by William Berczy (1744-1813) depicts the Mohawk leader in native dress, armed and accoutered with a rifle, powder horn, and bullet bag. Loyal to the British, he participated in the Cherry Valley massacre (1778) and subsequently ravaged New York's Mohawk Valley with Butler's Rangers. Courtesy of the National Gallery of Canada, Ottawa.

the Tuscarora who had joined the Iroquois in 1726 after the British had driven them from their Carolina domain, the Six Nations comprising the Iroquoian Confederation followed the wily Brant and were supported by the aggressive Delaware, Mingo, Shawnee, and Wyandot.

The Cherokees had not forgotten the depredations of the American frontiersmen despite the Treaty of Hard Labor, and the majority fought for the British, though Attakullaculla (Little Carpenter) embraced the patriot cause with 500 warriors.[45] The powerful Creeks and Seminoles also favored the British, primarily because trade goods were plentiful in East and West Florida.

The British continuously funneled war matériel to the Native Americans from their northern bases at Detroit, Mackinac, Oswego, and Niagara as well as their southern bases at Baton Rouge, Manchac, Mobile, Natchez, Pensacola, and St. Augustine. At Oswego, in a policy doubtlessly implemented elsewhere, Native Americans opposing the patriots were given a bonus consisting of a firearm, a tomahawk, gunpowder, a brass kettle, clothing, and unspecified amounts of currency.[46]

Against that awesome array of Native American might the Appalachian frontier could muster little more than raw courage and two towering figures whose individual and indefatigable efforts relieved a catastrophic frontier situation which could have placed Washington in the precarious if not impossible position of fighting a three-front war. The first was George Morgan, patriot agent to the Native Americans who demands and deserves a more detailed treatment by historians, and the second was George Rogers Clark.

While George Morgan sealed the front door of the Appalachians to a major British-Native American threat, Clark effectively blocked the rear entrance, permitting Washington to concentrate on mounting British pressure in the east. What the cunning and ruthless Brant was to the Native Americans supporting the British, the equally shrewd and ruthless Clark was to the frontier people.

And it was Clark's thin but determined line of buckskin-and-homespun-clad American riflemen who valiantly withstood eight years of unremitting frontier warfare, waged six victorious wilderness campaigns under the most adverse conditions, prevented the hostiles from invading and ravaging the populous eastern settlements as well as attacking the exposed flanks of the weary Continentals, participated in the only successful invasion of British territory by patriot forces, and procured for the infant United States a claim to all the land spread between the Appalachians and the Mississippi River; an unprecedented achievement never again surpassed on the American frontier.

For Clark it began in the summer of 1775 when he found himself in the same position as Washington at Cambridge: gunpowder, that essential ingredient of warfare, was in extremely short supply. Hurrying to Williamsburg, he convinced the council that the fate of Virginia rested upon the safety of Kentucky and the settlements there could be protected only if sufficient gunpowder was made available.

The Virginia Council reluctantly parted with 500 pounds of gunpowder and arranged for its shipment to Fort Pitt.[47] Clark promptly informed his Kentucky associates that they could pick up the powder there. The message, however, miscarried and the powder waited unclaimed until Clark learned of the delay and went to Fort Pitt after it. His troubles began when he left Fort Pitt on the hazardous 400-mile trip down the Ohio River to Kentucky.

Pursued by a mixed band of hostiles led by renegade Mohawk warrior Pluggy, Clark was forced to bury the gunpowder in five caches in the vicinity of Limestone Creek and hurry overland with his small party to seek help from Harrodsburg. Some of the men dropped out at McClelland's Station on the Great Buffalo Trace as Clark and the remainder went on. In the interim a survey party reached McClelland's, and Clark's men persuaded them to help recover the powder; the enormous risk superseded by dire necessity.

Returning to McClelland's with James Harrod and a strong party of Kentuckians, Clark learned that the recovery expedition had been ambushed on Christmas Day, 1776. Harrod, fearing the worst, quickly returned to defend his station from Pluggy's marauders and Clark stayed to help John McClelland. Shortly thereafter Pluggy attacked and was met with a furious defense which saw both McClelland and the Mohawk leader slain. The war party momentarily withdrew and Clark, outnumbered and anticipating another assault, abandoned McClelland's and made for Harrodsburg.

Harrod, meanwhile, had sent Simon Kenton, Benjamin Linn, Samuel Moore and several others to scout Pluggy's advance. They returned with the news that Harrodsburg was no longer threatened. Assembling 30 volunteers, Harrod led them on a circuitous route to Limestone Creek, located the five caches, and cautiously returned to his station with the vital gunpowder on January 2, 1777.

No less harrowing than Clark's adventure were the exploits of Virginia militia lieutenant William Linn, Benjamin's older brother. In July, 1776, Linn left Fort Pitt with George Gibson and 15 others to pick up 98 barrels of gunpowder at New Orleans which had been purchased from the Spaniards by Virginia agents.[48]

Linn, like Clark, reached his objective to find his party under British surveillance. Gibson, aware of the consequences if the mission failed, had himself arrested on charges of violating Spanish neutrality. The ruse confused the British and Linn's party slipped out of New Orleans on September 22 disguised as Spanish traders.

Again braving the perils of the Mississippi and eluding the hostiles, Linn reached Wheeling (now W. Va.) on May 2, 1777. He and his men had been gone nearly 11 months, traversed almost 4,000 miles of inhospitable wilderness, and delivered intact five tons of desperately needed gunpowder to a frontier then held in the frenzied grip of a terrifying Native American-Tory onslaught.

Clark also took advantage of the covert American-Spanish arrangement, for most of the gunpowder and other supplies used in his spectacularly successful 1778-1779 campaigns against Kaskaskia, Cahokia, and Vincennes in the remote, British-dominated Illinois coutry were procured at New Orleans; purchased in part with $74,087 in secret funds contributed by Bernardo de Galvez (1746?-1786), appointed governor of Spanish Louisiana in 1777.[49]

Of the numerous, literally "hair-raising" exploits performed by patriot frontiersmen in procuring sufficient gunpowder to defend the exposed wilderness settlements, few entailed a more personal risk as that experienced by a member of the storied Zane family who first crossed the mountains in 1769 to settle on the Ohio River at the mouth of Wheeling Creek where now stands Wheeling, W. Va.

The brothers Andrew, Ebenezer, Jonathan, and Silas Zane first built a log blockhouse to protect their station and it was subsequently expanded into a stockade known as Fort Henry, for several years the western-most outpost in Virginia and prior to the Revolutionary War it had withstood two major Native American assaults.

On September 11, 1777, the Zane enclave was struck again, this time by Tory frontiersman Simon Girty and a mixed band of 400 Native Americans. Among the 40-odd frontier riflemen defending the stockade were Silas and Ebenezer Zane and the latter's young sister Elizabeth, home from a Philadelphia finishing school.

Toward the end of the three-day siege the defenders were reduced to 12 riflemen in dire need of gunpowder. Ebenezer remembered a keg of gunpowder stored in a cabin approximately 60 yards from the stockade, yet for anyone to attempt to retrieve it was nearly impossible because Girty's band had an unobstructed field of fire across the clearing in front of the cabin. Ebenezer called for a volunteer. Aware that the loss of even one experienced rifleman could jeopardize the survival of all, 16-year-old Betsy Zane stepped forward.[50]

Barefoot and stripped to her petticoat in order to run faster, Betsy suddenly burst from the stockade and dashed across the clearing to the isolated cabin. Caught by surprise at the sight of a young woman ostensibly fleeing the stockade, Girty's marauders failed to fire a shot. A hot spate of rifle fire from the blockhouse attempted to pin the Native Americans down as Betsy, the powder keg clasped tightly to her breast, dodged a deadly gantlet of lead to reach safety. The grim defenders held on and the following day Girty and his band fled when 40 mounted riflemen arrived.

The Quest for Firearms

As Walter Millis has noted, 1776 saw more patriots under arms than any of the war years and even then only an estimated three percent of the American populace served, i.e., 89,661 including 49,901 Continentals, 26,000 state troops, and 16,700 short-term militia. As the conflict progressed the figures steadily declined, for in 1780 an estimated 43,076 were in patriot ranks, or approximately 1.5 percent of the population.[51] Thus it can be safely said that the American Revolution was sustained by an active minority in the military, government, commerce, and industry.

The diligent American effort expended to procure gunpowder was paralleled in the quest for firearms. Reliable estimates indicate that only ⅓ of the firearms employed in British America at the outset of hostilities were produced domestically; the bulk of the remainder imported from the mother country and an even smaller percentage procured from Germany, the Netherlands, and elsewhere on the Continent.[52] Significantly, most of those sources had been curtailed by the 1774 arms embargo, and patriot forces consequently embraced any firearms in shooting condition.

The majority of the Americans involved in the conflict, Whig and Tory alike, were poorly trained and equipped in comparison to British regulars. Though required by militia regulations to possess a suitable firearm, many patriots had weapons which did not conform to martial standards and, of the martial firearms available, it was found that large numbers of them were obsolescent or obsolete, while some were in need of repair.

Most of the firearms in the hands of the militia or seized by the patriots at the beginning of the conflict were British martial patterns and to those were added a small number of French martial firearms, captured relics of the French and Indian War which had been stored in colony armories and maga-

FOWLING PIECE (ca. 1775): Many local militia units reported for duty with non-martial firearms like this fowling piece emulating the pattern of the American rifle with its long barrel and full-length, pin-fastened stock. The 45½ inch barrel is a .75 caliber smoothbore. Furniture is brass and the ramrod is secured by two thimbles and a guide.

The design and beautifully figured grain of the stock of the fowling piece depicted indicates that it was made in Pennsylvania. Note (right) the rifle-type side-plate. The absence of a patchbox and the half-round barrel suggests the firearm was originally a fowling piece rather than a rifle which was rebored for the use of shot. Courtesy of the Morristown National Historical Park, Morristown, N.J. Charles L. Maddox, Jr., photographer.

zines for emergency use. A 1776 Pennsylvania Council of Safety report noted that because of the wide variety of firearms represented in the ranks of some militia companies as many as seven kinds of ammunition were required.[53]

In the principal combat theatre where warfare was basically orthodox, the venerable smoothbore musket with its socket bayonet was preeminent. On the frontier, however, the musket had been largely though not entirely displaced by the American rifle, and rifles were used by patriot and loyalist forces, some *jäeger* units incorporated with George III's Hessian auxiliaries, and small detachments of British regulars serving as special marksmen. Native Americans also used rifles, though for the most part they were given martial firearms by the belligerents seeking their assistance, or they employed various kinds of flintlock trade fusils.

Few pistols were domestically produced, for cavalry generally performed a minor role in the Continental Army, operating primarily in the southern campaigns, and preferred the carbine and blunderbuss to the sabre and the pistol. The need for pistols in the small but demonstrative Continental Navy was also slight and, in any event, there was subsequently an abundance of captured or imported British, Dutch, French, German, and Scottish pistols available. Also found in negligible quantities in patriot ranks were carbines, blunderbusses, musketoons, grenade launchers, and either rifled or smoothbore wall guns; most of them captured or imported, though small quantities were made domestically.

Gen. Washington's bold but disastrous New York campaigns in the latter part of 1776 resulted in a vast number of men and arms captured and both were extremely difficult to replace. In some instances the British confiscated militia firearms as happened at Boston (see p. 301).

The shortage of firearms remained a crucial factor in patriot ranks even as late as the desolate winter of 1777-1778 when the ragged remnants of Washington's army licked its wounds at Valley Forge, Pa., after suffering heavy losses at Brandywine (September 11, 1777) and Germantown (October 4), while Gen. Anthony Wayne's defeat at Paoli, Pa. (September 20), saw the British capture a major Continental supply depot.

Arriving at Valley Forge from Prussia early in 1778 and appointed inspector general of the Continental Army in February, a perturbed Baron Friedrich Wilhelm Ludolf Gerhard Augustin von Steuben (1730-1794) complained that ". . . muskets, carbines, fowling pieces, and rifles were found in the same company."[54]

A bewildering array of weaponry, combined with a harsh winter and distinct language barrier,

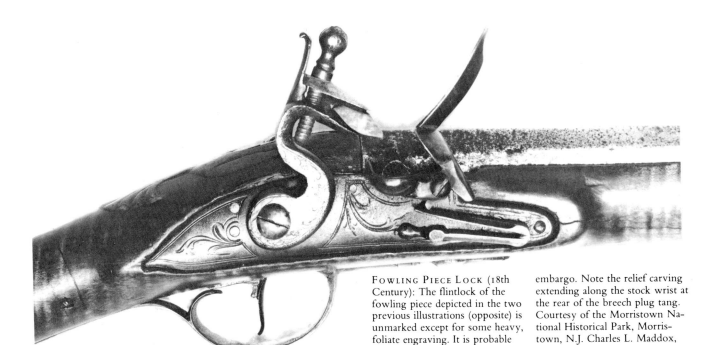

FOWLING PIECE LOCK (18th Century): The flintlock of the fowling piece depicted in the two previous illustrations (opposite) is unmarked except for some heavy, foliate engraving. It is probable that the lock was imported from Germany prior to the 1774 arms embargo. Note the relief carving extending along the stock wrist at the rear of the breech plug tang. Courtesy of the Morristown National Historical Park, Morristown, N.J. Charles L. Maddox, Jr., photographer.

made Steuben's immediate task of welding the battered rebels into an effective fighting force extremely difficult; yet in a few gruelling, anxious months he performed the remarkable if not miraculous feats of reorganizing the army, immeasurably improving discipline, instilling a sense of pride in the forlorn and demoralized ranks, and teaching them that the bayonet could be more gainfully employed as an offensive weapon than as a convenient spit for roasting what little meat came their way.

Under Steuben's salty tongue and experienced tutelage the Americans also gained confidence in their tactical movements, as well as a startlingly improved proficiency in loading their muskets. As 2nd Lt. George Ewing of the Third New Jersey Regiment noted in his diary on April 7, 1778:

This forenoon the Brigade went through the maneuvers under the direction of Baron Steuben. The step is about halfway betwixt slow and quick time, an easy and natural step, and I think much better than the former. The Manual [of arms] also is altered by his direction. There are but ten words of command, which are as follows:

1. Poise Firelock
2. Shoulder Firelock
3. Present Arms
4. Fix Bayonets
5. Unfix Bayonets
6. Load Firelock
7. Make Ready
8. Present
9. Fire
10. Order Firelock[55]

Steuben's simplification of musket drill, reducing by more than half the 21 commands normally given, was based on previously devised Prussian drill (see p. 149) and eliminated much of the former confusion accompanying the tedious routine because the words were readily understood by most of the untutored ranks; especially immigrants unfamiliar with English and unaccustomed to firearms of any kind.

Committee of Safety Firearms

It was not as though the Americans had entirely neglected to provide for the manufacture of firearms, for with war an inescapable fact in April, 1775, the various Committees of Safety (COS) drafted additional powers designed to stimulate the expansion of domestic arms-making and implement the procurement of firearms, munitions, and other war matériel from domestic and foreign sources either by contract or purchase from the open market. Neither can it be ignored that a profitable clandestine commerce emerged, dealing in a variety of stolen weapons and equipment.

In essence the COS were the solid link in an otherwise weak and rather long chain binding an infant, homespun, widely dispersed, and distinctly disorganized American industry to the myriad, burgeoning demands of an equally fledgling military establishment hastily created to meet an emergency situation.

Pl. III.
27
28
29
30
31
32
33
34
35
36
37
Art Militaire Exercice

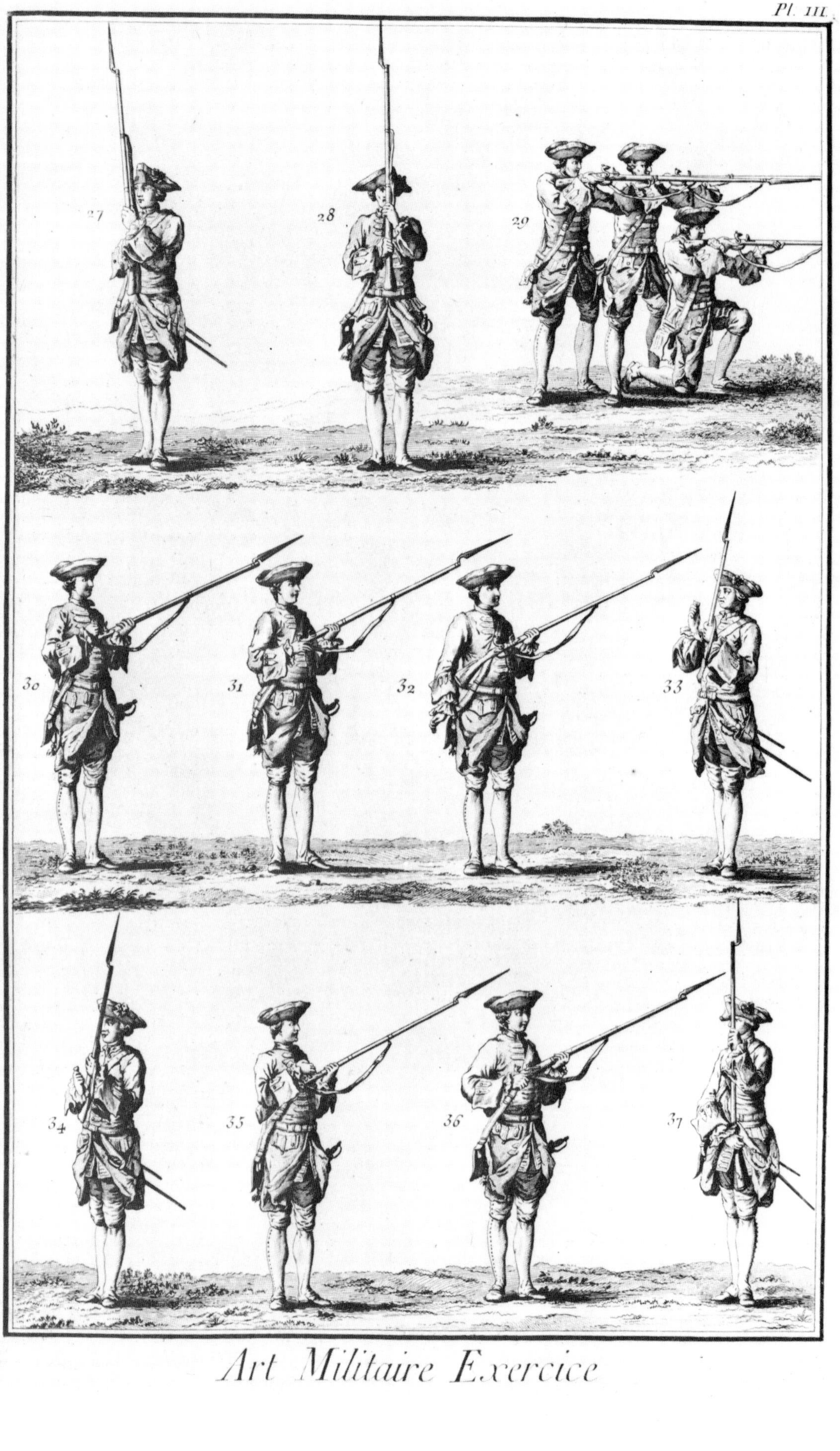

MUSKET DRILL (18th Century): This plate from Diderot's *L'encyclopédie* depicts French infantry musket drill. Figures 27 & 28 show the primed and loaded musket poised. Figure 29 illustrates the infantrymen prepared to fire, presenting their muskets. Figures 30, 31, 32, 33 (cartridge in hand), 34, 35 and 36 depict the infantryman priming the lock, while Figure 37 shows the musket in poised position prior to loading the powder and ball. The musket lock was normally primed first; thus ensuring sufficient powder for loading. Courtesy of Eleutherian Mills Historical Library, Wilmington, Del.

Despite numerous difficulties and shortcomings the various COS acquitted their purpose with efficiency and dispatch, and they can be regarded as the single, most significant factor in organizing eighteenth-century American industry; thus preparing the foundation for the future techonomic development of the United States.

Documentary evidence indicates that COS did not authorize any arms contracts prior to Lexington and Concord, consequently the firearms and other weapons produced under COS direction can be presumed to have been made between late April, 1775, and the latter half of 1778 when most COS functions had been absorbed by comparable agencies within the then newly formed state governments.

Though deeply involved in procuring all manner of essential war matériel, COS devoted considerable time and effort in contracting for muskets and rifles. To date, however, no pistol contracts or pistols have emerged indicating COS origin. Martial muskets produced under COS contract generally emulated the contemporaneous British Short Land or Short Land, New Pattern, muskets simply because the design was familiar to most patriot gunsmiths.

There are indications, however, that muskets of a kind as yet unidentified might have been supplied to COS contractors to use as pattern pieces though the majority of the COS muskets produced before and after November, 1775 followed the specifications then adopted by Continental Congress:

Resolved, That it be recommended to the several Assemblies or conventions of the Colonies respectively, to set and keep their gunsmiths at work, to manufacture good firelocks, with bayonets; each firelock to be made with a good bridle lock, ¾ of an inch bore [.75 caliber], and of good substance at the breech, the barrel to be 3 feet 8 inches in length, the bayonet to be 18 inches in the blade, with a steel ramrod, the upper loop thereof to be trumpet mouthed; that the price to be given be fixed by the Assembly or convention, or Committee of Safety of each Colony. . . .[56]

In May, 1775, Massachusetts COS contractors were paid £ three each for a musket complete with ramrod and bayonet, i.e., a stand.[57] Early in the war the average cost of a stand in most colonies was $12.50 though as hostilities progressed costs generally escalated. By March, 1776, inflation raised the price of a stand in Lancaster, Pa., to £4/15s (see p. 310).

Only Pennsylvania rivalled Massachusetts in firearms manufacture and throughout the American Revolution no other colony approached either in the number of COS contract muskets or the variety of

firearms otherwise produced, and Pennsylvania made at least 90 percent of all long rifles. Parenthetically, production figures for domestic firearms made during the conflict exist only in fragmentary form because much of the documentation was either lost to enemy action or the ravages of the intervening years.

Pennsylvania was heavily involved in COS musket production and in the seven-month period from October 1, 1775, to April 30, 1776, contractors in 11 counties were ordered to make 4,500 stands, i.e., an average of approximately 643 muskets per month which, if production levels had been sustained, would have yielded around 7,716 muskets annually; a singularly unimpressive figure.[58]

As with all firearms then made there were conspicuous variations, though not all of them were related to the idiosyncrasies of the gunsmith, for COS specifications deviated considerably as each committee or council recommended what it deemed suitable, while production was also effected by wartime exigencies.

Most COS muskets conformed to the 1775 Congressional specifications, though in Massachusetts barrels were an inch longer.[59] The barrels of Maryland COS muskets were two inches shorter and the bayonet had a 17-inch blade.[60] Connecticut COS muskets had barrels two inches longer, though the bayonet blade was shortened to 14 inches.[61] As far as it can be determined, Rhode Island did not award COS contracts either within the colony or elsewhere, relying on open market purchase or firearms run through the blockade.[62]

Of whatever origin COS muskets usually displayed 42 to 46 inch, round iron barrels of .75 caliber either browned or finished bright and pin-fastened to walnut or, infrequently, maple stocks. Furniture was iron though brass was used when available. Prewar British or continental European locks were preferred and they were generally superior to domestic specimens. Shortages often dictated the use of single bridle locks instead of the stronger and more reliable double bridle variety. Locks of any kind were difficult to procure early in the conflict.

Firearms manufacture, like powder-making, was fraught with obstacles throughout the war. Raw material shortages curtailed production and inflation escalated costs. There was a lack of skilled labor because many artisans sought more remunerative employment outside the industry or they had been recruited for military service. Limited financing restricted the construction of new facilities or the expansion of existing works. Distribution was hampered by poor or non-existant roads and there was a lack of transport for basic materials and the finished product. Theft, fraud, and peculation were rampant, while of paramount concern was the ubiquitous

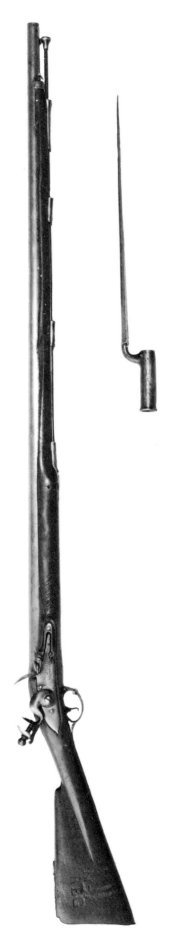

COMMITTEE OF SAFETY
MUSKET & BAYONET (ca. 1775):
On June 13, 1775, Henry Watkeys
(fl. 1770-1792) and Robert Boyd
of New Windsor, Ulster Co.,
N.Y., received a COS contract
for 1,000 muskets at £3/15s each.
The stock of this specimen is
branded N-Y REG in two lines and
though the lock is marked WAT-
KEYS beneath the pan the signature is believed to be spurious.
Courtesy of the Smithsonian Institution, Washington, D.C.

threat of British and Tory interference. Not only did
the destruction of vital arms-making installations
and machines impair or totally halt production, but
the capture of finished or partially finished weapons
and the capture or death of skilled craftsmen presented a series of blows from which an already over-
burdened armament industry could not hope to
recover.

On February 9, 1776, James Pollock and Samuel
Laird of the Carlisle, Pa., COS, wrote to Benjamin
Franklin then serving as president of the Pennsylvania COS, that "... we have engaged a number of
workmen to complete the full complement of
Muskets by the 1st of April next, for which we have
taken their obligations, with sufficient security [a
deposit or bond forfeited if the makers failed to fulfill
their contracts]. We have also done all in our power
to urge the workmen to their duty and Interests, but
some difficulties attended them, *particularly on account of the gun locks, which are not to be purchased at any
rate.*"*63

Also in Pennsylvania, where to meet the inordinate demand many riflesmiths were engaged in
musket-making, inflation was a primary concern as
exemplified in a letter sent to the Pennsylvania COS
by the Lancaster COS on March 16, 1776:

... We are apprehensive of meeting with
many obstacles in making ... a new contract.
Our workmen universally complain that the
sums already fixed [for muskets] are inadequate
to their Labours; *that the Sacrifice they made in
quitting their rifle business* is greater than they can
well bear without some equivalent ... [and] ...
they cannot in Justice to their families, provide
the muskets and bayonets at a less sum than £4
10s or £4 15s. We are very sensible that their
observations ... are not without foundation....64

Samuel Kinder and James Walsh, Philadelphia
gunlock-makers, also complained of escalating
prices and shortages of tools and materials in a letter
to the Pennsylvania COS in December, 1776:

... Files are now double what they have been,
and some treble; Vices, double; Steel, scarce any
to be found good; 30 to 40 shillings advance on
one hundred Bushels of Coal [see p. 239]; Journeyman's wages still rising; your Petitioners
limited; and the enormous Price of every other
necessity, too well known to trouble your
honors with a repetition....65

Of the approximately 500 known patriot gun-
smiths active in the various colonies (see APPENDIX
IX), at least 27 percent were COS contractors like
partners Henry Watkeys and Robert Boyd of New
Windsor, Ulster County, N.Y., who on June 13,
*Italics added.

1775, agreed to make 1,000 stands of muskets for the New York militia at £3/15s each.[66]

Samuel "Deacon" Barrett (1726-1800) of Concord, Mass., was also a COS musket contractor and at Cambridge the *New England Chronicle* of December 14, 1775, reported "We hear from Concord that a fine laboratory for gunmaking is set up there by Deacon Barrett, where every branch of the business is carried on. As the laboratory has the advantage of a stream, the boring, grinding, and polishing is performed by water."[67]

Documentary evidence indicates that each colony established a COS to which those within the colony were subordinate; thus opening lines of communication which fostered coöperation and the exchange of vital information concerning the armament industry, e.g., if a local COS required certain materials or firearms components which another possessed in abundance, transfer or swap arrangements could be made.

Colony COS frequently subsidized local COS and independent manufacturers. On December 5, 1775, gunsmith Samuel Wigfal of Philadelphia was advanced £100 by the Pennsylvania COS ". . . to enable him to prosecute the Business of Gun Lock Making . . ." and he received a contract to make 200 locks at 22s/6d each, to be delivered within three months.[68] Marmaduke Blackwood of Philadelphia received a similar contact though he was given six months to deliver the locks.[69]

The American rifle was also produced under COS contract, though rifle contracts were fewer in number than those for muskets. Pennsylvania riflesmiths in the Reading vicinity were especially fortunate, for pre-forged and pre-bored barrel blanks were readily available from the many mills operating along Wyomissing Creek (see p. 272), and when domestic firearms manufacture became mandatory with the onset of the American Revolution the barrel boring and welding mills were a boon of incalculable economic significance. The time saved with mill production increased the output of the rifle-maker and considerably diminished costs when wartime exigencies escalated labor and material expenditures.

In 1775 John Yost (Youste) of Georgetown, Md., received a COS musket and rifle contract, making the former for £4/5s and the latter for £4/15s each.[70] Gunsmith and expert engraver John Young of Easton, Pa., received a COS contract with Adam Foulkes to make 130 rifles in April, 1776.[71] Henry Young, John's brother, operated a gunsmithery ". . . in a large, one-story, stone building, near where the road crosses the northern boundry of Easton, going over Chesnut Hill."[72]

COS firearms contractors performed a vital techonomic role and in the first stages of the conflict
*Italics added.

it was of paramount significance, for they were the only domestic source in most instances and remained so until the infant states were able to establish and operate their own arms-making facilities. Manufactured early in the conflict, only a few COS firearms survived the vicissitudes of combat and cannibalization.

Independent and State Gun Factories

Virginia was among the first of the former British colonies to establish a public arms-making facility when the council approved the Act of July 4, 1775, and instructed Gen. Washington's brother-in-law Col. Fielding Lewis and Maj. Charles Dick ". . . to form, establish and conduct a Manufactory of Small Arms . . ." at Fredericksburg on the Rappahannock River.[73]

Known as the Virginia State Gun Factory, the Fredericksburg Gun Factory, and the Public Gun Factory, it was primarily supervised by Maj. Dick who was appointed director in 1781. Col. Lewis and Maj. Dick used their personal funds to help finance the installation which made muskets, bayonets, and small quantities of gunpowder; the latter probably used for proof testing.[74]

Col. Lewis resigned his position in 1781 and his son John assumed his duties. In 1782 the factory employed 19 workmen and five apprentices. By February, 1783, when increased production and an abundance of captured and imported firearms had created a diminishing demand, the number of employees was reduced to three.

Located at Falmouth across the river from the Virginia State Gun Factory was Rappahannock Forge, established in 1732 and operated in 1775 as the Hunter Iron Works by the brothers David and James Hunter. On September 28, 1776, the Virginia Council requested that David Hunter and Peter Light:

Appear in Council and Contract with the Board, to furnish, for the use of the State, two hundred Stand of Arms, to consist each of a good Musket, three feet eight inches in the barrel, three-quarters of an inch bore, steel rammers, the upper thimble trumpet-mouthed, the lower thimble with a spring to retain the ramrod, bridle lock, brass mounting, a Bayonet eighteen inches blade, with scabbard, one pair of bullet moulds to mould sixteen bullets to every forty guns; a priming wire and [pan] brush to each Musket; the Stand Compleat, well fixed & properly proved, to be delivered at Williamsburg at 6 pounds Virginia Currency each.[75]

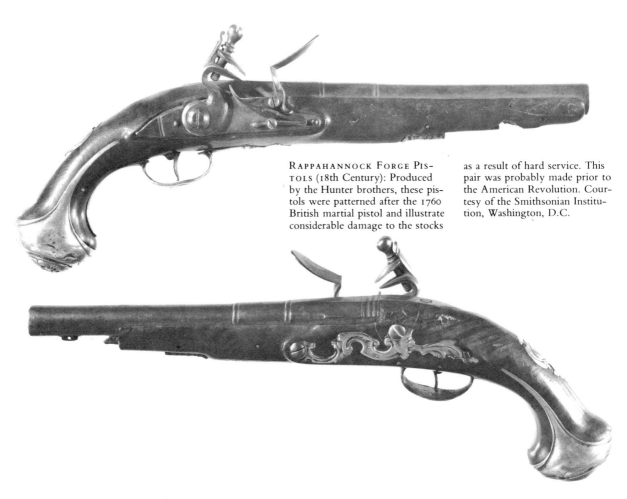

RAPPAHANNOCK FORGE PIS-
TOLS (18th Century): Produced
by the Hunter brothers, these pistols were patterned after the 1760
British martial pistol and illustrate
considerable damage to the stocks
as a result of hard service. This
pair was probably made prior to
the American Revolution. Courtesy of the Smithsonian Institution, Washington, D.C.

James Hunter also made contract muskets and David apparently received an additional contract, for on June 25, 1777, the Virginia Council ". . .agreed to take all the Muskets compleatly fitted which he [David Hunter] can make within Twelve Months of this time and allow him the price of £8 for each, providing they shall be as well filed and finished as those formerly purchased by this Board of the said James Hunter."[76]

The Hunter brothers also made cavalry pistols and carbines, camp kettles, spades, and shovels. They did not, as some historians have asserted, produce pistols for the Commonwealth of Pennsylvania.[77] They did, however, recruit a few Pennsylvania rifle-smiths and make rifled wall guns of which only four are known to currently exist; one with an octagonal barrel.[78]

The overall length of those massive, flintlock wall rifles fluctuates between 61 and 61 and ½ inches, while barrels are between 44 and ¼ and 44 and 5/16 inches with caliber ranging from one and 1/16 inch to one and 3/16 inch. The bores were rifled with 12 or 13 lands and grooves and a front and a rear sight are provided. The full-length, pin-fastened walnut stocks displayed a fore-end cap, swivel mount, cheekpiece, and a patchbox with a sliding wooden cover. Furniture is brass and the wood ramrod is secured by two thimbles and a rear guide.

There are no markings on the octagonal-barreled rifle and only one of the three round-barreled specimens is marked, stamped atop the breech thusly I HUNTER. The capital I is superim-posed by a slash (/) apparently intended to represent the J as in James. The locks are flat and chamfered, stamped behind the gooseneck cock in two un-derscored lines: RAPA FORGE. The rifles vary in weight from 48 and ½ to 57 pounds.

It is believed that the first rifled wall guns made by the Hunter brothers appeared late in 1775 or early in 1776 and they possibly inspired Col. Fielding Lewis of the Virginia State Gun Factory to consider making similar firearms, for in a letter to Gen. Wash-ington dated February 4, 1776, he remarked ". . . I propose making a Rifle next week to carry a quarter of a pound ball [4 bore]. If it answers my expecta-tions, a few of them will keep off ships of war from our narrow Rivers, and be useful in the beginning of an engagement by land. . . ."[79]

Whether the Virginia State Gun Factory made wall rifles remains moot though the caliber of con-temporary specimens is indicated in Col. Lewis' correspondence. Wall rifles of larger caliber were also known, for a letter dated May 10, 1776, and sent from Williamsburg by Gen. Charles Lee to Gen. Washington infers that Lee knew of Col. Lewis' intention to make a wall rifle and further notes:

... I am likewise furnishing myself with four-ounced [4 bore] rifle-amusettes, which will carry an infernal distance; the two-ounced [8 bore] hit a half sheet of paper 500 yards distance. . . .[80]

Rappahannock Forge ceased operations in the late spring of 1781, the reason explained in a letter dated May 30 which an apprehensive James Hunter sent to then Virginia governor Thomas Jefferson:

... [Lt. Col. Banastre] Tarleton with 500 Horse is reported to have been at Hanover Court yesterday & last night within five miles of Bowling Green, on his way to destroy my works. . . . At present I am removing my tools and . . . [have made] . . . a total stoppage of everything. . . .[81]

The Virginia COS had been sufficiently impressed by the rifled wall guns produced by the Hunter brothers to seek other gunsmiths willing to make them, approaching Col. Josiah Clapham who had "... made himself very popular by erecting a Manufactory of Guns ..." at Point-of-Rocks in Loudoun County.[82]

On March 27, 1776, the COS directed that "... a letter be written to Col. Josiah Clapham ... informing him that we have sent him 360 pounds to pay for the rifles mentioned by Chro. Perfect, That the Committee agree to take all the good muskets that shall be made by the 5 or 6 hands he mentioned, by the 1st of December next [1777], and desire for him to contract for the *12 large rifles also. mentioned.*"*[83]

Though having been somewhat reluctant to grant Clark's request for gunpowder, the Virginia Council did not hesitate risking colony assets in arms-making ventures, for on December 17, 1776, the COS authorized the "Issue of a warrant for 250 pounds to Robert Rutherford for the use of Thomas Rutherford, to be applied for the promotion of the gun factory established in the town of Mecklenburg in the County of Berkley."[84] Known as the Mecklenburg Manufactory of Arms, the facility was operating as late as January 15, 1778, for Thomas then received an additional 250 pounds "on account."

The raid by "Bloody" Tarleton's Legion which caused much of James Hunter's consternation and narrowly missed capturing Gov. Jefferson at Monticello, successfully destroyed the Virginia State Magazine located at the confluence of the James and Rivanna rivers. With the Act of July 4, 1783, the Virginia Council authorized the construction of three new buildings there and the site was redesignated Point-of-Fork Arsenal; the facility operating until 1803.[85]

The Pennsylvania Colony also moved quickly

*Italics added.

RAPPAHANNOCK FORGE RIFLED WALL GUN (18th Century): This Rappahannock Forge wall gun is one of four surviving specimens. The round, 1-3/16-inch caliber, 44¼-inch barrel is pin-fastened to the stock. Furniture is brass. The lock is marked RAPA FORGE in two lines behind the cock and the interior of the flat lockplate is marked IP, R (or P), and several roman numeral IV's; possibly indicating the fourth lock made. Note the heavy yoke or pintle. Courtesy of the U.S. Military Academy Museum, West Point, N.Y.

to establish suitable arms-making installations, for on March 6, 1776, the COS authorized Capt. John Wilcocks to establish the State Gun Lock Factory at a site on Philadelphia's Cherry Street and appropriated £950 for the purpose.[86] The facility was subsequently known as the State Gun Factory and the Provincial Gun Factory.

Early production there was supervised by Capt. Wilcocks, a Maj. Meridith, and a Capt. Peters though Philadelphia gunsmith Peter DeHaven managed the works.[87] Fiscal management, however, was directed by Nottingham, Pa., gunsmith Benjamin Rittenhouse who had previously manufactured COS muskets.[88] Originally making gunlocks, the factory also manufactured muskets and bayonets, and DeHaven hired Philadelphia gunsmith E. Ong to assist with the work.[89]

On December 13, 1776, as Howe's redcoats threatened Philadelphia, the Executive Council of Pennsylvania ordered DeHaven ". . . to procure Waggons to Carry the Tools belonging to the Gunlock Factory, and such arms as want repair, to some convenient place, not more than 30 miles from Philadelphia, there to erect the factory."[90] DeHaven relocated the factory on French Creek in Chester County, not far from the Continental Powder Mill.

DeHaven reported nineteen hands employed at French Creek as of January 3, 1777, and informed the COS that more funds were needed ". . . to Procure Provisions and Pay our men." Rittenhouse noted that it cost the factory 15 shillings for stocking a musket, 3s/9d for splicing a stock (making a buttstock from two pieces of wood), the same amount for "dressing the mountings" (filing or grinding and then polishing the furniture), and 1s/3d for sawing stocks.[91] In April, 1777, former COS musket contractor Hugh DeHaven[92] joined his brother at the factory, while in July stock-maker William Lane of Lancaster was engaged by Peter DeHaven as a subcontractor.[93]

When Lord Cornwallis occupied Philadelphia in late September, 1777, Peter DeHaven urgently requested a guard detachment to protect the factory. He was again ordered to move, however, and by late October operations resumed at Hummel's Town. On June 18, 1778, when Sir Henry Clinton ordered Philadelphia evacuated, DeHaven asked permission on July 12 to return to French Creek. The COS refused and on December 17 it ordered the factory dismantled and the property sold.[94]

Rittenhouse and the DeHaven brothers apparently decided to privately enter the arms-making business and offered to purchase the works though the council demurred, assigning Philadelphian George Henry the task of liquidation which he completed May 3 1779, though ". . . preserving the finished and unfinished arms."[95]

In late 1777 the Pennsylvania COS established the State Gun Repair Shop at Allentown and engaged former COS gunlock-maker James Walsh to supervise the works (see p. 310).[96] On May 11, 1778, Walsh reported that 800 muskets had been refurbished and 150 more were in the process. A similar repair facility was then active at Carlisle, Pa.,[97] while another was started at Reading Furnace.[98]

Though various arms-making installations were constructed and expanded during the American Revolution, others were proposed which failed to mature. One such was suggested by Philadelphia COS musket-maker John Nicholson.[99] On June 4, 1776, Nicholson presented to the Pennsylvania COS a "Plan for Carrying on a Gun Factory . . ." and recommended fellow gunsmith Joshua Tomlinson as the ". . . proper man to be charged with a Mill for boaring and grinding barrels. . . ."[100]

Nicholson apparently had high hopes for the project, for the June 26, 1776, *Pennsylvania Gazette* advertised:

WANTED IMMEDIATELY. Two or three good Hands, that understand welding Gun-Barrels; or good smiths, inclined to be instructed in the said business. Any such Persons may meet with good encouragement by applying to Joshua Tomlinson, at the Gulph Mill, near Lancaster Road, 14 miles from Philadelphia. For particulars apply to John Nicholson, Gunsmith, near the Drawbridge, Phila. N.B. An apprentice, not under 14 years of age, is wanted to learn the welding, boring and grinding of Gun-barrels. Apply as above.

Nicholson's proposed gun factory was never built and in April, 1777, Joshua Tomlinson, master barrel-maker, died.[101] Nicholson continued in the trade and on October 17, 1781, the *Philadelphia Journal* advertised:

For Sale, at John Nicholson's . . . A number of Small arms for Shipping, such as Muskets, short ditto for tops or close quarters, Blunderbusses with or without swivels, Pistols with ribs [belt hooks] or without, Cutlasses & c. upon the most reasonable terms.

In neighboring Maryland Colony the COS established the State Gun Lock Factory at Frederick in the spring of 1777 and appointed as commissioners Charles Beatty, John Hanson, and James Johnson. Samuel Boone, nephew of the storied Daniel, managed the installation.[102] In 1768 Samuel had returned from North Carolina to learn gunsmithing in Philadelphia. Daniel Boone's brother (?) Squire started a gunsmithery at Harrodsburg prior to 1800, while his first cousin Thomas was a riflesmith in Berks County, Pa., ca. 1790.[103]

On June 17, 1777, Samuel Boone was directed by the factory commissioners to deliver 110 finished gunlocks to Frederick COS musket-maker Nicholas White.[104] Eighteen months later, on November 10, 1778, the Maryland COS ordered the factory sold. Boone and White, in association with several others, purchased it for £765/10s/6d.[105] The partners continued to make gunlocks and firearms, for on January 12, 1781, they received a state musket contract which was followed by another on January 20, 1782.[106]

News of the rifled wall guns first manufactured in Virginia apparently reached Annapolis, for the Maryland COS subsequently contacted Frederickstown riflesmith Jacob Schley about making similar firearms. Schley doubtlessly encountered production problems and the delay obviously created some concern as indicated by the tone of the correspondence forwarded to him by the COS on July 30, 1776:

Sir: The publik service requires that you should send to this place [Annapolis] with all expedition you can, the rifles by you made for ... the Province; also, the ten large rifles contracted for by you to be made and delivered on the first day of August next.[107]

As far as it is known Schley fulfilled the COS rifle contracts, including the one for "the ten large rifles" which were described as "... heavy, brass-mounted, black walnut stocked and to carry a four ounce ball."[108] The COS reported that he received three payments for firearms between January 12, 1781, and June 7, 1783.

In North Carolina the Charlottsville Rifle Works, established to make public arms in 1740, produced COS muskets and bayonets from 1775 to 1777, though despite the designation it is doubtful if rifles were produced at that time.[109] With the Act of April 24, 1776, the COS authorized Christopher Dudley and Joseph John Williams to start construction on the North Carolina Gun Works at Halifax. Master Armorer James Ransom, until the COS closed the facility in 1778, supervised the production of:

... good and sufficient muskets and bayonets of the following description, to wit: Each firelock to be made of three-fourths of an inch bore, and of a good substance at the breech, the barrel to be 3 feet 8 inches in length, a good lock, the bayonet to be 18 inches in the blade, with a steel ramrod, the upper end of the upper loop to be trumpet mouthed; and for that purpose collect all gunsmiths and other mechanics who have been accustomed to make; or assist in making muskets.[110]

The Act of April 24 also approved the establishment of the Public Gun Factory on Black River,

Wilmington District, New Hanover County, N.C. The principals involved were gunsmiths John Devane[111] and Richard Herring.[112] Operations apparently began in late May, 1776, for on June 1 Devane's brother James was employed there.[113] James, a North Carolina minuteman in 1775, enlisted in the Continental Army in 1777 and reached the rank of captain. Following the war James resumed gunsmithing and was active until 1832.

A report on the North Carolina armament industry issued five years after the American Revolution (December 5, 1788) mentioned that "... the said John Devane and Rich'd Herring drew from the Treasury of this State the Sum of one thousand pounds to enable them to carry on a Gun Manufactory in the District of Wilmington. That by receipts from proper officers it appears they delivered one hundred muskets with bayonets, three rifles and six smooth [bore] guns. That afterwards the said Factory, with a quantity of gun barrels were destroyed by the Tories."[114]

The New Jersey Colony found it extremely difficult to preserve a viable arms-making industry because of its strategic position across the Hudson River from British headquarters on Manhattan Island, while it was also the scene of numerous campaigns throughout the conflict and a notorious hotbed of outlaw activity as exemplified by the Tory element known as Cowboys or Refugees and the self-styled patriots calling themselves Skinners; gun running the least of the many heinous atrocities and other crimes perpetrated by those renegade bands.

The New Jersey COS established the State Gun Lock Factory at Trenton late in 1775, though during most of the war the colony relied on firearms purchased from the open market, foreign sources, or neighboring colonies; particularly Pennsylvania.[115] By 1778, however, Pennsylvania banned the sale of war matériel beyond her borders because of intensified British, Tory, and Native American threats to the armament industry.[116]

The State Gun Lock Factory was forced to close shortly after December 8, 1776, when Washington hastily retreated beyond the Delaware River, hotly pursued by Lord Cornwallis. Hessian and Highland troops occupied Trenton when Cornwallis smugly settled into winter quarters at New Brunswick on the Raritan River approximately 20 miles to the northeast.

Gen. Washington realized he had been presented with an opportunity too great to ignore and on a snowy Christmas night which soaked most of the American cartridge and gunpowder supply he recrossed the ice-choked Delaware to strike Trenton at bayonet point. While Trenton emerged as a stunning patriot victory often hailed as the turning point of the American Revolution, it was little comfort to one of history's most tragic figures, John Fitch (1743-1798).[117]

Fitch, fleeing a disastrous marriage in East Windsor, Conn., established himself as a watchmaker on King Street in Trenton, and with the advent of the rebellion he began making muskets for the New Jersey COS. The Hessians burned him out in December, 1776, and he followed Washington's ragged rebels to Bucks County, Pa. During the desolate winter of 1777-1778 he is thought to have served as a lieutenant with New Jersey troops at Valley Forge, possibly as one of Henry Knox's ordnance officers.

Fitch apparently left the army, for in 1780 he was appointed deputy surveyor for Virginia. A year later he was in Philadelphia where in 1782 he emerged as a frontier trader; a career ending in near disaster when he was taken by hostiles at the mouth of the Muskingum River in the Ohio country. He escaped in the winter of 1783, making his way to Warminster, Pa., where he began experimenting with steam engines; an obsession haunting the remainder of his life.

By 1785 Fitch had devised the first practical vessel to be successfully driven across water by steam power, the project purportedly financed in part by the astute Lancaster riflesmith William Henry, Sr. (see p. 258).[118] In August, 1787, Fitch demonstrated his invention at Philadelphia to the delight and amazement of the dignified members of the Constitutional Convention meeting there.

As is often the fate of the product of genius, Fitch's brilliant concept was stolen by despicable men of fortune and influence who realized fame and profit from the assiduous labor of others. In July, 1798, a destitute, disillusioned, and forgotten John Fitch, gunsmith and inventor, took his life in Bardstown, Ky.

Though vindication does not console the dead, in 1817 a select investigating committee of the New York Legislature found that ". . . the steamboats built by [Robert R.] Livingston and [Robert] Fulton were in substance the invention patented to John Fitch in 1791, and Fitch during the term of the patent had the exclusive right to use the same in the United States."[119]

Congressional Arms-Making

In the hectic aftermath of Lexington and Concord an active Continental Congress found itself addressing innumerable questions regarding defense and made several recommendations, among them

one on July 18, 1775, concerning the proper equipment for militia which stated "That each soldier be furnished with a good musket, that will carray an ounce ball, with a bayonet, steel ram-rod, worm, priming wire and brush fitted thereto, a cutting sword or tomahawk, a cartridge box, that will contain 23 rounds of cartridges, twelve flints and a knapsack."[120]

Congress early evinced an interest in firearms manufacture and on February 23, 1776, appointed a committee ". . . to contract for the making of muskets and bayonets for the use of the United Colonies."[121] A move into the armament industry on the national level had been apparently considered somewhat earlier, for six days prior to the appointment of the contract committee a contract to make 1,000 muskets was awarded to John Young and Johnson Smith of Easton, Pa. (see p. 311),[122] while on March 8 the committee appropriated $10,000 for the establishment of the Continental Gun Factory at Lancaster, Pa.[123]

With the scarcity of gunlocks early apparent Congress evidently contracted with COS facilities to procure sufficient quantities and there is verification in one instance, for on May 23, 1776, Congress directed ". . . the manager of the continental factory of firearms at Lancaster, and the manager of the gunlock factory at Trenton to deliver . . . all muskets and gunlocks . . . for the more expeditious arming of the continental battalion. . . ."[124]

The martial muskets produced at the Continental Gun Factory or by individual U.S. contractors—Congress altering the United Colonies designation to United States on September 9, 1776—are believed to have been similar to contemporary British muskets and followed the specifications recommended in November, 1775 (see p. 309). There were, however, design changes of sufficient magnitude to warrant the manufacture of pattern pieces which Congress furnished the contractors; a superfluous and expensive gesture if Continental muskets had exclusively emulated the familiar British design. Though retaining the standard British caliber, nothing else is known regarding the other pattern specifications or who made the pattern muskets.

Early in 1776 Congress ordered the manufacture of 3,000 pairs of cavalry pistols of an unknown pattern, though it was probably similar to the 1760 British horse pistol.[125] In March, 1778, Congress requested that the Board of War suggest to the states the kinds of firearms needed to equip a cavalry troop, and the Board recommended that each horseman, in addition to his other accouterments, should be provided with:

1) A pair of pistols and holsters.
2) A carbine, fusee, or short blunderbuss; the

barrel of the blunderbuss not to exceed two
feet in length.

3) A belt for the carbine, with a running swivel
that will slip to any part of the belt.

4) A cartridge-box to buckle round the waist,
with twelve tin pipes for the cartridges.[126]

Gen. Washington had been favorably impressed
by the blunderbuss, for on April 4, 1779, he wrote to
the Board of War ". . . It appears to me that Light
Blunderbusses on account of the quantity of shot
they will carry will be preferable to Carbines, for
Dragoons, as the Carbines only carry a single ball
especially in the case of close action."[127]

Though the shotgun-effect of the blunderbuss
produced ruinous casualties at short range there was
a patriot gunsmith-inventor who was convinced that
a musket capable of rapid, continuous firepower
would be equally or more effective at a greater distance; thus in a letter dated April 11, 1777, Philadelphian Joseph Belton described to Congress a
method:

> . . . wherein a common small arm, may be
> maid to discharge eight balls one after another,
> in eight, five or three seconds of time, & each
> one to do execution five & twenty, or thirty
> yards, and after so discharg'd to be loaded and
> fird with cartrages as useal [usual], which I am
> ready to prove by experimental proof, and can
> with ease fix them so as to discharge sixteen or
> twenty, in sixteen, ten or five seconds . . .,
> which I have kept as yet a secret, thinking that in
> two or three Months we might have an armey
> thus equipt, which our enemy should know
> nothing of, till they should be maid to know it in
> the field, to their immortal sorrow. . . .[128]

Joseph Belton's "secret weapon" was based on
the superimposed charge concept originating in early
fifteenth-century Europe and brought to a limited
degree of perfection by Giuliano Bossi early in the
seventeenth century (see p. 104). Whether the Board
of War or Congress witnessed a demonstration of
Belton's musket remains moot. Congress, however,
apparently examined at least one musket altered to
the Belton design and favorably responded with
unaccustomed alacrity, for on May 3, 1777, the following resolution was passed:

> Resolved, That . . . Belton be authorized and
> appointed to superintend, and direct the making
> or altering of one hundred muskets, on the con-
> struction exhibited by him and called "the new
> improved gun" which will discharge eight
> rounds with once loading; and that he receive a
> reasonable compensation for his trouble, and be
> allowed all just and necessary expenses.[129]

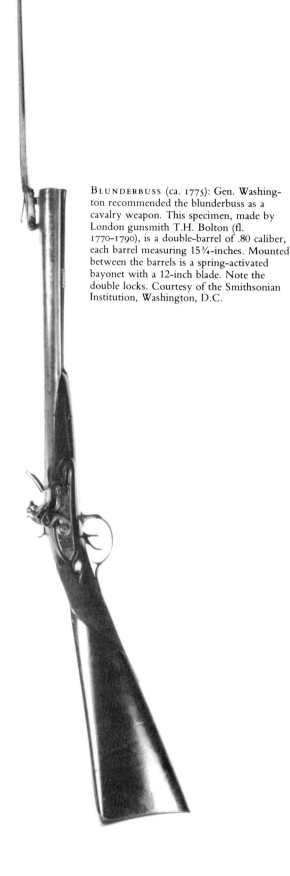

BLUNDERBUSS (ca. 1775): Gen. Washington recommended the blunderbuss as a
cavalry weapon. This specimen, made by
London gunsmith T.H. Bolton (fl.
1770-1790), is a double-barrel of .80 caliber,
each barrel measuring 15¾-inches. Mounted
between the barrels is a spring-activated
bayonet with a 12-inch blade. Note the
double locks. Courtesy of the Smithsonian
Institution, Washington, D.C.

There is no current evidence indicating that Belton fulfilled his exceedingly generous Congressional contract, and neither does history reveal the use of superimposed-charge muskets during the American Revolution. In 1784, a year after the war, Belton went to London and unsuccessfully attempted to interest the Board of Ordnance in the firearm.[130] He entered into a partnership with London gunsmith William Jover (fl. 1750-1810) in 1768 to make muskets for the East India Company featuring detachable breech chambers and sliding flintlocks.[131] It cannot be ascertained whether the sliding lock principle was used in the musket design Belton submitted to Continental Congress, for if any were made none survived the conflict.

Even before the war years the Connecticut Valley emerged as the center of the American armament industry with Massachusetts producing more firearms than the remaining colonies combined, and when hostilities began arms-making continued to flourish there. Pennsylvania, long the nucleus of rifle-making, established during the war an armament industry at least equal to that of the Connecticut Valley, while the Lancaster region became renowned as the Arsenal of America because of the wide variety of firearms made there and in the vicinity.

In 1777, at General Washington's behest, Continental Congress approved the establishment at Springfield, Mass., of an ordnance depot and manufactory for musket cartridges and cannon carriages.[132] The Springfield facility expanded as the war progressed, emerging as a vital firearms repair center and munitions laboratory. Congress broadened the scope of the installation on April 26, 1782, authorizing ". . . a good and efficient magazine for the reception of the public ammunition . . ." which was subsequently erected ". . . on the high ground known as the Training Field."[133]

There were a few large gunsmitheries operating in British America prior to the War of Independence; notably the facilities of Hugh Orr in Bridgewater, Mass., and William Henry in Lancaster, Pa. In addition the barrel mills established along Pennsylvania's Wyomissing Creek had proliferated since the French and Indian War. Though most of the labor was still performed by hand, the large gunsmitheries and barrel mills utilized trip hammers, grinding wheels, and boring machines driven by water power.

The existence of large gunsmitheries and barrel mills in British America by 1755 are conclusive evidence that a rudimentary factory system had early emerged; the factory designation subsequently appearing in the names of the various patriot arms-making installations active during the American Revolution, e.g., the Continental Gun Factory, the Pennsylvania Gun Factory, and the Maryland Gun Lock Factory, to note but few.

Thus in British America, as it was somewhat earlier in France and the Netherlands, arms-makers were employing relatively sophisticated manufacturing concepts and techniques at least 20 years before 1775 when many historians credit the factory system with industrializing the British textile industry and ushering in the so-called Industrial Revolution (see p. 31).

A typical patriot arms-making factory of the Revolutionary War period, according to a contemporary description, was equipped with ". . . 3 or 4 barrel forges, a grinding mill for grinding and polishing barrels, a lock shop with 7 forges, and benches for 40 filers, 10 benches for gunstock makers, a brass foundry for mountings [furniture] with several finishing benches, a couple of forges for bayonets and ramrods, together with a mill for grinding and polishing them, another forge for fittings [pins, screws, etc.], and an assembly shop."[134]

A gun factory of the size indicated was usually located on a suitable body of water to take advantage of a convenient power source and it occupied either a large building or several small ones; barrel boring and welding mills generally two-story structures to accommodate the requisite machinery. If personnel were available to fill all the positions delineated in the description a minimum of 70 craftsmen would have been employed; a generous figure because skilled labor was scarce and most factories were consequently short-handed.

While the factory system was certainly evident in the American armament industry during the period 1775-1783, it enjoyed a limited period of extensive operation because it was created by wartime exigency. By late 1778 most COS had been eliminated as state agencies assumed their functions, while many state and national arms-making facilities ceased production by late 1782 because of the large number of firearms then available, including foreign weapons and those repaired and returned to service.[135] A number of the large gun factories, however, continued to operate after hostilities terminated, preserving techonomic continuity.

The Blockade Firearms

Despite continuous, diligent, and in some instances extraordinary effort the fledgling American armament industry never produced sufficient firearms to meet the insatiable demand. Part of the demand was met by rebel sympathizers in Europe and they responded to the desperate need with the same enthusiasm and motivation displayed in supplying the patriots with gunpowder (see p. 300).

On September 26, 1776, Benjamin Franklin, Thomas Jefferson, and Silas Deane were appointed commissioners to France by a Continental Congress desperately seeking financial and material aid to continue prosecuting the rebellion; Deane already serving in France as a confidential agent.

In December an ailing Jefferson was replaced on the commission by Arthur Lee, youngest son of Thomas Lee whose family had been inextricably woven into the fabric of Virginia history since 1641. Arthur, however, was recalled from France in 1779 for conduct "... highly prejudicial to the honor and integrity of these United States ..." in that he cast suspicion on the motives and activities of Deane and the highly respected Franklin which, in the cold light of recent historical revelations, was probably more than justified.

In any event Franklin and Deane were extremely effective, securing from Louis XVI nearly $10,000,000 in loans and an equally generous spirit of coöperation. As a result Franklin was able to report in April, 1777, that "... We have purchased 80,000 fusils [muskets], a number of pistols, etc., of which the enclosed is on account, for 220,000 livres. They were King's arms and secondhand, but so many ... are unused and exceptionally good that we esteem it a great bargain if only half of them should arrive."[136]

In the wake of Franklin's welcome announcement the Americans received an unexpected gift of 250 M1763 French infantry muskets from the brilliant, 20-year-old Marquis de Lafayette (1757-1834).[137] Disobeying the king's orders to join the patriot cause, Lafayette brought with him Baron Johann de Kalb and eleven other officers when on June 14, 1777, he landed at Georgetown, S.C.

Available records indicate that direct French arms shipments to the American rebels began early in February, 1776 (three months before Hortalez et Cie. was formed, see p. 301), when Connecticut received 3,000 assorted firearms, and continued until late August, 1781, when the Resolue delivered to Boston 16,800 long arms.[138] Indirect arms shipments were continued by Hortalez until July 10, 1778, when France officially declared war on Britain and obviated the need for subterfuge.

From February, 1776, to February, 1779, Philadelphia received 14,156 French firearms, while 41,680 were delivered at Portsmouth, N.H., between October, 1776, and December, 1777.[139] In April, 1777, the brig Mercury out of Nantes arrived at Portsmouth, unloading 364 cases of arms (11,987 muskets), 1,000 barrels of gunpowder, 11,000 gunflints, large supplies of shoes and clothing, and her master reported no less than 34 other vessels clearing French ports for America.[140]

All did not go smoothly for the blockade runners, for on June 19, 1776, the Nancy with 191 firearms aboard was wrecked off Cape May as she made for Little Egg Harbor, N.J.[141] Of the many ships dispatched by Hortalez to West Indies ports, however, only one was intercepted by the British.[142]

Not all of the ships leaving European ports for America displayed foreign flags, for several patriot privateers were active. Capt. Tibbet of the Wild Duck reached Philadelphia in February, 1776, with 300 firearms, one of John Hancock's vessels docked at Bedford, Mass., with 3,000 more in November, 1777, and the Sally with Capt. Stocker arrived at Philadelphia on March 24, 1777, with 11,000 firearms.[143]

At least one gunsmith of record produced muskets for privateer use and he was Elisha Buell of Hebron, Conn. On October 11, 1776, he delivered 40 muskets to the privateer Oliver Cromwell. After the war he established at Marlborough, Conn., "... the principal gun factory in the vicinity, on the Turnpike Road, near the Methodist Church."[144]

Curiously, on February 15, 1777, approximately four months after Buell delivered the muskets to the Oliver Cromwell, the Connecticut COS directed Gen. Jabez Huntington to transport "... the chest of broken fire-arms ... from the ... Oliver Cromwell to [William] Williams who is ... to take care that the same are well repaired, fitted, and kept for the use of this State."[145] Whether the damaged firearms were the muskets made by Buell remains conjectural.

It has been reliably estimated that from 1776 to 1781 at least 102,000 French martial firearms had been sent to America, and while 1,110 are known to have been carbines, most of them were infantry muskets ranging in character from the obsolete M1717 to the M1768 though the M1763 was preeminent.[146] Most of the French muskets reaching the patriots were engraved CHARLEVILLE on the lock and in the ranks the word was applied to any French musket.

Pliarne, Penet et Cie, another French-subsidized firm, sent arms and munitions to the patriots in care of James Gruel & Co. A company ship, the Penet, reached Portsmouth, N.H., on June 11, 1777, with 13,333 muskets.[147] Many of the muskets reaching Gruel & Company were from Liège and were of inferior quality in comparison to Dutch, French, and Spanish muskets. A few M1752 Spanish muskets were bought by American agents in New Orleans for frontier militia use.

Netherlands arms merchants were extremely active in the brisk, lucrative armament trade and the firearms produced there were of excellent quality. Benjamin Franklin, representing Massachusetts, purchased small quantities of Dutch martial firearms

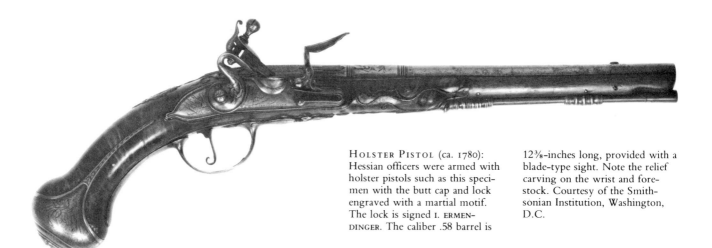

HOLSTER PISTOL (ca. 1780): Hessian officers were armed with holster pistols such as this specimen with the butt cap and lock engraved with a martial motif. The lock is signed I. ERMENDINGER. The caliber .58 barrel is 12⅜-inches long, provided with a blade-type sight. Note the relief carving on the wrist and forestock. Courtesy of the Smithsonian Institution, Washington, D.C.

and most of them were shipped to St. Eustatius. There is, however, the possibility that Dutch ships risked the British blockade directly, for in February, 1776, 2,100 firearms reached Williamsburg from Rotterdam though it is evident that they also could have been transported in an American vessel.[148]

Dutch martial muskets were shorter, lighter, and of smaller caliber (.65) than most imported firearms, emulating the pattern of the officers' fusils common in other European armies. An Amsterdam gunsmith known only as Thone appears to have been a major supplier, for his mark is conspicuous among surviving specimens; possibly indicating that he might have been working under a COS or state contract. Thone muskets display Amsterdam proof marks on the barrel and they have three brass barrel bands; the upper band distinguished by its eight-inch length to serve as a readily identified characteristic. The maker's surname and location is stamped on the flat lockplate in two lines.

Dutch cavalry and sea service pistols were also evident in patriot ranks, the latter displaying belt hooks. Most Dutch pistols exhibited round, ten-inch, pin-fastened barrels of .69 caliber, an iron ramrod, a brass priming pan, and a brass blade front sight. There was no rear sight and some pistols had no sideplates. The walnut grip had a pommel butt minus a cap, though the forestock was capped with brass.

An undetermined though probably small number of German pistols were purchased by Virginia agents in Prussia.[149] They were primarily obsolescent cavalry models displaying 11 and ¾ inch barrels of approximately .75 caliber pin-fastened to walnut stocks. Furniture was brass, like the blade front sight, and the forestock and the large pommel butt were capped. The lockplate and the sideplate were flat and the iron ramrod was attached to the barrel by a yoke-like swivel. The royal cypher appeared on the buttcap and proof marks are found on the barrel

and the trigger guard. Pistols marked POTZDAM-MAGAZIN on the lock were made at the famous Potsdam Arsenal.

Captured Firearms

Prior to and during the course of the American Revolution a large number of firearms were confiscated or captured by patriot forces and most of them were British. German and Scottish firearms were also taken as the spoils of war, though fewer in number; the latter primarily pistols. German firearms included martial muskets, martial-type *jäeger* rifles, and pistols similar to those purchased by Virginia agents in Prussia.

German muskets and rifles varied considerably in design because several patterns were provided by the callous Teutonic nobles who sold their subjects to the Hanoverian, King George III, though Prussia's Frederick the Great refused to indulge in that reprehensible commerce in human flesh. George III paid dearly for his German auxiliaries commonly known as Hessians, expending £4.7 million for 28,875 of them, or approximately £7/4s/4½d per head; many unfit for military service or inadequately trained and equipped.

Most of the so-called Hessian muskets displayed round, iron barrels of .75 to .80 caliber measuring 41 to 44 inches long with an elliptical brass front sight mounted either on the barrel or the upper barrel band. The barrel was either banded or pin-fastened to a walnut stock which illustrated a flat butt with a relatively high comb. Furniture was brass. A moulding surrounding the lock mortise was characteristic.

Hessian musket locks were of the conventional martial pattern, though the muskets carried by some of the Brunswick battalions displayed locks with a distinctly curved, flat lockplate blunted at either end, while the battery was also distinguished by a flat rather than pointed top profile. Iron ramrods were used exclusively. The socket bayonet displayed a straight socket with mounting and locking slots though the 13 to 13 and ½ inch hexagonal blade was atypical; differing from conventional bayonet blades because it could be used for slashing as well as stabbing.

The Highland regiments serving with the British were issued regulation Brown Bess muskets and were the only infantry normally armed with pistols, retaining the traditional Scottish pattern. Birmingham gunsmith Isaac Bissel (fl. 1775-1780) made elegant Scottish officers' pistols featuring a ramshorn butt design with an oval inlay displaying a petal motif.[150] London gunsmith John Waters (fl. 1775-1783) produced less ornate pistols.[151]

The Scottish emigrants inhabiting the Appalachian frontier had clung to their cherished traditions and firearms, consequently Scottish pistols were often found in patriot and loyalist ranks; an unknown number taken from the 900 Scottish Tories captured by North Carolina rebels in the Battle of Moore's Creek, February 27, 1776.

Old model British martial pistols, relics of King George's War (1744-1748), and new model holster pistols were common in patriot and loyalist ranks. As a rule American martial pistols followed the later British pattern; those made at Rappahannock Forge strikingly similar to the 1760 British pattern and of generally superior quality than most American martial pistols of the period.

Basically short range firearms used by the mounted and naval forces of the combatants, pistols were occasionally employed for duelling and in one notable incident in a somewhat unorthodox fashion by British fugitive John Paul who had added Jones to his name to protect his identity. The incident occurred during the epic sea battle of September 22-23, 1779, when Jones, spirited captain of the barely seaworthy *Bonhomme Richard,* engaged the powerful *Serapis* off the English coast.

The fiery Jones, angered by the cowardice displayed by three of his crew, was observed in the heat of battle as he bawled "... in a loud voice, 'what damned rascals are them—shoot them—kill them!' He was upon the forecastle when these fellows ... made their appearance upon the quarter-deck where he had just discharged his pistols at some of the enemy. The carpenter, and the master-at-arms, hearing Jones' voice, sculked below, and the gunner was attempting to do the same, when Jones threw both of his pistols ..., one of which struck him in the head, fractured his scull, and knocked him down ... where he lay till the battle was over."[152]

HESSIAN MUSKET AND BAYONET (18th Century): This Hessian musket is one of two captured from the Brunswick Grenadiers at Bennington, Vt., August 16, 1777. Note the high buttstock comb and arched lockplate. The ramrod is secured by three thimbles and a guide, while the bayonet lug is positioned beneath the barrel. The lock is unmarked. Courtesy of the U.S. Military Academy Museum, West Point, N.Y.

Other Firearms

In addition to the numerous kinds of martial firearms employed during the American Revolution, there were quasi-martial firearms like the American rifle and the American pistol, and a variety of non-martial firearms including fowling pieces and countless utilitarian pistols of domestic and foreign origin; most of the latter produced in Britain before the conflict.

General Washington and many other patriot officers used their personal firearms of which most had been purchased from fashionable London and Paris gunsmiths prior to hostilities, though a few had been bought from indigenous craftsmen. Washington, who owned as many as 50 firearms during his lifetime,[153] purchased a pair of silver-mounted, brass-barreled holster pistols from London gunsmith John Hawkins (fl. 1750-1775) and considered them among his favorite sidearms.[154]

In March, 1776, after inspecting patriot defenses at Dorchester Heights overlooking Boston, Washington was so disturbed by the loss of a pistol that it was mentioned in his General Orders of the ninth:

His Excellency the General lost one of his pistols yesterday upon Dorchester Neck. Who-

ever will bring it to him or leave it with General Thomas shall receive two dollars reward and no questions asked; it is a screwed barreled pistol mounted with silver and a head resembling that of a pug dog at the butt.[155]

It is not known if Washington recovered his "screwed barreled" pistol, though he apparently had a penchant for losing pistols, for yet another was misplaced, strayed, or possibly stolen as indicated in a letter dated July 2, 1777, and addressed to Capt. Charles Morley by one F. Braithewate of Stanford, Connecticut:

Sir:

His excellency Gen. Washington, desires you to look among his effects for a pistol which is mislaid or possibly lost. You will know it by being a large brass barrel and the lock is also brass, with the name of Gabbitas, the Spanish armorer, thereon. It also has a heavy brass butt. His Excellency is much exercised over the loss of this pistol, it being given him by Gen. Braddock, and having since been with him through several campaigns, and he therefore values it very highly. Also, it is a good pistol and serviceable. A speedy reply will greatly oblige, Your faithful and obt. servant. . . .[156]

Washington never found his prized pistol, though it appeared during the late nineteenth century in the collection (Inventory No. 494) of the U.S. Cartridge Company, Lowell, Mass., which was

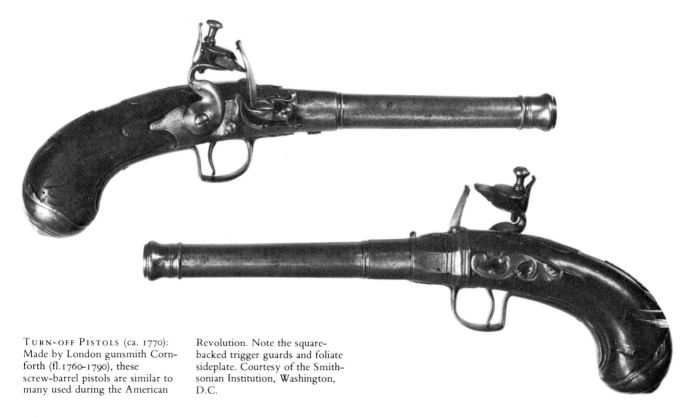

TURN-OFF PISTOLS (ca. 1770): Made by London gunsmith Cornforth (fl. 1760-1790), these screw-barrel pistols are similar to many used during the American Revolution. Note the square-backed trigger guards and foliate sideplate. Courtesy of the Smithsonian Institution, Washington, D.C.

GEN. GEORGE WASHING-
TON'S SADDLE PISTOLS (ca.
1770): Made by London gunsmith
John Hawkins (fl. 1750-1775),
these brass-barrelled, silver-
mounted pistols were among
Washington's favorites. Overall
length: 13½ inches, Barrel length:
8 inches, slightly flared at the
muzzle. The .66 caliber bore took
a .65 caliber ball. Note the sliding
safety behind the cock and the
ornate martial motif of the cast-
brass sideplate depicting the Lion
and Unicorn. A silver grip plate
extending to the butt cap straps is
engraved GEN. WASHINGTON.
Courtesy of the U.S. Military
Academy Museum, West Point,
N.Y.

active from 1869 to 1919. The pistol is described as a
.50 caliber "flint-lock horse-pistol" stamped BRIS-
TOL on the brass barrel, while the lockplate is engraved GABBITAS.[157] Gabbitas was active in Bristol,
Somerset, England, from ca. 1750 to ca. 1775.[158]

According to historian Milton F. Perry, Washington's lost pistol surfaced in the no longer intact
collection of the late William G. Renwick (1886-
1971), though he did not mention when or from
whom Renwick acquired it.[159] Though there is no
conclusive proof, it is likely that the Renwick specimen is from the U.S. Cartridge Company collection,
for that pistol also has a brass barrel and a brass
lockplate correspondingly marked, while a signature
plate in the walnut stock bears Gen. Braddock's
initials.

Before the rebellion most prosperous Americans, like Washington, procured many of their firearms from European agents. Robert Cary & Company of London served Washington in that capacity,
purchasing for him several fowling pieces, pistols,
and accessories. In a letter to Cary dated July 25,
1769, Washington ordered a large powder horn ". . .
bound tight with sml. brass wire from one end to the
other . . ." with the admonition that it be ". . . sec'd
[secured] in such a man'r as to prev't the wires slip-
ping." Also included was a request for ". . . as handsome a fowling piece 3½ feet in the Barl. as can be
bo't for 3 Guins [guineas]."[160]

SCREW-BARREL
(TURN-OFF) PIS-
TOLS (ca. 1750): These
silver-mounted pistols
were made by London
gunsmith B.B. Brooke
(fl. 1710-1760). The
6½-inch barrels are of
.50 caliber and the en-
graved trigger guards
are iron. Note the bar-
rel lugs for the spanner.
The butt caps are cast-
silver in the shape of a
pug dog's face. There is
the possibility that one
of the pair was the pis-
tol lost by Gen. Wash-
ington at Dorchester
Heights. Courtesy of
the Morristown Na-
tional Historical Park,
Morristown, N.J.

Washington's early frontier experience exposed him to the American rifle and he was purportedly armed with one at Fort Necessity. In any event a rifle was made for him in 1770 by Georgetown gunsmith John Yost for £6/10s Maryland currency; a considerable sum suggesting that the rifle was exceptionally fine because Yost produced extremely plain COS rifles at £4/15s each when costs had distinctly escalated during the war years (see p. 310).[161]

Thomas Jefferson (1743-1826), statesman, architect, inventor, and no less an avid sportsman than fellow Virginian and compatriot George Washington, philosophically advised "Let your gun be the constant companion of your walks . . .," and at age twenty-five ". . . won at shooting a shilling three-

pence."[162] Jefferson also acquired a number of firearms, among them a pair of elegant Turkish pistols previously owned by his friend Brig. Gen. Isaac Zane of the Virginia militia.[163]

Jefferson's personal account books not only illustrate the exemplary care he lavished upon his firearms, but serve as a contemporary economic index relating to the gunsmithing craft and a host of kindred items while including fragmentary identification regarding the several gunsmiths and merchants with whom he often dealt:

1775—Nov. 29. Pd. for repairing pistols £-3-0-6
1775—Dec. 23. Pd. Marshall for 2 cartridge boxes 9/
1776—Jan. 8. Pd. Robt. Dickerson stockg. a gun 34/
1776—July 15. Pd. Rob. Morris for 12 lb. powder £3
1776—Aug. 30. Pd. Nicholson for a double gun-lock 5-5
1777—Dec. 4. Pd. Archbd. Cary for 12 lb. powder £3-12
1780—Pd. for 1 lb. powder 24 pounds. 4 lb. shot 30 pounds.
1782—Sept. 23. Sent R. Dickerson 40/ of which 34/6 is for a gun he has stocked & the balance towards repairing one now sent
1783— Jan. 5. Pd. for mending gun lock 8/4[164]

A close examination of this partial listing of Jefferson's accounts reveals the extent inflation escalated the cost of gunpowder between July 15, 1776, and 1780; the amounts probably given in Virginia currency. The gunsmith Nicholson noted in the entry for August 30, 1776, possibly refers to the Philadelphia craftsman located on Front Street, for at that time Jefferson was attending the Congress and had recently written the Declaration of Independence.

That Jefferson clearly understood and championed individual rights is unquestioned and perhaps no more graphically demonstrated than in a provision he included in his original draft of the 1776 Virginia Constitution which proclaimed, "No freeman shall ever be debarred the use of arms."[165] That astute dictum, with his vigorous urging though in a substantially altered form, was subsequently included in the Second Amendment (Bill of Rights, 1791) to the Constitution of the United States of America:

A well regulated militia, being necessary to the security of a free State, the right of the people to keep and bear arms, shall not be infringed.

SADDLE HOLSTERS (19th Century): The saddle holsters depicted are missing the customary butt flaps and muzzle caps, though they are similar to martial pistol holsters which emerged during the early 16th Century. Courtesy of the Mercer Museum, Bucks County Historical Society, Doylestown, Pa. Charles L. Maddox, Jr., photographer.

Proof and Property Marking

The often repeated assertion that patriot arms-makers refused to mark their products in fear of British or Tory reprisals is refuted by historical evidence, for signature and property marks are found on domestic firearms as well as those captured or run through the blockade. Markings were die-stamped or engraved on the metal components, while in some instances the stock or grip was stamped or branded. In addition Continental Congress and the infant states appointed qualified arms inspectors.

Most COS and other firearms were signed by the maker and displayed in various forms the mark of the colony established by statute. Connecticut required all muskets to be ". . . marked with the name or initial letters of the maker's name . . ." and the letters S C (State of Connecticut); a mark not to be confused with firearms belonging to South Carolina.[166] The Rhode Island coat of arms and the letters C R (Colony of Rhode Island) appeared on all firearms purchased by the colony.[167] Massachusetts law ordered each musket stamped with the letters M B (Massachusetts Bay).[168]

Like most colonies Maryland assigned small arms inspectors to examine and test the firearms of contract gunsmiths as exemplified by Baltimore COS musket-maker Samuel Keener. On February 12, 1776, Capt. Thomas Ewing who provided his own inspector's stamp in the form of a crown or, perhaps, a tulip blossom,[169] informed the COS that he, ". . . with Major Cist and Van Bibber, proved all the guns made by Baltimore Gunsmiths. All the guns were charged with one ounce of powder and two balls, reports—Keener 32 guns, 13 good, 19 bad."[170]

Robert Towers served as Philadelphia's arms inspector and on October 27, 1775, he was ordered to stamp all muskets proved there with the letter P.[171] The COS amended the mark to P.P. prior to March, 1776.[172] On November 19, 1775, Towers was appointed Continental Armorer and Commissary of Military Stores, serving for the annual sum of $1,094 until May 19, 1777.[173]

Musket proof was apparently less stringent in Pennsylvania than Maryland, for on March 2, 1776, Philadelphia COS musket-maker Mathias Keeley delivered to the committee 31 of 100 contract muskets which were ". . . proved with the weight of the powder equal to the weight of the ball."[174]

One of the most prominent Connecticut arms inspectors was Isaac Dolittle, gunsmith and possibly a powder-maker, for on August 21, 1776, he was ordered ". . . to deliver 300 pounds of gun powder to the selectmen of Milford for their use in the fort."[175] The following October he was ". . . appointed as one of the inspectors to examine and approve all such firearms and locks as should be made within the State."[176]

The large gunsmithery of militia Lt. Col. Medad Hills (1729-1803) of Goshen, Conn., was also an arms inspection post for the surrounding area and the brothers Edmond and Miles Beach were the inspectors.[177] Hills received a Connecticut COS contract and on February 4, 1776, he delivered 40 muskets and bayonets. His father Benoni was an active gunsmith at Durham, Conn., from 1728 until 1741 when he moved to Goshen where he resumed the trade.[178]

As the American Revolution progressed and the demand for firearms commensurately escalated it was determined that a distinctive mark identifying them as "publik" property was necessary if not mandatory, for there was an alarming increase in the theft of weapons of all description. The stolen weapons were then sold to states desperately needing them to arm their militia, volunteers, or Continental levies, while they were also purchased from the gun runners by the British and distributed among the Tories and Native Americans supporting the crown.

After repeated and unsuccessful attempts to halt the nefarious commerce, Continental Congress adopted the recommendations of Robert Towers as Commissary of Military Stores and on February 24, 1777, declared that ". . . the several States . . . take the most effectual steps for collecting from the inhabitants, not in actual service, all Continental arms, and give notice of the number . . . to General Washington. That all arms or accoutrements, belonging to the United States shall be stamped or marked with the words 'United States': all arms already made to be stamped upon such parts as will receive the impression, and those hereafter to be manufactured, to be stamped with the said words on every part comprising the stand; and all arms and accoutrements so stamped or marked shall be taken wherever found for the use of the States, excepting they shall be in the hands of those actually in Continental service. That it be recommended to the legislatures of the several States to enact proper laws for the punishment of those who shall unlawfully take, secrete, refuse or neglect to deliver, any Continental arms or accoutrements which they may have in their possession."[179]

Those recommendations reached Washington at his Morristown, N.J., headquarters and in a letter dated March 31, 1777, he wrote to Lt. Col. Benjamin Flower, Commissary General of Artillery, requesting that he ". . . have several stamps made and sent by the earliest opportunity to Mr. French, Commissary of Stores here with directions to advise me of

BRITISH LONG LAND SERVICE MUSKET (1747): The lock on this specimen was signed by London gunsmith Jordan (fl. 1733-1762) and dated 1747. The tail of the lock is surcharged U S, signifying that it was used by patriot forces. Courtesy of the U.S. Military Academy Museum, West Point, N.Y.

their arrival that they may be immediately used."[180]

Writing to Washington on April 12 from Peekskill, N.Y., Brig. Gen. Alexander McDougall suggested that the words UNITED STATES be branded on all musket stocks; a suggestion apparently heeded in abbreviated form judging from the surviving muskets bearing the U. STATES brand.[181]

It is perhaps curious that Continental Congress procrastinated in the matter of marking American martial firearms when it had requested in 1776 that all gunpowder be identified (see p. 302), and while the U.S. mark was first used by gunpowder inspectors it was intended to delineate quality rather than property though it subsequently performed both functions.

On April 18, 1777, Washington issued the following General Order:

All Continental Arms, those in possession of the troops, as well as those in Store, to be marked immediately.

Commanding Officers of Corps to see this Order put in execution—they will get the Brand by applying to the Commissary of Military Stores.[182]

The widespread use of the shortened U. STATES brand or the abbreviated U.S. property mark was not immediate. The branding and marking plan was delayed by difficulties in procuring official stamps and brands though in some instances the markings were crudely executed by other means. Whether the marking plan effectively curtailed theft and gun-running remains unknown and it is an aspect of the American Revolution which deserves additional investigation.

Ammunition and Accouterments

While patriot forces often prepared paper cartridges as they rested between battles, large quantities were also produced at ordnance installations like the Springfield Magazine, and there were individuals engaged in their manufacture either independently or under COS or state contracts. The *Pennsylvania Journal* of August 23, 1775, carried the advertisement of an apparently independent cartridge-maker:

The Subscriber takes this method to acquaint his friends and the public . . ., that if proper encouragement be given, he will continue to make Cartridges for quickfire, likewise Balls for Artillery, and . . . they may depend on having their orders executed with care and dispatch, by their humble servant, John Langeay. N.B.

BAR (WROUGHT) IRON INGOT (ca. 1780): Six inches in diameter and 30 inches long, this bar iron ingot is marked HIBERNIA and was cast at the forge of that name located near Morristown, N.J. Courtesy of the Morristown National Historical Park, Morristown, N.J.

Would be glad to attend any country battalion who may need his assistance. Enquire of the Printer.

As early employed in colonial America the common, extremely effective practice of loading a number of buckshot with a regulation caliber ball was also evident during the War of Independence. Gen. Henry Dearborn apparently found compound cartridges useful, for he noted that during the brisk attack at Quebec on December 31, 1775, his piece "... was Charged with a ball and Ten Buck shott. . . ."[183] He was, however, frustrated when he attempted to shoot a British sentry with the lethal load and regrettably reported "... to my great mortification my Gun did not go off . . .;" a misfire caused by damp powder and doubtlessly attributable to the swirling snowstorm then in progress.[184]

Washington also recognized the efficacy of compound cartridges, early suggesting that the troops load their muskets "... with one . . . ball and four or eight buck Shott, according to the strength of their pieces."[185]

The imperative need for ammunition throughout the conflict precludes amplification, though the South Carolina COS was early sensitive to the demand, directing its Bermuda agents to procure "... musket, pistol, and blunderbuss ball, handgrenades, good flints and cartridge paper."[186] Such foresight was admirable in 1776 yet by 1780 the colony's fortunes had diminished and even the cunning Swamp Fox, Gen. Francis Marion (1732-1795), had reached the point where his men were forced to carry "... old saws that had been wrought at a country forge into the rude likeness of sabres, while many of the bullets were cast from melted pewter mugs and dishes."[187]

Like all combatants throughout history, those involved in the American Revolution expressed their frustrations with the burden of war in various ways and the brutalizing effect of combat often nurtured unmitigated atrocities with one gruesome horror instigating another in retaliation. Among rebels and redcoats there was a predilection to alter musket balls in a fashion designed to inflict upon each other the most ghastly wounds.

BRITISH MUSKET LOCK (ca. 1762): Obsolescent British muskets were used by many colonial militia companies before and during the American Revolution, and many were stored in colony armories. The Virginia Colony inventory of the Williamsburg Magazine listed 527 "old muskets." Courtesy of the Morristown National Historical Park, Morristown, N.J.

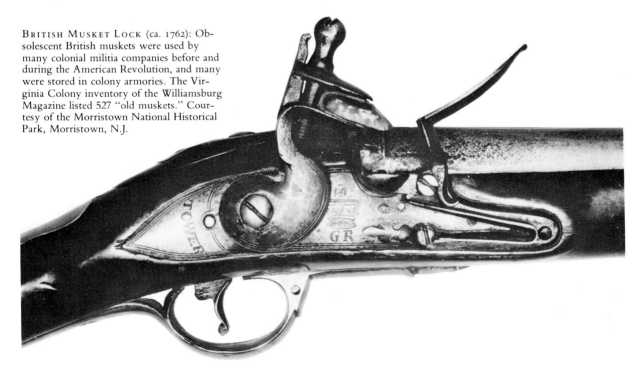

Lead musket balls ordinarily distorted some-what when they struck flesh and bone, however, they were often crosscut (X) with the idea that they would split in four pieces and scatter like buckshot or flatten even more on impact to create deliberately devastating wounds. A more murderous refinement was to pierce the ball with a nail or similar object which ripped as well as punctured. Numerous musket balls arranged in that lethal fashion have been recovered by archaeologists from various American and British encampments and battlegrounds. Not all atrocities, however, were confined to the mutilation of musket balls.[188]

Lead ingots and cast bullets were confiscated from British stores, taken in battle, purchased from abroad, and domestically produced. British and Tory prisoners and black slaves labored in patriot lead mines in Pennsylvania, New Jersey, and Virginia as well as in the extensive copper mines at East Granby, Conn.[189] Literally tons of bullet lead were cast in the many American forges and furnaces, and most of those facilities employed prisoners and deserters.

The Adventure Furnace (Hibernia Iron Works) near Morristown, N.J., cast lead ingots for bullet-making and Charles Hoff, the superintendent, wrote to Gov. Robert Livingston in a letter dated June 27, 1777, that the works produced 120 tons of shot ". . . in the last year for public service."[190] He also mentioned that he had attempted to procure Hessian deserters from Philadelphia to work at the furnace.

Powder horns, powder flasks, canteens, cartridge boxes, knapsacks, cleaning implements and the like as used by the combatants were not much

*Probably Native American trade fusils.

different than those commonly employed before the conflict, though there were innovations, while material shortages effected quality. An idea of the variety of arms and accouterments available to the patriots at the outbreak of hostilities is found in the June 3, 1775, inventory taken at the Williamsburg Magazine.[191]

Though the Williamsburg inventory is not specific regarding the firearms listed, it is possible that the tent was a bell-of-arms or bell tent; a small, circular field tent for storing various kinds of firearms to protect them from the weather or where soldiers kept their muskets when they slept.[192] The musket barrels rested on wood dowels protruding from the center pole of the tent like the spokes of a wheel. Bells-of-arms, like personnel tents, were scarce in patriot ranks and in permanent winter quarters small cabins were usually constructed. Also used for securing muskets were wooden racks similar to saw horses, though with a notched crosspiece to fit the barrels. The racks were covered by a tent or tarpaulin when available.

The bullet moulds used by patriot forces were brass or iron and of the single cavity or gang type with bare metal handles. Gang moulds usually cast more than one caliber ball and a few were designed for shot. The Virginia COS determined that one mould for every 40 muskets was sufficient and required each to cast a minimum of 16 one-ounce balls, though whether the mould was brass or iron was not specified.[193] Maryland, however, specified brass moulds each casting 12 musket balls on one side and as many buckshot as practicable on the other, while one mould was issued with every 80 muskets.[194]

Patriot cartridge boxes early emulated British patterns and were made of leather though capacity fluctuated. Infantry boxes generally carried more than cavalry and each was suspended from shoulder or waist belts; cavalry primarily using the latter. Early in the conflict most boxes were substantial though as the war progressed shortages occurred and

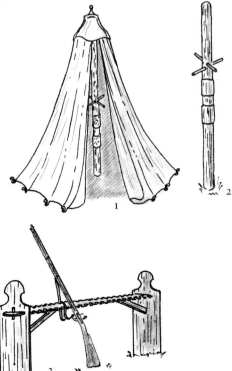

BELL OF ARMS (BELL TENT) AND MUSKET RACK (18th Century): (1) Bell tent or bell of arms for storing and protecting muskets. (2) Bell tent center pole. Musket barrels rested against dowels. (3) Musket rack. Crosspiece was notched to receive the barrel. Author's sketch.

CARTRIDGE BOX (ca. 1775-1783): Like the firearms produced for the war effort, patriot contractors frequently followed British patterns when making infantry accouterments. This American copy of a British cartridge box has a wood block with 26 compartments; the ten paper cartridges are original. Courtesy of the Morristown National Historical Park, Morristown, N.J.

quality deteriorated, exemplified by the following criticisms:

> Sir, the 300 cartouch boxes . . . are just come in. I . . . can assure you they are not worthy of the name. Numbers of them are without any straps, others without flaps, and scarce any . . . would preserve the cartridges in a moderate shower of Rain—What straps there are to the boxes are of linen.[195]

And:

> The arms . . . are good but the cartouch boxes bad, many of the old construction and wore out. Some with waist belts, others without any belts at all slung by pieces of rope or other strings. . . .[196]

On July 18, 1775, Continental Congress recommended that infantry cartridge boxes be of sufficient size to hold ". . . 23 rounds . . ." (see p. 316) and that cavalry be provided with boxes containing ". . . twelve tin pipes for the cartridges . . ." (see p. 317). In 1779 Massachusetts specified that cartridge boxes ". . . will hold fifteen Rounds . . . at least . . .,"[197] while different capacity standards were established by other colonies, ranging from as few as ten to as many as 30 cartridges.

By autumn, 1777, there appeared all metal cartridge boxes designed for infantry and they were described by the Board of War:

> The recommendation to provide cartridge boxes and tin cannisters for cartridges is given, because of the almost total want of them in the public stores, and the impossibility of making a number of them in any degree equal to the demands of the army, in public manufactories, where workmen are few, and it is impossible to encrease them: agreeable to the direction of congress, the board give the following description of the tin cannisters.
>
> They are to be six inches and a half deep, or long; three inches and three quarters of an inch broad (this breadth receiving the cartridges lengthways, as they lie in a horizontal position) and two inches and seven eights of an inch thick; (this thickness admitting four cartridges, to lay side by side) a box of these, in the clear, will well contain thirty six cartridges with ounce balls. A wire is to be fixed in all the edges at the top and then each side turned down (outwards) a full half inch and soldered. The cover is to be a full half inch deep, so that when fixed on the cannister the edges shall come close down to the ledge formed by the enclosed wire. This cover at one end turns on a hinge an inch and a quarter long, the wire (fixed as above mentioned) being laid naked, that space, for the purpose; and a piece of tin is run underneath the wire, doubled together, and soldered on the inside of one end

of the cover. The soldier carries a cannister by a shoulder belt, as he does a cartridge box: and for this reason the cannister has fixed to it three loops of tin, each half an inch wide, with the edges turned back, to be smooth and strong; one of them is placed underneath the middle of the bottom, and one on each of the narrowest sides, the latter at four inches distant from the bottom of the lower edges. The loops are to be sent down at each end and very well soldered, leaving a space to admit a leathern belt full one inch and a half wide, and nearly an eighth of an inch thick. The cover opens against one part of the belt, which causes it to fall down, after a cartridge is taken out, by wch means the rest are secured from accidental fire. If possible, the cannisters should be japanned [varnished], or

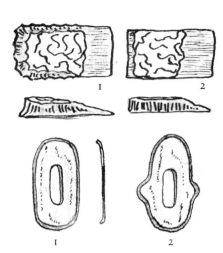

GUNFLINTS (18th Century): First row (left to right). (1) Top and profile of European (Continental) gunflint with rounded heel and curved sides. (2) English gunflint with square heel and straight sides. Second row (left to right). (1) Oval, cast-lead flint cap ca. 1740. (2) Oval, cast-lead flint cap with "ears" (mould sprue) attached ca. 1750. Author's sketch.

painted, to preserve them from rust; and all fixed to belts.

The boards are of the opinion that these cannisters are preferable to cartridge boxes, as they will infallibly secure the cartridges from rain, and their weight is so trifling as to be no burthern to the Soldier. And seeing leather is so scarce they will be a most excellent substitute for cartridge boxes.[198]

Gunflints, like other essential war matériel, were procured by patriot forces from a few domestic knappers, though the majority came from France. The number of gunflints issued was generally determined by the amount of ammunition carried, i.e., a ratio of one flint per 20 cartridges, though there were variations. Congress specified 12 flints per man (see p. 316), though Massachusetts resolved in 1779 that, in addition to his musket and bayonet, each militiaman was to have "... a cutting sword or a tomahawk or hatchet, a Pouch containing a cartridge box, that will hold fifteen ... cartridges ..., a hundred buckshot, a Jack Knife and Tow for wadding, six flints, one pound of powder, fourty leaden Balls ..., a Knapsack and Blanket a Canteen or wooden bottle sufficient to hold one Quart."[199]

Most accessories and accouterments were imported though some were made by COS contractors, state facilities, or individual craftsmen like James Weir who advertised in the *Pennsylvania Evening Post,* January 4, 1776:

Wires and brushes for Firelocks, after the best and most approved construction of the most experienced officers, Made and Sold ... at the corner of Church-alley, in Second Street, at the low rate of five shillings per dozen. Black Ball of the best quality may be had at said shop, with a reasonable allowance when purchased by the quantity. Orders from the country will be faithfully and punctually executed.[200]

CARTRIDGE CANISTER (1777): Patriot forces were issued lightweight tin cartridge canisters with a capacity of 36 paper musket cartridges. Loops were soldered to the bottom and sides of the canister for attaching a shoulder strap. The tin canisters provided more protection for the cartridges and permitted more to be carried. Courtesy of the U.S. Military Academy Museum, West Point, N.Y.

Notes

1. James Grant Wilson and John Fiske, ed., *Appletons' Cyclopaedia of American Biography,* 6 vols (New York, 1889), 6:364.

2. William R. Staples, ed., *Documentary History of the Burning of the Gaspee* (Providence), 1845, pp. 8-9.

3. U.S. Bureau of Census, *Historical Statistics of the United States* (Washington, 1961), Series Z 1-19, p. 756.

4. J. Leitch Wright, Jr., "Blacks in British East Florida," *Florida Historical Quarterly* (April 1976): 436.

5. George F. Scheer, ed., *Private Yankee Doodle* [Joseph Plumb Martin, *A Narrative of Some of the Adventures, Dangers and Sufferings of a Revolutionary Soldier, Interspersed with Anecdotes of Incidents That Occurred Within His Own Observations* (Hallowell, Me., 1830)] (New York, 1962), p. 6n.

6. Wilson and Fiske, 2:570.

7. Norman B. Wilkinson, *Explosives in History, The Story of Black Powder* (Chicago: Rand McNally & Company, 1966): 10.

8. Ibid., p. 11.

9. Ibid., p. 10.

10. Ibid.

11. Ibid., p. 11.

12. James E. Serven, "Massachusetts: Cradle of American Gunmaking," *American Rifleman* (March 1968): 27-28.

13. Henry B. Dawson, *Battles of the United States by Sea and Land,* 2 vols (New York, 1858), 1:22-23.

14. George F. Scheer and Hugh F. Rankin, *Rebels and Redcoats: The Living Story of the American Revolution* (New York, 1957), p. 30.

15. Dawson, 1:22-23.

16. Scheer and Rankin, p. 40.

17. Henry True, *Journals and Letters . . . Also an Account of the Battle of Concord by Captain Amos Barrett* (Marion, Ohio, 1900), pp. 34-35.

18. Bruce Lancaster and J.H. Plumb, *The American Heritage Book of the Revolution* (New York, 1958), p. 102.

19. John Barker, *The British in Boston* (Cambridge, 1924), p. 35.

20. Letter, author unknown, *William and Mary Quarterly,* 3rd ser., vol. 10 (1953): 106.

21. Wright, p. 435.

22. Sid Moody, "Slavery Was Widespread During Revolutionary War," *Tampa (Fla.) Tribune,* October 24, 1976, Sec. C, p. 4.

23. Walter Millis, *Arms and Men* (New York, 1956), p. 28.

24. Ibid.

25. Wilkinson, p. 11.

26. John Hyde Preston, *Revolution 1776* (New York, 1933), p. 62. The origin of the quote cited remains speculative though it is indicative of American tactics at Breed's Hill.

27. Wilkinson, p. 14.

28. Scheer, ed., *Private Yankee Doodle,* p. 287, n.4.

29. Clay Perry, "Big Guns for Washington," in *The American Heritage Reader* (New York: Dell Publishing Company, Inc., 1956), p. 89.

30. Wilson and Fiske, 3:566.

31. Perry, p. 97.

32. Lancaster and Plumb, p. 141.

33. Wilkinson, p. 14.

34. Col. Robert E. Gardner, *Small Arms Makers* (New York, 1962), p. 144.

35. Wilkinson, p. 11.

36. Ibid., p. 13.

37. Ibid.

38. Ibid.

39. Ibid.

40. Ibid.

41. Ibid., p. 14.

42. Maj. James E. Hicks, *U.S. Military Firearms, 1776-1956* (Alhambra, Cal., 1962), p. 11.

43. Ibid.

44. Wilkinson, p. 13.

45. Frederick Webb Hodge, ed., *Handbook of American Indians North of Mexico,* 2 vols (Washington, 1912), 1:115.

46. Dale Van Every, *A Company of Heroes* (New York, 1963), p. 102.

47. Ibid., p. 81.

48. Ibid., p. 107.

49. Ibid., p. 270.

50. Wilson and Fiske, 6:655.

51. Millis, p. 35.

52. George C. Neumann, "Firearms of the American Revolution, Part I," *American Rifleman* (July 1967): 17.

53. Ibid.

54. Ibid.

55. Thomas Ewing, *George Ewing, Gentleman, a Soldier of Valley Forge* (Yonkers, 1928), p. 34.

56. Harold L. Peterson, *Arms and Armor in Colonial America, 1526-1783* (New York, 1956), p. 183 (hereafter cited as *Arms and Armor*).

57. Ibid.

58. Col. Arcadi Gluckman, *United States Muskets, Rifles and Carbines* (Buffalo, 1948), p. 48 (hereafter cited as *U.S. Muskets*).

59. Peterson, p. 183.

60. Ibid.

61. Ibid.

62. Ibid., p. 184.

63. Gluckman, p. 44.

64. Ibid., p. 45.

65. Ibid., p. 43.

66. Gardner, p. 204.

67. A Merwyn Carey, *American Firearms Makers* (New York, 1953), p. 7; Gardner, p. 13.

68. Carey, p. 133; Gardner, p. 211.

69. Carey, p. 11; Gardner, p. 20.

70. Carey, p. 138; Gardner, p. 217.

71. Carey, p. 40; Gardner, pp. 67, 217.

72. Gardner, p. 217.

73. Gardner, p. 200.

74. Ibid. Also a letter to the author, January 19, 1971, from F.L. Greaves, Flagstaff, Ariz., citing Merrow Egerton Sorley, *Lewis of Warner Hall* (Columbia, Mo., 1935), n.p.

75. Carey, p. 58; Gardner, pp. 98, 157.

76. Gardner, p. 157.

77. Col. Arcadi Gluckman, *United States Martial Pistols and Revolvers* (Harrisburg, 1956), pp. 29-30. Gluckman mentions a single example of a pistol so marked though it has been exposed as a fake by Nathan L. Swayze, *The Rappahannock Forge* (Cincinnati: American Society of Arms Collectors Publication Number Two, 1976): 33.

78. Peterson, p. 208.

79. Ibid., p. 207.

80. Ibid., p. 208.

81. Gardner, pp. 98-99.

82. Ibid., pp. 37-38.

83. Ibid., p. 38.

84. Ibid., p. 167.
85. Ibid., p. 200.
86. Ibid., pp. 149, 211.
87. Carey, p. 28; Gardner, p. 50.
88. Carey, p. 104; Gardner, pp. 149, 153.
89. Carey, p. 90; Gardner, p. 143.
90. Gardner, p. 50.
91. Ibid., p. 149.
92. Ibid., p. 50.
93. Ibid., p. 112.
94. Ibid., p. 149.
95. Ibid.
96. Ibid., pp. 149, 202.
97. Gluckman, *U.S. Muskets*, p. 49.
98. Scheer and Rankin, p. 241.
99. Gardner, p. 140; Henry J. Kauffman, *Early American Gunsmiths, 1650-1850* (New York, 1952), p. 71.
100. Gardner, p. 140.
101. Ibid., p. 194.
102. Ibid., p. 22.
103. Ibid.
104. Ibid., pp. 126, 209.
105. Ibid., p. 126.
106. Ibid., p. 209.
107. Carey, p. 109; Gardner, p. 170.
108. Gardner, p. 170.
109. Ibid., p. 36.
110. Ibid., pp. 141-142, 157.
111. Ibid., p. 52.
112. Ibid., p. 91.
113. Ibid., p. 52.
114. Ibid., p. 91.
115. Gluckman, p. 49.
116. Peterson, p. 185.
117. Carey, p. 38; Gardner, p. 64.
118. Wilson and Fiske, 3:176, state that Henry ". . . was among those antecedents to Fitch and Fulton in the application of steam . . . to propel boats. His original drawings, made in 1779, were found among his papers after his death."
119. Ibid., 2:472.
120. Peterson, p. 333.
121. Gluckman, p. 48.
122. Gardner, pp. 181, 217.
123. Gluckman, p. 49.
124. Ibid.
125. Ashley Halsey, Jr., "Rarities of the Revolution," *American Rifleman* (July 1972): 42.
126. Peterson, p. 334.
127. Ibid., p. 205.
128. Ibid., p. 217.
129. Ibid., p. 218.
130. Howard L. Blackmore, *Guns and Rifles of the World* (New York, 1965), p. 78.
131. Ibid.
132. Gluckman, p. 65.
133. Gardner, p. 185.
134. Serven, pp. 26-27.
135. Gluckman, p. 49.
136. Gluckman, p. 60.
137. Ibid., p. 61.
138. Ibid., pp. 60-61.
139. Ibid.
140. Lancaster and Plumb, p. 210.
141. Gluckman, p. 60.
142. Peterson, p. 190.
143. Gluckman, pp. 60-61.
144. Gardner, p. 29.
145. Ibid., p. 212.
146. Gluckman, p. 61.
147. Ibid.
148. Ibid.
149. Peterson, p. 215; also Harold L. Peterson, "Pistols in the American Revolution," *American Rifleman* (October 1955): 31-33.
150. Gardner, p. 238.
151. Ibid., p. 327.
152. John S. Barnes, ed., *Fanning's Narrative, Being the Memoirs of Nathaniel Fanning . . . 1778-1783* (New York, 1912), pp. 34-48.
153. Milton F. Perry, "Firearms of the First President," *American Rifleman* (February 1956): 32.
154. Ibid., p. 35; Gardner, p. 270.
155. William Henshaw, *The Orderly Books . . . October 1, 1775 through October 3, 1776* (Worcester, 1948), p. 101.
156. Gardner, p. 263.
157. Ibid.
158. Ibid.
159. Milton F. Perry, p. 33.
160. Ibid.
161. Ibid.
162. Ashley Halsey, Jr., and John M. Snyder, "Jefferson's Beloved Guns," *American Rifleman* (November 1969): 17.
163. Ibid., p. 18.
164. Ibid., p. 19.
165. Ibid., p. 17.
166. Peterson, *Arms and Armor*, p. 183.
167. Ibid., p. 184.
168. Ibid., p. 183.
169. Ibid., pp. 185-186.
170. Carey, p. 64; Gardner, p. 105.
171. Gardner, p. 195.
172. Ibid., p. 144.
173. Ibid., p. 195.
174. Carey, p. 64; Gardner, p. 105.
175. Gardner, p. 54.
176. Ibid.
177. Carey, p. 54; Gardner, p. 92.
178. Gardner, p. 92.
179. Hicks, p. 12.
180. Ibid.
181. Ibid.
182. Ibid.
183. Peterson, p. 227.
184. Ibid.
185. Ibid.
186. Ibid., p. 333.
187. Wilson and Fiske, 4:208.
188. Peterson, p. 228.
189. Kent Britt, "The Loyalists: Americans With A Difference," *National Geographic* (April 1975): 538-539.
190. Spencer C. Tucker, "Cannon Founders of the American Revolution," *National Defense* (July-August 1975): 36-37.
191. Peterson, pp. 332-333.
192. Harold L. Peterson, *The Book of the Continental Soldier,"* (Harrisburg, 1968), p. 75.
193. Ibid., pp. 73-75.

194. Ibid.
195. Ibid., p. 67.
196. Ibid.
197. Peterson, *Arms and Armor,* p. 335.
198. Ibid., pp. 239-241.
199. Ibid., p. 335.
200. Kauffman, p. 89.

CONTINENTAL SOLDIERS AND FRONTIER RIFLEMEN (18 Century): Most American leaders considered the infantry musket superior to the rifle in orthodox warfare, though those who understood its capabilities and limitations frequently used riflemen to great advantage. Courtesy of the Library of Congress.

As the American Revolution progressed, the weary citizen-soldier, always a minority, was forced to carry an even heavier burden than ordinarily shouldered on the battlefield because the avarice of the many purporting to support the patriot cause with the requisites of war produced totally unnecessary hardships and privations.

The war profiteers created an atmosphere of suspicion, petit jealousy, and eventually despair. Enlistments consequently declined, desertions soared, and treason was an ogre which could not be ignored as exemplified by the Hickey Conspiracy (1775), the Conway Cabal (1778), and Benedict Arnold's defection after a brilliant and exemplary combat record.

The Year of the Three Gallows, as 1777 was then called, emerged as the decisive year of the conflict. The stupendous patriot victory at Trenton, snatched by Washington from the gaping jaws of defeat in the waning days of 1776, was immediately followed by the triumph at Princeton, January 3, 1777. And it was in the autumn of 1777 that the eventual patriot victory was determined when on October 17 Gen. John "Gentleman Johnny" Burgoyne surrendered at Saratoga, N.Y., and neither he nor his troops were again engaged in the war.

Trenton and Saratoga smashed George III's illusions of a quick victory and influenced the decision of France and Spain to intervene in the conflict on a more than salutory level. On February 6, 1778, the struggling United States concluded the Treaty of Commerce and Alliance with France and direct French support materialized on July 8, 1778, two days prior to the official French declaration of war against Britain and ten days after Washington's success over Sir Henry Clinton at Monmouth, N.J., when the fleet of Comte Jean d' Estaing appeared off the Delaware Capes.

Charles III made no formal alliance with the patriots as had Louis XVI, rather he had declared war on Britain June 16, 1779, because the French promised to assist him in recovering Gibraltar and *La*

Florida; both lost to Britain in the wake of the French and Indian War.

In September, 1779, the important British supply bases at Baton Rouge, Natches, and Manchac fell to Bernardo de Galvez and on March 10, 1780, he captured Mobile in West Florida. Four months to the day later Comte Jean Baptiste Donatien de Vimeur de Rochambeau arrived at Newport, R.I., with the first complement of French troops: 6,000 infantry armed with the M1777 musket.

The Spaniards continued their impressive string of victories and in January, 1781, British-held Fort St. Joseph in the Illinois country was taken by Don Eugenio Pourre in an action subsequently used by Carlos III to advance his claim to the entire Louisiana territory. From March 9 to May 8 Galvez beseiged the strong British bastion of Fort George at Pensacola. The outcome was decided when a Spanish shell struck the powder magazine in the Queen's Redoubt, killing 105 and forcing Gen. John Campbell's surrender.

The Rifle in the American Revolution

The romanticist nonsense purveyed over the years by numerous historians has exaggerated beyond credence the role of the American rifle in the War of Independence. The blanket contention that the American rifle "won the war" is no more valid or justified than the narrow view that its performance was insignificant. The truth is to be found between those extremes and, judged in the context of its milieu, the American rifle gave a stellar performance. The American rifle, however, was not the only rifle used by the combatants during the protracted struggle.

First and always a frontier firearm, the American rifle was suited to the game, terrain, and

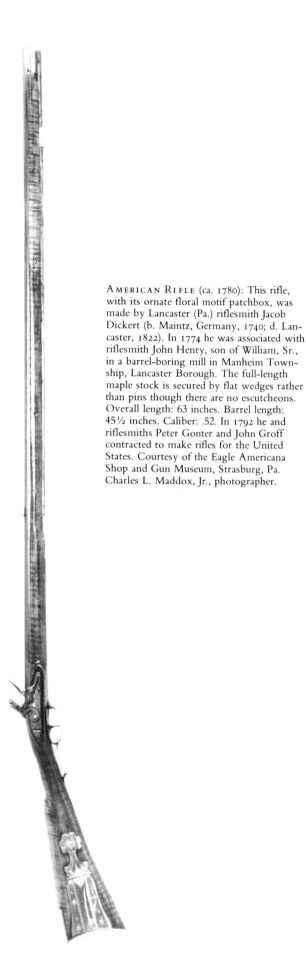

AMERICAN RIFLE (ca. 1780): This rifle, with its ornate floral motif patchbox, was made by Lancaster (Pa.) riflesmith Jacob Dickert (b. Maintz, Germany, 1740; d. Lancaster, 1822). In 1774 he was associated with riflesmith John Henry, son of William, Sr., in a barrel-boring mill in Manheim Township, Lancaster Borough. The full-length maple stock is secured by flat wedges rather than pins though there are no escutcheons. Overall length: 63 inches. Barrel length: 45½ inches. Caliber: .52. In 1792 he and riflesmiths Peter Gonter and John Groff contracted to make rifles for the United States. Courtesy of the Eagle Americana Shop and Gun Museum, Strasburg, Pa. Charles L. Maddox, Jr., photographer.

guerilla-style warfare of the wilderness. In the central combat arena of the Revolutionary War, however, orthodox tactics were dominant and the American rifle was subordinate to the smoothbore musket because it failed to meet the criteria for a suitable infantry firearm: (1) it was slower and more difficult to load, and (2) it had no bayonet. For those reasons the American rifle was almost completely misunderstood as a tactical weapon by patriot officers schooled in eighteenth-century European warfare; yet there were a few, like Col. Daniel Morgan and Gen. Nathaniel Greene, who learned to use it advantageously.

The American rifle was slowly integrated into patriot ranks and served the Tories and the Native Americans aligned with either side as well. Operating against the patriots in New York, New England, and Pennsylvania, John Butler's Rangers and Joseph Brant's followers recognized the value of the American rifle, chiefly through the influence of Sir William Johnson, who had prior to his death in 1774 persuaded a few Pennsylvania riflemakers to work in Canajoharie, Johnstown, Kingston, and Schenectady, N.Y.[1]

On the New England frontier rifle production was minimal before hostilities began, though rifles were familiar to Ethan Allen's Green Mountain Boys and other French and Indian War veterans. From Pennsylvania southward along the Appalachians the American rifle was known and respected by patriot, loyalist, and Native American alike. In the populous tidewater settlements, however, the American rifle and most other kinds remained virtually unknown prior to hostilities.

In any event rifles of some undetermined kind were available in New York City before the Revolutionary War, and while it is remotely possible that they were the American rifle, it is more likely that they were European, though the evidence is inconclusive, as indicated in the advertisement appearing March 16, 1775, in the *New York Journal and General Advertiser:*

> Gilbert Forbes, Gun Maker. At the Sign of the Sportsman in the Broad Way, opposite Hull's Tavern in New York. Makes and sells all sorts of guns, in the neatest and best manner; on the lowest terms; has for sale, Silver and Brass Mounted Pistols; Rifle Barrel Guns, Double swivel and double-roller gun locks; 50 ready made new bayonet guns, on all one size and pattern.[2]

Several of the Pennsylvania, Maryland, and Virginia rifle companies called for by Continental Congress had reached the Provisional Army at Cambridge by July, 1775, bringing to tidewater New Englanders and others their first glimpse of the

American rifle which was as alien to their eyes as the strangely though colorfully garbed frontiersmen carrying them. As one apocryphal story has it, the easterners surrounding Boston watched with considerable astonishment as a company of frontier riflemen placed all of its shots in a seven-inch target at 250 yards.[3]

Even if shooting conditions had been perfect the tale is extremely difficult to accept, for such accuracy at 250 yards is nothing short of phenomenal and it is likely that the story was concocted for propaganda in an attempt to impress the British with American prowess. A more plausible paean to American rifle accuracy was given by John Harrower, an indentured servant teaching at a Virginia plantation school. Harrower observed, as one company commander sought, without much success, to eliminate the worst marksmen from an overflow of volunteer riflemen seeking to accompany him to Cambridge:

> He took a board of a foot square and with chalk drew the shape of a moderate nose in the center and nailed it up to a tree at one hundred and fifty yards distance, and those who came nighest the mark with a single ball was to go. But by the first forty or fifty that fired, the nose was all blown out of the board, and by the time his company was [filled] up, the board shared the same fate.[4]

The shooting match recorded by Harrower at a much more realistic 150 yards was certainly a challenge compared to the customary frontier match range of 60 to 80 paces (see p. 270).

Largely unfettered by the customary amenities of civilized behavior and noted for an uncommon braggadocio, frontier riflemen were not the most popular troops comprising the infant Continental Army and at Cambridge their marksmanship and conduct suffered some justified criticism; the common sentiment expressed by Benjamin Thompson:

> . . . instead of being the best marksmen in the world and picking off every [British] regular that was to be seen, there is scarcely a regiment in camp but can produce men that can beat them at shooting, and the army is now universally convinced that the continual firing which they kept up by the week and month together has had no other effect than to waste their ammunition and convince the King's troops that they are not really so formidable . . . as they wish to be thought. . . . And to be sure, there never was a more mutinous and undisciplined set of villains that bred disturbance in any camp. . . .[5]

No more objective evaluation of the formidable accuracy and range of the American rifle came unsolicited from Maj. George Hanger whose comments on the efficacy of the smoothbore musket were previously noted (see p. 228). Hanger was captured at Saratoga in 1777, and after the war he recalled what was possibly his first encounter with the American rifle as he, Lt. Col. Banastre Tarleton, and a bugler reconnoitered an American position:

> . . . There was a rivulet in the enemy's front, and a mill on it, to which we stood directly with our horses' heads fronting, observing their motions. It was absolutely a plain field between us and the mill. . . . Our orderly-bugler stood behind us about three yards, but with his horses's side to our horse's tails. A rifleman passed over the milldam, evidently observing two officers, and laid himself down on his belly; for in such positions, they always lie, to take a good shot at a long distance. He took a deliberate and cool shot at my friend, at me, and at the bugle-horn man. Now observe how well this fellow shot. It was in . . . August, and not a breath of wind was stirring. . . . A rifle-ball passed between him and me; looking directly to the mill I evidently observed the flash of the powder. I directly said to my friend, 'I think we had better move, or we shall have two or three of these gentlemen shortly amusing themselves at our expense.' The words were hardly out of my mouth when the bugle-horn man behind me . . . jumped off his horse and said, 'Sir, my horse is shot.' The horse staggered, fell down, and died. . . . I have passed several times over this ground and ever observed it with the greatest attention; and I can positively assert that the distance he fired at us was full 400 yards.[6]

Hanger, doubtlessly impressed by the incident, attempted to learn more about the American rifle and the opportunity came after he had been taken prisoner, for he noted, "I have many times asked the American backwoodsman what was the most their best marksmen could do; they have constantly told me that an expert marksman, provided he can draw good and true sight . . . can hit the head of a man at 200 yards."[7]

It has been asserted that the American rifle was responsible for the patriot victory at Saratoga when Tim Murphy, a Pennsylvania rifleman in Col. Daniel Morgan's command, picked off Gen. Simon Fraser of the resolute 71st Highlanders, thereby stalling the British counterattack and forcing Bourgoyne's surrender.[8] While Morgan primarily used his riflemen in the fashion dictated by frontier warfare or as snipers instructed to eliminate enemy commanders, Gen. Nathaniel Greene more shrewdly assessed the advantages of the rifle.

Greene, for example, drew up his infantry line in three ranks and it was his habit, depending upon the tactical situation, to put his riflemen in the forefront where the range and accuracy of their weapons successfully thinned the advancing enemy. When the distance closed, however, he withdrew his riflemen and engaged the enemy with musketry from his second line usually comprised of state troops and militia. If necessary the second line also retired, exposing the enemy to the musketry and the bayonets of his experienced Continentals in the third line. When, as often happened, the enemy broke in the face of that formidable arrangement, Greene again advanced his riflemen to extract a deadly price from the fleeing remnants.

While the tightly fitting, patched ball requisite for accuracy and range made the American rifle slower and more difficult to load than the smoothbore musket and thereby curtailed its rapid fire capability, its fragile design precluded the use of a bayonet which was often the decisive factor in eighteenth-century warfare. Though the slim stock profile reduced the weight of the American rifle it also weakened the wrist and the butt which were easily damaged or broken when subjected to the hard physical abuse of bayonet fighting and hand-to-hand combat.

That muskets and rifles without bayonets were no match for muskets with them was a cruel lesson early learned by the patriots, for directly after Breed's Hill a letter from Samuel Webster to the New Hampshire COS bitterly lamented "... 'tis barbarous to let men be obliged to oppose Bayonets with only gun Barrels. ..."[9]

Webster's complaint was certainly valid and the absence of the bayonet among rebel riflemen was amplified disastrously in the hotly contested Battle of Long Island on August 20-21, 1776, as Gen. John Sullivan's rifle battalion was slaughtered by Col. von Heeringen's Hessians at Guan Heights. More than 600 Americans died there, and for years it was called, with good reason, The Wood of Horrors; the full meaning of the appellation conveyed by von Herringen's words:

> ... The greater part of the riflemen were pierced with the bayonet to the trees. These dreadful people ought rather to be pitied than feared; they always require a quarter of an hour's time to load a rifle, and in the meantime they feel the effects of our balls and bayonets.[10]

Accustomed as they were to the use of the bayonet, British and Hessian troops often overwhelmed patriot riflemen as they reloaded, though loading was somewhat faster than von Heeringen's contemptuous comment suggests, and they frequently waited for such an opportunity as happened at Princeton when Hugh Mercer's slow-loading

AMERICAN AND HESSIAN MUSKET Bayonets (18th Century): Left. American musket bayonet made under COS contract and marked U S, blade: 17¾ inches; socket: 2¾ inches. Right. Hessian musket bayonet, blade: 15 inches; socket: 2¾ inches. The socket is marked 57 near the elbow and the letters and numerals C VII: N 35 appear on the socket. Courtesy of the Morristown National Historical Park, Morristown, N.J. Charles L. Maddox, Jr., photographer.

riflemen were shredded by the cold steel of the 17th Leicesters and 55th Borderers.

Washington, several of his field commanders, and many patriot officials were extremely conscious of the inherent deficiencies of the rifle. Maryland, offering to supply a rifle company for the Continental Army, received a rather curt response from the Secretary of the Board of War:

> If muskets were given them instead of rifles the service would be more benefitted, as there is a superabundance of riflemen in the Army. Were it in the power of Congress to supply musketts they would speedily reduce the number of rifles and replace them with the former, as they are more easily kept in order, can be fired oftener and have the advantage of Bayonetts.[11]

As early as 1777 Gen. Washington sought to alleviate the bayonet problem, suggesting that spears with hinged shafts be issued to riflemen. The design initially submitted was unsuitable and an improved Rifleman's Pike was subsequently devised by Col. Benjamin Flower though whether any were made and used remains conjectural.[12]

The American rifle, while not a decisive factor in the conflict, performed admirably on the frontier and was used to good advantage on several occasions by those patriot officers familiar with its limitations and capabilities.

The British could not be considered ignorant concerning the American rifle or rifles in general. Many redcoat veterans of the French and Indian War and ensuing Native American confrontations had been introduced to the American rifle and a number of them had been sent to Britain for evaluation. A few select British marksmen were issued rifles of a special pattern during the American Revolution and one British unit was provided with sophisticated breech-loading flintlock rifles.

The approximately 4,000 jäeger light infantry among George III's Hessian auxiliaries were armed with rifles. Primarily from Anspach, Brunswick, and Hannau, the jäeger served as pickets and skirmishers and at least one mounted jäegers unit was active, facing the Americans at Pound Ridge, N.Y., on July 2, 1779. While most of the jäegers participated in the northern campaigns, some were engaged in the southern theatre; particularly at Wetzell's Mills, N.C., on March 16, 1781, and Guilford Court House nine days later.

The martial jäeger rifle employed in the American Revolution was a plain though somewhat heavier version of the popular German hunting rifle early brought to the Pennsylvania Colony. It was comparable to its offspring, the American rifle, in accuracy and range though displaying a shorter bar-

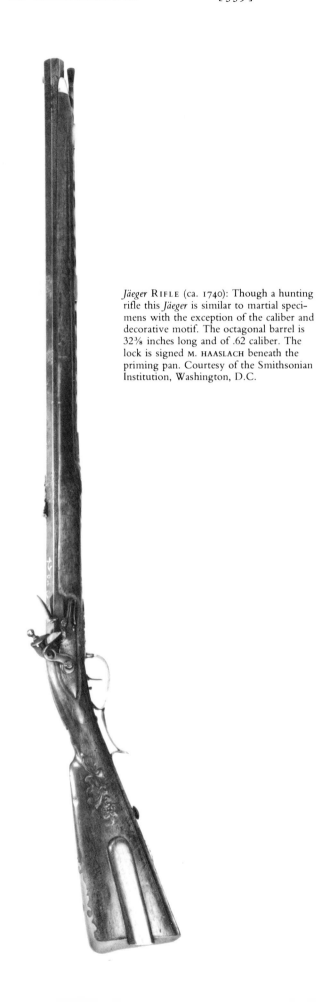

Jäeger RIFLE (ca. 1740): Though a hunting rifle this *Jäeger* is similar to martial specimens with the exception of the caliber and decorative motif. The octagonal barrel is 32⅜ inches long and of .62 caliber. The lock is signed M. HAASLACH beneath the priming pan. Courtesy of the Smithsonian Institution, Washington, D.C.

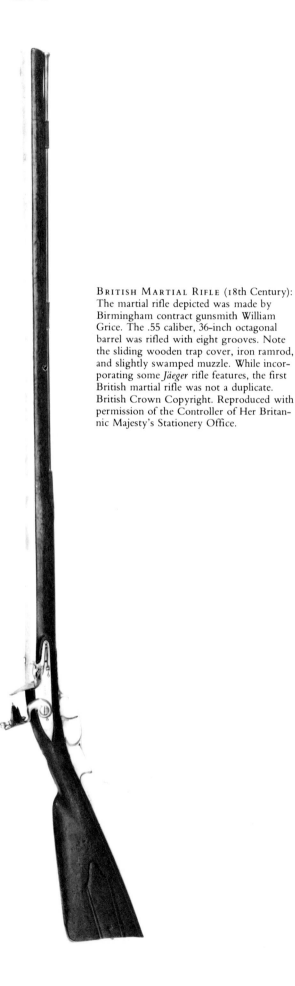

BRITISH MARTIAL RIFLE (18th Century): The martial rifle depicted was made by Birmingham contract gunsmith William Grice. The .55 caliber, 36-inch octagonal barrel was rifled with eight grooves. Note the sliding wooden trap cover, iron ramrod, and slightly swamped muzzle. While incorporating some *Jäeger* rifle features, the first British martial rifle was not a duplicate. British Crown Copyright. Reproduced with permission of the Controller of Her Britannic Majesty's Stationery Office.

rel and a larger caliber. Many of those recruited for the *jäeger* battalions, however, were stolid peasants who were as ignorant of rifles and marksmanship as they were of military service in general; a deplorable fact conveniently disregarded by British recruiters and the German nobles desperately seeking to fill enlistment quotas by any means to swell their coffers.

A small cadre of British officers, veterans of the frontier campaigns in the French and Indian War, intensified their efforts to convince the Board of Ordnance that the American rifle or rifles of a similar pattern could serve a useful role in the British Army (see p. 289); a view apparently given greater consideration in the aftermath of Lexington and Concord, for it was suggested by the board that five riflemen be assigned as marksmen to each company in the regiments posted to the fractious American colonies, and that a minimum of 1,000 rifles would be required to arm them.[13] The decision regarding what kind of rifles and who would make them was not immediate.

The Master General of the Ordnance, familiar with the *jäeger* rifles employed by some Hessian auxiliary units, requested a pair of them from Col. Faucitt, the British recruiting officer in Hanover. Following a thorough examination by the Board of Ordnance, Col. Faucitt was ordered to procure from reputable riflesmiths 200 *jäeger* rifles of good quality, for ". . . the advantages which these Pieces are supposed to have over Musquets will be lost if the exactness of their Construction and the goodness of the materials are not particularly attended to."[14]

The 800 remaining rifles of the 1,000 approved for procurement were contracted from four reputable Birmingham gunsmiths in January and March, 1776.[15] The first (January) contract was assigned to William Grice (fl. 1770-1790), an experienced martial musket contractor and formerly a volume exporter of gunlocks and other firearms components to British America.[16]

It is not known whether Grice had prior riflemaking expertise, though he was paid £ 3/3s/0d each for 200 rifles and instructed to make pattern pieces. He fulfilled his obligation and the pattern pieces were distributed to three other contractors in March: Matthew (Matthias) Barker (fl. 1775-1780),[17] Benjamin Wilets (Willets, fl. 1770-1789),[18] and Thomas Galton & Sons (fl. 1750-1785).[19] Wilets and the Galtons had previously produced contract muskets.

The Grice-pattern rifles did not exactly duplicate the *jäeger* design and one example, now in the Tower of London Armouries (No. XII-94), is 52 inches overall with a 36 inch, octagonal barrel of .55 caliber rifled with eight grooves and slightly swamped at the muzzle. The full-length walnut stock emulated the Brown Bess musket pattern. The brass furniture and sights as well as the butt trap with its sliding wood cover followed the *jäeger* design. There were no sling swivels and two thimbles and a guide secured the wood ramrod. The flat lockplate is engraved GRICE and the initials W G are stamped in the breech with the V (viewed) and P (proof) marks earlier designed by Galton (see Chapter VI, n. 16). Flanking those marks are two crossed scepters denoting Tower proofhouse acceptance; the design derived from the early Ketland proof symbol.

Galton & Sons produced 200 rifles, Wilets made 192, and Barker fabricated 78 before the Master General of the Ordnance abruptly ordered in late April that "... no more Rifles be made according to the present Pattern and that number wanted to compleat those already bespoke must be finished immediately. ..."[20] It is not known how many, if any, of the muzzle-loading rifles reached the American colonies though it is possible that a few were among the rifles issued to a special corps of 50 marksmen assigned to Gen. Burgoyne during his ill-fated 1777 New York campaigns.[21]

The sudden decision to halt muzzle-loading rifle production was influenced by the outcome of a series of trials initiated on April 27, 1776, when Capt. Patrick Ferguson (1744-1780), formerly serving with the 70th Foot at Tobago, West Indies, demonstrated the astonishing capabilities of a sophisticated breech-loading flintlock rifle he designed in 1774 and tested at his estate in Scotland the following year (see p. 189).[22]

In June, 1776, the *Annual Register* made the following comment on the Ferguson rifle demonstration:

Some experiments were tried at Woolwich before Lord Viscount [George] Townshend, Lord [Gen. Jeffrey] Amherst, Generals Hervey and Desaguilliers, and a number of other officers, with a rifle gun upon a new construction by Captain Ferguson, ... when that gentleman, under the disadvantage of a heavy rain and a high wind, performed the following four things, none of which have ever before been accomplished with any other small arms: First, he fired during four or five minutes at a target, at 200 yds. distance, at the rate of four shots each minute; second, he fired six shots in one minute; third, he fired four times per minute, advancing at the same time at the rate of four miles in the hour; fourth, he poured a bottle of water into the pan and barrel of the piece when loaded, so as to wet every grain of powder, and in less than half a minute fired with her as well as ever, without extracting the ball. He also hit the bullseye at 100 yds., lying with his back on the ground; and, notwithstanding the unequalness of the weather, he only missed the target three times during the whole course of the experiment.[23]

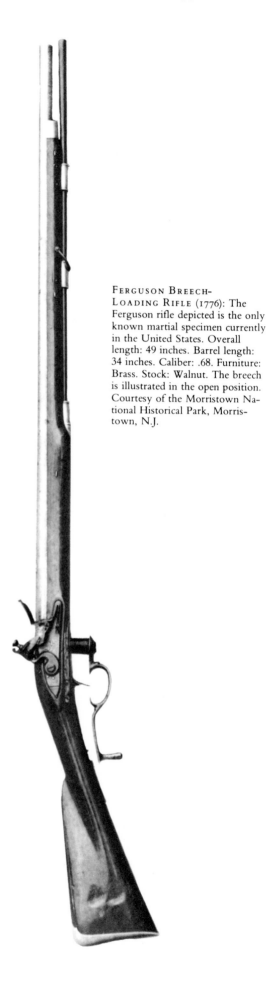

FERGUSON BREECH-LOADING RIFLE (1776): The Ferguson rifle depicted is the only known martial specimen currently in the United States. Overall length: 49 inches. Barrel length: 34 inches. Caliber: .68. Furniture: Brass. Stock: Walnut. The breech is illustrated in the open position. Courtesy of the Morristown National Historical Park, Morristown, N.J.

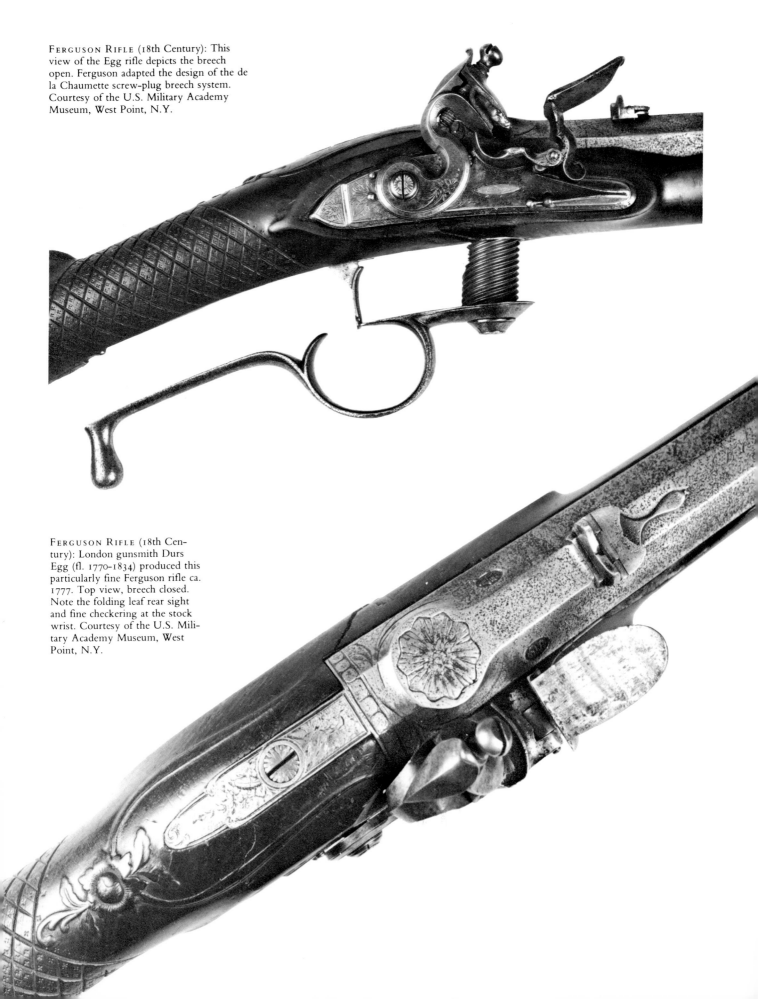

FERGUSON RIFLE (18th Century): This view of the Egg rifle depicts the breech open. Ferguson adapted the design of the de la Chaumette screw-plug breech system. Courtesy of the U.S. Military Academy Museum, West Point, N.Y.

FERGUSON RIFLE (18th Century): London gunsmith Durs Egg (fl. 1770-1834) produced this particularly fine Ferguson rifle ca. 1777. Top view, breech closed. Note the folding leaf rear sight and fine checkering at the stock wrist. Courtesy of the U.S. Military Academy Museum, West Point, N.Y.

FERGUSON RIFLE (18th Century): The breech is closed in this view of the Ferguson rifle. Egg's signature appears on the oval silver inlay mortised into the lockplate beneath the priming pan. The rear curvature of the pan acted as a fence, angling ignition flash away from the eyes. Courtesy of the U.S. Military Academy Museum, West Point, N.Y.

It was truly an amazing performance in the age of the smoothbore muzzle-loader and Ferguson subsequently duplicated many of his marksmanship feats for George III at Windsor Castle, while shortly thereafter he was assured that the rifle would be officially adopted and that he would be given command of an elite corps of marksmen armed with it so it could be thoroughly tested under combat conditions in the rebellious colonies.

Though Ferguson's rifle was never officially adopted the four Birmingham gunsmiths who had received the previous rifle contracts were awarded new contracts by the Board of Ordnance in May, 1776, for the manufacture of 100 Ferguson breech loading rifles "... with plugs and bayonets ..." at £4 each.[24] None of the contractors experienced production difficulties and all of them met their quotas of 25 rifles apiece, indicating that despite the mechanical sophistication of the Ferguson rifle it was well within the technological capability of the era.

On November 2, 1776, Ferguson received patent No. 1139 for his rifle though he never alluded to himself as its inventor, nor was it "... a rifle gun upon a new construction ..." as asserted in the *Annual Register*. Ferguson merely contributed a design modification to the innovative screw plug breech-loading system originally conceived by von Sprinzenstein and subsequently developed by others; notably Isaac de la Chaumette (see p. 189).

In the Ferguson design the screw plug was altered with a series of vertical channels interrupting the helical threads; the channels trapping excess powder residue which clogged the threads and made the breech difficult or impossible to open as happened in the de la Chaumette and prior systems. Combined with Bidet's quick-turn thread for rapid breech operation (see p. 189), Ferguson's design brought the screw plug breech-loading system to the apogee of perfection.

A particular advantage of the Ferguson system was that the soldier could load the rifle in virtually any position without a ramrod; thus limiting his exposure to enemy fire. It was, however, an advantage not fully realized until the widespread acceptance of metallic cartridge breech-loaders in the latter half of the nineteenth century.

Contracts were awarded for 200 additional Ferguson rifles in late 1776.[25] Officer and infantry models were made, each varying in dimensions. The infantry version weighed seven and ½ pounds and was approximately 50 inches long, displaying a round, iron barrel of 34 inches rifled with eight grooves, while caliber fluctuated between .60 and .63. The full-length walnut stock was fastened to the barrel by flat keys (wedges) rather than pins; an innovation reaching North America late in the century.

The furniture of the enlisted model was brass, including the three thimbles for the cleaning rod which could be used to knock a ball out of the breech when it was desired to unload. The rear sight was of the leaf type, adjustable in elevation from 100 to 500 yards. Birmingham gunsmith John Whatley (fl. 1770-1778) was apparently involved with Matthias Barker in making the infantry pattern Ferguson rifle, for the initials I W appear on a specimen made by Barker and now located in the Morristown (N.J.) National Historical Park collection.[26]

The officers' model Ferguson rifle was produced by such estimable gunsmiths as Durs Egg of London (fl. 1770-1834),[27] Francis Innes of Edinburgh (fl.1773-1777), and others.[28] It weighed approximately seven pounds, displaying a 24 to 26 inch octagonal barrel ranging from .58 to .60 caliber. The barrel was half-stocked in walnut, leaving clearance for a sliding, retractable, 25 and ½ inch bayonet. Officers' versions were similar to the lightweight fusil and were customarily given a better finish and were more elegantly appointed than infantry models, some displaying light scroll engraving on the lock and checkering at the stock wrist. Sights emulated the enlisted model.

Despite the advantages of accuracy, fast loading, and rapid firing there was a discernable weakness evident in the Ferguson rifle design, for the bulk of

the breech subjected the stock to excessive stress at that point. At least one Ferguson rifle—the Morristown specimen—illustrates a major stock repair, mended at the fragile breech with a piece of U-shaped iron.[29] A flint-ignition rifle, the Ferguson was also susceptible to the vagaries of the weather, though it was apparently less effected by rain than most contemporary firearms as indicated by the April trials noted in the *Annual Register*.

It has been frequently asserted that the Ferguson was the first rifle and the first breech-loader to be adopted for military use by any nation. It was, however, preceded as a martial rifle by the muzzle-loaders made in Birmingham prior to the Ferguson contracts, and as a martial breech-loader by the Crespi pivotal breech musket and carbine accepted by Austria in 1770 (see p. 191). Nevertheless, the Ferguson rifle can be considered the first screw-breech firearm successfully produced in quantity and the *first breech-loading rifle* adopted on a limited scale, for it did not officially replace the Brown Bess musket.

*Italics added.

FERGUSON RIFLE (18th Century): This view of the left side of the Ferguson rifle breech depicts the rear sling swivel arrangement and broken stock. The crown and crossed scepters mark at the breech/stock juncture denotes Tower acceptance. Further breech markings include the initials M b & I W; the former signifying Birmingham contractor Matthew Barker (fl. 1775-1780) and the latter John Whatley (fl. 1770-1778) who was apparently affiliated with Barker. Courtesy of the Morristown National Historical Park, Morristown, N.J. Charles L. Maddox, Jr., photographer.

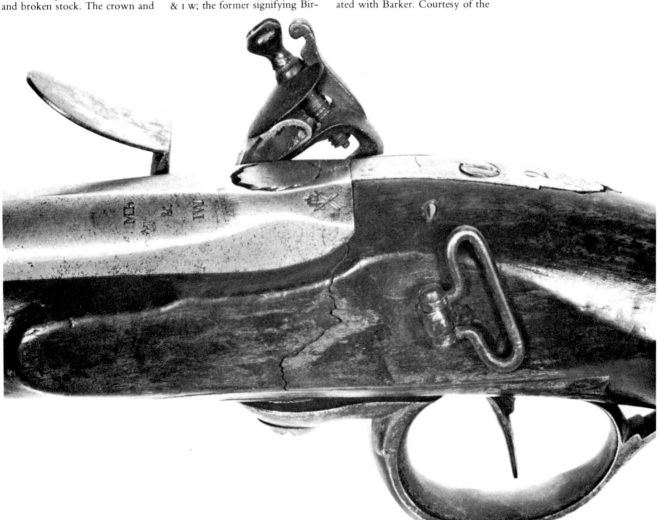

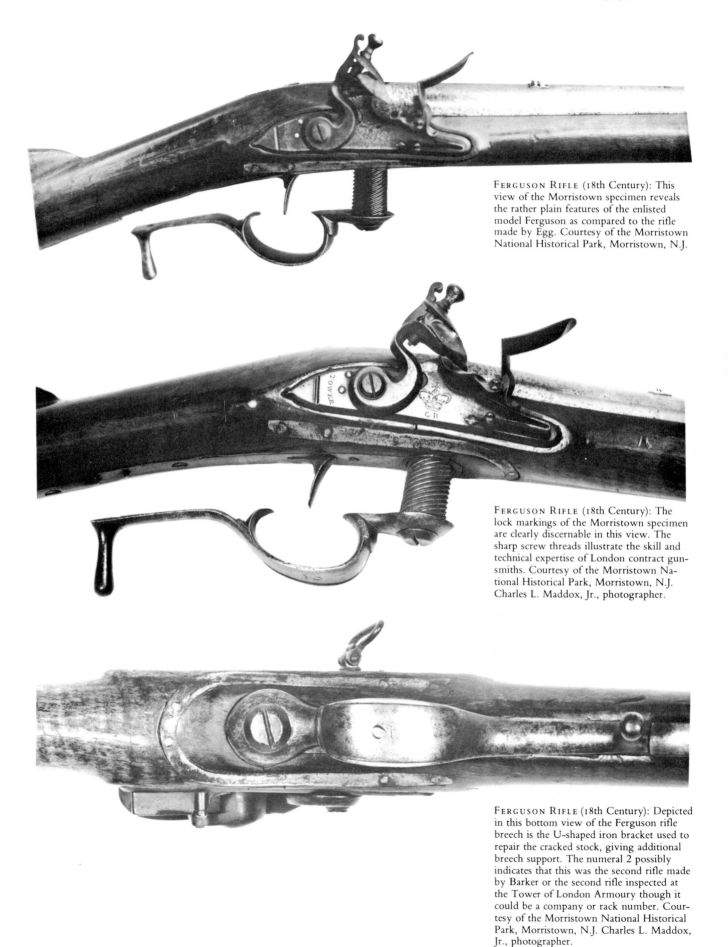

FERGUSON RIFLE (18th Century): This view of the Morristown specimen reveals the rather plain features of the enlisted model Ferguson as compared to the rifle made by Egg. Courtesy of the Morristown National Historical Park, Morristown, N.J.

FERGUSON RIFLE (18th Century): The lock markings of the Morristown specimen are clearly discernable in this view. The sharp screw threads illustrate the skill and technical expertise of London contract gunsmiths. Courtesy of the Morristown National Historical Park, Morristown, N.J. Charles L. Maddox, Jr., photographer.

FERGUSON RIFLE (18th Century): Depicted in this bottom view of the Ferguson rifle breech is the U-shaped iron bracket used to repair the cracked stock, giving additional breech support. The numeral 2 possibly indicates that this was the second rifle made by Barker or the second rifle inspected at the Tower of London Armoury though it could be a company or rack number. Courtesy of the Morristown National Historical Park, Morristown, N.J. Charles L. Maddox, Jr., photographer.

Despite the overwhelming technological superiority of the Ferguson rifle and the fact that it could be readily manufactured in quantity, the imponderable course of history seemingly conspired to prevent its large-scale adoption as the regulation British infantry arm and its fate and that of its inventor was sealed at King's Mountain, S.C.

For Capt. Patrick Ferguson, a municipal barrister's son born in Pitfour, Scotland, the curiously twisting road to King's Mountain began when at 14 he joined the British Army. The spring of 1777 found him in Pennsylvania, assigned to Gen. Simon Fraser's 71st (Highlanders) Regiment, and his journey thereafter was strewn with obstacles by Gen. William Howe, the British commander-in-chief, who resented the incursion of a 33-year-old captain with King's orders to form a special corps of marksmen drafted from his command.

Despite Howe, Ferguson organized and trained a small cadre of expert marksmen; a number of them loyalists familiar with the American rifle. On September 8, 1777, he and his riflemen were encamped at Kennet Square, Pa., as the British prepared to move against Gen. Washington across the Brandywine. And it was during the bloody engagement on the 11th that Ferguson, according to a tale now considered apocryphal by some historians, could have altered the entire course of the Revolutionary War and made Great Britain master of North America.

Scouting the British front, Ferguson and a few of his riflemen purportedly spied two American officers, one of them passing close enough to his position, as he later wrote, that "... I could have lodged half a dozen balls in or about him before he was out of my reach, but it was not pleasant to fire at the back of an unoffending individual who was acquitting himself very coolly of his duty, so I let him alone."[30] There is, however, no conclusive evidence that the two patriot officers were Gen. George Washington and his aide-de-camp, the Marquis de Lafayette, as often asserted.

Later that day Ferguson's right elbow was shattered by a rebel ball and while he was recuperating he learned that Gen. Howe disbanded his riflemen and shipped his breech-loaders to Nova Scotia; a spiteful act, though such vengeful and malicious ploys were prevalent in both the British and American high command throughout the conflict.

When sufficiently recovered from his wound, Ferguson retrieved some of the rifles from Nova Scotia and raised another force of marksmen, while his audacity at Stony Point, N.Y., on May 31, 1779, earned him a promotion to major. The British victory was of short duration, for in a midnight bayonet assault on July 16 Gen. Anthony Wayne recaptured the position, as well as a number of Ferguson's breech-loading rifles.

Shortly thereafter Ferguson took command of 300 New York and New Jersey loyalists known as The American Volunteers, though they soon merited the sobriquet Ferguson's Sharp-shooters. In March, 1780, Ferguson was again wounded, a bayonet piercing his good left arm during the attack on Charleston, S.C. With Gen. Benjamin Lincoln's surrender on May 12, Sir Henry Clinton ordered Lord Cornwallis and Tarleton's Legion to invade the interior.

Victorious at Camden, S.C., on August 16, 1780, Cornwallis failed to pursue the rebels and, contrary to Clinton's orders, decided upon a Virginia campaign rather than marching and counter-marching through the blistering South Carolina heat searching for an elusive enemy constantly nipping at his flanks; a problem growing more acute as summer drew to a close.

Fighting fire with fire, Cornwallis dispatched Ferguson and his riflemen to protect his western flank as his main body marched to Virginia and in so doing precipitated the Battle of King's Mountain. Bolstered by local Tories, Ferguson challenged the Carolinians, proclaiming he would "... march his army over the mountains, hang their leaders, and lay their country waste with fire and sword."[31]

The effect of Ferguson's haughty pronouncement was immediate.

By September 30 nearly 1,400 overmountain men gathered with their rifles on the Catawba River under the estimable leadership of Col. William Campbell, Col. Isaac Shelby, and Lt. Col. John Sevier. As the formidable host marched toward Cowpens, S.C., it was joined by 400 riflemen led by Col. James Williams. Now nearly 2,000 strong the frontiersmen were unified under Col. Campbell on October 6.

Ferguson, unsure of his loyalists and learning that his 1,110-man force was outnumbered, heeded the military axiom as valid then and now as it was in the days of Gaius Julius Caesar: Take the high ground. The highest and the most defensible ground in the vicinity was King's Mountain. There he and his loyalist riflemen waited, approximately 100 of them armed with his breech-loaders.[32]

The morning of October 7, 1780, dawned gray and overcast and by noon the Americans began silently filtering up the heavily wooded, boulder-strewn slopes made more treacherous by the light though incessant autumn rain which remains a harbinger of southern winter. Ferguson received no warning until the crack of American rifles rent the air, followed by the bull-voiced command of Col. Isaac Shelby, "Shout like hell and fight like devils!"[33]

The sharp encounter was a rifleman's contest, the whistling balls shattering flesh and bone with astonishing regularity. "Rifleman took off rifleman with such exactness," wrote a contemporary, "that they killed each other when taking sight, so instantaneously that their eyes remained open after they were dead, one shut and the other open, in the usual way of marksmen when levelling at their object."[34]

Blood and powdersmoke mingled freely as Ferguson, astride his plunging war horse, seemed everywhere at once, the checkered hunting shirt he habitually wore in battle a beacon for his men and a target for every patriot. Wiping the stinging sweat from his powder-blackened face, an American rifleman knelt behind a boulder to reload, searching the laurel and wild azalea thicket for a target. Snapping his long rifle to his shoulder, he squeezed the trigger and the flash in the priming pan was instantaneous with the shock of recoil as a British officer tumbled from his mount.

Patrick Ferguson, soldier-inventor, was dead.

The propitious American victory at King's Mountain was the turning point in the southern campaigns and validated the American rifle as a valuable instrument of eighteenth-century warfare. Shortly thereafter the rifle proved itself again, for now Gen. Daniel Morgan's riflemen devastated Tarleton's Legion at Cowpens on January 17, 1781.

Considering the varied role of the rifle in the American Revolution it is tempting to speculate about what might have happened had Ferguson not fallen at King's Mountain or had been previously incapacitated, for with his vigor and the confidence he expressed in his rifle it is possible that Britain would have adopted it on a large scale, thereby ultimately altering the outcome of the rebellion and doubtlessly upsetting the future balance of power in Europe.

That observation also lends itself to speculation, for Britain's rivals would have been forced in self-defense to devise comparable martial firearms or develop superior breech-loading systems; thus creating a situation not unlike the present armament race.

Yet another point to ponder is what happened to the firearms captured by the Americans at King's Mountain and were any of them Ferguson rifles?

On February 1, 1781, the North Carolina *Senate Journal* reported:

Whereas it is represented to the General Assembly by Col. Cleveland of Wilkes County, that he hath now in his hands 153 stands of arms taken from Major Ferguson's party at the Battle of King's Mountain. Fifty-three stands Colonel Cleveland considers his own property by purchase from the captors; the other 100 stands ready to be applied to public use.[35]

The *Senate Journal* subsequently noted that the 100 stands ". . . were branded upon the breech with the initials of the words North Carolina . . . ," and

were then turned over to the state. Of the 1,100 British and Tories engaged, it appears that more than 153 firearms would have been recovered and worthy of mention. That Col. Cleveland purchased 53 of the 153 stands taken indicates that they were a special kind, yet there is no conclusive evidence that they were Ferguson rifles and the *Senate Journal* does not provide a specific description of the remaining 100; thus unless more concrete evidence is forthcoming the question cannot be satisfactorily resolved.

Gunsmiths of the American Revolution

Just as the Ferguson rifle question remains unanswered there is no accurate data available pertaining to the number of gunsmiths in British America at the time of the struggle for independence. It has been estimated, however, that fewer than 2,000 were then active.[36] Of that arbitrary figure perhaps as many as 1,500 could be found in the tidewater settlements and the remainder scattered along the vast Appalachian frontier, while possibly two thirds of the estimated total embraced the patriot cause; a frightfully small number when compared to a population of more than two million.

Most patriot gunsmiths were independent craftsmen, toiling in their small shops, though a few established large factories employing skilled and semi-skilled artisans including journeymen, apprentices, free and enslaved blacks, and in some instances British and Hessian deserters. The majority accepted Congressional, Committee of Safety, and state contracts to produce various kinds of martial firearms and their components; some were employed by independent or government facilities manufacturing and repairing firearms; there were those serving as arms inspectors; and yet others engaged as public armorers or serving as militia, state, and Continental armorers.

Among the many gunsmiths variously serving the patriot cause was Richard Falley (1740-1808) born at George's River, Me.[37] In his teens during the French and Indian War, Falley was captured by Native Americans at Fort Edward, N.Y., and taken to Montreal where he was subsequently befriended by ". . . a lady who purchased him for 16 gallons of rum and sent him to Westfield, Mass."[38]

It was apparently there that Falley became an apprentice, and by late 1761 he had married and established his own gunsmithery. A militia captain, he served as a company commander at Breed's Hill while his son Frederick stood at his side as a drum-

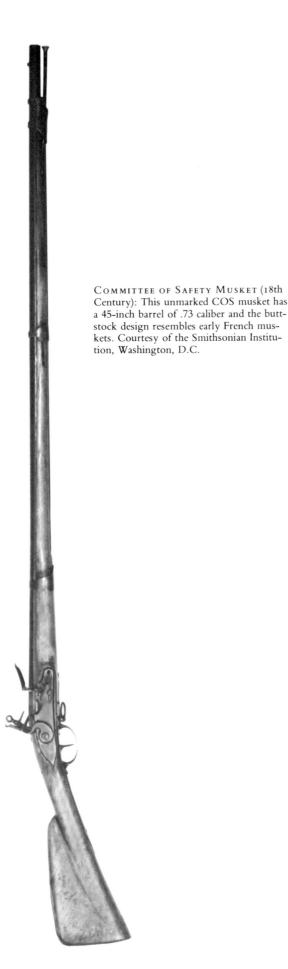

COMMITTEE OF SAFETY MUSKET (18th Century): This unmarked COS musket has a 45-inch barrel of .73 caliber and the butt-stock design resembles early French muskets. Courtesy of the Smithsonian Institution, Washington, D.C.

mer boy. He had been previously appointed Public Armorer for Massachusetts Bay with the Act of May 15, 1775; one of many serving in that capacity including Charlestown gunsmith Thomas Austin who was also a Massachusetts COS musket contractor.[39]

Another Massachusetts gunsmith, purportedly a "master gun-welter [barrel welder]" and known only by the surname Talley, was a militia ensign and on June 13, 1775, he was appointed Master Armorer to the Colony of Massachusetts Bay with a monthly salary of 40 shillings.[40]

Many gunsmiths were called up for militia duty, like Capt. Isaac Davis of Acton, Mass., and many others joined the Continental Army; several fighting and dying in the fiercest battles. John Ames (1738-1803) attained the rank of major in the army before returning in 1776 to establish a shovel and musket factory in Bridgewater, Massachusetts; the Ames Company currently producing farm and garden implements.[41] Gunsmith Ard Welton of Waterbury, Conn., served as a Continental Army lieutenant throughout the war.[42]

The riflesmithing brothers Abraham and Isaac Berlin of Easton, Pa., both entered Capt. Henry Alshouse's 5th Company, Northampton County Militia.[43] Abraham joined as an ensign in 1776 and was commissioned a lieutenant in 1782, while Isaac, also a swordsmith, enlisted as a private and advanced to company adjutant prior to his release from duty on November 10, 1781. The Berlin brothers were active gunsmiths throughout the conflict and thereafter.

The Annely brothers, Edward and Thomas, were New Jersey Colony armorers; the former from 1770 to 1777 and the latter from 1776 to 1777.[44] Shortly thereafter they moved to Pennsylvania and became riflesmiths. Cornelius Austin also served as New Jersey Colony armorer from 1776 to 1778,[45] while in 1775 Pennsylvania gunsmith Phineas Parmalee became a Continental Army armorer.[46]

Early in 1777 Continental Congress, recognizing the need, appointed Philadelphia gunsmith Thomas Butler as Chief United States Armorer.[47] Butler apparently assumed his duties prior to the date of the following advertisement appearing in the *Pennsylvania Evening Post*:

Water Street Armoury, July 19, 1777. Wanted two or three Gunlock Filers, and a good Stocker or two, who by applying as above, shall be properly encouraged by Thomas Butler, chief armorer of the United States.
N.B. Those who live at a distance, will do well to write first.[48]

Frontier gunsmiths also contributed heavily to the patriot cause and prominent among them was the Bean family. In 1759 Virginia gunsmith William

Bean (1720-1782) emigrated to the newly opened Watauga settlement and built a trading station and small gunsmithery in what is now Cumberland County, Tenn.[49] His first born, William Bean, Jr. (1745?-1799), learned the craft from his father and started Bean's Station in present Grainger County. He served as a captain in the conflict and his brothers Edmund, George, Jesse, John, and Robert were also gunsmiths; Jesse seeing action with the frontier militia at King's Mountain.

Capt. William Bean's son Russell was also a riflesmith and father of riflesmiths Baxter, Charles, Joseph, and Robert Bean who were active until ca. 1830. James Bean, a relative, was associated with Baxter, probably as an apprentice. Charles Bean, Jr., continued in the gunsmithing trade until ca. 1920.[50]

Powder-makers also served in the Continental Army, as exemplified by John Patton who operated a small powder mill on the Tennessee River.[51] In his absence his wife Mary operated the mill and materially assisted the spirited American effort at King's Mountain with a gift of 500 pounds of gunpowder; a considerably expensive donation, for gunpowder then sold for the equivalent of $1.00 per pound.

The acute shortage of skilled gunsmiths, coupled with the fact that their valuable expertise would be irretrievably lost if they were killed in battle, sufficiently worried Congress to the extent that it requested the newly formed states to exempt gunsmiths and their workmen from military duty. The states apparently did not grant automatic deferments, for in the majority of the records studied the individuals involved applied for exemptions or they were requested by officials seeking to preserve their respective armament industries.

North Carolina COS musket-maker Timothy Bloodworth was granted an exemption for himself and his workmen in June, 1776.[52] On December 5, 1777, the Executive Council of Pennsylvania excused gunsmiths John Eberly,[53] Henry Gingerich,[54] and George Rathfong,[55] all of Lancaster, to work there in William Henry's large gunsmithery. Gunsmith Jacob Reaser of Frederick, Md., applied on June 9, 1778, to Gov. Thomas Johnson for an exemption for himself and fellow gunsmiths Jacob Dunkle, Woodward Evitt, Henry Fisher, and Thomas Lawrence; noting also that his apprentice was then guarding prisoners of war.[56]

In a letter dated August 3, 1781, Henry Delong of Mecklenburg County, Va., wrote to Gov. Thomas Jefferson that "Richard Meanly a good gun-smith has been, by the County Court Martial, excused from a Tower [tour] of duty in the Militia to the Southward, provided he set upon making guns for the public."[57] Delong subsequently provided Meanly with ". . . one or two hundred weight of Iron and some Steel . . ." and reported that he ". . . has a British deserter, a gunsmith, working with him."[58]

Though Lancaster riflesmith William Henry had conscientiously served the crown during the French and Indian War, he embraced the rebellion with characteristic vigor and on March 23, 1776, the Provincial Council of Pennsylvania "Resolved, That Mr. Owen Biddle, Mr. Alex'r Wilcock be a committee to agree with William Henry for making 200 rifles."[59] As far as it can be determined that resolution guaranteed Henry's first martial rifle contract. The rifles were made at his Lancaster works, then employing 14 hands and described as ". . . a large Manufactory and Ironmongery . . ." located on the southeast corner of Center Square.[60]

In addition to rifles, Henry's factory produced muskets and bayonets for the Pennsylvania COS, a body he served unstintingly while also supervising the manufacture of firearms, clothing and munitions as assistant commissary general for the Lancaster District. Early in 1776 Henry became a member of the American Philosophical Society founded in 1743 by Benjamin Franklin. He befriended fellow member David Rittenhouse whose brother was a director of the Pennsylvania Gun Factory (see p. 314). In 1769 David constructed the first astral telescope in North America and in 1777 served as president of the Pennsylvania COS.

In April, 1778, Continental Congress abolished Thomas Butler's post as Chief United States Armorer and created instead the position of Superin-

WILLIAM HENRY, JR., Pistols (18th Century): This pair of silver-mounted, brass-barreled flintlock pistols depict the gunsmithing skills of William Henry's son whose surname appears on the lock (left). The initials F B in script appear on the signature plate of the pistol (right) and its barrel is marked *Nazareth* in script. Note the relief carving surrounding the breech plug tang and the annulus at the muzzle. A single thimble and guide secured the hickory ramrods. Courtesy of the Historical Society of Pennsylvania, Philadelphia.

BRITISH MUSKETOON (18th Century): The initials P H are carved in the buttstock of this British martial musketoon. Many captured British firearms were used by patriot forces and repaired by patriot gunsmiths. Courtesy of the Morristown National Historical Park, Morristown, N.J. Charles L. Maddox, Jr., photographer.

tendent of Arms and Accoutrements to the Continental Congress, appointing William Henry to the task. His son William operated a gunsmithery at Nazareth, Pa., making COS muskets.[61]

The Lancaster factory also repaired firearms and Henry hired gunsmith Adam Deterer for the work (see Chapter VI, n. 72). On September 20, 1777, Henry received £173/12s/06d from the Sublieutenant of Lancaster County for firearms made and repaired,[62] while in 1779 the Pennsylvania COS paid him the not inconsiderable sum of £11,867/5s/1d ". . . on account of arms repaired and manufactured."[63]

Many other patriot gunsmiths repaired firearms, working independently or for state and national facilities, and not the least of their problems was receiving prompt payment. In 1776 Pennsylvania COS musket-maker John Handlyn asked the Provincial Council to pay him for repairing the several muskets from a Capt. Dorsey's company.[64] Philadelphian John Tyler repaired public arms from 1776 to 1779 and apparently had no difficulty receiving payment,[65] yet in 1776 John Fox of Reading Borough, Berks County, Pa., was forced to petition the Provincial Council for payment ". . . for repairing firelocks belonging to Captain Allens, Williams and Jones Companys."[66]

Prompt payment for newly manufactured firearms was also difficult to procure, for Hebron, Conn., gunsmith Samuel Dewey "Showed to the Assembly that after the 15th day of May, 1775, to May, 1776, he had made 46 gun barrels and 21 bayonets, and that they are all in the public service, and the premium of 3 shillings and 6 pence on each gun so made, amounting to 8 pound: 1 shilling lawful money was ordered paid."[67]

COS musket-maker Richard Dallam of Hartford County, Md., was beset with a number of difficulties which undoubtedly incurred production delays and he explained his problems in a letter to the Maryland COS dated July 16, 1776:

Sirs: In answer to yours of the 10th instant, which I received yesterday, I inform you I have twenty-two muskets finished complete and fifteen more ready for stocking, six of which will be finished this week. Harvest, and the sickness of two of my best hands and the bursting of twelve or thirteen of my barrels in my absence, have disappointed my expectations. Twelve of the guns finished have been proved with two ounces of powder and one ball, the remainder with one ounce of powder and one ball.

P.S. I have not the least doubt that my arms will please, and will be found as good as any made in Maryland. R.D.[68]

Partnerships between patriot gunsmiths, like that of Samuel Boone and Nicholas White, were frequently entered and many gunsmiths made arrangements with stock-makers. John Doud, a Connecticut COS musket-maker who had learned the gunsmithing craft in the shop of Benoni Hills (see p. 325), took as a partner stockmaker Ebenezer Norton.[69] Just prior to the conflict a two-room gunsmithery was built by Doud on the west side of East Street in Goshen, Conn. Doud made barrels in the forge room and they were stocked in the other by Norton.[70]

A similar partnership was agreed to by John Shaw, an Annapolis gunsmith who also served as Maryland state armorer from 1780 to 1781,[71] and Archibald Chisholm (1755?-1810) who was an experienced cabinetmaker and first settled in Annapolis ca. 1773.[72] The partnership apparently began prior to February 23, 1776, for on that date the minutes of the Maryland COS noted that "Messrs John Shaw and Archibald Chisholm agreed with the Council of Safety to stock the Gun Barrels made by Mr. Isaac Harris [a Savage Town, Md., gunsmith] for the use of this Province at the price the same are done in Philadelphia.[73]

"Ordered that the Treasurer of the Western Shore deliver to Messrs John Shaw & Archibald Chisholm 50 of the Gun Barrels left with him by Mr. Isaac Harris to be stocked by said Shaw & Chisholm and take receipt for the same."[74]

The partners apparently performed their work satisfactorily, for at an April 16 meeting the COS "Ordered that the said Treasurer pay to Messrs John Shaw and Archibald Chisholm twenty two pounds six shillings and eight pence for stocking Musquets as per account."[75]

Whether the sum was full or partial payment cannot be determined, just as it is not known whether Shaw and Chisholm delivered all of the stocked muskets by that date. On May 8, 1776, however, the COS "Ordered that the said Treasurer pay to Messrs John Shaw and Archibald Chisholm twenty three pounds sixteen shillings and six pence for stocking Musquets."[76]

It is possible that the May disbursement was payment for stocking additional muskets, while on June 19 the partners received £29/7s/8d ". . . for stocking Musquets and for other services as per account."[77]

An indication of what those "other services" were is supplied by a memorandum signed by Shaw and Chisholm and submitted to the COS on August 28, 1776, for it refers to a number of firearms components purchased by the partners:

Firm accounts for gun mountings: 74 complete sets, also 9 breechpieces [breech plugs], 4 [trigger] guards, 9 tail-pipes [ramrod guides], 12 middle pipes [thimbles], 150 [forestock] caps, 10 sideplates, 5 thumbpieces; it is noted that 500

sets [of furniture] were in the [Annapolis] magazines; Horn [?] brought from Philadelphia, guards breechpieces, caps and pipes.[78]

Archibald Chisholm dissolved his partnership with John Shaw on December 5, 1776, and apparently returned to cabinet-making. The split was doubtlessly amicable, for in November, 1784, Shaw and Chisholm were engaged in the mercantile business.[79]

Many eighteenth-century American gunsmiths could trace their ancestry to the early colonial epoch and such a craftsman was Seth Pomeroy: son of Ebenezer, grandson of Medad, and great-grandson of Eltweed.[80] Born May 20, 1706, In Northampton, Mass., Seth Pomeroy had served in the French and Indian War and his gunsmithing reputation was so widespread that Native Americans from Canada journeyed hundreds of miles to visit his shop.[81]

Seth Pomeroy fought at Breed's Hill and was shortly thereafter chosen by Gen. Washington as one of the eight brigadier generals to serve in the Continental Army. On February 19, 1777, while on his way to join Washington in New Jersey, Gen. Pomeroy died at Peekskill, N.Y. His son Lemuel continued in the gunsmithing trade.[82]

Like the Henry family of Pennsylvania the eminent Bridgewater, Mass., gunsmith Hugh Orr also embraced the American cause and, with his son Robert, manufactured COS muskets and bayonets.[83] Orr subsequently established a large cannon foundry in association with Louis de Maresquelle.

Equally prominent Massachusetts gunmakers were the brothers Asa and Andrus Waters of Sutton, near Millbury.[84] The Waters' made COS muskets and it is likely that they were descendants of Salem gunsmith Richard Waters active in 1632. Andrus died in 1778, and Asa served as a lieutenant in the Lexington Alarm. The Waters gunsmithing dynasty flourished until ca. 1856.

Not all of the gunsmiths in British America worked for the patriot cause, though the percentage loyal to the crown remains unknown. Some of them, however, availed themselves of the opportunity offered by British officials to return to England with paid fare and assured employment, others stayed in the colonies with the tenuous promise of crown protection, and a number fled in exile to Nova Scotia, the Bahamas, and British Florida.

Loyalist gunsmiths Thomas Allen,[85] William Tunx,[86] and John Woods[87] were persuaded to leave the colonies by Royal Governor William Tryon of New York. William Allen, possibly related to Thomas, remained in New York City until November 25, 1783, when the British evacuated, though he resumed gunsmithing there in January, 1784.[88]

Gunsmith Michael Genter also stayed in New York City during the British occupation and possibly regretted the decision, for on January 13, 1777, the *New York Gazette* reported "The shop of Michael Genter of this city, Gun Smith, was broke open and robbed of five rifle guns and two fuzees, some bayonets and a lock of a gun." Three years to the day later the *Royal Gazette* recorded his obituary.[89]

Also among those choosing to stay was Tory gunsmith Gilbert Forbes (see p. 336). Described as ". . . a short, thick man . . . ," Forbes established his gunsmithery in 1767 and it prospered. Unlike many loyalists, Forbes became deeply involved in opposition to the patriot cause and was ensnared in the Hickey Conspiracy; a diabolical scheme designed to destroy simultaneously the city magazines, kill the general officers of the Continental Army, and either kidnap or murder Gen. Washington.

The plot was uncovered on June 26, 1776, and among those arrested were Thomas Hickey, a member of Gen. Washington's personal guard who was purportedly bribed by a British agent; Mayor David Matthews, Gilbert Forbes, and approximately 15 others.[90] Hickey was court-martialled, found guilty on Forbes' testimony, and hanged. Forbes cheated the noose, his fate swallowed up in the sweeping panorama of the American and British struggle for New York.

On September 7, 1776, nine days after Sir Henry Clinton forced Washington's withdrawal from Long Island, David Bushnell of Saybrook, Conn., was at last afforded an opportunity to test his remarkable technological innovation on Lord Admiral Richard Howe's fleet anchored in the Hudson River. Bushnell christened his novel invention the *American Turtle* in November, 1775; an apt descriptive because it was designed not only to cruise the surface, but to manoeuvre when submerged.[91] The *Turtle,* in essence, was the first practical submarine, though the concept had originated in Leonardo da Vinci's fertile imagination.

It was Bushnell's dream to deliver undetected a lethal explosive charge to the hull of an enemy ship. Filled with approximately 150 pounds of gunpowder, the explosive container carried by the *Turtle* was known as a torpedo, though it was nothing more sophisticated than an oak keg fitted with an auger designed to be turned into the wooden hull and detonated by a device permitting the submersible to leave the scene with a reasonable safety margin.

To meet that criterion Bushnell designed a time-delay mechanism consisting of a clock and a flintlock ". . . with a good flint that would not miss fire." A stout cord linking the main gear axel of the clock to the lock's trigger was slowly wound around the axel as the minutes ticked off until sufficient pressure on the sear effected ignition; an ingenious

contrivance which could trace its ancestry to the complex alarm guns and other "infernal devices" conceived by Italian gunsmiths and clock-makers early in the sixteenth century.[92]

Little more than a submersible coffin, the *Turtle* was piloted by a 27-year-old Connecticut militia sergeant, Ezra Lee, whose objective was the 64 gun *Eagle* serving as Lord Howe's flagship. Though a multitude of problems forced Lee to abort the *Turtle's* first combat assignment and a subsequent mission, he was successful in his attack on the British frigate *Cerberus* at Black Point Bay west of New London, Conn., in 1777.

Whether Sgt. Lee again attempted a submarine attack remains unknown, though during the British occupation of Philadelphia the wily Bushnell managed to snap the redcoats out of their complacency by sowing the Delaware River with a number of explosive devices similar to the torpedo used by the *Turtle.* The detonator, however, was of a kind yet to be identified.

What transpired on the Philadelphia waterfront was a tragicomedy painted with a broad stroke of sarcasm by an unknown resident whose letter dated January 9, 1778, was excerpted and appeared February 19 in the Boston *Continental Journal & Weekly Advertiser:*

This city has lately been entertained with a most astonishing instance of the activity, bravery, and military skill of the royal navy of Great Britain. . . . last week two boys observed a keg . . . floating in the river opposite the city. They got into a small boat, and attempting to take up the keg, it burst with a great explosion and blew up the unfortunate boys.

On Monday last several kegs of a like construction made their appearance. An alarm was immediately spread. . . . Various reports prevailed, filling the city and the royal troops with unspeakable consternation. Some reported that these kegs were filled with armed rebels, who were to issue forth in the dead of night, as the Grecians did of old from their wooden horse . . . at Troy, and take the city by surprise, asserting that they had seen the points of their bayonets through the bung holes of the kegs. Others said they were charged with . . . combustibles to be kindled by secret machinery and setting the whole Delaware in flames were to consume all the shipping in the harbor; whilst others asserted that they were constructed by art magic, would of themselves ascend the wharves in the night time and roll flaming through the streets of the city, destroying everything in their way.

Be this as it may, certain it is that the shipping in harbor and all the wharves of the city were fully manned. The battle begun, and it was sur-

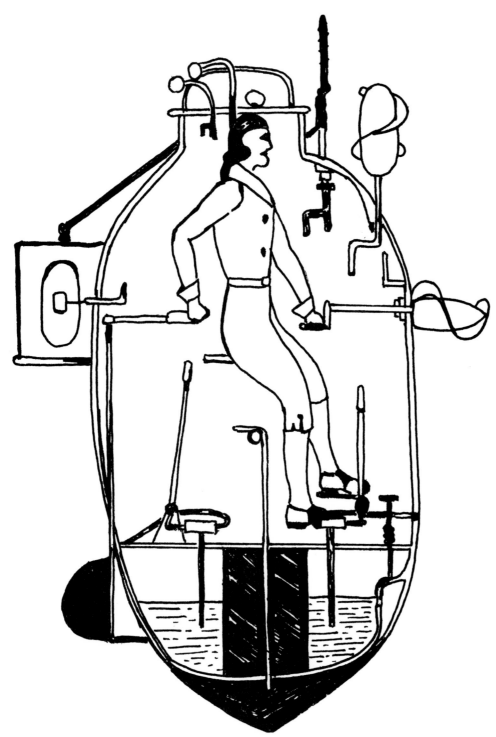

American Turtle (18th Century): Invented by David Bushnell, the first practical submarine served during the American Revolution and Sgt. Ezra Lee of Connecticut can be considered the first combat submariner. Author's sketch.

prising to behold the incessant blaze that was kept up against the enemy, the kegs.

. . . From the Roebuck and other ships of war whole broadsides were poured into the Delaware. In short, not a wandering chip, stick, or drift log but felt the vigor of British arms.

The action begun about sunrise and would have been completed . . . by noon had not an old . . . woman . . . unfortunately let a small keg of butter fall overboard, which . . . floated down to the scene of the action. At the sight of this unex-

pected reinforcement . . . , the battle was renewed with fresh fury; the firing was incessant till evening closed the affair.

The kegs were either totally demolished or obliged to fly, as none of them have shown their heads since. It is said . . . Lord Howe has dispatched a swift sailing packet with an account of this victory to the court of London. In a word, Monday, the fifth of January, 1778, must ever be distinguished in history for the memorable BATTLE OF THE KEGS.

The Road to Victory

The road to victory was long, arduous, and generously obstructed with hardships for the improperly fed, poorly clothed, and rarely paid Americans struggling for independence; a concept few of them could readily grasp. The conditions under which they valiantly fought and desperately died were cruel to the extreme though armies are not by natural inclination predicated upon personal indulgence, freedom, justice, or other democratic principles, and the Continental Army was certainly no exception.

Pay was a particular sore point with patriot officers and men alike and especially sensitive was a problem faced by many American militiamen as exemplified in a letter from Gen. James Potter to Thomas Wharton, Jr., President of the Board of War:

H.Q., Wilmington [Del.], September 1, 1777

I have this day ordered the Militia at Lancaster to this place. One reason why the militia of our State coming so ill armed is, they are afraid that if they lose their arms they will not be paid for them; and as proof of the fears, they give an instance, the arms they lost with the loss of Fort Washington [N.Y., November 16, 1776], for which they have as yet never been paid or received any satisfaction. Therefore, if the Council would be pleased to issue orders to their County Lieutenants, to apprise the people's muskets & assure them that if they are lost in actual service, they shall be paid for them.[93]

The decisive patriot victories at Trenton (1776), Saratoga (1777), Monmouth (1778), Vincennes (1779), and King's Mountain (1780) set the stage for the immutable drama at Yorktown in 1781 and the villain of the piece, Lord Charles Cornwallis, trapped himself with ambition and expectations unfulfilled. Marching up from the devastated Carolinas to implement his grandiose scheme for the conquest of Virginia, Cornwallis ran afoul of the spirited Lafayette.

Forced into a defensive posture Cornwallis ensconced his weary, 7500-man army on the Yorktown peninsula, expecting reinforcements and supplies from Gen. Clinton in New York via the Royal Navy. Sir Henry vacillated in the face of Washington's nominal threat to the city and then quite unexpectedly the vital sea lanes were severed on August 30, 1781, when from the West Indies arrived Comte Françqis Joseph Paul de Grasse with a substantial French fleet to block Chesapeake Bay.

On August 17, anticipating De Grasse's arrival off Virginia, Washington feinted against Clinton and crossed the Hudson River with the bulk of his forces three days later. By September 2 the Continentals had passed Philadelphia and on the fifth Washington waxed ecstatic when learning that the French had sealed the bay, simultaneously crippling Admiral Sir Thomas Graves' fleet.

Cornwallis found himself in a decidedly untenable position, rendered even more desperate when on September 11 Comte Louis de Barras joined De Grasse with a sizeable fleet from Newport, R.I. Three days later Washington arrived at Williamsburg with 16,000 American and French troops, linking up with Lafayette. The pincers were closed in a remarkable 30-day troop movement accompanied by the loss of only ten French infantrymen.

The Siege of Yorktown began on September 28, 1781, and Cornwallis capitulated 21 days later on October 19. For the British in America it was the beginning of the end.

Yorktown was as joyful and significant a triumph to the Americans and their allies as it was frustratingly painful to Cornwallis' disheartened redcoats who, a regiment at a time, resentfully lay down their arms in an open field surrounded by French hussars. Capt. Samuel Graham of the 71st Highlanders, part of Yorke's Brigade, poignantly recalled:

. . . the mortification and unfeigned sorrow of the soldiers will never fade from my memory. Some went so far as to shed tears, while . . . a corporal, who stood near me, embraced his firelock and then threw it on the ground, exclaiming, 'May you never get so good a master again!'[94]

The corporal's sentiments were obviously shared and readily displayed elsewhere, for as Surgeon James Thacher of a Massachusetts regiment observed, a number ". . . of the [British] platoon officers appeared to be exceedingly chagrined when giving the word 'ground arms,' and I am witness that they performed this duty in a . . . sullen temper . . . throwing their arms on the pile with violence, as if determined to render them useless. This . . . was checked by . . . General [Benjamin] Lincoln."[95]

Neither Gen. Washington nor Continental Congress had entertained any illusions concerning the significance of Yorktown, for the Lion and Unicorn remained rampant elsewhere and the conflict sputtered on for another 19 months.

Continental Congress proclaimed an end to the monumental struggle for independence eight years after Lexington and Concord and, in a rare spate of gratitude, voted to let the patriots retain their muskets and other firearms as a farewell gift; a magnanimous gesture, for that august body had too frequently neglected those resolute veterans who had suffered every intolerable privation spawned by war.[96] Not until September 3, 1783, however, was a definitive peace treaty concluded in Paris.

The American Revolution, aside from resolving the issue of independence, established during those tormented years the permanent techonomic foundation upon which the infant United States of America was built, and it was the patriot gunsmith and the inspired employment of the factory system which made it possible; the former providing the technological expertise and the latter enhancing productivity.

Independence was finally won not only by the courage displayed on the grim field of battle, but by the singular determination of a small segment of the populace working in conjunction toward a common goal of uncommon human aspiration. The magnificent contribution to the ultimate triumph generated by those who left bloody footprints in the drifting snow was no more vital than what had been given by the many who toiled endless hours in the blistering heat of a barrel forge or who with numbed and calloused fingers sat painfully hunched over a lock filer's bench.

Notes

1. Capt. John G.W. Dillin, *The Kentucky Rifle* (Washington, 1924), p. 25.
2. Col. Robert E. Gardner, *Small Arms Makers* (New York, 1962), p. 66.
3. Harold L. Peterson, *Arms and Armor in Colonial America, 1526-1783* (New York, 1956), p. 196.
4. John Harrower, "Diary . . . 1773-1776," *American Historical Review* (October 1900): 100.
5. George F. Scheer and Hugh Rankin, *Rebels and Redcoats: The Living Story of the American Revolution* (New York, 1957), p. 86.
6. Peterson, pp. 197-198.
7. Ibid., p. 198.
8. Joe Kindig, Jr., *Thoughts on the Kentucky Rifle in its Golden Age* (New York, 1960), pp. 4, 36.
9. Peterson, p. 199.
10. Long Island Historical Society, *Memoirs*, 2 vols (New York, 1869), 2:433.
11. Peterson, p. 200.
12. Ibid., pp. 292-293.
13. Howard L. Blackmore, "The British Rifle in America," *American Rifleman* (June 1963): 28.
14. Ibid.
15. Ibid.
16. Gardner, p. 268.
17. Blackmore, p. 28.
18. Gardner, p. 329.
19. Ibid., p. 263.
20. Blackmore, p. 29.
21. Anthony D. Darling, *Red Coat and Brown Bess* (Ottawa: Museum Restoration Service Historical Arms Series No. 12, 1970): 61. Darling notes (p. 59) that the riflemen were selected at random from the marksmen in Burgoyne's own regiments.
22. Jac Weller, "Breechloaders in the Revolution," *Gun Digest* (Chicago, 1959): 55.
23. Maj. Reginald Hargreaves, M.D. (Ret.), "The Fabulous Ferguson Rifle and its Brief Combat Career," *American Rifleman* (August 1971): 34.
24. Blackmore, p. 29.
25. Ibid. Blackmore notes that at least 700 Ferguson rifles were made; none of them reaching America except those initially taken by Ferguson.
26. Gardner, p. 329.
27. Ibid., p. 257; Weller, p. 57.
28. Gardner, p. 273.
29. Author's examination of the Ferguson rifle (Accession No. 175) in the museum collection, Morristown National Historical Park, Morristown, N.J.
30. Hargreaves, p. 35.
31. Ibid.
32. Author's estimate based on available documentary evidence. The number of Ferguson rifles available at King's Mountain, if any, remains controversial. Blackmore (p. 29) avers that after Brandywine (1777) the rifles were "forgotten." Weller (p. 56) suggests two hundred or fewer were in Ferguson's possession in late 1778. Hargreaves (p. 35) indicates fewer than 100 served at King's Mountain and Weller (p. 57) concurs.
33. John Hyde Preston, *Revolution 1776* (New York, 1933), p. 362.
34. Hargreaves, p. 36.
35. Gardner, p. 260.
36. The estimate does not include gunsmiths active in British Florida, Spanish Louisiana, the Illinois country, or Canada, including those working in the Hudson's Bay Company factories.
37. A. Merwyn Carey, *American Firearms Makers* (New York, 1953), p. 37; Gardner, p. 61.
38. Gardner, p. 62.
39. Carey, p. 4; Gardner, p. 9.
40. Carey, p. 122; Gardner, p. 191.
41. Carey, pp. 2-3; Gardner, p. 6.
42. Gardner, pp. 205-206.
43. Carey, p. 99; Gardner, p. 18.
44. Carey, p. 3; Gardner, p. 7.
45. Carey, p. 4; Gardner, p. 9.
46. Gardner, p. 147.
47. Ibid., p. 32.
48. Henry J. Kauffman, *Early American Gunsmiths, 1650-1850* (New York, 1952), p. 16.
49. Gardner, p. 15.
50. Ibid. Also, Charles E. Hanson, Jr., *The Plains Rifle* (Harrisburg, 1960), p. 14.
51. Bates M. Stovall, "American Gunpowder Makers," *American Rifleman* (May 1964): 50.
52. Gardner, p. 21.
53. Ibid., p. 57.
54. Ibid., p. 74.
55. Ibid., p. 157.
56. Ibid., pp. 157-158.
57. Ibid., p. 129.
58. Ibid.
59. Kauffman, p. 49.
60. Gardner, p. 90.
61. Henry J. Kauffman, *The Pennsylvania-Kentucky Rifle* (Harrisburg, 1960), p. 258.
62. Gardner, p. 90.
63. Ibid.
64. Ibid., p. 83.
65. Ibid., p. 197.
66. Ibid., p. 68.
67. Ibid., p. 52.
68. Ibid., p. 47. In a letter to the author January 14, 1971, John Dallam Hill, San Diego, Cal., revealed that the day following the cited correspondence (July 17, 1776) Continental Congress appointed a Richard Dallam to the post of ". . . deputy paymaster general for the flying camp."
69. Gardner, p. 55.
70. Ibid., p. 143.
71. Ibid., p. 175.
72. Biographical data anent Archibald Chisholm supplied by Joseph Suess, Rockville, Md., in a letter to the author January 22, 1971 (hereafter cited as *Suess*).
73. Gardner, p. 85.
74. William H. Browne, et al, ed., *Archives of Maryland* (Baltimore, 1884-   ), Vol. 9, 9:180 *(Suess)*.
75. Ibid., p. 333 *(Suess)*.
76. Ibid., p. 417 *(Suess)*.
77. Ibid., p. 499 *(Suess)*.
78. *Maryland State Papers, the Brown Books*, Vol. 5, pp. 64-65 *(Suess)*.
79. *The Maryland Gazette*, December 5, 1776, and November 11, 1784 *(Suess)*.
80. Carey, p. 96; Gardner, p. 153.

81. Felicia Johnson Deyrup, *Arms Making in the Connecticut Valley* (York, Pa., 1970), p. 34, n. 3.
82. Gardner, p. 153.
83. Carey, p. 90; Gardner, p. 144.
84. Carey, p. 130; Gardner, p. 203.
85. Gardner, p. 4.
86. Ibid., p. 197.
87. Ibid., p. 4.
88. Ibid.
89. Ibid., p. 72.
90. James Grant Wilson and John Fiske, ed., *Appleton's Cyclopaedia of American Biography,* 6 vols. (New York, 1889), 3:195.
91. There are numerous accounts of Bushnell's *American Turtle* and the author has chiefly relied on Steward H. Holbrook, *Lost Men of American History* (New York, 1946), pp. 64-70.
92. Lewis Winant, *Firearms Curiosa* (New York, 1954), pp. 95-97.
93. Col. Arcadi Gluckman, USA, Ret., *United States Muskets, Rifles and Carbines* (Buffalo, 1948), p. 46.
94. *Virginia Historical Register,* Vol. 6, No. 10 (1853): 205.
95. James Thacher, *A Military Journal during the American Revolutionary War* (Boston, 1827), pp. 346-347.
96. George F. Scheer, ed., *Private Yankee Doodle,* (New York, 1962), p. 279, n. 3.

UNITED STATES OF AMERICA (18th Century): The map depicted was printed February 9, 1783, by London cartographers R. Sayer and J. Bennett according to the preliminary articles of peace signed at Versailles in January, 1783. Courtesy of the Library of Congress.

THE INFANT UNITED STATES of America, deliciously intoxicated by the elixir of freedom from British rule, staggered under the complexities involved in establishing a new nation. The fledgling Republic was not only caught in the powerful grip of a prolonged economic depression—a recurring phenomenon in the climactic aftermath of warfare throughout the ages—but also squeezed in the vise-like jaws of a then enormous foreign debt totalling nearly $13,000,000; most of it incurred by the purchase of vital war material.

France alone claimed $10,352,000 of the American debt, the Netherlands another $1,304,000, and Spain a nominal $174,017. Though what was owed to Spain was meager by comparison, Charles III promptly raised a more significant claim jeopardizing the security of the American frontier.

Under the terms of the Treaty of Versailles (September 3, 1783) Spain regained control of British Florida and, with some justification, proposed to occupy the vast Illinois country which she had successfully invaded in 1781. The threat became reality on June 26, 1784, when four years prior to his death Charles III closed the vital Mississippi River to all United States commerce and attempted to halt the burgeoning influx of the frontier people no longer restrained by the intangible Proclamation Line or the formidable Appalachian barrier.

Neither had the maritime and technological might of Great Britain diminished in the wake of the recent American conflict and she remained a potential threat, occupying neighboring Canada and preserving her influence among the Native Americans there and in her former Illinois dominions, while maintaining an authorative position in Spanish Florida through the lucrative trade monopoly established in 1783 at St. Augustine and Pensacola by Panton, Leslie & Company (see p. 289); a politically-oriented commercial concession which had mollified the restive Creeks, Seminoles, and other Native Americans hostile to Spain during the brief British period while continuing to incite them against the Americans in an effort to halt United States expansion in the vast southeast.

Significantly, the end of the American Revolution saw the Tory element suffer inescapable and irreparable economic disaster, for with Britain's improbable defeat the influential Americans who had supported the crown lost their assets and were hastily forced to vacate the United States and Spanish Florida; many of them relocating in Canada, the mother country, or the British possessions in the West Indies.

With Spain's signal victories in West Florida and the Illinois country in 1781, Governor General Bernardo de Gálvez magnanimously permitted most of the Illinois Tories to go to New York, while those in West Florida were also allowed to leave; the majority electing the Bahamas, though some preferred East Florida. With the conclusion of the conflict in 1783 the East Florida Tories, like the Spaniards who had 20 years earlier fled British rule, were forced to evacuate and they were joined in the exodus by many loyal Native Americans and numerous blacks, free and slave.

In September, 1784, the *Bahama Gazette* reported:

... there has arrived here from St. Mary's [East Florida] several Transports and Ordnance Vessels, with the Garrison and Stores of St. Augustine, and a number of the late inhabitants of East Florida.[1]

Like their brethren elsewhere the East Florida Tories took with them as many of their possessions as possible. The *Countess of Darlington,* a brigantine hired by Panton, Leslie & Company, reached Nassau from St. Mary's on October 4, 1784, bringing with her 72 slaves, freight, and Tory household effects including 22 firearms described on her cargo manifest as 16 muskets, four pistols, and two blunderbusses.[2]

The New Nation Grows

There were no significant technological developments in American firearms evolution during the period 1775-1792. Even the innovative multi-shot flintlock musket designed during the war by Philadelphia gunsmith Joseph Belton incorporated principles known to European gunsmiths for more than three centuries, while the novel shot tower known in Britain by 1769 did not appear in the United States until 1794 when Stephen Austin built the first one in Philadelphia ". . . below Walnut street wharf."[3] And though the American Revolution drew considerable attention to the efficacy of the rifle as a martial firearm, the disadvantages remained distinctly apparent and the rifle failed to have any drastic or significant impact on orthodox infantry tactics in North America or Europe until the nineteenth century.

RIFLING ENGINE, STOCKMAKING TOOLS AND POWDER CANISTER (18th/19th Century): The rifling engine depicted is similar to those devised ca. 1790 and it was used during the period 1800-1840. The plank serving as the base for the barrel clamps measures 109 × 10 × 2¾-inches. The master barrel (right) was the guide for the lead collar on the wood guide head of the rifling rod. The collar followed the grooves of the master barrel, duplicating the rifling there in the barrel blank (left). Also depicted are two stockmaking planes, a spokeshave, and a copper powder canister of the 1825-1840 period. Courtesy of the Eagle Americana Shop and Gun Museum, Strasburg, Pa. Charles L. Maddox, Jr., photographer.

Technological innovation in gunpowder manufacture also remained stagnant in the United States and accidental explosions in several mills significantly reduced production, forcing the young Republic to rely on imports from Britain, France, and the Netherlands; a tenuous prospect in the event of war with any of those nations because an immediate embargo could be expected.

Though gunpowder production perceptibly declined in relation to the demand, several mills continued to operate and the majority were located in eastern Pennsylvania which had remained the center of United States powder-making since the American Revolution. A 1791 survey ordered by then Secretary of the Treasury Alexander Hamilton (1757-1804) noted that there were five mills operating in and around Philadelphia, seven in Berks County, two each in the counties of Lancaster and York, and one in Montgomery County; each producing approximately a ton of powder a week.[4]

Hamilton, recognizing the need, attempted to stimulate the gunpowder industry by placing a ten percent tax on imported powder and recommending that sulphur and saltpeter be considered duty free imports; a suggestion subsequently heeded by Congress.[5] And in his 1791 report to the House of Representatives on the condition of American manufacture, Hamilton reiterated his concern about gunpowder:

No small progress has been made in the manufacture of this very important article. It may, indeed, be considered as already established, but

its high importance renders its further extension very desireable.[6]

The American situation in the article of gunpowder, however, failed to measurably improve until the perceptive protégé of the brilliant Lavoisier, Éleuthère Irénée du Pont (1771-1834), introduced the sophisticated manufacturing techniques employed in France and in 1802 established on Brandywine Creek near Wilmington, Del., the first modern gunpowder mills in America, though production did not commence until two years later.[7]

United States firearms manufacture also dramatically declined with the end of the exigent wartime demand and most state facilities ceased production during the postwar depression. Nevertheless the young Republic found itself virtually inundated with a surplus of martial firearms; most of them stored at ordnance installations in Massachusetts (Springfield), Connecticut (New London), New York (Fort Rensselaer), Pennsylvania (Carlisle), and Virginia (Manchester).[8] Carlisle and Springfield had served as arms depots since the American Revolution.

Between October 7, 1789, and December 16, 1793, there were a number of transactions involving surplus martial firearms sold or transferred by the United States.[9] During that period 7,619 replacement muskets were forwarded to the U.S. Army and 1,000 more were sent to American forts on the northern and southern frontier increasingly threatened by Native American raids emanating from Canada, Louisiana, and Florida.

The United States also transferred 2,000 muskets to Georgia and another 600 to South Carolina to arm the militia; a practical expedient designed to fortify the defensive posture of the border states and alleviate a lack of storage space in some of the more crowded ordnance depots. The transfer or sale of surplus martial firearms to the states worked sufficiently well to become a standard federal practice.

In addition the United States sold 1,000 muskets to her former French ally on October 4, 1791, and some of them were French muskets employed by patriot forces during the American Revolution.[10] France ostensibly purchased the muskets for use in her Caribbean and South American possessions; several of them torn by bloody revolution.

In 1792 Congress, further alarmed by increasing British and Spanish activity along the vast frontier, raised a battalion of riflemen consisting of four companies each comprised of 82 privates which were to be armed with the American rifle.[11] And it is perhaps appropriate that the first firearm made under United States contract was the American rifle.

The contract rifles, devoid of ornamentation, were purchased from Pennsylvania riflesmiths be-

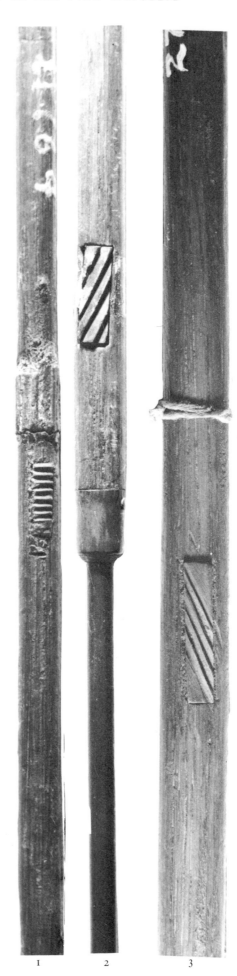

RIFLING RODS AND GUIDE HEADS (18th/ 19th Century): Left to right. (1) Hickory rifling rod with integral lead collar and mortised rifling bit (saw) for straight-groove rifling. Rod length: 65½ inches. Saw length: 1 inch. Saw teeth: 8, straight. (2) Rifling rod with wood guide head (collar not shown) for helical rifling. Iron rod length: 62½ inches. Guide head length: 12 inches. Saw length: 1 inch. Saw teeth: 4, angled. (3) Rifling rod with wood guide head for helical rifling. Rod length: 63¾ inches. Guide head length: 12 inches. Saw length: 1¼ inches. Saw teeth: 4, angled. Courtesy of the Mercer Museum, Bucks County Historical Society, Doylestown, Pa. Charles L. Maddox, Jr., photographer.

1   2   3

U.S. CONTRACT MARTIAL RIFLES, 1792-1793

Name	Date	Locale	Contract No.	Amt. Received	Quantity
Jacob Welshans	9/17/1792	York, Pa.	2059	$72.00	7
Adam Angstadt	11/26/1792	Berks Co., Pa.	2256	$204.00	20
John Nicholson	11/27/1792	Philadelphia, Pa.	2262	$312.00	31
John Nicholson	12/31/1792	Philadelphia, Pa.	2329	$156.00	15
John Nicholson	1/31/1793	Philadelphia, Pa.	2435	$120.00	12
Abraham Morrow	5/28/1793	Philadelphia, Pa.	2815	$312.00	31
Jacob Dickert	9/12/1792	Lancaster, Pa.	2055	$1,200.00	120
Peter Gonter, Jr.	10/18/1792	Lancaster, Pa.	2173	$1,200.00	120
John Groff	11/26/1792	Lancaster, Pa.	2260	$804.00	80

tween September 12, 1792, and May 5, 1793, at an average cost of $10.00 per stand, though prices varied throughout the period.[12] Jacob Dickert (fl. 1771-1809),[13] Peter Gonter, Jr. (fl. 1778-1818),[14] and John Groff (fl. 1780-1795)[15] were partners, receiving the first contract and two others. John Nicholson (see p. 314) was given three contracts, while Jacob Welshantz (Welshans, fl. 1777-1799),[16] Adam Angstadt (fl. 1770-1795),[17] and Abraham Morrow (Murrow, fl. 1771-1795)[18] each received a single contract. A total of nine government contracts worth $4,380.00 produced an estimated 436 rifles as noted in the Table.

While many riflesmiths continued to use the traditional techniques and had duplicated the venerable rifling engines brought to colonial America early in the eighteenth century, there emerged in Pennsylvania ca. 1790 an innovative variation which was less complicated and produced rifling equally as good at a much faster pace.

GUNSMITHING IMPLEMENTS (18th/19th Century): (1) .75 caliber bristled bore cleaning brush. (2) Barrel boring rod with integral bit. (3) Wood guide head with lead collar. (4) Bullet worm. (5) Barrel boring rod with integral bit. (6) Barrel boring rod with integral bit. (7) Tip of tapered barrel mandrel. (8) Mandrel tip. (9) Barrel boring rod with integral bit. (10) Barrel boring rod with integral bit. (11) Barrel boring rod with integral bit. (12) Wood guide head with lead collar, rifling saw missing. (13) Barrel boring rod with integral bit. (14) Barrel lapping rod (iron). (15) Polishing rod and head. (16, 17, 18) Mandrel tips. (19) Boring drill gauge (holes represent precise bore diameter), tapered, 22 inches long; the holes represent 32 distinct calibers. The average length of the boring rods depicted is 36 inches. Courtesy of the Pennsylvania Farm Museum of Landis Valley, Lancaster, Pa. Charles L. Maddox, Jr., photographer.

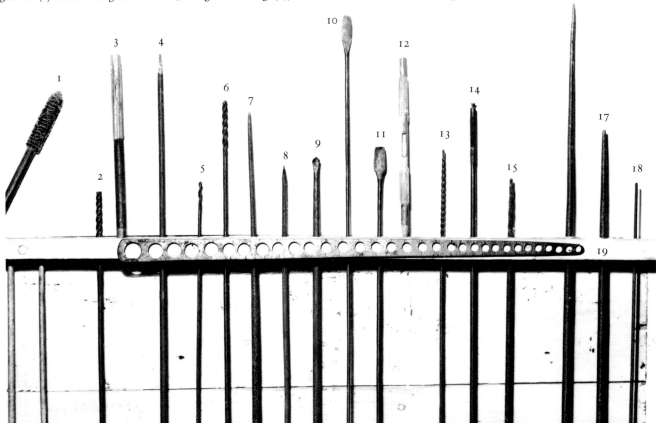

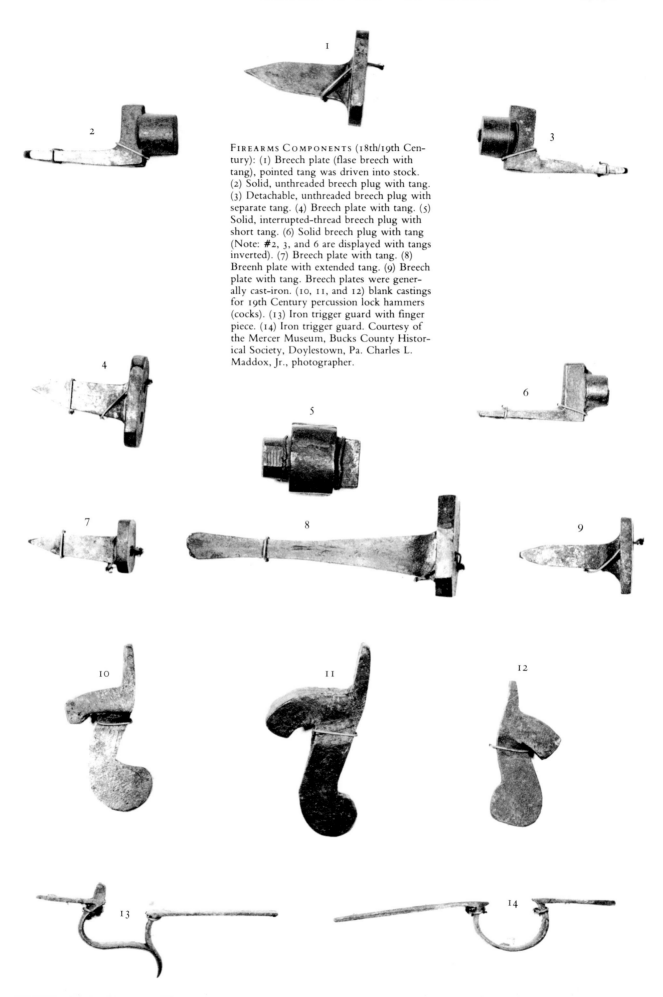

FIREARMS COMPONENTS (18th/19th Century): (1) Breech plate (flase breech with tang), pointed tang was driven into stock. (2) Solid, unthreaded breech plug with tang. (3) Detachable, unthreaded breech plug with separate tang. (4) Breech plate with tang. (5) Solid, interrupted-thread breech plug with short tang. (6) Solid breech plug with tang (Note: #2, 3, and 6 are displayed with tangs inverted). (7) Breech plate with tang. (8) Breenh plate with extended tang. (9) Breech plate with tang. Breech plates were generally cast-iron. (10, 11, and 12) blank castings for 19th Century percussion lock hammers (cocks). (13) Iron trigger guard with finger piece. (14) Iron trigger guard. Courtesy of the Mercer Museum, Bucks County Historical Society, Doylestown, Pa. Charles L. Maddox, Jr., photographer.

In the improved rifling engine the wood rifling guide with its helical grooves and index plate, supported by the heavy rifling bench (see p. 271), was supplanted by a previously rifled barrel serving the same purpose. The guide barrel and the pre-bored barrel blank to be rifled were rigidly clamped to a long plank generally placed on the riflesmith's workbench for convenience.

The innovative rifling engine, however, demanded two modifications: (1) the length of the hickory rifling rod was increased to project through both the guide barrel and the blank, and (2) in addition to the rifling bit or saw mortised into the head of the long rod, a short lead collar was cast around the rod near the saw and a somewhat longer collar was positioned on the part of the rod inside the guide barrel. The rod was initially forced through the guide barrel; thus "printing" the exact depth, width, and twist of the guide barrel rifling on the lead collars.

The rifling rod was rotated by hand rather than a crank as in the earlier rifling engine, the lead collars correctly positioning and guiding the rifling saw in the barrel blank because they precisely followed the guide barrel lands and grooves. Though the improved rifling engine was a significant technological innovation, it did not replace the traditional engine until the late nineteenth century in the individual gunsmithing shop, while in some instances the ancient rifling engine is currently used (see Chapter I, n 59).

The new Republic remained in an almost constant state of turmoil following the American Revolution, for Britain and Spain surrounded the infant states and conspired to limit their freedom to expand geographically. There was, however, a climate ripe for the propagation and exploitation of practically unlimited techonomic development in the struggling United States.

Inspired by Britain and Spain with delusions of political and economic gain, hostile Native Americans continuously ravaged the American frontier and many of the settlers were as thoroughly disenchanted with the treatment they received from officials in the eastern states as they had been with crown administrators prior to the American Revolution. Particularly disillusioned were the North Carolinians inhabiting the Watauga settlement in what is now eastern Tennessee, for they faced the same problems which had given rise to the War of Regulation (1768-1771).

Consequently and in desperation the Watauga settlers drafted a constitution on August 23, 1784, and organized the independent state of Franklin named for then U.S. Minister to France, Benjamin Franklin. They elected as governor John Sevier (1745-1815) who had served at King's Mountain and had in 1781 defeated the marauding Chickamauga.

The state of Franklin was considered an affront to North Carolina sovereignty and in May, 1787, Gov. Richard Caswell proclaimed Sevier's government in open revolt. Hostilities commenced shortly thereafter and continued sporadically until 1789 when the North Carolina militia put an end to the bold experiment in frontier autonomy.

The Watauga settlers were not the only Americans disillusioned in the aftermath of independence. In Massachusetts there emerged increasing discontent in the western counties hard hit by the post-war depression and what the inhabitants considered poor legislative representation, extortionate taxation, exorbitant salaries paid to indifferent state officials, and various other socio-economic grievances.

Petitions for redress were ignored and early in 1786 uprisings occurred in several Massachusetts counties, the demonstrators employing many of the tactics successfully used against the British prior to Lexington and Concord. Daniel Shays (1747?-1825), a veteran of Bunker Hill, Fort Ticonderoga, Saratoga, and Stony Point who had resigned his captaincy in the Continental Army, joined the movement and in August, 1786, marched on Springfield with approximately 1,000 angry dissidents attempting to prevent a state supreme court session.

Gen. William Sheppard's militia broke up the demonstration and thereafter Shays and his followers were branded insurgents. Early in December the persistent Shays led another protest at Worcester and when the militia was again mustered he fled to Vermont. In January, 1781, Shays organized three insurgent groups and planned to strike the U.S. Magazine at Springfield on the 25th where they hoped to capture large quantities of firearms and ammunition. The magazine was guarded by Gen. Sheppard's militia and as a precaution Gen. Benjamin Lincoln stood encamped nearby with 400 additional troops.

Insurgent leader Luke Day sent a message to Shays informing him that his group would not reach Springfield until the 26th. The message was intercepted by Sheppard and the militia was prepared. Rather than wait for Day, Shays attacked the magazine with Eli Parson's group on the afternoon of the scheduled date, oblivious to repeated warnings from Gen. Sheppard.

The militia fired two volleys over the heads of the attackers, though the third caught them as they stormed the magazine doors, killing three, wounding one, and putting the remainder to flight with Gen. Lincoln in pursuit. Shays' Rebellion abruptly ended in the drifting snow of a raging blizzard about two miles beyond Petersham, Mass., on February 3, 1787. Shays and several of his cohorts escaped during the storm and they were sentenced to hang in absentia, though all were subsequently pardoned.

SPRINGFIELD ARMORY (1794): On April 26, 1782, Congress authorized the establishment at Springfield, Mass., of "a good and efficient magazine for the reception of the public ammunition." Springfield was subsequently expanded and the production of firearms there was provided for by the Act of April 2, 1794; thus establishing the first national armory in the infant United States. In 1964, after 170 years of continuous service, Springfield Armory was closed in a Department of Defense economy move. Courtesy of the Library of Congress.

Delegates from the fledgling United States convened on May 25, 1787, at already historic Independence Hall in Philadelphia and on the 13th agreed ". . . that a national government ought to be established," and on August 23 recognized the amended Articles of Confederation (March 1, 1781) as the United States Constitution.

On July 13, 1787, Congress adopted the controversial Northwest Ordinance which established a non-slave government for the Ohio territory and on October 5th appointed as governor Gen. Arthur St. Clair. The Ohio Company, organized at Boston on March 1, 1786, established Marietta at the mouth of the Muskingum River as the first permanent settlement in the Northwest Territory on April 7, 1788.

Americans voted in the first national election on January 7, 1789, and on April 30 in New York City former rebel leader George Washington assumed the role of President of the United States and the Constitution simultaneously became ". . . the supreme law of the states."

Initially created as the United States Department of Foreign Affairs, the State Department was formed on July 27, 1789, and on August 7 the second monolithic bureaucracy established in the Republic was the Department of War with affable Bostonian Maj. Gen. Henry Knox sworn in as its first secretary on September 12.

In 1789 the U.S. Army, under the aegis of the Department of War, represented the only active military force at the national level of government and had a total strength of 718, of whom 46 were commissioned officers. Congress had been empowered to request additional troops from the states which retained the venerable militia system, while in an emergency volunteers bolstered the ranks.

In the early years of the Republic the U.S. Army was kept deliberately small, for the spectre of British power still haunted the founding fathers who distrusted a large military establishment, because it could be readily utilized as an instrument of oppression if concentrated in the hands of totalitarian leadership.[19]

The first national census in 1790 reported a population grown to 3,929,214 and the national debt stood at $54,124,464.56. Between 1789 and 1791 the federal budget reflected expenditures of $4,269,000 with $2,349,000 applied to reduce the interest on the debt. Another $1,286,000 was appropriated for government operation though the sum did not include the cost of maintaining the Department of War at $633,000 or an expenditure of $176,000 for veterans' compensation and pensions, and an additional $1,000[20] for the then newly created Department of the Navy with its 150 officers and 1,076 ratings; an entity separate from the Department of War.[21]

The Native American Trade

With the advent of the American Revolution in 1775 there was a conspicuous increase in British commercial and military activity among the Native Americans, for the crown had hoped to gain the exclusive allegiance of the powerful nations against the rebellious colonists. Most of that accelerated activity was centered on the Iroquoian Confederation under the influence of Sir William Johnson's heirs and Mohawk leader Joseph Brant (see p. 302); however, the British did not neglect the mighty Creek Confederacy influenced first by Kelsall and Spaulding operating from Georgia and then by Panton, Leslie & Company in East and West Florida.

During the Revolutionary War the British regarded the fur industry secondary to the need for Native American military assistance, though despite the frontier turmoil the procurement of furs and pelts escalated. Canada, touched only briefly by hostilities, preserved a lucrative fur trade maintained in part by the French populace under British rule since 1763 and primarily by the venerable Hudson's Bay Company which in 1770 had observed a century of commerce with the Native Americans. By 1775, however, the company was forced to expand its operation because of the competition then established at Montreal by several independent English and French traders banding together as the Northwest Company.[22]

Gooding's estimable research has revealed a number of Hudson's Bay Company gunsmiths active during the 1770-1792 period, among them Richard Barnes who on May 23, 1770, received a standard five-year contract at £25 per annum and replaced armorer Thomas Lingard upon his resignation from the company at Severn House.[23]

Serving in the company factories at York Fort, Churchill, and Albany Fort was armorer William Bews who had several contracts with the company between 1777 and 1800.[24] Also at York Fort from ca. 1779 to 1781 was James Carmichael and part of the time he served aboard the sloop SR visiting remote Native American villages on the shores of Hudson's Bay and repairing firearms.[25]

Between 1773 and 1778 Charles Higgins was a company armorer at Albany Fort,[26] and from 1778 to 1787 armorer David Kirkness worked at Albany River and Moose Fort.[27] Serving at Prince of Wales Fort with a five-year contract beginning in 1773 was armorer John Smith who was paid £25 yearly and received a £15 bonus when his term expired.[28]

Several independent gunsmiths also worked in Canada during the 1770-1792 period, among them at least two United States emigrés though the majority were French or of French or English descent. In the former category were the brothers Antoine (1728-1788) and Augustin LeMire (1737-1797) of Province Quebec.[29] Another French-Canadian gunsmith was Charles Chauvin (1702-1772), born in Quebec though relocating at Detroit Mission in Ontario prior to 1727.[30]

Most independent English gunsmiths or those of English extraction working in Canada, like Samuel Nunn of Shelburne, N.S.,[31] appear to have been widely dispersed throughout the provinces after Britain acquired New France in 1763. The French gunsmiths, however, thereafter congregated at Montreal and Quebec, among them Pierre Castagnet (fl. 1790-1805),[32] Joseph Gaulin (fl. 1791-1798),[33] Andre Moffette (fl. 1790-1791),[34] Charles Nolin (fl. 1790-1798),[35] Jean Parent (fl. 1790-1792),[36] and Antoine Richeaux (fl. 1791-1795).[37]

TRADE FUSIL MARKINGS (18th/19th Century): Left to right. (1) Fox-like animal or so-called sitting fox facing right as on Northwest Company trade fusils ca. 1775-1780. (2) A variant of the sitting fox known as the fox-in-circle mark used by the Hudson's Bay Company and subsequently counterfeited by other trade fusil makers. (3) Tombstone Fox mark found on Hudson's Bay Company and Northwest Company trade fusils ca. 1790 and thereafter. Author's sketch, not to scale.

1   2   3

Also active in Quebec in 1790 was German gunsmith Philip Braun, believed to have been a Hessian mercenary who had immigrated from the United States after the American Revolution and anglicized his surname to Brown.[38] Gunsmith Henry Watkeys and his son of New Windsor, N.Y., were also emigrés, moving to Halifax, N.S., ca. 1792 (see p. 310).

At some undetermined time in the 1775-1792 period the Hudson's Bay Company adopted a distinctive mark which was stamped on the trade fusil lock, its form suggesting a fox or fox-like animal in the sitting position.[39] Though probably an inspector's view mark, there is the possibility that it conveyed another meaning yet there is no documentary evidence in company records explaining either the origin or significance of the stamp.

A similar mark depicting a fox or fox-like animal sitting in a circle is found on Native American trade fusils made in England for the Northwest Company ca. 1790.[40] The so-called fox-in-circle mark is stamped on the lock below the pan and on the top breech flat. Again, there is no valid explanation except the hypothesis that the mark was meant to deceive the Native Americans familiar with the quality of Hudson's Bay Company fusils because Northwest Company fusils were similar in most respects.

A variation of the fox stamp appeared on Hudson's Bay Company fusil locks ca. 1790 and it is now referred to as the Tombstone Fox, for the seated animal is framed with a border resembling the outline of a tombstone.[41] The animal faces left rather than right as in the Northwest Company fox-in-circle design.

Another distinguishing feature of the Tombstone Fox mark is that the figure often surmounts a pair of letters. There is, however, no indication of what the letters signify, though it is possible that they were originally the initials of either a now unknown maker or company inspector. Nineteenth-century examples of the mark surmounting the letters E B or P A are available; the former possibly the initials of London gunsmith Edward Bond whose family made trade fusils for the Hudson's Bay Company ca. 1822 and thereafter.[42]

Like the earlier sitting fox and fox-in-circle marks the Tombstone Fox mark was subsequently pirated by other trading companies as the fur industry became more competitive and those marks or variations continued to be used by English and American trade fusil makers until the late nineteenth century.

Known for more than 100 years as a fusee or a Hudson's Bay fuke, the trade fusil began to be referred to as a Northwest gun by ca. 1790; an appellation probably stemming from its association with

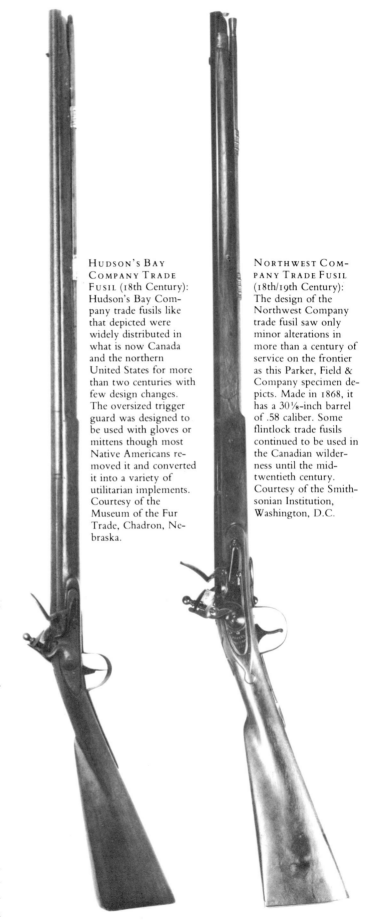

HUDSON'S BAY COMPANY TRADE FUSIL (18th Century): Hudson's Bay Company trade fusils like that depicted were widely distributed in what is now Canada and the northern United States for more than two centuries with few design changes. The oversized trigger guard was designed to be used with gloves or mittens though most Native Americans removed it and converted it into a variety of utilitarian implements. Courtesy of the Museum of the Fur Trade, Chadron, Nebraska.

NORTHWEST COMPANY TRADE FUSIL (18th/19th Century): The design of the Northwest Company trade fusil saw only minor alterations in more than a century of service on the frontier as this Parker, Field & Company specimen depicts. Made in 1868, it has a 30⅛-inch barrel of .58 caliber. Some flintlock trade fusils continued to be used in the Canadian wilderness until the mid-twentieth century. Courtesy of the Smithsonian Institution, Washington, D.C.

the Northwest Company in lower Canada, though equally appropriate because it continued to be used on the rapidly expanding North American frontier until the late nineteenth century.

It was also ca. 1790 that a special fusil was produced in Britain for the so-called medal chiefs cultivated by commercial and military interests. Patterned after the common trade fusil, those special firearms can be termed presentation fusils, for they were given as gifts by the British to ensure the loyalty of their powerful Native American allies like the exquisitely engraved medals presented to influential chieftans by Britain, France, and Spain since the late seventeenth century.[43]

Most presentation fusils displayed a round, 36-inch, .60 caliber barrel with an octagonal breech and a front and a rear sight. The full-length stock was chosen from select walnut and the lock was of sporting quality, while the brass furniture was lightly engraved. Conspicuously absent is the serpent side-plate associated with other trade fusils.

A number of presentation fusils were marked with the fox-in-circle stamp and all have British proof marks; the lockplate stamped with a crown and the broad arrow denoting government ownership. The most distinguishing characteristic, however, is the silver, Indian head medallion of about 7/16-inch diameter illustrating a detailed profile and mortised into the stock wrist in lieu of the thumbplate found on most sporting firearms.[44]

It is known that presentation fusils were made under crown contract until ca. 1815 and it is probable that they enjoyed widespread distribution in North America, though no record is available delineating the number produced.[45] Most of the presentation fusils were made by London gunsmiths Thomas and Samuel Galton (see p. 340), Henry Morris (fl. 1785-1815),[46] and Thomas Moxham (fl. 1780-1812),[47] while also involved were Birmingham gunsmiths John, Thomas, and William Ketland (see Ch. VI, n. 16) and W.J. Rolfe (fl. 1780-1815).[48] John and Thomas Ketland were active in Philadelphia from 1797 until 1800 where they contracted to supply American gunsmiths with various firearms components imported from their Birmingham factory.[49]

In 1784 the Ohio country Iroquois expressed a desire to negotiate with the United States because their former commercial arrangements with the British had been abrogated by the unexpected American victory in the War of Independence. Delegates from the Six Nations assembled at Fort Stanwix on October 22 and they ceded to the United States all of their land in the vast, vaguely defined wilderness which came to be called the Northwest Territory.

The Iroquoian precedent, much to the dismay of the British, influenced many of the other Native Americans in the region and, not fully comprehending the implications, they signed a treaty with the United States at Fort McIntosh in the Ohio country on January 2, 1785. The Shawnee, however, having recovered some of their power after their disastrous defeat in Lord Dunmore's War, steadfastly refused to part with their land and the territory remained in the throes of conflict for nearly a decade; the Shawnee and their allies procuring trade fusils and ammuntion from the expanding Northwest Company and martial firearms and other war material from British bases in Canada, primarily Fort Detroit.

Emerging coevally as part of the United States Department of War (see p. 365) was the Office of Indian Affairs (OIA) and it served with that designation until March 11, 1824, when it became the Bureau of Indian Affairs (BIA). The BIA continued under Department of War aegis until it was transferred to the then newly created Department of the Interior on March 3, 1849, where it has since remained to stain the honor and integrity of a great nation.

In the early years of the Republic the OIA closely cooperated with the U.S. Army in dealing with the political and socio-economic aspects of Native American relations with the federal government. Initially embracing a conciliatory policy, the OIA can be assessed as a successful failure; the amicable relationship early fostered with the Native Americans subsequently hampered in part by poor organization, limited funding, public apathy, pressure from commercial interests, government bureaucracy, and the surreptitious British and Spanish manipulations of the Native American trade on the frontier abetted by the Northwest Company and Panton, Leslie & Company.

Much of the initial success of the OIA occurred during the years immediately beyond the purview of this study and it is attributable to the United States factory system advocated by President Washington in 1793. Administered by the OIA, the factory system provided the Native Americans with quality trade fusils, trade rifles, gunpowder, and other goods which could be purchased at cost from a chain of government stations scattered along the frontier; the first factory established among the Cherokee in 1798 at Tellico on the Little Tennessee River.[50]

By 1782 most of the Native Americans under British influence realized that their ancestral land would be thrown open to American encroachment if the Lion and Unicorn suffered defeat in the War of Independence. Consequently, in November, Native American delegates from as far away as the Great Lakes region congregated at St. Augustine in British East Florida seeking assurances of military protection and trade concessions.[51] The St. Augustine Congress was headed by Royal Governor Patrick

Tonyn, serving in that capacity from 1774 to 1783, and the Superintendent of Indian Affairs for the Southern District, Thomas Brown (see p. 298).

Tonyn and Brown expressed equal concern about the potential American threat, promising the Native Americans more assistance than they could guarantee or deliver under the circumstances. They were also aware that the Creeks were particularly vulnerable because their domain abutted Spanish possessions and the war-torn colonies. Partly to assuage Creek fears and to broaden Britain's economic foundation in East Florida, Tonyn and Brown encouraged the establishment of trading stations within reasonable reach of the Creek villages.

On January 15, 1783, Gov. Tonyn licensed William Panton to represent Britain's commercial interests with the Creeks, Seminoles, and other southeastern nations.[52] Panton's partners in the profitable venture were prominent East Florida merchants John Leslie, Thomas Forbes, and William Alexander; the latter pair more financially than physically involved.

With the Spanish conquest of British West Florida in 1781 Arturo O'Neill was appointed governor and served until 1793. Remembering past Spanish treatment the Creeks preferred to deal with the British and did so until they were forced out in 1783 and East Florida was returned to Spain with Vincente Manuel de Zéspedes serving as governor until 1790; Spain retaining the former British political demarcations to preserve administrative continuity. The Creeks then faced the alternative of relations with Spain or the United States and chose the former as the lesser of two evils; the first overture made to Gov. O'Neill at Pensacola by a rising star in the powerful Creek Confederation, Alexander McGillivray (1759?-1793).

Son of a Creek princess and a Scottish trader, McGillivray was educated in Charleston and Savannah and, like Joseph Brant, remained staunchly loyal to the British during the American Revolution. An able, enterprising leader, McGillivray early recognized Creek and Spanish empathy in preventing American incursions and also realized, as he wrote Gov. O'Neill on January 1, 1784, that ". . . Indians will attach themselves to & Serve them best who Supply their Necessities."[53] Governors O'Neill and Zéspedes were determined that aggressive American traders would not have the opportunity.

Bernardo de Gálvez, Captain General of Louisiana and the Floridas, was also vitally interested in the Native American trade as a means to limit American encroachments in the Mississippi Valley and to keep peace among the Choctaw and Chickasaw; an interest further extended to the Alibamons and McGillivray's Talapuche Creeks following the Spanish triumph in West Florida.

Shortly after the fall of Fort George at Pensacola in May, 1781, Gálvez sent to Spain his wealthy father-in-law, veteran New Orleans trader Gilberto Antonio de Maxent, with the object of securing commercial concessions from the crown.[54] His proposals were accepted and on January 22, 1782, Charles III opened Louisiana and West Florida to direct trade with the French through Maxent.

Spain had developed no substantial fur industry in North America and consequently had no reason to establish facilities to manufacture trade goods, however, her arrangements were financially and politically rewarding because she received a six percent duty on the flow of French trade fusils, gunpowder, and other goods into Louisiana and West Florida; thus preserving a relatively placid relationship with the Choctaw and Chickasaw while they and their allies protected the Spanish frontier from American incursions.[55]

Maxent, however, suffered severe financial reverses and was subsequently arrested for smuggling specie. When his mercantile empire collapsed it left a discernable void in the Louisiana and West Florida trade. Esteban Miró, as temporary governor of Louisiana, filled the gap in April, 1784, when he arranged for the commerce to continue under the direction of British merchants James Mather and Arthur Strother of New Orleans.[56] Miró also contacted McGillivray and initiated negotiations with the Creeks, scheduling a meeting at Pensacola on May 30.

Governors Miró and O'Neill attended the Pensacola Congress and on June 1 successfully concluded a treaty with the Talapuches. The Creeks, among other things, promised to defend Spanish territory from any threat in return for firearms, gunpowder, and other trade goods at reasonable prices. Eight Talapuche chiefs were awarded Great Medals and six received Small Medals, and all of the delegates and their families were given sufficient gunpowder, rum, and provisions for the ten-day return trip to their villages.[57] McGillivray was appointed Creek agent with an annual stipend of $600.

On June 21 Miró sat with the Choctaw, Chickasaw, and Alibamon at Mobile and negotiated a pact with each nation; the stipulations similar to those accepted by the Talapuches. In East Florida, meanwhile, William Panton had convinced Gov. Zéspedes that only his firm could preserve Creek friendship and to solidify his position he enlisted McGillivray's aid, promising him a generous 1/5 share of the profits if the company trade arrangements were approved.[58]

At Panton's request Gov. Zéspedes endorsed the company proposals on July 31, 1784, and recommended to the crown that Panton be permitted to continue the Native American trade in both Floridas ". . . on the same basis as formerly under the British government. . . ."[59] While waiting for a response from Madrid, Zéspedes encouraged Panton, Leslie & Company to operate freely in East Florida.

An aggressive, avaricious entrepreneur who would not be considered a managerial anachronism in the corporate structure of the current conglomerate interests manipulating international commerce, Panton was not content with the East Florida concession. By March, 1785, he and McGillivray, despite the latter's agreement with Miró and O'Neill, were actively seeking to destroy the Mather and Strother monopoly.

In the summer of 1785 Panton was provided with a powerful lever when Mather and Strother found themselves in financial difficulty. They attempted to circumvent their losses by increasing prices on their trade goods. Their poor credit, however, denied them sufficient merchandise and both factors contributed to the dissatisfaction expressed by the Alibamon, Choctaw, and Chickasaw. As Gov. Miró feared, the Native Americans began looking to American traders for relief.

In September, 1785, Panton grasped his opportunity. Deliberately cutting prices for a temporary loss on what he considered a monumental gain, he successfully convinced Spanish officials to permit him to import trade goods worth 125,000 *pesos* into Pensacola; thus establishing a toehold in the West Florida and Louisiana market by bartering quality trade goods for less which elated and mollified the restive Native Americans.[60] Mather and Strother loudly protested and they were heard in Madrid.

Panton was chagrined to learn that while the crown had approved some of his earlier proposals on May 8, 1786, the company was still confined to the East Florida market. Miró, now permanently confirmed as governor, further informed Panton that his trade goods would be confiscated if the firm persisted in attempting to eliminate Mather and Strother from the Louisiana and West Florida trade.

Temporarily stymied, Panton nevertheless continued his campaign to capture the profitable commerce and elicited McGillivray's assistance, for the mendacious Creek leader was increasingly disturbed by American expansion in Georgia and a growing pro-United States faction among the Upper Creeks. In late 1786 he initiated a general frontier uprising which continued until mid-1788 when Spain became increasingly reluctant to escalate the conflict in fear of massive American retaliation.

Panton, Leslie & Company, whose role in the Spanish trade was ostensibly one of preserving peace to promote an uninterrupted and thus lucrative commerce, profited either way because the firm capitalized on pedestrian trade goods as well as the Native American demand for firearms, gunpowder, and the other accouterments of war.

And neither was Panton inclined to halt Creek depredations. To the contrary he violated his arrangement with Spain by covertly acting on behalf of British interests which fortunately coincided with his own, going so far as to personally inform the Creeks that the firearms and ammunition his firm supplied were to be used to kill Americans.[61]

By 1789 Panton achieved his ambitious goal, for on March 23 the crown authorized the company to conduct the West Florida and Louisiana commerce. Shortly thereafter company flatboats left New Orleans for Choctaw Bluff (present Vicksburg, Miss.) and other stations north and west, while long trains of pack horses and mules, averaging 25 miles daily with each animal carrying 80 pounds of merchandise, penetrated the southern heartland from Mobile and Pensacola.[62]

The checkered performance of Panton, Leslie & Company in the convoluted drama of the restive southern frontier is replete with political and socioeconomic chicanery spanning more than 50 years and includes innumerable acts of bribery, espionage, murder, treason, and other crimes involving Britain, France, Spain, the United States, and various Native Americans.

Almost from the beginning William Panton's crafty machinations in the firearms and gunpowder traffic were deliberately calculated to foment unrest along the expanding United States frontier during Britain's continuing efforts to regain a strong foothold in her former American colonies, and they are inextricably woven into the web of intrigue cloaking the secret Treaty of San Ildefonso whereby Spain ceded the vast Louisiana Territory to France on October 1, 1800.

It also can be said that the rapacious mercantile empire established by Panton and promoted by his equally shrewd successors after his death at sea on February 26, 1801, figured prominently in the tumultuous events which subsequently led to the purchase of the Louisiana Territory by the United States on April 30, 1803.

As Panton insidiously promulgated unrest in the vast southeast other British agents were active in the Northwest Territory, inciting the Shawnee and their allies. Gov. St. Clair attempted to placate the hostiles and on January 9, 1789, reaffirmed the earlier Fort McIntosh Treaty. Many of the Native Americans remained dissatisfied however, and the British nurtured their discontent.

St. Clair was forced to mount a punitive expedition against the refractory nations and he was handsomely defeated on the Wabash River, November 4, 1791. In April, 1792, President Washington appointed Gen. Anthony Wayne as commander-in-chief of the army with orders to subdue the hostiles.

An experienced Revolutionary War veteran,

Gen. Wayne for more than a year mercilessly hammered his force of 1,000 regulars, Ohio militia, and volunteer riflemen into shape for the arduous campaigns he envisioned, earning him the irreverent sobriquet Mad Anthony. The final defeat of the Northwest Territory malcontents came on August 20, 1795, when Gen. Wayne's seasoned troops struck them on the Maumee River near present Toledo, Ohio, at a place called Fallen Timbers.

Significantly, the profitable Native American trade was at least partially responsible for the controversial War of 1812 (1812–1815) when the factious and fragmented United States was forced to declare war on Great Britain to preserve the fledgling "republican experiment" growing out of the American Revolution.[63]

Not until Fallen Timbers was the Northwest Territory relatively safe for settlement, and not until the conclusion of the War of 1812 had the chaotic southern frontier been neutralized, and the monumental significance of those historic events was that they set the stage for the immutable and epochal drama of Manifest Destiny.

As the American frontier moved relentlessly west during the early nineteenth century, civilization immediately followed to take from the restless frontier people their most cherished possession and, paradoxically, it had been the frontier people who had struggled so fiercely for more than 200 years to deprive the Native Americans of that one precious and intangible attribute they had so desperately desired; that one indefinable commodity that had driven them beyond the capricious Atlantic and into the wilderness; that one unfulfilled promise that had forced them into bloody revolt; and that one improbable dream that had created a nation: freedom.

Old World Technological Innovation

Spain's successful colonization of California during the latter half of the eighteenth century managed to halt the Russian advance along the Pacific strand and some progress was also made in establishing missions and settlements in what is now Arizona, New Mexico, and Texas despite the ubiquitous threat posed by the fierce Navaho, Apache, and Comanche nations.

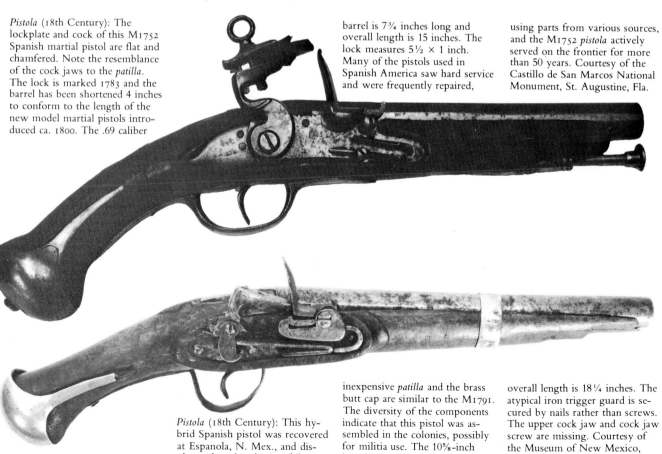

Pistola (18th Century): The lockplate and cock of this M1752 Spanish martial pistol are flat and chamfered. Note the resemblance of the cock jaws to the *patilla*. The lock is marked 1783 and the barrel has been shortened 4 inches to conform to the length of the new model martial pistols introduced ca. 1800. The .69 caliber barrel is 7¾ inches long and overall length is 15 inches. The lock measures 5½ × 1 inch. Many of the pistols used in Spanish America saw hard service and were frequently repaired, using parts from various sources, and the M1752 *pistola* actively served on the frontier for more than 50 years. Courtesy of the Castillo de San Marcos National Monument, St. Augustine, Fla.

Pistola (18th Century): This hybrid Spanish pistol was recovered at Espanola, N. Mex., and displays a barrel and grip of the M1752 cavalry model, while the inexpensive *patilla* and the brass butt cap are similar to the M1791. The diversity of the components indicate that this pistol was assembled in the colonies, possibly for militia use. The 10⅝-inch barrel has a .72 caliber bore taking a .69 caliber ball and the overall length is 18¼ inches. The atypical iron trigger guard is secured by nails rather than screws. The upper cock jaw and cock jaw screw are missing. Courtesy of the Museum of New Mexico, Santa Fe. David Stein, photographer.

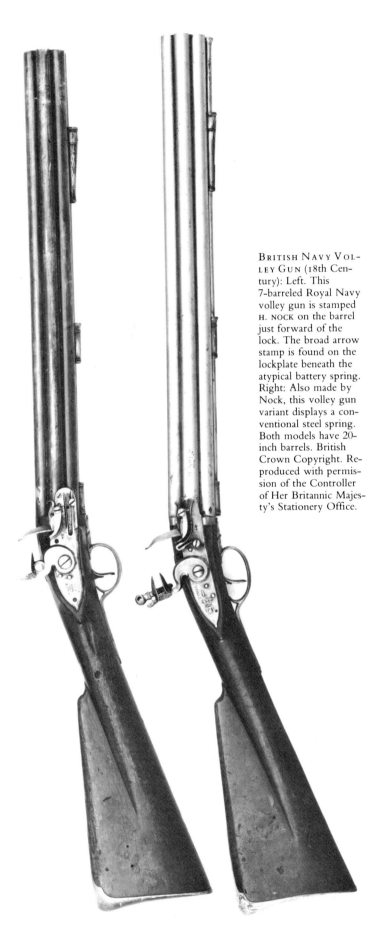

BRITISH NAVY VOL-
LEY GUN (18th Cen-
tury): Left. This
7-barreled Royal Navy
volley gun is stamped
H. NOCK on the barrel
just forward of the
lock. The broad arrow
stamp is found on the
lockplate beneath the
atypical battery spring.
Right: Also made by
Nock, this volley gun
variant displays a con-
ventional steel spring.
Both models have 20-
inch barrels. British
Crown Copyright. Re-
produced with permis-
sion of the Controller
of Her Britannic Majes-
ty's Stationery Office.

In 1791 Spain again made evident though minor alterations in her basic martial firearms, most of them confined to the lock. The French martial flint-lock introduced in Spanish martial firearms in 1752 was supplanted by the earlier *patilla (miquelet)* which was less fragile. The M1791 *patilla* was provided with a detachable brass priming pan and a pivotal fence secured by the battery screw.[64]

A more substantial sideplate was found on the M1791 musket, carbine, light infantry *escopeta,* and pistol; the latter also incorporating a single brass barrel band and a belt hook. Otherwise the primary character of Spanish martial firearms remained the same as the 1752 models.[65]

In any event the craftsmanship characterizing eighteenth-century European firearms was vastly superior to that representative of the firearms made in North America and it is evident that English gun-smiths were more concerned with design innovation than either their American or Continental contemporaries; particularly after midcentury and especially in relation to sporting firearms.

If any craftsman could be chosen to represent the innovative aspects of eighteenth-century English gunmaking it would be the celebrated London gun-smith Henry Nock (1741-1806), one of the foremost firearms inventors of any era.[66]

Nock began his distinguished career as a gun-lock maker in 1762 and by 1775, in association with gunsmith William Jover (see p. 318) and John Green (fl. 1770-1778),[67] he patented a concealed or so-called waterproof flintlock in which the lock was installed in a stock cavity directly behind the breech and it was provided with a tube or chimney for drawing off the powder smoke resulting from ignition (see p. 192).

In 1776 Nock contracted to produce Ferguson-pattern flintlock muskets for the East India Company and the following year he received an Ordnance Board contract to make Brown Bess musket locks. His involvement in government arms-making sub-sequently resulted in a contract to manufacture vol-ley guns for the Royal Navy and between 1780 and 1788 he produced 655 of them at £13 each.[68]

The unusual design of those navy volley guns was conceived by Royal Marine Capt. James Wilson who on July 29, 1779, submitted his ". . . new in-vented Gun with seven barrels to fire at one time . . ." to the Ordnance Board for trials and it was adopted by the Admiralty in October while a second model was introduced in 1787.[69]

The innovative Wilson volley gun consisted of a single, 20-inch, .65 caliber barrel around which six others of equal length were brazed. The vent channel leading from the priming pan was connected by six vents radiating like the spokes of a wagon wheel from the center barrel to the others. The overall length of the volley gun was approximately 36 inches

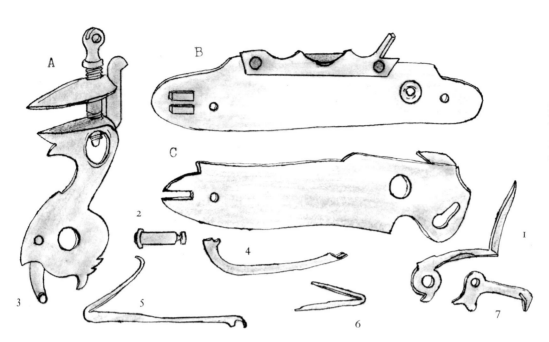

HENRY NOCK'S SCREWLESS LOCK (18th Century): (A) Cock. (B) Lockplate. (C) Retaining plate. (1) Battery. (2) Retaining pin. (3) Cock/Mainspring link. (4) Pan cover lever. (5) Mainspring. (6) Sear spring. (7) Sear. Author's sketch, not to scale.

and it displayed a musket-pattern stock, conventional lock, and steel ramrod secured by two thimbles and a guide.

Late in 1779 Nock submitted a pair of prototype Wilson volley guns with rifled bores to the Admiralty. Each cost £15, though as far as it can be determined all of those ordered by the Royal Navy were smoothbores. The volley guns were intended for the use of sailors and marines stationed in the rigging of H.M. warships to repel boarders and eliminate enemy gunners.

There is a single recorded instance of the volley gun used in combat and it occurred in September, 1782, when Admiral Lord Richard Howe successfully lifted the three-year siege of Gibraltar by the French and Spanish.[70] Shortly thereafter the Admiralty discontinued the use of volley guns because they were inordinately expensive, difficult to load, frequently misfired, and no more effective than the naval blunderbuss.

Long involved with volley gun manufacture, Nock nevertheless pursued other interests and in 1768 produced two significant design innovations, one incorporating the other, though neither exerted a profound influence on firearms technology. The first was a breech-loading musket and the second was a variation of the so-called screwless lock.

In 1784 Lewisham gunsmith Jonathan Hennem invented a flintlock mechanism in which the components were secured to the lockplate by clips and pins rather than screws, i.e., the first practical screwless lock.[71] Two years later Nock improved the concept, employing it as a concealed lock in the breech-loading musket.[72] The only screw in the locks designed by Hennem and Nock was the cock screw which transversed the lock, securing it to the stock.

In Nock's design the lock components were incorporated in a single, box-like unit comprised of the lockplate and the retaining plate. Excluding the external cock components (A), the lockplate (B), and the retaining plate (C), there were seven functional parts: (1) the combined battery and pan cover, (2) the pan cover retaining pin, (3) the pivotal cock link, (4) the pivotal pan cover lever, (5) the mainspring, (6) the sear spring, and (7) the sear. The cock was positioned between the lockplate and the retaining plate, i.e., centrally-hung.

While Hennem's lock required a special disassembly tool, Nock's mechanism could be readily dismantled. The cock screw was first removed with a screwdriver or any implement which fit the slotted cock screw head; thus freeing the lock unit from the stock. A projecting catch on the retaining plate (C), engaging a slot at the front of the lockplate (B), was easily disengaged by pushing forward with the fingers which pivoted the retaining plate down to release the tension on the sear spring (5).

Releasing the tension permitted the lockplate to be removed and the sear (7) and the sear spring disassembled from their respective positions. Compressing the mainspring (6) disengaged it from the pivotal cock link (3), freeing the cock (A) and the mainspring. The retaining pin (2) then could be removed from the combined battery and pan cover (1), releasing it and the pivotal pan cover lever (4) to complete disassembly. The lock was assembled in reverse order.

Nock's screwless lock was incorporated in the .75 caliber musket he also designed in 1786, a variation of the pivotal chamber devised by Bicknell (see p. 145) and others. The overall length of the musket was 42 and ½ inches and the loading chamber was

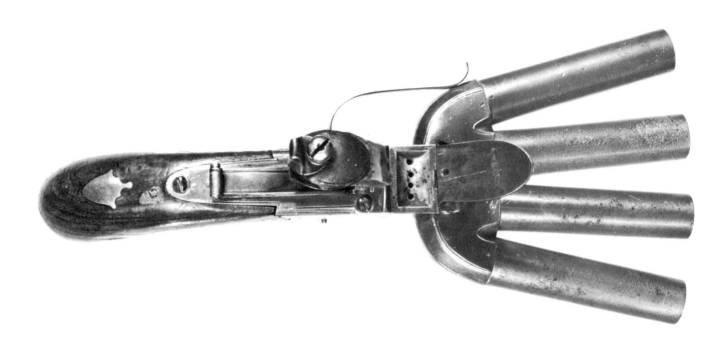

DUCK'S FOOT PISTOL (18th Century):
This variant of Henry Nock's design was
made by London gunsmith Jaques ca.
1795-1800. Note the splayed barrel arrangement and the four vents in the priming pan (top view). Each .37 caliber barrel
measures 2 13/16-inches and all barrels fired
simultaneously. The cock is centrally-hung
and a belt hook is provided. Courtesy of the
Glasgow Art Gallery and Museums, Scotland.

hinged at the rear to a retractable slide and secured in the breech by a lock pin provided with a finger ring. A short chain attached to the sliding breech cover prevented the loss of the lock pin. Withdrawing the lock pin permitted the slide to move rearward, extracting the chamber from the breech and it pivoted upward for loading.[73]

Henry Nock also devoted considerable time to pistol manufacture, producing a variety of pocket models and several multi-barreled specimens; one of the latter a peculiar, four-barreled pistol employing a vent system like the Wilson volley gun and popularly called a duck-foot pistol because of the distinctly splayed barrel arrangement.[74] The duck-foot pistol served the same purpose as the blunderbuss and volley gun though it was not a martial firearm. Nock, however, did produce several kinds of martial pistols, designing a cavalry model with a detachable butt in 1783; the length of the buttstock converting the pistol to a carbine.[75] A decade later he designed a double-barreled pistol for the Royal Horse Artillery.[76]

What can be considered Nock's greatest triumph was conceived in 1787 and on April 25 he was issued Patent No. 1598 for his celebrated patent breech; a technological innovation of major significance. The patent specifications illustrated two improved breech plug designs, either of them adaptable to the false breech introduced in England ca. 1745-1750 and common throughout Europe 20 years later (see p. 192).[77]

Nock's patent breech plugs eliminated the obvious time lapse characterizing chamber breeching which had been introduced ca. 1750 (see p. 193) and he achieved the purpose with two radical design concepts: one breech plug incorporating a short, wide antechamber and the other a long, narrow antechamber. In either plug variant the powder-filled antechamber was adjacent to the vent and the priming flash entered it directly from the pan, therefore ignition was practically instantaneous because it was not delayed in the long, L-shaped vent channel which characterized chamber breeching. The antechambers were provided with small, threaded plugs readily removed for cleaning the vent channel and the antechambers.

The patent breech system eliminated the traditionally long barrels associated with most sporting guns. The 39 to 48-inch barrel common to fowling pieces earlier in the century was relegated to obscurity throughout most of Europe by ca. 1795. Thereafter most European flintlock sporting guns displayed barrels ranging from 22 to 32 inches. The shortened barrel reduced the weight of the fowling piece as well as the length of the forestock which became little more than a convenient handgrip by the turn of the century.

Despite the popularity of Nock's patent breech system in Europe it found little use in the United States; however, the patent breech combined with Henry Nock's other inventions resulted in his appointment as gunmaker-in-ordinary to the King in 1789.[78]

Sir Charles Lennox (1735-1806), the Third Duke of Richmond and Master General of the Ordnance, sought a new pattern British infantry musket and authorized the Ordnance Board to advance £100 to Henry Nock for a suitable design. In 1790 Nock produced a prototype incorporating his screwless lock and shortly thereafter began manufacturing the muskets under an exclusive contract.[79]

Known as the Duke of Richmond pattern, the Nock martial musket was a muzzle-loader with an overall length of 62 inches. The .75 caliber barrel was 46 inches long and the stock emulated the Brown Bess design. Weighing ten pounds and 12 ounces, the innovative musket was provided with a 17-inch socket bayonet.

The Duke of Richmond musket, difficult to make because of the screwless lock and consequently expensive, was then considered to be the finest martial musket made anywhere and at least 1,000 were manufactured before the devastating nineteenth-century Napoleonic wars forced the Ordnance Board to abandon the project and return to the less expensive Brown Bess pattern musket.[80]

It was also during the late eighteenth century that the pins or bands formerly used to secure the barrel of sporting guns to the stock were gradually superseded by a metal wedge or key provided with escutcheons. While Nock's patent breech system improved the shooting quality of the sporting gun, the weight reduction commensurate with the shorter

HENRY NOCK'S PATENT BREECH (1787): The loading charge also filled the offset antechambers and was instantly ignited by the flash from the priming pan transversing the vent channel; thus increasing ignition speed. The screws could be removed for cleaning the antechambers. bauthor's sketch, not to scale.

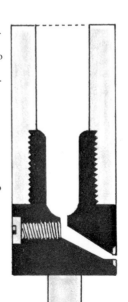

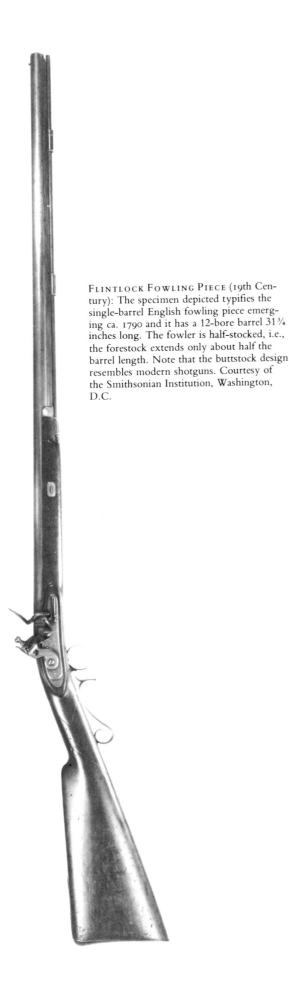

FLINTLOCK FOWLING PIECE (19th Century): The specimen depicted typifies the single-barrel English fowling piece emerging ca. 1790 and it has a 12-bore barrel 31¾ inches long. The fowler is half-stocked, i.e., the forestock extends only about half the barrel length. Note that the buttstock design resembles modern shotguns. Courtesy of the Smithsonian Institution, Washington, D.C.

barrel made it easier to handle. And those innovations subsequently permitted a second barrel of equal length to be mounted at the breech without sacrificing manageability; thus giving the hunter an extra shot and introducing the first examples of the justly famed English double gun. In essence, by the final decade of the century the basic characteristics of the modern shotgun had evolved.

The quest for a suitable method of choke boring the fowling piece was revived in France during the final quarter of the century, for in 1781 G.F. Magne de Marolles described a method used by Parisian gunsmiths which produced an effect on the shot pattern earlier demonstrated by Paczelt (see p. 192), though it was accomplished by other means:

An iron or wooden mandrel, fitting the bore, is furnished at one end with small files [similar to the rifling saw], which cut transversely only. This tool, put into the muzzle . . . and turned round by means of a cross-handle, forms a number of superficial scratches in the metal, by which the defect of scattering the shot is remedied. One effect . . . is that of destroying the smoothness of the barrels within, rendering them liable to foul, and causing them to lead [see p. 12] sooner, after the discharge.[81]

In 1789 a London gunsmith named Mellor, located in Greyhound Lane, Whitechapel, advertised:

To Gentlemen Sportsmen.—Guns matchless for shooting to be sold, or twisted barrels bored on an improved plan, that will always maintain their true velocity, and do not let the birds fly away after being shot, as they generally do with guns not properly bored. The shortest of them will shoot any common shot through a whole quire [25 sheets] of paper at 90 yards with ease. . . .[82]

Though the range and shot penetration claimed by Mellor were doubtlessly exaggerated, his statement concerning ". . . barrels bored on an improved plan . . ." suggest that some form of choke boring, if not like the Paczelt or French method, was evident in Britain at least a decade before the advent of the nineteenth century.

The efficacy of the flintlock mechanism was further enhanced ca. 1770 when London gunsmiths introduced a bearing (roller) to the battery spring or the pan cover tail and a small link or swivel between the tumbler and the mainspring.[83] The roller practically eliminated friction and wear at the crucial conjunction of the pan cover tail with the battery spring; thus increasing lock speed in respect to ignition because when the flint struck the battery the pan cover opened smoothly and rapidly. The tumbler swivel also reduced friction drag on the sear shoulder

FLINTLOCK FOWLING PIECE LOCK (19th Century): This close-up of the lock from the fowling piece in the previous illustration shows the elegantly simple craftsmanship of London gunsmith E. Bond (fl. 1790–1838) who also made trade fusils; the Bond gunsmithing family active from ca. 1765. Note the roller bearing mounted on the top leaf of the battery spring; an innovation appearing on quality sporting firearms prior to 1775. Courtesy of the Smithsonian Institution, Washington, D.C.

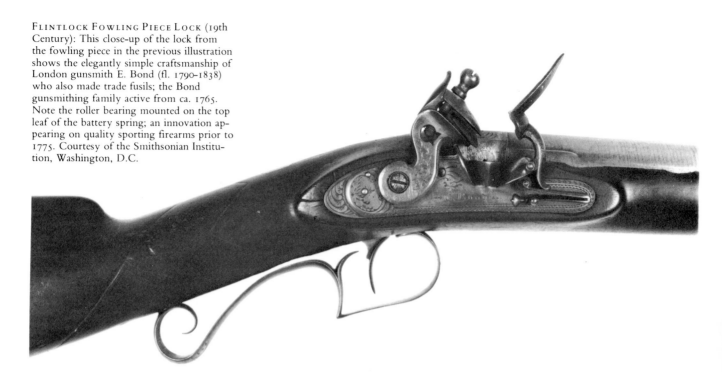

and each of those innovations improved lock performance.

By 1775 double-roller locks were advertised by New York City gunsmiths (see p. 336), while a decade later the roller and swivel were incorporated on most quality European locks except martial specimens; those innovations considered too fragile and not a prerequisite for performance.

The waterproof priming pan, gold and platinum vent bushings, friction bearings, tumbler swivels, and Henry Nock's patent breech plugs had measurably improved flintlock performance by the end of the eighteenth century. A standard quality English or continental European lock of ca. 1780 could be depended upon to discharge 200 times in succession without a misfire provided the best gunpowder was used and the flint changed and properly adjusted in the cock jaws when necessary. If the same criteria were followed a superior quality lock delivered at least 1,000 shots without a misfire.[84]

Regarding ignition speed, i.e., the elapsed time from the release of the cock to discharge, a quality European flintlock would register between 3/1000 to 6/1000 of a second; a performance unapproached in eighteenth-century American gunlocks, though it must be taken into consideration that American gunsmiths found it nearly impossible to procure the steel necessary to make quality lock springs until the nineteenth century.[85]

Coincidental with the advent of the American Revolution there appeared in London a kind of pistol as yet in rudimentary form which was expressly designed for the then fashionable though pernicious human foible known as dueling.

Predating the dawn of recorded history and persisting in one form or another until the present, dueling represented a common method of rectifying real or imagined personal wrongs and it was almost universally recognized as an "honorable" solution to many problems, despite the obvious fact that it defied all concepts of rational human behavior. However, the adherents of dueling were more numerous than its detractors.

A 1657 epistle titled "A Circulatory Letter of the Gentlemen Governors of the Hospital of Paris to the Governors of Other Hospitals of France" contains what is perhaps the first reference to the use of firearms for dueling, mentioning that for the purpose ". . . there are carried Swords, Daggers, Knives and of late Pistols or other Firearms."[86]

While on the Continent firearms came to be acceptable for dueling in the latter half of the seventeenth century, they failed to alter the empirical rules of the *Code Duello* in Britain until the first half of the eighteenth century; a delay attributed more to tradition than common sense. Curiously, however, no one apparently bothered to develop a firearm specifically designed for those ghastly meetings on the so-called field of honor for more than a century.

The pistols usually employed in the duel were martial horse pistols familiar to most "gentlemen," an elite group representing the aristocracy from which the military officer corps was drawn, though subsequently amended to include anyone of sufficient financial means. The majority of those educated, often talented individuals subscribed to the Code and, as the opponents of dueling so poignantly noted, many of them were sacrificed to a deadly

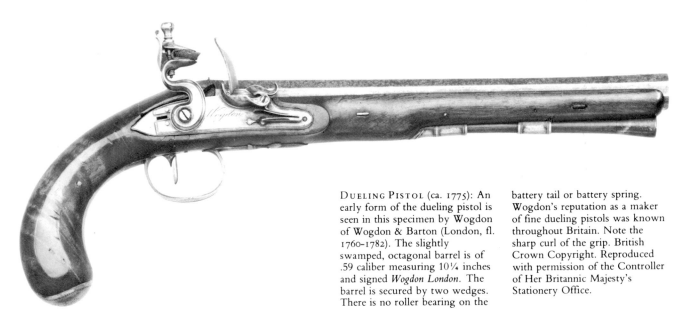

DUELING PISTOL (ca. 1775): An early form of the dueling pistol is seen in this specimen by Wogdon of Wogdon & Barton (London, fl. 1760-1782). The slightly swamped, octagonal barrel is of .59 caliber measuring 10¼ inches and signed *Wogdon London*. The barrel is secured by two wedges. There is no roller bearing on the battery tail or battery spring. Wogdon's reputation as a maker of fine dueling pistols was known throughout Britain. Note the sharp curl of the grip. British Crown Copyright. Reproduced with permission of the Controller of Her Britannic Majesty's Stationery Office.

ounce of lead which robbed more than one nation of its most precious asset: the potential of its younger generation.

During the Seven Years' War (1756-1763) British officers' holster pistols were produced in three calibers to take advantage of the standard martial ammunition then in abundance: 12 bore (approximately 14 balls to the pound), 16 bore (20 balls to the pound), or 20-/24 bore (34 balls to the pound).[87]

Most popular was the 16 bore used in martial carbines and pistols. The weight of the medium-bore pistol with its natural balance and familiarity appealed to those desiring a pistol suitable for military use and dueling, while for the latter the pistol was generally loaded with a patched ball in the manner of rifled firearms to deliver maximum accuracy and velocity.[88]

By 1775 a number of London gunsmiths had become aware of the popular demand for suitable dueling pistols and began producing 16-bore prototypes.[89] In the early development stage the martial-dueling pistol displayed hybrid characteristics, though by ca. 1795 the prototypes had transcended the martial influence to emerge as true dueling pistols.

A composite description best illustrates the design of the hybrid or transitional dueling pistol, for no two were alike despite the fact that they were smoothbores and made in pairs like the horseman's pistols. The octagonal breech extended half way down the 12 inch barrel which terminated with a baluster (cannon-barrel) moulding in most instances though in later specimens it was eliminated. The ramrod was wood, carried separately as most pistols were cased, and there were no sights, while the barrel was pin-fastened to the forestock.

The dueling pistol grip demonstrated a more distinct curvature than the martial holster pistol and was flattened on either side to better fit the hand; the heavy pommel butt gradually abandoned. A raised moulding usually surrounded the lock mortise and, to prevent distractions, there was little or no ornamentation. Barrels were generally browned to reduce glare, for the duelist could ill-afford to have his vision impaired by reflected light.

Particular attention was given to the balance of the dueling pistol to improve its pointing qualities and the lock also received special notice. A smooth, crisp trigger pull was an obvious prerequisite and the timing of the lock was of the utmost importance because a heavy trigger pull could put the duelist off his aim and poorly timed springs could cause a misfire; neither conducive to the longevity of the duelist at a crucial moment and, in most instances, he would be in no position to complain to his gunsmith. Nor could the gunsmith afford to make inferior dueling pistols, for while his life was not in jeopardy his reputation certainly was, and the esteem he garnered often determined his economic survival.

While throughout history duels have been fought with an extraordinary variety of weapons, perhaps none was as bizarre or succinctly illustrated the sheer stupidity of dueling as those chosen by doughty Israel Putnam when serving as a militia officer in the French and Indian War (see p. 289). His often brusque, abrasive manner saw him challenged by a British officer and he readily accepted, choosing as weapons two barrels of gunpowder each provided with a long fuze.

The pair mounted their respective barrels and the fuzes were ignited. Putnam, grimly rooted to the lethal perch, glared at his antagonist as the fuzes swiftly ran their deadly course. The anxious British

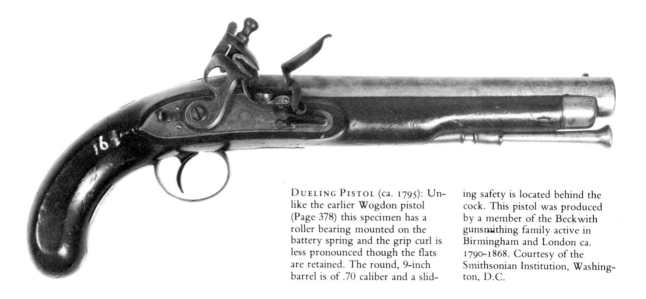

DUELING PISTOL (ca. 1795): Unlike the earlier Wogdon pistol (Page 378) this specimen has a roller bearing mounted on the battery spring and the grip curl is less pronounced though the flats are retained. The round, 9-inch barrel is of .70 caliber and a slid-ing safety is located behind the cock. This pistol was produced by a member of the Beckwith gunsmithing family active in Birmingham and London ca. 1790-1868. Courtesy of the Smithsonian Institution, Washington, D.C.

officer lost his nerve and dignity, running just before the fuze reached his barrel. Putnam, conscious of the American militia and British regulars watching from a safe distance, remained stoically seated and suddenly laughed uproariously as both fuzes entered the barrels and sputtered out. Cheerfully vaulting from his seat, Putnam exposed the contents of the barrels to his embarrassed and humiliated challenger—onions![90]

Additional research into the percussive properties of fulminating compounds also continued in the eighteenth century (see p. 147). In France Dr. Bayen, formerly the personal physician to Louis XV, purportedly conducted experiments with fulminate of mercury in 1774.[91] More progress was made in 1785 by Count Antoine François de Fourcroy (1755-1809) and his assistant, Louis Nicholas Vaquelin (1763-1829); both disciples of the eminent Lavoisier.[92]

Claude Louis Berthollet (1748-1822), also involved with Lavoisier and noted for his brilliant work with textile dyes, isolated fulminate of silver in 1788; a compound even more sensitive than fulminate of mercury.[93] Berthollet also discovered that sulphur and charcoal, when mixed with chlorate of potash (potassium chlorate) in the proper ratio, produced an extremely powerful explosive and he offered it as a substitute for black powder.

Shortly thereafter the *Régie des Poudres* attempted to manufacture Berthollet's substitute powder with disastrous consequences, for the volatile compound demolished part of the huge government gunpowder mill and laboratory at Essonnes.[94] Despite the holocaust in France, chlorate of potash experiments were conducted in Britain under the auspices of the Society for Philosophical Experi-ments and Conversations, organized in London in 1794. The society also concluded that the substance was highly unstable, demonstrating that it could be detonated by simply grinding or pulverizing.[95]

British chemist Edward C. Howard discovered a safe process for making fulminate of mercury in 1799, though he was convinced that because of its violent nature ". . . no gun could confine a quantity of the mercurial powder sufficient to project a bullet," and he was extremely doubtful if it could be successfully employed as an ignition agent for gunpowder.[96] Howard's hypotheses, perhaps prejudiced because he had been seriously injured when experimenting with the compound, were figuratively exploded in 1807.

It was then, after 14 years of fulminate research, that the Reverend Alexander John Forsythe (1768-1843) of Belhelvie, Aberdeenshire, Scotland, invented the first gunlock successfully using minute quantities of fulminate of mercury rather than flint as the ignition agent.[97]

Forsythe's lock eliminated the priming pan and the flint, while the cock was replaced with what came to be termed a hammer. Substituted for the pan was a small vial of fulminate of mercury. Rotating the vial permitted a tiny drop of fulminate to enter a small chamber atop the vial. The chamber was provided with a stemmed anvil. When the hammer struck the anvil the fulminate was detonated, flashing through the vent channel to ignite the powder charge.

Subsequent developments in the radically innovative percussion ignition system rendered flintlock firearms obsolete by 1840, ushering in what is commonly referred to in firearms evolution as the Percussion Era. The Percussion Era introduced what can be appropriately termed The Age of Modern Firearms, for a more sophisticated and innovative form of the percussion system is currently employed as the ignition agent.

A major factor in the rapid evolution of machine tools in Great Britain was the widespread acceptance of Benjamin Huntsman's improved steel-making technique by 1776 (see p. 240), while an innovative method of refining wrought iron was patented there in 1784 by Henry Cort (1740-1800). Cort's process improved the quality of wrought iron and also increased production; thus preserving it as the most important product of the iron-maker's furnace for another 75 years.[98]

In the Cort or puddling process large quantities of wrought iron were produced in a coke-fired reverberatory furnace equipped with a separate chamber which isolated the ore from the fuel in contrast to earlier furnace designs. The oxygen provided by the bellows and required to burn out the excessive carbon was rapidly introduced to the molten iron by continuously agitating it with an iron paddle known as a rabbling bar. The rabbling technique made a more ductile wrought iron because most of the carbon was removed, and as the iron became hotter it formed a so-called puddle ball with a paste-like consistency. The puddle ball was removed from the furnace chamber with large tongs then processed by tilt hammers or grooved rolling mills.

Cort's puddled wrought iron was considered by some to be too weak for many purposes, though it was faster and more economical to make. Subsequent investigations into the chemical properties of the ore improved quality and puddled iron was frequently used in arms-making.

Though known in the United States prior to the nineteenth century, puddled iron was not accepted by American iron-makers or manufacturers who apparently preferred traditional techniques and less ductile wrought iron. Wrought iron continued to be used for making martial gun barrels in the United States until 1873 and neither was it superseded by steel in commercial barrel-making until the early twentieth century.[99]

The mandrel lathes conceived by Plumier, La Lievre, and Duval (see p. 195) saw minor improvements late in the eighteenth century, though significant innovations were introduced in France by Jacques de Vaucanson (1709-1782) in the period 1770-1780.[100] Vaucanson devised a sliding tool carriage running parallel to the axis of the workpiece and it was advanced into the work by a manually-operated devise called a lead screw. The innovative lead screw permitted the lathe operator to move the tool carriage, known as the slide, to any position along the work and regulated the depth of the cutting tool. Vaucanson also transformed machine tools from wood-frame to metal construction.[101]

Additional lathe improvements emerged during the final decade of the century, though they are beyond the purview of this study; particularly the innovative gearing system contributed in 1795 by French inventor Senot[102] and the improved tool rest devised in 1796 by David Wilkinson of Pawtucket, R.I.[103] Two years later Wilkinson's innovative rest was overshadowed by one conceived by Henry Maudslay (1771-1834) of Woolwich, Eng.[104] Maudslay began working in London machine shops at age 12 and subsequently achieved fame as the greatest designer and builder of machinery and machine tools in Britain.

Significantly, many of the sophisticated machine tools spawned throughout the centuries of European technological evolution were either initially employed in or subsequently adapted to firearms manufacture and, during the eighteenth century, they had a resounding impact on the rapid development of other innovative machine tools; an impact which would be even more pronounced in the United States during the early nineteenth century.

The inordinate technological growth of the French armament industry after ca. 1750 was predicated in part upon an abundance of natural resources, an economy bolstered by a nearly perpetual involvement in warfare, innovative machine-tool development, and a liberal intellectual atmosphere which stimulated scientific and technological achievement.

While the aristocracy and consequently the national government supported science and technology the need for humanitarian social reform was blithely ignored; thus the smouldering discontent of an impoverished and persecuted populace violently erupted in Paris on July 14, 1789, as the French Revolution (1789-1795).

Unrecognized, however, was that an even more significant revolution had occurred in France by 1784, for it was then that Honoré Blanc, an obscure Paris martial musket contractor, unceremoniously introduced the radically innovative technological concept of manufacturing muskets with interchangeable parts produced by machine; a concept of inestimable techonomic impact throughout the globe.[105]

Blanc's concept had been anticipated in the manufacture of cannon cartridges in 1764 by his countryman Gen. Jean Baptiste de Gribeauval (see p. 217), and it had also emerged in Britain ca. 1780 when the Taylors of Southampton had partially mechanized the manufacture of wood pulley blocks for the Royal Navy; pulley blocks an essential part of a sailing vessel's rigging.[106]

Not until ca. 1810, however, was the Taylor system perfected with the introduction of innovative machines designed by civil engineer and French Revolution refugee Marc Isambard Brunel (1769-1849) and Samuel Bentham (1757-1831), an English naval architect and also a civil engineer.[107] Supervised by Burnel and Bentham, Henry Maudslay built 34 precision block-making machines for the Taylors, installing them at the Portsmouth dockyard.

In any event Honoré Blanc's principles were sound and by 1785 he had devised a successful system, aware that it could be advantageously employed in the national armories. Blanc optimistically approached the government, however, for reasons never fully explained French officials failed to recognize the exceptional merit or the nearly limitless potential of the concept.

Early in 1785 then United States Minister to France Benjamin Franklin, now in his 79th year after a long, active, and distinguished career of public services sought from Congress the interminably delayed respite he had indisputably earned, and Thomas Jefferson was approached to shoulder the task.

The erudite architect of American independence accepted the appointment with some reluctance on March 10, 1785, and when he reached Paris any misgivings he had entertained abruptly vanished, for his innate and unlimited curiosity was intensely aroused by French accomplishments in science and technology.

Jefferson quickly became a habitué of the elegant Parisian salons where gathered the intelligensia of Europe and he penned long, glowing letters to fellow Virginian George Washington and his other intimates describing the wonder of the phosphorous match, the amazing propellers using air to drive boats along the scenic Seine, and the huge, thumping steam engines which provided power for French factories, mills, and water works.

On one of his frequent excursions into the depths of the city Jefferson chanced to meet musket-maker Honoré Blanc and visit his factory; an encounter of incalculable significance for the future development of American industry. Visibly impressed, Jefferson recognized the immense value of Blanc's concept and submitted a detailed report, informing Congress that he had observed musket components ". . . ga[u]ged and made by Machinery,"[108] and added that he had personally assembled 50 musket locks ". . . taking pieces at hazard as they came to hand."[109]

Congress, like the French officials approached by Blanc, was not particularly interested. Jefferson, however, enthusiastically urged Blanc to establish a musket manufactory in the United States. Blanc politely but firmly refused and apparently faded into obscurity or was lost in the revolutionary fever sub-sequently gripping France, for a doubtlessly disappointed Jefferson later wrote "I do not know what became of him."[110]

Like many others whose dazzling display of genius flashed all too briefly across the cosmic countenance of history, Honoré Blanc reaped no reward for his invaluable contribution to posterity, nor did he receive the recognition he so richly deserved until recent research revealed his vital role in the often enigmatic course of technological evolution, and had it not been for a discerning Thomas Jefferson the radical manufacturing concept introduced by Honoré Blanc might have been forever lost in the cataclysm of rebellion.

Epilogue:
The Technological Impact

Of all the varied socio-economic changes in the cultural structure of the United States which emerged in the wake of independence there were two of monumental significance. The first is what Walter Millis has brilliantly defined and described as "the democratization of war,"[111] while the second can be appropriately termed the liberation of commerce and industry.

From the outset the American Revolution had been entirely supported by volunteers rather than a standing military force conscripted from a coerced populace as distinctly evident in Europe. Consequently the new Republic unequivocally owed its existence to its free citizenry and therefore Americans had the inalienable right to demand that the government they had created provide for their needs arising as a consequence of war. The democratization of war was a doctrine slow to materialize in Europe because of the inordinate power wielded by the aristocracy.

The parasitic mandate initiated by Spain to take from rather than give to her New World possessions was subsequently emulated by Britain, France, and the Netherlands. Despite a growing technology, Britain had deliberately restrained commerce and industry in her North American dominions and the result was unexpectedly shattering.

The evident divergence of American and European technology was also a result of that pernicious Old World mandate, for in the New World technology had not been permitted to expand naturally, despite its European roots and a burgeoning proclivity for invention and innovation. Significantly, the American rifle had been the single, major technological innovation spawned in the New World

U. S. MUSKET, M1795 (18th Century): The M1795 was the first U.S. martial musket and the first to be produced in a U.S. national armory (Springfield). Overall length: 59½ inches. Stock length: 56⅜ inches. Barrel length: 44⅝ inches. Caliber: .69, taking a 16 gauge ball weighing one ounce. Average weight: 8 lbs., 14 oz. Furniture: iron, finished bright. Bayonet: 15 inch blade 1⅛ inches wide. The walnut stock is secured by three bands, each retained by a spring. The front sight is a brass blade mounted on the rear strap of the front barrel band. Courtesy of the Smithsonian Institution, Washington, D.C.

prior to the War of Independence and even that portentous achievement was based upon previous European technological expertise.

Not surprising, therefore, is that throughout the eighteenth century Europe retained its preeminent role in the evolution of science and technology, each in many instances supportive of the other, with Britain, France, and the Netherlands making significant if not prodigious contributions in chemistry, metallurgy, and the development of innovative machine tools and novel manufacturing techniques.

In eighteenth-century France the factory system as applied in the government armament industry had reached a high plateau of sophistication and was relatively widespread at the time of the revolution, and until the aristocratic Lavoisier fell victim to the guillotine blade during the Reign of Terror (1793-1794) he had been led down many rewarding paths of scientific inquiry by his gunpowder experiments.

By 1755 the factory system came to be employed on a minor scale in the British American firearms industry, and it was considerably expanded during the Revolutionary War, though as in France it was still confined to the armament industry; yet just as the American Revolution had freed a nation, so also was commerce and industry liberated; set free to exploit and expand its techonomic prerogatives and potential.

In 1794 the spectre of war between the United States and her former ally, France, clouded the future of the struggling Republic and on April 2 Congress acted to ensure an adequate supply of firearms and other war matériel, approving the purchase of 7,000 martial muskets from Britain and Germany, while authorizing the construction of two national armories; the first to be erected at the site of the U.S. Magazine established during the American Revolution at Springfield, Mass. (see p. 318), and the other at the confluence of the Potomac and Shenandoah rivers in Harpers' Ferry, Va.[112]

Significantly, after some heated debate, the fledgling Ordnance Office of the War Department selected the familiar M1763 French infantry musket used in the American Revolution as the production pattern for the first martial muskets manufactured in the new Republic: the U.S. Musket, M1795.[113] As work on the Springfield Armory continued the threat of war with France fortunately evaporated and late in 1795 the facility produced 245 muskets under the supervision of Master Armorer Robert Orr (see p. 351).[114]

The few muskets manufactured at Springfield Armory during its first years of operation and the prolonged delay in completing the Harpers' Ferry Armory—production did not begin until 1801—prompted Secretary of War James McHenry (1753-1816) to ask Congress to approve the purchase

WHITNEYVILLE ARMORY (ca. 1815): Located at East Rock on the Mill River near New Haven, Conn., Eli Whitney's armory—a factory by another name—was initially constructed and equipped to make martial muskets, though firearms for the commercial market were also made there, while it was used as a model for several national armories. Courtesy of the Sterling Memorial Library, Yale University.

of 40,200 M1795 muskets from independent gunsmiths.[115]

Congress authorized McHenry's request with the Act of July 5, 1798. Seven months prior to the official pronouncement, however, Secretary of the Treasury Oliver Wolcott (1760-1833) made arrangements with 27 gunsmiths in seven states to produce the muskets under government contract.[116]

Among the independent contractors were prominent Revolutionary War gunsmiths Richard Falley, William Henry, Jr., Ard Welton, and Nicholas White. Curiously, one of the M1795 musket contractors had never received any training as a gunsmith nor had he ever produced firearms of any kind; yet on January 14, 1798, he procured the largest contract which called for 10,000 muskets at $13.40 per stand. Equally peculiar is that despite stipulations requiring him to deliver 4,000 muskets by September, 1799, and the balance within the following year, he failed to complete the contract until January, 1809; a more than ten-year lapse. His name was Eli Whitney (1765-1825).[117]

Government contracts represented a lucrative source of income which was extremely appealing to the practical, imaginative, 33-year-old Massachusetts-born Yale University graduate, for he was thoroughly disillusioned with the costly and prolonged court battles clouding the invention and marketing of his celebrated, innovative cotton gin.

Thus in 1798, 13 years after Thomas Jefferson's report to Congress, the interchangeable parts system began to find expression in the infant United States and, significantly, it was again applied to martial musket manufacture.

Though it has never been conclusively ascertained whether Eli Whitney knew of Jefferson's comprehensive report concerning Honoré Blanc's concept of making interchangeable musket components by machine, there is little reason to doubt that a man of Whitney's catholic interest in technology would have remained unaware of it.

In any event, Whitney apparently failed to anticipate many of the pitfalls involved in creating the requisite tools and machines to implement Blanc's innovative technique and several of them were subsequently recounted by Col. Decius Wadsworth of the Ordnance Office in a letter to Secretary of War John Armstrong (1758-1843) dated June 6, 1814:

. . . I have been well acquainted with the establishment [Whitney's factory] at New Haven [Conn.] from its origin. . . .

Many of the individuals of small property who engaged in these [U.S. musket] contracts were absolutely ruined thereby, and the difficulties were so much greater than had been apprehended, it proved in general a losing business to the concerned. Mr. Whitney having never before engaged in such a business, and not having workmen brought up to the trade, was under the necessity of contriving original tools and modes of executing various parts of the work adapted to the inexperience of his hands,

ELI WHITNEY'S MILLING
(PLANING) MACHINE (19th
Century): In his quest to produce
martial firearms with inexperi-
enced labor and interchangeable
components, Eli Whitney designed the milling machine or
slabber depicted ca. 1818. The
flywheel and moveable work
plate are missing. The geared
wheel rotating the work plate

shaft was turned by the belt attached to the two wood pulleys.
The cutting head at the end of the
drive shaft (also missing) rapidly
rotated against the work held on
the work plate which moved
horizontally, feeding the work
into the cutter. Courtesy of the
Smithsonian Institution, Washington, D.C.

and calculated to obviate the necessity of employing men alone who had been bred to the
trade. Some of the inventions I speak of have
been confirmed to be valuable improvements to
the art, and have been disseminated in different
parts of the United States, and it is not too much
to say the manufacture of arms is more indebted
to him than to any other individual in this country. A great deal of patient attention, of reflec-
tion, and of time were employed by him at the
onset; his progress for a time was but slow,
apparently. The advances the Government had
made were heavy, amounting, I think, to

$20,000 or more. His abilities not so generally
known and acknowledged then as they have
since been, his friends, and even the Secretary of
the Treasury, Mr. Wolcott, felt a little uneasi-
ness and doubt at one time about his ultimate
success. . . .

. . . He fulfilled the contract to the satisfaction
of the government, refunded the money which
had been advanced, and secured his establishment, not the most extensive, but in my judg-
ment the most perfect and complete existing in
the United States. . . .

. . . It may not be amiss to state that I think his
arms as good, if not superior, to those which
have in general been made anywhere else in the
United States, not excepting those which have
been made at the public [national] armories. . . .[118]

Though Eli Whitney did not originate the interchangeable parts concept or the idea of making
musket components by machine as several historical

MILLING MACHINE (19th Century): The working model of Eli Whitney's slabber depicted illustrates the flywheel (left) which was driven by a waterwheel via a belt-and-pulley arrangement. The flywheel drove the cutting head shaft. Such machines were initially designed for firearms manufacture and were subsequently adapted to make other complex products, their efficacy enhanced by the subsequent application of steam power. Courtesy of the Do All Museum, Des Plaines, Ill.

studies have indicated, he certainly can be credited with establishing the system in the United States, and many of his innovative contributions to machine-tool evolution had a profound effect on the widespread development and acceptance of the system in the United States and elsewhere during the early nineteenth century.

Also relevant is that scythe-maker Simeon North (1765-1852) of Berlin, Conn. applied the machine-made interchangeable parts system to the manufacture of the U.S. Pistol, M1799. The M1799 was the first martial pistol adopted by the fledgling Republic and, like the M1795 musket, it also derived from a French design, the M1777 pistol.[119]

Equally significant is that the interchangeable parts system pioneered by Whitney and North in martial firearms manufacture was subsequently employed by them in making commercial firearms, while it was also early adopted by the national armories and came to be used by other arms-makers as well.

During the early years Whitney and North experienced numerous problems with the machines they had devised to implement the system and much of the work continued to be performed by hand. Not until the nineteenth century was the system entirely perfected and most of the credit can be given to Maine gunsmith-inventor John Hancock Hall (1778-1841) who achieved that remarkable accomplishment when developing his innovative breech-loading rifle for the U.S. Army at Harpers' Ferry Armory during the period 1816-1824.[120]

Nourished by the rapid geographic expansion of the young Republic as well as the War of 1812 and the First Seminole War (1817-1818), the interchange-

U.S. PISTOL, M1799 (18th Century): On March 9, 1799, Simeon North received a U.S. contract to produce 500 martial pistols patterned after the M1777 French design. Like Whitney, North was a pioneer in the manufacture of firearms with interchangeable parts. His brother-in-law Elisha Cheney made pins and screws for the M1799. The .69 caliber barrel was an inch longer than the French pistol barrel. Courtesy of the U.S. Military Academy Museum, West Point, N.Y.

U.S. RIFLE M1819 (19th Century): Patented by Capt. John H. Hall and William Thornton on May 21, 1811, the pivotal breech system used in the M1819 had been anticipated during the 17th Century. The breech is in the open position for loading. Hall contracted to make 100 rifles at $25.00 each in 1817, though production was delayed until 1824 because he had to design and build the requisite tools and machines at Harpers' Ferry Armory. The M1819 HALL was the first martial breech-loading rifle adopted by the U.S. and the first firearm in the world entirely mass produced with precision-made, interchangeable parts. Overall length: 52¾ inches. Stock length: 49½ inches. Barrel length: 32¾ inches. Caliber: .52. Average weight: 10 lbs., 12 oz. Courtesy of the Smithsonian Institution, Washington, D.C.

able parts system began to flourish in the government and commercial firearms industry which was primarily responsible for the development of precision measurement and the accelerated growth of the United States machine-tool industry.

The intimate and unique relationship of the interchangeable parts system to the burgeoning United States firearms and machine-tool industry during the second quarter of the nineteenth century is the foundation upon which rests our currently preeminent technology, for the relationship continuously expanded to include other industrial applications. As Felicia Johnson Deyrup has noted, interchangeability was not employed in other than the United States firearms and machine-tool industry until 1846 when it was introduced in manufacturing sewing machines.[121]

By 1850 the innovative interchangeable parts system successfully pioneered on a limited scale in France by musket-maker Honoré Blanc in 1785 had lost its radical character and was universally known as the American system of manufacture.

Significantly, the American system had a more profound effect on the mechanization of industry than either the machines or techniques employed in the late eighteenth-century British textile industry, for those machines were primarily constructed of wood and did not materially contribute to the evolution of precision machine tools from which other sophisticated machines and products could be created, while the manufacturing techniques employed in the textile mills were literally borrowed intact from the factory system previously established in the venerable armament industry.

Thus it can be said with some precision that the firearms industry, especially as it evolved in the United States during the late eighteenth-and early

GUNSMITHING/BLACK-SMITHING FORGE (19th Century): The forge depicted is typical of the small forges found in the colonies and the infant United States. The charcoal-fired, brick and fieldstone forge (80×43×33 inches) was provided with a large, leather bellows (60×35 inches) pumped by the long, overhead pole. Note the quenching tub and charcoal bin (right), the various anvils and the bending vise with its foot pedal (center, foreground). Tree sections were used as anvil bases. White spaces (background) are windows. The forge illustrated is in the J.W. Epley Blacksmith Shop of ca. 1860 which was moved from Gettysburg (Pa.) and reconstructed at the Pennsylvania Farm Museum of Landis Valley, Lancaster, Pa. Courtesy of the Pennsylvania Farm Museum of Landis Valley, Lancaster, Pa. Charles L. Maddox, Jr., photographer.

nineteenth century, generally exerted a greater economic and technological impact on civilization than any other dynamic human endeavor since the dawn of recorded history.

The currently evident technological revolution began at some unrecorded time in history when a premordial primate of indistinct origin fashioned the first rudimentary tool to ensure survival in an uncompromising environment. Since that distant millennium technology has been the companion of civilization.

Seven centuries have passed since the first crude gun hurled the first primitive missile by the powerful force created by the first explosive chemical compound, and there subsequently emerged countless technological innovations of major significance which can be directly attributed to either the manufacture of firearms or gunpowder, and the techonomic impact of those frequently radical innovations

on the entire cultural structure of civilization remains incalculable.

It cannot be denied that firearms performed a distinctive role in the course of human endeavor and an equally monumental role in the evolution of existing technology. Neither can it be denied that technology has exerted an unremitting influence upon the diverse paths of scientific investigation, engendering profound changes which will continue to effect humanity, for the wonder of technology is not confined to the past.

Notes

1. Thelma Peters, "The Loyalist Migration From East Florida to the Bahamas," *Florida Historical Quarterly* (October 1961): 133 (hereafter cited as *FHQ*).
2. Ibid., p. 134.
3. Henry J. Kauffman, *Early American Gunsmiths, 1650-1850* (New York, 1952), p. 5.
4. Norman B. Wilkinson, *Explosives in History: The Story of Black Powder* (Chicago: Rand, McNally & Company, 1966): 17.
5. Ibid., p. 16.
6. Ibid.
7. Du Pont de Nemours, E.I. & Co., Inc., *Du Pont: The Autobiography of an American Enterprise* (New York, 1952), pp. 3-8.
8. Col. Arcadi Gluckman, *United States Muskets, Rifles and Carbines* (Buffalo, 1948), Appendix I, p. *i*.
9. Ibid.
10. Ibid.
11. Maj. James E. Hicks, *U.S. Military Firearms, 1776-1956* (Alhambra, Cal., 1962), p. 14.
12. Ibid.
13. Col. Robert E. Gardner, *Small Arms Makers* (New York, 1962), p. 53.
14. Ibid., p. 75.
15. Ibid., p. 79.
16. Ibid., p. 205.
17. Kauffman, p. 4.
18. Gardner, p. 136.
19. Walter Millis, *Arms and Men* (New York, 1956), p. 48.
20. U.S. Bureau of Census, *Historical Statistics of the United States* (Washington, 1951), Series Y 350-356, p. 719.
21. Ibid., Series Y 763-775, p. 737.
22. Carl P. Russell, *Guns on the Early Frontiers* (New York, 1957), p. 300 *n.* 50.
23. S. James Gooding, *The Canadian Gunsmiths, 1608-1900* (West Hill, Ontario, 1962), p. 63.
24. Ibid., p. 66.
25. Ibid., p. 74.
26. Ibid., p. 110.
27. Ibid., p. 120.
28. Ibid., p. 162.
29. Ibid., p. 124.
30. Ibid., p. 78.
31. Ibid., p. 142.
32. Ibid., p. 76.
33. Ibid., pp. 96-97.
34. Ibid., p. 135.
35. Ibid., p. 142.
36. Ibid., p. 146.
37. Ibid., p. 156.
38. Ibid., p. 72.
39. Charles E. Hanson, Jr., "Trade Guns," in *Encyclopedia of Firearms*, Harold L. Peterson, ed. (New York, 1964), p. 318.
40. Ibid.
41. Ibid.
42. Gardner, p. 239; also, S. James Gooding, "Gunmakers to the Hudson's Bay Company," *Canadian Journal of Arms Collecting* (February 1973): 20.
43. Frederick Webb Hodge, ed., *Handbook of American Indians North of Mexico,* 2 vols (Washington, 1912), I:829-833.
44. Hanson, *Encyclopedia*, p. 318.
45. Ibid.
46. Gardner, p. 263.
47. Ibid.
48. Ibid., p. 311.
49. Ibid., p. 276.
50. Russell, p. 57.
51. Thomas D. Watson, "Continuity in Commerce: Development of the Panton, Leslie and Company Trade Monopoly in West Florida," *FHQ* (April 1976): 548.
52. Ibid., p. 549.
53. Jack D.L. Holmes, "Spanish Treaties With West Florida Indians, 1784-1802," *FHQ* (October 1969): 140.
54. Watson, p. 550.
55. Ibid., p. 551.
56. Ibid., p. 552.
57. Holmes, p. 142.
58. Watson, p. 551.
59. Ibid., p. 554.
60. Ibid., p. 555.
61. J.A. Brown, "Panton, Leslie and Company Indian Traders of Pensacola and St. Augustine," *FHQ* (April 1959); 328.
62. Leeila S. Copeland and J.E. Dovell, *La Florida, Its Land and People* (Austin, 1957), p. 121.
63. Roger H. Brown, *The Republic in Peril: 1812* (New York: W.W. Norton & Company, Inc., 1971), gives an outstanding interpretation of the issues involved.
64. Sidney B. Brinckerhoff and Pierce A. Chamberlain, *Spanish Military Weapons in Colonial America, 1700-1821* (Harrisburg, 1972), pp. 31, 35.
65. Ibid., p. 31.
66. Gardner, p. 297.
67. Ibid., p. 267.
68. Howard L. Blackmore, *Guns and Rifles of the World* (New York, 1965), p. 74 (hereafter cited as *Guns and Rifles*).
69. Harold L. Peterson, *The Treasury of the Gun* (New York, 1962), p. 191.
70. Blackmore, p. 74.
71. Geoffrey Boothroyd, *The Handgun* (New York, 1970), pp. 38-39; Blackmore, p. 43.
72. Blackmore, p. 43.
73. Ibid., p. 66.
74. Howard L. Blackmore, "Nock, Henry," *Encyclopedia of Firearms*, p. 224.
75. Ibid.
76. Ibid.
77. Robert Held, *The Age of Firearms* (New York, 1957), p. 137 (hereafter cited as *Firearms*); Boothroyd, pp. 39-40.
78. Blackmore, *Encyclopedia*, p. 224.
79. Ibid.
80. Ibid.
81. W.W. Greener, *The Gun and its Development* (New York, 1967), p. 225.
82. Ibid.
83. Held, *Firearms,* p. 136.
84. Robert Held, "Kentucky Rifle: Fact—and Fiction," *Gun Digest* (Chicago, 1962): 197.
85. Ibid.
86. Held, *Firearms,* p. 99.
87. Boothroyd, p. 34.
88. Ibid., p. 33.
89. Ibid.
90. John Hyde Preston, *Revolution 1776* (New York, 1933), p. 49. The incident is possibly apocryphal. Many flamboyant figures like Putnam inspired folk tales based in fantasy rather than fact.

91. Herschel C. Logan, *Cartridges* (Harrisburg, 1959), p. 2.
92. Blackmore, *Guns and Rifles,* p. 45.
93. Ibid.; also, Logan, p. 2.
94. Blackmore, p. 45.
95. Ibid.
96. Ibid.
97. Ibid.; also Boothroyd, pp. 56-61; Logan, p. 2.
98. Eugene S. Ferguson, "Metallurgical and Machine-Tool Developments," in *Technology in Western Civilization,* Melvin Kranzberg and Carroll W. Pursell, Jr., ed. 2 vols (New York & London, 1967), 1:267-268.
99. Charles H. Fitch, *Report on the Manufacturers of Interchangeable Mechanisms* (Washington, 1883), p. 8.
100. Ferguson, 1:275; also W. Steeds, *A History of Machine Tools, 1700-1900* (Oxford, 1969), p. 20.
101. Steeds, p. 20.
102. Ibid., pp. 21-22.
103. Ibid., p. 22.
104. Ibid., p. 23; Ferguson, 1:275.
105. Edwin A. Battison, "Eli Whitney," in *Those Inventive Americans,* Robert L. Breeden, ed. (Washington, 1971), p. 59.
106. Ferguson, 1:276.
107. Ibid., pp. 277-278.
108. Battison, p. 59.
109. Arnold Whitridge, "Eli Whitney, Nemesis of the South," *The American Heritage Reader* (New York: Dell Publishing Co., Inc., 1956), p. 83.
110. Ibid.
111. Millis, p. 27.
112. Hicks, pp. 14-15.
113. Ibid., p. 16. The designation "U.S. Musket, M1795" is a collector's term designed to avoid confusion regarding the terminology used to describe the first U.S. martial musket and it is so employed herein. Official government records generally refer to the M1795 as "Charleville Pattern," "Charleville Muskets," or "New Muskets Charleville Pattern."

114. Ibid.
115. Ibid., p. 19.
116. Gluckman, *U.S. Muskets,* pp. 69-81; Hicks, 19.
117. Gluckman, pp. 78-79.
118. Ibid., pp. 79-81.
119. Col. Arcadi Gluckman, *United States Martial Pistols and Revolvers* (Harrisburg, 1956), pp. 31-34.
120. Gluckman, *U.S. Muskets,* pp. 205-208; Hicks, p. 59; Gardner, p. 82.
121. Deyrup, *Arms Making in the Connecticut Valley* (York, Pa., 1970), p. 11. Professor Deyrup's regional investigation of Connecticut Valley arms-making during the period 1798-1870, originally titled *Arms Makers of the Connecticut Valley,* initially appeared in 1948 as Vol. XXXIII, Smith College Studies in History. It is the most comprehensive study available to date pertaining to the relationship between Connecticut Valley arms-makers and the United States government, while it also delves deeply into the economic and technological history of the national armories. For those reasons alone Professor Deyrup's masterful treatment of the origin and growth of what is now termed the military-industrial complex certainly deserves more careful scrutiny than it has received from those interested and involved in the study of firearms evolution and industrialization in the United States.

APPENDICES

Appendix I

BORE NUMBER AND CALIBER EQUIVALENTS

Bore number—number of balls per pound of lead. Caliber—diameter of the ball in inches.

Bore Number	Caliber	Bore Number	Caliber	Bore Number	Caliber	Bore Number	Caliber
4	1.052	24	.577	44	.473	108.49	.350
5	.983	25	.571	45	.469	118.35	.340
6	.924	26	.564	46	.466	129.43	.330
7	.884	27	.560	47	.463	140	.323
8	.883	28	.557	48	.458	141.95	.320
9	.804	29	.554	49	.456	142	.319
10	.786	30	.546	50	.454	149	.313
11	.762	31	.532	51.05	.450	156.14	.310
12	.747	32	.525	54.61	.440	172.27	.300
13	.734	33	.520	58.50	.430	190	.290
14	.713	34	.515	60	.429	200	.285
15	.703	35	.510	62.78	.420	210	.280
16	.662	36	.506	64	.416	220	.275
17	.654	37	.501	67.49	.410	232	.270
18	.649	38	.497	72.68	.400	244	.265
19	.643	39	.491	78.41	.390	256	.260
20	.630	40	.488	84.77	.380	270	.255
21	.627	41	.484	87	.375	285	.250
22	.622	42	.480	91.83	.370		
23	.610	43	.476	100	.360		

Appendix II

GUNMAKERS' RATES

Job Description	Rate: £/s/d*	Job Description	Rate: £/s/d*
1. For a new musket with mould, worm and scouwer	0/15/6	15. For making clean a square fyled [filed] musket white [burnishing to a bright finish]	0/1/8
2. For a new wolnut-tree stock for a musket, plated at the butt end with iron	0/2/6	16. For the yearly dressing and keeping clean a musket that needs not new russetting, with the furniture and rest	0/0/10
3. For a musket stock of beech plated at the butt end with iron	0/1/8	17. For powder and shot for proving every musket	0/0/0
4. For a match-tricker [trigger] lock compleat	0/1/0	18. For stamping every musket proved and allowed	0/0/0
5. For a whole worke [lock] consisting of the pan, cover of the pan, the scutchion [side plate], and the screw pynn	0/0/0	19. For a new bandalier with twelve charges, a prymer [charger], a pryming wyre [vent pick], a bullet bag, and a strap or belt of two inches in breadth	0/2/6
6. For a stick [ramrod], worme, socket, scowrer and bone	0/1/0	20. For a pair of firelock [wheellock] pistols, furnished with a key [spanner], mould, scowrer, worm, flask, and case of leather, of length and boar [bore] according to the allowance of the councel of war	3/0/0
7. For a handle or guard of a tricker	0/0/6		
8. For a new cock fitted	0/0/8		
9. For a new breech [plug]	0/1/0		
10. For furnishing a setting of a tricker lock in place of a sceare [sear] lock, with a handle, tricker, and tricker pynnes	0/2/6	21. For a pair of horsemans pistols furnished with snaphaunces, mouldes, worms, scowrer, flask, charger and cases	2/0/0
11. For a new touch hole screwed	0/0/10		
12. For a new barrel of a musket, only forged and bored, fower [four] foote in length, the bore according to the bullet of ten in the pound [.78 caliber] standing, and twelve roweling [rolling]	0/8/0	22. For a harquebuze with a firelock and belte, swivel, flask, key, moulde, worme and scowrer	1/16/0
13. For making clean and new russetting [browning] of a musket	0/0/4	23. For a carbine with a snaphaunce, belt, swivel and flask & c. as aforesaid	1/0/0
14. For a musket rest	0/0/10		

*£ (pounds), s (shillings), d (pence).

Appendix III

VALUE OF FURS EXPORTED
TO ENGLAND FROM BRITISH AMERICA: 1700-1775*

	1700	1710	1720	1725	1730	1739[1]	1750[2]	1760	1765	1770	1775
Colony Total £	**16,280**	**7,840**	**19,377**	**23,541**	**22,348**	**25,196**	**22,817**	**19,985**	**49,293**	**47,758**	**53,709**
Continental Colonies	13,710	5,165	19,128	21,903	19,804	22,536	17,491	14,637	45,925	44,394	51,058
Canada								1,930	24,512	28,433	34,486
Carolina	570	27	4	46	57	9	12	20	491	26	128
Florida										68	108
Georgia								3	53	9	63
Hudson's Bay	2,360		9,839	11,180	12,335	13,452	8,143	8,321	9,770	9,213	5,640
New England	2,430	1,595	2,119	1,862	2,010	2,481	1,015	946	2,811	2,453	1,642
Newfoundland	220	553	457	452	500	551	420	470	648	403	1,913
New York	4,960	2,148	5,393	6,952	2,611	5,073	5,710	1,023	5,565	2,340	3,939
Nova Scotia					156			24	78	132	210
Pennsylvania	720	88	849	923	1,642	329	1,909	1,879	1,927	1,148	2,866
Virginia & Maryland	2,430	754	467	488	493	641	282	21	70	169	63
All other colonies	2,570	2,675	249	1,638	2,544	2,660	5,326	5,348	3,368	3,364	2,651

*Figures represent pounds sterling
[1]English customs records for 1740 incomplete, records for 1739 used.
[2]As value figures indicate, the French and Indian War (1754-1763) caused a decline in the fur industry because of the disrupted frontier situation.
Reference: U.S. Census Bureau, *Historical Statistics of the United States* (Washington, 1961) Series Z 108-121, p. 762.

Appendix IV

FLINTLOCK MUSKET & SOCKET BAYONET NOMENCLATURE GUIDE

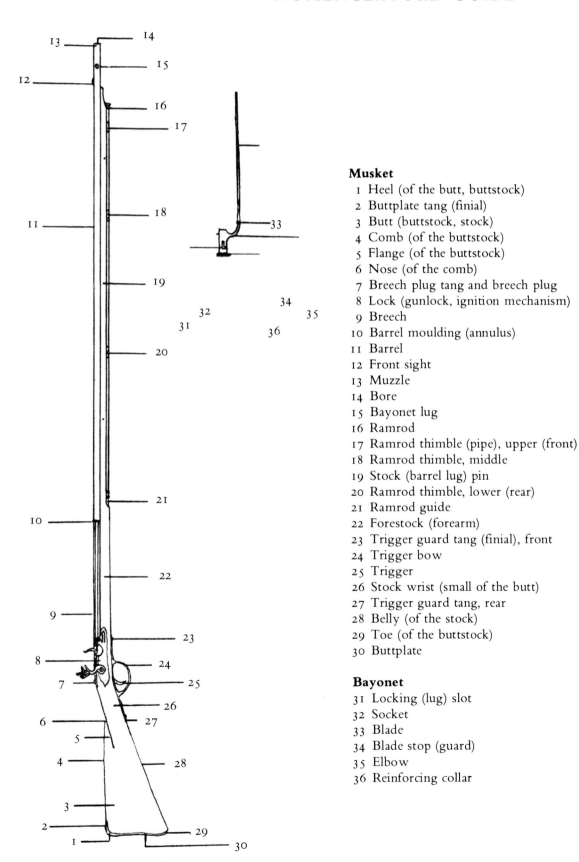

Musket
1 Heel (of the butt, buttstock)
2 Buttplate tang (finial)
3 Butt (buttstock, stock)
4 Comb (of the buttstock)
5 Flange (of the buttstock)
6 Nose (of the comb)
7 Breech plug tang and breech plug
8 Lock (gunlock, ignition mechanism)
9 Breech
10 Barrel moulding (annulus)
11 Barrel
12 Front sight
13 Muzzle
14 Bore
15 Bayonet lug
16 Ramrod
17 Ramrod thimble (pipe), upper (front)
18 Ramrod thimble, middle
19 Stock (barrel lug) pin
20 Ramrod thimble, lower (rear)
21 Ramrod guide
22 Forestock (forearm)
23 Trigger guard tang (finial), front
24 Trigger bow
25 Trigger
26 Stock wrist (small of the butt)
27 Trigger guard tang, rear
28 Belly (of the stock)
29 Toe (of the buttstock)
30 Buttplate

Bayonet
31 Locking (lug) slot
32 Socket
33 Blade
34 Blade stop (guard)
35 Elbow
36 Reinforcing collar

Appendix V

SPANISH MILITARY FIREARMS
AND RELATED MATÉRIEL*

Item	Quantity	Issued	Surplus	Unservicable
Ball, fusile, cal. .665[1]	2400	218	2152	—
Ball, fusile, cal. .637[2]	40	100	—	60
Bayonet, fusile, complete	168	—	168	—
Bayonet, *escopeta*	56	—	56	—
Bullet mould, fusile	100	100	—	100
Carbines, cal. .65[3]	360	—	360	—
Carbines, cal. .69[4]	100	—	100	—
Cartridge boxes, w/straps	14	—	14	—
Cartridge boxes, w/o straps	12	—	12	—
Cartridges, fusile, w/ball	126,000	123,000	—	237,360
Cases, tin, matchcord	2	—	2	—
Flasks, powder	194	—	194	—
Flints, fusile and pistola	2,101,534	28,224	2,073,000	—
Fusiles, new, cal. .69 w/bayonets[5]	1983	800	1183	—
Fusiles, new, cal. .65 w/bayonets[6]	85	—	85	—
Fusiles, old, cal. .69 w/bayonets[7]	263	—	263	—
Fusiles, old, cal. .65 w/bayonets[8]	98	—	98	—
Lead (ingots)	132	—	132	—
Paper, cartridge (reams)	—	132	—	132
Pistolas, pair, cal. .69[9]	800	50	750	—
Ramrods, fusile, iron (reserve)	—	50	—	50
Rests, musket, complete	128	—	128	—
Rests, musket, w/o shaft	3	—	3	—
Slings, fusile (20 boxes)	4691	—	4691	—

*Partial inventory of the military stores available at Havana, Cuba, December 31, 1771, as reported by Don Nicólas Devis, *Commandante de Artilleria.*

1 Cast undersized for .69 bore.	6 M1752 light infantry fusiles.
2 Cast undersized for .65 bore.	7 M1728 or M1752 early issue.
3 Cavalry carbine, M1752.	8 M1728 *escopetas* or M1752 early issue light infantry fusiles.
4 Dragoon carbine, M1752.	9 M1752 cavalry pistols, enlisted model.
5 M1752.	

Appendix VI

BRITISH MARTIAL FIREARMS: 1740-1790*

Type	Caliber	Barrel Length	Overall Length	Weight (Pounds/Ounces)
MUSKET				
Long Land	.75	46''	5'2''	10/12
Short Land	.75	42''	4'10''	10/8
Sea Service	.75			
Long	.75	37''	4'5''	9/10
Short	.75	27''	3'6''	8/7
New Pattern				
Short Land	.75	42''	4'10''	10/6
CARBINE				
Heavy Dragoon	.65	42''	4'9''	8/14
Light Dragoon	.65	36''	4'3½''	7/10
Light Infantry	.65	42''	4'9''	7/12
Artillery	.65	37''	4'4''	7/12
PISTOL				
Heavy Dragoon	.65	12''	1'7''	3/2
Light Dragoon	.65	12''	1'7''	3/2
Light Dragoon	.56	9''	1'3''	3/0
Sea Service				
Long	.56	12''	1'6''	3/7
Short	.56	9''	1'3''	3/0

*All models and variants not listed; measurements fluctuate.

Rates Paid To British Martial Contract Gunsmiths: 1775-1785*

Description	Barrel	Lock	Rough Stocking	Barrel Filing	Assembly
MUSKET					
Long Land	7/6	6/0	4/0	/5	6/3
Short Land	7/6	6/6	4/0	/5	6/5
Sea Service	5/10	5/0	2/10	/5	5/0
MUSKETOON					
Sea Service	7/0	5/0	2/10	/4	4/0
CARBINE					
Artillery	6/6	6/2	3/4	/8	6/0
Light Dragoon	6/6	8/0	5/0	/8	9/0
PISTOL (pair)					
Land, cal. .65	5/6	7/6	3/9	1/0	7/0
Land, cal. .56	5/8	7/6	3/9	1/0	7/0
Sea, cal. .56	5/6	7/6	3/6	/8	5/0

*Rates given in shillings/pence (s/d). Does not include all rates or all kinds of martial firearms.

British Martial Firearms Stored in the Tower Armouries: 1754-1763

Description	Quantity	Description	Quantity
Muskets, Long Land, w/iron ramrod	50,000	Muskets, Marine or Militia	50,000
Muskets, Short Land, w/wooden ramrod (Dragoon)	10,000	Musketoons	2,000
		Carbines, Artillery, w/bayonet	50,000
Muskets, Sea Service (blackened), w/bayonets	10,000	Carbines, Dragoon, w/bayonet	2,000
		Pistols, Land (pairs)	2,000
Muskets, Sea Service (bright), w/bayonets	10,000	Pistols, Sea Service (pairs)	10,000
		Total	**196,000**

Appendix VII

BRITISH AMERICAN IRON FURNACES
AND FORGES: 1702-1775*

Date	Forge or Furnace Name	Other Name(s)	Location
1702	Despards		Pembroke, Mass.
1720	Christine	Redding	Chester Co., Pa.[1]
1720	Coalbrookdale		Berks Co., Pa.
1723	Gwynns Falls		Maryland
1723	Mount Royal		Maryland
1724	Kings		Taunton, Mass.
1724	Principio		Cecil Co., Md.
1725	Keith's		Christiana Creek, Del.[1]
1726	Kurtz's		Lancaster Co., Pa.
1727	Abington		Christiana Creek, Pa.[1]
1727	Germanna		Virginia
1727	Fredericksville		Virginia
1727	Durham		Bucks Co., Pa.
1730	Plympton		Carver, Mass.
1730	Mount Holly	Hanover	Hanover, N.J.
1732	Massaponax		Virginia
1732	Rappahannock		Virginia
1733	Popes Point		Carver, Mass.
1734	Patuxent		Maryland
1735	Hope		Rhode Island
1735	Three Furnace		Rhode Island
1738	Mount Pleasant		Berks Co., Pa.
1738	Warwick		Chester Co., Pa.
1740	Valley Forge	Mount Joy	Chester Co., Pa.
1740	Ringwood	Ogden's	Greenwood Lake, N.J.
1740	Lime Rock		Litchfield Co., Conn.
1742	Oxford		Warren City, N.J.
1742	Cornwall		Lebanon Co., Pa.
1744	Kingsbury		Baltimore Co., Md.
1745	Popadickon	Potts Grove	Pottstown, Pa.
1750	Union		Hunterdon Co., N.J.
1750	Ancram		Ancram Creek, N.Y.
1750	Elizabeth		Lancaster Co., Pa.

Date	Forge or Furnace Name	Other Name(s)	Location
1750	Accokeek	England's Iron Mines	Virginia
1751	Martic		Lancaster Co., Pa.
1751	Lancashire		Principio Co., Md.
1751	Sterling Iron Works	Ward and Coulton's	Orange Co., N.Y.
1753	Hereford		Berks Co., Pa.
1755	Roxborough	Berkshire, Reading, Robesonia	Berks Co., Pa.
1759	Hopewell		Berks Co., Pa.
1760	Isabella		Page Co., Va.
1760	Old Hampton		Emmetsburg, Ma.
1760	Andover		Andover, N.J.
1760	Mossy Creek		Augusta Co., Va.
1760	Bush		Hartford Co., Md.
1760	Northampton		Baltimore Co., Md.
1760	Legh		Westminster, Md.
1760	Charlotte		South Carver, Mass.
1761	Mary Ann		York Co., Pa.
1762	Carlisle		Cumberland Co., Pa.
1762	Unicorn		Queen Anne Co., Md.
1763	Deep Creek		Sussex Co., Del.
1764	Pine Grove		Sussex Co., Del.
1765	Bloomingdale		Bloomingdale, N.J.
1765	Codorus	Hellam	York Co., Pa.
1765	Lenox		Berkshire Co., Mass.
1765	Hibernia	Adventure	Morristown, N.J.
1766	Atsion		Mullica River, N.J.
1766	Taunton		New Jersey
1768	Batsto		Mullica River, N.J.
1768	Long Pond		Greenwood Lake, N.J.
1768	Pompton		Pompton, N.J.
1769	Gunpowder River		Maryland
1770	Mount Etna		Antietam Creek, Md.

Date	Forge or Furnace Name	Other Name(s)	Location
1770	Franklin		Franklin, N.J.
1770	Queensborough		New York
1770	Green Spring		Washington Co., Md.
1770	Pine Grove		Cumberland Co., Pa.
1770	Holly		Mount Holly Springs, Pa.
1772	Oley		Berks Co., Pa.
1772	Mount Hope		Mount Hope, N.J.
1773	Furnace Village		Furnace Village, Mass.
1774	Catoctin		Frederick Co., Md.
1774	Shearwell		Berks Co., Pa.
1775	Amenia Furnace & Foundry		Dutchess Co., N.Y.
1775	Charlottenburg		Pequannock Creek, N.J.
1775	Craigsville		New York
1775	Haverstraw		New York
PR	Elk Ridge		Patapsco River, Md.
PR	Forest of Dean		Orange Co., N.Y.
PR	Zane's		Virginia
n.d.	Bergen		Monmouth Co., N.J.
n.d.	Phillipsburg		Westchester Co., N.Y.
n.d.	Shapleigh		York Co., Me.
n.d.	Stemmer's Run		Baltimore Co., Md.
n.d.	Windsor		Lancaster Co., Pa.

*Partial listing. Some furnaces and forges ceased operations prior to 1775 and others continued thereafter, while many have escaped historical notice.

[1]Unsettled boundary between Delaware and Pennsylvania resulted in disputed location.

PR: Pre-Revolutionary War period, date uncertain.

n.d. (no date): Believed operating prior to or during American Revolution (1775-1783).

General Note: Firearms and other weapons were often produced at forges and furnaces and they also cast cannon, cannon balls, cannon shot, and ball and shot for firearms. Colonial gunsmiths purchased wrought iron and steel from forges and furnaces, some of the latter specializing in making barrel skelps of predetermined specifications.

Appendix VIII

IRON AND STEEL IMPORTS: BRITISH AMERICA, 1710-1776

Wrought Iron Imported from Britain by Colony: 1710-1773

Year	New England	N.Y.	Penn.	Va. & Md.	Carolina	Georgia	Florida	Total
1710[1]	4597	567	988	3014	1143	—	—	10,309[2]
1715	5796	1380	988	8947	691	—	—	17,802
1718	3110	1396	887	6735	969	—	—	13,097
1729	7394	1904	851	4866	1342	—	—	16,357
1730	7330	2775	2629	6390	1480	—	—	20,604
1735	8598	2380	2208	7446	2168	—	—	22,800
1740	7105	1610	2420	8815	2693	—	—	22,643
1745	6192	2291	3150	8641	2881	—	—	23,155
1750	6544	2137	2102	9709	3353	—	—	23,845
1755	7884	4384	4765	8684	3733	—	—	29,450
1760	3455	6280	8687	10,128	6849	58	—	35,457
1765	6290	4883	5303	4866	7993	385	—	29,720
1770	2907	620	1565	21,734	5773	878	208	33,685
1771	2250	3860	176	7664	4393	1402	11	19,756
1772	4209	11,497	—	38,546	13,212	1068	654	68,186
1773	2634	5972	19,652	12,544	12,155	1855	2166	56,978

[1]Includes imports for 1711.
[2]In hundredweights (cwt.).

Ref. U.S. Bureau of Census, *Historical Statistics of the United States* (Washington, 1961), Series Z 203-210, p. 765.

Bar Iron Imported from Britain by Colony: 1710-1750

Year	New England	N.Y.	Penn.	Va. & Md.	Carolina	Total
1710[1]	201	10	13	2	—	226
1715	373	111	8	17	2	511
1720	150	92	—	2	6	250
1725	243	102	5	4	11	365
1730	413	58	3	5	9	488
1735	371	55	2	12	25	465
1740	263	90	—	2	8	363
1745	101	108	—	3	6	218
1750[2]	1	—	—	3	1	5

[1]In tons of 2240 lbs.
[2]Bar iron imports sharply dropped after 1750 because of limitations imposed on colonial manufacture by the Iron Act.

Ref: U.S. Bureau of Census, *Historical Statistics of the United States* (Washington, 1961), Series Z 153-158, p. 763.

Bar Iron Imported by British Colonies from Other Continental Colonies: 1768-1772

Year	N.H.	Mass.	R.I.	Conn.	N.Y.	N.J.	Penn.	Md.	Va.	N.C.	S.C.	Ga.	Fla.	Total
1768	1500	7977	2322	271	236	145	684	45	71	1401	1775	317	161	16,905[1]
1769	2390	8648	1175	1734	710	—	530	97	1546	1352	3127	525	28	21,860
1770	3717	13,052[2]	1240	2295	120	—	166	—	2105	1186	3961	324	172	28,338
1771	3079	10,869	2240	2351	880	—	494	47	2420	2604	2590	419	91	28,064
1772	4169	14,367	2304	1588	220	6[3]	940	16	4540	1749	2278	352	127	33,156

[1]In hundredweights.
[2]Plus 154 bars.
[3]New Jersey Colony was self-sufficient in iron production, importing only sporadically after 1768.

Steel Imported from Britain by Continental Colonies: 1768-1771.

Colonial bloomeries produced limited quantities of blister steel for specific purposes on an "as needed" basis.

Year	Amount
1768[1]	—
1769	1599[2]
1770	1578[2]
1771	2126

[1]In hundred weights
[2]Plus 1 bundle and 41 faggots in 1769 and 4030 bars, 12½ faggots, and 36 long tons of steel in 1770.
Ref: U.S. Bureau of Census, *Historical Statistics of the United States* (Washington, 1961), Series Z 165-202, p. 764; Series Z 211-222, p. 764.

Appendix IX

PATRIOT ARMSMAKERS

Legend   All of the arms-makers listed contributed to the manufacture of firearms or related war matériel for the patriot cause during the American Revolution (1775-1783) and their activity or activities are indicated by the letter designations below:

A—Colony (State) Armorer

B—Bayonet Maker

BS—Barrelsmith

CA—Continental Armorer

COSGL—Committee of Safety Gunlock Maker

COSM—Committee of Safety Rifle Maker

COSR—Committee of Safety Rifle Maker

CMM—Continental Musket Maker

CPM—Continental Pistol Maker

CRM—Continental Rifle Maker

CTGM—Cartridge Maker

CUSA—Chief United States Armorer

G—General Gunsmith

MA—Master Armorer

MB—Musket Ball Maker

MM—Musket Maker

MILA—Militia Armorer

PS—Pistolsmith

RS—Riflesmith

SAI—Small Arms Inspector

SM—Stock Maker

WBM—Wire and Brush Maker

Name	Locale	Activity	Name	Locale	Activity
Acfield, Jacob	Pa.	B, G	Austin, Cornelius	New Jersey	A, G
Adkins, Josiah	Conn.	G, MM	Austin, Thomas	Charlestown, Mass.	A, COSM
Agy, _____	Pa.	RS			
Albrecht, Andreas			Babcock, Moses	Charlestown, Mass.	B, MM
(Andrew)	Lancaster Co., Pa.	RS	Backhouse,		
Albright, Henry	Lancaster, Pa.	RS	Richard	Easton, Pa.	BS, G
Aldenderfer, M.	Lancaster, Pa.	RS	Bailey, Nathan	New London, Conn.	B, COSM
Ames, David	Bridgewater, Mass.	B, COSM	Bailey, Robert	York, Pa.	G
Ames, John, Maj.	Bridgewater, Mass.	B, COSM	Baker, John	Montgomery Co., Pa.	B, COSM
Anderson, James	Williamsburg, Va.	A, COSM	Baker, Melchoir	Fayette Co., Pa.	RS, MM
Angstadt, Peter	Lancaster, Pa.	RS, CPM	Baldwin, Elihu	Branford, Conn.	G, MM
Angush, James	Lancaster, Pa.	RS	Baldwin, Jacob	Pa.	COSM
Annely, Edward	New Jersey	A, G	Balsley (Paulsley),		
Annely, Thomas	New Jersey	A, G	Christian	Cumberland Co., Pa.	G, MM
Antes (Antis),	Northumberland		Banks, Uri [ah]	Conn.	G, MILA
William	Co., Pa.	B, MM, RS	Bard, George	Lancaster Co., Pa.	RS

Name	Locale	Activity	Name	Locale	Activity
Barrett,			Burger & Smith	Charleston, S.C.	G
Samuel "Deacon"	Concord, Mass.	B, COSM	Burnham, Elisha	Hartford, Conn.	A, G
Bartlett, A.	Mass.	G	Burnham, George	Conn.	A, G
Bauer, George	Lancaster, Pa.	G	Burt, John	Lancaster Co., Pa.	RS
Beach, Edmond	Goshen, Conn.	SAI	Busch, F.L.	Lancaster, Pa.	RS
Beach, Miles	Goshen, Conn.	SAI	Butler, John	Lancaster, Pa.	COSM
Bean, Edmond	Bean's Station, Tenn.	RS	Butler, Thomas	Lancaster, Pa.	CUSA
Bean, Jesse	Bean's Station, Tenn.	RS	Byers, James	Southwark, Pa.	G
Bean, John	Bean's Station, Tenn.	RS			
Bean, Robert	Bean's Station, Tenn.	RS	Campbell, William,		
Bean, Russell	Bean's Station, Tenn.	RS	Capt.	Annapolis, Md.	COSM, SM
Bean, William	Bean's Station, Tenn.	RS	Carlisle, Henry	Carlisle, Pa.	RS
Bean, William,			Carpenter, John	Lancaster Co., Pa.	RS
Jr., Capt.	Bean's Station, Tenn.	RS	Carpenter, Nicholas	Pa.	G
Beck, Gideon	Lancaster, Pa.	RS, COSM	Carroll, Lawrence	Philadelphia, Pa.	G
Beck, John	Bethabara, N.C.	RS	Cave, Christopher	Philadelphia, Pa.	RS, MM
Valentine			Chandler, Stephen	Conn.	G, MM
Beeman (Beman),			Chapman, _____	Amelia Co., Va.	G
_____	Mass.	COSM	Chapman, James	Bucks Co., Pa.	B, COSM
Belton, Joseph	Philadelphia, Pa.	CMM	Chapman, John	Amelia Co., Va.	G
Bemis, Edmond	Boston, Mass	MM	Chapman, Josiah	Fredericktown, Md.	COSM
Berlin, Abraham	Easton, Pa.	B, MM	Cherrington,		
Berlin, Isaac	Easton, Pa.	B, MM	Thomas P., Sr.	Cattawissa, Pa.	RS
Berry, Peter, Jr.	Lancaster Co., Pa.	RS	Child, Elisha	Conn.	G, MM
Best, _____	Lancaster, Pa.	G	Chisholm,		
Beyer, N.	Lebanon, Pa.	RS	Archibald	Annapolis, Md.	SM
Bidwell, Oliver	Hartford, Conn.	B, COSM	Chittenden,		
Bielry, _____	Philadelphia, Pa.	CPM	Ebenezer	Conn.	G, MM
Blackman, Elijah	Middletown, Conn.	G, MM	Christ, Daniel	Lancaster, Pa.	RS
Blackman, J.	Pa. (?)	PS	Christ, Jacob	Lancaster, Pa.	RS
Blackwood,			Cist, _____ Maj.	Baltimore, Md.	SAI
Marmaduke	Philadelphia, Pa.	COSGL	Clallch, H.M.	Pa.	RS
Blaisdel,			Clapham,	Point-of-Rocks,	COSM, RS
Jonathan	Amesbury, Mass.	A, COSM	Josiah, Col	Va.	
Bloodworth,			Clark, Francis	Pa. .	B, COSM
Timothy	N.C.	COSM	Clark, William	Philadelphia, Pa.	CPM
Blymire, George	York, Pa.	RS	Cobb, John	Taunton, Mass.	G
Bobb, Anthony	Reading, Pa.	G, MILA	Coon, Levi, Sr.	Ithica, N.Y.	RS, MM
Bollinger, Peter	Lancaster Co., Pa.	RS	Coutty, Samuel	Philadelphia, Pa.	CPM
Bolton, Robert	Georgia	A, G	Cowell, Ebenezer	Allentown, Pa.	COSM
Bond, Richard	Cecil Co., Md.	COSM	Cowell, Joseph	Boston, Mass.	G
Boniwitz, John	Lebanon, Pa.	RS, MM	Cowell, P.	Pa.	RS
Boone, Samuel	Berks Co., Pa.	MA	Craig, Robert	Philadelphia, Pa.	COSGL
Bosworth, _____	Lancaster, Pa.	RS	Crawford, Hugh	Charleston, S.C.	G, MILA
Boyd, Robert	New Windsor, N.Y.	COSM	Crouch, Richard	Richmond, Va.	G
Breidenhart,			Cunningham,		
Christopher	Pa.	COSR	_____	Va.	G
Brice (Bryce), John	Philadelphia, Pa.	MB	Cunningham,		
Brong, Joseph	Lancaster, Pa.	RS	John	Hartford Co., Md.	COSM
Brong, Peter	Lancaster, Pa.	RS	Curry, William	Carlisle, Pa.	G
Bronoup, James	Philadelphia, Pa.	G	Curtis, Jesse	Waterbury, Conn.	G, MM
Buckwalter,					
Abraham	Lancaster Co., Pa.	G	Dallam, Richard	Hartford Co., Md.	B, COSM
Buckwalter,			Dana, J.	Canton, Mass.	G
Henry,	Lancaster Co., Pa.	G	Davis, Isaac, Capt.	Acton, Mass.	G
Buckwalter, John	Lancaster Co., Pa.	G	Deberiere		
Buell, Elisha	Hebron, Conn.	G, MM	(Debarrier),		
Bulow, Charles	Lancaster, Pa.	G	Henry	Philadelphia, Pa.	CPM
Burger, David	Charleston, S.C.	G	Dechard, Jacob	Philadelphia, Pa.	RS

Name	Locale	Activity	Name	Locale	Activity
Deeds, H.	Reading, Pa.	COSM, RS	Faulk, Adam	Pa.	RS, MM
DeHaven, Hugh	Philadelphia, Pa.	COSM	Feree, Jacob	Lancaster Co., Pa.	RS
DeHaven, Peter	Philadelphia, Pa.	MA	Feree, Joel	Lancaster, Pa.	RS, COSM
DeHuff, Abraham	Lancaster, Pa.	RS	Feree, Manuel	Lancaster, Pa.	RS
DeHuff, Henry	Lancaster Co., Pa.	RS	Fesig, Conrad	Reading, Pa.	G
Dereiner, Michael	Lancaster, Pa.	COSM, COSR	Fetter, William	Pa.	G
			Few, Richard	Chester Co., Pa.	G
Deringer, Henry, Sr.	Philadelphia, Pa.	PS, MM	Figthorn, Andrew	Reading, Pa.	G
			Fishburn, Philip	Dauphin Co., Pa.	G
Deterer, Adam	Lancaster, Pa.	B, COSM	Fisher, Henry	Frederick, Md.	G, MILA
Devane, James	Wilmington, N.C.	COSM	Fitch, John	Trenton, N.J.	CA, COSM
Devane, John	Wilmington, N.C.	COSM	Foher (Fohrer),		
Devernay, Francis	Charleston, S.C.	G	Ludwig	Pa.	COSM
Dewey, Samuel	Hebron, Conn.	B, COSM	Folleck, John	Johnstown, N.Y.	RS
Dick, Walter	Charleston, S.C.	G	Fondersmith,		
Dickerson, Robert	Va.	G	John	Lancaster Co., Pa.	RS, COSM
Dickert, Jacob	Lancaster, Pa.	RS	Fondersmith,		
Dickey, David	Cumberland Co., Pa.	RS	Valentine	Lancaster Co., Pa.	RS
Dieberger,			Foster, Joseph	Pa.	COSM
Heinrich	Pa.	G	Fottrell, Patrick	Philadelphia, Pa.	COSM
Diffenderfer, John	Lancaster Co., Pa.	RS	Foulkes, Adam	Easton, Pa.	COSR, COSM
Diffenderfer,					
Michael	Lancaster Co., Pa.	RS	Foulks, William	Lancaster, Pa.	RS
Dike, Anthony	Bridgewater, Mass.	COSM	Fox, John	Reading, Pa.	G
Dippeberger,			Fraily, Henry	Pa.	COSM
Henry	Pa.	G	Franck, _____	Pa.	RS
Doolittle, Isaac	Milford, Conn.	SAI	Frink, Nathan	Conn.	G, MM
Doud, John	Goshen, Conn.	G	Frost, Gideon	Mass.	COSM
Douglas, John	Conn.	A, G	Fundersmith,		
Drayton (Draton),			Ludwig	Lancaster Co., Pa.	RS
John	Charleston, S.C.	G			
Drepperd,			Gander, Peter	Lancaster, Pa.	RS
Christian	Lancaster, Pa.	RS	Gaspard, _____	Lancaster, Pa.	RS
Drepperd, Jacob	Lancaster, Pa.	RS	Gautec, Peter	Lancaster, Pa.	G
Drepperd,			Getz, John	Lancaster, Pa.	RS
John Michael	Lancaster, Pa.	RS	Gilbert,		
Dunkle, Jacob	Frederick, Md.	G	Daniel, Capt.	Brookfield, Mass.	COSM
Dunwicke, William	Philadelphia, Pa.	COSM	Gilman (Gillman),		
			Daniel	Lancaster Co., Pa.	G
Earle, Thomas	Leicester, Mass.	G	Gingerich, Henry	Lancaster, Pa.	COSM, RS
Eberley, John	Lancaster, Pa.	COSM	Glass, Michael	Northampton Co., Pa.	G
Eby, Abraham	Lancaster Co., Pa.	RS	Golcher (Goulcher),		
Edmanson, Jacob	Charleston, S.C.	G	John	Easton, Pa.	BS, COSGL
Elton, Thomas	York, Pa.	G, MILA	Gonder, _____	Georgia	A, G
Elwell, H.	Liverpool, Pa.	RS	Gonter, Peter	Lancaster, Pa.	RS
Ely, Martin	Springfield, Mass.	B, COSM	Goodwin, Jonathan	Lebanon, Conn.	G, MM
Ernst, J.	Frederick, Md.	RS	Goucher, Thomas	Philadelphia, Pa.	COSM
Evans, Thomas	Lancaster, Pa.	G	Graeff, John	Reading, Pa.	RS
Evitt, Woodward	Frederick, Md.	G	Grant, Lewis	Philadelphia, Pa.	COSM
Ewing, Thomas	Baltimore, Md.	SAI	Grave, John	Lancaster Co., Pa.	G
Eyster, George	York, Pa.	RS	Green,		
			James, Capt.	Conn.	G, MM
Falley, Richard	Westfield, Mass.	A, COSM	Greentree,		
Fancher, Thomas	Waterbury, Conn.	G, MM	Alexander	Philadelphia, Pa.	COSM
Farnot (Fainot),			Gresheim, J.	Lancaster, Pa.	RS
Frank	Lancaster Co., Pa.	RS	Grove, Samuel	York Co., Pa.	RS
Farnot, Frederick	Lancaster Co., Pa.	RS	Guest, John	Lancaster, Pa.	CRM
Farnot, George	Lancaster Co., Pa.	RS	Guilliam,		
Farnot, Jacob	Lancaster Co., Pa.	RS	Benjamin	Massachusetts	COSM, MA

Name	Locale	Activity	Name	Locale	Activity
Haga, Wolfgang	Reading, Pa.	RS	Jost (Yost), _____	Pa.	G
Haines, Isaac	Lancaster Co., Pa.	RS	Jost, Caspar	Dauphin Co., Pa.	RS
Halbach & Sons	Baltimore, Md.	PS			
Halburn, Caspar	Lancaster, Pa.	COSM	Kashline, Peter	Northampton Co., Pa.	COSM
Hall, Samuel	East Haddam, Conn.	G, MM	Kearling, Samuel	Berks Co., Pa.	RS
Handlyn (Handlin),			Keeley, Jacob	Chester Co., Pa.	G
John	Pa.	COSM	Keeley, Jacob, Jr.	Chester Co., Pa.	G
Hardinger, Peter	Berks Co., Pa.	G	Keeley, Mathias	Philadelphia, Pa.	COSM
Harris, Henry	Lancaster Co., Pa.	G	Keeley, Sebastian	Philadelphia, Pa.	B, COSM
Harris, Isaac	Savage Town, Md.	BS, COSM	Keener, Peter	Baltimore, Md.	COSM
Hawken, Henry	Lancaster, Pa.	RS	Keener, Samuel	Baltimore, Md.	B, COSM
Hawkins, Henry	Schenectady, N.Y.	RS	Keesports, George		
Heckert, Philip, Sr.	York Co., Pa.	RS	Peter	Baltimore, Md.	A, G
Heckert, Philip, Jr.	York Co., Pa.	RS	Kenster, John	Georgetown, Md.	G
Heinhold, Simeon	Lancaster Co., Pa.	RS	Kerlin (Kirlin),		
Henry, John	Lancaster Co., Pa.	RS	John, Sr.	Chester Co., Pa.	G
Henry, William Sr.	Lancaster, Pa.	RS, COSM	Kern, Daniel	Northampton	RS
Henry, William, Jr.	Nazareth, Pa.	RS, COSM		Co., Pa.	
Herring, Richard	Wilmington, N.C.	COSM	Kern, Peter	Northampton	RS
Hertzog, Andrew	York Co., Pa.	A, G		Co., Pa.	
Hewes, Josiah	Pa.	COSM	Kerr, John	Carlisle, Pa.	G
Hide, Elijah	Conn.	A, G	Kinder, Samuel	Philadelphia, Pa.	GOSGL
Hill, William	Albany, N.Y.	G, MILA	Kleist, Daniel	Bethlehem, Pa.	RS
Hills, Medad, Col.	Goshen, Conn.	COSM	Koffler, Adam	Wachovia, N.C.	G, MILA
Hoadley, Lemuel	Conn.	G, MM	Kraft, Jacob	Lancaster Co., Pa.	RS
Hoghen, Wolfgang	Northumberland	COSM			
	Co., Pa.		Lane, William	Lancaster, Pa.	SM
Hollingshead,			Langeay, John	Philadelphia, Pa.	CTGM
William	Philadelphia, Pa.	G	Lawrence, Thomas	Frederick, Md.	B, COSM
Hollingsworth,			Layendecker,		
Henry	Elkton, Md.	B, COSM	George	Allentown, Pa.	G
Horn, Stephen	Easton, Pa.	G	Lefevre, Samuel	Lancaster Co., Pa.	RS
Houston, James	Philadelphia, Pa.	G	Leitner, Adam	York Co., Pa.	RS
Humberger,			Leman, Peter	Lancaster Co., Pa.	G
Peter, Sr.	Lancaster, Pa.	RS	Leonard, Eliphalet	Easton, Mass.	BS, COSM
Humble, Michael	Kentucky	RS	Lether		
Humphreys,			(Leather), Jacob	York, Pa.	BS, RS
Joshua	Virginia	B, COSM	Light, Peter	Berkeley Co., Va.	COSM
Hunter, David	Falmouth, Va.	B, COSM	Littig (Lydick),		
Hunter, James	Falmouth, Va.	COSR	Peter	Baltimore, Md.	COSM
Huntington,			Loesch, Jacob, Jr.	Salem, N.C.	RS, MM
Hezekiah	Windham, Conn.	G, MM	Lowery (Lawrey),		
Huntington,			David	Wethersfield, Conn.	G, MM
Simon	Conn.	B, COSM	Ludington, _____	Lancaster Co., Pa.	RS
			Ludwick, John	Pa.	G
Isch, Christian	Lancaster, Pa.	B, COSM			
Imhoff, Benedict	Lancaster Co., Pa.	RS	McCoy, Alexander	Philadelphia, Pa.	G
			McCoy, Kester	Lancaster Co., Pa.	G
Jankofsky,			Malcolm, John	Pa.	COSM
Anthony	Charleston, S.C.	G	Maus, Philip	Berks Co., Pa.	RS
Jasper, _____	Boston, Mass.	G	Mayesch, _____	Lancaster, Pa.	RS
Jenks, Stephen	Providence, R.I.	G	Meanly, Richard	Mecklenburg Co., Va.	COSM
Johns, Isaac	Philadelphia, Pa.	G	Merckley, Jacob	Philadelphia, Pa.	G
Johnson, Seth	Old Rutland, Mass.	COSM	Meriam, Silas	Concord, Mass.	G
Jones, Amos	Colchester, Conn.	G	Merriman, Silas	Conn.	G, MM
Jones, Charles	Lancaster, Pa.	G	Messersmith,		
Jones, Robert	Lancaster, Pa.	RS	Jacob	Lancaster Co., Pa.	RS
Jones, William	Bedford Co., Pa.	A, G	Messersmith, John	Lancaster Co., Pa.	COSGL
Jones, William	Kent Co., Del.	COSGL	Messersmith,		
			Samuel	Baltimore, Md.	COSM

Name	Locale	Activity	Name	Locale	Activity
Metzger, Jacob	Lancaster Co., Pa.	RS	Phelps, Silas	Lebanon, Conn.	G, MM
Mey, James	Maryland	COSM	Pincall, Emanuel	Pa.	G
Miles, Thomas	Philadelphia, Pa.	COSM	Pole, Edward	Philadelphia, Pa.	SM
Miller, Jacob	Lancaster Co., Pa.	RS	Pollard, Jno.	Pa.	G
Miller, John	Lancaster Co., Pa.	G	Poorman, M.	Lancaster Co., Pa.	RS
Miller, John, Jr.	Lancaster Co., Pa.	RS	Pomery,		
Miller, Mathias	Easton, Pa.	G	Lemuel	Northampton, Mass.	COSM
Miller, Simon	Hamburg, Pa.	RS	Pomeroy,		
Moll, John	Allentown, Pa.	RS	Seth, Gen.	Northampton, Mass.	G
Moore, Abraham	Chester Co., Pa.	COSM	Prahl, Lewis	Philadelphia, Pa.	COSM
Morgan, George	Philadelphia, Pa.	G	Pringle, John	Philadelphia, Pa.	COSM
Morgan, Joseph	Morristown, N.J.	G	Putnam, Enoch	Granby, Mass.	A, G
Morrow (Murrow)					
Abraham	Philadelphia, Pa.	CRM	Raffsnyder, John	Reading, Pa.	G
Moster (Morter),			Ransom, James	Halifax, N.C.	MA
George	Lancaster Co., Pa.	RS	Rathfong,		
Mullen, Joseph	Salem, N.C.	G	Frederick	Lancaster Co., Pa.	G
Myer, Henry	Lancaster Co., Pa.	COSM	Rathfong, George	Lancaster, Pa.	RS, CA
			Read (Reed),		
Nelson, Alexander	Philadelphia, Pa.	COSM	Robert	Chestertown, Md.	COSM
Nelson, Francis	Philadelphia, Pa.	SM	Read, William	Chestertown, Md.	COSM
Newcomer,			Reaser (Reasor),		
Abraham	Lancaster, Pa.	RS	Jacob	Frederick, Md.	COSM
Newcomer,			Reasor, David	Lancaster, Pa.	RS
John, Jr.	Lancaster, Pa.	RS	Reasure, John	Lancaster Co., Pa.	RS
Newcomer,			Reddick, _____	Baltimore, Md.	COSM
John, Sr.	Lancaster, Pa.	RS	Reed, James	Lancaster, Pa.	RS
Newhardt, Jacob	Allentown, Pa.	RS	Reigart, Peter	Lancaster, Pa.	COSM
Newton, Moses	Conn.	G, MM	Resser, Peter	Lancaster Co., Pa.	RS
Nicholson, John	Philadelphia, Pa.	RS, COSM	Riggs, Joseph	Derby, Conn.	G, MM
Norton, Ebenezer	Goshen Conn.	SM	Rittenhouse,		
Nunnemacher,			Benjamin	Philadelphia, Pa.	COSM
Abram	York, Pa.	G	Ritter, Jacob	Philadelphia, Pa.	G
Nunnemacher,			Roesser, Peter	Lancaster, Pa.	RS
Andrew	York, Pa.	RS	Roop, John	Allentown, Pa.	RS
			Rugert, Peter	Lancaster, Pa.	B, COSM
Oberholser,			Rupp, Herman	Lancaster Co., Pa.	RS
Christian	Lancaster, Pa.	COSM	Rupp, John	Allentown, Pa.	PS
Ong, E.	Philadelphia, Pa.	G	Ruppert, William	Lancaster, Pa.	G
Orr, Hugh	Bridgewater, Mass.	COSM	Rush, William	Philadelphia, Pa.	G
Orr, Robert	Bridgewater, Mass.	COSM	Rutherford, Robert	Mecklenburg Co., Va.	COSM
Osborn, Lot	Waterbury, Conn.	G, MM	Rutherford,		
			Thomas	Mecklenburg Co., Va.	COSM
Page, John	Preston, Conn.	G, MM	Rynes, Michael	Lancaster Co., Pa.	RS
Palm, Frederick	Ulster Co., N.Y.	RS			
Palm, Jacob	Ulster Co., N.Y.	RS	Saltonstall, Gurdon	Conn.	G, MILA
Palmer, Amasa	Conn.	G, MM	Saylor, Jacob	Bedford Co., Pa.	G
Palmer, Thomas	Philadelphia, Pa.	COSR	Sager, John	Lancaster Co., Pa.	RS
Parker, Henry	Liverpool, Pa.	RS	Scheaner, William	Reading, Pa.	RS
Parker, Samuel	Philadelphia, Pa.	COSM	Schley, Jacob	Frederickstown, Md.	COSR
Parkhill, Andrew	Philadelphia, Pa.	G	Schorer, Andrew	Bethlehem, Pa.	G
Parmalee, Phineas	Pa.	CA	Sell, Frederick	Maryland	RS
Pearson, James	Pa.	BS, COSM	Sever, Joseph	Framingham, Mass.	A, COSM
Peebles, Robert	Cumberland Co., Pa.	COSM	Sever, Shubabel	Framingham, Mass.	A, COSM
Pennypacker,			Shaffer, Baltzer	Baltimore, Md.	G
Daniel	Berks Co., Pa.	COSM	Shannon, William	Philadelphia, Pa.	G
Perkins, Joseph	Philadelphia, Pa.	COSM	Sharpless, Daniel	Philadelphia, Pa.	COSM
Perkins, Joseph	Little Rest, R.I.	G, MM	Shaw, _____	Mass.	COSM
Phelps, Jedediah	Lebanon, Conn.	G, MM	Shaw, John	Annapolis, Md.	COSM, A

Name	Locale	Activity	Name	Locale	Activity
Sheets, Adam	Sheperds Town, Va.	CA	Waters, Asa	Sutton, Mass.	COSM
Sheets, Henry	Sheperds Town, Va.	CRM	Waters, John	Carlisle, Pa.	G
Sheets, Philip	Sheperds Town, Va.	CRM	Watkeys, Henry	New Windsor, N.Y.	COSM
Sheetz,			Weaver, Adam	Lancaster Co., Pa.	RS
T. Christian	Lancaster Co., Pa.	RS	Webb, Joseph	Pa.	COSM
Sheffield, Jeremiah	Rhode Island	G	Weir, James	Philadelphia, Pa.	WBM
Shell, Martin	Dauphin Co., Pa.	CMM	Welshantz, David	York Co., Pa.	RS
Shell, Martin, Jr.	Dauphin Co., Pa.	CMM	Welshantz, Jacob	York Co., Pa.	CRM
Shell, Samuel	Tennessee	RS	Welshantz, Joseph	York, Pa.	RS
Sherrit, Joseph	Philadelphia, Pa.	G	Welton, Ard	Waterbury, Conn.	CA
Shomo, John	Berks Co., Pa.	G	West, Stephen	Woodward, Md.	G
Skellhorn, Richard	New York	G	Whetcraft, William	Annapolis, Md.	COSM
Sloan, Robert	Conn.	G, MM	White, Horace	Springfield, Mass.	COSM
Smith, Anthony	Northampton		White, Nicholas	Fredericktown, Md.	COSM
	Co., Pa.	RS	Whitehead,		
Smith, Jeremiah	Lime Rock, R.I.	G, MILA	Mathew	Pa.	COSM
Smith, Johnson	Northampton		Whittemore, Amos	Boston, Mass.	COSM
	Co., Pa.	COSM	Whittemore,		
Smith, Thomas	North Carolina	A, G	William	Boston, Mass.	COSM
Smith, _____	Charleston, S.C.	G	Wickham, T.	Philadelphia, Pa.	COSM
Spitzer, _____	Newmarket, Va.	COSM	Wigfall, Samuel	Philadelphia, Pa.	COSGL
Steel, John	Mass.	A, G	Wigel, Peter	York Co., Pa.	A, G
Steel, _____	Mass.	G	Wilcox, John	Deep River, N.C.	RS
Stephens, John	Pa.	COSM	Wiley, Theodore	Pa.	COSM
Sterewith, _____	Maryland	COSM	Williams, Edward	Conn.	G, MM
Stevenson, George	Cumberland Co., Pa.	BS	Williams, William	Conn.	A, G
			Willis, John	Philadelphia, Pa.	COSM
Talley, _____	Mass.	A, BS	Willis, Richard	Lancaster, Pa.	G
Taylor, George	Northampton		Willis, William	James City Co., Va.	COSM
	Co., Pa.	BS	Winger, Christian	Lancaster Co., Pa.	RS
Taylor, John	Pa.	COSM	Wingert, Richard	Lancaster, Pa.	COSM
Teff, George	R.I.	G	Winters, Elisha	Chester Town, Md.	COSM
Thomas, Isaac	Hartford Co., Md.	COSM	Withers, Michael	Lancaster, Pa.	COSM
Tomlinson, Joshua	Philadelphia, Pa.	BS	Wood, John	Roxbury, Mass.	COSM
Towers, Robert	Pa.	CA	Wood, Josiah	Pa.	COSM
Town, Benjamin	Pa.	COSM	Wyley (Wylie),		
Trumbull, David	Lebanon, Conn.	G, MM	Thomas, Capt.	Carlisle, N.J.	MA
Tyler, John	Philadelphia, Pa.	A, G			
Tydich, Peter	Baltimore, Md.	COSM	Yard, Benjamin	Trenton, N.J.	G
			Yost (Youste),		
Unseld, John	Maryland	COSM	John	Georgetown, Md.	RS, COSM
			Youmans, _____	Lancaster, Pa.	RS
Van Bibber,			Young, Henry	Easton, Pa.	COSR
_____	Baltimore, Md.	SAI	Young, John	Easton, Pa.	COSR
Van de Water,					
Hendrick	New York	G	Zorger, Frederick	York, Pa.	RS
Vogler, Philip	Salisbury, N.C.	RS	Zorger, George	York, Pa.	RS
Voight, Henry	Pa.	COSGL			
Volvert, _____	Lancaster, Pa.	RS			
Vondergrift, John	Bucks Co., Pa.	COSM			
Vondersmith,					
_____	Lancaster, Pa.	RS			
Walker, John	Lancaster Co., Pa.	RS			
Walsh, James	Philadelphia, Pa.	COSGL, MA			
Walsh, John	Philadelphia, Pa.	SM			
Waters, _____	Dutchess Co., N.Y.	COSM			
Waters, Andrus	Sutton, Mass.	COSM			

Ref: M.L. Brown, "Early Gunmakers Met War Woes," *American Rifleman* (January, 1971); 92-97. Author's abridgement. Reprinted with permission.

Archives

North Carolina Spanish Records Collection, Department of Archives and History, Raleigh.

Stetson Collection, P.K. Yonge Library of Florida History, University of Florida, Gainesville.

Books

Baker, John. *The British in Boston.* Cambridge, 1924.

Barado y Front, Francisco. *Museo Militar: Historia de Ejército Español; Armas, Uniformes, Sistemes de Combate, Instituciones Organizacion del Mismo.* 3 vols. Barcelona, 1889.

Barnes, John S., ed. *Fanning's Narrative, Being the Memoirs of Nathaniel Fanning . . . 1778-1783.* New York, 1912.

Blackmore, Howard L. *British Military Firearms, 1650-1850.* London, 1961.

——————. *Guns and Rifles of the World.* New York, 1965.

Blair, Claude E. *Pistols of the World.* New York, 1968.

Bonaparte, Charles Louis Napoleon and Favé, Col. Íldefonse. *Études sur le Passé et l' Avenir de l'Artillerie.* 6 vols. Paris, 1862.

Boothroyd, Geoffrey. *Guns Through the Ages.* New York, 1962.

——————. *The Handgun.* New York, 1970.

Bowman, Hank Wieand. *Famous Guns from the Smithsonian Collection.* Greenwhich, Conn., 1966.

Brandon, William. *The American Heritage Book of Indians.* New York, 1961.

Breeden, Robert L., ed. *Those Inventive Americans.* Washington, 1971.

Brinckerhoff, Sidney and Chamberlain, Pierce. *Spanish Military Weapons in Colonial America, 1700-1821.* Harrisburg, 1972.

Brown, Roger H. *The Republic in Peril: 1812.* New York, 1971.

Browne, William H., et al., eds. *Archives of Maryland.* Baltimore, 1884.

Carey, A. Merwyn. *American Firearms Makers.* New York, 1953.

Cary, Lucian. *Guns and Shooting.* Greenwhich, Conn. 1952.

Champlain, Samuel de. *The Works of Samuel de Champlain.* H.P. Biggar, ed. 6 vols. Toronto, 1922.

Chapel, Charles Edward. *Guns of the Old West.* New York, 1961.

Chatelain, Verne E. *The Defenses of Spanish Florida, 1565 to 1763.* Washington, 1941.

Chinn, Col. George M., USMC. *The Machine Gun.* 6 vols. Washington, 1951.

Cipolla, Carlo M. *Guns, Sails and Empires: Technological Innovation and the Early Phases of European Expansion, 1400-1700.* New York, 1965.

Colonial Williamsburg Foundation. *Colonial Williamsburg Official Guidebook & Map.* Williamsburg, 1970.

Conner, Jeanette Thurber. *Colonial Records of Spanish Florida.* 2 vols. De Land, 1925-1930.

Copeland, Leeila S., and Dovell, J.E. *La Florida, Its Land and People.* Austin, 1957.

Cottrell, Leonard. *The Anvil of Civilization.* New York, 1957.

Dawson, Henry B. *Battles of the United States by Sea and Land.* 2 vols. New York, 1858.

Deyrup, Felicia Johnson. *Arms Making in the Connecticut Valley.* York, Pa., 1970.

Diderot, Denis. *Encyclopédie ou Dictionnaire Raisonné des Sciences, des Arts et des Méitiers.* 17 vols. Paris, 1751-1765.

——————. *Recueil de Planches sur les Sciences, les Arts Libéraux, et les Arte Méchanique avec leur Explication.* 11 vols. Paris, 1762-1772.

Dillin, Capt. John G. W. *The Kentucky Rifle.* Washington, 1924.

Du Pont, E.I. de Nemours & Co. *Du Pont: The Autobiography of an American Enterprise.* New York, 1952.

Ewing, Thomas. *George Ewing, Gentleman, A Soldier of Valley Forge.* New York, 1928.

Feldhaus, F.M. *Die Technik.* Berlin and Leipzig, 1914.

Ferris, Robert G., ed. *Explorers and Settlers.* Washington, 1968.

——————. *Founders and Frontiersmen.* Washington, 1967.

Ffoulkes, Charles. *The Gun Founders of England, XIV-XIX Centuries.* Cambridge, 1937.

Force, Peter, ed. *American Archives,* 4th Series, 6 vols. Washington, 1837-1846.

——————. *Tracts and Other Papers.* 4 vols. Washington, 1836-1846.

Frith, James, and Andrews, Ronald. *Antique Pistol Collecting.* New York, 1960.

Gardner, Col. Robert. *Small Arms Makers: A Directory of Fabricators of Firearms, Edged Weapons, Crossbows and Polearms*. New York. 1962.

Gibbon, Edward. *The Decline and Fall of the Roman Empire*. 3 vols. New York, n.d. (Modern Library edn).

Gluckman, Col. Arcadi. *United States Martial Pistols and Revolvers*. Harrisburg, 1956.

———.*United States Muskets, Rifles and Carbines*. Buffalo, 1948.

Gooding, S. James. *The Canadian Gunsmiths, 1608 to 1900*. West Hill, Ontario, 1962.

Greener, W.W. *The Gun and its Development*. New York, 1967.

Hanson, Charles E., Jr. *The Plains Rifle*. Harrisburg, 1960.

Harris, Clive. *History of the Birmingham Gun-Barrel Proof House*. Birmingham, 1946.

Held, Robert. *The Age of Firearms*. New York, 1957.

Henshaw, William, ed. *The Orderly Books . . . October 1, 1775 through October 3, 1776*. Worcester, Mass., 1948.

Herodotus. *Histories*. New York, 1934.

Hicks, James E. *U.S. Military Firearms*. Alhambra, 1962.

Hindle, Brooke. *Technology in Early America*. Chapel Hill, 1966.

Hodge, Frederick Webb, ed. *Handbook of American Indians North of Mexico (Bulletin 30)*. 2 vols. Washington, 1912.

Holbrook, Stewart H. *Lost Men of American History*. New York, 1946.

Innis, Harold L. *The Fur Trade in Canada*. New Haven, 1930.

Jackson, Herbert J., and Whitelaw, Charles E. *European Hand Firearms of the 16th, 17th and 18th Centuries*. New York, n.d. (Bramhall House edn.).

Kaempffert, Waldemar, ed. *A Popular History of American Invention*. 2 vols. New York, 1924.

Kauffman, Henry J. *Early American Gunsmiths, 1650-1850*. New York, 1952.

———. *The Pennsylvania-Kentucky Rifle*. Harrisburg, 1960.

Kennard, A.N. *French Pistols and Sporting Guns*. Feltham, Eng., 1972.

Kindig, Joe, Jr., *Thoughts on the Kentucky Rifle in its Golden Age*. New York, 1961.

Kist, J.B., Puype, J.P., Van Der Mark, W. and Van Der Sloot, R.B.F., *Dutch Muskets and Pistols*. York, Pa., 1974.

Kranzberg, Melvin, and Pursell, Carroll W., Jr., eds. *Technology in Western Civilization*. 2 vols. New York and London, 1967.

Kull, Irving S., and Kull, Nell M. *An Encyclopedia of American History*. New York, 1952.

Lahontan, Baron de. *New Voyages to North-America*. Reuben Gold Thwaites, ed. Chicago, 1905.

Lamb, Harold. *Hannibal: One Man Against Rome*. New York, 1963.

Lancaster, Bruce, and Plumb, J.H. *The American Heritage Book of the Revolution*. New York, 1958.

Lavin, James D. *A History of Spanish Firearms*. New York, 1965.

Lenk, Torsten. *The Flintlock, Its Origin and Development*. New York, 1965.

Lindsay, Merrill. *One Hundred Great Guns*. New York, 1967.

Logan, Herschel C. *Cartridges*. Harrisburg, 1959.

Long Island Historical Society. *Memoirs*. New York, 2 vols. 1869.

Long, Luman, ed. *The 1970 World Almanac*. New York, 1970.

Lowery, Woodbury. *The Spanish Settlements Within the Present Limits of the United States*. 2 vols. New York, 1901-1905.

Miers, Earl Schenck. *Where the Raritan Flows*. New Brunswick, N.J., 1964.

Miller, John C. *The First Frontier: Life in Colonial America*. New York, 1966.

Millis, Walter. *Arms and Men*. New York, 1956.

Mueller, Chester, and Olson, John. *Shooter's Bible Small Arms Lexicon and Concise Encyclopedia*. New York, 1968.

Neilson, William Allen, et al., eds. *Webster's Biographical Dictionary*. Springfield, Mass., 1972.

Olin Mathieson Chemical Corporation. *Winchester-Western Ammunition Handbook*. New York, 1964.

Orr, Charles. *History of the Pequot War*. Cleveland, 1897.

Pargellis, Stanley, ed. *Military Affairs in North America, 1748-1756*. New York, 1936.

Parkman, Francis. *Count Frontenac and New France Under Louis XIV*. Boston, 1888.

Peterson, Harold L. *Arms and Armor in Colonial America, 1526-1783*. New York, 1956 (Bramhall House edn.).

———. *The Book of the Continental Soldier*. New York, 1968.

———., ed. *Encyclopedia of Firearms*. New York, 1964.

———. *Pageant of the Gun*. New York, 1967.

———. *The Treasury of the Gun*. New York, 1962.

Pope, Dudley. *Guns*. New York, 1965.

Pratt, Fletcher. *The Battles That Changed History*. New York, 1956.

Preistley, Herbert Ingram. *The Luna Papers*. 2 vols. De Land, 1928.

Preston, John Hyde. *Revolution 1776*. New York, 1933.

Reed, H. Clay. *The Delaware Colony*. New York, 1970.

Riling, Ray. *The Powder Flask Book*. New York, 1953.

Roberts, Ned. *The Muzzle-Loading Cap Lock Rifle*. New York, 1942.

Russell, Carl P. *Guns on the Early Frontiers*. New York, 1957.

Sanz, Vincente Murga. *Juan Ponce de León*. San Juan, 1959.

Sarles, Frank B., Jr., and Shedd, Charles E. *Colonials and Patriots*. Washington, 1964.

Scheer, George F., ed. *Private Yankee Doodle*. New York, 1962.

———., and Rankin, Hugh F. *Rebels and Redcoats: The Living Story of the American Revolution*. New York, 1959.

Smith, W.H.B., and Smith, Joseph E. *The Book of Rifles*. Harrisburg, 1963.

Staples, William R., ed. *Documentary History of the Burning of the Gaspee*. Providence, 1845.

Steck, Francis Borgia. *Marquette Legends*. New York, 1960.

Steeds, W. *A History of Machine Tools, 1700-1900*. Oxford, 1969.

Strassman, W. Paul. *Risk and Technological Innovation: American Manufacturing Methods during the Nineteenth Century*. Ithaca, 1959.

Tawney, R.H., and Powers, E. *Tudor Economic Developments*. 2 vols. New York, 1953.

Thacher, James. *A Military Journal during the American Revolution*. Boston, 1827.

Thucydides. *The Peloponnesian War*. London, 1954.

True, Henry. *Journals and Letters . . . Also an Account of the Battle of Concord by Corporal Amos Barrett*. Marion, Ohio., 1900.

Van Every, Dale. *A Company of Heroes*. New York, 1962.

——————— . *Forth to the Wilderness*. New York, 1961.

Viardot, Louis. *Historie des Arabes et Maures d'Espagne*. Paris, 1832.

Walker, Kenneth, ed. *Love, War and Fancy*. New York, 1964.

Wellman, Paul I. *Glory, God and Gold*. New York, 1954.

Wigginton, Eliot, ed. *The Foxfire Book*. New York, 1972.

Williamson, Scott Graham. *The American Craftsman*. New York, 1940.

Willison, George F. *Saints and Strangers*. New York, 1945.

Wilson, James Grant, and Fiske, John, eds. *Appletons' Cyclopaedia of American Biography*. 6 vols. New York, 1899.

Wilson, Mitchell. *American Science and Invention*. New York, 1960.

Winant, Lewis. *Firearms Curiosa*. New York, 1954.

Woodward, William E. *The Way Our People Lived*. New York, 1965.

Periodicals

Anonymous. *William and Mary Quarterly*, 3rd Ser., Vol. 10. October, 1953.

Arana, Luis R. "The Day Governor Cabrera Left Florida," *Florida Historical Quarterly*. July, 1961.

Baird, Donald. "The Flintlock Whaling Gun," *Canadian Journal of Arms Collecting*, August, 1968.

Blackmore, Howard L. "The British Rifle in America," *American Rifleman*. June, 1963.

Blair, Claude. "A Further Note on the Early History of the Wheellock," *Journal of the Amrs and Armour Society*. April, 1964.

Boyd, Mark F. "The Expedition of Marcos Delgado from Apalachee to the Upper Creek Country in 1686," *Florida Historical Quarterly*. June, 1937.

Britt, Ken. "The Loyalists: Americans With A Difference," *National Geographic*. April, 1975.

Brown, J.A. "Panton, Leslie and Company, Indian Traders of Pensacola and St. Augustine," *Florida Historical Quarterly*. July, 1954.

Brown, M.L. "Early Gun Makers Met War Woes," *American Rifleman*. January, 1971.

——————— . "Firearms in Frontier America: The Economic Impact, Part I—1560 to 1800," *Gun Digest*. 1976.

——————— . "Matchlocks in Spanish Florida," *Gun Digest*. 1978.

——————— . "Muskets for Liberty," *Ordnance*. July-August, 1973.

——————— . "Muskets, Powder and Patriots," *Gun Digest*. 1973.

Caranta, Raymond. "A History of French Handguns," *Gun Digest*. 1969.

Covington, James W. "Migration Into Florida of the Seminoles, 1700-1820," *Florida Historical Quarterly*. April, 1968.

Darling, Anthony D. "A Late 17th Century French Military Matchlock Musket," *Canadian Journal of Arms Collecting*. May, 1971.

Dieckmann, Edward A. Sr. "Those Thundering Clerics," *Gun Digest*. 1965.

Du Mont, John S. "American Silver-Mounted Kentucky Pistols," *American Rifleman*. August, 1962.

Engelhardt, A. Baron. "The Story of European Proof Marks," *Gun Digest*, 1954.

Feldhaus, F.M. "Das Radschloss bei Leonardo da Vinci," *Zeitschrift für Historische Waffendunde,"* Dresden. June, 1906.

Gillaspie, William R. "Sergeant Major Ayala y Escobar and the Threatened St. Augustine Mutiny," *Florida Historical Quarterly*. October, 1968.

Gooding, S. James. "Gunmakers to the Hudson's Bay Company," *Canadian Journal of Arms Collecting*. February, 1973.

Gordon, Robert B. "Early Gunsmiths' Metals," *American Rifleman*. December, 1959.

Grancsay, Steven V. "Colonel Klett, Hofbuchsenmacher," *Gun Digest*. 1955.

——————— . "The Emperor's Pistol," *Gun Digest*. 1957.

Halsey, Ashley, Jr. "Rarities of the Revolution," *American Rifleman*. July, 1972.

———————, and Snyder, John M. "Jefferson's Beloved Guns," *American Rifleman*. November, 1969.

Hamilton, T.M., "Indian Trade Guns," *Missouri Archaeologist*. Vol. XXII. 1960.

Hanson, Charles E., Jr. "The Indian Trade Fusil," *Gun Digest*. 1959.

Hargreaves, Maj. Reginald, MC (Ret). "The Fabulous Ferguson Rifle and its Brief Combat Career," *American Rifleman*. August, 1971.

Harrower, John. "Diary . . . 1773-1776," *American Historical Review*. October, 1900.

Held, Robert. "Kentucky Rifle—Fact and Fiction," *Gun Digest*. 1962.

Hoffman, Paul E., and Lyon, Eugene. "Account of the *Real Hacienda,* Florida, 1565 to 1602," *Florida Historical Quarterly*. July, 1969.

Holmes, Jack D.L. "Spanish Treaties With West Florida Indians, 1784-1802," *Florida Historical Quarterly*. October, 1969.

Jones, B. Calvin. "A Semi-Subterranean Structure at Mission San Joseph de Ocuya, Jefferson County, Florida," *Bulletin No. 3,* Division of Archives, History and Records Management, Tallahassee, Fla. 1973.

Jordan, Chester A. "Powder Horn Recalls Bicentennial History, *The Gun Report*. June, 1975.

Keim, Charles J. "Beaver Pelts and Trade Muskets," *American Rifleman*. February, 1958.

Landis, Henry Kinzer, and Landis, George Diller. "Lancaster Rifles," *The Pennsylvania German Folklore Society*. Vol. VII. 1942.

Lasson, Tage. "Hand Cannon to Flintlock," *Gun Digest*. 1956.

Lecuyer, Bernard. "The Arquebusier: 1765," *Canadian Journal of Arms Collecting*. May, 1964.

Lyon, Eugene. "The Trouble With Treasure," *National Geographic*. June, 1976.

McLeod, Don. "Marines Won Their First Fight in the New Providence Raid," *Tampa (Fla.) Tribune*. February 29, 1976.

Mateo, Lt. Col. Luis Martinez. "Guns of the Conquistadores," *Guns*. April, 1961.

Matter, Robert Allen. "Missions in the Defense of Spanish Florida," *Florida Historical Quarterly*. July, 1975.

Moody, Sid. "Slavery Was Widespread During Revolution," *Tampa (Fla.) Tribune*. October 24, 1976.

——————. "Undersea Warfare Got Tryout in American Revolution," *Tampa (Fla.) Tribune*. October 3, 1976.

Muir, Bluford. "The Father of the Kentucky Rifle," *American Rifleman*. January, 1971.

Neumann, George C. "Firearms in the American Revolution, Part I," *American Rifleman*. July, 1967.

Perry, Clay. "Big Guns for Washington," *The American Heritage Reader*. 1956.

Perry, Milton. "Firearms of the First President," *American Rifleman*. February, 1956.

Peters, Thelma. "The Loyalist Migration from East Florida to the Bahamas," *Florida Historical Quarterly*. October, 1961.

Peterson, Harold L. "Did it Work?" *American Rifleman*. February, 1955.

——————. "Pistols in the American Revolution," *American Rifleman*. October, 1955.

Pickering, R.A. "The Plug Bayonet," *Canadian Journal of Arms Collecting*. February, 1972.

Renwick, William G. "The Earliest Known Rifle," *American Rifleman*. March, 1953.

Serven, James E. "Powder Horns With A Message," *American Rifleman*. December, 1960.

——————. "Massachusetts: Cradle of American Gunmaking," *American Rifleman*. March, 1968.

——————. "The Shotgun," *Gun Digest*. 1963.

Sprague, Richard K. "Early French Muskets in America," *American Rifleman*. January, 1958.

Stovall, Bates M. "American Gunpowder Makers," *American Rifleman*. May, 1964.

Tucker, Spencer C. "Cannon Founders of the American Revolution," *National Defense*. July-August, 1975.

Watson, Thomas D. "Continuity in Commerce: Development of the Panton, Leslie and Company Trade Monopoly in West Florida," *Florida Historical Quarterly*. April, 1976.

Weller, Jac. "Breechloaders in the Revolution, *Gun Digest*. 1959.

Wettendorfer, Eduard. "A Wheellock Automatic," *American Rifleman*. March, 1954.

Whitridge, Arnold. "Eli Whitney: Nemesis of the South," *The American Heritage Reader*. 1956.

Witthoft, John. "A History of Gunflints," *Pennsylvania Archaeologist*. January-February, 1966.

Monographs

Arnade, Charles W. *The Siege of St. Augustine in 1702*. Gainesville, 1959.

——————. *Florida on Trial*. Coral Gables, 1959.

Darling, Anthony D. *Red Coat and Brown Bess*. Ottawa, 1970.

Farnham, Alexander. *Tool Collectors Handbook*. Stockton, N.J., 1972.

Gooding, S. James. *The Gunsmiths of Canada*. Ottawa, 1974.

Gunnion, Vernon S., and Hopf, Carroll J. *The Blacksmith, Artisan Within the Early Community*. Harrisburg, 1972.

Hamilton, T.M. *Early Indian Trade Guns, 1625-1775*. Lawton, 1968.

Hudson, J. Paul, and Cotter, John L. *New Discoveries at Jamestown*. Washington, 1957.

Manucy, Albert. *Artillery Through the Ages*. Washington, 1949.

Mayer, Dr. J.R. *The Flintlocks of the Iroquois, 1620-1687*. Research Records of the Rochester Museum of Arts and Sciences, No. 6, Rochester, 1943.

Parker, Ellen. *Historical Sketch of the Old Powder Magazine, Charleston, S.C.* Charleston, 1924.

Riley, Edward M., and Hatch, Charles E., Jr., ed. *James Towne in the Words of Contemporaries*. Washington, 1955.

Sloan, Eric. *A Museum of Early American Tools*. New York, 1973.

Smith, Elmer L. *Early Tools and Equipment*. Lebanon, Pa., 1973.

Swayze, Nathan L. *The Rappahannock Forge*. The American Society of Arms Collectors. Cincinnati, 1976.

Webster, Daniel B., Jr. *American Socket Bayonets, 1717-1873*. Ottawa, 1964.

Wilkinson, Norman B. *Explosives in History, The Story of Black Powder*. Chicago, 1966.

Leaflets

Wilkinson, Norman B. *The Pennsylvania Rifle*. Leaflet No. 4, Pennsylvania Historical and Museum Commission. Second edn., Harrisburg, 1970.

Newspapers (Current)

Tampa Tribune (Florida), February 29, 1976; October 3, 1976; October 27, 1976.

Newspapers (18th Century)

Bahamas Gazette (Nassau), September 25, 1784.

Boston Gazette (Mass.), April 12, 1756.

Continental Journal and Weekly Advertiser (Boston, Mass.), February 19, 1778.

Maryland Gazette (Annapolis), February 25, 1773; May 6, 1773; December 5, 1776; November 11, 1784.

New England Chronicle (Boston, Mass.), December 14, 1775.

New York Gazette (N.Y., N.Y.), June 26, 1776; January 13, 1777.

New York Journal and General Advertiser (N.Y., N.Y.), March 16, 1775.

Pennsylvania Evening Post (Philadelphia), January 4, 1776; July 19, 1777.

Pennsylvania Gazette (Philadelphia), June 26, 1776.

Pennsylvania Journal (Philadelphia), August 23, 1775.

Royal Gazette (N.Y., N.Y.), January 13, 1780.

South Carolina Gazette (Charleston), August 18-25, 1739.

Virginia Gazette (Williamsburg), July 8, 1737; April 30, 1775.

Reports

Fitch, Charles H. *Report on the Manufacturers of Interchangeable Mechanisms.* U.S. Census Bureau. Washington, 1883.

U.S. Bureau of Census. *Historical Statistics of the United States.* Washington, 1961.

State Documents

Senate Journal (North Carolina), February 1, 1781.

Correspondence to the Author

January 14, 1971: John Dallam Hill, San Diego, Cal.

January 19, 1971: F.L. Greaves, Flagstaff, Ariz.

January 22, 1971: Joseph Suess, Rockville, Md.

November 13, 1972: J. Paul Hudson, Curator, Jamestown Colonial National Historical Park, Jamestown, Va.

September 5, 1975: Lena Rängstrom, Skokloster Armory, Stockholm, Sweden.

ACKNOWLEDGEMENTS

I N THE MORE THAN EIGHT YEARS devoted to researching and writing this exposition I have relied on resources derived from many sources and I therefore extend my profound gratitude and sincere appreciation to the numerous individuals and to the staffs of the various facilities who have in boundless ways contributed generously to its preparation and presentation.

Archives

Division of Archives and Manuscripts, Pennsylvania Historical and Museum Commission, Harrisburg.

Division of Archives, History and Records Management, Bureau of Historic Sites and Properties, Department of State, Tallahassee, Fla.

Florida Photographic Archives, Robert Manning Strozier Library, Florida State University, Tallahassee.

National Archives and Records Service, General Service Administration, Washington, D.C.

North Carolina Spanish Records Collection, Department of Archives and History, Raleigh.

Stetson Collection, P.K. Yonge Library of Florida History, University of Florida, Gainesville.

U.S. Census Bureau, Department of Commerce, Washington, D.C.

Associations

Fort Ticonderoga Association, Ticonderoga, N.Y.
National Rifle Association of America, Washington, D.C.
New York State Historical Association, Cooperstown.

Foundations

Colonial Williamsburg Foundation, Williamsburg, Va.

Historical Societies

Arizona Historical Society, Tucson.
Bucks County Historical Society, Doylestown, Pa.
Chicago Historical Society, Chicago.
Florida Historical Society, Gainesville.
Historical Society of Pennsylvania, Philadelphia.
Lexington Historical Society, Mass.
Longmeadow Historical Society, Mass.
Massachusetts Historical Society, Boston.
New York Historical Society, New York City.
St. Augustine Historical Society, Fla.
South Carolina Historical Society, Charleston.

Institutes & Institutions

American Iron and Steel Institute, Washington, D.C.
Smithsonian Institution, Washington, D.C.

Libraries

Bayerische Stäatsbibliothek, Munich, Germany.
Biblioteca Ambrosiana, Milan, Italy.
Bibliothèque Nationale, Paris, France.
Christ Church Library, Oxford, Eng.
Eleutherian Mills Historical Library, Greenville, Wilmington, Del.
Library of Congress, Washington, D.C.
New York Public Library, New York City.
Österreichische Nationalbibliothek, Vienna, Austria.
Robert Manning Strozier Library, Florida State University, Tallahassee.
Sterling Memorial Library, Yale University, New Haven, Conn.
Tampa Public Library, Tampa. Fla.
U.S. Army Military History Research Collection, Carlisle Barracks, Carlisle, Pa.
University of Florida Library, University of Florida, Gainesville.
University of North Carolina Library, University of North Carolina, Chapel Hill.
University of South Florida Library, University of South Florida, Tampa.
University of Toronto Library, University of Toronto, Ontario, Canada.

Museums

Anthropological Museum, University of Aberdeen, Scotland.
Arizona State Museum, Tucson.
Bayerisches Nationalmuseum, Munich, Germany.
Bayerisches Stäatsgemaldesammlungen, Munich, Germany.
British Museum, London.

Do All Museum, Des Plaines, Ill.
Eagle Americana Shop and Gun Museum, Strasburg, Pa.
Germanisches Nationalmuseum, Nuremburg, Germany.
Glasgow Museums and Art Galleries, Scotland.
Johnson Hall, Johnstown, N.Y.
Kungl. Armémuseum, Stockholm, Sweden.
Kungl. Livrustkammaren, Stockholm, Sweden.
Kunsthistorisches Museum, Nuremburg, Germany.
Mercer Museum, Doylestown, Pa.
Metropolitan Museum of Art, New York City.
Musée de l' Armée, Paris, France.
Museum of Anthropology, Louisiana State University, Baton Rouge.
Museum of the Fur Trade, Chadron, Nebraska.
Museum of the Great Plains, Lawton, Oklahoma.
Museum of New Mexico, Santa Fé.
Pennsylvania Farm Museum of Landis Valley, Lancaster.
Royal Ontario Museum, Toronto, Canada.
Skoklosters slott Styrelsen, Stockholm, Sweden.
Stäatliche Kunstsammlungen, Dresden, Germany.
State Hermitage Museum, Leningrad, USSR.
Statens Historiska Museum, Stockholm, Sweden.
Tøjhusmuseet, Copenhagen, Denmark.
Tower of London Armouries, London.
U.S. Military Academy Museum, West Point, N.Y.
U.S. National Museum (Smithsonian Institution), Washington, D.C.
Vienna Army Museum, Austria.
Winchester Gun Museum, New Haven, Conn.

National Monuments & Parks

Castillo de San Marcos-Fort Matanzas National Monuments, St. Augustine, Fla.
Fort Frederica National Monument, St. Simons' Island, Ga.
Jamestown Colonial National Historical Park, Jamestown, Va.
Morristown National Historical Park, Morristown, N.J.

Translators

Evelia F. (Mrs. George) Beiro, Tampa, Fla.
Estrella (Mrs. Ulysses) Perez, Tampa, Fla.

Universities

Florida State University, Tallahassee.
Louisiana State University, Baton Rouge.
Princeton University, New Jersey.
University of Aberdeen, Scotland.
University of Arizona, Tucson.
University of Florida. Gainesville.
University of New Mexico, Santa Fé.
University of North Carolina, Chapel Hill.
University of South Florida, Tampa.
University of Toronto, Ontario, Canada.
Yale University, New Haven, Conn.

Other Facilities

DBI Books, Inc., Northfield, Ill.
Deutsche Fotothek, Dresden, Germany.
Holland Press Limited, London.

National Gallery of Canada, Ottawa, Ontario.
National Portrait Gallery, Smithsonian Institution, Washington, D.C.
New York State Parks and Recreation, Waterford.
Yale University Art Gallery, New Haven.

Special Thanks To:

Helen C. Adamson, Depute Keeper, Department of Archaeology, Ethnology and History, Glasgow Museums and Art Galleries, Glasgow, Scotland.
John T. Amber, *Editor Emeritus, The Gun Digest,* Chicago, Ill.
Luis Rafael Arana, Chief Park Historian, Castillo de San Marcos-Fort Matanzas.
James R. Arnold, Pennsylvania Historical and Museum Commission.
Donald Baird, Director, Museum of Natural History, Princeton University.
Jacqueline Bearden, St. Augustine Historical Soceity.
George D. Berdnt, Chief, I & RM, Fort Frederica.
Paul E. Camp, Assistant Librarian, University of South Florida Library, Tampa.
Bertis E. Capehart, Director, Educational Department, American Iron and Steel Institute.
Astrid Carbonnier, Assistant Curator, *Livrustkammaren,* Stockholm.
Pierce A. Chamberlain, Chief Curator, Arizona Historical Society.
Capt. A. de Roubetz, M.A., Curator, *Kungl. Armémuseum,* Stockholm.
Jay B. Dobkin, Executive Secretary and Librarian, Florida Historical Society.
Robert G. Ferris, Book Series Editor, National Park Service, Department of the Interior, Washington, D.C.
Craddock R. Goins, Jr., Curator, Division of Military History, Smithsonian Institution.
F.L. Greaves, Flagstaff, Ariz.
Vernon Gunnion, Preparator, Pennsylvania Farm Museum of Landis Valley.
Carol B. (Mrs. Donald) Hallman, Research & Reference, Eleutherian Mills Historical Library.
Charles E. Hanson, Jr., Curator, Museum of the Fur Trade.
George J. Heckman, President, Longmeadow Historical Society.
John Dallam Hill, San Diego, Cal.
Kenneth A. Hinde, Assistant Curator, Mercer Museum.
Monika Jägos, Assistant Curator, *Österreichische National-bibliothek.*
B. Calvin Jones, Bureau of Historic Sites & Properties, Division of Archives History and Records Management, Tallahassee, Fla.
George Kladis, Tampa, Fla.
Susan A. Kopczynski, Park Historian, Morristown National Historical Park.
Dr. James D. Lavin, College of William and Mary, Williamsburg, Va.
James B. Levy, Jr., Restoration and Conservation Laboratory, Bureau of Historic Sites & Properties, Division of Archives, History and Records Management, Tallahassee, Fla.
Laine Liivrand, Curator, *Statens Historiska Museum,* Stockholm.

Prof. R.D. Lockhart, Curator, Anthropological Museum, University of Aberdeen.

Terry A. McNealy, Librarian, The Bucks County Historical Society.

Charles L. Maddox, Jr., Photographer, Doylestown, Pa.

Gary A. Matthews, American Consul, Leningrad, USSR.

James E. Morgan, Photographer, Tampa, Fla.

Daniel T. Muir, Curator of the Pictorial Collection, Eleutherian Mills Historical Library.

Robert W. Neumann, Curator, Museum of Anthropology, Louisiana State University.

Carl R. Nold, Registrar, New York State Historical Association.

Vincent W. Nolt, Owner-Curator, The Eagle Americana Shop and Gun Museum.

Arthur L. Olivas, Photographic Archivist, Museum of New Mexico.

Arne Orloff, Curator, *Tøjhusmuseet*.

Gunvor Palmborg, Curator, *Kungl. Livrustkammaren,* Stockholm.

Lynn F. Poirier, Curator, Mercer Museum.

Sol Polansky, Deputy Director, Office of Soviet Union Affairs, Department of State, Washington, D.C.

Mary B. (Mrs. Granville T.) Prior, South Carolina Historical Society.

Lena Rangström, Curator, *Skokloster slott,* Stockholm.

Edward F. Rivinus, Director Emeritus, Smithsonian Institution Press, Washington, D.C.

Peter T. Rohrbach, Potomac, Md.

George F. Schesventer, Superintendent, Castillo de San Marcos-Fort Matanzas.

Jack Scott, Keeper of Archaeology, Ethnography and History, Glasgow Museums and Art Galleries.

Walter K. (Ken) Seitz, Master Gunsmith, Tampa, Fla.

Joseph Suess, Rockville, Md.

Towana Spivey, Curator of Anthropology, Museum of the Great Plains.

John S. Tris, Curator of the Graphics Collection, Chicago Historical Society.

Ken Warner, Editor, *The Gun Digest*.

Col. Jacques Wemaëre, Curator, *Musée de l' Armée*.

Dr. Leonie von Wilckens, Curator, *Germanisches National-museum*.

Thomas L. Williams, Photographer, Williamsburg, Va.

In Memoriam
Harold L. Peterson
Chief Curator, National Park Service, Washington, D.C.
Board of Governors, Company of Military Historians.
Life Member, National Rifle Association of America.

INDEX

Name Index
Asterisk denotes gunsmith
Bold face numbers denote illustrations

influenced by flintlock musket
and socket bayonet, 140, 166
influenced by iron ramrod, 149
influenced by rifle, 263
Native American, 41, 43, 88-89,
98, 126, 263
skirmishers, 263
Tainos, resist Spaniards, 35-36, 98
Tampa Bay, 43
Tannenberg gun (see also
Handcannon), **8,** 9, 18-19, 35,
101, 193
Tap. See Tools: hand
Technological Revolution (see also
"American system," Factory:
manufacturing, Factory system,
Industries Revolution,
Interchangeable components,
Mass production, Specialization
in firearms industry,
Standardization, Tools: hand,
Tools: machine), 1, 31-32, 48,
66, 143, 188-189, 199-222, 236,
242, 244, 264, 272, 318, 355,
380-387
Telescope (see also Sights), 148, 349
Tellico (see also Cherokees, Indian
factory system), as U.S. trading
post, 368
Tenedors de bastímentos y
munitíones, 48
Tennessee, 124, 264; gunpowder
mill in, 302, 349
Termites, as threat to gunstocks and
powder horns in Spanish
Florida, 116
Testorero de la Casa de la
Contractacíon, 38
Tewa (see also Pueblo Revolt), 114
Texas, 43, 371; commerce with
Comanches and Apaches in,
119, 178
Spanish settlements in, 124,
178, 181
Textile industry (see also Industrial
Revolution), 31, 318, 386
Thalj al-Sin (see also Saltpeter), 3
The Hague (see also Dutch
Republic), and State Gun
Foundry, 91, 96
Thimbles (see also Ramrod), 42, 97,
133, 135, 262, 283
Tiller. See Gunstock
Timing (of gunlock), 72, 74, 77,
192, 376-377
Timucua, 43-44, **45,** 46, 126
Tin, 11, 30, 245, 259
Tinder lighter, **53,** 54
Tlaxcalans (see also Aztecs,
Otomi), 40
Tompion, 138, **249**
Tools: hand (see also Accessories,

Cleaning implements,
Measurement, Mould, Table IV,
Table VI), 200-201, **204,**
244-255, 258
anvil (buffalo head), 1, 19, **243,**
248, **252,** 258, **387**
armorers', 201-202, **204,** 287
arquebusiers', See armorers',
gunsmiths'
auger, 200, **204, 244,** 251
awl, 200, **204, 244,** 251
ax, **121,** 245, 258
ball (bore) gauge, **362**
barrel-straightening bow, **28,** 30
bellows, 1, 17, **64, 243,** 258, **387**
bits: boring, 18, 194, 244, **245,**
258, **362**
lathe, 195
rifling rod, 28-29, 258,
361-362
bore gauge, 91, 248, 258
bow drill, 1, **18, 28,** 60, 201,
204, 244
casting, **249, 254,** 258
checkering, 270
chemise. See mandrel
cherry, 201, **204, 254,** 258
chisel, 200-201, **204,** 251
combination. See
Combination tools
countersink, 201, **204**
die, 60, 201, **204,** 245, 325-326
draw knife (snitzel), **250**
drift, 248, **249**
file, 18, 201, **204,** 244-245, 258,
267, 310
flint striker (knapping tool), **247**
gimlet, **244**
gouge, 201, **204, 249,** 251
gunsmiths', 201-202, **204,**
243-251
hacksaw (see also saw), 248, 258
hammer, 1, 248, **249,** 258
hatchet, 132, 140, 177, 258
hide scraper, 157
jig (template), 200-201, **204,** 248
knapping. See flint striker
lapping rod, 30, **362**
mallet, 30, 248
mandrel, 18-19, 30, 194, **252,**
362, 376
maul, 208, **209, 253**
mortar and pestle, 10, **11,** 20-21,
Native Americans make from
firearms components, 157
patch cutter, 257
plane: forming, 251, 258
inletting, 201, **204, 250,** 251
rounding (hollow), 201,
204, 250
pliers, 248, 258
polisher (bone), 251, **275**
powder-making (see also mortar
and pestle), 10, **11,** 20-21,
208, **209, 211, 214, 219-220**

punch, 248, **249,** 258
rabbling bar, 380
rasp, 200, **204,** 258
reamer, 200, **204,** 258
sandpaper, 251
saw, **249,** 258
screwdriver, **55,** 248
screwplate, **28,** 60, 201, **204,** 245,
246, 253, 258
spokeshave, 251, 258
soldering iron, 245, 258
swedge, 12, 245, **246-247,**
248, 269
swedge hammer (see also
hammer), **247,** 248
tap, 60, 201, **204,** 245, **246,** 258
tongs, 194, **248,** 258
vise: bench, 243, **252,** 253-254,
310, **387**
mainspring, 201, **204, 247,**
253, 255, 258, 279
wire, **253**
Tools: machine (see also Mills,
Power sources, Tools: hand),
barrel boring, **28,** 29, 200, **201,**
243, 258, **271,** 272, 318
cannon boring, 196, **197**
cylinder boring (steam engine),
198-199
file-making, 61
glazing (tumbling), 217, **221**
grinding, 18, 201, **202,** 243, 258,
267, 318
lathe: lens-grinding, **148**
mandrel, **61,** 195, **196,** 380
pole, 1, **61**
milling (planing), 195-196,
202-203, 384-385
potter's wheel, 1, 60-61
rifling engine, 29, 258, **271, 360,**
362-364
rolling mill, 130, **215,**
216-217, 241
slabber. See milling
slitting mill, 130, 241
stamping mill, **21, 60, 214,** 216
treadmill, 60
trip-hammer, **17,** 259, **260,**
272, 318
tumbling, 21, **221**
Tory (Tories). See Loyalists
Torpedo (see also American Turtle,
Lock), 352
Touch-hole. See Vent
Tow (see also Obturation, Sabot,
Shot, Wadding), 13, 30, 42,
52, 330
Tower of London, 7, 11, 80-81,
140, 340
Tower Wharf (see also Proof), 236
Trade fusil. See Fusil,
Northwest gun
Trade rifle. See Rifle
Trajectory (see also Ballistics), 261